Being Catholic,
Being American

The Mary and Tim Gray Series for the Study of Catholic Higher Education

*By this gift
Mary and Tim Gray
support the appreciation and understanding
of the richness and tradition of Catholic higher education*

VOLUME I

*Being Catholic, Being American:
The Notre Dame Story,
1842–1934*

1999

VOLUME II

*Being Catholic, Being American:
The Notre Dame Story,
1934–1952*

2000

Being Catholic, Being American

The Notre Dame Story, 1934–1952

VOLUME II

Robert E. Burns

UNIVERSITY OF NOTRE DAME PRESS
Notre Dame, Indiana

Copyright © 2000
University of Notre Dame Press
Notre Dame, Indiana 46556
http://www.undpress.nd.edu
All Rights Reserved

Designed by Wendy McMillen
Set in 10.5/12.5 Minion by Em Studio Inc.
Printed in the U.S.A. by Sheridan Books

All photos are courtesy of the Notre Dame Archives.

The Library of Congress has catalogued this multivolume work as a set.
The catalogue record for the set is as follows:

Library of Congress Cataloging-in-Publication Data
Burns, Robert, E., 1927–
    Being Catholic, being American : the Notre Dame Story /
Robert E. Burns.
        p.   cm.
    Includes bibliographical references and index.
    ISBN 0-268-02156-2 (hardcover : alk. paper) volume 1
    ISBN 0-268-02163-5 (hardcover : alk. paper) volume 2
    1. University of Notre Dame—History.   I. Title.
 LD4113.B87   1999 v.2
 378.772'89—dc21
                                                              98-31553
                                                                  CIP

∞ *This book is printed on acid-free paper.*

For

M. A. Fitzsimons

and

all the courageous twenty-nine

Contents

Preface

This volume continues the work begun in my earlier volume *Being Catholic, Being American: The Notre Dame Story, 1842–1934*, volume I. Like that book, this second volume views the history of the University of Notre Dame as a mirror of the travails and triumphs of Catholics in mid-twentieth-century America.

Much of the story told in the first volume focused on repeated efforts by American Catholic leaders generally to demonstrate to an indifferent, sometimes hostile, public that Catholic religious beliefs and practices were absolutely compatible with contemporary American notions of religious freedom and political democracy. How many Protestants, Jews, and other Americans actually believed that was true during the 1920s and early 1930s is anyone's guess.

Be that as it was, most American Catholics who had time to think about such matters were convinced that the very strong loyalties which they publicly and enthusiastically gave to their church and country were entirely appropriate and completely free of contradiction or hypocrisy. That other Americans might think otherwise astonished them or was dismissed as a long-standing invincible prejudice.

Within that context, the Holy Cross priests running Notre Dame during the first third of this century insisted repeatedly that the predominantly Catholic faculty and student body attending Notre Dame were as loyal and patriotic as any other group of Americans. They insisted also that the kind of morally and philosophically secure education delivered here to the sons and grandsons of nineteenth- and early twentieth-century immigrants was very supportive of the existing social and economic order and in other ways very good for the country.

How many Americans even were aware of such arguments, let alone convinced by them, is problematic. Yet during the 1920s Notre Dame became one of the best-known American universities in the country, commanding fierce loyalties from Catholics and other Americans alike. Neither academic excellence, a morally secure educational environment, nor a reputation for social and economic conservatism accomplished that. Notre Dame became famous throughout the country because of athletic glory.

Rockne's highly successful football teams during those years made Notre Dame a household word across America. Even those parts of our general population at that time hostile to a large and increasingly assertive Catholic presence in America had to admit that Notre Dame football was a great American Catholic success story. Certainly, its legendary coach and many talented players were treated in the press and accepted in popular culture as genuine American heroes. Moreover, all of America knew that it was the special Catholic environment of Notre Dame that had produced them.

By 1934, when the first volume of this study ends, it is fair to say that Notre Dame was widely perceived by the public generally as a university where young men with Irish, German, Italian, and Polish surnames who excelled in sport were educated for success in middle-class America. It was also seen as a place where religion was taken seriously and patriotism highly valued. Indeed, Notre Dame was a university looked upon by those who managed and attended it, as well as by most of the public who read about it in the country's sports pages, as an institution that was in all things very Catholic and very American.

Most of the story told in the second volume is very different. The idea that American Catholics were as loyal and as patriotic as any other group of Americans was seriously challenged during the years before, during, and immediately after World War II.

Generally, American Catholic religious beliefs and practices were not special objects of challenge or of suspicion during this period. Religion was a private matter entirely, and how and where persons worshipped God was no one's business. However, during the immediate prewar years, fierce foreign policy controversies deeply divided the country. A few Catholic bishops with foreign policy agendas and a few like-minded lay Catholic leaders were both major and minor players in these controversies.

During that time, several American bishops issued some widely publicized official Catholic positions on highly contentious American foreign policy questions that appeared to be more focused on protecting special interests of the Catholic Church in Europe than supportive of our country's foreign policy objectives. For example, in their capacities as moral teachers, some of the leaders of the American Catholic hierarchy advocated such controversial public policy positions as support for the Franco nationalist party during the Spanish civil war, opposition to President

Roosevelt's policy of massive aid for Britain in its war with Nazi Germany, and withholding military aid from the Communist government of the Soviet Union and not cooperating with them in the war even after the United States had become a full-scale participant.

To be sure, a great many other Americans publicly had supported positions identical with those advocated by the bishops and had severely excoriated President Roosevelt and his policies in the process. Nonetheless, public advocacy of such positions by most, by no means all, of the American Catholic bishops became everyone's business because of the widely held but mistaken assumption that most American Catholics took their politics from their bishops as completely as they took their religion. That American Catholics would take their bishop's advice on matters of domestic and foreign policies very seriously and then do what they had been told to do was scarcely doubted by media pundits or by any of the reigning self-proclaimed authorities on the Catholic problem in America.

Within the context of prewar and war-time controversies, being both a patriotic, loyal American supportive of our president's foreign policy and an obedient, loyal Catholic supportive of Church interests abroad became harder and harder to do. Before the war was over, some American Catholics who thought seriously about such matters would have to decide which of those possibly conflicted loyalties was the strongest.

Until 1940 no one at Notre Dame actively participated in these intense controversies. It was true that administrators and many faculty held strong views on whether a policy of isolation or intervention into the affairs of Europe was an appropriate national policy, but those who did rarely ever expressed their personal views in a public way. A strict rule established during the presidential election in 1928 prohibited faculty from doing so. Fearful that personal opinions of faculty publicly expressed on national policy issues might be misinterpreted as official university positions, only the president of Notre Dame was authorized to speak for the university on such matters.

Because he was preoccupied with improving the quantity and quality of research activities at the university and involved in an ambitious building program, Father John F. O'Hara, C.S.C., president of Notre Dame from 1934 to 1940, generally left public discussion and comment on American policy issues to others. Except for some expressions of support for Franco and the nationalist cause during the Spanish civil war and occasional very strong anti-Communist statements, neither O'Hara nor the university were publicly identified with one side or the other in policy debates.

O'Hara's successor, Father J. Hugh O'Donnell, C.S.C., president of Notre Dame from 1940 to 1946, would have preferred to pursue the same institutional neutrality on policy issues but could not. The hiring of Father John A. O'Brien, a wealthy priest with a history of poor relations with his bishop, as a professor of religion in the fall of 1940 turned O'Donnell's comfortable world of controversy avoidance upside down. In the person of O'Brien, the intense, deeply divisive debates over isolationism and interventionism then raging throughout the country came to Notre Dame.

O'Brien joined the America First Committee immediately after arriving at Notre Dame and became a frequent and popular speaker for that isolationist organization. He quickly emerged as a strident critic of Roosevelt's foreign policy and as one of the most widely known Catholic isolationists in the country. Always identified as a Catholic priest and as a Notre Dame professor whenever speaking at America First functions, O'Brien simply shredded the university's rule prohibiting faculty from addressing controversial national issues in a public way, and the president of Notre Dame did nothing about it.

O'Brien's example inspired other members of the Notre Dame faculty to speak out for the other side. First, a small group of lay professors publicly disassociated themselves from O'Brien's anti-Roosevelt rhetoric and isolationist views. Next, one of that group, Francis E. McMahon, a devout Catholic and an associate professor of philosophy, joined Fight for Freedom, Inc., spoke regularly throughout the Midwest for them strongly defending Roosevelt's foreign policy of unlimited aid for Britain in the war, and quickly emerged as one of the most widely known Catholic interventionists in the country.

Because the isolationist/interventionist controversy so deeply divided Americans in 1940–41, the public advocacy activities of O'Brien and McMahon inspired an enormous amount of negative mail for O'Donnell to read and answer, including a very strong complaint against McMahon from John T. McNicholas, O.P., archbishop of Cincinnati. Convinced that the good name of the university was being compromised by the negative publicity of his two celebrity professors and ever respectful and obedient to higher religious authority, O'Donnell asked Father O'Brien to be a bit more circumspect in his public statements and to apologize to a U.S. senator who had been offended by them. Next, O'Donnell threatened McMahon with non-renewal of his annual employment contract if he did not cease his public advocacy activities.

Neither of these strategies worked. The U.S. senator was even more offended by O'Brien's apology than by his original statements. O'Donnell's threat to fire McMahon was reported in the Chicago press and elsewhere as a blatant and absolutely unAmerican violation of the professor's First Amendment rights. McMahon rescued O'Donnell and the university from a major public relations disaster by denying that a serious threat of that nature really had been made. Chastened by these two experiences, O'Donnell left O'Brien alone but pressed McMahon once again in the late fall of 1941 to curtail some of his more spectacular on-campus interventionist activities. After that, events took charge.

Ironically, after the Japanese attack on Pearl Harbor and our entry into World War II, peace of a sort was restored to the Notre Dame campus. With isolationism now discredited and the America First organization dissolved, O'Brien followed other former isolationist leaders into the more promising politics of anti-Communism. However, for most of the war years, the well-known priest from Notre Dame generally withdrew from public policy advocacy. Except for occasional public statements attacking Roosevelt's policy of demanding nothing less than unconditional surrender from the Axis powers as being immoral and likely to prolong the war, O'Brien turned away from politics and devoted his considerable energies to highly successful ecumenical activities.

McMahon followed another course. Much in demand as a pundit who had been proved right by events, McMahon continued to pursue a very full agenda of public advocacy activities. He insisted that the policy of unconditional surrender complied absolutely with the tenets of Christian morality as he understood them. McMahon condemned fascism utterly and argued in liberal journals that Catholicism had no special affinity for authoritarian fascist states. He attacked anti-Semitic doctrines and practices at home and abroad and defended Pius XII from allegations of insensitivity to the terrible plight of European Jews. Though strongly anti-Communist himself, in speech after speech McMahon urged close collaboration with the Soviet Union in the war and afterwards in order to secure a peaceful and better postwar world.

Preoccupied with keeping the university financially viable when virtually all potential students were bound for the armed forces, O'Donnell was distressed by the negative mail generated by some of McMahon's speeches but did nothing about it until August 1943. At that time, a higher religious authority directed a complaint against McMahon's public advocacy activities and against him as an employee of a Catholic university that O'Donnell interpreted as an order to silence the man. O'Donnell did his best to comply. He tried to impose a system of censorship upon McMahon's off-campus appearances and speeches which the professor refused to accept. Thereupon, in midsemester, O'Donnell terminated McMahon's ten years of employment at the university.

By admitting publicly that outside pressure of a sort had forced his decision to fire McMahon and then by refusing to disclose the source of that outside pressure, O'Donnell brought a firestorm of negative publicity upon the university that lasted six months. To persons on-campus and off, it appeared that McMahon had been fired for publicly defending in speeches and in writing the official foreign policy of our country. On-campus, in an entirely unprecedented action, twenty-nine courageous Notre Dame faculty members led by M. A. Fitzsimons and Willis Nutting of the history department publicly protested O'Donnell's action against McMahon and urged the president to define for them and for the American academic world generally how much free speech Notre Dame faculty members could enjoy and keep their jobs. That was one trap that O'Donnell refused to run into.

Occurring as it did in the midst of a terrible war against authoritarian fascist regimes, this unexplained arbitrary firing of McMahon occasioned the greatest public relations disaster in the history of the university. In a short-lived but intense media frenzy, the integrity of Notre Dame as an authentic American university was challenged and the commitment of Notre Dame officials responsible for the action against McMahon to American political and constitutional values was scorned. Off-campus, a petition prepared by George Shuster, a Notre Dame graduate, former Notre faculty member, and now president of Hunter College, and signed by a group of sixty-nine celebrity professors, intellectuals, and scientists urged O'Donnell to correct a terrible mistake by reinstating McMahon. The professor was not reinstated.

O'Donnell coped with this devastating public relations situation by saying as little about the McMahon affair as possible and doing nothing to prolong media interest in it. In public statements O'Donnell took full and sole responsibility for the action taken against the professor and publicly denied that higher religious authority had been involved in any way. As president of the university, O'Donnell took no action against the twenty-nine faculty protestors and even refused to acknowledge that a written and signed formal faculty protest had ever been received. Confident that war news would soon drive the entire McMahon affair out of public memory, O'Donnell absolutely refused to discuss or dispute with anyone the reasons for his action or any details relating to it. In the end, his strategy worked. War news in the spring of 1944 was spectacular, and active public interest in the most outrageous academic freedom incident in modern Notre Dame history disappeared. Moreover, university officials scrupulously avoided repetition of any incidents that might revive interest in it.

At war's end and in the immediate postwar years, American patriotism became equated in the public mind with anti-Communism. During the last year and a half of his tenure as president of Notre Dame, O'Donnell recovered much of the university's patriotic image lost during the aftermath of the McMahon affair by assuming public and very inelegantly stated anti-Communist stances whenever possible. He also managed successfully to show himself and the university on one very important postwar higher education issue to be more American than Catholic.

O'Donnell broke with the long-standing American Catholic tradition of opposition to any and all schemes of federal aid to higher education. He did so on the grounds of national security. O'Donnell publicly supported and played a role in the creation of a new federal agency, known later as the National Science Foundation, established to fund scientific research and science education in American colleges and universities. For that service, O'Donnell was awarded a seat on the national advisory board of the new agency.

O'Donnell's successor as president of the university, Father John J. Cavanaugh, C.S.C., a man endowed with extraordinary personal charm as well as great political skills tempered by an active conscience, worked even harder than his predecessor to enhance the university's patriotic image and succeeded grandly in doing so. Cavanaugh's public patriotic/anti-Communist stances were perhaps more deliberate and roughly stated than those of his predecessor. Cavanaugh's reputation in this regard made him a special favorite of military organizations and veterans' groups as a public speaker.

Beyond that well-intended public relations activity, within the university Cavanaugh successfully managed the enormous influx of postwar students into Notre Dame. He did so by hiring new faculty, encouraging development of new academic programs, and expanding facilities. More than that, Cavanaugh reorganized the upper levels of the university's administration, established a new permanent professional fund-raising organization, and initiated a major reform of the athletic department while at the same time successfully covering up a crisis or two in the football program.

Most important of all for the long term, Cavanaugh understood clearly that with himself an era in the history of Notre Dame was coming to an end. He believed strongly that a new style of leadership, sensitive to the rapidly changing environment of postwar American higher education and skilled in public relations and permanent fund raising, was required if Notre Dame were to grow and prosper as an authentic modern research-based American university.

With that end in mind, during the second term of his presidency Cavanaugh identified an heir apparent, Father Theodore M. Hesburgh, C.S.C., fortuitously much endowed with those needed sensitivities and skills. Cavanaugh provided his protégé with extensive practical experience as executive vice president and then quietly withdrew from active management of university affairs. As a former president, Cavanaugh offered counsel when asked, was always supportive, and generously applauded the triumphs of the new generation of leaders that he had installed. Cavanaugh initiated the modernization of Notre Dame that his better-known and very long-serving successor completed.

No book is ever completed without help from many people. The most generous with ideas, insights, and references to overlooked sources has been my longtime friend and colleague, J. Philip Gleason. He has educated me greatly with his many published works on American Catholic higher education and on American Catholic intellectual history generally. More than that, he has given me years of great conversation and encouragement, always listening patiently and sympathetically as I developed and redeveloped my story.

I must repeat here what I have written elsewhere about the resources of the Notre Dame archives. The amount and value of relevant material on deposit there for this story as well as for American Catholic history generally is enormous, and I make no claim to have exhausted all of it. However, some files of documents produced within the last fifty years are either closed or are subject to review before access is allowed. Consequently, this researcher has relied more in this volume than in his earlier one on available public records and newspaper accounts of events described or upon interviews with persons who had participated in them to tell his story.

Within the rules of access which in most cases are liberal, the staff of the Notre Dame archives has been extraordinarily helpful and cooperative. Special thanks are owed to Wendy Clauson Schlereth, university archivist, and to her assistants, Charles Lamb, Peter Lysy, and Sharon Sumpter, who have responded to my endless queries and requests with dispatch and good humor.

Finally, a few words must be said about the person to whom this volume is dedicated. Simply stated, M. A. Fitzsimons was a great man. Along with professors James A. Corbett and Willis Nutting of the Notre Dame history department and the rest of the courageous twenty-nine faculty petitioners in 1943, Fitzsimons publicly defended the integrity of Notre Dame as an authentic American institution of higher education. He did so at a time when the president of the university chose not to demonstrate that it was and when many American academics and media people doubted whether Notre Dame or any other Catholic university ever could be authentic because they were Catholic.

Beyond that courageous and timely stance in 1943, Fitzsimons was an inspiration then and later to everyone fortunate enough to know him. He was a devout Catholic, superb teacher, distinguished scholar, prolific writer, and in all things a man of honor. Fitzsimons enriched the university with his presence for over thirty years. Happily, in 1998 Notre Dame officials formally recognized his many contributions to the intellectual life and academic reputation of the university by establishing an endowed professorship in the College of Arts and Letters in his name.

PART I

NOTRE DAME DURING THE 1930S

In 1934, when Father John F. O'Hara, C.S.C., became the thirteenth president of Notre Dame, the university had been in existence for over nine decades. During that period the institution had evolved from a small-town Catholic boys' boarding school staffed almost exclusively by Holy Cross priests and brothers into the largest residential Catholic men's university in the country. Over 2,600 students studied in classroom buildings and laboratories at Notre Dame and lived in campus residence halls permeated by a strong religious atmosphere. These students were taught by a faculty of about two hundred fifteen, of whom in 1934 less than one-third were Holy Cross priests.

The university was organized into four undergraduate colleges: arts and letters, science, engineering, and foreign and domestic commerce. In addition, there was a law school and since 1931 a number of small but ambitious graduate programs. While virtually all of the upper-level administrative positions in the university were held by Holy Cross priests, priest/professors were not evenly distributed throughout all of the colleges. The College of Science listed only a few. There were no priests at all in the Colleges of Engineering and Commerce. Priest/professors were concentrated in the College of Arts and Letters, particularly in the departments of religion, philosophy, and history. Moreover, virtually all of the priests on campus, whether faculty members or not, had responsibilities in the residence halls as rectors or assistant rectors for maintaining an easily accessible quality spiritual life and acceptable social behavior.

Virtually any graduate of an accredited American high school qualified for admission, and very few students of acceptable moral character
were ever turned away. As a matter of fact, during the early 1920s it was
university policy to admit everyone who applied. Most students attending Notre Dame during the 1930s were drawn from middle-class American Catholic families of Irish, German, Italian, and Slavic descent. These
young men came to Notre Dame to mature emotionally, socially, and
intellectually in a morally and philosophically secure Catholic environment while preparing for successful careers in business or the professions.

As a representative Catholic university in 1934, Notre Dame was not a
place where all points of view on controversial issues would be expressed
or cultural, racial, social, or religious diversity encountered. In 1934 slightly
less than half of the Notre Dame student body pursued traditional liberal
arts courses of study. A majority of the undergraduate students at this
time were enrolled in academic programs with a strong professional orientation—business, engineering, pre-medical, and pre-law. In practice
then, the formal substantive education delivered to most Notre Dame
students during these years was pre-professional or professional. Among
Notre Dame students of this era, generally the most remembered and
valued common intellectual experience was not reading or recitation; it
was learning how to write coherent sentences.

The rest of the education provided at Notre Dame at the time tended
to be protective. Required courses in neo-scholastic philosophy were
thought sufficient to contain and, if the mechanics of Thomistic reasoning and analysis could be mastered, perhaps even refute the errors of
materialism and skepticism. Instruction in Christian doctrine by persons
professing the Catholic faith and practicing it in their own lives was best
taught through virtuous example. Finally, no Catholic education could
be authentic if it was not also a moralizing experience. Prefects and rectors were expected to watch over the morals of their charges. Young men
thus placed under observation, it was believed, should turn out to be better persons for having been watched. All of this was reasonably priced. A
Notre Dame education in 1934 cost residential undergraduate students
$650 a year for tuition, room, board, and laundry. Day students paid $275
a year for tuition.

For the lay faculty employed at Notre Dame as well as for those working in most other Catholic colleges, pay was low and job security was
problematic. In 1934 lay academic deans were paid about $6,000, the
most prestigious lay professors earned about $5,000, ordinary professors
accepted $2,500 for their efforts, and young assistant professors and
instructors received about $1,800 for the year. As a point of reference, the

head football coach in 1934 was paid $8,000 while his assistants earned $3,000. Because of cost controls imposed after Coach Rockne's death in 1931, the salaries paid to coaches in 1934 were significantly less than in previous years.[1]

With regard to job security for lay faculty, modern academic tenure did not exist at Notre Dame in 1934. All lay professors at Notre Dame, regardless of length of service or status as teachers or scholars, were employed under one-year contracts renewable at the discretion of the president. The only Notre Dame employees ever given contracts running for more than one year were the head football coaches. It must be said, however, that neither voluntary nor involuntary lay faculty turnover has ever been very high at Notre Dame at any time; so given the economic uncertainties of the 1930s, it was minimal during those years. Modern academic tenure and multi-year contracts did not become the norm at Notre Dame until 1954.

Much anecdotal evidence suggests that the insecurity of annual contracts negatively affected lay faculty morale. For example, the annual mailing of contract renewals to lay faculty in the spring was very much a party time for those who received them and was celebrated accordingly. That tradition of celebrating annual contract renewals continued long after academic tenure and multi-year contracts had diminished the anxiety associated with that fearsome event. Instead, the cause for celebration was transferred to the spring arrival of salary increase notifications.

As the institution expanded and evolved toward a modern university between 1920 and 1940, there were some things that lay faculty at Notre Dame simply did not do. While private criticism of university administrators, procedures, policies, or programs could be and was often savage in private, going public with such matters was risky and rarely done. Furthermore, any activity or behavior, private or public, having the effect of embarrassing the university, discouraging students from coming to Notre Dame, or offending financial contributors was job threatening.[2]

Even more important, lay faculty were frequently admonished to refrain from addressing current political or controversial policy issues in a public way while under contracted employment with the university. This policy had been set during the stridently anti-Catholic Republican presidential campaign of 1928. It was imposed at that time in order to discourage Coach Rockne, who for personal business reasons wanted publicly to endorse Herbert Hoover for the presidency. Such an endorsement by the most famous man at Notre Dame would have embarrassed the university greatly and infuriated millions of Al Smith's Catholic supporters as well as no small number of the university's financial contributors.

Since that narrow avoidance of a public relations disaster in 1928, university administrators insisted and virtually every lay faculty member understood and accepted the principle that the slightest association of the name of Notre Dame with personal views should be scrupulously avoided. One was not supposed to assert or claim a connection with Notre Dame when speaking publicly or writing about current political, social, economic, or foreign policy issues. Only the president of the university was authorized to speak for the university or give an impression that he was speaking for the university on such matters. The simple meaning of this policy was that ideally the only views on political or controversial public policy issues to be aired by persons employed or otherwise connected with the university were those approved by the president.

Because there was no way that a faculty member could prevent any newspaper from reporting speech or writing on matters of public controversy and then identifying the author as an employee of the university, strict compliance with this principle was virtually impossible. To comply strictly was to say nothing publicly that the president feared would embarrass the university. It would appear as well that no one at the university at this time, administration or faculty, was prepared to argue that serious application of this principle was censorship and denial of freedom of speech to American citizens in their own country.

— ii —

When O'Hara became president of Notre Dame in July 1934, he selected as his vice president Father J. Hugh O'Donnell, C.S.C., former prefect of discipline (1924–31) and president of St. Edward's College in Austin, Texas (1931–34). The rest of O'Hara's leadership team included Father John J. Cavanaugh, C.S.C., an assistant advertising manager for the Studebaker Corporation before joining the Congregation of Holy Cross, whom O'Hara appointed prefect of religion in 1934, and the long-serving Father J. Leonard Carrico, C.S.C., who continued as director of studies. Of this leadership team brought together by O'Hara in 1934, described by faculty wits as being headed by an evangelist, assisted by a Rotarian, and aided respectively by a ward heeler and an adding machine, one or more of them would direct the affairs of the university for the next eighteen years.

O'Hara and his team were very fortunate. By 1934, the university had managed to survive the worst ravages of the Great Depression. For Notre Dame, the academic years 1932–34 had been the most threatening ones.

Overall university enrollments had fallen from a high of 3,227 in 1930–31 to 2,617 in 1933–43, their lowest levels in fifteen years. During the first academic year of O'Hara's presidency, 1934–35, overall university enrollment rose to 2,709, driven by a freshman registration increase of 23 percent.

During these very difficult years, the strength of university finances followed enrollment trends. After 1933 no teachers were dismissed because of economic conditions. Draconian measures put in place in 1932 to reduce faculty did not have to be implemented. Actually, in three of the six years between 1930 and 1936, normal salary increases were provided. The value of the conservatively invested, modest university endowment ($1,100,000) first fell and then rose with general financial markets. The largest paper loss incurred during the worst of the Depression years amounted to only 13 percent. By 1937 those paper losses had been recouped.[3]

A similar pattern occurred with regard to profits from intercollegiate football during the early Depression years. Football profits had paid for much new construction and contributed generally to university development during the late 1920s. After Coach Rockne's death in 1931 football profits declined precipitously. The impact of the Depression along with inept coaching by Rockne's successor, Heartley "Hunk" Anderson, and poor team play combined to reduce football profits in 1933 to only one-third of what had been earned in 1930. That amount of income loss was unsustainable.

Largely through O'Hara's influence, Anderson was replaced by Elmer Layden in late 1933. The change of head coaches turned out to be good for Notre Dame football and for the athletic department's balance sheet. Not only did Layden's team perform much better in 1934 than had Anderson's squad the previous year, winning six games and losing only three, but football profits increased modestly as well. While football profits would never reach the spectacular levels of 1929 and 1930, the sharp decline in those profits occasioned by the impact of the Depression and by the poor performance of Anderson's teams was over.

In the three very important matters of enrollment, endowment safety, and football profits, O'Hara had been very lucky. When he became president in 1934, the financial condition of the university was not a matter of special concern. Thus relieved, notwithstanding the deteriorating state of international affairs and continuing evidence of fragility in our national economy, O'Hara turned at once to what was to be his principal activity, transforming Notre Dame into a modern university while remaining in all things a thoroughly Catholic institution.

There is no doubt that Father John F. O'Hara was one of the most extraordinary men ever to be associated with Notre Dame as his later career as auxiliary bishop of the Military Ordinariate, bishop of Buffalo, and cardinal archbishop of Philadelphia testified. It is impossible to overestimate the positive and negative influences of this most unusual man upon the administrative, religious, social, and intellectual life of the university between 1920 and 1940.

Most people who had known John O'Hara as a founder and sometime dean of the College of Commerce and later as a long-serving prefect of religion and highly successful religious journalist would never have described him as an intellectual or as in any way enamored with the life of the mind. Certainly, O'Hara would never have described himself as an intellectual. Yet, despite deep prejudices against much of the critical and evaluative work undertaken by intellectuals in contemporary state universities, O'Hara, almost in spite of himself, when president succeeded in bringing more of them to the university than had any of his predecessors.

In politics, O'Hara professed to be nonpartisan, but he had close personal relations with Notre Dame alumni holding influential positions in the Roosevelt administration. He often served as a conduit to Democrat influentials for local Republican businessmen seeking changes or relief from New Deal legislation or administrative policies. O'Hara was also a perfervid anti-Communist and valued loyalty to church, country, and Notre Dame as a standard by which all students and faculty ought to be measured.

O'Hara was blessed with a high level of intelligence, an enormous capacity for work, an unshakable optimism about any project undertaken, and a most retentive memory. He was also a man usually free of all vestiges of false dignity, vainglory, or pretension. For people he liked and knew or even did not know personally but respected, O'Hara spared no effort to insure that their time at Notre Dame was pleasant and productive. Toward such people, he found much pleasure in being thoughtful and kind. In interpersonal relations, O'Hara could be either the best of friends or the worst of enemies.

To most people who knew O'Hara with any degree of intimacy, he appeared always supremely self-confident and ever optimistic. Difficulties did not intimidate him, and problems were matters to be resolved. For others who did not know O'Hara well, that self-confidence could acquire the sting of arrogance. On most matters and in most situations, he was a decisive man; but when pressed by time and circumstances that otherwise admirable quality sometimes appeared uncomfortably arbitrary. On occasion, he is remembered for abruptly terminating discussion in faculty meetings by ordering discussants, priests or laymen, to "sit down and shut up."[4]

With the decline of football profits arrested and with general university finances more or less under control, O'Hara could be decisive about continuing the facilities improvement programs of predecessors. A new laundry and post office building were erected in 1934. An infirmary was put up in 1935. Three self-amortizing residence halls were built — Cavanaugh in 1936, Zahm in 1937, and Breen-Phillips in 1939. Of these, only Breen-Phillips had donor support. A new biology building was begun in 1936, and an extension was added to chemistry hall in 1939. Finally, in 1937 after a delay of six years, construction of the Rockne Memorial was started. Though only $135,000 had been raised for this project during the very poor fund-raising years of 1931–32, O'Hara managed to find an additional $200,000 in the athletic department account to proceed with the project.[5] In the long term, however, more important than building residence halls and science facilities was what O'Hara did in six short years to improve the quality of instruction and research at the university.

— iii —

Though not trained in science or in any other academic discipline for that matter, O'Hara highly valued scientific and scholarly research. Notwithstanding his prejudices against intellectuals, O'Hara greatly respected scientists and published scholars who had done their work well, that respect becoming near adulation if such scientists and scholars were Catholic. He was interested in history, especially Latin American history, and was fascinated by economics. O'Hara accepted all contemporary American Catholic assumptions about the centrality of Thomistic philosophy in Catholic higher education and its presumed value in developing clear thinking.

O'Hara's understanding of the nature of a Catholic education was conventional. For him it was much more than required courses in Thomistic philosophy and in religion. It was instruction in a full range of academic and vocational-oriented subjects provided to young Catholic men in the presumed religiously and morally correct environment of a residential Catholic university. It was not an educational setting where all sides of religious or morally controversial issues were presented. A Catholic education was delivered through a curriculum wherein error had no right to exist or to be heard.[6]

The creation and maintenance of that sort of a religious and morally correct Catholic educational environment in contemporary America was not easy. However, in these matters as in others, O'Hara was up to the task. Enforcement of *Index Librorum Prohibitorum* regulations and operative canon law provisions dealing with dangerous books was strict. In addition, if banning the sale of magazines such as the *American Mercury, Time,* and *Life* in university facilities because of what O'Hara believed were politically incorrect articles or purient photographs seemed appropriate, he did it.[7] In the case of *Life,* the magazine had published anti-Franco editorials and photographs of scantily clad females.

Indeed, for O'Hara purience was everywhere. He tended to see it in places and in activities where others did not. Always informed and kept current about the so-called occasions of sin in South Bend that might attract Notre Dame students, O'Hara strove mightily to eliminate them or otherwise limit their effects.[8] Consequently, if imposing the severe penalty of expulsion upon all students who attended South Bend public dance halls and styling the young women who frequented such places in an official university religious newsletter as "pigs" were necessary as deterrents, O'Hara would do it.[9]

With regard to the subject matter of a Catholic education, O'Hara had no patience with and considerable antipathy toward sociology and other social and behavioral sciences.[10] He absolutely abominated the name and concept of social studies. Unless literature provided some sort of moral inspiration, he saw little value and much danger in it.[11] O'Hara had no use whatsoever for contemporary American literature. He regarded a writer such as Hemingway as little more than a purveyor of pornography, and insisted that Hemingway's works had no place in libraries or in courses taught at Catholic colleges and universities.[12] As a matter of fact, on occasion while serving as president of the university he would make visits, usually during the hour after lunch, to the Notre Dame library and personally purge it of books thought by him to be dangerous or morally suspect. After such visits O'Hara would always send the librarian the title pages of the books removed so that he could pull the cards from the library catalogue.[13]

Though O'Hara had not a serious ecumenical thought in his head[14] and was a man of many strong views that bordered on prejudice, he was, nonetheless, totally possessed by the idea that Notre Dame could and should become a great university. O'Hara was convinced that an essential part of the process of becoming a great university was developing at Notre Dame the kind of research orientation in science and in a few other fields that was so characteristic of the best American and English universities.

For O'Hara, moving from thought to action on the matter of developing a serious research orientation at Notre Dame turned out to be relatively uncomplicated. It was uncomplicated because in the administrative environment of Notre Dame at that time, there simply was no way for an opposition to organize and act against the president once he had decided to pursue a policy or undertake a project. In this particular instance, O'Hara had support from a few energetic Holy Cross priests lately returned from graduate schools. [15]

— iv —

Given the level of affluence of most Notre Dame alumni in 1934 and general economic conditions, resources for new construction were easier to find than funds for expanding and improving research activities and facilities. Results following from the former were immediate and obvious while outcomes from funds given for the latter purpose tended to be generalized and long range. O'Hara began his search for such new resources by going to people most likely to appreciate and favor what he was trying to do. He turned to the General Education Board (which later became the Rockefeller Foundation) to look for advice and possible financial assistance in the fall of 1935.

The staff at the General Education Board knew and admired Father James A. Burns, a former president of the university and now the serving provincial of the American province of the Congregation of Holy Cross. He had successfully obtained a grant from the board in 1920 and had managed the matching fund-raising campaign that followed. The staff also knew O'Hara's predecessor, Father Charles L. O'Donnell, from his unsuccessful visits to their New York offices in 1931 seeking funds for the development of graduate education at Notre Dame. O'Hara was entirely new to them and charmed everyone there with his candor and lack of pretension. Even though the board had no programs in place in which Notre Dame was interested or which it could qualify for, a staff member, Trevor Arnett, visited the university, interviewed Burns and O'Hara, and then commented favorably (in a report filed with the board in September 1935) about the progress of the institution since the grant award in 1920. In this interview with Arnett, O'Hara had mentioned that many of the university's largest givers had made their first gift to the university in the fund-raising campaign of 1920–22 and had continued to be generous to Notre Dame in succeeding years.[16] O'Hara stated also that the university was able to live within its budgets and improve important scientific facilities. For example, some of the newly hired physics professors "were engaged in building a sphere for the bombardment of the atom. It was their opinion that it would furnish a larger amount of electric power than the one used at MIT for a similar purpose."[17]

About a month later, O'Hara visited the board's offices in New York and had another interview with Arnett. After this interview, Arnett commented positively on the work of the Notre Dame physics, zoology, and chemistry departments but offered no encouragement about the prospects for a grant. The board had committed all of its resources to specific programs. No funds were available at this time to assist Notre Dame or any other university in developing their scientific programs.

Though O'Hara was disappointed with the board's narrow focus, he was not dismayed and decided to maintain contact with its staff members. O'Hara corresponded with the board off and on over the next two years, apprising them of scientific and scholarly developments at the university. For example, he informed the board in 1937 about the improved condition of university finances, mentioning that all of the income from the faculty salary endowment established with the General Education Board grant in 1920 and with matched funds raised thereafter was now being used to support professors teaching graduate courses.[18] With no immediate prospect in sight for a foundation grant to assist development of scientific and scholarly research at Notre Dame, however, O'Hara decided that the university would have to find funds for such projects from internal sources. As his predecessors had done to finance new buildings, O'Hara turned to football profits for the monies needed to establish research and publication as a normal expectation from newly hired Notre Dame faculty.

As has been noted earlier, during 1934 Coach Layden's team won six games and lost three. Although Layden's win and loss record for 1934 was his worst during seven years as head coach, it was a vast improvement over Anderson's final year of only three wins, five losses, and one tie. Not only did Layden win more games than Anderson, but the style of team play indicated much better coaching as well. Most important of all, the steady decline in football profits from the highs of $540,000 during the glory years of 1929 and 1930 to only $177,000 in Anderson's last year had been checked. Receipts had increased significantly in 1934, but so had expenses. Football profits for 1934 rose slightly to $192,000. Stopping a negative trend and increasing profits ever so slightly was a good beginning.

Over the next six years, Layden's teams performed well, winning forty-one, losing ten, and tieing three. In no season did Notre Dame lose more than two games, and in one season, 1938, the team remained undefeated until losing their season-ending clash against the University of Southern California. Layden's teams achieved some memorable victories. For example, in 1935 against Ohio State in Columbus before 81,000 people,

Notre Dame scored three touchdowns in less than fifteen minutes in a magnificent come-from-behind win regarded by many sports' authorities as perhaps the greatest intercollegiate football game of the century. Yet, throughout the Layden years, the glory of an undefeated season and a national championship eluded his teams. Clearly, Layden was a much better coach than Anderson but he was not the equal of Rockne.

However, in the very important area of relations with the Big Ten Conference, Layden performed much better than had Rockne. Layden succeeded in scheduling games with the University of Illinois, whose coaches had scrupulously avoided playing Rockne teams, and with diplomacy and charm managed to end the athletic boycott of Notre Dame by the University of Michigan that extended back to incidents occurring in 1909. Fielding Yost, athletic director of the University of Michigan and a bitter personal enemy of Rockne, agreed to schedule a football series with Notre Dame beginning in 1942.

Unlike Rockne, Layden understood the value of prudent silence. In the mid-1930s, the most corrupt intercollegiate football program in the country was directed by Jock Sutherland at the University of Pittsburgh. Sutherland not only paid his athletes on a regular salary scale but arranged free off-campus housing and other amenities for them. Sutherland's system of professionalization worked and brought his teams four times into the Rose Bowl. Layden had coached at Duquesne before coming to Notre Dame and knew all about Sutherland and his professional players, despising both the man and his system.[19] Layden said nothing publicly about the situation at the University of Pittsburgh, but he joined with Navy and other schools which dropped the University of Pittsburgh from their schedules, thereby forcing a major reform of that university's athletic program and the departure of Sutherland to the National Football League.[20]

Similarly, in 1936 Layden and other university officials opted for prudent silence respecting scandalous activity in the Ohio State football program. Information that some Ohio State athletes were being subsidized with nominal jobs as state employees was passed on to the commissioner of the Big Ten Conference by Notre Dame officials with a request to investigate the situation there. The commissioner, Major John Griffin, made inquiries in Columbus and found that indeed some very good football players were on the state payroll. However, since those jobs had been arranged by state representatives and state senators, the commissioner persuaded himself that Ohio State University had not broken conference rules. The commissioner urged Notre Dame officials to keep all information about the situation at Ohio State confidential, which they did.[21] There would be no advantage for Notre Dame in antagonizing the commissioner of the Big Ten Conference by leaking such news to the press. Instead, Layden simply dropped Ohio State from the schedule without telling the reasons why. After appearing in the Notre Dame stadium in a losing effort in 1936, Ohio State and Notre Dame did not play another football game until 1995.

However tactical and successful was Layden's management of football relations with other institutions, his tenure as head coach at Notre Dame would depend upon the bottom line of the athletic department's budget at year's end. As long as football profits trended upward providing resources for university development, Layden's position would be secure. Only when football profits trended downward, would Notre Dame officials begin to take seriously complaints about the coach's perceived increasing petulance and his alleged slavish adherence to Rockne's system of football play that many regarded as outmoded by southwestern and West Coast innovations.

As has been noted earlier, football profits during Layden's first year increased modestly. They rose again in 1935 and 1936, peaking to over $300,000 in 1938 and 1939, and then dropped precipitously to $207,000 after a season of seven wins and two defeats in 1940. By and large, while O'Hara was president, Layden's football profit margins were acceptable. They were sufficient to allow O'Hara to proceed with his plans to improve the instruction and research activities at the university. However, O'Hara left the presidency and the university in late 1939 to become a bishop. His successor, Father J. Hugh O'Donnell, troubled by the decline of football profits in 1940 and by Layden's lack of cooperation in other matters, decided to look for a replacement.

— v —

Separate from the very important issue of the available resources, which Layden's football profit margins had helped resolve, O'Hara was able to move ahead with his academic development program because his predecessor, Father Charles L. O'Donnell, had prepared the way. Unlike some future presidents of Notre Dame as well as a few other future high-placed university officials, O'Hara never took credit for another person's ideas and initiatives. As president, O'Hara continued what O'Donnell had started and freely admitted to having done so.

Having authorized the building of the new Notre Dame football stadium in 1929, O'Donnell had become very defensive about accusations of an overemphasis on athletics. Generally disposed to encourage and support programs that would enhance the academic reputation of the university, O'Donnell provided modest funding and some personnel for Father Julius Nieuwland's acetylene chemistry research and for James Arthur Reyniers' germ-free laboratory animal research. Moreover, as a poet and student of literature, O'Donnell had tried to raise the level of literary interest and taste at Notre Dame by inviting English and Irish writers to lecture at the university. O'Donnell paid G. K. Chesterton the princely sum in 1930 of $5,000 plus expenses for a highly successful six-week lecture series.[22]

Even more important, given O'Donnell's absolute faith in the special place of Thomistic philosophy in Catholic higher education, was his support of efforts by O'Hara and others to start development of a graduate program in that subject at Notre Dame. Once the university's financial situation had stabilized in the fall of 1932, O'Donnell was ready to begin adding bright young Catholic men with recent doctorates to the philosophy department. In 1933, Francis E. McMahon, a doctoral recipient from the Catholic University of America, vice president of the Catholic Association for International Peace, and lately returned from a year of graduate study at the University of Munich, was hired primarily to teach Thomistic philosophy to graduate students.

Also in 1933, Father Philip S. Moore, C.S.C., trained in Thomistic philosophy and holding a doctorate from the Catholic University of America, returned to the university in 1933 after three and a half years of graduate study in Paris. He agreed to serve as secretary of the Committee on Graduate Study and teach philosophy and medieval studies to graduate students. Though not chairman of the committee, Moore's influence on policy was very strong; under his informal but powerful leadership new graduate programs were initiated or existing ones expanded in the Colleges of Science, Engineering, and Arts and Letters.

Moore also influenced the hiring of well-credentialed young Catholic scholars who could contribute to the expansion of graduate work in medieval studies. One such hire was James A. Corbett, a layman whom Moore had met while pursuing medieval studies at the Ecole National des Chartres in Paris. Moore urged O'Hara to hire and bring this very promising young scholar to Notre Dame. When in Paris, O'Hara looked up Corbett and was impressed. In due course, O'Hara hired Corbett to take up a newly created post of university archivist and teach some graduate courses in medieval studies.[23]

When Corbett completed the requirements for his certificate as an *Archivististe-Palaeographe* and arrived with his family at Notre Dame in the late summer of 1935 to assume his new post, he discovered that

O'Hara's plans for him had changed. A post such as university archivist was too sensitive for a layman to hold and a Holy Cross priest had been appointed before Corbett arrived. Instead of assuming the duties of university archivist, Corbett was assigned to the history department to teach courses in Western civilization and medieval history. At the same time, O'Hara charged Corbett to collect, organize, and research materials for a centennial history of Notre Dame that he would write and the university would publish in 1942. Corbett was satisfied with his changed assignment and began teaching classes to undergraduates and collecting materials for the centennial book forthwith.[24]

In recruiting lay faculty, the Corbett change of assignment notwithstanding, O'Hara broke entirely with the past. Gone was the long-standing fear of hiring laymen as regular teachers. Gone also were former President Burns' concern about finding money to pay for lay teachers and scholars and former President Walsh's determination to hire only as many as the lay faculty salary endowment could support. While O'Hara would still insist, as his predecessors had done, that positions be found for Holy Cross priests returning from graduate schools, his plans for Notre Dame included well-credentialed laymen as an essential, expanding, and increasingly important part of the Notre Dame academic enterprise. Once O'Hara had made this decision and began acting upon it, there could be no turning back.

The extent of O'Hara's efforts to improve the quality of scientific and scholarly research undertaken at Notre Dame is perhaps best illustrated by the fact that the number of students enrolled in 1940 was about the same as it had been in 1930; but the size of the faculty had increased by 40 percent. To be sure, and as will be seen, that circumstance was no accident. Even more important than the overall faculty expansion was the increase in the number of Notre Dame faculty holding doctoral degrees. That percentage rose from 18 percent in 1930 to 27 percent in 1940. However, this increase in doctorates was not evenly distributed among the four colleges. The College of Commerce employed none in 1930 and only had one in 1940. The College of Engineering added two during that time. In the College of Arts and Letters, the percentage of faculty holding doctorates rose from 20 percent in 1930 to 24 percent a decade later. In the smaller College of Science, over the same period of time the percentage of doctorates held by the faculty rose from 25 percent to 60 percent.

Within the College of Arts and Letters, most of the new doctorates were recruited for the departments of religion, philosophy, and politics. As a matter of fact, in 1940 with two-thirds of the department of politics faculty holding doctorates it was the best credentialed department in the college. The department of philosophy was second with half of its members having doctorates, and the English department with only one doctorate out of a faculty of thirty was the least credentialed.

In the College of Science virtually everyone hired during O'Hara's presidency had or very quickly received a doctorate. However, the most spectacular recruitment of doctorates in this college occurred in the departments of mathematics and of physics. Not one out of the eight faculty holding full or part-time appointments in the mathematics department in 1930 had received a doctorate. Ten years later, four out of ten held doctoral degrees. In the department of physics the number of doctorates increased from none out of seven in 1930 to six out of eight in 1940. Only one faculty member teaching physics and only one teaching mathematics at Notre Dame in 1930 were still doing so in 1940. Clearly, the beneficiaries of O'Hara's research encouragement program were the departments of politics and philosophy in the College of Arts and Letters and mathematics and physics in the College of Science.

In the College of Science, O'Hara did more than simply recruit additional faculty. He took advice from some men relatively new to Notre Dame who knew what scholarship and research was and the value of doing it for the educational mission of the university. These were men who believed in the general educational value of doing specialized research. Though they were a distinct minority in the Notre Dame faculty and in the Congregation of Holy Cross, O'Hara listened to them.[25]

While the department of chemistry was able to attract some outside funding needed to develop and sustain its research programs, some very important programs were not. For example, O'Hara continued to find internal support for Reyniers' germ-free animal experiments. The president also committed university funds—that is, in part football revenues—for the construction in 1937 of a new biology building which would provide space in twenty-three basement laboratories for germ-free animal research.[26] However, it was in the department of physics that some of the newest and more spectacular advances were made.

Between 1930 and 1940, the department of physics was transformed from a service department for pre-medical students and chemistry programs into a research-oriented department with active projects in nuclear and polymer physics. This transformation was led initially by Dr. George B. Collins and Edward A. Coomes, who received funds and encouragement from O'Hara in 1935 to purchase materials and themselves build an accelerator for nuclear research. However, the principal instrument of change in the physics department was Father Henry J. Bolger, C.S.C., lately returned to the university after three and a half years of graduate study at the California Institute of Technology. Bolger was appointed chairman of the physics department in 1937, a position that he held for the next thirty-six years.

Coincident with Bolger's return to the university in 1937 occurred what O'Hara described to the officers of the General Education Board as "a nice expansion of the faculty."[27] This expansion was to be of a very special sort. O'Hara had decided to try to hold undergraduate enrollment at a level of about three thousand, so that new faculty could be hired without regard to undergraduate teaching needs. He intended that most of the new faculty hired in 1937 and thereafter would be deployed in graduate work.[28]

Finding the resources to hire research-oriented professors was only one aspect of the larger problem of raising the level of scholarship and research productivity at Notre Dame. Another was finding such trained and qualified persons who were Catholic and who would be willing to come and live, research, and teach in an aspiring Catholic university located in northern Indiana.

There were only two sources where such trained and qualified people could be found. The first source was of course doctoral students completing degree requirements in American graduate schools. However, even among the strongest candidates from the best graduate schools scholarly productivity and scientific achievement were prospective and in no way assured. In any case, very few graduate students entering the academic market in 1937 were Catholics. A second source of research-oriented academic people was the growing body of refugee scholars and scientists from German and Austrian universities. To meet the needs of his planned faculty expansion for 1937, O'Hara turned his attention to both of those sources.

Altogether, fifteen laymen and ten clerics were appointed as instructors in September 1937. This group of young Catholic academics was the most talented and extraordinary group of entry-level faculty ever recruited at Notre Dame in a single year in the history of the university up to that time. Men such as M. A. Fitzsimons, John J. Fitzgerald, and Father Albert Schlitzer, C.S.C., in the College of Arts and Letters; Robert L. Anthony, Arthur N. Milgram, and Brother Columba Curran, C.S.C., in the College of Science; Lawrence Stauder in the College of Engineering; and James Dincolo and Bernard Finnan in the College of Commerce all came to Notre Dame as faculty for the first time in 1937. All of these men contributed enormously to the future growth and development of the university, giving many productive years of service as teachers, scholars, research scientists, and administrators.

O'Hara's decision to try and recruit refugee Austrian and German research-oriented scientists and scholars for the university was a logical one for him to make. The university had established scientific contacts of a sort with the University of Vienna. Father Francis J. Wenninger, C.S.C., had studied biology at Vienna and had received a doctorate from that institution in 1928. Moreover, after Wenninger had returned to Notre Dame, he facilitated the appointment of Dr. Theodore H. Just, another biologist trained at the University of Vienna, to the Department of Biology at Notre Dame in 1929. Therefore, reaching out through Wenninger to other scientists on that faculty was a natural way to proceed.

The first refugee scientist from Vienna to come was Dr. Arthur E. Haas. This well-known physicist had been a faculty member at the University of Vienna for thirteen years. Haas left Austria early. He came to the United States and to Bowden College as a visiting professor in 1935, where he stayed only a year, moving into a permanent position in the physics department at Notre Dame in the fall of 1936. Haas remained at Notre Dame as one of the leading teachers and researchers in the physics department until his death in 1941.

Haas was followed out of the University of Vienna to Notre Dame in January 1937 by Dr. Karl Menger, an eminent mathematician who had lectured at Harvard and the Rice Institute in 1931. Then, in the fall of 1937, Dr. Emil Artin, also a mathematician, and Dr. Eugen Guth, a young physicist with interests in synthetic rubber, joined their former colleagues from Vienna at Notre Dame. Menger remained until 1946, Guth stayed until 1955, while Artin was at the university only a year.

Menger was an enormous asset to the mathematics department and to the university. He served as chairman of that department for several years and did much to awaken and strengthen research interests among his colleagues. Most important, Menger organized a symposium on the Calculus of Variations in April 1938 that was a major event in the intellectual history of the university. This symposium brought such distinguished mathematicians as Solomon Lefschetz, president of the American Mathematics Society, and Marston Morse of Princeton to the university for the first time. As O'Hara reported to a friend, the combination of Menger and Haas and this symposium had the effect of establishing very friendly relations between Notre Dame's mathematics department and mathematicians at Princeton and Chicago.[29]

With regard to the College of Arts and Letters, the custom at Notre Dame of engaging foreign celebrity writers as guest lecturers had been going on for some time. O'Hara continued the practice of inviting visiting professors and guest lecturers to the university, believing that it was an effective way of raising intellectual standards and cultural awareness among both students and faculty. However, O'Hara changed the subject-matter focus of those invited, turning from celebrity creative writers of the past toward English Catholic and Irish Catholic academics and religious writers.

At first, the president sought out English-speaking foreigners to help staff a proposed two-year program in advanced Catholic apologetics that he favored and strongly believed that the country needed. O'Hara envisaged Notre Dame becoming the place in the United States where the foremost defenders of orthodox Catholic doctrine and practices could study and explicate the mysteries and wonders of the true faith. He expected that regular Notre Dame faculty could contribute something to this enterprise, but the strength of it had to come from distinguished European visiting professors. Only established scholars, of which Notre Dame had very few at this time, could provide the research, instruction, and religious counseling required for such a program to succeed. As later events determined, this program had a very short life at the university, 1938 to 1941. However, while in place the program turned out to be an extremely important vehicle for O'Hara to bring a succession of European Catholic scholars and writers to Notre Dame. This was the group known later and celebrated as O'Hara's "foreign legion."

A frequent traveler to England and the Continent himself, O'Hara looked there, particularly to England to find the priests and Catholic laymen experienced and skilled in apologetics who could provide the expertise needed for his intended new program. As early as 1934, O'Hara had met and established a close friendship with Frank G. Sheed of the Catholic publishing house of Sheed and Ward of Paternoster Row, London.

Sheed was in his own right a much-published writer on Catholic themes as well as a leading publisher of Catholic books. He was also deeply interested in O'Hara's advanced apologetics project. Not only did O'Hara invite Sheed to come to Notre Dame as a visiting lecturer, but he used Sheed as a contact and as a recruiter of well-known English, Irish, and European Catholic writers and academics for short-term visiting and eventually for permanent appointments at Notre Dame. At first, Sheed looked for men who could contribute to the apologetics program but quickly his search broadened to include talented Catholic scholars working in any of the disciplines represented in the College of Arts and Letters.

Sheed recommended as visiting professors: Christopher Hollis, Arnold Lunn, and David Mathew from England and Shane Leslie and Desmond Fitzgerald from Ireland. He also recommended Jacques Maritain, Etienne Gilson, and Charles De Bos from France.[30] All of these men came. Sheed's awareness and knowledge of these writers and scholars rested on the solid ground of personal acquaintance and on the fact that many of them had published books with Sheed and Ward.

Moreover, in 1936 Sheed had directed O'Hara's attention to another Sheed and Ward author, Waldemar Gurian, a Russian-born German-educated scholar and publicist presently living in Switzerland as a stateless refugee from Nazi Germany. A recipient of a doctorate from the University of Cologne in 1923, Gurian was a person of enormous learning and intellectual accomplishment. He had published widely on Russian, German, and French political and religious affairs. A devout Catholic, Gurian had left Germany in 1934 and supported himself in Switzerland by editing and publishing a newsletter devoted to analyzing and interpreting contemporary German politics.

O'Hara was so impressed with what Sheed had told him about Gurian that he wrote a strong letter of recommendation to the Catholic Worker's College in Oxford, England. O'Hara urged the rector there to consider hiring Gurian for a post at the college. In turn, the rector thanked O'Hara for the recommendation but regretted that at the moment there were no openings to fill.

O'Hara may have thought about offering Gurian a visiting position for a year at Notre Dame at that time but refrained from doing so. In early 1937 O'Hara had already made up his mind, again on the strong recommendation of Sheed, to try to engage another Sheed and Ward author, Edward I. Watkin, to come to Notre Dame for a year. Watkin was a much-published writer on religious, cultural, and historical subjects, who, as a matter of fact, had translated two of Gurian's books for Sheed and Ward. Watkin was a man who could add strength to several departments needing it in the College of Arts and Letters. However, Watkin's health was not good, and apparently decision making was not a mental process that he did easily or quickly. Negotiations with Watkin dragged on until early July 1937, when O'Hara received the man's definitive refusal.

At that point, O'Hara asked Sheed to find out if Gurian would be willing to come to Notre Dame for the academic year, 1937–38. Sheed reported that Gurian was interested, and O'Hara responded with an offer of a position that he expected would be made permanent in the department of politics.[31] Gurian agreed. A contract was sent, a visa was arranged, and Gurian departed for the United States on September 23, 1937.

O'Hara completed his extraordinary faculty recruitment program for 1937 by hiring still another German Catholic refugee scholar. Ferdinand Alois Hermens had received his doctorate from the University of Bonn in

1930 and had made electoral processes and proportional representation his academic specialty. Hermens had left Germany in 1935, spending a year at the Catholic University of America before returning to Germany as a John Simon Guggenheim Fellow in 1936–37. When the fellowship expired, Hermens came directly to Notre Dame with an appointment in the department of politics.

Though other European scholars would continue to come to Notre Dame as visitors and for permanent appointments in subsequent years, most notably Yves Simon to the philosophy department in 1938, by the end of 1937 O'Hara's foreign legion had been recruited up to strength. Very quickly these European-trained Catholic scholars with strong commitments to research and publication made a significant impact on the intellectual life of the university. Of this group, Menger and Gurian were the most important. Of these two, probably Gurian contributed the most, if for no other reason than Menger left the university in 1946 and Gurian remained there until his death in 1954.

— vi —

To be sure, Gurian was an extraordinary man and an entirely new experience for the administration, faculty, and students of Notre Dame. No one like him had ever lived and worked in this community before. One contemporary, Hannah Arendt, described Gurian as a "walking library of information" and marveled at his enormous capacity "to absorb, digest and communicate information," the like of which she had never seen in anyone else.[32] Others remember Gurian's love of ideas, his abiding concern for principles, and unfailing analytical prowess. Certainly, Gurian's interpretation of the appeals of Bolshevism and German National Socialism as twentieth-century social and political secular religions was strikingly insightful and original when published in the early 1930s.

What distinguished Gurian most from so many contemporary scholars and writers was not so much intellectual power, store of knowledge, or even originality; it was his active and all-pervasive Catholicism. Simply stated, Gurian was Catholic through and through and could not imagine serious personal intellectual activity independent of service to the Church.

Regarded as something of a prodigy in German university circles in the 1920s,[33] Gurian made an early and profound impact on the intellectual life of his generation. Between 1927 and 1932 he wrote and published significant books about the Church and the *Action Française*, the social

and political ideas of French Catholics, Bolshevism, and National Socialism. However, being a scholar working among other scholars was not
enough. Gurian worked for a time as an editor of a German Catholic
newspaper in Cologne and wrote articles for the German Catholic press
elsewhere. He saw himself as a scholar who was also a Catholic publicist,
that is, a missionary in the modern world confronting the contemporary
crises of the European mind and confident that answers to the great
questions of the times could be found in Church teachings.[34]

Gurian's concept of a Catholic publicist was a sophisticated one. Propaganda and polemical party journalism were not for him.[35] His thinking
on this matter involved much more than engaging in mere defensive
activity, providing information about Church positions, or trying to
influence public opinion on behalf of the Church. In Gurian's mind, the
task of the Catholic publicist was first of all to serve the Church by telling
the truth about her and then by explaining and interpreting the events
and great crises of the day against the timeless standards of Catholic
morality and ethics. One mechanism for doing so was to raise questions
about meaning and about the unscrupulous use of slogans as substitutes
for principles. Above all else, a Catholic publicist always tried to tell the
truth, no matter what the state of public opinion, without retreating into
relativism or succumbing to despair.

To be sure, Gurian never contended that only practicing Catholics
were capable of telling the truth. Yet he believed deeply that the particular Catholic intellectual quality of making distinctions made telling the
truth in the face of state power or established public opinion a bit easier.
As Gurian himself put the matter in a lecture delivered in Germany in
1931, only sons and daughters of the Church possessed the qualities of
mind and spirit required to do the work of a Catholic publicist. Only if in
one's own life one followed Him who is the Savior of the World and Lord
of all ages could one go beyond the bounds of his own subjectivity.[36]
Only then would it be possible to avoid the danger of using one's self as a
source of norms and standards of conduct and instead maintain a healthy
skepticism about personal wishes and prejudices.

Clearly, Gurian's concept of a Catholic publicist would be neither
attractive to nor realizable by everyone. It was, however, a scholarly and
journalistic role that he had thought about for a very long time. So
important, in fact, was this role to Gurian that he delayed hardly at all
after arriving at Notre Dame in the fall of 1937 to begin finding some way
of playing it. What Gurian discovered was that his concept of the role and
activities of a Catholic publicist appealed very much to O'Hara, a religious journalist of no small accomplishment in his own right. In the

administrative environment of Notre Dame in 1937, O'Hara's attraction to Gurian's concept turned out to be very important.

Things began to happen in early 1938. Menger's celebrated symposium on the Calculus of Variations held in the College of Science in April 1937 proved to be a powerful precedent. The holding of that mathematics symposium at Notre Dame insured that a similar one would be organized for the College of Arts and Letters sometime in 1938. What O'Hara had allowed Menger and the department of mathematics to do, he could not and did not deny to Gurian, Hermens, and the department of politics.

Gurian and Hermens moved with dispatch in the spring of 1938. Joined by Father Leo R. Ward, C.S.C., of the philosophy department and Frank O'Malley from the English department, Gurian and Hermens pressed O'Hara and his University Council to authorize and fund a symposium on political and social philosophy to be held at Notre Dame in early November 1938.

The organizers of this symposium, conceived as a major intellectual event, intended to invite the most renowned scholars and thinkers presently working in the fields of politics and social thought in European and American universities. Because Gurian knew many of the best prospects personally, the likelihood of putting together a spectacular program for this symposium was very strong. O'Hara was perhaps more pleased by the long-term public relations value of Gurian's symposium to the university than by what in the short-term faculty and students might learn from attending it. More important, O'Hara was particularly attracted by the idea that this symposium would go far to insure the success of another Gurian project that he favored.

Supported again by Hermens, O'Malley, and Father Ward, Gurian had submitted a proposal to O'Hara and the University Council for the establishment at Notre Dame of a periodical that would be a vehicle for the kind of work that Gurian believed Catholic publicists ought to undertake. To be called the *Review of Politics,* this periodical was not modeled after any existing American scholarly journal. (As a matter of fact, O'Hara always referred to the *Review* in correspondence with Gurian as a periodical, not as a journal.) The model for the *Review* were the German Catholic periodicals[37] that Gurian knew so well and whose purpose O'Hara understood and approved. In practice, the *Review* turned out to be scholarly in purpose, given the quality of the people who wrote for it, but it was broader in scope and much less specialized in content than any American scholarly journal then published.

Gurian's symposium was intended to be an occasion for publicizing and launching the *Review.* It was his hope that several of the better papers presented at the symposium attended by such eminent thinkers and scholars as Jacques Maritain, Mortimer Adler, Carl J. Friedrich, Goetz Briefs, and Donald Davidson would appear as articles in the first number of the *Review*. O'Hara was much impressed by the entire concept and apart from some concerns about university's responsibility for the articles published in it which were quickly resolved,[38] he was a strong supporter of the entire project. The University Council agreed to appropriate funds for the *Review of Politics* on a continuing basis at the end of July 1938.

Another Gurian and Hermens project proposed in 1938 fared not so well. Both Gurian and Hermens in the short time they had been at Notre Dame had experienced difficulties with Father Francis J. Boland, C.S.C., chairman of the department of politics, over teaching assignments, departmental obligations, research initiatives, and graduate students. Gurian actually appealed to O'Hara to intervene. Ever wise in such matters, O'Hara refused to do so directly; instead, he advised Gurian and Hermens to meet with Boland and work out their differences through discussion. There is no doubt that O'Hara had a conversation of his own about this matter with Boland. In any case, when the two professors met with their chairman, misunderstandings vanished and quiet discussion left all parties satisfied.

Though Gurian thanked O'Hara for his wise and effective counsel, the experience of dealing with Boland had been distracting. To avoid future problems and to secure administrative autonomy for himself and his enterprises, Gurian proposed that the university create an institute with himself as director. This proposed institute would require special university funding. Gurian justified the expense on the grounds that the institute would be an effective vehicle for training graduate students, seeking research funds, organizing scholarly conferences, and in the absence of a university press, publishing books. O'Hara received the institute proposal along with the *Review of Politics* prospectus and in the end approved the latter but not the former. The president told Gurian at the end of July 1938 that funds were not available for an institute and that the University Council believed that his full program could be implemented through the department of politics.[39]

However, as evidence of continuing support despite this refusal, O'Hara promised to search out and find larger quarters for Gurian so he could better house his programs. On the matter of graduate students for Gurian and Hermens, which seemed to be a particularly sensitive issue in their relations with Boland, O'Hara reported the possibility of a major change in the way graduate students were supervised at Notre Dame. The president advised Gurian that during the forthcoming academic year, 1938–39, he hoped to be able to transfer jurisdiction over graduate students "from a graduate committee to a graduate school." He would proceed in this matter, O'Hara continued, as soon as a few details were worked out.[40] Those few details turned out to be formidable indeed, especially the conviction of Father J. Leonard Carrico, long-serving director of studies at the university and chairman of the Committee on Graduate Study that the time for such a change was inopportune. Formal establishment at Notre Dame of a graduate school headed by a dean was delayed until 1944.

Despite disappointment over rejection of the institute project in 1938, both Gurian and O'Hara had reasons enough to be pleased by the symposium in November and by the reception of the first number of the *Review of Politics* in January 1939. The symposium had been planned as a great intellectual event, and such it turned out to be. Maritain and other distinguished writers and scholars came and most of them performed up to expectation. Maritain's paper, "Integral Humanism and the Crisis of Modern Times?" became the lead article in the first number of the *Review*. The articles in that issue as well as others that Gurian published in subsequent numbers quickly established the *Review* as unique among both university-based and learned society-based scholarly journals.

The *Review* was unique first of all because it had a single editor who had a clear idea of what he wanted the journal to be. Moreover, Gurian had contacts with scholarly writers and journalists who could write the kind of articles that he wanted to publish. The *Review* was unique also in its dedication to politics in the broadest sense. All aspects of political life were fit subjects for publication in the *Review*, and the perspectives of all disciplines, be they cultural, religious, philosophical, social, or economic, were welcome.

Despite the wide range of subject matter attracted by the *Review*'s nonspecialized character, it was a fact that articles rooted solidly in the traditions of political democracy and Catholic Christianity were well represented among those accepted and published. In practice, about the only type of article generally absent from the *Review* were technical quantitative studies of political behavior. The *Review* was Gurian's creation, and it remained very much a reflection of his personality and interests throughout the fifteen years of his editorship. Furthermore, it would be fair to say that at no time during that period was the *Review* ever a refereed journal (where publication decisions are made by an outside board of editors).

If the very high scholarly and journalistic ideals of telling the truth about the Church and of explaining and interpreting modern crises against standards of Catholic morality and ethics were achievable and sustainable for a period of time anywhere, the *Review* was the journal that came closest to doing so. Gurian published frequently in the *Review* himself—eleven articles during the fifteen years of his editorship—and distinguished scholars regularly submitted quality work to him. Although a list of authors published in the *Review*'s early years reads much like a directory of leading European and American scholars, Gurian's periodical did not become an outlet exclusively for celebrity writers and established scholars. By 1940 and increasingly so in the postwar years, young scholars newly arrived at Notre Dame and anxious to publish would send their best work to the *Review* first, and frequently Gurian would publish it.

In the end, Gurian's presence on campus, the enormous respect afforded his books and articles here and at other universities, and the success of the *Review* in scholarly circles impacted powerfully upon the College of Arts and Letters in several ways. First, Gurian's intellectual interests and the type of articles published in the *Review* deeply impressed John U. Nef and the group of scholars associated with the Committee on Social Thought at the University of Chicago. Nef saw Gurian and the *Review* as advocates for a new scholarship of synthesis, independent of established academic specialties but absolutely essential in any serious search for truth in the modern world.[41]

Nef began publishing in the *Review* as early as 1938, and quickly developed a close personal relationship with Gurian and some of the other Notre Dame faculty connected with the *Review*. Out of these relationships close ties developed between several of the academic departments in the College of Arts and Letters and Robert Hutchin's University of Chicago. Consequently, over the years a succession of young scholars with doctorates from Chicago joined the Notre Dame faculty and promising undergraduates from this university were directed to the University of Chicago for graduate study.

Finally, even more important than facilitating ties with the University of Chicago, Gurian's presence at Notre Dame helped produce a major change in faculty attitudes toward the role of research and publication in the life of the College of Arts and Letters. Gradually but surely, the idea of doing research and publishing entered the culture of the College of Arts and Letters as a desirable and expected faculty activity.

During the 1930s a great many interesting things had happened at Notre Dame. Under O'Hara's leadership, the direction of institutional development was turned irreversibly toward that of a modern university. Research and publication increasingly became a required faculty activity in several departments in the Colleges of Science, Engineering, and Arts and Letters. Frequent scientific and scholarly conferences and the publication of their proceedings, and a growing number of scholarly articles and books written by Notre Dame faculty, all powerfully abetted by the quality articles consistently published in the *Review of Politics,* broadcast to American higher education and to the public at large that football ability was not the sole form of excellence at Notre Dame.

— vii —

In addition to appointing Gurian, Menger, other refugees, and the stellar American faculty recruitment class of 1937, O'Hara made an appointment in 1939 that would profoundly affect the tranquility of the Notre Dame community for four years and thereby seriously damage for a decade the academic reputation of the university so carefully built up. Actually, O'Hara was cleverly manipulated into this appointment by the appointee himself, Father John A. O'Brien from the Diocese of Peoria. This energetic and enterprising priest was a popular religious writer, a renowned convert maker, former pastor of St. John's Church, former chaplain to the Catholic students attending the University of Illinois, and director of the Newman Foundation in Champaign, Illinois.

Over the years, O'Brien had run afoul of Catholic religious authorities many times. As a matter of fact, when O'Brien approached O'Hara for a teaching position at Notre Dame in the spring of 1939, he was in very serious trouble with his bishop, Joseph T. Schlarman, of the Diocese of Peoria. Bishop Schlarman had lately removed O'Brien from the pastorate of St. John's and from the Catholic chaplaincy at the University of Illinois. Schlarman had also suspended O'Brien from performing priestly functions in the Diocese of Peoria and had ordered the suspended priest to remove himself to some other ecclesiastical jurisdiction.

Indeed, O'Brien had a long and well-documented history as a troublemaker. However, there is no evidence that O'Hara knew anything about it. All that the president of Notre Dame appears to have known about O'Brien was his reputation as a convert maker and as a popular Catholic writer. O'Hara had met O'Brien a few times during the previous ten years. Some of those meetings were in situations that loudly proclaimed the priest's connections and regional celebrity status. For example, O'Hara shared a box with O'Brien in the company of Governor Henry Horner of Illinois and Dr. A. C. Willard, president of the University of Illinois, at the Notre Dame/Illinois football game in Champaign in 1937.[42]

Getting an appointment at Notre Dame in 1939 was largely a matter of persuading O'Hara that a specific candidate was worth hiring. O'Brien started that process at once. He made his first approach to O'Hara in the spring of 1939 about obtaining some sort of position at the university that would begin in the fall of 1940. O'Brien intended to spend the intervening year, 1939–40, in England studying at Oxford part of the time and traveling elsewhere in that country and occasionally to the Continent whenever possible.

O'Brien began his campaign for an appointment at Notre Dame by inviting O'Hara to come to Champaign and preach at St. John's Church. Next, O'Brien sent O'Hara a copy of *Catholics and Scholarship,* a collection of essays about the state of Catholic higher education that he had edited. Along with the book O'Brien sent a letter complimenting O'Hara on how much Notre Dame had prospered under his leadership and how significantly the university had contributed to the cultural life of the Church.[43]

O'Hara responded on May 22, 1939, with a polite rejection of the invitation to preach but thanked O'Brien profusely for sending the book.[44] O'Hara was very pleased to find that James Arthur Reyniers, a Notre Dame bacteriologist, had contributed a chapter to *Catholics and Scholarship* and in it had dwelt upon the strong support given by the Notre Dame administration to scientific research.[45] Shortly thereafter, O'Brien visited Notre Dame and obtained a meeting with O'Hara. He told O'Hara that after spending the next year at Oxford, he would like to be able to come to Notre Dame to retire, do some research and writing, and perhaps give a lecture a week in what he called philosophy of religion to advanced students. In this conversation, O'Brien casually had asked for a teaching load and leisurely set of working conditions that no other faculty member, priest or layman, could have imagined as possible at Notre Dame at that time. O'Hara did not terminate this conversation because of what O'Brien said next.

O'Brien indicated a willingness to do more for the university than just teach. He made very clear to O'Hara that he was a man of considerable and growing financial means and that he intended to become a financial contributor to the university. He wanted to be able to "help in a small way in aiding Notre Dame to achieve the intellectual and spiritual leadership among all of the institutions of higher learning in America." O'Brien had offered to come to Notre Dame not to earn money but to give it. Moreover, as a mark of good faith, he promised to send off to the university his personal library of more than a thousand volumes containing apologetics literature and a large quantity of educational books and articles collected while serving as superintendent of schools for the Diocese of Peoria.[46]

This was an offer that O'Hara could not refuse. Always impressed by men who had spent time at Oxford and certainly not offended by O'Brien's stated disposition to share his wealth, O'Hara made a verbal offer to O'Brien about coming to Notre Dame in the fall of 1940, staying for a few years, and perhaps playing a role in the Institute for Advanced Apologetics that the president much favored at that moment.[47] No salary, rank, or departmental affiliation appears to have been discussed at that time. Delighted with the offer however vague, O'Brien accepted it forthwith; and upon returning to Champaign he sent a confirming letter to O'Hara thanking the president for welcoming him to Notre Dame.[48]

Throughout O'Hara's very friendly encounter with O'Brien at Notre Dame in the spring of 1939, there can be no doubt that the president was charmed by the wealthy priest and much moved by his potential generosity to the university. What is also very clear is that O'Hara rather quickly and easily persuaded himself that the presence at Notre Dame of this well-known priest, popular religious writer, and potential financial contributor would make the university a better place. Apparently, O'Hara entertained no suspicions at all about O'Brien's near-compulsive attraction to controversy. The possibility that this wealthy, charming priest could or would in the near future disrupt and divide the university community and cause serious damage to the academic reputation of his beloved Notre Dame never seemed to have entered O'Hara's mind.

In any case, O'Hara was not fated to remain at Notre Dame and cope with the consequences of the changes he had wrought. Events were to take him away from Notre Dame and raise him to one of the highest stations in the American Catholic Church. Precisely when that ascent began is difficult to specify, but it was well underway when Notre Dame defeated Army, 14 to 0, in a dull, poorly played football game in Yankee Stadium in early November 1939. As was the custom at that time, O'Hara attended that game and paid his respects to the recently appointed archbishop of New York, Francis J. Spellman.

When Spellman, a relatively unknown auxiliary bishop in the Archdiocese of Boston who also happened to be a long-standing personal friend of the newly enthroned Pope Pius XII, vaulted over all contenders for the most coveted and most powerful archdiocese in the country in April 1939, he was also installed as Military Vicar to the United States armed forces. With international relations deteriorating everywhere and war breaking out in Europe in September 1939, Spellman's appointment as Military Vicar became increasingly important. The prospect of rapidly increasing American military and naval establishments and even enactment of a conscription law made it so.

Spellman needed a formidable Catholic cleric with demonstrated political skills who was also a tested manager of men and money, doctrinally sound, and morally alert to watch over and protect Catholic interests during this inevitable enormous expansion of the country's armed forces. At some point during summer of 1939, Spellman decided that Father John F. O'Hara, C.S.C., of Notre Dame was his man. Indeed, for his part, O'Hara enthusiastically embraced the role of being Spellman's man. As protégé and close friend of the increasingly powerful archbishop of New York, O'Hara chose a career path that led ultimately though circuitously to the exalted American Catholic ecclesiastical station of archbishop of Philadelphia.

Most likely, final arrangements about when and how to release the news of O'Hara's appointment as auxiliary bishop to the Military Ordinariate was settled during the Notre Dame/Army football weekend in New York City. In any case, during the first week of December, O'Hara left the university ostensibly for a vacation in the western states. On December 11, 1939, while O'Hara was absent from Notre Dame, news of the appointment was released in New York. The appointment had been a well-kept secret and surprised everyone.

Even Bishop John F. Noll of Fort Wayne, the diocese in which Notre Dame was located, had not known about it. Noll wrote to O'Hara offering congratulations and explaining that he certainly would have recommended him for episcopal rank except for a belief that his friend wanted to remain president of Notre Dame until his term expired in July 1940. Consecration ceremonies followed quickly at Notre Dame on January 15, 1940, with Archbishop Spellman officiating. Spellman was assisted by the bishops of Fort Wayne and of Indianapolis. No less than forty-five other bishops and archbishops braved the cold, snowy South Bend weather to attend the ceremonies and witness the creation of a new American ecclesiastical star.

O'Hara immediately left for New York to take up his new post wherein he displayed the same tireless activism that had characterized his years as president of Notre Dame. He remained an auxiliary bishop assigned to the armed forces for five years, whereupon Spellman facilitated his appointment as bishop of Buffalo. From Buffalo, O'Hara's powerful friend in New York obtained for him first the post of archbishop of Philadelphia and then later, the status of cardinal. While in Buffalo and Philadelphia, O'Hara acquired a well-deserved reputation as a school builder. However, after leaving Notre Dame and serving as bishop and archbishop, he had very little to do with Catholic higher education and was not identified with intellectual activities or causes of any sort.

When O' Hara left Notre Dame in January 1940, he was succeeded by his vice president, Father J. Hugh O'Donnell, C.S.C., who served as acting president until July 1940, when he was appointed to a presidential term in his own right. O'Donnell chose a close friend, Father John J. Cavanaugh, C.S.C., the serving prefect of religion, to be vice president. O'Donnell and Cavanaugh faced the difficult task of succeeding a very popular president who had improved faculty quality and raised instructional and research standards to their highest levels in university history. O'Hara's record of accomplishments would be very hard for any successor to equal.

Not only did O'Donnell and Cavanaugh have to manage the increasingly self-assertive and demanding lay faculty that O'Hara had hired, but they had to do so during the extraordinarily challenging wartime years, 1940–46. All of this required attention to lay faculty needs, to their increased scholarly activities, and especially to their greater participation in public policy controversies, was new to O'Donnell and Cavanaugh. Coming to terms with the realities of O'Hara's faculty meant that precedents from the past and old assumptions about what administrators could do or get away with had to be reexamined and administrative styles changed. Making changes of this sort is never easy, and as events would show, O'Donnell did not do it very well.

However, before figuring out how to manage an ambitious faculty during very difficult times, the new president found himself being expertly managed by a charming new faculty member who had not yet set foot in a Notre Dame classroom, Father John A. O'Brien. After having successfully charmed and manipulated a man as administratively astute as O'Hara, O'Brien found O'Donnell to be a very easy mark.

— 2 —

FATHER JOHN A. O'BRIEN AND HIS BISHOPS, 1916–1939

F ather John Anthony O'Brien was a most unforgettable man. He was very good at doing many things, most of all, creating controversy and aggravating ecclesiastical authorities. For that reason, O'Brien enjoyed celebrity status throughout his entire professional life. Among American Catholic priests of his generation, Johnny O'Brien, as his friends called him, was very much a star. For most of the Catholic prelates that had to deal with him, O'Brien was at times a headache, a loose cannon, or an utter rogue.

Born into a Catholic family of solid middle-class respectability and affluence in Peoria, Illinois, in 1893, John A. O'Brien attended parochial schools in that city and enrolled in St. Viator's College in Bourbonnais, Illinois, in 1910. While in college, O'Brien decided to become a priest. Obtaining an A.B. in philosophy in 1913, he entered the seminary program at St. Viator's in the same year. O'Brien finished all requirements for an M.A. in philosophy in 1914, completed his theology studies at St. Viator's, and was ordained as a priest of the Diocese of Peoria in 1916.

Blessed with obvious academic talents, the young Father O'Brien was allowed to spend a year studying Thomistic philosophy at the Catholic University of America. He did not enjoy the experience there, disliked the subject, and in time came to loathe some of its best-known American practitioners. Then at the age of twenty-four, O'Brien was assigned to St. John's Church, Champaign, Illinois, as pastor and also as the Newman chaplain for the Catholic students attending the University of Illinois. Notwithstanding the burden of these responsibilities, O'Brien sought and obtained permission from his bishop to begin doctoral studies in educational psychology at the University of Illinois, which he did in the fall of 1917. Thus began a relationship with the administration, faculty, and students of the University of Illinois that lasted for twenty years. It was the experience of living and working in the environment of a large midwestern state university that shaped O'Brien's interests and commitments during the 1920s and provided him with many causes to serve.

O'Brien completed his studies at the university specializing in speed reading and received his Ph.D. in 1920. As a matter of fact, O'Brien was the first diocesan priest ever to earn a doctorate at the University of Illinois. O'Brien's dissertation, *Silent Reading with Special Reference to Method*, appeared as a book in 1921. While O'Brien was a true believer in the value and efficacy of the discipline of educational psychology, he had no disposition to pursue personal study and research in that field beyond what had been required for his degree. To be sure, O'Brien was fully persuaded that methodology in education as taught and studied at the University of Illinois in 1920 had risen from a condition of "crude empiricism to the solid basis of objective fact, scientifically tested and verified."[1] However, O'Brien was never much tempted to engage in that sort of testing and verifying himself. He much preferred reading about the research and theories of others and then communicating what he believed were the possibilities and implications of that work to audiences that professional and scholarly journals never reached. Throughout his long career, O'Brien was in most things a simplifier and a popularizer. Consequently, on many occasions the sheer audacity of some of his simplifying got him into trouble.

For all of O'Brien's mastery of technical vocabulary and professional jargon, educational psychology was for him only a means to a much more important end. That important end was the saving of souls by winning converts to Catholicism. From the moment of ordination, O'Brien committed himself to an apostolate of presenting the truths of the Catholic religion to the non-Catholic people of America. As he stated many times, his professional specialty was presenting and demonstrating the credentials of Catholic religion. For that life-long activity O'Brien drew heavily upon his academic background in educational psychology. He believed that convert making was more of a science than an art, that there were effective methods of convert making that could be identified, analyzed, taught, learned, and replicated. In this most important work science was a welcome complement to religion.

As a simplifier of some very complex historical, religious, and scientific ideas, frequently O'Brien was carried away by the logic of his purpose to positions that were highly controversial at the time made and appeared just plain silly later. O'Brien's short pamphlet *Modern Psychology and the Mass,* published with all of the appropriate imprimaturs in 1927, is a case in point. He came to his subject with the perspectives of one who had some formal training in psychology and who was very active in the convert movement. O'Brien's purpose in writing *Modern Psychology and the Mass* was to demonstrate that the central act of Catholic worship, the sacrifice of the Mass, was neither meaningless gestures savoring of superstition, primitive magic, nor some unconscious representation of ancient tribal taboos.[2] Much to the contrary, O'Brien insisted, the ceremonies of the Mass were not only sacred and beautiful, but they "exemplified in a superb manner the basic principles of modern psychology in the domain of religious worship." The ceremonies of the Mass were "the supreme achievement of the whole human personality in the rendering of public worship to Almighty God."[3] *There was no way to do it better.*

According to O'Brien, the fundamental laws of mind-body relationships described by modern psychologists found generous recognition and splendid embodiment in the ceremonies of the Mass. Every gesture of the celebrant and every responding movement by members of the congregation had the effect of drawing those present into "an active participation, affording suitable expression for the aroused emotions, thus completing what was called in technical psychology the sensory-motor arch."[4] Since states of consciousness were effected by changes in the conditions of intercranial blood supply,[5] O'Brien contended that body movements in religious worship aroused appropriate mental states and strengthened and intensified religious feelings.[6] However, not all body movements in religious worship were similarly efficacious. The way such body movements were integrated into a total liturgical design was important. Just as there was a world of difference between the discord produced by a novice violinist sawing away on the strings of his instrument and the rare melody teased from the strings by a concert artist, so there was a corresponding difference between "the clangorous reverberations produced on the bodily sounding board by the haphazard movements and bodily swaying of the amateur evangelist" and the "delicate concord of emotional tones" swelling into the great psychic symphony of the Catholic Mass.[7] No race or tribe, concluded O'Brien, was alien to the Esperanto of the liturgy of the Catholic Church.[8]

Indeed, there were many occasions in his life in controversy when Father John O'Brien would say or write more than he meant or perhaps more than he understood. *Modern Psychology and the Mass* was clearly one of them. Yet, whenever this happened, O'Brien never had regrets or thoughts about retraction. Embarrassment was just not an emotion that bothered John A. O'Brien very much. Neither was fear.

— ii —

In 1919, while both a pastor and a student in Champaign, O'Brien joined with some Protestant chaplains at the University of Illinois and obtained the right to offer courses in religion at the university.[9] Such courses could not be taught in buildings owned by or rented from the university, but if offered in privately owned facilities appropriate for instruction of university students and taught by persons holding Ph.D. degrees, such courses would receive from the university the same sort of academic credit accorded secular subjects.[10]

For O'Brien this opportunity to teach the principles of Catholicism at the state university in fully accredited courses was a new and extraordinary articulation of American church-state relations. It was, as O'Brien immediately pointed out to Catholic bishops throughout Illinois, an opportunity to establish a Catholic college at the very door of the state university where there was a ready-made constituency of at least eight hundred and fifty Catholic students. O'Brien wasted no time in seeking out resources for what he chose to call the Catholic Foundation at the University of Illinois.[11]

Obtaining $10,000 from his family, O'Brien purchased and renovated an old house in Champaign for a temporary location for his Catholic Foundation.[12] He had plans prepared for a new and much larger facility, and then organized a fund-raising group of prominent Catholic laymen in early 1922 styled "The Million Dollar Campaign for the Catholic Foundation of the University of Illinois" headquartered in the Hotel Sherman in Chicago.[13]

In fund-raising speeches and brochures, O'Brien insisted that his proposed Catholic Foundation would provide the heart of a Catholic education in a state university setting. In O'Brien's view, a Catholic education consisted essentially in the teaching of the Catholic religion. Remove the teaching of the Catholic religion from the curriculum of the Catholic College, he wrote, "and you would have but a secular education." Instill the teaching of the Catholic religion into the secular curriculum, he continued, "and you preserve the essential features of Catholic education."[14]

As a fund-raising argument for the Catholic Foundation project, O'Brien's concept of what constituted a Catholic education was effective because funds sufficient to begin planning, site acquisition, and site preparation were raised. However, to many in the Church, O'Brien's concept of Catholic education was an absolute anathema. By representing his Catholic Foundation at the University of Illinois as the heart of a Catholic education and by implication as a viable alternative to the expensive system of Catholic schools and colleges in place and growing larger day by day, he casually ignored long-standing arguments about the necessity of educating young people in the totally secure religious and moral environment of Catholic educational institutions.

Though O'Brien had probably never thought through the implications of his argument that general replication of his Catholic Foundation plan at other state universities or for that matter at public elementary and secondary schools throughout the country might make most existing Catholic educational institutions superfluous, several important persons well connected in the Catholic educational establishment did.

In August 1925, O'Brien's Catholic Foundation project was attacked first by Father Herbert C. Noonan, S.J., former president of Marquette University, as a totally inadequate substitute for an authentic Catholic education.[15] In the same month and continuing until January 1926, Claude Heithaus, S.J., a Jesuit scholastic teaching at St. Louis University, began publishing a series of eight articles in *America* denouncing the Catholic Foundation plan. Heithaus accused O'Brien of misrepresenting the intentions of his bishop and of falsely claiming approval of his project by other Illinois prelates. He argued that the Foundation plan was contrary to Catholic educational ideals and contrary to canon law, as well as a threat to all Catholic schools and colleges.[16] No Illinois bishop publicly contradicted Heithaus' charge of misrepresentation.

What Noonan and Heithaus began, others continued. The Catholic Education Association passed a resolution in August 1926 rejecting O'Brien's now infamous concept of Catholic education.[17] Some of the Heithaus articles were reprinted in Rome by the Jesuit newspaper *Civilta Cattolica* in the spring of 1926, and early in the following year those pieces were serialized in three issues of the Vatican daily *L'Osservatore Romano*.[18] The Jesuits — or as O'Brien sardonically styled them many years later, those "sons of Loyola"[19] — had made the enthusiastic young priest from Champaign, Illinois, a celebrity in international clerical circles.

Opposition to O'Brien's Catholic Foundation was by no means limited to some members of the Jesuits. Archbishop Michael J. Curley of Baltimore denounced the plan in March 1926 when it appeared to him to threaten expansion of the parochial school system.[20] On March 8, 1926, Archbishop Curley addressed the International Federation of Catholic

Alumnae meeting in Washington, D.C., and though not mentioning O'Brien by name, attacked the Catholic Foundation plan as "one of the most dangerous movements in the entire field of Catholic education."[21] As reported in the news release of the speech issued by the National Catholic Welfare Conference, Archbishop Curley described the foundation plan "as destructive of our whole educational work of three centuries." The plan was dangerous to the Faith, dangerous to the mind and morals of youth, and opposed to the mind of the Church,[22] that is, in this instance contrary to formal positions taken by the American Catholic hierarchy on the nature of a Catholic education.

Before the attacks of *America* and Archbishop Curley, O'Brien had few public defenders. Although the initial basis of the archbishop's attack had been philosophical, it quickly became personal.[23] He accused O'Brien of saying one thing in public and another in private and of excessive cooperation with ministers and rabbis in common enterprises in Illinois. Curley suggested that O'Brien may have fallen into indifferentism or perhaps even "a sheer denial of Catholic teaching."[24]

O'Brien responded to such innuendos by publicly complaining about harassment by the archbishop and challenging him to file charges against him with the appropriate ecclesiastical authorities. Archbishop Curley obliged. He sent documentation of his relations and problems with O'Brien to the Holy Office in Rome where he expected that curial officials would settle the matter which they seem to have done in early 1927.[25] All parties desisted from further public discussion of this matter.

Bishop Edmund P. Dunne of Peoria, O'Brien's ordinary and protector, in effect, neutralized some of the arguments of the embattled priest's enemies by appointing him superintendent of the Catholic schools of the Diocese of Peoria in the same year. Archbishop Curley could not have been pleased by the resolution of this affair. While His Grace of Baltimore was a forgiving man, he was not a forgetful one. Henceforth, in the Archdiocese of Baltimore and elsewhere as well, O'Brien was very much a marked man. Whenever he spoke or wrote about a subject on which the mind of the Church had been expressed, his words were scrutinized carefully. If O'Brien spoke or wrote in ignorance of received opinions or in contravention of them, he would be answered.

With regard to the status of the Foundation project itself, fearing some sort of stop order from ecclesiastical authorities, O'Brien speeded up construction. He was determined that, no matter what, the project would be completed and it was. A new chapel seating over one thousand people was completed in September 1927 and dedicated a year later. In the fall of 1929 the rest of the buildings in the project were completed, including reading rooms, a social center, a dining room, and dormitory space for

325 male students. How funds for construction of this large and costly project had been raised is not entirely clear. All of O'Brien's energy, ingenuity, and no small part of his recklessness were required. The intense controversy surrounding the Foundation plan during 1925–27 must have made fund raising through the Knights of Columbus or other Catholic organizations very difficult. Even before that controversy became public in 1925, O'Brien had suspended the fund drive in Chicago for several months in early 1922.[26] It was reopened, however, and of the total project cost of $750,000, perhaps no more than $300,000 was raised by the fund-raising campaign or from family and friends.

What is fairly certain is that sometime in June 1927, O'Brien obtained sufficient funds from Bishop Dunne to proceed with construction of the chapel.[27] Using personal and family assets as security, O'Brien went ahead and borrowed sufficient money to complete construction of the rest of the project. Then on February 15, 1928, O'Brien issued and sold 5 percent serial real estate first mortgage gold notes in the amount of $375,000. These 5 percent notes were issued in $500 and $1000 denominations maturing serially between 1938 and 1943. On August 15, 1928, he issued and sold 5.5 percent gold debentures totaling $50,000. These debentures were also issued in $500 and $1,000 denominations maturing serially on annual dates to August 15, 1938.[28]

Money raised by the sale of these notes and debentures were used to repay the funds borrowed to finish the project.[29] O'Brien expected that income from the dining hall and dormitory operations would be sufficient to pay the interest and reduce the principal, as well as provide for proper building maintenance. It is also fairly certain that the individuals and institutions purchasing these bonds and debentures assumed that they had been approved by the bishop and were secured by the faith and credit of the Diocese of Peoria. That assumption was false.

The timing for such a project could not have been worse. O'Brien's friend and protector Bishop Dunne died on October 17, 1929, and the great stock market collapse began a week later. The stock market crash and the Great Depression that followed it impacted severely on O'Brien's ability to service this very large personal debt. Even by cutting back on operating expenses and deferring needed maintenance, Foundation income was insufficient to meet the interest payments due on February 15, 1932.[30] O'Brien's situation was by no means uncommon at that time, and matters did not get critical until note holders organized, obtained attorneys, and pressed for legal relief.

In the meantime, to protect family assets and obtain tax advantages, O'Brien, his family, and their lawyers decided to establish the Elizabeth T. O'Brien Charitable Trust. Over the next several years real estate and other assets including royalties from O'Brien's writings were transferred in and out of the trust as circumstances required.[31] During 1933 and 1934, O'Brien was much distressed by the financial affairs of the Foundation and by his inability to pay the interest due on the notes and debentures. As a matter of fact, in April 1934 while trying to negotiate a higher than normal royalty schedule for one of his books with Benzinger Brothers, he admitted that "I have a very large debt of several hundred thousand on our church plant, it is for that purpose that I am seeking to use the royalty."[32]

By year's end, the prospect of legal action by the note and debenture holders and some sort of forced sale of Foundation property including the chapel in an extremely depressed real estate market grew stronger day by day. The prospect of foreclosure on a functioning Catholic church building was too scandalous to ignore. At this point, Bishop Joseph H. Schlarman, Dunne's successor in Peoria, intervened. In effect the bishop bought the chapel building from O'Brien. He borrowed $75,000 in the summer of 1934 from the Metropolitan Life Insurance Company, secured by a mortgage on the chapel building.[33] Presumably that money was in all or in part used to reduce the overall Foundation debt then being held by O'Brien.

Next, on January 14, 1935, O'Brien and his lawyers established the Newman Foundation at the University of Illinois as an Illinois corporation with Rev. John A. O'Brien as president and conveyed to it all remaining Foundation property. In exchange for receiving the property, this new corporation assumed the obligations of paying the interest due and the principal of the notes and debentures, which by January 1935 had been reduced to $372,000.[34] Under the law, O'Brien and the Newman Foundation were jointly and severally liable for the outstanding debt.[35]

Later in 1935 the newly created Newman Foundation found itself in bankruptcy court. The corporation sought protection under section 72-B of the Bankruptcy Act and prepared a reorganization plan for submission to the U.S. District Court under the provisions of that act. For O'Brien, a moment of truth had arrived.

The first reorganization plan prepared by O'Brien's financial advisor in November 1935 proved to be impractical. It involved negotiating with the note and debenture holders to extend the life of the loans, deferring principal payments, and lowering interest rates to market levels in 1935. This plan was impractical even if the debt holders could have been persuaded to agree because, even assuming an 80 percent occupancy rate in the dormitory facilities at the Newman Foundation, income was insufficient to pay interest at the proposed new and lower rates and cover operating costs.[36]

O'Brien's lawyer put the issue to his client clearly and succinctly: If you "remain personally obligated upon the notes, then there is only one outcome to be expected and that is your eventual bankruptcy."[37] The scandal and loss of property attendant upon such an outcome was too horrendous to consider. Drastic measures had to be taken to reduce the interest and principal payments on the Newman Foundation debt to a level where the income from the dining hall and dormitory operations was sufficient to service it.

O'Brien's lawyers recommended two courses of action. First, the obligations of note and debenture holders were reduced through refinancing. Money was borrowed at lower interest rates for longer periods of time from insurance companies [38] and used to pay deferred interest and redeem past due notes and debentures. Second, the overall debt of the Newman Foundation was reduced by cash transfers from O'Brien family assets. How much money was actually transferred is not clear,[39] but it probably exceeded $100,000 and was sufficient to enable the Newman Foundation to remain open and pay its bills.

The financial crisis at the Newman Foundation had been severe, and O'Brien was fortunate indeed to have weathered it as well as he did. No untoward legal consequences followed from any misleading representations made at the time that the notes and debentures were sold. However, major damage was done to O'Brien's relationship with Bishop Schlarman. The bishop could not forgive O'Brien for burdening the diocese with a heavy debt at a time when none was needed.[40] To be sure, Schlarman could not turn O'Brien out of his place as president of the Newman Foundation, but he could relieve him from all duties as chaplain to the Catholic students at the University of Illinois. The bishop resolved to take that action as soon as the financial affairs of the Newman Foundation were securely settled and when a replacement for O'Brien could be found. Simply stated, Bishop Schlarman wanted O'Brien out of that job and, if possible, out his diocese. For the bishop, that happy prospect did not become realizable until the spring of 1939.

— iii —

While deeply involved in the philosophical and financial controversies of the Foundation project in Champaign and while serving as school superintendent of the Diocese of Peoria, O'Brien never put aside even temporarily what was for him the principal objective of his priestly life — convert making. Despite his continuing celebrity status and many personal and professional problems, he was in his own mind a Catholic priest with a special calling, or as he said on many occasions, an earnest fisher of souls. With that special calling always in mind, O'Brien had convinced himself and tried to convince others that missionary opportunities in the United States during the 1920s were enormous. He put his thoughts on this subject into a collection of essays on the techniques of convert making, *The White Harvest: A Symposium on Methods of Convert Making,* published in 1927.[41]

At the time, he estimated that 60 percent of the entire American population—70 million people—were unaffiliated in an active way with any church. All that was needed to initiate a massive movement of unchurched and lightly churched Americans into a new "Promised Land," declared O'Brien, was the capture of individual reason by a skillful presentation of Catholic truth.[42]

In the face of such favorable "circumstances for convert work, the number of them accepted into the Church each year was pitiably small— only 35,000 during 1927. That number represented slightly less than two converts per year per priest. Since some priests, O'Brien insisted, averaged more than fifty converts a year, it was clear that many simply failed to undertake this very important religious work. Moreover, that failure was derived in large part from the fact that seminary education gave very little curriculum time to the techniques of effective convert making and also because the American hierarchy had neither prepared nor seemed anxious to prepare some sort of a national convert-making strategy.[43]

Even more responsible for this tragic failure to attract converts to the Church was the apathy of the great mass of lay Catholics to convert work. American Catholic laymen, O'Brien asserted, do not "seem to be even dimly conscious of any obligation on their part to spread the Kingdom of Christ in the Souls of men." For O'Brien, the potentialities of convert making realizable through a large-scale organization of American Catholics into an active lay apostolate were incalculable.[44]

Assuming the presence of 10 million adult Catholics in America, if each adult would convert but a single soul for the Catholic Church in the course of one year, O'Brien contended, the conversion of the whole nation would be effected in less than four years. Even with only a mere one million Catholics organized into such a lay apostolate, if each of those Catholics won but a single convert a year, he argued, the conversion of America would be a fact in less than seven years.[45] Indeed, O'Brien had a way of simplifying the most complex phenomena that must have made even his closest friends wince.

O'Brien's collective arraignment of the bishops, priests, and Catholic laity for disinterest and non-support of the convert movement incurred no response from the hierarchy or elsewhere. However, when O'Brien turned his attention to the other and more controversial side of the growth problem of the Catholic Church in America, namely, the reasons for the drift of practicing Catholics out of the Church, a response from ecclesiastical authority was certain. This phenomenon—or leakage as it was called at the time—was difficult to quantify because of unreliable statistics and estimates about American Catholic demography. Those difficulties as well as a limited knowledge of statistical applications and analysis intimidated O'Brien not at all.

As early as 1929, O'Brien had written a short article on the extent of leakage from the Church in America and suggested that the Church's strong prohibition against divorce was a major cause of it. No Catholic journal or paper would publish that article.[46] Next, in late 1931 O'Brien sent questionnaires to about forty priests, bishops, and interested laymen seeking their views about the extent of leakage and the reasons for it. On the basis of the data thus collected, O'Brien prepared a short article in December 1931 for the *American Ecclesiastical Review* arguing that the Church had lost over a half-million Catholics during 1930. At that rate of loss, the future of the Church in America promised to be a short-lived one. For that catastrophic loss, the priests, bishops, and Catholic people of America stood indicted. There was no doubt, wrote O'Brien, that "we have unwittingly and unwillingly contributed vast annual quotas of Catholics to swell the ever growing army of the churchless around us."[47] Once again, driven by the logic of his position, O'Brien said more than he meant and much more than he understood.

Responses to this article were immediate. As might have been expected, the most important one came out of Archbishop Curley's Archdiocese of Baltimore in the person of Father Gerald Shaughnessy, S.M., the leading expert on Catholic religious statistics and demography. O'Shaughnessy was direct and personal. According to Shaughnessy, O'Brien's computations were "unscholarly in that they are based on inaccurate and untrustworthy statistics." O'Brien simply had not proved his case. Moreover, Shaughnessy declared, if O'Brien persisted in maintaining a view of leakage that "attacks the good faith of bishops, priests, and people in one blanket indictment, he must adduce better proof and more scholarly treatment" than was evidenced here.[48]

O'Brien argued no further with Shaughnessy. Perhaps a half-million defectors from the Church in a single year was an exaggeration, but none of his critics denied that leakage to some extent was occurring. The only real controversy about leakage was the amount of it. Within a year, O'Brien was back in print addressing the causes of leakage rather than its extent.[49] He was convinced that the strict moral code of the Catholic

Church—in particular the Church's absolute prohibition of divorce and her teachings on birth control—accounted for most of the leakage. O'Brien attributed 18 percent of defections to divorce-remarriage problems and most of the rest to what he believed was the generally misunderstood official Catholic position on birth control.[50]

— iv —

The issue of birth control was an extremely important public concern in 1933. During a time of severe economic dislocation and very high unemployment, most American Catholics along with the rest of their countrymen did not want or could not afford large families and were not having them. Evidence of widespread birth control practices by Catholics in the United States and in foreign countries was significant; disregard of Church discipline in this matter could not be denied. However, in 1933 the Catholic press abounded with articles and stories about a method of birth limitation that was at once natural and morally acceptable. This method was derived from the researches of two gynecologists—one in Japan and the other in Austria working independently—into the fertility cycles of women. K. Ogino had published his findings in Japan as early as 1923 and H. Knaus' work appeared in German medical journals in 1930.

The Ogino-Knaus theory of birth limitation rested on assumptions and data that normal women experienced periods of fertility and infertility during a menstrual cycle. It was also assumed that these fertile and infertile periods could be predicted and dated. The method depended therefore upon observing periodic continence during fertile periods and normal sexual activity during infertile ones. Discussion of the Ogino-Knaus method in the Catholic press was initiated by the publication of a small book, *The Rhythm*, by Dr. Leo M. Latz in Chicago in 1933. Dr. Latz was a member of the medical faculty of the Loyola University School of Medicine and the book appeared with "Ecclesiastical Approbation in the Archdiocese of Chicago" and also with an introduction by Father Joseph Reiner, S.J. Most of the accounts of the Ogino-Knaus method in the Catholic press came in the form of reviews or as observations on Dr. Latz's book.[51]

Father Reiner's introduction to Latz's *The Rhythm* set the style and tone of public discussions in Catholic circles about the discovery and applications of the Ogino-Knaus method. According to Father Reiner, the discoveries of Ogino and Knaus were monumental. Divine Providence, Reiner wrote, "has come to the assistance of mankind at critical periods by unfolding the secrets of nature." Providence had demonstrated that wonder once again "by enabling scientists to discover the rhythm of sterility and fertility in women. Doctors Ogino and Knaus show us the way out of a difficulty, without compromise of principle."[52] In enthusiasm for the method, O'Brien was only a step or two behind Father Reiner, less cosmic perhaps, but a bit more practical.

In a series of articles published in the *Homiletic and Pastoral Review* during the spring of 1933, O'Brien assured his clerical readers that the Ogino-Knaus discoveries about fertile and sterile periods indicated that whenever there were grave reasons why additional children were inadvisable—mother's health, dire poverty—nature herself had provided a means of family limitation without recourse to any artificial means of birth control.[53] In the same article, O'Brien stated categorically that no violation of Catholic moral law occurred if married Catholics restricted sexual activity to the sterile period of the menstrual cycle.

Elsewhere O'Brien insisted that the Catholic Church did not view self-control or complete abstinence as the only means by which married people could regulate the number or frequency of their children.[54] The value of one of the secondary ends of marriage—promotion of mutual love—was clearly recognized by the Church and due provision had been made for its achievement.[55] On this matter, O'Brien and a few others went further than ecclesiastical authority in America was prepared to follow. Clarification from the theologians of the Catholic University of America was required. Too many hopes had been raised too high. The possibilities of the Ogino-Knaus method had been oversold.

Because so much had been written during 1933 in the Catholic press about the providential gift of the Ogino-Knaus discoveries, the moral and ethical ramifications of the rhythm method had to be explained. The very Reverend John A. Ryan undertook the task of doing so, but Ryan's display of official Catholic reasoning O'Brien found boring and irrelevant. According to Ryan, the moral and theological arguments of the Ogino-Knaus method were simple and conclusive. Limiting marital intercourse to the sterile period was in itself quite as lawful as intercourse during pregnancy or when the wife had passed the menopause.[56] In all three such cases, conception was impossible and so the primary aim of marriage and intercourse, that is, procreation of offspring, was impossible. However in all three of those cases, Ryan declared, one or both of the secondary ends of marriage and intercourse, that is, promotion of mutual love and satisfaction of concupiscence, were attainable. Either of those secondary ends was sufficient reason for performing the marital act. Yet, one must always bear in mind that the secondary ends of marriage were not only secondary, they were also subordinate. Ryan sharply dissented from the view that sensual satisfaction was as important, normal, and on the same plane of nobility and as worthy a motive as procreation of offspring.[57]

The simple and direct meaning of Ryan's clarification was that even though restriction of intercourse to the safe period was not in itself wrong, the practice was not justifiable for all couples at all times. If the practice were adopted by free mutual agreement for the purpose of preventing the birth of any and all children without a serious justifying reason, such as danger of death or grave injury, or degrading poverty, it was surely sinful, perhaps mortally so. If the practice were directed toward limiting the family to two or three children, it was at least venially sinful.[58] While Ryan's clarification of the moral aspects of periodic abstinence according to Ogino-Knaus calendars had not been written for O'Brien's benefit alone, it was a very long way indeed from O'Brien's contention that the Ogino-Knaus method was legitimate birth control according to natural law in harmony with Catholic morality. O'Brien neither completely understood Ryan's clarification nor was he in any way persuaded from his own views by it.

In future pamphlets and books, O'Brien simplified virtually all of Ryan's distinctions and reservations. For O'Brien, not only was the Ogino-Knaus method morally acceptable, but it was medically safe and unerringly effective. During the 1930s, it would appear that several distinct voices spoke to American Catholics for the Church on the Ogino-Knaus method. While O'Brien was only one of those voices, his was always loud, clear, and unambiguous, and because of his celebrity status he probably reached the largest audiences.

— v —

O'Brien's intense and enduring commitment to convert making underlay virtually everything he thought about and did. The experience of doing convert work in the Champaign area had taught him that potential converts were moved more by appeals to intellect than to emotion. According to O'Brien, faith should never be represented as resting on authority or as being opposed in any way to reason or to the intelligence of young people. Moreover, familiarity with modern scientific thought and contemporary intellectual movements was absolutely essential for successful missions among university students. He insisted that if preachers of the Christian gospel were to touch modern minds, such preachers had first to know what that modern mind was thinking.[59] In the late 1920s that modern mind seemed to be doing a lot of thinking about the religious implications of the concept of human evolution.

Like so many of his contemporaries, O'Brien had been intrigued by the Scopes trial and had followed newspaper and magazine accounts of it with great interest. In the issues raised by this trial and in the enormous publicity attendant upon it, O'Brien saw great new convert making opportunities. To make the most of such opportunities, O'Brien believed that first one would have to demonstrate the relative open-mindedness of the Catholic Church on any real or imagined conflicts between modern science and biblical revelation.

As early as 1930 in an article appearing in the *American Ecclesiastical Review* and in a twenty-four page pamphlet, *Evolution and Religion,* brought out by the Paulist Press in the same year and in a book also entitled *Evolution and Religion* published in the Century Catholic College Text series by the Century Company in 1932, O'Brien strode unhesitatingly into the philosophical and theological thicket of conflicts between religion and science.[60] In all of these publications, O'Brien made a case for acceptance by Christians of the general findings of anthropology, archaeology, paleontology, psychology, and other related disciplines. O'Brien drew heavily with acknowledgement upon both the personal correspondence and published works of a French authority on Darwinism and religion, Canon Henri Dorlodot, and also upon the condemned evolution doctrines[61] of the late nineteenth-century excommunicated English scientist and Modernist religious writer, St. George Jackson Mivart.

In his pamphlet, O'Brien distinguished between what he called the fact of evolution—a progressive development from simple to higher and more complex forms of life—which most scientists accepted, and the particular causal agency of natural selection advanced by Darwin to explain evolution, which commanded no such unanimity of scientific opinion.[62] Following Mivart, Dorlodot, and H. H. Newman—a professor of zoology at the University of Illinois—O'Brien recognized that while natural selection as a causal theory explaining the origin of species presented great problems for some scientists as well as for most Christians, the fact of evolution, the age of the earth, and the antiquity of life on it should not. There was nothing in the findings of paleontology that should "disturb any principle of the Christian faith or of the Biblical revelation when the latter is properly understood."[63] Again, following Mivart and Dorlodot, he was ready to argue that far from minimizing the Creator's power, the concept of evolution gave a grand and more exhalted manifestation of it.[64]

In 1930, O'Brien wanted very much to believe that the official Catholic Church was open-minded on scientific questions and that it would welcome every wise thought and useful discovery whatever the origin of such thoughts and discoveries might be.[65] However, the strength of that conviction was severely tested by the difficulties experienced while trying to obtain an imprimatur for this pamphlet. At first, the Paulist Press approached the Chancery of the Archdiocese of New York for the required approvals. So confident were they about getting an imprimatur that they proceeded with the first printing of covers carrying a notice that one had been obtained from Archbishop Hayes.[66] It is not clear whether the censors in the New York Chancery were aware how closely O'Brien had followed Mivart and that recantations had been exacted between 1895 and 1899 from an English bishop as well as from French and American clerical writers for publicly supporting Mivart's position that evolution, not natural selection, was a principle of nature compatible with Christian belief.[67]

In any case, there was a great deal of nervousness about recommending an imprimatur. After a quick study of the pamphlet and the supporting expert testimony submitted by the Paulist Press, the Chancery responded in a highly tortuous fashion by stating that although O'Brien's work was probably orthodox, his treatment was quite a departure from the orthodox view.[68] The Chancery suggested that instead of proceeding with the matter and seeking an imprimatur from Archbishop Hayes, a better strategy would be to try to obtain one from O'Brien's brand-new Ordinary, Joseph H. Schlarman, bishop of Peoria.[69]

Joseph Mendez, director of the Paulist Press, recognized sound advice when he received it. In the interest of maintaining a good relationship with the Chancery in New York, Mendez urged O'Brien to get the needed approval from Peoria.[70] In office only a few months, Bishop Schlarman saved all concerned from embarrassment by quickly issuing an imprimatur. Much relieved, Mendez reprinted the covers with Schlarman's imprimatur and released the pamphlet.

More frustrated than intimidated by his experience in dealing with ecclesiastical bureaucracy, O'Brien was of no mind to drop a subject that interested him and also one to which he had devoted so much time and energy. While preparing the pamphlet for the Paulist Press, he had published articles on the subject of evolution theory and religion in *Our Sunday Visitor* and had been hard at work on a book-length manuscript on that subject for the Catholic Text series published by the Century Company. This book, *Evolution and Religion,* was O'Brien's most serious effort to do scholarly writing.

In general, as published, *Evolution and Religion* extended and amplified what he had said in his pamphlet. As a matter of fact, the pamphlet was incorporated as the first chapter of the book. While denying any intent to persuade anyone to accept or reject evolution as a validated scientific hypothesis, O'Brien proceeded to argue very strongly for the evolutionist point of view by reporting that "convergent data from many fields are amply sufficient to establish evolution as a generalization of science accepted by over 99 percent of the authorities in those fields."[71]

In writing *Evolution and Religion,* there were few veterans of the nineteenth- and early-twentieth-century wars between science and religion that O'Brien overlooked. As in the pamphlet, O'Brien depended heavily upon Mivart, Dorlodot, and H. H. Newman. The enemies of understanding were also identified. They were the presumptuous theologians of all denominations who mistook their own opinions for the word of God.[72] For such persons, O'Brien had little use. He used even stronger language against them in another place. While reviewing Father Ernest C. Messenger's *Evolution and Theology: The Problem of Man's Origin* for *Commonweal* on March 9, 1932, O'Brien complained bitterly about that species of theologian who hysterically tried by a "factitious flourish of authority" to compel others to accept their opinions.[73]

As originally written, O'Brien's manuscript had been divided into ten chapters. When published, the book appeared with only the first nine chapters. On the advice of Father John M. Cooper, an anthropologist at the Catholic University of America, a chapter of sixteen pages entitled "Origin of the Soul" had been put aside. After having read that chapter, Cooper believed that although it contained nothing that had been formally condemned by Church authorities, there was material in the chapter open to misinterpretation and likely to create difficulties for the book and also for the author.[74] While Cooper did not specify precisely what parts of the chapter were dangerous, O'Brien's critical remarks about theologians along with his central point that the question of the origin of the soul was "far from being a definitely closed or settled one"[75] were challenges which the reigning theological authorities at the Catholic University of America in 1932 would not have let pass. O'Brien had trespassed into well-protected territory and could not have escaped from such a foray without wounds.

By denying the possibility of what he called some refined form of generationism as an explanation of soul-origin as opposed to the common teaching of direct and immediate creative acts by God of every individual human soul, O'Brien suggested that some theologians were in effect limiting God's infinity and omnipotence. Where is the theologian, questioned

O'Brien, "who would seek by injunction to limit the expression of His power or restrict Him by syllogisms from acting in any manner other than that ordained by human minds or envisaged in the childhood traditions of the race."[76]

If that sort of explication of theological tradition was not enough to provoke a response from the American Catholic theological establishment, nothing was. In the same pages where O'Brien berated contemporary theologians, he also gave some attention to Thomistic philosophers. O'Brien implied that many of the Thomists that he had read were really closet evolutionists. The meaning that Thomists had applied to the word creation with regard to the soul, he asserted, did not differ in any substantial way from the meaning scientists attached to the word evolution.[77]

Without the radical nature of the deleted chapter, the rest of the book presented no special problems for ecclesiastical authorities. As O'Brien stated in his application to the Chancellor of the Peoria Diocese for an imprimatur, the book was actually more limited in scope than his earlier pamphlets, and in it he had carefully avoided any of the "problems which would be somewhat ticklish, such as the problem of the emergence of consciousness and the problem of the human soul."[78]

Because the book came into the marketplace equipped with an imprimatur, a preface by a retired Catholic seminary professor of philosophy, an introduction by a scripture professor and president of a Catholic seminary, and a foreword by the head of the department of Zoology at the University of Illinois,[79] it was generally well received in Catholic circles. Though the Jesuit periodical *America* ignored the book, a sometime colleague from the Newman Foundation in Champaign reviewed it for *Commonweal*. Father J. Elliot Ross pointed out what would have been obvious to most informed readers of *Evolution and Religion*. There was really not much new and nothing really controversial in the book. Ross claimed that by 1932 inorganic evolution was generally accepted in Catholic circles, and organic evolution, in spite of some opposition, was generally regarded as not essentially in conflict with Church teachings.[80]

O'Brien had dealt only with old issues and had rehearsed old arguments which was after all probably appropriate for a college text. Though O'Brien received many letters praising his work from Catholic friends and admirers,[81] he knew the truth about himself and what he had done. Already in serious trouble with his bishop over the financial crisis at the Catholic Foundation, he needed peace, not another war. Those presumptuous theologians who had assumed for themselves the sole right to read the mind of God had frightened him off. Sometime, perhaps after reflecting on the paucity and perfunctory character of the reviews of *Evolution and Religion* appearing in the Catholic press, O'Brien decided that next time, if there were a next time, things would go differently. Of course, there was a next time; and indeed, things did go very differently.

— vi —

For almost fifteen years O'Brien had been a party to a succession of controversies on behalf of one cause or another. Too often, O'Brien had annoyed or offended important men and powerful interests in the American Catholic Church. Sooner or later his habit of overstatement and exaggeration was bound to get him into trouble with ecclesiastical authority. That O'Brien should find himself in difficulty with the Holy Office in 1935 was not surprising considering how close to censure he had come with his pamphlets and book on evolution; that he would be disciplined for writing about the traditional theological concept of hell was unexpected.

In June 1934 while in the midst of complex financial negotiations for the Catholic Foundation and while still very active in the convert-making field, O'Brien published a short commonplace article in *The Homiletic and Pastoral Review* urging priests engaged in convert work to adopt what he described as a saner treatment of hell when speaking to prospective converts.[82] The idea that reprobates would suffer the pains of material hell fire for an eternity, O'Brien believed, struck many prospective converts as too severe to attribute to an all-loving, beneficent God. The traditional doctrine of eternal damnation and hell fire offended reasonable judgment, and O'Brien contended that the spiritual conquest of America by the Catholic Church had been much delayed because of it.

In this article, O'Brien did not himself try to deal with the theology of the concept of hell. Instead, he quoted from a book by Sir Arnold Lunn, who had argued that Catholics were free to reject the view that individual souls were eternally damned and that the fires of hell were real. Using Lunn as an authority, O'Brien argued the importance of being able to separate matters of faith from those of speculation. Much harm could be and had been done, he added, by presenting the teaching on hell with a severity not warranted by official pronouncements of the Church.[83]

Three months later, the eminent professor of theology from Mount St. Alphonsus, Father Francis J. Connell, C.Ss.R., took the time and the trouble to respond in the same journal to O'Brien's piece on a saner treatment of hell. Connell was very careful not to criticize Lunn for ignorance of theological details.[84] No such consideration was given to O'Brien.

Connell made very clear that metaphorical interpretations of the fires of hell or a concept of hell without eternal suffering were heretical ideas or very close to being so.[85] In Connell's professional judgment, there was simply no scriptural warrant for the Lunn-O'Brien view. Moreover, Connell provided O'Brien with an explanation of the role of Catholic theologians in the Church and the basis of their authority. Clearly, because of what O'Brien had written about presumptuous theologians in *Evolution and Religion* and elsewhere, Connell had no doubts at all that he needed one.

While theologians possessed no teaching authority in the Church in their own right, Connell admitted, they were reliable and recognized witnesses of what the teaching authority proposed.[86] If Catholic theologians during the course of several centuries unanimously held that a certain doctrine was an article of faith or an indubitable theological truth, Catholics were obliged to accept their decision and assent to the doctrine. Moral unanimity among theologians, stated Connell, was sufficient in this matter of a concept of hell. If any Catholic writer proposed a view that was contrary to the long-standing and unhesitating consent of all those who had written on this particular matter, Connell added, the strength of the argument of the standing consensus was in no way impaired.[87] In what appeared to be a special message to O'Brien, Connell declared, "The Catholic Church has never made any compromise with the doctrine of eternal hell fire in order to make it less repugnant to her own members or to those outside of the Fold."[88]

Connell's discourse on the role of theologians in the Church and his attribution of heretical ideas about hell to O'Brien hurt and angered the beleaguered priest from Champaign. Notwithstanding all of the problems facing him at the Newman Foundation, on this matter O'Brien simply could not turn the other cheek. He decided to challenge Connell in his own field. For such a challenge, however, O'Brien needed expert help, and he knew exactly where to find it. Having read several of St. George Mivart's books and articles on evolution, O'Brien was well aware that Mivart had also engaged in a celebrated and bitter controversy over traditional Catholic views of hell and eternal damnation in 1892–93. In the end, Mivart's moderate views about hell were rejected by ecclesiastical authority and his articles on that subject were placed on the Index. That outcome deterred O'Brien not at all from initiating and vigorously pursuing the same sort of controversy in 1934–35 or from using ideas, arguments, and details borrowed from Mivart's proscribed articles.[89] Because of the availability of Mivart's work in the University of Illinois libraries, O'Brien needed less than a month to prepare and write a fourteen-page response to his adversary's article. In "Father Connell's Ideas of Hell," O'Brien tried very hard to be scholarly and packed his work with all of the knowledge of scripture and of all other authorities that he could collect from friends, specialists, and the University of Illinois libraries. O'Brien listed no fewer than fourteen points in Connell's argument that were open to objection.[90] Also, in what turned out to be his most direct attack upon Connell's position, he argued that his opponent's notion of the role of theologians in the Church and their authority on doctrinal matters was not sustainable by historical fact. To make that argument, O'Brien listed twenty points, ranging from ideas about the physical location of heaven and hell to the teaching that the Pope, *jure divino,* must be a civil ruler which theologians had held to be true for long periods of time but later were reversed or rejected.[91]

What had begun as a minor correction of some alleged misstated theological details had escalated into a full-blown controversy about the role and authority of theologians in the Church. It would appear that on this matter of a saner concept of hell, O'Brien's day of judgment had come. In this controversy O'Brien had engaged one of the most learned and well-connected doctors in the American Catholic Church. A safe and sound escape from this encounter was impossible.

In two months' time Connell wrote a carefully prepared fifteen-page refutation of all of O'Brien's arguments on the doctrine of hell which he mistakenly hoped would put an end to this entire matter. First, Connell denied the accuracy of the title of O'Brien's article. The theologian insisted that his personal opinions about the concept of hell were not at issue. What Connell had argued against in O'Brien's moderated view of hell was no more and no less than the long-standing, undoubted doctrinal position of the Holy Catholic Church. Personal speculations, Connell insisted, were not involved in this controversy in any way. Next, Connell berated O'Brien for sloppy scholarship and urged him to designate exactly the passages in scripture or in other authorities under discussion. O'Brien's habit of asserting that St. Augustine said this or St. Thomas said that "tends to favor inexactness."[92] In any case, even when passages were properly referenced, Connell declared, O'Brien usually misread or misinterpreted them.[93] Clearly, Doctor O'Brien was no theologian. What followed thereafter was a point by point rebuttal of O'Brien's position.

Before concluding his article, Connell returned to the business of the role of theologians in the Church. It was from theologians, wrote Connell, "that future priests and bishops derive their knowledge of Catholic teachings."[94] Theologians were the voice of the teaching Church. To dispel all ambiguities and make matters perfectly clear, Connell stated directly for O'Brien's benefit, that "The voice of the teaching Church is the proximate rule of faith for all Catholics, learned as well as ignorant, priests as well as laity."[95] One of those "factitious flourishes of authority" about which O'Brien had written so derisively had been displayed, and this controversy was supposed to be over. However, O'Brien chose not to heed that authority however threateningly flourished; he did not know that he had been refuted or that he had been warned.

Before responding to Connell's article, O'Brien felt compelled to answer a less sophisticated attack on his theological knowledge and reasoning. Father Albert A. Chevalier, O.M.I., accused O'Brien of reviving the condemned opinions of Modernism and Americanism and of adopting a near-Protestant attitude toward theological authority.[96] By elevating private opinions—his own—over those of recognized theological authorities, Chevalier insisted, O'Brien had revived and repeated some of the errors of sixteenth-century heretics. In Chevalier's judgment, O'Brien was a would-be theologian who had ventured beyond the limits of his own knowledge and ability. O'Brien's misunderstanding of the concept of hell and his fierce attachment to that misunderstanding was unpardonable in a Catholic priest.[97]

O'Brien simply denied Chevalier's charges of Modernism and Americanism and implied that Father Chevalier was closer to near-Protestant attitudes about theological authority than he was. By pushing reason out of theological inquiry, O'Brien suggested, Chevalier stood more deeply in Luther's shadow than himself. In any case, O'Brien argued, the Church gets her teachings from God, not from theologians. As far as faith was concerned, theologians got their teachings from the Church. For all Catholics, O'Brien declared, the rule of faith "is founded in the public authority of the Church, not in the private views of Doctors however learned."[98] O'Brien could give as good as he had received.

Chevalier was only a minor player in this affair, and O'Brien spent three months writing a two-part article which he expected would be the last word in this controversy. His expectation was reasonable because the editors of the *Homiletic and Pastoral Review* had become very nervous about the way the controversy had escalated. Certainly the involvement of a theologian as eminent, influential, and well connected as Connell should have made them apprehensive. Encounters with such powerful guardians of orthodoxy and doctrinal purity in the post-Americanist and post-Modernist American Church were risky matters indeed. The editors, Fathers C. J. Callan, O.P., and J. A. McHugh, O.P., agreed to publish one more rebuttal from O'Brien and then close off the pages of their journal to further discussion of this subject.[99] For Callan and McHugh, hell had become too hot.

Believing that he was to have the last word in this controversy, O'Brien was not disposed to be either magnanimous or compassionate toward his adversary. He affected a sincere regard for his opponent's learning and competence, observing that he had defended a very weak case as well as could be done.[100] On the substantive matter of the proper concept of hell, O'Brien insisted that Catholics worshipped no Moloch but rather a God of love and mercy. Being all-holy and good, God must hate and punish sin, but He would not be angry forever. The Holy Church, O'Brien concluded, had not made and would not make solemn pronouncements about God punishing human souls with excruciating tortures. The Church "knows what harm can be done to faith and to souls by picturing God not only as undivine, but as actually inhuman and worse than brutal."[101]

With regard to what had become the most serious issue in this controversy, that is, O'Brien's observations about the authority of theologians, O'Brien was candid. Connell had complained about his lack of deference for the non-definitive statements of the Church—the views of theologians—and to that charge, O'Brien pleaded guilty. It was true that he had criticized the views of theologians when they spoke for themselves as theologians, even though there had been agreement among them for a long period of time. However, "It is clear that majorities were often wrong, even in theology." In any case, theologians "do not constitute the *Teaching Church,* but rather belong to the *Learning Church,* and hence not all of their pronouncements about what is *de fide* are official." O'Brien insisted that his criticisms had not been directed against all theologians, but only against those who have "indulged in exaggeration, imaginative speculations, lurid descriptions, and heartless assertions that would make God appear as a monster."[102] Once again, O'Brien had said much more than the situation required.

Indeed, O'Brien had the last word on this controversy in the pages of the *Homiletic and Pastoral Review,* but the final disposition of the matter was to be left to others. In an earlier article attacking O'Brien's position on the concept of hell, Connell had denied any intention of "casting discredit on Dr. O'Brien's sincerity."[103] After O'Brien's final word on hell and theologians had been published, it would appear that Connell and others decided that a little discredit was exactly what the situation called for. O'Brien was denounced to the Holy Office as a propagator and defender of rash (*sententiae temerariae*) and unsound theological opinions. The Holy Office reviewed the case and in the end agreed with the charges against O'Brien. They proceeded to discipline O'Brien and also the editors of the *Homiletic and Pastoral Review* who had accepted and published the offending articles. O'Brien and the editors were required to publish apologies and full recantations of three specific theological points relating to the concept of hell. Moreover, O'Brien was obliged to admit publicly in print that he had been unaware of what he had done. He had not known that he had taught and defended objectionable opinions.[104]

O'Brien's recantation was dated June 22, 1935, and appeared in the August number of the *Homiletic and Pastoral Review.* O'Brien's association with that journal ended, as did his career as a speculative theologian. For a priest who had devoted so much of his life to dispelling anti-Catholic myths about the inquisition and infallibility, the action of ecclesiastical authority against him was devastating. In a university town such as Champaign, O'Brien's courage was and would continue to be much admired,[105] but what had happened to him did little to support his credibility or promote his mission in that community.

— vii —

Notwithstanding O'Brien's brief and very humiliating experience as an amateur theologian in 1934–35, he was a well-known, popular religious writer. His pamphlets on marriage, birth control, the conversion of prominent intellectuals, and the role of the priesthood in a changing world all had been commercially successful. Given O'Brien's desperate need for money during those years, the idea of a major Catholic popular apologetics book for a mass market came very easily to him. He discussed such a project with Bishop John F. Noll of Fort Wayne and the editors of Our Sunday Visitor Press. Noll and the editors were easily convinced that a very large market for Catholic popular apologetics existed and that O'Brien was the person to exploit it. The bishop knew that O'Brien was a skillful phrase turner and that he wrote quickly and never missed deadlines. In view of the vast market available, those qualities counted for more with Noll than O'Brien's recent recantation and public apology for teaching and defending objectionable theological opinions. All things considered, Noll decided that O'Brien was a proper person to do a book intended to explain the principles of Catholicism to a mass market. *The Faith of Millions,* begun in 1937 and published by Our Sunday Visitor Press in 1938, became O'Brien's most commercially successful work.

Noll and O'Brien hoped that this book would do for the present generation of American Catholics what Cardinal Gibbons' apologetics classic *The Faith of Our Fathers,* published first in 1876, had done for previous ones. In a book such as this where so many controversial subjects had to be examined and explained the problem of how to be doctrinally correct, readable for the entire American Catholic community, and interesting to prospective converts was not easily resolved. O'Brien knew how to make anything readable and was very experienced in dealing with prospective converts. A theologian or church historian, he was not; and he certainly should have known it. He had to figure out some way of obtaining insurance against accidental doctrinal error and possible renewal of harassment from the American Catholic theological establishment. Finding ways to get that sort of insurance turned out to be easy, if not entirely honest.

First, O'Brien took much more than the idea of a title for his own book from Cardinal Gibbons' *The Faith of Our Fathers.* He simply borrowed sections of Gibbons' book without specific citation and presented what he had borrowed as his own work. To be sure, O'Brien modernized and improved the writing style of the cardinal's book, but he plagiarized much of its substance. One could hardly fall into accidental theological error on such controversial subjects as papal infallibility and indulgences by heavily plagiarizing from the late cardinal.

An egregious example of O'Brien's plagiarism is in the matter of Gibbons' treatment of unworthy popes. Writing in 1876, Gibbons admitted that perhaps five or six pontiffs in the entire history of the Church had been unworthy men. However, Gibbons argued, "Seventy-nine of the two hundred and sixty-one that sat on the Chair of St. Peter are invoked upon our altars as saints eminent for their holiness." That ratio of good to bad was very good: "We have forty-three virtuous to one bad Pope, while there was a Judas Iscariot among the twelve Apostles."[106]

Writing in his book in 1938, O'Brien dealt with the same problem with the same words even down to the number of popes appropriate for the year, 1876. "Out of two hundred and sixty-one who have sat upon the chair of Peter, seventy-nine are invoked upon our altars as saints of God because of their eminent holiness." To complete the unattributed borrowing, O'Brien added, "It is remembered that one of the twelve chosen by Christ himself was a Judas Iscariot."[107]

Second, obtaining prior public endorsement of the book from powerful members of the American Catholic hierarchy was another way of avoiding new encounters with the likes of Ryan, Shaughnessy, Connell, or others in or close to the American Catholic theological establishment. When O'Brien's *The Faith of Millions* appeared in 1938, it carried an imprimatur from Bishop Noll, a preface by William Cardinal O'Connell, and an introduction by Dennis Cardinal Dougherty. Who would dare suggest that anything in a book thus endorsed could be in any way theologically suspect?

During its very long life *The Faith of Millions* was an outstanding commercial success, running through twenty-seven editions and translated into nine languages. The book earned a great deal of money for Our Sunday Visitor Press, fostered a long-standing business relationship between Bishop Noll and O'Brien, and contributed significantly to the large personal fortune amassed by O'Brien over the next thirty years.[108] Yet this commercial success came too late to affect the refinancing of the Newman Foundation debt or repair O'Brien's now dreadful relationship with Bishop Schlarman. The outcome of the controversy with Connell simply intensified the bishop's growing distrust and dislike of O'Brien.

— viii —

Living and working in the environs of the University of Illinois for so many years, O'Brien could not avoid discussions about the nature and importance of scholarship and scientific research even if he personally was not to be a serious practitioner of either. Out of these discussions, which included several with David Kinley, president of the University of Illinois, came the realization that very few American Catholics held teaching or research appointments at that university. Kinley regretted this situation, insisting that discrimination was virtually no factor and that the university would be delighted to consider qualified Catholics for positions if they would only apply.[109] Unaware that he was resurrecting a question that had been addressed several times before, O'Brien decided to try to find out why more American Catholics did not qualify as scholars and why so few who did qualify failed to seek employment at the University of Illinois.

O'Brien began his critique and analysis of American Catholic underachievement in scholarship and science with an action that was in itself an exemplification of the whole problem. As a Catholic priest whose past encounters with religious authorities on doctrinal and moral issues had been painful and embarrassing, O'Brien did not proceed with this project without first obtaining prior approval and an endorsement from leading members of the American Catholic hierarchy. After what he had been through with the Jesuits, Archbishop Curley, Connell, and others, O'Brien would not dare venture into such potentially stormy waters without having on board as pilots some archbishops and bishops. He approached two distinguished ones early on and found them willing. Archbishop John T. McNicholas, O.P., of Cincinnati agreed to provide a preface, and Bishop Hugh C. Boyle of Pittsburgh promised to write an introduction for a book on this subject.

Thus protected against future clerical squalls, O'Brien contacted persons whom he believed were prominent Catholic scientists, educators, social scientists, writers, and journalists, and obtained commitments from fifteen of them to prepare short papers on the general subject of American Catholics and scholarship. O'Brien's personal contributions to the project included four short articles of his own, brief summarizing introductions to each of the solicited articles, and a very brief final summation. When completed, the book, *Catholics and Scholarship: A Symposium on the Development of Scholars,* was presented as if the papers in it had been read at a symposium and critiqued by participants. No such symposium had ever been held. The papers were collected by O'Brien, edited in a haphazard fashion, and sent off to Our Sunday Visitor Press in the summer of 1938 for publication in early 1939. O'Brien promised to donate all royalties for the support of a proposed National Catholic Council on Research to encourage scholarship and research by Catholics.[110] In the end, not many people read the book and there were very few royalties for any purpose.

Apart from descriptions of some on-going projects, rehearsals of personal experiences, and complaints about a lack of money and resources, there was very little in *Catholics and Scholarship* that was new. Except for a few extreme statements by O'Brien and a frank and forceful indictment of some of the values and many of the practices of contemporary Catholic higher education by Jerome G. Kerwin, the book did not move the subject of Catholics and scholarly achievement very far. Moreover, the quality and depth of analysis displayed in the book was perhaps a measure of how serious the problem of American Catholic intellectual and scholarly performance really was.

Catholics and Scholarship was seriously flawed in two ways. First, it was poorly edited and marred by printing errors. Second, the book presented a totally inadequate notion of what scholarship was. For O'Brien and for most but not all of the other contributors to the volume, scholarship was scientific research only. Unstated but strongly implied throughout was the idea that research in the natural, life, and engineering sciences was more important certainly, and perhaps safer than undertaking studies in humanities and social science disciplines.

O'Brien's contributions to *Catholics and Scholarship* were mainly concerned with what he viewed as a gross under-representation of American

Catholics on the faculties of the great state universities of the United States. In O'Brien's view, Catholics paid their full share of the taxes that supported such institutions, but they played virtually no role in the administration or in the teaching and research activities carried on in them.[111] American Catholics, O'Brien concluded, had "a rare genius for aloofness from the public tax-supported institutions which are so largely directing scholarly thought in America."[112]

According to O'Brien, the consequences of that genius for aloofness had been disastrous. The prestige of Catholics in America was very low. Catholic influence upon American public opinion was minimal. To the majority of Americans, in O'Brien's judgment, Catholics appeared fit only to be "hewers of wood and drawers of water—just a step higher in the intellectual scale than the Salvation Army."[113] To be sure, American Catholics had more than a proper share of "pugilists, star football players, home run swatters, and child movie actors," but no more than half a dozen professors of distinction in all fields of scholarship in any university or college public, private, or Catholic.[114]

O'Brien saw the need for a research orientation for American Catholic universities and colleges as essential. The reputation of an educational institution, he continued, depended in final analysis "not upon buildings or equipment, much less upon its athletic teams, but upon the scholarship of its faculty."[115] Expanding on ideas about the important role of research in major universities borrowed with full attribution from an article in *The Tabloid Scientist* by his old friend Father John Cooper, O'Brien questioned the integrity of the entire system of Catholic higher education. Unless the faculties of American Catholic universities and colleges did research themselves, he wrote, they could not even claim to be educators.[116] In view of the atrocious research record of the American Catholic professorate, O'Brien wondered "just what our Catholic educational institutions have done to rate the name of colleges and universities."[117]

Though O'Brien offered no special insights into why American Catholics appeared to be so apathetic about learning and scholarship, his contributors suggested that perhaps certain attitudes and cultural characteristics exhibited by many American Catholics were at the root of the problem.

For example, George N. Kramer, a professor of history at Loyola University at Los Angeles and a free-lance writer, argued that Catholic intellectuals and scholars were in short supply because American Catholics were simply not interested in producing them. He supported that assertion by arguing that Catholic laymen engaged in educational work at

Catholic universities and colleges were underpaid, overworked, and denied the leisure, facilities, and means required to do scholarly work.[118]

Even more damaging to the cause of scholarship at Catholic universities and colleges than the lack of resources and time was the fact that neither the work itself nor the persons performing it were highly valued. Lay professors at Catholic universities and colleges were generally without influence on the policies of those institutions and not respected by the larger Catholic community. According to Kramer, such men and women were without honor among their own people, and like barren unwatered trees produced nothing.[119]

Jerome G. Kerwin, an associate professor of political science at the University of Chicago and also perhaps the most eminent and best-known American Catholic scholar of that time, echoed some of Kramer's sentiments. Kerwin attributed the scarcity of American Catholic scholars to a deliberate rejection of scholarship and university teaching as careers by the best and the brightest of that community. Catholic students were more interested in pursuing lines of work that brought the quickest and largest monetary gains.[120] Business, law, medicine, and dentistry were far more financially attractive than teaching and research. Catholic students inclined toward a scholarly life usually entered the priesthood or religious orders, and once committed to that vocation, scholarly or scientific development had to give way to priorities set by bishops and religious superiors.[121]

Kerwin believed also that Catholic educators had stretched available intellectual and material resources beyond their limits. In his judgment, there were just too many Catholic colleges and universities competing for students and resources. He estimated that no more than 40 percent of existing Catholic colleges in 1938 were capable of undertaking more than junior college work.[122]

Furthermore, most of the colleges counted in that 40 percent were addicted to the worst sort of athleticism. In order to field winning teams, too many Catholic colleges seemed ready and perhaps even eager to lower scholarship standards and allow athletic practices not tolerated at the best secular institutions. It was the twin evils of too many vocational and preprofessional courses in Catholic college curricula and uncontrolled athleticism that had brought Catholic colleges and universities to their present level of mediocrity.[123]

Another serious problem at most Catholic colleges were assumptions about individual student irresponsibility and potential antisocial behavior that underlay rules regulating student life at such places. Kerwin questioned, "How long are our Catholic colleges going to be run like institutions for children and delinquents." He insisted that at long last the time had come to terminate the system of "prefects of discipline, official snoopers, faculty spies, student stool pigeons, and the multifarious rules and regulations which . . . [led] to assorted subterfuges, conspiracies, and minor villainies." If young people who had reached the age of seventeen or eighteen years could not conduct themselves with prudence and discretion in the college community, elaborate rules, no matter how ingenious or systematically enforced, would not make a difference. Correcting the behavior of social misfits was no proper application of college time and energy. Paternalism would never be a substitute for personal responsibility and self-reliance.[124]

Finally, Kerwin urged Catholic college administrators to seek out contacts and find ways of cooperating with secular universities. Catholic colleges were not improved by demoniacal denunciations of secular education. Kerwin hoped for the development of some sort of affiliation between the better Catholic colleges and the great private and public American universities in the image of such affiliations presently operative at Toronto and Oxford.[125] In the end, Kerwin assigned the major responsibility for American Catholic underachievement in scholarship and science to the weaknesses of Catholic higher education. The Church and the country needed Catholic scholars. Academic leadership, courage, time, and money would be required to produce them.

Neither O'Brien's extreme statements about whether most Catholic colleges were worthy of the name or Kerwin's general indictment of many Catholic higher education practices and values generated much of a response in the Catholic press or anywhere else. Other current events seemed far more important to American Catholics than the problems and weaknesses of their higher education system.

Appearing when it did during the anxiety-laden months of early 1939, *Catholics and Scholarship* did not have much chance of reaching a large audience. In any case, Our Sunday Visitor Press made no special efforts to get the book reviewed. *America* and the *Commonweal* ignored it; the *American Ecclesiastical Review* provided only a brief perfunctory notice.[126] The *Homiletic and Pastoral Review* published the only serious review. Father Virgil R. Stallbaumer, O.S.B., pointed out the sloppy editing and faulted O'Brien for embracing the current popular idolatry of science. Nonetheless, Stallbaumer insisted that the depressed state of Catholic scholarship and higher education described in *Catholics and Scholarship* was undeniable and that the future of the Church in America might be at risk because of the apathy of American Catholics toward learning and scholarship. Stallbaumer quoted Pius X about the danger of ignorance to the Church in America and Cardinal Newman about the weaknesses of Catholic educational efforts.[127]

Though public reaction to the book was disappointing to O'Brien, the publication of it was a credential of sorts that might help him find an academic post somewhere. As 1939 progressed, Bishop Schlarman made O'Brien painfully aware that the present year in the Diocese of Peoria would be his last. *Catholics and Scholarship* was the only potential passport into academe at hand for O'Brien and he used it shamelessly in his campaign to get an academic appointment at the University of Notre Dame.

— viii —

By 1939, O'Brien had grown weary of his student services role in the Newman Foundation and of his awkward status of being at the University of Illinois but not part of it. There was not and could never be a place for him there. To be sure, the initiative for turning O'Brien out of Champaign came from Bishop Schlarman, but the priest was ready to leave. Eighteen years in one place was long enough.

Relieved at last from the anxiety and burden of the Newman Foundation debt and fortified by a steady stream of royalty payments as well as rising rents from his mother's Peoria properties, O'Brien was well on his way to becoming a very rich man. Because of this, O'Brien was also independent. He could afford to go anywhere in the summer of 1939, and he chose England. O'Brien wanted to spend a least a year abroad observing and perhaps writing about the great events occurring in Europe. However, before leaving for England he wanted to be certain that he had some place to return. The question for him in the spring of 1939 was where?

What O'Brien wanted most of all was a position at some respectable Catholic college or university. Opportunities open to him for such an appointment were very few. Because of past controversies, Jesuit institutions were largely closed to him. O'Brien had some friends but also some very powerful enemies at the Catholic University of America. By process of elimination, his best prospect appeared to be at the University of Notre Dame. He had no known enemies there and believed that under the current university leadership his convert work and popular apologetics writings would be respected and his money and celebrity status appreciated.

As has been already noted, O'Brien's campaign to obtain the promise of an appointment at Notre Dame from O'Hara succeeded grandly.

Though O'Hara had been marvelously unspecific about what O'Brien would be expected to do, the priest did not care. He had at long last an authentic academic identity at an institution located in a diocese administered by a bishop with whom he had a highly profitable business relationship. For a priest with O'Brien's record, things could not get much better than that. He was free of Schlarman; his time of tribulation was over. No surprise then that O'Brien went off to England in the early summer of 1939 pleased with himself and in a spirit of high adventure. He had a fair prospect of being an actual witness to the occurrence of historic events.

— ix —

Once disembarked in England, O'Brien wasted no time in seeking out the rich and powerful. He quickly established a social relationship with the American ambassador, Joseph P. Kennedy. Before settling in at Greyfriars, Oxford, O'Brien managed a short trip to Spain and a brief but interesting interview with General Franco.[128] Arriving in England when he did, O'Brien experienced all of the popular anxieties and euphoria associated with the beginning of the war.

Though life and work in the fall and winter of wartime Oxford was disturbed by mobilization and other measures, the architecture of the town and university, the libraries, the formality and gentility of social life, the kindness and openness of the Catholic community there to a visiting American priest with an Irish name persuaded O'Brien to live in Oxford during most of his time in England and perhaps to visit Ireland in the summer of 1940 on his way back to the United States and to Notre Dame. Even during those ominous days of late 1939, Oxford fascinated O'Brien. For him, it was an absolutely perfect environment for writing and research.[129]

While mentioning in several letters to O'Hara how much he missed hearing radio accounts of Notre Dame football games and professing great expectations about next year settling down and doing "some writing amidst the stimulating companionship of the saints and scholars at Notre Dame,"[130] O'Brien tried to take full advantage of the many opportunities for intellectual stimulation available at Oxford. He went to hear Christopher Dawson lecture and arranged to have a short visit with him.[131] In addition to matters intellectual and cultural, there were priestly activities as well. O'Brien met a number of English Catholic families in the Oxford and London areas. He was a frequent visitor in their homes and often acted as a friend and spiritual counsellor to persons confused and agitated by war time dangers.[132]

However, in March 1940, O'Brien's own anxiety level rose significantly when he learned that the now Bishop O'Hara had left Notre Dame. O'Brien had only O'Hara's promise of a position at Notre Dame. He had neither contract nor written confirmation of his intended status. O'Brien had met the new president, Father J. Hugh O'Donnell, on occasions in the past but really did not know him. With O'Donnell a new beginning had to be made, and O'Brien proceeded to do so at once. O'Brien wrote to O'Donnell in early March 1940 offering congratulations on his promotion to the presidency, observing that "Your friendly smile and warm hand clasp will have even a larger scope to win more friends for Notre Dame."

Next, O'Brien explained his present situation, his arrangement with O'Hara, enclosed an outline of a course in philosophy of religion, and assured O'Donnell that "If the sea be not shredded with mines, I'll be at ND in September."[133] O'Brien made a very good beginning with O'Donnell, and in the months and years ahead they would become friends.

O'Donnell responded at the end of April in a thoroughly friendly manner and confirmed in writing O'Brien's understanding with O'Hara. It was too late to list O'Brien's proposed course in the university catalogue but precisely what O'Brien would teach could be worked out with Father Carrico, director of studies, whenever O'Brien arrived on campus.[134] O'Brien was to be appointed a professor of religion with a salary of $2,500 plus full room and board.

After O'Brien had arrived on campus, he would be given status in the department of politics and would be listed to teach a course to graduate students and advanced undergraduates entitled The Principles of World Peace. O'Brien had persuaded himself and O'Donnell that time spent in England during the fall and winter of 1939–40 had qualified him as a political scientist and as an expert on foreign policy and European affairs.

Emotionally and psychologically, if not academically, one can see how and why a switch from Catholic apologetics to international affairs and American foreign policy had been managed. For O'Brien, keeping America out of this distant European conflict became a moral and patriotic duty. In wartime England, O'Brien had discovered the great and powerful cause of American isolationism. Upon returning to the United States in August 1940, he found an exciting arena in which to pursue that cause and quickly emerged as the country's most popular Catholic isolationist.

PART II

— 3 —

BRITAIN AT WAR AND
ISOLATIONISM IN AMERICA,
1939–1940

American isolationism was very much on the minds of the men charged to manage Britain's war effort in 1939. The clearest manifestation of that isolationism were the neutrality laws enacted between 1935 and 1939. Despite the name attached to this legislation, these laws had very little to do with defining neutrality or protecting traditional neutral rights in a war-torn world. This legislation was in part a reaction to the way America had been brought into World War I as a full participant and in part a belated effort by Congress to resume greater influence over American foreign policy. These laws had the single objective of preventing the United States from being drawn into wars waged in Europe and Asia.

As a whole, the neutrality laws enacted between 1935 and 1939 authorized the president to impose embargoes on arms sales and shipments to belligerents and placed the sale of other strategic materials to them on a cash-and-carry basis. Arming of United States vessels was prohibited. Travel by American citizens to war zones or in vessels of belligerents was restricted as were the rights of Americans to lend money to belligerent governments. British ministers watched the enactment of this legislation with utter horror.

As early as December 31, 1936, the permanent under secretary of state for foreign affairs, Sir Robert Vansittart, complained in his end-of-year review that "We scrambled through the last war by importing in its early stages some 500 million dollars' worth of American munitions. To date in the event of war we can count on getting nothing."[1] Vansittart added the very sobering observation, "We must act and state our case in such a way as to retain American sympathy at all times."[2]

That advice was much easier to give than to act upon. Isolationism in America was much more than a matter of law. Remaining aloof from the politics of Europe was a long-standing element in American politics. Contemporary American isolationism was driven by the deeply disappointing experience of full belligerency in World War I, by profound regional and generational forces, and by anti-British attitudes among the country's Irish, German, and Italian ethnics.[3] According to Nicholas J. Cull's study of the British government's response to American isolationists, by 1939 the elements of American isolationism had blended into an all-pervasive culture, rarely challenged and highly resistant to change. So dominant in American politics were isolationist spokesmen during 1937 and 1938 that the Chamberlain government abandoned all hope of getting American aid if war came. Chamberlain was not disposed to try to placate American public opinion in order to get aid and he acted accordingly during the international crises of those years.

The Munich Agreement of 1938, wherein Britain and France agreed to satisfy all current German demands for Czechoslovakian territory in order to avoid war, initially was well received in the United States. However, by early 1939 when the failure of the Munich Agreement to settle anything had become increasingly apparent, the worst suspicions of anti-British Americans seemed confirmed. Britain had offered little more than pompous rhetoric and compromises as responses to German adventurism in central Europe. Czechoslovakia had been sacrificed.

In particular, Prime Minister Chamberlain was viewed in America as a man who was weak, untrustworthy, almost effeminate and whose ever-present umbrella became an object of comedic derision. He was for Americans a caricature of aristocratic government in action. Something had to be done quickly to recapture American respect and thereby assure material support in another great war with Germany that was only months away. Britain and France had to exhibit some degree of willingness to resist German aggression or face the strong possibility of being totally abandoned by the American government and people.

Something was done. Even before a shot was fired in Europe a grand campaign to win the hearts and minds of the American people and the votes of their congressmen to the Allied cause had begun. It started quite properly at the top with a state visit of King George VI and Queen Elizabeth to the United States in the first week of June 1939.

The tour of the king and queen from Canada to Washington, then to New York City with a stop at the World's Fair and a weekend with the

Roosevelts at Hyde Park was a public relations triumph. Americans in the areas visited simply could not see enough of them. Cheers, bells, and horns greeted the royal couple wherever they went. However, all of this immense popular applause did not translate into policy changes. The prospects for American aid to Britain when war broke out had not been improved.

To be sure, while at Hyde Park, the president expressed deep personal sympathy for the Allied cause and tried to explain his problems with isolationist opinion in the Midwest and with isolationist congressmen and senators in Washington. At the same time, during the discussions at Hyde Park Roosevelt spoke expansively about schemes for future Anglo-American naval cooperation in the western Atlantic where American warships would shoot German U-boats on sight. He even assured the king that if London was bombed, the United States would come into the war.[4]

In these private moments with the king and queen, Roosevelt's enthusiasm clearly got the better of him. The President had said too much too soon. The heavy bombing of London a year hence raised no great clamor for American intervention, and not until September 1941 did Roosevelt actually order the U.S. Navy to fire at German submarines whenever sighted. A much more realistic appraisal of American opinion about involvement in a European war and of the prospects for aid could have been read in the *New York Times*. While the crowds cheered the king and queen in New York City and Roosevelt raised royal hopes in Hyde Park, a bill to amend the neutrality laws died an embarrassing public death on the Senate floor.[5] Their majesties had come and gone. Not much had changed.

Indeed, there was much to change. Because immediate American aid and eventual participation in the approaching war as a full belligerent was so vital to the Allied cause, changing American public opinion about how important that cause was to United States' national interests became an urgent priority. At that time, there were only two ways that American public opinion could be reached. One way was by cultivating American radio and press correspondents on assignment in England, and the other was through opinion-influencing activities undertaken in the United States. However, both of these strategies encountered a formidable obstacle, namely, a powerful fear of British propaganda deeply rooted in America's public consciousness.

This near paranoid fear of British propaganda effectiveness had developed during the mid 1930s following published revelations of British propaganda coups during World War I. Large numbers of Americans in academic circles, in the media, and in politics had convinced themselves that British propaganda had brought America into the Great War in

1917 and they were determined that history would not be repeated in 1939 and 1940. For Americans of such a mind, the very idea of mass propaganda by a foreign power, especially Britain, in the United States was an absolute anathema. Of course, in the real world this widespread American fear of British propaganda was fed by a clever and successful German-orchestrated propaganda campaign in America against British propaganda.

For British ministers, the stakes were high, and the problems of reaching and changing American public opinion were complex and not easily resolved. British officials had to organize and mount propaganda campaigns in the United States without appearing to do so. Alarmed by America's fear of propaganda, the British Foreign Office, as long ago as 1924, had proclaimed an official policy of no propaganda in the United States. British official policy in such matters in America was "to tell the truth, to eschew secrecy except when publicity would prejudice delicate negotiations or do harm to others, and to let the facts speak for themselves."[6]

This official policy of no propaganda, operative in 1939, was only a starting point and open to all sorts of interpretations and applications. Moreover, in a very short period of time the policy would change. By the summer of 1939, the policy of no propaganda had come to mean that British messages to the American people were best communicated in American accents by American messengers.

In that anxiety-laden summer, British propaganda responsibilities in the United States were shared among the Ministry of Information (MOI) operating through its London-based American division, and the Foreign Office operating through its embassy in Washington, D.C., and the British Library of Information (BLI) located in New York City. During that summer, in addition to working with Anglo-American cultural organizations, producing films, books, and pamphlets for distribution in the United States and organizing lecture tours, the American division of MOI concentrated on managing and facilitating the work of American radio and press reporters in London.

In the United States, the British embassy and BLI handled press relations and public relations generally, and responded quickly and efficiently to requests for a wide range of information about Britain, British policies at home and in the Empire, and, of course, the royal family. In addition to performing public relations activities of all kinds, the embassy and BLI also collected intelligence information, both solicited and unsolicited, about American public opinion and politics. To help the embassy and BLI cope with their responsibilities and escalating work load, both organizations received additional personnel in June 1939.

In Washington, the new ambassador to the United States, Lord Lothian, was given John Wheeler-Bennett, an Oxford don who was expert in German politics and also knowledgeable about American affairs. Wheeler-Bennett, presently lecturing at the University of Virginia, brought the ambassador a facile pen, sharp wit, and contacts within the American academic community. Wheeler-Bennett added the duties of press attaché to those of personal assistant.

In New York, a wealthy Welshman, well-established in social circles there, was recruited for the press intelligence unit of the BLI. Aubrey Morgan's new duties included monitoring American public opinion on a daily basis. In addition to the advantages of wealth, good looks, and social standing, Morgan had the additional one of being married into the family of the well-known American diplomat and financier Dwight W. Morrow. By marrying Constance Morrow, Morgan became brother-in-law to Charles A. Lindbergh, famous aviator, husband of Anne Morrow, and now strident isolationist. The great issue of American neutrality in the European war that so dominated American politics and divided Americans during 1940 and 1941 had special significance for the Morrow family.[7]

So it was in the fateful summer of 1939, the American division of MOI had the special care and contentment of American correspondents working in England in their charge, whereas the embassy and BLI in the United States had a more general responsibility for public relations and for information collection in America. However, because the directors of MOI had great ambitions to launch new propaganda programs in the United States and actually succeeded in doing so during the summer and fall of 1940, this early sharing of American propaganda responsibilities was neither happy nor efficient. However fragile, strained, and under-staffed Britain's propaganda apparatus in the summer of 1939, it was to be severely tested sooner than most British ministers suspected.

On August 24, 1939 when Soviet officials signed a nonaggression pact with Germany, the outbreak of war awaited only the final offensive positioning of German forces along the Polish border. On September 1, German troops invaded Poland and declarations of war by Britain and France followed two days later. No one in the British or French governments was prepared to forecast how or where the war would be fought or how long it would last. Yet, two circumstances were clear enough.

First, the Allies could not wage a prolonged war against Germany without war materials and other resources from the United States. Second, access to those resources depended upon what American public opinion and Congress would allow the president to do. As German tanks pushed deeper into Poland, Roosevelt dutifully declared a state of war existing in Europe and initiated enforcement of America's neutrality laws.

— ii —

The war in Poland was vicious but brief. In the West, the only actions of note in the early months occurred at sea. On the Franco-German border, troops on both sides maneuvered behind their respective defensive fortifications and occasionally fired an artillery piece. So quiet was the western front that a leading American isolationist, Senator William E. Borah (R-Idaho), speculated publicly on September 17, 1939, that there had to be something phoney about a war in which neither side attacked. Unwittingly, Borah provided a name, "phoney war," for the entire seven-month period of formal belligerency, September 1939 to April 1940, that stuck.

What Senator Borah did not suspect and would have been delighted to know was just how confused the Chamberlain government's policy toward the United States was. Moreover, that particular confusion was a reflection of a much broader uncertainty over general war aims. During the entire seven months of the phoney war there was no official statement of why Britain was in the war or what their leaders hoped Britain and the world would be like after the conflict. As a matter of fact, no formal statement of British war aims appeared until the joint issuance of the Atlantic Charter by President Roosevelt and Prime Minister Churchill in August 1941, almost two years after the war had begun.

The lack of policy objectives for America during this critical time was a serious matter. As Frank Darvall, deputy director of the American division of MOI, complained to a foreign office official in December 1939 in the convoluted prose style for which he was so well known, the objectives of British publicity in the United States needed clear definition. If Britain's secret policy objective was to bring America into the war, MOI ought to pursue one line. If the policy objective was to stop short of winning full American belligerency and only to obtain financial credits and modification of the cash-and-carry provisions of the neutrality laws, then MOI should pursue another line. The American division of MOI, Darvall concluded, was as ignorant of Britain's policy objectives toward America in December 1939 as it had been on the day the war started. Official policy in so far as Darvall understood it was "the creation of general good will."[8]

In so far as MOI had a strategy for turning American public opinion away from its isolationist base, it was simply to supply American correspondents with a steady stream of high drama news from the battle fronts which could be reported to their respective American publics. Alas, there was nothing of high drama to report from the western front.[9] The only possibilities for high drama news were incidents occurring at sea and most of that happened to be bad. In any case, the Admiralty was extremely reluctant to provide details of their operations to reporters, American or otherwise.

As early in the war as the end of September 1939, Lord Lothian wrote to the foreign secretary from the embassy in Washington urging the Admiralty to be more forthcoming with American correspondents.[10] A few months later, Darvall returned to the same problem. He complained that although the Admiralty agreed in principle with the need to provide American correspondents with information, they were very slow to do so. Their lordships failed to appreciate how difficult it was for MOI to dramatize British naval actions if nine-tenths of them were done in secret.[11]

T. North Whitehead, an official in the American department of the Foreign Office, was even more explicit about dealing with American correspondents. The fighting services, North Whitehead insisted, must constantly appreciate the importance of American correspondents as political instruments.[12] Britain could not obtain the quantity of support from America required for survival without them.

After so many high-level admonishments to cooperate with American journalists and broadcasters, some impatient officers in Admiralty leadership positions must have wondered when the MOI and Foreign Office would ask that naval actions be staged so that American correspondents would have some high drama news to report to their American readers. Indeed, such a moment actually came in April 1941 when Britain committed 60,000 troops from the forces in North Africa to resist the German invasion of Greece.

No one believed that the Greek campaign had any chance of success. It was a calculated display of gallantry in a hopeless cause undertaken to impress American public opinion. Only American correspondents were supplied with combat information. American public opinion was certainly moved, but not very far, by Britain's determination to fight for democracy. In this glorious defeat, Britain lost 13,000 troops.[13]

In London, the policy of creating a general good will toward Britain in America was forwarded by an assiduous cultivation of American broadcasters and journalists. The principal agents in this activity were the MOI and the British Broadcasting Corporation (BBC). As early as 1938, a few members of the American media community in London were well connected in the highest levels of British society.[14] Vincent Sheean, John

Gunther, Quentin Reynolds, and Edward R. Murrow ate in the best restaurants, were welcome in most of the London clubs, and were frequent guests in country homes.

So important to the British war effort were Edward R. Murrow of the Columbia Broadcasting System (CBS), Fred Bate of the National Broadcasting Company (NBC), and John Steele of the Mutual Broadcasting System (MBS) that they were treated as American royalty. In August of 1939, they were invited to a confidential meeting at MOI to have British censorship regulations personally and privately explained to them. Calls to government offices by these men were passed on at once to the person sought or were quickly returned, and of course, their social calendars were never empty.

So friendly were the relations between NBC and CBS representatives in London with the MOI that Darvall claimed they were keeping him informed about conditions in Berlin relayed by their broadcasting representatives there.[15] Murrow became such a close friend of Darvall that Janet Murrow spent most of the summer of 1940 in the country as a guest of Mrs. Darvall.[16]

Newsmen of lesser notoriety were treated a bit less splendidly but grandly indeed. The Savoy Hotel was a home away from home for most of them; actually, some prepared their best copy in its elegant bar. So important was the Savoy as a social center for American correspondents that the MOI moved its nightly press briefings there where MOI spokesmen delivered the briefings cocktail in hand.[17]

All of this was a delightfully new experience for American journalists whose status in their own country had not risen much above that of an ordinary employee. Passing directly into an under secretary's office suite while industrialists, financiers, and even representatives from occupied countries cooled their heels in an outer waiting room did much for ego and self-esteem. For American broadcasters and journalists of all ability levels and degrees of notoriety working in London in 1939 and 1940, it was no ordinary time.

It was no ordinary time because they were the conduits through which American public opinion was to be reached and changed. The importance of these broadcasters and journalists to the British war effort cannot be overestimated. British ministers and lesser officials knew how important they were, and very quickly so also did the broadcasters and journalists themselves. Consequently, their demands, both professional and personal, upon officials in the MOI and other departments were constant, often extraordinary, and usually satisfied.

One memorable example was provided by Quentin Reynolds of *Collier's* magazine. During the height of German air raids on London in mid-September 1940, Reynolds agreed to provide an American-accented commentary for MOI's highly successful propaganda film produced for American audiences, *London Can Take It*. However, Reynolds refused to leave the security of the Savoy bar and basement air raid shelter to report eyewitness accounts of German nightly air raids. The directors of the film had to make their way with all of their equipment through blacked-out London streets to the Savoy bar where they recorded Reynolds' commentary on the terrors of that night's bombing.[18] Despite the great difficulties of that wondrous moment, Reynolds did not disappoint. Addressing the Savoy's celebrated array of Scotch whisky bottles, Reynolds provided for the film an unforgettable American-accented account of what Londoners experienced during the worst nights of the Blitz.

What was reported about Britain at war to the American people was one measure of the success of the MOI's policy of cultivating American broadcasters and journalists. What those broadcasters and journalists did not report was another. Coverage of the woefully inadequate access to air raid shelters in working-class areas of London was one glaring example of sympathetic self-imposed censorship.

While wealthy London neighborhoods had much better shelter access than poorer ones, working-class housing areas in the East End were very badly served. That situation was made even worse by the fact that the government had closed the very deep Underground railway stations in the evenings, preventing them from being used as shelters. The reason was fear that development of a so-called deep shelter mentality might prevent London's working classes from "carrying on." Closing these stations in the evenings was calculated to make working-class upper lips a bit stiffer. British censors did not suppress stories about these closings or shelter inadequacies. Although the evening closing of Underground stations and stories about the shortage of shelters were all well known to American correspondents, they were not generally reported.[19]

As a matter of fact, the most spectacular shelter incident occurred right under the noses of those American correspondents living and drinking at the Savoy Hotel. In the evening of September 15, 1940, a stylishly dressed English gentleman strode into the lobby of the Savoy and asked if he could inspect the air raid shelter there on behalf of an American businessman who was planning to move into the hotel. As the gentleman entered the basement area, he darted to a side door, opened it, and about eighty East Enders and two dogs poured into the Savoy's shelter.

The police were summoned but could do nothing. The air raid siren had sounded and the interlopers had a legal right to shelter for the duration of the raid. The East Enders remained in the Savoy shelter for the night drinking tea for which they would pay only East End prices. When the all clear sounded at daybreak, these uninvited guests, having had their night at the Savoy, left the hotel and went about their daily business. The man who had arranged this East Ender's evening at the Savoy was Phil Piratin, a Communist counselor from Stepney.[20]

Though many American broadcasters and reporters lived at the Savoy and many more drank and ate there, none of the major American news services carried the story. Murrow dealt with the broader issue of shelter access. Only James Reston of the *New York Times* covered the story in depth. Apparently, the Savoy crowd of American correspondents assumed that somehow the incident reflected negatively on them for living there or that reporting such a story would in some fashion give aid and comfort to the enemy, though British censors did not.

Two days later, Piratin gave American correspondents another opportunity for a story which most found much more appealing. In the late afternoon of September 17, Piratin and his friends broke into the Goodge Street Underground station and directed crowds into it for safety from an expected night air raid. Even though the War Cabinet had already decided that working-class upper lips were stiff enough and were ready to open the Underground stations for shelter use, Piratin's second audacious escapade forced immediate action.

Goodge Street station was far enough from the Savoy to cause no personal guilt problems for the American correspondents living there, and the idea of Londoners living underground during the nightly air raids captured the imaginations of most American reporters working in the city at that time. Pictures and stories of families living on Underground station platforms in front of Cadbury chocolate vending machines and Whitbread's beer advertisements were splashed across America's front pages. Even though only 4 percent of London's population ever used Underground stations for air raid shelter purposes, the image of families doing so became one of the most enduring and moving ones of the entire war.[21] Most working-class Londoners unable to evacuate elsewhere found shelter wherever they could, in basements of their apartments and homes, under tables and work benches, and in makeshift setups in back-garden sheds.

— iii —

Meanwhile, in the United States during the fall and winter of 1939–40, the embassy and BLI tried to fulfill its public relations and information collecting responsibilities. The official no propaganda policy of those two agencies made difficult the task of creating general good will toward

Britain in America. His Majesty's government's policy line in America within the boundaries of the no propaganda rule had two principal objectives. The first was to present a picture of Britain-at-War painted in Britain through American press, radio, films, lecturers, and other publicists calculated to please American public opinion.[22] The second was to counter German propaganda in the United States.

If this picture of Britain-at-War painted in Britain was to have any significant impact on American public opinion, it had to emphasize Britain's commitment to political democracy. Points must be made that despite necessary wartime controls, Britain and the Empire had remained essentially democratic, allowing freedom of movement, speech, publication, and political organization. Another important point to be emphasized was the freedom of the Dominions to enter the war or not. Attention should also be directed toward the progress of self-government and spread of democratic institutions in India, Burma, and elsewhere in the Colonial Empire.[23]

Some past faults in Britain's imperial record had to be admitted, but countered by an argument that the old type of imperialism was rapidly disappearing. At the same time, the point must be made that imperial territories were neither owned by Britain nor exploited for profit as if they were pieces of property. Finally, because there was such great hostility in America toward Japan and the Soviet Union for their respective invasions of China and Finland, there could be no suggestion that Britain was even considering buying war materials from either of those two states.[24]

Second, the problem of successfully countering German propaganda efforts in the United States was a formidable one. The Germans had implemented a highly successful propaganda program intended to prevent the United States from giving material aid to the Allied cause. German propagandists made no attempt whatsoever to praise the Hitler regime. Instead, they represented the war as a conflict between two imperialisms in which America could have no interest.[25] That German propaganda line was encountered everywhere in the United States and was being delivered by many American messengers.

In the United States, the public relations and information collecting functions of the embassy and BLI were complicated in part by the picture of Britain-at-War trumpeted by the MOI. The embassy and BLI were sometimes severely embarrassed by public statements from visiting academics and celebrities. Though exit visas were required for travel from wartime Britain to the United States in order to protect and proclaim the democratic value of freedom of movement, the visas appear to have been freely given. Apart from people with strong Indian nationalist opinions, most persons with legitimate business in the United States were allowed to go.

There was one elderly academic, however, that the Foreign Office and several angry members of Parliament wished had never been given an exit visa. Sir George Paish was seventy-two years old and an accomplished economist compulsively driven to express strong opinions on virtually any subject. He came to the United States to pursue lecture tour dollars. Paish first attracted the attention of the embassy in August 1940 when the American press attributed defeatist statements to him.[26]

Paish became a major public relations problem when he encountered Senator Burton K. Wheeler (D-Montana). Paish provided this leading isolationist with enough foolish small talk to justify a full-scale condemnation in a speech during the Senate debates on the conscription bill. According to Wheeler, Paish had boasted to him that information provided by him in 1916 had brought the United States into the last war and that information in his possession now would bring America into the present one. On the Senate floor, Wheeler quoted Paish: "I am going to cross the United States on a speaking tour and I am going to get this country into the war."[27] When Lothian read an account of Wheeler's speech, he immediately cabled the substance of the incident to the Foreign Office and then released a statement to the press emphatically denying that Paish was in this country on any sort of official mission.[28] The Foreign Office responded forthwith by cable urging Lothian to contact Paish and persuade him to return to Britain as soon as passage could be arranged.[29]

Lothian found Paish and interviewed him at the embassy. The ambassador was not gentle with the old man. Lothian told him that if the public defeatist statements reported in the American press had been made in Britain, Paish would have been given six months in prison. Above all else, Lothian insisted, under no circumstances should a visiting Englishman ever privately or publicly dispute with a United States senator.

Next, Lothian told Paish that Secretary of State Cordell Hull had informed him that the attorney general had given a pledge to the Senate that deportation proceedings against Paish would be seriously considered on the grounds that he was a foreign propagandist seeking to nullify the neutrality of the United States and to create disturbances in the country. To save the United States government the embarrassment and trouble of initiating such proceedings, Lothian directed Paish to leave the country as soon as possible.[30] Indeed, Paish found himself in an impossible situation. He faced harassment by the British government for making defeatist statements and was threatened with deportation by the American government for being a British propagandist. No mean accomplishment for a man seventy-two years old.

After interviewing Paish, Lothian concluded that the man was so vain, so anxious to obtain notoriety for his opinions and to maintain his status as an economist that prudence meant nothing to him. Paish was, Lothian added, in a sense senile and had no judgment or sense left.[31] To quiet angry members of Parliament who had heard about the Paish incident, Lothian urged the prime minister to use the senility argument as a response to inquiries certain to be raised in the House of Commons at question time about who had authorized an exit visa for Paish.[32] In Washington, D.C., the last word on the Paish affair appeared in the *Washington Post* on August 27, 1940. The paper reported an observation attributed to an unnamed official in the British Embassy: "We wish someone would drop Sir George over Germany as a [propaganda] pamphlet."[33]

Almost a month after putting an end to the embarrassing Paish affair, Lothian had to deal with what he described as another visiting "self-appointed interpreter of British thought." This time Britain's latest visiting apostle of imprudence was H. G. Wells, celebrated author, agnostic, and social critic.[34]

During the last war Wells had lent his pen to the war effort by joining Sir Gilbert Parker's London-based stable of patriotic celebrity writers who fed American correspondents with interviews and articles about the virtues of the Allied cause. Wells was asked to join a similar group in 1939 but refused.[35] However, Wells was in New York City in October 1940 and managed to obtain front page coverage in several of that city's newspapers. The issue was an incident occurring at Columbia University. Nicholas Murray Butler, president of Columbia, had started an anti-totalitarian heresy hunt at the university, and Wells publicly took him to task for doing so.[36] From the point of view of the embassy, Butler and Columbia University were absolutely the wrong targets for criticism of any sort at this time. Butler was a rabid supporter of Britain and the British war effort and some of his faculty members were leaders in a small but increasingly active American interventionist group.

Wells compounded this problem for the embassy by expounding his socialist views and anti-monarchical prejudices to American audiences, contending that the British government was not totally committed to winning the war.[37] Thereupon, George Sokolsky, a labor columnist for the Hearst newspaper chain, attacked Wells for justifying the Soviet Union's attack on Finland and for other positive comments about Stalin's Russia. Senator Arthur Vandenberg (R-Michigan) criticized Wells and wondered what he was doing in the United States.[38] So did Lothian.

The ambassador complained bitterly to the Foreign Office that "these egotistic and somewhat senile half-extinct prophets are much better kept at home where their importance is generally correctly estimated."[39] Again, inquiries about Wells' presence and activities in the United States were raised in the House of Commons.[40] All British officials agreed that public relations damage of this sort within a month of the American presidential election was counterproductive to British policy objectives in the United States and to President Roosevelt's re-election campaign. In the fall of 1940, nothing was more important for Britain's survival in this war than Roosevelt's re-election. All prospects for increased aid and possible American intervention turned on that event.

— iv —

The busiest information-collecting program mounted in America in the fall and winter of 1939–40 was the BLI's American press-monitoring work conducted by its survey section under the direction of Aubrey Morgan. The survey section acquired a small staff and offices in Rockefeller Center. The staff collected press clippings and other materials from consulates around the country. A team of writers, supervised by the director's wife, Constance Morrow Morgan, collated incoming materials and prepared short reports on current trends, issues, and political personalities making news in the American press. The finished reports were transmitted over the Reuters' line to London.

The quality of these transmitted reports varied greatly. All reflected the haste, four or five hours, with which they had been prepared. Some of the reports suggest that the preparers had little understanding of American politics and were grossly ignorant of its details. Though the reports seldom traveled father than the upper levels of the Foreign Office, a few were passed on to the War Cabinet and, whether based on facts or fancy, became the basis for policy decisions.[41]

In addition to receiving information from consulates, Morgan and others in the BLI established friendly contacts with American journalists, with individuals with tales to tell and information to sell, and with the very small but growing number of American interventionist groups. Throughout late 1939 and 1940, a steady stream of opinion, observations, hearsay, and gossip flowed into the survey section which after collation and refinement was passed out and upward to other departments of the Foreign Office as intelligence information.

Free-lancers provided both the embassy and BLI with some of the most interesting as well as most bizarre and untrustworthy information.

The principal problem with regard to such information facing the survey section and the officials to whom it reported was assessment of source credibility. These officials had to avoid the equally dangerous pitfalls of gullibility and extreme cynicism while learning how to distill insight from information that might be special pleading and self-serving.

For example, a report prepared in New York in December 1939 on the impact of anti-British propaganda on American public opinion by H. Hessell Tiltman, an itinerant British free-lance journalist/adventurer, old China hand, and Spanish civil war reporter, now living in the United States, was discouraging reading. Angus Fletcher, director of the BLI, disliked Tiltman and disparaged his report. For Fletcher, Tiltman was a "self seeker, a faker pure and simple."[42] Though highly opinionated, Tiltman's report showed a broad knowledge of American affairs, familiarity with American extremist publications, and awareness of the latest public opinion polling data.

According to Tiltman, anti-British propaganda was strongest among the "Keep America out of the war gangs." Among those gangs subversive pro-Fascist publications abounded. The worst of the lot was a weekly, *Social Justice,* published in Detroit by the Catholic priest Father Charles E. Coughlin. Tiltman insisted that Coughlin had followed and continued to follow the propaganda line put out by Dr. Joseph Goebbels in Berlin, that is, Britain was fighting to preserve its oppressive, ill-gotten empire.[43] *Social Justice,* Tiltman reported, was thoroughly dangerous. It was anti-British, anti-Semitic, and after its own fashion, anti-capitalist. In Tiltman's judgment, *Social Justice* was the worst threat to decency in the United States. Paradoxically, the anti-British, pro-Nazi, anti-Semitic line of Coughlin was also reflected in the strongest of all American anti-Catholic publications *The Monitor,* a successor to the older, widely known but now defunct *Menace.*[44] This was neither the first nor last time in this decade or later that traditional enemies would find themselves saying the same things and supporting the same causes.

No less paradoxical, wrote Tiltman, was the editorial behavior of the American Communist and Communist-inspired publications, *Daily Worker* and *New Masses.* Prior to the announcement of the Berlin-Moscow Pact in August 1939, both of those publications had attacked Coughlin, and *Social Justice* savagely "took Coughlin's shirt off regularly."[45] However, since that pact and the beginning of the war, those publications calmed down and paid no attention to Coughlin. Instead, they adopted an anti-British stance and slavishly followed whatever Moscow's line happened to be at a given moment.[46]

About public opinion in the United States generally, Tiltman estimated that Americans were 80 percent anti-Hitler, 30 percent pro-

British, 100 percent suspicious of concealed propaganda, and 90 percent opposed to entering the war. According to him, there were a small number of prominent American isolationists who were at heart pro-Fascist. Among them Tiltman listed Charles A. Lindbergh, Henry Ford, Senator William E. Borah, and Congressman Hamilton Fish. Of those men, probably only Congressman Fish had accepted money from the German government, but Lindbergh, Ford, and Borah had all been strongly influenced by the current German propaganda line. They were saying and saying persuasively the things that Dr. Goebbels wanted them to say.[47]

From a British perspective, Tiltman's account of the state of American public opinion was discouraging. However, there was a bright side even to this dismal picture that British policymakers needed to consider exploiting. The bright side was the strongly pro-British attitude of so many editors and reporters working on the large and influential eastern newspapers. Tiltman described the editors and desk men employed by the *New York Times* and the *New York Herald-Tribune* as "95 percent sympathetic to the British cause." They were ready, he continued, to lean over backwards to help the Allies, but while doing so "they must be able to keep their integrity." Precisely how that feat of ethical gymnastics was to be achieved, Tiltman did not say.[48] At this moment, Tiltman concluded, given adequate personal contacts between British officials in the United States and the American press, "the British Ministry of Information could get away with murder—always providing that the murder was served up with a clear [American] label."[49]

Whatever doubts Fletcher or others may have had about Tiltman's authenticity and credibility, his report found its way into the Foreign Office files and was certainly read by advisors of policymakers if not by the policymakers themselves. Exactly how influential the Tiltman report was can only be guessed. Yet, during the winter and early spring of 1940, the official British policy of no propaganda in America, though challenged, had evolved into one of no propaganda in the United States without clearly labeling it as coming from American sources.

— v —

Throughout the critical months of late 1939 and early 1940, the most serious problem for British ministers responsible for developing and implementing a policy for America was trying to understand how American politics worked, that is, determining what sorts of political behaviors were predictable and which were not. British political models and experience were no help. As a matter of fact, when Foreign Office analysts prepared brief reports on American politics for cabinet and subcabinet officials, the combination of general unfamiliarity and British political assumptions sometimes produced bizarre results. J. O. Perowene's official Foreign Office Minute on James J. Farley and Ambassador Joseph P. Kennedy is a case in point.

Farley was a native of Rockland County, New York, born into an upper-middle-class Catholic family. He was himself not an office seeker. Instead, Farley chose the role of political manager and enjoyed extraordinary success. By 1928, he had become the elected secretary of the New York State Democratic Committee where he helped direct Franklin D. Roosevelt's winning gubernatorial campaigns in 1928 and 1930. Recognizing Farley's charm and organizational skills, Roosevelt chose him to direct the successful presidential campaign of 1932 and then put him in his cabinet with an appointment as postmaster general. In 1936, Farley once again directed Roosevelt's campaign and helped win the greatest landslide presidential victory in modern American history. However, by early 1940, relations between Roosevelt and Farley had cooled noticeably because of the latter's widely known opposition to a third term for any American president.[50]

Farley's opposition to a third term was compounded and intensified by Roosevelt's refusal to say whether or not he wanted to be nominated. The president had hoped to cast his renomination for a third term as a draft by the convention and, accordingly, made no plans to attend the Democratic National Convention in Chicago in mid-July to lobby for it. Roosevelt did not indicate to Farley that he wanted the nomination until July 9, 1940, a week before the convention opened. Believing that the president's silence on this matter was damaging the Democratic party by making impossible the emergence of any other candidates, token or otherwise, Farley told Roosevelt to his face on July 9 that he would allow his own name to be put before the convention. The close personal friendship between the two men could not continue. In the end, Roosevelt was nominated for a third term, and Farley's career as a national Democratic party leader was over.[51]

Farley's deteriorating relationship with Roosevelt over the issue of a third term in a presidential election year was of vital interest to the British War Cabinet. The ministers understood clearly that nothing was more important for Britain's survival in the present war than the reelection of President Roosevelt. J. O. Perowene prepared a Foreign Office Minute explaining why Farley behaved as he had.

According to Perowene, it was difficult indeed for ordinary English men to appreciate just how dishonest and inefficient American executive government officials, civil servants, and politicians really were. Corruption was an essential part of the American political system. The influence of the present administration in the country depended on an elaborate spoils system. Senior civil servants were appointed on the basis of their affinities with those electoral groups with whom the administration wanted to stand well.[52]

The East Coast Catholic Irish were such a group, Perowene continued, and were of very great importance to the present Democratic administration. The principal problem in all of this, said Perowene, was that among the East Coast Catholic Irish were included "the most dirty politicians in the country."[53] At the center of this elaborate almost elegantly corrupt political system stood Farley. As a past governor of Massachusetts and several times mayor of Boston, according to Perowene, Farley controlled large blocks of East Coast Catholic Irish votes. That was the source of his power and the reason for his central position in the Roosevelt administration.[54] Implied but not stated was the point that defection of Farley from the administration would be a most serious matter for the president in this very uncertain election year.

The best that can be said for this collection of misunderstanding, nonsense, and prejudice is that Perowene managed to confuse the charming James J. Farley of New York with the indefatigable James Michael Curley of Boston. Farley had never been mayor of Boston or governor of Massachusetts while Curley had been elected to both of those offices. Actually, Farley and Curley had no use for one another at all. About all the two men shared in common were their first names, ethnicity, and religious backgrounds, nothing else.

Perowene was not much better in his analysis of Ambassador Joseph P. Kennedy's American political background and of the effect of that background on his political behavior in England. Perowene simply did not research his subject in any detectable way but made judgments about the man based on his bizarre assumptions about the Irish American dimensions of American politics. If Perowene had done any research or even interviewed Kennedy, he would have discovered how distant were Kennedy's ethnic attachments and that major American ambassadorial posts were generally awarded to large financial contributors to winning presidential campaigns.

Perowene described Joseph P. Kennedy in his Foreign Office Minute as owing his present appointment as ambassador "to the fact that he represents a Catholic Irish, anti-English group . . . [and] must therefore continue to exhibit this type of attitude."[55] That sort of judgment could be made only by someone who knew virtually nothing about Kennedy as a man or about his personal history.

Though Joseph P. Kennedy was as familiar with the antics and corruption of Boston's Catholic Irish American politicians as anyone through the experiences of his father and father-in-law, that political culture had little personal appeal for him. As a young business man, Kennedy tried very hard in life and work to distance himself from that milieu and from his ethnic background, complaining frequently that he was as American as any Protestant born in this country.

Obsessed with the idea of becoming a millionaire before turning thirty-five and later making enough money to leave each of nine children a million dollars, Kennedy succeeded grandly. He entered national public service at the top in 1934 but as a rich Catholic financial contributor to the Democratic party rather than as the type of Catholic politician with a large following among Irish Americans as Perowene imagined him to be. Access to the Roosevelt circle had been facilitated by a contribution of $25,000 to the presidential campaign in 1932 and by a loan of $50,000 to the Democratic National Committee. Kennedy continued as a contributor to the Democratic party giving both time and money to the presidential campaign in 1936. With his status as a financial contributor firmly established and after some delay and reflection upon the public relations value of appointing an Irish American to be ambassador to the Court of St. James, Kennedy was given the post in late December 1937.

When British experts on American affairs such as Perowene put such gross misunderstanding and egregious factual errors into reports passed on to policymakers in early 1940, the great unstated value of the official no-propaganda-in-America policy becomes clear. That policy effectively prevented implementation in the United States of propaganda programs and activities based on ridiculous assumptions and flawed information that might have damaged Britain's cause in America beyond repair.

To be sure, the no propaganda policy was strongly challenged in February 1940 by Alfred Duff-Cooper, an influential, out-of-office, anti-Chamberlain Tory.[56] It was challenged again in the same month by Sir John Reith, the founding director of the BBC, when he replaced Lord Macmillan as minister of information.[57] These challenges notwithstanding, Foreign Office officials argued strongly and repeatedly against involving MOI in direct propaganda work in America.

T. North Whitehead insisted that "Influential Americans are saying all the things we want them to say, varying from demands for unlimited help to the Allies to demands for intervention."[58] Dorothy Thompson, Walter Lippman, the *New York Herald-Tribune,* Raymond Gram Swing of MBS, H. V. Kaltenborn of NBC, and Edwin C. Hill of CBS were all doing their part, and doing it very well.[59] North Whitehead added that a reversal in American thinking about the war was well underway. There would be no greater futility, he concluded, than to send British propagandists to the United States "to add their mite of grit to this well-oiled 100 percent American propaganda machine."[60]

While the Foreign Office strongly opposed involving MOI in direct propaganda work in the United States, ministers in London as well as Lord Lothian in Washington were by no means averse to expanding propaganda activities of their own in America within the limits of the existing no propaganda policy. How this was to be done was not easily explained, so in March the Foreign Office looked for outside assistance and considered an elaborate plan prepared by the J. Walter Thompson advertising agency.

The plan prepared by J. Walter Thompson emphasized the limited nature of the amount of aid needed from the United States. It was based on a theory of reverse psychology, contending that Americans would be more generous with their aid if assured that their troops would never be needed.[61] Foreign Office officials were not convinced by this argument and were disappointed with other parts of the plan as well. Though this J. Walter Thompson plan died aborning, there would be others.

In any case, during February and March of 1940 the Foreign Office and MOI were on the way toward direct confrontation over the issue of doing direct propaganda in the United States. As a matter of fact, one could argue that during February and March, the most serious aggressive actions of the war did not occur between Allied and German forces on the western front. During those two months, the real war in the West was waged between the British Foreign Office and MOI over what an appropriate propaganda policy in America ought to be and which government agency ought to direct it. All of this came to a frightening end when German forces invaded Denmark and Norway in early April.

Britain's immediate naval response to this invasion and the subsequent disastrous amphibious operations in Norway dominated the news throughout April and early May. The Chamberlain government could not recover from the military and naval failures of this campaign, and the prime minister was forced to resign. Churchill replaced Chamberlain as prime minister on May 9 and formed a national government to take charge of the war effort. Out-of-office Tories were added to the cabinet as well. Anthony Eden became minister of war and Anthony Duff-Cooper replaced Reith as minister of information. The new government enjoyed no respite at all. The German assault on the Low Countries and the opening of the Battle of France began on May 10, 1940, and quickly became the most compelling emergency of the war.

About a week before the Chamberlain government fell and before German tanks roared into the Low Countries and into France, the small war between MOI and the Foreign Office over control of propaganda in America ended. On May 2, representatives of the Foreign Office and MOI met to clarify the status of a new MOI presence in America. The issue between these two government departments was no longer whether to expand propaganda activities in the United States, but when and how.[62] The official policy of no propaganda in America was over. Rae Smith of the J. Walter Thompson advertising agency was ready with another plan which this time was presented to MOI instead of to the Foreign Office.

Smith's plan was derived from similar ones which the agency had developed for use in Rumania and in Latin America.[63] The agency proposed establishing a subsidiary in Canada that would distribute articles and drawings for magazines and newspapers throughout the United States. Whether this subsidiary would go beyond simply providing articles and pictures to other forms of propaganda would be decided later. Materials developed for the subsidiary would be distributed through the BLI in New York or through "some existing American body . . . with which . . . [J. Walter Thompson] were on confidential terms."[64] The timing for submission of Smith's plan could not have been worse. The rush of events in early May postponed all serious consideration of it.

The last weeks of May and the first week of June were an extraordinary time. German penetration of the Ardennes broke through the center of the French armies, cut off all of the northern Allied forces from southern communications, and forced the British Army and half of the French First Army to withdraw to the Dunkirk bridgehead. Evacuation from Dunkirk began on May 26, and by the time it was completed on June 4 over 338,000 Allied troops had been landed in England. Twelve days later, the French government sought terms for an immediate armistice. The Battle of France was over; the Battle of Britain was about to begin.

— vi —

It was a desperate time and desperate measures had to be taken. Churchill began his celebrated inspirational broadcasts directed as much toward American listeners as to his own people. The prime minister pleaded with Roosevelt for a loan of fifty destroyers. Those ships were needed to replace the six British destroyers lost and nineteen damaged at Dunkirk and to help repel an anticipated German invasion. The British government published the text of a declaration of indissoluble political union between Britain and France. Though in itself an utterly meaningless document, it was drafted and released in order to persuade Americans that Britain had not really abandoned France to save itself.[65]

On the specific issue of doing direct propaganda in America, one incredibly over-optimistic tactic was considered and some practical ones were adopted. Because a wall of censorship surrounded operations at Dunkirk, virtually no one outside of the prime minister and service departments knew what was happening there or what the outcome would be. While those heroic events were underway, Rae Smith of J. Walter Thompson returned to MOI on May 30 with another propaganda plan.[66]

In order to find propaganda advantage in the present military crisis in Belgium, Smith proposed a radio blitz of America's vast listening audience. Smith intended that once the military situation in Belgium stabilized, British propaganda broadcasters could declare that while the Germans have won a battle, in doing so they have lost the war. Hitler's fatal error of judgment, his biggest blunder, was to drive through to the channel ports leaving the French army intact. Historians will describe the Battle of Flanders as the greatest military victory in British history.[67]

Scripts had been written for Churchill, members of the cabinet, service commanders, the head of Chrysler Corporation in Britain, a wounded and burned tank driver, a fighter pilot, and refugees. Smith submitted a program budget of £100,000 for a radio campaign lasting six months.[68] Of course, the military situation in Flanders never stabilized, the French army was split, and Hitler's fatal blunder was to have his forces pause outside of Dunkirk to regroup before overrunning and occupying the town.

What Churchill thought about the plan or about the radio scripts written for him and others is unknown. However, no further references to Rae Smith or to the J. Walter Thompson agency appear in Foreign Office or MOI files for the rest of the war. However, the Smith propaganda plan was not entirely without effect or historical consequences. Though Smith's specific scheme for deriving some sort of propaganda benefit from Germany's spectacular victory in Belgium and northern France was rendered obsolete by events, his idea about finding glory in defeat was not. If there were no glory or propaganda advantage in the Battle of Flanders, perhaps some could be found in Operation Dynamo, the evacuation from Dunkirk.

By any measure, this evacuation was an ignominious event. So ignominious was it that the British concealed news about what was happening there from their Belgian and French allies for several days. However, the bravery of the pilots of Fighter Command who successfully disrupted German bombing of the beaches and the heroism of the destroyer crews who brought off most of the men from the Dunkirk quays, aided by a handful of civilian volunteers in vessels of all sizes, excited editorial imaginations on both sides of the Atlantic, and the Dunkirk spirit of experiencing defeat but never recognizing or admitting it was born.

The idea of civilian volunteers spontaneously responding to the military crisis in Dunkirk harbor and on nearby beaches by participating in the rescue of thousands of troops from destruction and capture was overpowering. The *New York Herald-Tribune* expressed the emotive power of this as yet unnamed Dunkirk spirit on May 31, 1940, in an editorial proclaiming, "Defeat sustained with such fortitude is no disaster."[69] The *New York Times* did the same, declaring that the rages and blemishes hiding the soul of British democracy had fallen away in the hell and horror of Dunkirk harbor, "There, beaten but unconquered, in shinning splendor she faced the enemy."[70] Here was an image of Britain that Americans could admire. Here was a nation of kindred people that Americans must help survive.

However, the Dunkirk spirit and image throughout the summer of 1940 was one that required constant reinforcement. From the British perspective, there were sinister forces at work in America against the British cause. Most of these sinister forces appeared to be driven in part by information supplied by the American ambassador in London, Joseph P. Kennedy. The Foreign Office advised Lothian in a coded telegram on June 25, 1940, that Kennedy had reported to Washington a very low state of morale in Britain about continuing the war. Lothian was directed to counter such reports by calling on State Department officers with a clear message that Britain was determined to prosecute the war to a victorious conclusion.[71] In such meetings with State Department officials, Lothian was instructed to make the point that Britain would never follow the French path. Serious consideration was being given to the idea of bombing Berlin "in spite of reprisals which are recognized as inevitable."[72]

Lothian went directly to the State Department to mention the Kennedy matter and to deliver his message. He also sent a personal statement to the president expressing the British government's determination to fight on to the end.[73] Next, Lothian urged the prime minister to make a "cheering" broadcast directed to the Empire but really intended for the United States. He also urged that the prime minister of Canada make a "stouthearted statement" of the same sort.[74] While at the State Department, Lothian was told by the under secretary that Kennedy had sent no reports about low morale in Britain. All that Kennedy had reported was that the British public had not yet grasped the seriousness of their position.[75]

Churchill responded to Lothian's request for a "cheering" broadcast by promising to make one but he did not believe that words counted for very much at the present moment. Up to April, Churchill declared, the

Americans were so sure the Allies would win that not much help was thought necessary. Now, most of America, he continued, was so sure that Britain would lose, that help of any sort was thought to be futile. Though twelve ships loaded with war materials were on their way from Raritan, New Jersey, to Britain, Churchill was correct on June 28, 1940, when he complained that "we have not had any help worth speaking from the U.S. so far."[76]

About responding to what Churchill called the "eddies of U.S. opinion," too much attention should not be paid to such shifts and changes as "only the force of events can govern them."[77] We know, Churchill added, "the president is our best friend, but it is no use to try to dance attendance upon the Republican and Democratic conventions." What really matters "is whether Hitler is master of Britain in three months or not. I think not." The prime minister believed strongly that Britain could "repel invasion and keep alive in the air. Any how we are going to try. . . ." As ambassador, Churchill advised Lothian, "Your mood should be bland and phlegmatic. No one is down-hearted here."[78]

Yet decisions about increasing propaganda activities in the United States had to be made in June 1940. Among the practical ones made at that time were more public speeches and private communications to influential people by Lothian himself, the addition of press liaison personnel to the British consulate in New York, and the dispatch of the Hungarian-born British film director Alexander Korda to Hollywood. Most important of all was the decision to assign William Stephenson to New York as head of British secret intelligence operations in the Western hemisphere.

Lothian increased his own public speaking activities. The ambassador addressed repeatedly the theme of sea power and how much the security of the United States depended on the Royal Navy. At the same time, in private communications to influential Americans Lothian pointed out how tenuous that very important dependence really was. In the event of disaster, a neutral America should not expect that the Royal Navy would be turned over to them.[79] In addition to those public speeches and private communications, Lothian used Aubrey Morgan, Lindbergh's brother-in-law, as a conduit to American interventionists such as Henry P. Van Dusen of the Union Theological Seminary in New York, and John Balderston, a playwright and journalist who had spent many years living and working in London.[80]

As Lothian read the present state of American public opinion at the end of 1940, the need for additional skilled press liaison people in New York was self-evident. Since the fall of France, the ambassador wrote to the Foreign Office, a wave of pessimism had passed over the United States. There was widespread fear that Britain would be defeated. With that discouraging outcome almost certain, there was no reason why America should entangle itself in European affairs.

Moreover, Lothian continued, the "Isolationist Brigade" was still extremely formidable and included important elements in the Republican party.[81] Senator Robert A. Taft (R-Ohio) had delivered a speech in St. Louis on May 20, setting forth carefully considered isolationist views which possibly might be swept aside by a flood of public opinion, if indeed, such a flood could be generated.[82] Other Republican politicians at their national convention in Philadelphia in June had managed to "confuse thoroughly the whole European issue with the lowest type of party politics."[83]

Given this situation, Lothian insisted, British representatives in the United States could not afford to lose a single opportunity to reinforce a discernable trend in American public opinion toward regarding Britain as America's first line of defense. Opportunities to do so occurred on a daily basis. Each hydra-headed isolationist argument needed to be cut off whenever and wherever it appeared.[84] Experienced press personnel were needed to do this. Lothian's argument to the Foreign Office was accepted completely. Press personnel were quickly recruited and sent off to New York.

Alexander Korda was a special friend of Churchill and apparently had done work for the British Secret Intelligence Service during the 1930s. When war broke out in September 1939, Korda abruptly stopped production of his feature adventure film *The Thief of Baghdad*, borrowed money, and quickly produced a propaganda film, *The Lion Has Wings*, based on a story about an RAF raid on the Kiel Canal. The film was ready for release in late October. The American version carried a commentary by Lowell Thomas, veteran American foreign correspondent and regular narrator for Fox newsreels. Though shot from an uninspired script and hastily produced, the film and story appeared authentic to American audiences and was highly successful.[85]

Korda went off to Hollywood in 1940 because he needed to finish *The Thief of Baghdad* and because his wife, Merle Oberon, had signed a contract with a studio there. His presence in Hollywood insured a steady parade of motion pictures with a definite pro-British message as well as films that were direct propaganda. Among the best of those with a pro-British message was *That Hamilton Woman*, a story about Lord Horatio Nelson's relationship with his mistress during the Napoleonic wars given contemporary reference by including speeches about never making peace with dictators. A highly successful Korda-financed direct propaganda film was the entertaining comedic assault on Hitler's image, *To Be or Not to Be.*[86]

More important, Korda joined with other British producers, directors, and actors already in Hollywood and helped enlist the American film industry into the British war effort in 1940 and 1941. Churchill rewarded Korda for his artistic achievements and other services in the United States prior to the attack on Pearl Harbor by giving him a knighthood in 1942.[87]

William Stephenson was also a special friend of Churchill. A Canadian by birth, a fighter pilot during World War I, and an industrialist during the inter-war years, Stephenson was familiar with the United States and was well-connected there through business contacts. Stephenson had also done work for British intelligence services during the 1930s monitoring the German rearmament program.[88] Arriving in New York on June 21, 1940, Stephenson began exploring the possibility of contact and cooperation between the British Secret Overseas Service (MI6) and the Federal Bureau of Investigation (FBI). Stephenson successfully established direct relations with J. Edgar Hoover, director of the FBI, and obtained Roosevelt's approval of close cooperation between the FBI and MI6. Stephenson acquired a small staff, set up offices in Rockefeller Center near the BLI and BBC, and began operations under the name, suggested by Hoover, of British Security Coordination (BSC).[89]

Though Stephenson's mission charge was vague, he understood it to be that of investigating enemy activities and organizing American public opinion in favor of giving more aid to Britain. Once Stephenson's BSC was in place, it became the coordinating center for a whole range of overt and covert activities. The real importance of the BSC was not so much undercover activities as it was developing cordial relations with American security services.[90]

Stephenson became a close and trusted friend of Colonel William Donovan, Roosevelt's new intelligence aide, and provided much welcomed advice and assistance for what came to be the American Office of Strategic Services (OSS). However, with that help came some enormous risks. Major Dick Ellis, Stephenson's deputy, provided the Americans with valued information about techniques of undercover work. At the same time, however, as he confessed later, he also sold secrets to both the Germans and the Russians, an achievement unmatched by any agent on any side during World War II.[91]

Though Stephenson's BSC obtained some significant successes in 1940, he was inclined, later, to claim credit for every advance of the British cause in America. His claims about arms procurement from the

American government during the critical days following the Dunkirk evacuation is a case in point. The evacuated British soldiers had left virtually all of their weapons and equipment in France for the Germans to capture or destroy. The weapons lost could not be replaced from existing inventories in England but only by newly manufactured arms which took time or were obtained from the United States. Because of the threat of possible invasion, the arms and munitions situation in Britain during the summer of 1940 was truly a desperate one.

The only legal way for the American government to transfer arms and munitions from their military inventories to Britain quickly and without congressional approval was to make use of an old statute and declare such needed arms and munitions to be surplus. Once declared surplus, government arms and munitions could be sold to a private American corporation which in turn would sell them to Britain for cash. The arms and munitions would then be transported across the Atlantic on British ships. The middle man for such a transaction in the summer of 1940 was the U. S. Steel Corporation.[92]

Given the legal and many practical problems related to transferring arms and munitions to Britain and the fact that American military leaders were strongly opposed to raiding their inventories in order to do so, there was not much that lobbying efforts by BSC or any other organization could do to facilitate such a project. As a matter of fact, the less people knew about the project the better. Nonetheless, Stephenson claimed after the war that his group was responsible for the delivery of one million rifles, 30 million rounds of ammunition, and 100 Flying Fortress heavy bombers to Britain in the summer and fall of 1940. Stephenson's recollections of this transaction were flawed, inaccurate about what had been sent, and self-serving.

The reality was that about 500,000 rifles of World War I vintage, most of British design and manufacture, were released for export along with perhaps 100,000 machine guns, fewer than 200 tanks, 895 75mm field guns, large quantities of ammunition, and ninety-three light and medium bombers. Since the U.S. Army Air Force only had fifty-two Flying Fortresses in active service, only twelve or one quarter of the entire inventory were authorized to be declared surplus and sent to Britain. Altogether 600 freight cars brought materials from army depots and arsenals scattered about the country to the central loading station at Raritan, New Jersey.[93] Twelve British ships were at Raritan to receive the material and loading began on June 11, 1940, ten days before Stephenson arrived in New York. This massive project had been driven by President Roosevelt and succeeded only because he followed every detail of it, brushed aside opposition from the military high command and the secretary of war, and intervened constantly to see that schedules were met.[94]

Stephenson's claims about BSC propaganda coups were strongly put but generally accurate. He took full credit for exposing German efforts to break the American oil embargo. Stephenson supplied the *New York Times* and *New York Herald-Tribune* with details about German contacts with American oil executives. On another occasion, he provided Donovan and the journalist Edgar Ansel Mowrer with material on pro-German groups and their activities in the United States. The material provided by Stephenson became the basis for a series of articles in the *New York Herald-Tribune* and an alarmist national radio broadcast by Donovan.[95]

In early 1941, Stephenson and BSC received new and greater responsibilities. BSC became the American office of Britain's internal security service (MI5). Also, for about six months a branch of the Special Operations Executive (SOE) in the United States, a covert propaganda unit reported to Stephenson. In July 1941, control of SOE in the United States passed from BSC to the Foreign Office.

In addition, Stephenson claimed to have a stable of both British and American intellectuals, writers, academic, and actors at his beck-and-call ready and willing to do whatever they could to try and bring America into the war. Stephenson claimed also to have contacts with New York liberal publications such as *PM*, the *Nation*, and the *New Republic* which were anxious to publish articles derived from materials regularly provided by BSC.

Most important, during 1941, BSC developed links with existing American interventionist groups and claimed to have helped found and fund new, much more militant ones such as the Non-Sectarian Anti-Nazi League, Friends of Democracy, and the Fight for Freedom Committee. According to BSC documents, none of these groups were aware of just how pervasive British influence was upon them. Permanent officials in those organizations had no direct contact with BSC; all contact was carried through third party cutouts.[96]

With Lothian regularly communicating with American interventionists through Morgan, with so many supportive contacts in the New York press, and with all of Stephenson's experienced, well-funded intelligence assets in place, in early 1941 a full-scale propaganda assault on American isolationism could begin and did. On June 28, 1940, the war cabinet formally decided to undertake propaganda in the United States. It was time, the War Cabinet Minute stated, "to take more active steps to make our point of view more widely known in the U.S. and to counteract German propaganda."[97] Among the first of many celebrities recruited and employed to work for the embassy, BLI, and BSC charged to help bring America into the war were Gilbert Highet, renowned classicist from Columbia University and his wife Helen MacInnes, author of mysteries and thrillers; the brilliant young Oxford philosopher with contacts in the American Jewish community Isaiah Berlin; and the actor and playwright Noel Coward.[98]

As Churchill had predicted, during the late summer and early fall of 1940 events drove everything, and the British government was able only to respond to the most important of them. On July 16, 1940, Hitler directed that preparations for invading Britain should go forward. The Battle of Britain began in earnest on August 13 when German bomber fleets attacked potential invasion landing sites in southeast England, losing more than twice as many planes as the British in the process. After five days, the Germans changed tactics and set out to destroy British fighter bases in Kent, nearly succeeding. About the same time, the British began night bombing of German towns, including an attack on Berlin that been under consideration since June.

Embarrassed and infuriated by the attack on Berlin, the Germans shifted tactics again. They turned away from attacks on airfields, and on September 7 began bombing London. The Germans made their last great air offensive as a prelude to invasion on September 15 and failed to win control of British airspace. On September 17, German invasion plans were postponed only to be cancelled on October 12 which was, in effect, final.

The nightly air raids on London begun on September 7 intensified and continued for fifty-seven nights. Having abandoned invasion plans, Hitler decided to try and bomb Britain into insignificance while looking for military victories elsewhere. As German air assaults on London continued and spread to industrial centers in the Midlands, Churchill waited for any sort of positive reaction from the United States. He had hoped that bombing of London, Oxford, Coventry, and Canterbury would cause a wave of indignation in America and a popular clamor for intervention on Britain's side. That did not happen.

Churchill and others in the British government had to admit to themselves that President Roosevelt had been wrong in 1939 when he told the king that bombing London and other British cities would bring America into the war. On September 27, 1940, the British War Cabinet acknowledged that their country could never win the war without American participation as a full-scale belligerent.[99] That fortuitous event could not be left to chance. Only after waging and winning a campaign against isolationism in the United States and obtaining American intervention could a victorious war against Germany begin.

— vii —

Americans had been following with great attention the course of the war since September 1939 through newspaper, radio, and film accounts. None had followed it more closely, however, than President Roosevelt and his White House staff. After May 10, 1940, when the Germans invaded the Low Countries, war news flowed into the White House on a minute-by-minute basis and none of it was good. Clearly, a major Allied defeat was building, an international crisis of historic importance was at hand, and the American people would have to be told what the great events occurring in the Low Countries and France meant to them. A major presidential address was scheduled to be delivered to a joint session of both houses of Congress on May 16, 1940.

More than major speeches were required in London. When German forces smashed through French defenses at Sedan and there were no French reserves at hand to oppose them, the full magnitude of a rapidly unfolding military disaster was clear to both the French and British high commands. On May 16, when Roosevelt addressed Congress, Churchill flew to Paris and heard first hand from French generals that the Germans probably would be in Paris within a week. The prime minister returned to London and issued orders to his field commanders to extricate as many British troops as possible from a situation becoming more hopeless hour by hour.

Roosevelt went to the Capitol in the early afternoon of May 16 and addressed Congress and the country on the dangerous prospects facing the nation. The president noted flying times from Greenland, the Azores, and Caribbean islands to American cities, making the point that the Atlantic and Pacific oceans in this age of flight were no longer the protective barriers they once had been. Moreover, Germany had more war planes than all of the Allies put together as well as a much greater weekly productive capacity to replace aircraft lost.

America could respond to this changed and ever changing world in only one way. Security and salvation in this very dangerous time were obtainable only through preparedness. "No old defense is so strong," Roosevelt insisted, "that it requires no further strengthening, and no attack is so unlikely or impossible that it may be ignored."[100] He asked for appropriations to recruit an additional 500,000 men for the army, to buy guns and equipment, to manufacture modern tanks, and to build more ships for the navy.

His most striking request was to call upon Congress for funds and upon American industry for a manufacturing capacity to produce 50,000 war planes a year, more than ten times current annual production. That goal, seemingly so utterly impossible, stirred the imagination of the country, inspired confidence, and persuaded millions of Americans that they could do anything. Actually, this apparently impossible goal was not so far-fetched. It was almost achieved by 1942 and was greatly surpassed a year later.[101] No where in Roosevelt's speech was there any mention of how much this massive proposed preparedness effort would cost or how the government would pay for it.

When the president finished his speech, senators and congressmen rose and gave him a ringing ovation. The leader had spoken, and most of the people wanted to believe what he had said. Though costs and taxes had not been mentioned, Republican leaders generally, including former President Herbert Hoover, stated publicly that in the matter of preparedness, Roosevelt was right. However, the ringing ovation of Congress and the praise of Republican leaders was short-lived. The cheers stopped and criticism began after Charles Lindbergh delivered a trenchant and pessimistic response to the president's speech in a nation-wide radio address two days later.

Actually, Lindbergh built upon what other isolationists had been saying for some time. Senator Bennett Clark (D-Missouri) had complained bitterly that over $6 billion had already been spent on preparedness, and according to the White House, the country was still supposedly woefully unprepared. It must be said that at this stage of Senator Clark's life, one could never be certain whether he was drunk or sober. Whether in his cups or not, Clark made the point that the existence of an emergency in Europe could not justify turning over billions more to bunglers who had already wasted $6 billion.[102]

On May 18, 1940, Lindbergh berated the president for creating what he described as a "defense hysteria," insisting that the United States was not threatened by foreign invasion and would never be unless Americans brought it on themselves by meddling in Europe's affairs. That line of argument could be heard also from any German official in the United States. What Lindbergh said next was original with him and probably derived from his knowledge of the activities of his brother-in-law and sister-in-law, Aubrey Morgan and Constance Morrow Morgan, and their friends at the BLI.

Lindbergh told his national radio audience that the only reason why there was any danger of America getting into the European war was because powerful elements in American society wanted us to become involved. According to him, those powerful elements were a small minority of affluent influentials who had ready media access and were determined to move American public opinion toward eventual intervention in the war as a full belligerent.[103] Lindbergh wanted his listeners to know where this minority was trying to lead them.

Isolationists rallied to a new champion of their cause. Senator Gerald P. Nye (R-North Dakota) described Lindbergh as a voice of sanity at "this wild moment—engineered by the president."[104] Congress John Rankin (D-Mississippi) said much the same. Lindbergh's speech so infuriated Roosevelt that he privately expressed his conviction that that man had become a Nazi.[105] Even Henry Stimson, a life-long Republican, described Lindbergh's speech as "not . . . better put if it had been written by Goebbels himself."[106] Though Lindbergh would argue his cause in much stronger and more accusatory terms over the next year and a half, for the president and those around him the man had crossed a very important line on May 16, 1940. Indeed, while congressional isolationists were delighted by finding such a well-known and highly regarded champion, the president, not a man easily driven to anger, had discovered an absolutely unforgivable enemy.

Up until the fall of France in May 1940, public opinion polls in this country heavily favored Britain and France over Germany and most Americans expected that in the end the Allies would win the war.[107] As a matter of fact, in polls taken in March 1940 before the Germans invaded Denmark and Norway, almost seven out of every ten respondents believed that the United States would not be drawn into the war at all.[108]

After the fall of France that sense of relative complacency was shattered. Polls taken in June 1940 showed an almost complete reversal of public opinion on the prospect of the United States staying out of the war. Sixty-five percent of those polled in June expected the United States to enter the war sometime.[109] In polls taken two months later, at the height of the Battle of Britain, the number of respondents expecting future American involvement in the war rose to 67 percent.[110]

This major shift of American public opinion toward an expectation of formal involvement in the war was a direct consequence of the course of that conflict. German military successes had greatly raised anxiety levels in the United States about the inevitability of American participation in the war. At the same time that the dramatic events occurring in the skies over London were changing American public opinion about the war, several small but influential pro-British groups of American citizens working out of New York and Washington, D.C., organized themselves to try and do the same thing.

Shortly after the war began in September 1939, at the behest of President Roosevelt, Clark Eichelberger, sometime director of the League of

Nations Non-Partisan Association in New York, and James T. Shotwell, a Columbia University historian, asked William Allen White, celebrated editor of the Emporia, Kansas, *Gazette,* to head an organization committed to obtaining revision of the Neutrality Act.[111] While White was for many a symbol of mid-American homespun values, he was best remembered by American Catholics as a strident opponent of Alfred E. Smith's presidential candidacy in the very bigotted anti-Catholic Republican campaign of 1928.

By the end of October 1939, Eichelberger and White had decided to call this group the Non-Partisan Committee for Peace through Revision of the Neutrality Law and had managed the establishment of a rudimentary structure of chapters in thirty states. In addition, Eichelberger and White managed to obtain endorsements and expressions of support from prominent Democrats and Republicans for the cause of neutrality law revision.[112]

With the enactment of the Pittman Amendments or "cash-and-carry" provisions of the Neutrality Law in November 1940 permitting belligerents to pay cash for arms and transport them out of this country in their own ships, the Non-Partisan Committee disbanded. However, interested participants maintained communication with one another and in effect preserved the basis of a network of like-minded influentials for some future public policy organization.

As early as December 1939, President Roosevelt had invited White to spend a night at the White House. The president wanted White to help him persuade the American people to think more seriously about the consequences of the wars in Europe and Asia for this country. He was alarmed that important American interests in Europe and Asia might be sacrificed because of panic inspired by a fear of being dragged into either of those conflicts.[113] From that presidential overture to White much was to follow, but first events had to justify organization and action.

The fall of Denmark and Norway in April 1940 provided such a justification. White and several other influentials who had participated in the Non-Partisan Committee at last had become convinced that more active measures were required to assure an Allied victory. By drawing heavily upon Non-Partisan Committee mailing lists, Eichelberger and White managed to put together in about one month's time a nationwide organization to promote all-out aid to Britain and France.[114]

This new organization appropriately named the Committee to Defend America by Aiding the Allies (CDAAA) went public on May 20, 1940. White became national chairman but remained in Kansas. Eichelberger was appointed executive director of the committee and handled daily operations out of its New York City headquarters.[115] The CDAAA enjoyed a phenomenal success during the next few months. Under White's leadership the committee recruited a sponsoring board of prominent persons, raised funds, and established over six hundred local branches.[116] Most important, the CDAAA carried out an effective "Stop Hitler Now" campaign in newspaper advertisements across the country.[117]

The creation and progress of CDAAA or the White Committee as it came to be known was carefully monitored by the British Embassy and BLI. The rapid spread of local branches across the country also attracted the attention of Douglas Williams, new head of the American division of MOI in London. On October 4, 1940, Williams sent a telegram to Lothian requesting that an offer of collaboration be sent from the embassy directly to White. Williams wanted White to select an MOI official to open up direct negotiations with him by transatlantic telephone. Williams' proposal almost gave Lothian apoplexy.[118]

The ambassador communicated immediately with Duff Cooper, the minister of information, and Lord Halifax, foreign secretary, urging that the Williams proposal be dropped at once. If it were ever known that the White Committee was communicating and collaborating with any branch of His Majesty's government, Lothian insisted, the result would be utterly disastrous. Such charges were already being made indirectly against the White Committee on a daily basis by German and isolationist propagandists.[119]

At the moment, Lothian continued, Britain's standing in the United States was "astonishingly good but could be severely damaged by any further shocks of this character. The enemy is already organizing the America First Committee to counter the William Allen White movement."[120] Duff Cooper responded to Lothian immediately. He agreed that all plans for collaboration between Williams and the White Committee should be abandoned, adding that anything of this nature, everything in New York, must be deferred until after the presidential election in November.[121]

While there was no formal connection between the CDAAA and the Roosevelt administration, it quickly became something of an unofficial public relations organization for the President's foreign policies.[122] White and other leaders of CDAAA frequently consulted with the president and his cabinet members, but there was not always complete agreement between the committee and the administration.[123] White in particular was very difficult to move further than he was ready to go.[124] To be sure, White believed that defeat of the Axis powers was essential for the survival of western civilization, and he was ready to support all necessary aid to Britain short of war. Nonetheless, White was firmly opposed to American intervention as a full-time belligerent.

At this time, however, some members of CDAAA were of a different mind. A few influentials in the committee and several like-minded individuals who were not members had persuaded themselves that defeating the Axis was more important than keeping the United States out of the war. As a matter of fact, a very small group of such persons came together during the dark days of June 1940 and actually issued a public letter to major newspapers across the country urging a declaration of war against Germany.[125]

This one-and-a-half page letter entitled "A Summons to Speak Out" had been drafted by Whitney Shepardson from the Council on Foreign Relations with assistance from Francis Pickens Miller, also from the Council, and Helen Hill Miller, Washington correspondent for *The Economist* of London.[126] This public letter urged Americans to recognize that Nazi Germany was the mortal enemy of American ideals, institutions, and way of life.

Moreover, if the Allies were defeated, the United States would have to fight Nazi Germany alone. The facts and logic of this situation, the letter continued, required that the United States should declare war on Germany and dispatch immediately all disposable air, military, naval and material resources to the Allies.[127]

"The Summons to Speak Out" was released on June 10, 1940, and appeared with thirty signatures led by Shephardson and the Millers and followed by Herbert Agar, author, editor of the *Louisville Courier-Journal*, and former correspondent residing in London; Henry W. Hobson, Episcopal bishop of Cincinnati; the ubiquitous John Balderston; Stringfellow Barr, president of St. John's College; and Walter Millis, historian and editorial writer for the *New York Herald-Tribune*.[128]

The appearance of the "Summons to Speak Out" was a very small matter indeed amidst the momentous events occurring between the Dunkirk evacuation and the surrender of France. While the "Summons to Speak Out" was not unnoticed by major American newspapers, the impact of it upon American public opinion was minimal. Probably nothing further would have been heard from the group that issued the "Summons to Speak Out" had it not been for the zeal and industry of Dr. Henry Pitt Van Duesen, dean of students at the Union Theological Seminary.

As a sincere and committed Christian minister, Van Duesen had very strong views about the moral necessity of immediate American intervention in the war against Nazi Germany, and had been personally offended by not having been solicited to sign the "Summons to Speak Out." This very energetic man persuaded the Millers and others that a group of influentials favoring immediate American participation in the war ought to be organized and that a public relations campaign to attain that end should be undertaken.[129]

Van Duesen and the Millers agreed to approach some man of means who favored intervention and who would be willing to act as a dinner host for a group of a dozen or so persons who would discuss the present crisis situation and plan a course of action.[130] The first of such dinners was given by Lewis W. Douglas, president of the Mutual Life Insurance Company and former director of the budget, in New York in early July. Other dinners followed, soon to be regularized on a weekly basis. About twenty-eight prominent and influential persons became informally associated to educate the American people about the necessity for United States participation in the war.

Known as the Century Group because so many of their weekly sessions were held on the premises of the Century Association, a private men's club in New York, a core of regulars was always present, although attendance varied from meeting to meeting. Among this core were those signers of the "Summons to Speak Out" living in the New York metropolitan area as well as Van Duesen; Douglas; Henry Sloan Coffin, president of the Union Theological Seminary; Robert Sherwood, playwright and presidential speech writer; Ulric Bell, on leave from the *Louisville Courier-Journal;* Ward Cheney, wealthy New York silk manufacturer; and James Warburg, writer and banker. In and out of the Century Group were men as talented and celebrated as Allen Dulles, Dean Acheson, Joseph Alsop, Elmer Davis, and James B. Conant.[131]

The Century Group decided to pursue three courses of action during the summer and fall of 1940. First, members intended by public endorsements and personal influence to persuade the public to support a policy of massive aid to Britain, especially the sale or transfer of as many destroyers, fifteen years of age or older, as possible. Those destroyers as well as some of the new high-speed motor torpedo boats and new four-engine, long-range B-17 heavy bombers, leaders of the Century Group insisted, would be needed to repulse the German invasion of England which they believed would be underway in a few weeks.

Second, the group planned a program of news releases, public letters, and radio broadcasts to attack what they believed were the perils and fallacies of continued American neutrality. In their view, the voices for interventionism had to be louder and heard more often than those of neutrality.

Third, the group agreed to advocate and promote a series of government policies and actions such as convoying British merchant vessels and even dispatching American naval units to assist the Royal Navy. The objective of such policies was no more and no less than eventual full-scale American belligerency in the war.[132]

During the summer and fall of 1940 all of these activities were undertaken by the Century Group and enjoyed varying degrees of success and failure. It became clear enough while the Battle of Britain was being fought over London and southeast England in September that in America more than public letters and celebrity statements were needed to move public opinion toward an interventionist position. While the Luftwaffe had not been much impressed by statements and radio addresses of prominent Americans for the British cause, American public opinion had not been much moved by them either.

Anti-interventionist public statements were widespread and anti-interventionist organizations were multiplying. A wider and more intense public discussion of the need to go to war was required than either the Century Group or the White Committee had been able to achieve. In the fall of 1940, some members of the Century Group, in contact with Stephenson and BSC, began to think and talk about establishing a new nationwide interventionist organization. Francis Miller, Van Duesen, Bishop Hobson, Warburg, Agar, Bell, and Douglas all gave time and energy to the creation of this national organization. It was Francis Miller who on January 11, 1941, contributed the name Fight for Freedom; and three weeks later James Warburg wrote the organization's founding declaration.[133]

According to Warburg, the proper goal of American statesmanship was not to keep America out of the war but to keep the military phases of the war out of America. All of America's strength and resources should be fully deployed as soon as possible to defeat the Axis powers.[134] The founders of what came to be Fight for Freedom, Inc. (FFF), had taken a very long step past the White Committee's position of all aid short of war.

Even with assistance and funds from BSC, organizational problems took time to resolve, and not until April 19, 1941, were the leaders ready to go public and begin establishing local chapters on a nationwide basis. Senator Carter Glass of Virginia, chairman of the Senate Finance Committee, agreed to serve as honorary chairman while Bishop Hobson assumed the post of national chairman. A stellar list of Fight for Freedom sponsors including university presidents, religious leaders, Hollywood personalities, authors and playwrights, representatives from the media, the bar, and the business world was released as a qualitative indicator of support for the new organization. Day-to-day operations fell into the hands of F. Peter Cusick, a New York advertising executive and a close friend of Wendell Willkie. As chairman of the executive committee, Ulric

Bell became the principal policymaker and the person most responsible for coordinating the efforts of local Fight for Freedom chapters and keeping in touch with the Roosevelt administration and the BSC.[135]

Organizing local chapters proceeded apace with the help of teams of professional organizers. Within a month those teams had established 273 local chapters in various stages.[136] By the time of the attack on Pearl Harbor the number of local chapters had risen to 372, and in perhaps a dozen states there were statewide organizations.[137] While the quality and effectiveness of the local chapters varied greatly, strength was concentrated in the northeast and south, and in virtually all of the major cities there was an FFF presence.

The growth of local FFF chapters notwithstanding, even when abetted by CDAAA activities for all aid short of war and Century Group campaigns, interventionist opinions in the country up to October 1941 never exceeded 21 percent of all Americans polled.[138] When the conversion of American opinion came on December 7, 1941, it was the rush of events that had managed it. Nonetheless, the proliferation of pro-British organizations and the mounting of interventionist public relations campaigns made many Americans wonder where their country's foreign policy was being made and who was making it.

A major reaction to CDAAA and Century Group activities was inevitable. What Lothian had referred to on October 4, 1940, as America First, the enemy's counter to the White Committee began first in the late spring of 1940 on college campuses among draft-age young men.

At that time, a group of law students at Yale University began meeting regularly to discuss their fears that America was drifting slowly but surely toward full belligerency in the European war. This group was led by Robert Douglas Stuart, Jr., son of a vice president of the Quaker Oats Company. Stuart, aided by Kingman Brewster, Jr., editor of the *Yale Daily News;* Gerald R. Ford, a future president of the United States; and Potter Stewart, a future justice of the Supreme Court, sent anti-interventionist petitions to friends on other eastern college campuses urging them to collect signatures from students opposed to American involvement in the European war.[139]

Another future president was among the early financial contributors to this cause. John F. Kennedy contributed $100 in April 1941, indicating to Stuart that he believed that this work was vital. Stuart responded by asking Kennedy to join their group and work full time for the cause when he returned from a trip to Latin America.[140] Kennedy did not chose to do so, but his future brother-in-law, R. Sargent Shriver did. Shriver joined College Men for Defense First (CMDF), a committee organized later by the Stuart group.[141]

When the petitions sent to other colleges were returned with requests for still more petitions, Stuart and his friends at Yale realized that they had touched a groundswell of popular opinion and decided to take more definite steps to organize and direct it.[142] From these modest beginnings came the America First Committee (AFC), the largest and most influential anti-interventionist organization of the time.

Working through business connections of his father, Stuart solicited support from midwestern business leaders, held a luncheon for interested Chicagoans in July, and obtained rent-free space in the Quaker Oats section of the Chicago Board of Trade building. By the end of July, General Robert E. Wood, chairman of the board of Sears, Roebuck, and Company, and a friend of Stuart's father, accepted the chairmanship of what was to be a nationwide anti-interventionist public relations organization. Wood's acceptance of the chairmanship greatly facilitated recruitment of a national committee of prominent business leaders, churchmen, and public figures. Also in July, Stuart became executive director.[143]

The principles of AFC as developed during the summer of 1940 were simple, clear-cut, and four in number. First, AFC sought an impregnable defense for America. Second, the leadership of AFC insisted over and over again in their releases and statements that no nation or group of nations could or would ever successfully attack a prepared America. Third, preservation of American democracy and civil liberties required that the country stay out of the European war. Fourth, the policy of aid short of war to any of the belligerents would weaken national defense at home and in the end would involve America in the war.[144] Later, a fifth principle was added which urged American humanitarian aid for Britain and also for the occupied countries of Europe, even if delivering such humanitarian aid meant breaching the British naval blockade of Germany and the occupied countries.[145]

The overall objective of AFC was to bring together and provide national leadership for Americans of all political persuasions, economic levels, and social backgrounds who wanted to keep their country out of the war. Specifically excluded from space under the AFC umbrella were Nazis, Fascists, Communists, and members of other groups that placed the interests of other nations ahead of those of the United States.

This exclusion of Communists from AFC membership was especially important because American Communists were stridently anti-interventionist until the Germans invaded Russia in June 1941. Even though the foreign policy objectives of the American Communists and the AFC were similar between August 1939 and June 1941, the AFC leadership rejected any and all thoughts of association or cooperation with them in the common enterprises of anti-interventionist campaigns.

With regard to the scope and depth of public relations activities, the AFC committed itself to a systematic presentation of anti-interventionist opinions to the president, Congress, and the public at large. The leadership also promised to exert themselves mightily to resist and abate the rising war hysteria that swept over the country during times of crisis.[146] The AFC announced itself to the American public on September 4, 1940, and two weeks later was formally incorporated as an Illinois corporation.

The principal AFC public relations efforts in the fall of 1940 concentrated on placing advertisements in major newspapers and in sponsoring radio broadcasts. AFC projects during this period were not much different from those undertaken by the Century Group—endorsements from influential people, advertisements, and public letters. However, from the beginning, Stuart had the idea of organizing local chapters on the model of the White Committee and creating a nationwide network of anti-interventionist enthusiasts. In early November, AFC temporarily suspended its advertising campaign, and the national committee authorized the formation of local chapters in important urban centers.[147]

The growth of AFC local chapters initially was slow but steady. By December 7, 1941, approximately 450 local chapters had been established and total national membership exceeded 825,000.[148] About two-thirds of the membership was located within 300 miles of Chicago, but strong chapters existed in New York, Massachusetts, Pennsylvania, Connecticut, New Jersey, California, and Maryland.

In terms of leadership, size, and effectiveness of organization, some of the best chapters were in Chicago, New York, Cincinnati, Washington, D.C., San Diego, Los Angeles, and Fort Wayne.[149] By the end of 1940, the AFC organization was sufficiently in place and developed to challenge the White Committee and its interventionist allies in a spirited public relations struggle mostly for the hearts but also for a few of the minds of the American people. The great national debate over what America's role in the war ought to be lasted from September 1940 to December 7, 1941. During those fifteen months, it was carried on by both sides with great intensity and for much of the time without many scruples.

Hostile congressional reaction to interventionist activities started about the same time that Stuart and his Yale friends began preparing their first anti-interventionist petitions. Senator Rush D. Holt (D-West Virginia) publicly derided the "Summons to Speak Out" on the floor of the Senate two days after it had been released, noting the ages and occupations of the signers and observing that virtually all of them were well past draft age.[150]

On subsequent occasions, Holt also attacked the CDAAA and styled White as a front for eastern financial and industrial magnates anxious to protect their interests in England and profit as much from this war as they had from the last one.[151] Holt was particularly outraged by the "Stop Hitler Now" full-page advertisements written and promoted by Robert Sherwood that appeared in many papers on June 10.

What annoyed Holt the most about these advertisements was not only that the president had publicly approved them in a press conference, but that he had described Sherwood's work as an appropriate method for educating the American people about the extent of the Nazi threat to America. For this former West Virginia school teacher that sort of calculated arrogance was too much. He angrily pointed out connections between the "Stop Hitler Now" advertisement sponsors and New York law firms and financial houses.

Holt then described those so-called educational materials as having been paid for with blood money, that is, money earned or expected to be earned from the blood of millions of war victims.[152] For the rest of the summer, Holt and other senators continually railed against the ever-increasing volume of pro-war propaganda in the United States and urged adoption of a senate resolution authorizing an investigation of it. In Holt's view, Nazi, Communist, or British propaganda was all equally reprehensible and dangerous and ought to be exposed.[153]

That exposure or at least the British part of it began in earnest on September 26, 1940, when Senator Bennett Clark (D-Missouri) attacked pro-British pressure groups operating in the United States in a speech delivered to a nearly full Senate and a crowded gallery. Clark was delightfully sober and in excellent form. On this occasion he was joined by Holt and Senators Gerald P. Nye, Burton K. Wheeler, Hendrik Shipstead, John Danaher, and David I. Walsh.

Individually and severally these senators denounced the activities of the White Committee and the Century Group. The senators perceived the White Committee and the Century Group as de facto agents of the British government and charged them with being part of a conspiracy to bring America into the war.[154] The senators based this charge primarily on an article written for the *St. Louis Post-Dispatch* by Charles Ross.

This article was an objective account of the origin and activities of the White Committee and the Century Group. The piece had been written with the cooperation of Shepardson and when published on September 22, 1940, it had not displeased or disturbed the leadership of those organizations.[155] The senators, however, used the Ross article in their speeches as proof positive of a British conspiracy to bring America into the war.

John Balderston was singled out by Holt for special excoriation as a British agent.[156] Though Balderston professed no intention of suing Holt for slander because of congressional immunity, he replied to the senator's allegations in a twenty-three page memorandum and attacked him for employing "copperhead smear tactics" and aiding Hitler's cause.[157] This memorandum entitled "Smear Campaign in the Senate" was sent to several major newspapers and found its way into print in several of them.

In addition, Herbert Agar was identified by Holt as the author of the radio address delivered by General Pershing on August 4 to mobilize support for the transfer of fifty destroyers to England and considered the principal exploiter of the gallant old soldier's reputation.[158] Joseph Alsop was identified as the person responsible for arranging Pershing's appearance on the radio broadcasting network.[159]

All in all, the Ross article, speeches on the Senate floor, and the Balderston-Holt controversy directed public attention in late September 1940 toward a pro-war public relations campaign whose organizers hitherto had been largely unidentified. Among those shocked and angered by the revelations about interventionist propaganda activity in the United States was Father John A. O'Brien. Lately returned from England where he had lived for the past year, O'Brien had experienced most of the anxieties and some of the terrors of modern war. He was present at the outbreak of the conflict and observed from Britain the great German victories in France, the Dunkirk evacuation, and British civilian reactions to the start of German air attacks. Back in the United States, O'Brien's response to the revelations about pro-war propaganda in America was absolutely in character. That response was quickly prepared, derived from what others had already written, and as events would soon show, it would be extreme and long lasting.

— 4 —

THE WAR CONTROVERSY: ISOLATIONISM AND INTERVENTIONISM AT NOTRE DAME, MAY 1940 TO JUNE 1941

T he sudden and spectacular German military successes on the western front in May 1940 persuaded O'Brien and many other Americans living and working in England to think seriously about leaving the country. As early as May 17, 1940, the United States embassy in London advised all American citizens in Britain to return to America by way of Ireland as soon as possible.[1] On June 7, following the completion of the Dunkirk evacuation, Ambassador Joseph P. Kennedy issued a sterner warning to the estimated 4,000 Americans still in England. Kennedy stated unequivocally, "This may be the last opportunity for Americans to get home until after the war."[2] The BBC carried the ambassador's warning on its early afternoon broadcast.

Initially, the ambassador's warning did not cause undue excitement within the American community living in England. Actually, some Americans formed their own Home Guard unit complete with uniforms bearing a red eagle shoulder patch. However, as news from France revealed the full extent of the military disaster occurring there, most Americans living in England heeded Kennedy's warning and made preparations to travel to Ireland and America as soon as possible.[3]

O'Brien took the ambassador's advice very seriously and prepared to leave England at once. Not only did O'Brien admire Joseph P. Kennedy as a highly successful person, but he also agreed completely with the ambassador's views on the course of the war and America's relation to it. O'Brien accepted Kennedy's assumptions that Britain's defeat or capitulation was only a matter of time and that America could not make the situation in England or in Europe any better by getting into the war. Along with Kennedy and others, O'Brien convinced himself that keeping America out of the European conflict was a moral and patriotic duty. His later passionate commitment to the cause of isolationism in America was total and had been derived directly from his observations and experiences while in Britain during 1939 and 1940.

Sometime before June 20, O'Brien left Oxford for America without providing the British post office with a forwarding address.[4] O'Brien was extremely anxious about arriving in the United States and at Notre Dame in time for the opening of the new school year. He left Oxford and England quickly because transatlantic bookings on American or other neutral ships were so difficult to obtain in late June and early July. The rush of Americans out of London to Dublin and then on to Galway in order to meet the SS *Washington,* scheduled to depart for New York from there on July 6, was so heavy that special trains had to be added for the run from Euston Station to Holyhead.[5]

However, there may have been reasons other than transportation difficulties why O'Brien left Oxford so precipitously. As the threat and reality of German air attacks intensified, O'Brien found himself in an awkward personal situation in Oxford that appears to have been occasioned by his old habit of saying more than he meant.

Quite understandably, during May and June the entire country seemed obsessed with the dangers of air attack and invasion. Parents from all social classes in every part of Britain were extremely fearful for the safety of their children. There was little doubt at that time that much of England was about to become a battlefield, and everyone agreed that a battlefield was no place for children, especially one's own children.

Of that cast of mind were some of O'Brien's closest English Catholic friends in the Oxford area.[6] Helen and Charles Bruce-Jones and their two children were a very observant English Catholic lower middle-class family. O'Brien had been a frequent visitor at their home and was well acquainted with many of their friends and relatives.

This family, like so many others in Britain during the summer of 1940, had no difficulty imagining what bombing attacks would be like. For five years eye witnesses and photographers from Ethiopia, China, Spain,

Poland, Norway, and France had prepared their minds for the terrors of the new, deadly, indiscriminate form of attack. Now that Britain's turn had come, the Bruce-Jones family along with many thousands of others were overwhelmed by a wave of panic that swept through all levels of British society. British parents feared for the safety of their children.

Initially, the new Churchill government responded to this wave of panic in a predictable way. In early June an interdepartmental committee was created to study the possibilities of evacuating English children overseas.[7] By mid-June the Children's Overseas Reception Committee was in place as an official government agency and began receiving applications for placement of children in America, Canada, and elsewhere in the Dominions. Applications poured into the committee, exceeding 200,000 by early July, whereupon receipt of additional ones was temporarily suspended.[8] The panic and the wave of applications for overseas placement had been driven in large part by aristocratic example and parliamentary rhetoric.

As early as June 13, 1940, J. Rolland Robinson, M.P., arrived in New York to act as a liaison between the Children's Overseas Reception Committee and cooperating American private agencies. Though Robinson denied that only the children of the rich and well-born were being sent to North America and insisted that 75 percent of the children embarked would be selected from working-class applicants,[9] most of the early arrivals were children from England's best families.

On July 4, 1940, the *New York Times* reported the arrival in Montreal of 300 aristocratic children destined for the homes of relatives and friends in America. Among this group were three nieces and a nephew of the queen, accompanied by the grandmother of the children and two governesses, all bound for a country estate in Virginia and arriving under the sponsorship of Mr. J. P. Morgan. Other notable refugee children included sons and daughters of the Duke of Richmond, the Earl of March, the Earl of Bessborough, and the Cavendish family.[10]

At the same time, in Parliament, Josiah Wedgewood III and Lady Astor berated the Churchill government for not addressing the problem of overseas evacuation of British children with sufficient dispatch. Wedgewood urged the government to seek help from the U.S. Navy to convoy floating nurseries across the Atlantic, and Lady Astor declared that five million English children could be sent to North America.[11]

Clearly, among some English politicians during the summer of 1940, rhetoric and emotion on this matter had gone too far. Churchill took corrective action. Never himself a supporter of schemes to evacuate children overseas,[12] he delegated Deputy Prime Minister Clement Attlee to address the matter in the House of Commons. Attlee did so by deploring what he described as the absurd notion that everyone except fighting men should leave the country.[13]

Meanwhile in the United States, preparations for the reception of refugee children proceeded apace. On June 20, Mrs. Roosevelt accepted the temporary chairmanship of the U.S. Committee for the Care of European Children, an organization created to coordinate activities and resources on behalf of refugee children and to lobby for a relaxation of immigration laws and financial responsibility requirements.[14]

Winthrop Aldrich announced the establishment of the Allied Relief Fund to raise $5 million to provide shelter in the United States for refugee children presently in England. This project obtained endorsements from Lord Lothian, the British ambassador, and prominent U.S. government officials. Mrs. Roosevelt agreed to serve as permanent co-chairman.[15] For his fund-raising efforts in this cause, Aldrich, a conservative Republican and strident opponent of the New Deal, expected to be named as the other permanent co-chairman, but President Roosevelt vetoed his selection. Instead, the post went to Marshall Field, a Chicago philanthropist and New Deal loyalist.[16] Offers of housing flooded into the Committee's New York headquarters, and the *New York Times* reported that the type of children in greatest demand were six-year-old blond English girls.[17]

If the demand to receive refugee children in New York were large and growing, the pool of applicants in London seeking placement in North America had become enormous. The American embassy in London was so beset with inquiries about how to make contact with American placement agencies that they opened an annex in the Mayfair Hotel for that purpose and from that annex issued about a hundred visas a day.[18] Moreover, 90 percent of all space on transatlantic liners leaving the British Isles for North America had been reserved for refugee children.[19] Such was the background and context for the decision by the Bruce-Jones family to ask O'Brien to help them get a placement in an American refugee children's program for their two children.

By late June 1940, Helen Bruce-Jones had persuaded herself that, as a priest and as a friend, O'Brien would do his utmost to rescue her children from their present dangerous circumstances. "I truly believe," she wrote, "God meant you to befriend my children."[20] During his visits and time with the Bruce-Jones family, O'Brien appeared once again to have said more than he meant, leading them to believe that he had actually promised to do more than he was capable of delivering. In her most anxiety-laden state, Mrs. Bruce-Jones seemed to have mistaken expressions of kindness and sympathy for commitment. On the radio on June 20 she had learned about the evacuation program being mounted by the U.S.

Committee for the Care of European Children and immediately sent a telegram to O'Brien's Oxford address. The wire was brief and to the point, "Please accept Douglas and Mary under Roosevelt scheme."[21]

O'Brien had left Oxford before June 20, and the wire was returned as undeliverable because no forwarding address had been filed with the post office.[22] Next, Mrs. Bruce-Jones went to Campion Hall where O'Brien had lived and looked up Father Watts, who provided her with the address of Notre Dame. Before leaving Campion Hall, Father Watts took Mrs. Bruce-Jones into the chapel, where they prayed together and asked God to bless her quest. Returning to her home in Headington, Mrs. Bruce-Jones wrote to O'Brien at Notre Dame requesting his help at this moment of great danger.[23]

"I ask you," she wrote, "Will you offer a home to my two children for the duration of this terrible war? If you are not making a settled home, please ask one of your friends to take my two treasures into their home and love and care for them."[24] She reported hearing on the radio that Mrs. Roosevelt was organizing a fund and that all transatlantic expenses would be paid out of that fund if a home in America were guaranteed. Their only worry was the fare from Oxford to Liverpool or Galway from where the liners were supposed to depart.

Mrs. Bruce-Jones asked O'Brien if he would help with those expenses because as he well knew they had not been able save anything during the past few years. She promised that her husband would refund a little of that money in every letter sent to the children in their new American home. The extent of this English mother's desperation was revealed in her account of air attacks on Oxford during the week of June 24. She described hearing the roar of seven consecutive bomb explosions and a fearful four hours of sitting in a shelter. That sort of "mental misery was not for children," so most of them in Oxford were leaving.[25]

Mrs. Bruce-Jones urged O'Brien to obtain all of the particulars about the evacuation project from Washington and let her know what was required as soon as possible so she could complete the necessary formalities at the education office in Oxford. She concluded with a plea, "Please, please Father, make or find a safe haven for my children, that I may know they may live."[26]

O'Brien did not receive Mrs. Bruce-Jones' letter until after he had arrived in South Bend and had settled in at Notre Dame. Whether he maintained any contact with the family in later years is unknown. In this instance, however, O'Brien had been unable to do anything for the family, but it is clear enough that he did not forget them, because he preserved Mrs. Bruce-Jones' very sensitive and moving letter.

There is no doubt that this whole episode touched O'Brien very deeply. Perhaps psychologists can find in this experience or in the guilt feelings derived from it some explanations for his pessimistic attitude toward Britain's survival in the war, and his subsequent passionate attachment to the cause of American isolationism and to breaking the British blockade to deliver food to European children. Not many persons lately back from Britain in the fall of 1940 reacted to the war and to the Battle of Britain as did O'Brien.

For the Bruce-Jones family and for thousands of other British families, the prospect of an American sojourn for their children for the duration of the war diminished with the ever-increasing confidence of the Churchill government and the intensifying U-boat campaign. Confidence in the new government took some time to build, but grow it did. Along with growing confidence came also hope and determination. As time passed, the case for keeping the children at home became easier to make. Certainly, among the older children there was evident a very strong feeling that evacuation overseas was shameful.[27]

Whatever the reasons, the panic-driven exodus of English children out of the country in May and June had slowed to a trickle when all government-sponsored overseas evacuation of children was stopped on October 2, 1940.[28] After the sinking of the *Vollendam* in August and the fortuitous rescue of 320 refugee children without a loss,[29] it was arguable that there might be more risk in traveling to America than in remaining in Britain.

That point was tragically demonstrated on September 17, 1940 when the *City of Benares* was torpedoed in a raging storm 600 miles from the British Isles with a loss of 293 lives. Of the ninety refugee children on board, seventy-six, including twenty pairs of brothers perished. Six of the surviving thirteen refugee children had to endure eight days in an open boat before being rescued.[30] Further overseas evacuation efforts seemed much too dangerous to continue.

By the time government-sponsored programs had ended, fewer than 5,000 children between the ages of five and fifteen had been evacuated to the Dominions, and fewer than 2,000 went to the United States. Of the 5,000 children evacuated overseas, about 2,700 went abroad under government-sponsored schemes.[31] The sinking of the *City of Benares* did not put American relief organizations out of business. The Allied Relief Fund sent remittances to London for the care of children in England and for the relief of homeless air raid victims.[32]

How O'Brien reacted to the *City of Benares* tragedy is not known. He certainly knew about it. Secretary of State Cordell Hull denounced the sinking in very strong language.[33] Berlin dismissed the whole incident as nothing more than British propaganda.[34] If O'Brien thought about what might have happened to the Bruce-Jones children if they had been on board, he did not do so for very long. He was much involved in all of the busyness associated with the opening of a new school year and the start of another football season. O'Brien had to find a house somewhere near the university, prepare lectures for a required course in religion, and of course pay a courtesy call on the president of the university. He moved into a house on St. Peter Street and had his visit with O'Donnell on September 12.

O'Brien had met O'Donnell occasionally in the past and had corresponded with him but really did not know the man. In his meeting with the president, O'Brien talked at length and with much animation about his experiences while in England. What O'Brien learned about his new boss at this meeting was what most people, lay or cleric, already knew about him. O'Donnell was very different from his famous predecessor, clearly not as able or energetic, but on a priest-to-priest basis cultivatable as a good friend. O'Brien left this meeting satisfied that at last he had found some good work in a new and interesting home.

For his part, O'Donnell must have been impressed by his meeting with O'Brien. After the priest had left his office, O'Donnell wrote a short note to Tom Barry, university press relations officer, instructing him to put out a publicity release on the new appointment of Father John A. O'Brien to the Notre Dame faculty. O'Donnell believed that there was enough material in hand about O'Brien to write a full story, perhaps even enough to begin another one about non-C.S.C. priests teaching and studying at the university for the forthcoming academic year.[35]

Within two months, O'Brien would begin providing Barry with materials for more stories than he ever wanted to write and O'Donnell with more releases than he ever wanted to read. O'Brien had become a Notre Dame professor, and as a professor he was ready to say or do anything that would keep American young men out of this terrible European war. In O'Brien's opinion, the war was not winable, and as German propagandists kept repeating, the British Empire for which it was being waged was not worth saving.

— ii —

What manner of man was Father J. Hugh O'Donnell, the president of Notre Dame, who would have to cope with and try to manage the storm of controversy that O'Brien would bring to the university? O'Donnell had been born in Grand Rapids, Michigan, in 1895. He entered Notre Dame as an undergraduate in 1912, played center on the football team, and acquired the nickname "Pepper." According to one widely accepted tradition, O'Donnell had caused a fumble which lost a close football game to Yale, the one and only time that Notre Dame played Yale. O'Donnell graduated in 1916, entered the Holy Cross novitiate immediately, studied for a few years at the Holy Cross House of Studies at the Catholic University of America, and was ordained in 1921. He obtained a doctorate in American church history from Catholic University in 1922 and returned to Notre Dame to teach American history. He served as prefect of discipline at Notre Dame between 1924 and 1931. He went to St. Edward's College in Austin, Texas, as president in 1931 where he remained until 1934, returning to Notre Dame at that time to serve as Father John F. O'Hara's vice president during a very active period of intellectual and physical development at the university. O'Donnell succeeded to the presidency in an acting capacity in early 1940, when O'Hara resigned to become auxiliary bishop of the Military Ordinariate. He was appointed to a regular three-year term as president in his own right in July and selected Father John J. Cavanaugh, C.S.C., then serving as prefect of religion, to be his vice president.

Father O'Donnell had the misfortune of following a vigorous, popular, and highly successful president. As a person, O'Donnell was pleasant and affable, an experienced administrator, but one who did not bear the responsibilities and burdens of his office lightly. O'Donnell was a worrier, and in 1940 and 1941 there would be much for him to worry about. There was, of course, the war and the state of the world. As president of the university, O'Donnell was never free of worries about money problems, now made more serious and urgent by uncertainties about the impact of the draft on student enrollment. Balancing the real need for additional faculty against the justice and necessity of salary increases for lay faculty already here was never easy. Soliciting funds from contributors was endless. O'Donnell neither enjoyed that special presidential responsibility nor did it well.

In addition to worries about the university, as local religious superior O'Donnell had to be attentive to the interests and welfare of members of the Congregation of Holy Cross and ever mindful of its internal politics. For example, O'Donnell felt obligated to write what turned out to be an unenthusiastic letter to a friendly congressman in a vain attempt to secure reinstatement of a brother of a Holy Cross priest who had been dismissed from the U.S. Postal Service.[36]

O'Donnell also responded to pressure from members of the congregation to require a lay history professor to stop all work on a history of
Notre Dame intended to be published as part of the centenary celebration of the founding of the university in 1942. Though charged by O'Hara
to begin such a project in 1935, O'Donnell directed Professor James A.
Corbett to stop work on this project in September 1941 and turn over
what he had written to date as well as all research notes—ten file drawers—
to a Holy Cross priest, never trained as a historian, but interested in completing the project.[37] Though demeaned and angered by O'Donnell's
order, Corbett had no other real choice than to comply. That was the way
Notre Dame was at that time.

Another project begun under O'Hara that became O'Donnell's to
complete was the Warner Brothers film, *Knute Rockne—All American,*
released in the fall of 1940. This project was much more complicated than
Corbett's proposed history of Notre Dame and much more difficult for
university leaders to insure that the university's best interests would be
well served by the content of the film and the manner of promoting it.
O'Donnell could tell a faculty member what to do and expect immediate
compliance. The president quickly learned that was not the case with
Warner Brothers executives.

As biographical motion pictures became increasingly popular during
the 1930s, a number of people proposed ideas for a film about the life of
Knute Rockne. However, no Hollywood studio became seriously interested in a Rockne film project until after DuPont's Calvacade of America
radio show broadcast episodes drawn from Rockne's ghost-written *Auto-
biography* in December 1938. Warner Brothers bought the radio script
and began negotiating shortly thereafter with Notre Dame and Mrs.
Rockne for the necessary permissions and rights to produce a film.

University leaders had neither sought out Warner Brothers to make a
Rockne film nor welcomed the film proposal when it came. Because the
film had every prospect of reinforcing the public image of Notre Dame as
a football factory, O'Hara was reluctant to approve the project. In the
end, both O'Hara and O'Donnell agreed to cooperate with Warner
Brothers because of the great financial benefit the film would provide for
Mrs. Rockne. She had asked for $50,000 for the rights to make a film
about her husband's life.[38]

Fearful of criticism that Notre Dame was attempting to profit from
the life and tragic death of their famous football coach, O'Hara insisted
that the university be paid nothing for its cooperation. Moreover, he
demanded as part of the contract with Warner Brothers that a foreword

to the film specifically state that Notre Dame had cooperated in the film project "without compensation." In addition, O'Hara did not want the name of the university or members of the university community exploited in any way. He refused to allow the name Notre Dame to appear in the title of the film or in scenes where that could be avoided. Beyond those two stipulations and a very strong objection to casting James Cagney as Rockne, the university generally accommodated the studio.[39]

Among the several actors seeking the Rockne role, Cagney was the one most preferred by Warner Brothers. As a box office attraction, Cagney was perhaps rated third or fourth among all male actors in the industry. More importantly, Cagney was under contract to Warner Brothers. However, O'Hara would not even consider Cagney for a role in a film associated with Notre Dame. O'Hara's reasons were clear enough. Cagney had taken a strong public anti-Franco stance during the Spanish Civil War. The American Catholic hierarchy had been strongly pro-Franco and anti-Communist during that conflict, and O'Hara was of no mind to risk damaging the reputation of the university among American Catholics by approving the casting of an outspoken anti-Franco actor in a film about Rockne and Notre Dame.[40]

After learning of O'Hara's objection to Cagney, Warner Brothers threatened to drop the project if Cagney was not cast in the role.[41] O'Hara was not intimidated and refused to withdraw his objection to Cagney; the project was actually suspended for about five months. In the end, Pat O'Brien was given the role, notwithstanding the great difficulty of making this middle-aged actor look young enough to play Rockne as a Notre Dame student. The university was indifferent about the other actors and actresses cast in supporting roles, including Ronald Reagan as George Gipp. Production began in late January 1940.[42]

Except for the Cagney matter, the university had been generally accommodating to Warner Brothers. Mrs. Rockne was not. Bonnie Rockne would not admit that her husband had been only a college football coach. She insisted that he be portrayed in the film as an educated person, as a man of influence and culture, and as an inspirer of youth. In order to get Mrs. Rockne's approval of the screen play, the studio added an utterly improbable scene where the president of the university conversed with Rockne at graduation time about life choices. In this ridiculous scene, the university president exhorts this young man with a degree in pharmacy and passable grades in elementary chemistry courses to decide whether he should devote his life to chemistry or become a football coach.

Perhaps the most absurd scene in a film with many of them presents this absolutely unbelievable, fictitious university president urging Rockne to go to New York and voluntarily appear at a hearing conducted by a committee of American educators to defend himself and other college football coaches from charges of football overemphasis and corruption. The idea of Rockne ever going to such a meeting at the urging of the president of the university to attack in a public way intercollegiate football reformers goes far beyond anything justifiable by dramatic license.[43]

In still another totally out-of-character scene, the studio has Rockne denouncing gamblers who bet on collegiate football games and spurning an offer from a sporting goods manufacturer to endorse their products. Those sorts of behaviors were simply incredible to people in the Notre Dame community who had known Rockne and put up with him as a football coach for thirteen years. Of course, there was the now famous but certainly fictitious deathbed "Win one for the Gipper" speech delivered by Ronald Reagan that thereafter entered American public consciousness as a genuine historical event. That phrase "Win one for the Gipper" became a much used and abused symbol of valiant underdogs triumphing over adversity. Generally, however, Mrs. Rockne got her way with the studio.

The most uncooperative person at Notre Dame essential for completion of the film turned out to be the serving head football coach, Elmer Layden. The studio needed Layden's approval for use of his name in the film and for an appearance with the other famous Four Horsemen in a final scene. O'Donnell had assured the studio that he would obtain signed releases from Layden as well as from Stuhldreyer, Crowley, and Miller. Layden refused to sign his release, whereas the others did. Layden feared that a picture about Rockne at Notre Dame would reflect poorly upon him as the present coach. As Layden saw the thrust of the film, it clearly implied that no successor coach could ever equal the performance of the master. Layden was also angry over the fact that Stuhldreyer had been given the best lines in the closing scene.[44]

Layden was so stubborn about these points that he delayed signing his release for over a month. The studio reacted to this delay by threatening to eliminate all references to and scenes involving the Four Horsemen from the screen play.[45] In the end, Layden finally signed his release, but relations between the coach and O'Donnell had been irreparably damaged. The president regarded Layden's obstinacy on this matter as a personal insult. This embarrassing affair contributed to O'Donnell's determination to replace Layden as head football coach at the end of season in late

1940.[46] In this matter the president had been able to deal with the coach because, after all, he was an employee. But O'Donnell found himself unable to deal effectively with Mrs. Rockne or with Warner Brothers, once permission to make the picture had been given, because they were not in any way beholden to him.

In that regard, the studio actually broke its contract with Notre Dame about stating explicitly in a foreword that the university had cooperated in making the film without compensation. Mrs. Rockne had objected to the use of such explicit language, fearing that if the public knew that Notre Dame had been unpaid for its cooperation, she would appear extremely avaricious for having demanded and received $50,000. In this matter, Warner Brothers sided with Mrs. Rockne and put language into the film foreword that thoroughly obscured the issue of whether or not the university had been paid for its contributions to the film.[47] O'Donnell was angered by this blatant breach of a written agreement; but unlike O'Hara's firm stand on the Cagney issue, he allowed the incident to pass without initiating or even threatening to initiate legal action to enforce the agreement.

Similarly, O'Hara had been adamantly opposed to the film representing Notre Dame as being nothing more than a football factory. The title of the film chosen by the studio after much correspondence with university officials, *Knute Rockne—All American,* appeared to have communicated precisely that unwanted message. Though O'Donnell and Cavanaugh both detested the title chosen and let the studio know it, their objections counted for nothing with Warner Brothers executives. *Knute Rockne—All American* was their film and as long as the words "Notre Dame" did not appear in the film title or in advertising, the studio insisted that they could title the film as they saw fit.[48]

Indeed, during the course of the project, on occasions O'Donnell had been very roughly handled in ways that were new experiences for him. At that time, however, he could not have imagined that even rougher experiences awaited him over the next three years. When those moments arrived, the president behaved much as he had with Warner Brothers, that is, let embarrassing matters pass and hope for the best. Both O'Donnell and Cavanaugh were delighted when at long last the Rockne film project was completed in the summer of 1940. A near intolerable distraction from important university business, from the intense excitement of a national presidential election campaign, and from the progress of the war finally had come to an end.

As the new academic year began and the presidential election campaign heated up, there were many pressing matters to decide and to avoid. During the past year, unlike O'Hara, O'Donnell had revealed himself to be an uncertain crisis manager. In most situations, O'Donnell greatly valued authority and power, whether religious or secular, as the making of *Knute Rockne—All American* had demonstrated; later events would show he was easily intimidated by displays of both. Yet no matter how much O'Donnell respected authority and power, he did not himself always exercise them wisely or well.

O'Donnell exhibited an extraordinary inability to comprehend or anticipate the probable effects of difficult decisions made by him upon people under his authority, as in the Corbett case. At the same time, O'Donnell had neither the skills nor much luck in anticipating possible negative public relations damage to the university from actions intended to be beneficial. This is not to say that O'Donnell made important decisions too easily, because he did not.

The problem was that there never was much of him in them. After thinking about an issue, in the end he tended to defer to authority or accept and act upon the opinions of persons he liked and trusted. Moreover, once a decision had been made, he would stay with it no matter what. O'Donnell was rarely ever disposed to reconsider a decision in the light of unanticipated events or negative reactions.

— iii —

When Father John J. Cavanaugh recommended contacting Frank Leahy, then a highly successful football coach at Boston College, to replace Elmer Layden as head football coach and athletic director at Notre Dame, O'Donnell authorized an approach to Leahy before Layden was told that he would be replaced. O'Donnell also agreed that officials at Boston College should not be informed of Notre Dame's serious interest in Leahy. Though Leahy had signed a new contract with Boston College less than two weeks before, he accepted a contract with Notre Dame on the grounds that the signed contract with Boston College contained an alma mater escape agreement. When Boston College officials learned about Leahy's intentions from the press, they insisted that no written or verbal alma mater escape agreement had ever existed. Leahy was unable to produce any written confirmation or verbal corroboration that one ever had.

In the press Notre Dame was represented as trying to steal a successful coach from another Catholic institution. Officials at Boston College were outraged by the whole affair, but after some delays released Leahy from the contract which he clearly intended to repudiate. In an acrimonious correspondence lasting more than six months and reaching Father Albert F. Cousineau, C.S.C., superior general of the Congregation of Holy Cross, Father Maurice Dullea, S.J., president of Boston College, brought the controversy to an end by acidly stating to Cousineau, "Your men have Leahy. Let them keep him. We have no desire to have him back."[49]

Once this matter had been set in motion, O'Donnell stepped back and let events take charge. He had supported his vice president's project even though it rested on an obvious and undeniable falsehood. Moreover, O'Donnell did nothing to try and restore the image of lost integrity widespread in Catholic circles as well as in the public at large. The experience of having acted in this instance, as well as in another one involving Leahy a year later and in several other similar situations over the next decade based upon falsehoods for a perceived greater good of the university, haunted Cavanaugh for the rest of his life. O'Donnell was never thus affected. His public statements when such situations arose would be as brief and uninformative as possible, secure in the belief that, no matter how painful, such instances would pass and the institutional life of the university would continue.

In the business of the hiring of Frank Leahy away from Boston College, such was the case. Leahy's performance as head football coach at Notre Dame between his first season in 1941 and when he went into the navy in early 1944 was so spectacular that the manner of bringing him to Notre Dame passed quickly out of the public memory. In 1941 Leahy's team went through the season undefeated, winning nine games and playing Army to a scoreless tie in Yankee Stadium before 74,000 people. Not only did Leahy manage the first undefeated season since 1930, but he was chosen Coach of the Year by the American Football Coaches Association.

To be sure, Leahy owed much of his success in 1941 to the fact that Layden had recruited an extraordinarily gifted passing quarterback, Angelo Bertelli. Though playing out of Rockne's now outdated box formation offensive set, wherein quarterbacks blocked and ran more than they passed, Bertelli electrified the football world as a sophomore in 1941 by passing for over a thousand yards and eight touchdowns. That amazing feat for a first-year varsity player earned Bertelli a second place in Heisman Trophy voting behind Bruce Smith of Minnesota.

While Bertelli accounted for a large part of Leahy's success in the coach's first season at Notre Dame, the fortuitous presence of a great quarterback was by no means the full explanation. Leahy's style of coaching was much different from the one practiced by his predecessor. Layden had been a teacher and a believer in observing rules. Leahy was a perfectionist determined to win by any means. Leahy trained his players mercilessly, resorting to verbal and frequently even to physical chastisement to make coaching points.

Moreover, to ensure the position of his team as perennial contenders for national championship status, Leahy was a ferocious recruiter, ready to do almost anything to bring outstanding football prospects to Notre Dame. For example, in the summer of 1942 Leahy virtually kidnapped John Lujack, a highly regarded football prospect from Connellsville, Pennsylvania, and persuaded him to break a formal commitment to enroll in the U.S. Military Academy at West Point and come to Notre Dame. In effect, Leahy persuaded Lujack to do to West Point what he himself had done to Boston College. Even in the generally corrupt world of intercollegiate football recruiting, Leahy's seduction of Lujack set a new standard for predatory recruiting.

What Leahy did to West Point in the Lujack matter was certainly immoral but was, in a historical sense, also poetically just. Throughout the 1920s and for much of the 1930s, the U.S. Military Academy ran one of the most corrupt football programs in the country. West Point regularly recruited players who had completed undergraduate football careers in other colleges and universities and enrolled them for up to four more years of intercollegiate football competition as players on Army teams.

Because West Point had so openly flaunted the three-year standard eligibility rule, the Army team became a pariah in intercollegiate athletics. Even though several prominent intercollegiate football teams, including the U.S. Naval Academy, dropped Army from their schedules for rules violations, the leaders of the West Point football program refused to see the error of their ways. They refused to operate under a three-year eligibility rule until President Roosevelt ordered them to do so in 1938.

Earl Blaik, head football coach at Army since 1940, had served as an assistant football coach at West Point, 1927–1933, when Army's celebrated two running backs "Light Horse" Harry Wilson and Red Cagle completed seven and six years respectively of intercollegiate football competition. Blaik's rules violation past notwithstanding, the Army head coach became absolutely incensed when Leahy managed to recruit John Lujack away from West Point in the summer of 1941. Blaik would never forgive Leahy and Notre Dame.

The West Point version of this so-called Lujack kidnapping represented Leahy as an unprincipled villain and O'Donnell and Cavanaugh as perhaps unwilling but thoroughly intimidated collaborators. As described in a memorandum prepared by the Army athletic council in 1946 for General Maxwell D. Taylor, superintendent of the U.S. Military Academy, 1946–1949, the Lujack story began in 1942 when Congressman

Schneider appointed the young man, a star football player, to West Point. Lujack was a superb all-round athlete who had demonstrated extraordinary football skills as a passer.[50]

Congressman Schneider actually visited Connellsville and personally presented the letter of appointment to Lujack in a widely reported public ceremony. At this ceremony Lujack publicly accepted the appointment and, according to the West Point memorandum, began preparing for the West Point entrance examinations. At some point after Lujack had formally committed himself to West Point, Leahy renewed contact with Lujack and persuaded the young man to abandon West Point for Notre Dame. Part of Leahy's method of persuasion included the usual football scholarship plus a well-paid summer job and living accommodations in Chicago. The West Point memorandum stated further that Lujack went off to Chicago that summer without informing his mother why or where he had gone. Hence, the styling of this affair in the West Point memorandum as a kidnapping.[51]

West Point authorities brought the Lujack matter to the attention of Father Cavanaugh at Notre Dame. The vice president informed Leahy about the West Point accusations, and the coach simply denied any knowledge of what had been alleged. Determined to protect the good name and reputation of the university in such matters, Cavanaugh compelled Leahy to travel with him to West Point where the coach's accusers could be confronted and an exoneration of the coach and of Notre Dame accomplished. According to the West Point memorandum, when Leahy was confronted with evidence provided by Lujack's mother, the coach broke down and admitted to all present that he had lied about the matter and that events had transpired as represented by the West Point authorities.[52]

The West Point memorandum concluded with the observation that Cavanaugh was visibly distressed by what had happened, but after returning to Notre Dame took no known corrective action. Lujack kept his football scholarship. However, he did not play in intercollegiate competition until he had attained sophomore status in the fall of 1943; the young man performed brilliantly then and throughout his college career, winning the Heisman Trophy in his senior year.

Of course, Leahy continued as head football coach, and, as best as he could, put this humiliating episode behind him. As a matter of fact, Leahy proceeded to make himself absolutely indispensable to the Notre Dame football program. Notwithstanding the undefeated season of the past year, Leahy changed completely the offensive set of the team for the season of 1942. The coach abandoned Rockne's box formation and dominant running offense for the wide-open, T-formation passing offense borrowed from the Chicago Bears. If O'Donnell and Cavanaugh had ever considered replacing Leahy because of the Lujack affair or because of this major change in offensive football tactics made in the summer of 1942, the present moment was not the time to do it.

Actually, Leahy had a solid football rationale for changing his offensive system. In Bertelli and Lujack, Leahy had two brilliant passing quarterbacks who could lead Notre Dame teams over the next four years. Leahy built an entirely new T formation offense to exploit their passing skills. While both O'Donnell and Cavanaugh knew that real harm had been done to the West Point football program, regrettably the harm done was irreparable. Punishing Lujack for what Leahy had done seemed pointless. In 1942, forcing Leahy to resign would have generated a public relations storm that the university did not want. In any case, at the time, Leahy's egregious recruiting excesses seemed to be a high but otherwise affordable price to pay for the much valued revenue increases and public relations advantages accruing to the university from football success.

Over the long term, O'Donnell and Cavanaugh believed that institutional embarrassments of the sort following from the Leahy hiring would pass, and the life and growth of the university would go on. Though not a courageous or always a morally defensible institutional strategy, O'Donnell's disposition to do what he believed was in the best interests of the university and then not worry too much about either the morality of a particular action or of short-term public relations damage turned out to be generally successful. In the life of an institution such as Notre Dame, public relations damage, particularly if derived from football incidents, was short-lived and simply did not matter in the long run.

— iv —

As a crisis manager during the previous year O'Donnell had shown himself to be deficient, and with John A. O'Brien settling in at the university, Notre Dame would have a need for an effective crisis manager over the next few years. By the time O'Brien began meeting classes at Notre Dame in September, American public opinion was being polarized by spirited public relations campaigns mounted by pro-British White Committee on one side and isolationist America First Committee on the other. Each side had powerful spokesmen in Congress and their respective points of view were aired daily in the press and on the radio.

Theologically liberal in most things, politically conservative in some things, and stridently anti-Roosevelt in everything, O'Brien became affiliated with America First sometime during the presidential election campaign and offered his services as a speaker. Most likely O'Brien was brought into America First by Clarence P. Manion, dean of the Notre Dame Law School, who had been an early member and was well-connected with several of the Chicago businessmen serving on its national committee.

Appalled by the fact that President Roosevelt, without congressional approval, transferred fifty old destroyers to Britain in exchange for naval and air bases on British-held territory in the Western hemisphere in September 1940 and distressed by Roosevelt's re-election for a third term, O'Brien enthusiastically embraced America First and the anti-war cause. Anxious to reach the Catholic community, the midwestern leaders of America First welcomed Father O'Brien into their organization with open arms and made him a member of their governing national committee. When those same midwestern leaders—Robert Wood, General Thomas S. Hammond, and Clay Judson—decided in late November to accuse the White Committee of leading America into war,[53] O'Brien was sufficiently a part of the America First organization to begin implementing that decision in the South Bend area.

The start of a nationwide campaign by America First speakers attacking the White Committee had been noted by Lord Lothian in late November and was duly reported to the Foreign Office at that time. Lothian described this new America First campaign as well thought out and intended to discredit the White Committee's representative character. The strategy employed, Lothian continued, was to identify the White Committee with the Roosevelt administration and thereby avoid countering its main argument that aiding Britain was in America's national interest. As yet, Lothian happily reported, there was no frontal attack on the issue of aid to Britain.

However, all of that was to change in December. For example, forty South Bend businessmen, joined by five from Mishawaka, six from Elkhart, and eight from Goshen, paid for a "No gas masks for America" advertisement published in the *South Bend Tribune* on December 1. This advertisement urged all citizens of the region "to vote for men who will oppose the paid propagandists at work night and day to tear down faith in American institutions and breed discontent ... to establish some sort of dictatorship here."[54]

On the same day, the *South Bend Tribune* editorialized strongly against the White Committee without specifically naming it. According to the editors, at least one of the formally organized groups advocating U.S. assistance to Britain had intensified its campaign for all necessary aid "short of war." The frontal attack on aid to Britain that Lothian had feared was now underway. The editorial writers admitted that such organizations "had not yet urged a declaration of war against Germany but analysis of . . . [their] propaganda suggests that by next spring . . . [they] will."[55]

The American people must face the fact, the editorial writers insisted, "that much of the short of war talk is only a screen for a determination to use American men as well as American munitions and money in another foreign military crusade." We are being "led into war by a minority that talks as if it had a monopoly on wisdom, foresight, and humanitarianism. It is the 1914–1918 war to make the world safe for democracy again."[56]

Inspired by the strong isolationism of the *South Bend Tribune* and perhaps driven also by an attack by the White Committee on Ambassador Kennedy, Father O'Brien stridently assailed both the White Committee and the great cause of supplying aid for Britain. He went further in that direction than had any other America First speaker up to that time.[57]

O'Brien disappointed none of his new friends in America First with a speech delivered in Washington Hall on December 16, 1940. He denounced the White Committee in his best all-out attack style, urging a proper renaming of it as "The Mass Murder Committee." O'Brien's stylization of the Committee to Defend America by Aiding the Allies was no slip of the tongue uttered in a moment of extreme passion. It was an entirely appropriate description, O'Brien insisted, because that committee would willingly sacrifice the blood of millions of American boys and bring bankruptcy to the country in order to perpetuate Britain's hold on one-fifth of the world. Instead of asking Americans to fight Europe's wars, he concluded, we should do battle with the war mongers and the alien pro-pagandists who, more than the European dictators, are threatening the peace and safety of our country.[58]

A story about this speech was carried in newspapers throughout the country. That a priest from the University of Notre Dame had denounced the White Committee as being a mass-murder committee was news. The day after delivering the speech Father John A. O'Brien was a national celebrity. After delivering only this one speech, he had become America First's most important Catholic isolationist spokesman. Congratulatory letters, telegrams, and telephone calls flooded into O'Brien's house on St. Peter Street.

One of the most valued was a letter from the now former Ambassador Joseph P. Kennedy. O'Brien had great respect for the former ambassador and treasured the memory of socializing with him in London during

1939, but Kennedy's reported positions on the value of a negotiated peace, on aid to Britain, and on the president's policies must have puzzled the priest from Notre Dame.

Since the fall of France in June, Kennedy was reported in the press as saying many different things. In private, he had become increasingly defeatist. Overawed by German military prowess and the devastating power of the German air force which he had witnessed at first hand, Kennedy believed that a negotiated peace with Germany was Britain's only hope for survival. Kennedy's views were definitely not shared by the president nor by the state department. Because of the uncertainties attendant upon the presidential election and the strength of isolationist opinion in the country, Roosevelt was of no mind to dismiss Kennedy and perhaps provide isolationists with a new champion.

Instead, the president pursued a policy of excluding Kennedy from both policy formation and implementation. For example, Kennedy played no role in arranging the exchange of destroyers for bases deal. Roosevelt dealt directly in Washington with Lord Lothian and conducted important business in London through special envoys dispatched for specific purposes. Kennedy was aware of what was being done to him and objected vociferously and often.

By threatening to release a scathing indictment of Roosevelt's secret promises to the British government and of his policies in Britain, Kennedy forced the president and state department to grant him leave to return to the United States before the presidential election.[59] He arrived in New York on October 22, 1940, determined not to return to London as ambassador.

Avoiding all questions from reporters about his future plans, Kennedy proceeded directly from the airport to the White House for a meeting with the president. At this meeting with Roosevelt and with a long-time Kennedy friend, Senator James F. Byrnes (D-South Carolina) in attendance, this disgruntled ambassador recited a well-prepared litany of complaints and stated his intention to resign. After listening sympathetically for several moments, the president asked Kennedy to make a national radio broadcast endorsing the Roosevelt presidential candidacy in the election two weeks hence. By the time this meeting was over, Kennedy had agreed to do so.[60]

Kennedy's reasons for making the broadcast are not clear. One account has Kennedy moved by the possibility that Roosevelt would give him his blessing for the presidential nomination in 1944. Another account has Kennedy confronted with transcripts of some of his indiscreet London conversations acquired from British intelligence which could be leaked to the press. Still another account, attributed to Kennedy himself and made known many years after the event, says a deal was struck: Kennedy agreed to endorse Roosevelt for president in 1940 if Roosevelt would support his son, Joseph P. Kennedy, Jr., for governor of Massachusetts in 1942.[61]

Whatever his reasons, Kennedy made the radio broadcast on October 29, giving the president a solid endorsement in his campaign for a third term. Though confessing differences with the president on some issues, Kennedy stated that the times were too dangerous to consider training a new and inexperienced man for this critical office. Franklin D. Roosevelt was the best man for the job and ought to be re-elected president of the United States.[62]

Press reactions to the speech were extremely positive. As might be expected, *Life* magazine, owned by a long-time friend of Kennedy, Henry Luce, described it as the most effective vote-getting speech of the campaign. The Democratic National Committee purchased newspaper advertisements across the country featuring lines from the speech. Wendell Wilkie regarded Kennedy's speech as a turning point in the campaign after which all chances of defeating Roosevelt slipped away.[63]

Isolationists were chagrined by Kennedy's performance. General Robert E. Wood of America First tried to find some comfort in the hope that after the election the ambassador might be able to speak a bit more freely and frankly.[64] At Notre Dame, O'Brien must have been utterly confused by Kennedy's endorsement of Roosevelt. In both tone and substance, the speech was far different from what O'Brien and others had heard from Kennedy about the president in London during the winter and spring of 1940. However, a few days after Roosevelt had won re-election, part of the confusion of O'Brien and other isolationists was dispelled. Kennedy publicly restated old views that had been put aside for the election.

On November 9, while in Boston, Kennedy gave a highly indiscreet interview to Louis Lyons, a *Boston Globe* columnist, that in effect ended his career as a member of the Roosevelt administration. In that interview, Kennedy stated that getting America into a war that Britain could not win would drain our country of resources and probably end democracy here as we know it, much the same as organizing for war had already ruined democracy in Britain.[65]

For good measure, Kennedy also complained to Lyons about Mrs. Roosevelt bothering Washington officials "to take care of little nobodies who hadn't any influence." The Lyons interview was a journalistic coup of the highest order. Kennedy made headlines across the country. Whatever had been Kennedy's intentions about returning to London, the British would never accept him back as ambassador, and President Roosevelt wanted him out of his administration. In due course, on December 1, Kennedy submitted his resignation as ambassador to the president. Roosevelt accepted it without much regret and appointed John Gilbert Winant—a Republican, former governor of New Hampshire, and a man with years of experience in international organizations—to the London post.

Publication of the Lyons interview irretrievably damaged Kennedy's reputation in Democratic circles. Even many of Kennedy's conservative friends in London expressed shock and dismay over what he had said. The White Committee petitioned the president to repudiate Kennedy "as a threat to the democratic way of life."[66] Though White apologized later for such a strong statement, that petition was a fair measure of the outrage among liberal-minded folk against Kennedy when the *Boston Globe* published the Lyons interview.

Catholic isolationists such as O'Brien who knew and respected Kennedy were much more annoyed by William Allen White's attack on the ambassador than by the revelations of the interview. White appeared to them to be trying to do to Kennedy in 1940 what he had done to Al Smith in 1928. Generally Catholic isolationists were pleased that at long last their wandering ideological prodigal son had come home.

Other isolationists sympathized with Kennedy as well. On December 11, General Wood of America First actually offered Kennedy the chairmanship of that organization. After thinking about the advantages and disadvantages of speaking from such a platform, Kennedy decided on December 17 to turn down General Wood's offer.[67] Kennedy justified his refusal on the grounds that he had not yet decided how he could work best in the anti-interventionist cause.

Two events seem to have given Kennedy pause about accepting Wood's offer. The first was Father O'Brien's savage attack on the White Committee in a speech delivered at Notre Dame on December 16. Apparently Kennedy read O'Brien's speech as a powerful riposte against the White Committee for its attack on him following publication of the Lyons interview. He wrote to O'Brien just before Christmas and congratulated the priest for making such an excellent speech and asked for advice from him about how to bring the anti-interventionist message to more people.[68] Whether O'Brien ever responded or gave any advice cannot be determined for certain.[69] It is unthinkable, however, that O'Brien would not have answered someone as important as Kennedy and have given some sort of suggestions. In any case, whether inspired by O'Brien or not, Kennedy decided to purchase radio time and bare his mind and soul to a national audience on January 18, 1941.

Second, in a press conference on December 17, President Roosevelt announced a billion-dollar aid program for Britain that came to be known as Lend-Lease. Kennedy wasted little time after the president's press conference on Lend-Lease to criticize it publicly. He described the scheme as wrongly conceived and untimely, because our own weak defenses limited what we could do for Britain.[70] Twelve days later, Roosevelt proceeded to explain Lend-Lease to the American people in his famous "Arsenal of Democracy" speech broadcast on December 29.

Actually, the necessity for something like Lend-Lease had become a major concern of the president following receipt of a special message from Churchill as early as December 9.[71] In this letter, Churchill listed many of Britain's most pressing immediate needs and admitted that his country no longer had the funds to pay for what was required. He entreated the president, acting in the name of the American people, to find ways and means to ensure Britain's survival and gain the time needed for America to become fully armed.[72]

Roosevelt was profoundly affected by this candid statement of the state of things and appeared to have come up with Lend-Lease idea himself. Roosevelt's new approach to providing aid for Britain was highly unconventional but ingenious in its simplicity. As developed by the president, the American government would provide weapons and supplies to Britain without charge and then, after the war, be repaid not in dollars but in kind. An essential part of the president's argument for Lend-Lease was that such a program was an alternative to going to war.

Roosevelt and his advisors reckoned that as an alternative to war, Lend-Lease would attract wide support, which it did. After the president mentioned the program to the press on December 17, the Germans knew what the president would say in his announced speech on December 29. On that night, in order to lessen the impact of Roosevelt's speech on British morale, the Germans subjected London to the heaviest bombing attack of the war. During that terrible raid, Londoners crowded around their radios at 3:30 A.M. to hear what the president would say. Though much of London was ablaze that night, those Londoners listening to Roosevelt's speech knew that relief would be coming and that survival was possible.[73]

On January 6, 1941, the president presented his Lend-Lease program to Congress in the annual State of the Union address. He began solemnly by stating that America's present security and future safety were at risk because of the war in Europe. American security, present and future, the president declared, depended on the defeat of the Axis powers. Next, Roosevelt asked Congress for authority and funds to continue sending aid to Britain and to other democracies fighting the Axis powers even if those nations could no longer pay for such aid with ready cash.

The president made this speech one of the most memorable of his entire career with a magnificent, moving peroration. He spoke eloquently about a future world based on four essential human freedoms: freedom of speech, freedom of worship, freedom from want, and freedom from fear.[74] On this memorable day, the concept of Four Freedoms was born.

This speech was widely acclaimed in the press and certainly set the national mood for the congressional debate over Lend-Lease. However, Roosevelt and his advisors tempered their optimism about the prospects for Lend-Lease. They were uncertain about the impact of the president's speech on the conservative and isolationist congressmen who held the fate of the measure in their hands. More importantly, they did not know what Kennedy intended to say in his national radio broadcast on January 18.

Fearful that Kennedy might damage the prospects for Lend-Lease, the president invited him to a meeting on January 16 in the White House which lasted ninety minutes. Kennedy once again complained about bad treatment from the press and from the men around Roosevelt. Once again, Roosevelt hinted at the prospect of an interesting job for Kennedy as a special envoy to Ireland. Next, they talked in a general way about Lend-Lease; and when the meeting was over, Kennedy had decided not to break with Roosevelt on that issue or on any other for the time being.[75]

As scheduled, Kennedy went on the air to speak to a national audience on January 18. Isolationists were hopeful that finally the one man who most certainly knew details about the president's assumed intervention-ist intentions would tell all. Alas, he did not. Kennedy began by referring to his endorsement of Roosevelt for president in the recent election and declared his sincere judgment was at that time that England ought to be given all possible aid, short of American entry into the war. He insisted that questioning the likelihood of a British victory in the war which he had done was not defeatism.

Kennedy condemned what he described as a smear campaign being waged against him and pleaded guilty to the charge of being an appeaser if that meant opposing America's participation in the war. On the subject of Lend-Lease, Kennedy disappointed his isolationist friends. He refused to denounce the measure as unnecessary or as dangerous to American democracy.

Instead, Kennedy supported aid to Britain but admitted reservations about the specific Lend-Lease program advocated by the president. He doubted whether the national danger was sufficient to justify empowering the president with the extraordinary powers that Lend-Lease would authorize. There ought to be less drastic ways of resolving the problem of presidential power, Kennedy added, but he suggested none. He concluded his radio talk by urging all Americans to rally behind the president in this very difficult time.[76]

Anxious to exculpate himself from past actions and from the consequences of the Lyons interview, Kennedy had tried to do so by providing something for everyone. He supported both aid to Britain and the isolationist imperative of keeping America out of the war. Something like Lend-Lease was acceptable, but not the specific measure sought by the president. Wherever one stood on these questions, all Americans should rally behind their elected national leader.

Kennedy's radio performance was, as Dorothy Thompson wrote, one wherein he had out-Hamleted Hamlet, wanting "to be and not to be" at the same time.[77] Given the intensity and passion of the war controversy, one could find in Kennedy's talk something to praise but a great deal to blame. Most press comments on the broadcast found more blame than praise. At this moment in America on these highly emotional issues, one could not support both sides. Even the leadership of America First was divided about the Kennedy talk. General Wood thought the speech struck just the right note but others in the organization believed that Kennedy had straddled too much.[78]

In any case, as HR 1776, the Lend-Lease bill was introduced in early January 1941. Hearings on the measure before the House Foreign Affairs Committee began at once. Though Wendell Willkie, Roosevelt's Republican opponent in the recent election, agreed to support the bill and testify for it, Kennedy, the president's former ambassador to Britain, volunteered himself to appear on January 21 before the committee as the first witness to testify against the bill.

Kennedy's appearance before the committee lasted five hours. He made a presentation and then responded more or less to questions put by members. At the end of that day, he had satisfied no one. Pressed by isolationist members during questioning to provide some unambiguous criticism of the Lend-Lease concept and program, Kennedy simply would not oblige. He expressed no special anxiety over the extraordinary powers provided to the president by the bill but thought that some sort of consultation when exercising that power would be desirable. When questioned by Congressman Richards (D-South Carolina) about his faith in the integrity and patriotism of the president, Kennedy responded by saying that he had complete faith in the president. On the much repeated isolationist charge that a measure as sweeping as Lend-Lease could lead to a dictatorship in America, Kennedy chose not to speculate on such a hypothetical outcome.[79]

By taking no public stand decisively either for or against Lend-Lease, Kennedy did no service to himself or to the isolationist cause. He exasperated both supporters and opponents of Lend-Lease while adding nothing to the great national debate over whether enactment of this measure would be a step toward or away from war.[80] Once the hearings were over, Kennedy would require another three months to admit to himself that no job of any sort would be forthcoming from the Roosevelt administration. Moreover, during those same three months, enormous British shipping losses to U-boats in the North Atlantic plus a string of military defeats in Greece, Crete, and North Africa convinced Kennedy that the war could not be won and that continuing to oppose intervention while supporting the president were irreconcilable positions. For Kennedy, the month of May 1941 was to be the end of ambiguity about his relations with Roosevelt and total public commitment to isolationism.

However, in January, what Kennedy had been unwilling to say publicly about Lend-Lease because of an understandable fear of offending Roosevelt and losing all prospects for a posting to Ireland or some other appropriate assignment in the administration, others were anxious to do. Prominent isolationist Republicans vigorously attacked the concept and program of Lend-Lease. Senator Robert A. Taft (R-Ohio) attacked HR 1776 on the grounds that it invested the president with dictatorial powers to wage undeclared wars all over the world and inexorably would bring America into the war.[81] Charles A. Lindbergh described the bill as another step closer to war and away from democracy.[82] At Notre Dame, O'Brien, puzzled by Kennedy's ambiguity, chose to follow the Taft-Lindbergh line on Lend-Lease. As was his custom, O'Brien intensified that line in ways that must have made even the most perfervid isolationists blink.

— v —

O'Brien's attack on the White Committee, especially the nationwide reporting of it, had been a new experience for the Notre Dame community. Faculty of this university simply did not address current political, social, economic, or foreign policy controversies in a public way and identify themselves as being associated with the university. This was a convention of long standing made into a rule in 1928 to prevent Coach Rockne from publicly endorsing Herbert Hoover over Alfred E. Smith in the bitterly anti-Catholic presidential campaign of that year.

University administrators insisted and virtually all faculty understood and accepted the principle that the slightest association of the name of Notre Dame with personal views on contemporary controversial public issues was to be scrupulously avoided. Only the president of Notre Dame was authorized to speak for the university on such matters, meaning that ideally the only views on public controversial issues to be aired by persons connected with the university were those approved by the president.

Strict compliance with this rule was virtually impossible, because there was no way that a faculty member could prevent newspapers from reporting speeches or writing on matters of public controversy and then identifying the author as an employee of the university. Moreover, no one at the university at this time, administrator or faculty member, contended that serious application of this principle was censorship and denial of freedom of speech to American citizens in their own country.

For all of these reasons, only a week before O'Brien's speech, five Notre Dame professors—Francis J. O'Malley, Francis E. McMahon, Edward Coomes, T. Bowyer Campbell, and Robert Anthony—had joined a protest group of thirty-eight other Catholic laymen and women organized in New York by interventionist-minded Catholics there—William Agar, Carleton Hayes, Ross Hoffman, and Chancellor James Byrne of New York University.[83] This group of forty-three well-known Catholics sent a common letter drafted by Agar but signed by them to the *New York Herald-Tribune* opposing the efforts of Herbert Hoover and others to force open the British blockade of Europe in order to feed the people of the conquered countries. The signers of this letter could not believe that much of whatever might be allowed through the blockade would ever reach those needing help. Neither Christian ethics nor American interests, they argued, would be served by Hoover's plan. Though these five professors from Notre Dame had identified themselves only as Catholic laymen, the reporter writing this story mentioned that five of the signers were Notre Dame professors.[84]

To be sure, over the years presidents of Notre Dame had spoken out in the name of the university on a variety of public issues ranging from the loss of papal temporal power in the nineteenth century to Irish nationalism, opposition to women's suffrage, the Mexican Revolution, and international communism in the present century. But always it was the president who spoke for Notre Dame. In one evening, Father John A.

O'Brien had changed all of that. He either did know about the principle of never associating the name of Notre Dame with public controversy or could not imagine that it would apply to him. However, only a few of the faculty and no one in the administration at that time realized what had happened.

Local reaction to O'Brien's speech was not long delayed. The large and heavily Catholic South Bend Polish-American community was appalled and shocked by what they interpreted as an apologia for the destruction of Poland. O'Brien had to respond to their angry protests at once. South Bend Polish-American leaders were particularly disturbed by O'Brien's condemnation of the Versailles Treaty, which in their view had been responsible for the resurrection and reconstitution of Poland. In a written response sent to the *South Bend Tribune*, O'Brien expressed sympathy for the present plight of Poland and praised that nation as the eastern rampart of Christian civilization and protector against the spread of Bolshevism. The Versailles Treaty, even though that treaty had given rightful liberty to Poland and Czechoslovakia, was nonetheless an instrument of hate and vengeance.[85]

O'Brien simply repeated the standard German propaganda line about the treaty with a few unique embellishments of his own. According to O'Brien, that treaty was invidious because it took away Alsace-Lorraine from Germany, stripped the country of all of its colonies, and starved thousands of German children. In addition, that treaty authorized and caused the French occupation of the Rhineland. That whole episode O'Brien styled as "a stench upon history."[86] The French had employed "Senegalese Negro" troops in this occupation and their assaults upon German girls and women should have outraged the conscience of the Allies. Instead, the French compelled Germany to pay for the quartering of that army while its soldiers ravaged the wives and daughters of German men.[87] So much for the Versailles Treaty.

Faculty reaction to the O'Brien speech and to the national publicity attendant upon it was equally swift. Fifteen Notre Dame professors drawn from all of the colleges of the university signed and sent a common letter dated December 18, 1940, to the *New York Times, Chicago Tribune,* and other newspapers, disassociating themselves from the isolationist views of O'Brien. Because so much publicity had been given to O'Brien's Washington Hall speech and to the fact that he was a member of the Notre Dame faculty, these fifteen men identified themselves as members of the same faculty and declared their unconditional opposition to his stand. They believed strongly that American interests would be best served by a national policy of aid to Britain.[88] One of the signers of this letter,

Dr. Francis E. McMahon, did more than disassociate himself from O'Brien's views. He decided to follow O'Brien's example and enter the lists as a public advocate.

Francis E. McMahon had joined the Notre Dame faculty in 1933. He was Chicago-born and had graduated from DePaul in 1927. McMahon received a doctorate in Thomistic philosophy from the Catholic University of America in 1931. He spent 1931 and 1932 in Europe as a Penfield scholar visiting and studying in Louvain, Rome, and Munich. As a child McMahon had suffered a polio attack that left him afflicted with a severe limp. During his career at Notre Dame, McMahon was unmarried.

McMahon's recruitment to Notre Dame in 1933, along with other Thomists later, was a recognition of the centrality of Thomistic philosophy in Catholic higher education at that time. McMahon had been hired to teach metaphysics to seniors and to add strength to the new graduate program in philosophy. As a vice president of the Catholic Association for International Peace, soon to be elected president, his interest in international affairs was understandable. What is unusual for some one of McMahon's background was not that he had such an interest but the direction which that interest took.

When the war broke out in September 1939, McMahon was making speeches on campus denouncing unbridled nationalism and idolatry of the nation-state as causes of war. According to McMahon, the prospect of perpetual war stood before the world unless nations were able to divest themselves of national pride and could agree upon specific procedures for peaceful settlement of international quarrels. What he called world fraternalism was the only effective cure for war.[89] With regard to the current crisis, McMahon added, we should remain neutral but not indifferent to the present conflict, that is, try to form a neutral bloc with other nonwarring states, collectively mitigate as much as possible the horrors of this war and actively work for a just and charitable peace.[90]

A year later in October 1940, McMahon's mood had changed but his language had not. In a pamphlet, *The Rights of the People,* published by the Catholic Association for International Peace, he condemned isolationism as folly, arguing that no nation, especially the United States, was exempt from an obligation to seek world peace. A national policy of withdrawing behind the protective barriers of our ocean borders and observing the carnage of Europe from a safe distance was, in McMahon's judgment, immoral and unChristian. A policy more compliant with Christian morality would be one of working—in some unspecified way—to defeat nationalism and establish a world order based on the spirit of Christian charity.[91]

Elated by the election victory of Roosevelt but distressed by the steady spread of isolationism in the country, especially in the Midwest, McMahon's views about the nature of the present crisis began to change and harden. Observations about the evils of nationalism and the spirit of Christian charity vanished from his statements and speeches about the war and Hitlerism. This exemplary Catholic gentlemen, so representative of Notre Dame lay professors of that time, turned away from his beloved St. Thomas Aquinas and faced the terrible reality of a possible triumph of Hitlerism in Europe and in the world. Very quickly after O'Brien's Washington Hall speech, McMahon moved from a position of passively supporting all aid to Britain short of war to one in early 1941 of actively advocating immediate American intervention in the war.

Clearly, by the time Lend-Lease became law on March 11, 1941, and effectively ended American neutrality, McMahon was a fully committed interventionist, a zealous member of the Fight for Freedom organization, and the most prominent Catholic interventionist in the Midwest. However, McMahon's personal war against Hitlerism had begun on December 16, 1940, and in that war any means of waging it were justifiable.

One of McMahon's first public moves in his capacity as the new president of the Catholic Philosophical Association was to join with 169 other prominent persons on December 26, 1940, to urge Roosevelt to be aggressive in dealing with the dictators and to be as generous as possible in helping Britain.[92] Moreover, in his presidential address to the association on December 30, 1940, McMahon declared that at this moment of world crisis forces were at work in Europe which, if unchecked, would ultimately destroy the cultural and religious values they all held so dear. He concluded by urging his audience to stand fast with President Roosevelt and support his armament and aid to Britain programs.[93]

In speeches and public statements attacking isolationism in early 1941, McMahon did not shrink from a heavy-handed employment of the tactic of guilt by association. He tried to make very clear just whose party line America First and other isolationists were following. According to McMahon, the most outspoken exponents of isolationism were the Communists and surely every intelligent American knew the nature of their game. He argued that the leading Communist newspaper in America, the *Daily Worker,* consistently asserted that the present war was not our affair and warned Americans not to repeat the mistakes of 1917.[94] Even though Communists and Fascists had been by name specifically and publicly barred from membership in America First branches, McMahon pointed out how strikingly similar were their objectives and language.

Thus did the most powerful and divisive foreign policy controversy occurring in the United States come to Notre Dame. O'Brien and McMahon became the university's two best-known professors and frequent regional and national speakers for their respective causes and organizations, O'Brien for America First and McMahon for Fight for Freedom.

The intrusion of a public controversy of such intensity into the daily life of the university was a new experience for the entire Notre Dame community. The person most concerned about consequences and possible problems arising from this new situation was, of course, the president of the university. O'Donnell's initial reaction to O'Brien's Washington Hall speech and McMahon's emergence as an interventionist advocate was to instruct his secretary to open a special file entitled War Controversy. He anticipated, quite correctly, that O'Brien's speech and local and national responses to it would generate a substantial number of letters to the president of Notre Dame. After opening this file and preparing form letter responses for correspondents, O'Donnell then turned his attention to other matters, but not for long. The war controversy, as Father Hugh O'Donnell had described it, absolutely dominated public discourse at the university until December 7, 1941.

— vi —

By February 1941, the combination of two very active public policy advocates clearly identified as Notre Dame professors addressing opposing sides of a major national issue frightened and puzzled O'Donnell. Two of his professors were very important regional players in the largest and most expertly managed propaganda campaigns in the history of the country. This new public relations situation was absolutely unprecedented in the history of the university. O'Donnell did not know what to do but believed that his obligation to protect the reputation of the university required him to do something. One faculty member in the education department, Walter L. Wilkins, related his view of O'Donnell's ability to manage this new and escalating public relations problem at Notre Dame to a longtime friend, Father John Tracy Ellis, a professor of history at the Catholic University of America.

According to Wilkins, at the heart of the matter was the fact that, like the country as a whole, the local Holy Cross congregation was divided on the war controversy issue. Some of the priests supported O'Brien's position, while others believed that McMahon was correct. Insofar as Wilkins could tell, the present Notre Dame administration, like administrations generally, had no convictions on this issue. Another complicating factor was the fact that Father Cavanaugh, regarded as being much brighter than O'Donnell, was "very thick with O'Brien." O'Donnell was probably a decent person, Wilkins concluded, but impressed faculty as a "facade of pomposity" and gave "a perfect impression of a stuffed shirt."[95] Perceived thus by who knows how many, there simply was not much that O'Donnell could do that had much chance of inspiring confidence or winning support.

Because O'Brien had become an instant anti-war celebrity and America First star after the Washington Hall speech, he had many more outside speaking engagements than McMahon during the first six months of 1941. O'Brien spoke often in the Chicago area. He was popular with Catholic organizations, unaffiliated peace groups, and some business-oriented political conservatives.

In all of his winter and spring appearances, O'Brien never disappointed his audiences. The denunciations of the Washington Hall speech were repeated and anti-Roosevelt rhetoric intensified. Always identified as a Catholic priest from the University of Notre Dame, O'Brien's attacks on President Roosevelt and his policies inspired a flood of negatively critical letters to the university from alumni, donors, friends, and ordinary people.

O'Donnell answered most, not all, of these letters with a form letter asserting that the controversial views complained of belonged to Father O'Brien alone and should not be attributed in any way to the university, adding also that only the president of Notre Dame could speak for and in the name of the university. Nonetheless, as the War Controversy file in O'Donnell's office thickened, he began to worry seriously about public relations damage to the university from the public advocacy activities of his two celebrity professors. That worry became near panic in March and April when O'Brien seemed to have gone too far and when McMahon became an unabashed interventionist.

In the early weeks of 1941, the biggest issue driving the war controversy across the country was President Roosevelt's Lend-Lease plan. O'Brien followed the Taft-Lindbergh line on this issue rather than the puzzling, ambiguous one of his friend former Ambassador Kennedy. In speech after speech across the Midwest, O'Brien relentlessly attacked Lend-Lease. In one speech delivered at a "Pro-America Peace Rally" in Dubuque, Iowa, on March 4, 1941, under the approving eye of the strongly isolationist Archbishop Francis J. Beckman, O'Brien not only excoriated Roosevelt and all of the pro-war groups in his usual fashion, but he also attacked Senator Clyde L. Herring, (D-Iowa) for refusing to take a stand on the Lend-Lease bill. According to O'Brien, Herring's non-position was "evasive, non-committal, straddling, cowardly," and if the senator went ahead and voted for the war-dictator measure, he would be "a second Judas Iscariot."[96]

In this instance as in some others, O'Brien was totally wrong about his facts. Herring had announced his support for Lend-Lease as early as January and had delivered a nationwide radio broadcast on behalf of the measure the same night that O'Brien had appeared in Dubuque.[97] Herring was outraged by O'Brien's speech when he read about it in the *Dubuque Telegraph-Herald* and wrote to O'Donnell asserting a close friendship with Bishop Bergan of Des Moines and demanded a public apology from O'Brien and a correction by the newspaper. The senator affected disbelief that "a great institution like the University of Notre Dame would approve such intemperate utterances from a man considered to be the representative of the university."[98]

In the end, opposition of the sort voiced by Taft, Lindbergh, and O'Brien was futile. Lend-Lease passed both houses of Congress with handy majorities on March 11, 1941, and was signed into law by the president on the same day. Hours after the enactment, Churchill described the Lend-Lease law as "the most unsordid act in the history of any nation."[99] Taking an entirely different view of the enactment of Lend-Lease, O'Brien was not discouraged by the outcome. The priest from Notre Dame was more determined than ever to intensify his contributions to the great struggle to keep America out of the war. If anything, O'Brien became more reckless about what he said and what the immediate consequences of his strong words might be.

For example, on April 15, O'Brien spoke in Chicago at a Clark Street meeting of the Lincoln Park chapter of America First where his strident anti-Roosevelt and anti-Churchill remarks provoked a near riot. Police had to rescue an elderly gentleman, Patrick Quinn, who had been severely beaten after protesting the priest's disparagement of the president.[100]

This incident was widely reported in the Chicago area and inspired a number of strongly worded protest letters to O'Donnell. One Chicago woman, Mrs. Julia Robinson, was so shocked at the physical assault on Quinn that she could not resist writing to O'Donnell. Poor Mr. Quinn, she wrote, was almost murdered for trying to say a few words in defense of the president of the United States in Chicago. "All of this disloyal activity and publicity at Notre Dame," she added, "has so angered me. . . . I have always had the greatest feelings of esteem and love for Notre Dame, but this is one thing I cannot as a true loyal American Catholic uphold."[101]

After receiving the Herring and Robinson letters, O'Donnell had to do something. He asked O'Brien to stop at his office for a visit. That visit took place probably on April 26, and it would appear that the meeting was polite and friendly. Though no memorandum of this meeting was ever written, undated handwritten notes about what O'Donnell intended to say to both O'Brien and McMahon have survived.[102] It is very clear that O'Donnell mentioned the Herring matter and the Bishop Bergan connection and asked O'Brien to apologize to the senator. Most likely O'Donnell also made the point that in speeches on the war controversy O'Brien was popularly perceived as speaking for Notre Dame and that mistaken perception was damaging the reputation of the university.

According to O'Donnell's notes, he would have preferred that both O'Brien and McMahon had given the time and energy expended on public controversy to their classes. However, as members of the faculty they were entitled to express their views about any subject of current interest in American life so long as the basic philosophy of Catholic education was preserved. They were entitled to express their views in conformity with the basic policy of academic freedom with full, free, and complete discussion.

Having made those points, O'Donnell next intended to ask respectfully that O'Brien and McMahon "refrain from addressing any large mass meeting or assembly."[103] If O'Brien or McMahon wanted to participate in any other forum under university auspices "where both sides of the present question are presented, I have no objection." Moreover, if either professor received any speaking invitations before the end of academic year, either O'Donnell or Cavanaugh "should be glad to review [them] with [either of] you before giving your final decision."[104]

With regard to writing, O'Donnell asked his two faculty members "to refrain from writing to newspapers, altho I have no objection to your contributing to outstanding periodicals provided you state specifically that your opinion is purely your own as an American citizen and that reference to your university connection be omitted. Give your South Bend address as reference."[105] As O'Brien probably pointed out, he had no control over how reporters covering a speech or editors publishing an article would identify him. O'Donnell recognized this practical problem and reluctantly settled for prefatory disclaimers that the opinions expressed were the speaker's own and not those of the Catholic Church or of the university.

O'Brien left the meeting with O'Donnell a bit disappointed but not outraged, believing either that he could live with the new arrangements or that they would not work or last. In any case, after some additional badgering, O'Brien sent a written apology to Senator Herring and a correction to the *Dubuque Telegraph-Herald*. However, O'Donnell found little comfort in this. O'Brien's written apology ran to four single-spaced typewritten pages. Because Herring had voted for Lend-Lease and because the senator had sent his complaint to the president of the university instead of directly to O'Brien, the apology was far more censorious than had been the original misrepresentation.[106] Already, as a mechanism for protecting the university from popular identification with one side in public controversy, and even before O'Donnell's meeting with McMahon, the new arrangements had begun to fall apart.

— vii —

In March and April 1941, British shipping losses in the North Atlantic were so bad that imports into Britain actually fell below what was needed to feed the people and keep the factories running. Britain simply did not have sufficient ships to protect the convoys sailing from North America.[107] Without immediate American naval support all the way across the Atlantic, the prospect of Britain being starved into submission was real. Churchill pleaded with American officials to employ the American warships as convoy escorts.

With a clear eye on American public opinion, Roosevelt was not ready to go quite that far. If American warships were to be employed as convoy escorts, that mission would have to be given another name. Instead of assigning American sailors and warships to convoy duty, the president proposed instead to employ them on extended patrols far out into the Atlantic. The mission of these patrols was to detect the presence of German submarines and report their locations to British ships. Though the president refused to describe such patrols as convoy duty,[108] the press regularly referred to them as convoys, and most people found the president's distinction incredible. That was the issue that O'Brien addressed at an America First rally in Chicago on May 1, 1941.

When O'Brien began his speech, he certainly went out of his way to make the point that he spoke that night for himself as an ordinary citizen and not as a Republican or Democrat and not in an official way for the University of Notre Dame or for the Roman Catholic Church.[109] It was well that he did, because this speech was his strongest attack to date on the truthfulness of the president of the United States.

O'Brien accused Roosevelt of intending to employ the U.S. Navy on convoy duty in the North Atlantic and calling it by another name. The idea of using American warships to convoy merchant ships loaded with munitions and weapons of war to a point near Britain where the Royal Navy could make contact and escort them into British ports, O'Brien declared, was the next thing to a declaration of war against Germany. In his Chicago speech of May 1, O'Brien accused the president of the United States of adopting this convoy scheme for no other purpose than to stage an incident that would bring America into the war.[110]

In the same speech, which was vintage O'Brien from beginning to end, he declared the American people "sick at heart at the spectacle of an American administration, elected on a platform of keeping us out of war, proceeding by every form of camouflage and indirection to drag us into the ever-erupting volcanoes of European feuds and hatreds."[111] He ended by urging Americans everywhere to send ten million letters and telegrams demanding that the convoy scheme be dropped.[112]

This speech inspired another packet of letters to O'Donnell. One woman from Chicago asserted that her son would never attend a school that proudly boasted of a man of God with such un-American ideas, noting that when Father O'Brien's picture appeared in a newsreel shown in a Chicago movie house, "the priest was booed immensely."[113] A man also from Chicago complained that Catholic clergymen such as O'Brien and Charles E. Coughlin were hurting all Catholics. We are getting an awful name from Protestants, he declared, because they see in the views of such priests a forecast of what might happen if Catholics ever became a majority in this country. "For God's sake," he concluded, "stop O'Brien or issue a statement to the press denying any approval of his speech."[114] O'Donnell noted on this letter, "File but don't acknowledge."[115]

At this moment of mounting desperation, O'Donnell could scarcely believe and could not account for what happened next. Someone in the university office of publicity obtained copies of O'Brien's Chicago speech against the convoy scheme and sent them folded in Notre Dame envelopes, to newspapers across the country.[116] Despite all that O'Donnell had said and tried to do, it appeared to the press and to much of the public that O'Brien was indeed speaking for the university when he attacked President Roosevelt and his policies. If more proof of that judgment was needed, some students and a dean provided it.

A junior in the College of Engineering, John I. Mahler of Scarsdale, New York, released to the press an anti-war petition addressed to the president of the United States. This petition, signed by one thousand Notre Dame students, appeared in the *South Bend Tribune* on May 20, 1941, and in the *Chicago Tribune* on the next day. Copies were sent to the president, Senator Burton K. Wheeler, and the chairman of the appropriate Senate and House committees.

The one thousand signatures on the petition had been collected in about two weeks' time by a student committee organized for that purpose. Mahler was the student chairman of the committee. This petition was part of the America First project that O'Brien had mentioned in his Chicago speech on May 1. The purpose of the project was to flood the White House with anti-war mail and telegrams on the eve of an announced presidential fireside chat on war dangers and the convoy proposal.[117] The timing of the release, May 20, was also influenced by the appearance of Senator Gerald P. Nye at an outdoor anti-war meeting in South Bend's Playland Park. Presiding over this meeting, introducing Senator Nye, and clearly associating Notre Dame with the senator's isolationist position was James E. McCarthy, dean of the College of Commerce and member of the local chapter of America First.[118]

Father James E. Trahey, C.S.C., prefect of discipline, was charged to look into the origins of this petition but could discover nothing unusual about it despite all of the local and national America First activity. Apparently, Father Trahey regarded all of this organized America First activity as coincidental. He made no mention of outside influences affecting Mahler's action in his report to the president. Mahler took sole responsibility for drafting the petition, obtaining the one thousand signatures, and choosing the time to release the document to the press. He denied receiving assistance from any faculty administrator or outside organization.[119]

To be sure, Mahler may have written the petition, but most likely he had a copy of O'Brien's recent Chicago speech in front of him when he did. The petitioners urged the president not to turn his back on solemn promises made during the last presidential campaign to keep American boys out of foreign wars and thus betray the millions of Americans who had elected him to a third term. The signers also attested to their collective hope that the president would resist the hysteria of war, the alien-minded propagandists who would lead our nation into national suicide, and all those seeking the butchery of American youth.[120] If the author of the petition had not actually borrowed language from O'Brien's recent Chicago speech, he was certainly inspired by what the priest had been saying on campus and around the country for five months.

There was no doubt that administration, faculty, and student anti-war and anti-Roosevelt activities in April and May had severely tested the credibility of the official university policy of neutrality in the war controversy. However, the severest test of all from the other side was yet to come. O'Donnell himself would be part of it, and McMahon would be the cause.

— viii —

While O'Brien had been speaking in Dubuque and Chicago and Mahler had been collecting student signatures for his petition, McMahon had been increasingly active for the other side. He had spoken often in the South Bend and Chicago areas, but his main work in March and April was participating in a BSC-inspired project directed out of New York that targeted Catholics and Irish Americans. The object of this project was to try and moderate Catholic and Irish American opinion in the United States on the highly emotional issue of Ireland's neutrality in the war.

The very practical aspect of this issue was the exclusion of the Royal Navy from using Ireland's southern ports. Given the extraordinary success of the German U-boat campaign in the North Atlantic, access to those ports by anti-submarine forces would provide the Royal Navy with a significant tactical advantage. The matter of getting access to Irish ports had been raised in Foreign Office correspondence as early as November 12, 1940, and at that time a judgment had been made that "Americans were the best people to put pressure on the Irish."[121]

Indeed, Churchill had requested that American officials try to persuade the Irish government to open southern Irish ports to regular use by the Royal Navy,[122] but more pressure was needed. McMahon was brought into this effort by his interventionist Catholic friend in the New York Fight for Freedom organization, William Agar. With help from a few other Americans and strongly encouraged by George Stephenson of BSC, Agar drafted an open letter to Prime Minister DeValera urging him to allow the Royal Navy access to southern Irish ports. They hoped prominent Irish Americans would sign it and send it out as their own.[123]

McMahon obliged his new New York friend. Asserting his identity as a Catholic and as an Irish American, McMahon sent his version of the Agar open letter to DeValera to the *New Republic,* (where it was published on May 12, 1941, and then condensed for the *Reader's Digest* that same month) urging the prime minister to allow the British use of southern Irish ports.

Aroused to action, McMahon went far beyond the question of opening the Irish ports. The time for America to be in the war was now. He drafted "A Letter to Americans" for distribution to newspapers across the country. In this "Letter," he identified himself as an Irish American, a Catholic, a professor at the University of Notre Dame, and a vice president of the Catholic Association for International Peace. Notwithstanding his twelve years in the peace movement, McMahon realized that there were some things worse than war and announced his conviction that America ought to be in the war fighting alongside other free men against the forces of destruction.[124]

According to McMahon, the issue facing the country today was not war or peace. The real issue was whether we fight Hitler in alliance with the British today or allow them to be defeated and then face the Hitler menace alone tomorrow. The first of these choices was really the only choice. Isolationists, he concluded, may call me a war monger. If to be a war monger means a willingness and determination to fight for ideals when there is no other way of preserving them, then "list me as a war monger. I shall glory in the title."[125]

Both of these public letters generated quantities of mail to O'Donnell. The open letter to DeValera produced outraged responses from sons, daughters, and even granddaughters of long-suffering Irish patriots. While it is not certain that O'Donnell even saw such letters, his secretary replied with the usual form letter stating that McMahon's opinions on this matter were his alone and that only the president of Notre Dame could speak officially for the university on controversial subjects. However, one response to McMahon's "A Letter to Americans" was so thoughtful and from such an important person that O'Donnell had to think very carefully about how to respond. A form letter to Muriel Benziger of the well-known Catholic publishing house of Benziger Brothers, a donor to past Notre Dame fund drives, and a longtime friend of the university, would not do. (As a matter of fact, Notre Dame's celebrated Father John A. Zahm had died at a Benziger villa in Munich while visiting members of that family in 1921.)

Living in Washington, D.C., and aware of official perceptions of persons and institutions, Miss Benziger wrote not to condemn McMahon for his "A Letter to Americans" but to praise him. "Thank God," she wrote, "there is someone at Notre Dame who at last vindicates the reputation that Notre Dame University has gained through its members being so pro-Irish [and] anti-English to see a Nazi victory so long as England is licked. Notre Dame is today classified as an isolationist, very anti-English and pro-German University."[126]

Next, she referred to Father Zahm's vision of what the role of Notre Dame in American Catholic life ought to be, for which "all sacrifices had been worth struggling for, all prayers worth praying for." Notre Dame ought to be a place, Benziger continued, "that we American Catholics could depend on for its sure guidance and its dependability in this moment of world crisis."[127] Referring to McMahon's "A Letter to Americans," she added, "Any nation that can persecute its own as has Nazi Germany is unfit to carry the torch of civilization. Dr. McMahon's article clearly shows just what the world faces in the event of such a victory."[128]

Benziger could not understand why and how Notre Dame had changed from a place that had been doing so much to help German refugee scholars during Father O'Hara's presidency to such an isolationist, anti-English, pro-German institution today, "excepting that a group of rabid men had gotten within your walls to harm the college."[129] Benziger's reference to rabid men was clearly directed toward O'Brien. It is not certain that she knew O'Brien personally, but she certainly must have had read newspaper reports of his anti-war speeches.

Given the intensity of anti-war activities at Notre Dame in May 1941, O'Donnell had great difficulty responding to the Benziger letter. He did not know what to say, so he said nothing. O'Donnell's secretary acknowledged receipt of the letter and replied that the president was out of town and would respond when he returned, which he never did.[130]

A day or two before O'Donnell received the Benziger letter, he had received another one from Arthur T. O'Leary, a lawyer from New York City. O'Leary was neither an alumnus nor a donor, but he was prominent in Catholic affairs in New York and had been a leading advocate for Nationalist Spain during the Spanish civil war—a member of the General Committee of the American Union for Nationalist Spain. O'Leary sent O'Donnell a clipping from the *New York Daily News* containing McMahon's "Letter to Americans" and in an accompanying letter argued convincingly that McMahon was damaging the reputation of Notre Dame.

Specifically, O'Leary complained about McMahon using his association with Notre Dame for war propaganda purposes.[131] O'Leary admitted that he differed with McMahon over the war and that McMahon was entitled to hold and spread whatever views he liked. What O'Leary resented most and complained most earnestly against was that a man such as McMahon who had made "such a questionable public exhibition of himself should be in a position to shame those of us who are jealous of the good repute of Catholic education institutions."[132] That argument made perfect sense to O'Donnell. His intended meeting with McMahon could be delayed no longer. An end had to be put to McMahon's exploitation of his Notre Dame connection for partisan purposes.

O'Donnell's meeting with McMahon occurred on May 14 or 15, and it went very badly. The only account of what happened is a brief note sent to Arthur O'Leary by O'Donnell's secretary acknowledging receipt of O'Leary's recent letter. The secretary informed O'Leary that O'Donnell "has ordered Dr. McMahon not to discuss the European war situation before assemblies as he has done in the past and also to refrain from using his professional rank and the name of the university in this connection."[133]

That account is entirely consistent with what O'Donnell's notes indicate he intended to say. Clearly, O'Donnell had taken a much stronger line with McMahon, the layman, than he had done with O'Brien, the priest. Unfortunately, the president of the university had taken such a line precisely at the moment when O'Brien's recent Chicago speech was being received by newspapers all over the country in envelopes marked Office of Publicity, University of Notre Dame.

McMahon's reaction to O'Donnell's order was predictable. He wrote at once, probably on May 16, 1941, to Morrison, chairman of the Chicago chapter of the CDAAA, advising him about what O'Donnell had said, and that he, McMahon, had been banned from speaking and writing against isolationism and for the anti-Hitler movement. Evidently, Morrison contacted friends in the local press, because rumors about official action being taken against McMahon began appearing in Chicago newspapers. All of the worst fears expressed in Muriel Benziger's letter seemed about to be realized. Moreover, for the university a major public relations disaster was at hand. It would appear that Cavanaugh intervened to orchestrate and coordinate a damage control operation that began on May 18.

First, O'Donnell put out a statement denying that any sort of ban had been imposed on McMahon or anyone else. At the same time, O'Donnell made clear that the recent dissemination of copies of O'Brien's speech by the University publicity department had been unauthorized.[134]

That dissemination had occurred, O'Donnell continued, because of a misunderstanding on the part of the director of publicity, Tom Barry, and was contrary to a previously issued instruction confirming a long-established university policy. No member of the university staff, O'Donnell added, had ever been "asked to curtail the right of free speech which he enjoys as an American citizen." No one, O'Donnell concluded, "but the president, however, ever may speak or give the impression that he is speaking officially for the university on controversial subjects."[135]

Next, McMahon himself spoke out to rescue the university from the highly embarrassing situation that O'Donnell had created. McMahon issued a statement which he cleared with Cavanaugh before releasing[136] that he had been "assured personally by the president of the university, Father O'Donnell, that the university had never contemplated the least interference with my activities. I was assured that I was free to speak and write without any hindrance."[137]

The critical element in this highly successful cover-up was the price that McMahon had exacted from Frank Smothers, the *Chicago Daily News* reporter covering this story, for an exclusive. Smothers would get O'Donnell's statement and McMahon's confirmation of it only if Smothers would agree not to quote anything from McMahon's earlier letter to Morrison, chairman of the Chicago chapter of the CDAAA.[138] Smothers agreed, and both statements were released. On May 18, McMahon reported to O'Donnell the details of his arrangements with Smothers, indicated his satisfaction that all misunderstandings had been cleared up, and assured the president of his "intense loyalty to Notre Dame and personal affection for you."[139]

Indeed, the crisis was over. Though all thoughts of a ban on writing letters to newspapers or of O'Donnell or Cavanaugh reviewing speaking invitations for McMahon or O'Brien vanished completely, O'Donnell persuaded himself that his two notorious public advocates had learned a lesson and henceforth would be prudent and mend their ways. Both McMahon and O'Brien assumed that the new arrangements about outside speaking and writing that O'Donnell had tried to impose were dead letters. In any case, Tom Barry, a relative of Bishop O'Hara, kept his job as director of publicity, and life was to go on as if these two members of the Notre Dame family had a clear understanding about what they could or should not do as public advocates.

For the next few weeks both O'Brien and McMahon were very careful about making disclaimers that they spoke for themselves and not for the university. However, their association with Notre Dame was never in doubt and that association was what made their speeches and public statements newsworthy. While O'Donnell had been deeply disturbed by his recent experience with McMahon and the *Chicago Daily News*, he showed very little gratitude for the lies McMahon had told to rescue the president and the university from a bad public relations situation. However, during the summer months, O'Donnell was disposed to leave O'Brien and McMahon alone and hope for the best. Yet, at no time did O'Donnell even think about abdicating one iota of his resposibility to protect the good name of the university from whatever damage the public activities of these two advocates might do.

— ix —

As had been the case during the first six months of the year, O'Brien was more active than McMahon on the platform during the rest of May. It was final examination time at Notre Dame, and McMahon's advocacy efforts were limited to writing a long letter to the *New York Times* wherein he dissected current isolationist arguments and then identified them as part of an increasingly effective Nazi propaganda campaign in the United States.[140]

Meanwhile, back at Notre Dame in late May for a special event, O'Brien must have been pleased by what he read in the press about his celebrity friend Joseph P. Kennedy finally separating himself publicly from the president's interventionist policies. For some time Kennedy had wanted to talk about the policy reasons for his long-overdue break with Roosevelt. However, he wanted to do so at a well-covered event such as a Harvard or Princeton commencement, but neither of those institutions wanted him. Instead, Kennedy had to settle for commencement speaking invitations and honorary degrees from two institutions where the revelations of the Lyons interview had not mattered—Oglethorpe University in Atlanta on May 24 and Notre Dame on June 1.

In the Oglethorpe University speech, Kennedy publicly signed on to the complete isolationist agenda. He tried to diminish the importance of Lend-Lease as a strategy for winning the war and of a British victory for future American security and prosperity. According to Kennedy, America had no authentic self-interest in assuming a role of guardian of world peace. A British victory in the present war, he continued, "would be helpful from the viewpoint of our foreign markets—but it is nonsense to say that an Axis victory spells ruin for us."[141] This theme of coexistence with the dictators was not a new one for Kennedy. He had presented it long ago in his infamous Trafalgar Day address to the Navy League in London in 1938, shortly after Chamberlain had returned from Munich. However, coexistence was not a theme that Kennedy had said much about in public over the past three years.

In addition to this now intensely heretical theme of coexistence, Kennedy spoke about his great fear of what preparing for war and actually waging it would do to the country. As Kennedy saw the future, increased government spending, more taxes, and more federal regulations would limit production and consumption in the private sector forever. Consequently, the country would be extremely vulnerable to perilous social and economic transformations of the Utopian sort that would never work. While Kennedy did not mention Roosevelt by name, it was clear enough who was meant when he stated that essential facts had been and were being withheld from the American people to further the interventionist cause.[142]

Because Notre Dame was so widely perceived at that time as a bastion of isolationist and anti-British sentiments, Kennedy's speech there on June 1 promised to be even more severe than the one delivered at Oglethorpe University. However, events intervened, forcing Kennedy to change the tone and substance of what he was expected to say at Notre Dame. The intervening event was the president's national radio broadcast on May 27 explaining that he had issued that night a proclamation declaring the existence of an unlimited national emergency. Under law, the president could take this step only when he believed the outbreak of war was imminent.[143]

Several situations had been building for sometime that led to the proclamation. Certainly the nearly desperate situation in the North Atlantic contributed to it. Equally important, however, was the unwillingness or inability of American business leaders to make the kinds of decisions about allocating resources and capital to the national defense effort. Though men were being conscripted, capital was not. There was a powerful disposition to continue business as usual within corporate and small business America that hurt the preparedness effort. In the end, to effect conversions to defense work and for companies to become fully engaged in it, profits would have to be guaranteed in government contracts, and in many cases, capital for expansion provided from government agencies.

After issuing the proclamation, the president had authority to increase the size of the army and navy. He could place compulsory defense orders in factories, assign priorities to producers and suppliers for scarce materials, and direct manufacturers to fill defense orders ahead of private ones.[144]

When the president made his broadcast, sixty-five million people in twenty million homes listened to him. His tone was deadly serious. The country was in danger, and though not stated, it was clear that the country was only a step or two from entering the war. Responses to the president's broadcast were overwhelmingly favorable. Discussion of the many implications of the new state of national emergency dominated the news for the next week.

With such a tense and anxiety-laden public opinion atmosphere, it was clearly no time for Kennedy to go to Notre Dame and denounce increased government spending, government regulations limiting production and consumption in the private sector, or presidential credibility. There was not much that Kennedy's speech writers could think of saying against the president at this time that could be put into the Notre Dame speech. Kennedy dared not publicly criticize the commander-in-chief when the country stood poised on the brink of war. Dutifully, he told his Notre Dame audience that the president's proclamation was "a most historic and most solemn pronouncement" that required the "unlimited loyalty" of all Americans.[145]

Instead of attacking the president as many had hoped, Kennedy spoke about traditional Catholic values and the need for Western societies to return to them. He suggested that Notre Dame students should reflect on some contemporary conventions of Western civilization that were not worth saving, namely, education without religion and morality, monopolistic capitalism, and a corrupt and racketeering labor movement. He warned about an evident shift of responsibility from individuals to government and about the dangerous tide of collectivism sweeping all before it.[146]

America was the light of the world, Kennedy insisted, and Americanism was a magnificent concept. It was not revolution. Americanism was a belief in the sacredness of human personality and in the inherent inalienable rights which every man possessed independent of the state. Remembering where he was, Kennedy concluded by praising the stern manly sense of the fortitudes of faith taught at Notre Dame, congratulating the Congregation of Holy Cross for what they had accomplished here, and, of course, paying homage to the university's glorious tradition of athletic prowess. That tradition, symbolized by the emblem of the "Fighting Irish," had never failed to stir the nation in the past and would do so again and again.[147] Kennedy's speech writers had written a speech that Catholics would like, and the ambassador had delivered it in a workmanlike fashion, not great but not badly either.

At the Notre Dame commencement, Kennedy had disappointed many of his admirers there by fleeing from the front lines of the anti-war struggle to the safety of patriotism and pious platitudes. Few other prominent isolationists were intimidated by the declaration of national emergency and followed Kennedy's example. Taft, Lindbergh, and O'Brien did not. On June 20, O'Brien went to California to participate in a massive anti-war rally in the Hollywood Bowl. His appearance that night on the same platform with Charles A. Lindbergh, the most popular America First speaker in the country, was the high point of the priest's anti-war activist career. What had been planned as a maximum impact anti-war event, however, turned out to be otherwise. Although the Hollywood Bowl was packed with anti-war enthusiasts, and reporters attended in large numbers, the stories filed from Hollywood that evening and the next day did not make many front pages in other parts of the country.

Alas, similar to Kennedy's Notre Dame speech, the isolationist celebrities at the Hollywood Bowl were upstaged by an event much greater in historical importance than Roosevelt's proclamation of a national emergency. The German invasion of Soviet Russia in the early hours of June 22, 1941, made virtually all other news unimportant during the week that followed.

That event was momentous. It changed the whole course of the war in Europe and had a profound impact in the United States on the ways people thought about it. For observant American Catholics, the German attack upon the Soviet Union raised very serious issues. Despising and opposing Communism in every possible way had become such a habit for them that some officials in Washington and London doubted whether even the very powerful national interest politics of defeating Hitler's Germany could break it. After June 22, 1941, American Catholics might have to decide which was more important, being a patriotic American or an obedient Catholic.

— 5 —

THE WAR CONTROVERSY: ISOLATIONISM AND INTERVENTIONISM IN THE COUNTRY AND AT NOTRE DAME, JUNE TO OCTOBER, 1941

fter April 15, 1941, when the chief objective of British foreign policy was formally declared to be "at the present moment . . . to get America fully into the war,"[1] British propaganda activities in the United States intensified. All past reservations about establishing a regular and direct liaison with CDAAA and Fight for Freedom disappeared. Sir Gerald Campbell, director and coordinator of British propaganda efforts in the United States, advised MOI officials in London that those two organizations operated "nationwide programs on our behalf."[2] Campbell proposed to appoint two special assistants located in New York with a staff of two secretaries and a typist to work with those organizations and give them direction as well as information. The men appointed and charged with these new responsibilities were John Wheeler-Bennett and Aubrey Morgan, Lindbergh's brother-in-law.[3]

Following approval of these two new appointments to work with American interventionist organizations, Campbell received new guidelines respecting two propaganda points that ought to be made as often as possible and two older ones that should never be mentioned. First, the idea that the war was as much America's as Britain's should be stressed repeatedly. Second, the certainty that, in the event of a British defeat, America would never be able to come to terms with Hitler. Third, no British propaganda materials should state or imply that the British government did not want or need America to come into the war. Fourth, no British propaganda materials should state or imply that the British government wanted or needed an American expeditionary force. At the same time, however, Americans should not be discouraged from preparing public opinion for that eventuality.[4]

Thus reinforced with more staff and new guidelines, Campbell and his new assistants, along with Robert Wilberforce, an English Catholic attached to BLI in New York, set themselves to finding ways of reaching and influencing American Catholics. As a matter of fact, ever since the outbreak of the war in September 1939, the American sections of the Foreign Office and of MOI had been seriously interested in this group. American Catholics were such a large and important part of their country's political culture that ways of changing that group's largely negative attitudes toward Britain and the war had to be found.

To achieve that end, British intelligence services had been collecting information about American Catholics from their usual sources in Rome and in America. Among the pieces of information collected in Rome as early as October 1940 were reports of dissatisfaction by high-placed Vatican officials with the publicly expressed pacifist and isolationist tendencies of American Jesuits. To counter those public positions, Father Wlodomir Ledochowski, superior general of the Jesuits, and Eugene Cardinal Tisserant, prefect of the Congregation of Oriental Churches, dispatched a certain Father Coffey from Rome to America with detailed instructions for American Jesuits about how they should mend their ways.[5]

While the information of this sort from Rome and other material gathered in America over the years was never summarized into a proper profile for any sort of general policy preparation, judgments by Foreign Office and MOI personnel were made about American Catholic attitudes, intergroup relations, and personalities. Those judgments became a basis for the American sections of those departments to develop programs about how to reach and influence American Catholics.

Among the more detailed and insightful reports about the state of American Catholic affairs collected by the Foreign Office was one prepared by a German Catholic refugee sometime in late 1941 or early 1942.[6]

He believed that the American Catholic Church was the strongest and most affluent in the world and that after the war Anglo-American ideas would be a powerful influence on the Vatican. From his point of view as a European, this almost certain development would be a mixed blessing. The American Catholic Church was much different from anything that contemporary Europeans had known. For example, the American hierarchy exercised much tighter control over Catholic lay organizations than had been the case in Europe; thus Catholic laymen in America were much less independent-minded than their European brethren. Being different was not necessarily bad, but what this significant difference might mean for the Church as a whole when American influences predominated in the Vatican, no one could tell.[7]

According to this report, the Catholic hierarchy and clergy in the United States had managed to obtain tight control over the Catholic masses in many matters not strictly related to those of faith and morals.[8] While there was some evidence of anti-clericalism inside and outside of the Catholic Church in America, Catholics in this country generally believed and behaved on public policy issues as their bishops directed. Moreover, there was no secret about how this present formidable clerical influence over public policy issues among Catholics had been established and was sustained.

Over the years, anti-British sentiments nourished by Irish influences in the seminaries had produced an overwhelmingly isolationist clergy. Leading Catholic publications such as the *Catholic World* and especially the Jesuit periodical *America* had been consistently and persuasively isolationist in tone and content. American Catholics had simply followed their clerical leaders into isolationism. Any criticism of this leadership, the report continued, had to be private instead of public because the hierarchy controlled all organizations and publications.[9] Whether the picture of the American Catholic Church as presented in this report and in others was accurate or an offensive caricature did not matter to British ministers in 1941 and 1942. The picture before them, whether true or false, was the one upon which they proceeded to act.

During the summer of 1941, the MOI intended to have in place an American religious division specializing in American religious groups and charged to reach and influence as many of them as possible. The Protestant section of this division proposed to reach their targeted population through a committee of influential religious leaders assembled by Dr. Henry Van Dusen of the Union Theological Seminary, a strong supporter of a wide range of interventionist activities. Apparently, under Van

Dusen's leadership the committee performed in an exemplary fashion, described in a confidential MOI memorandum as giving "magnificent cooperation in many ways."[10]

With American Catholics, the problems of communication and influence were much more complicated and less amenable to direct management. Nonetheless, the fact that structurally as well as practically the American Catholic Church was such a top-down organization suggested an easily implemented tactic for changing American Catholic opinion on a number of issues important to the British war effort. Only the hierarchy had to be courted and converted. That done, Foreign Office and MOI officials assumed the masses would follow their natural leaders anywhere they chose to lead them. The American divisions of the Foreign Office and MOI built their propaganda policies on a belief that American Catholic laymen and laywomen had given their minds away to their bishops and priests.

Among the few Catholics in New York sympathetic to the British cause, no one was as devoted and influential as Van Dusen was among Protestants. There was not and never could be the kind of direct contact between MOI officials and American Catholic bishops as there was with Van Dusen, although there was minimal contact of a sort between Robert Wilberforce of BLI and some local sympathetic Catholic leaders. Trying to replicate the Van Dusen model, Wilberforce had managed to organize a small committee of American Catholics around William Agar.

However, Agar and his friends were utterly incapable of influencing Catholics to the extent Van Dusen was able to influence Protestants. MOI was advised that the position of this small committee of American Catholics was "too delicate to allow direct communication."[11] In addition to Wilberforce, the chief MOI contact with American Catholic leaders was O'Hara's old friend and foreign faculty recruitment advisor, Frank Sheed of the Sheed and Ward publishing house. In America during most of the war, Sheed had maintained regular and close contact with those few American Catholic leaders, lay and clerical, sympathetic to the British cause.[12]

To assist Wilberforce and Sheed in New York, MOI organized tours of America by celebrity English Catholics such as Father Martin D'Arcy, S.J., Monsignor Ronald Knox, and Richard Downey, archbishop at Liverpool. The special message to be emphasized on these tours was that great moral and spiritual issues were at stake in this war and only a British victory would ensure preservation of them.[13]

In addition to celebrity Catholic tours, MOI created a weekly Catholic newsletter, the *Catholic Bulletin,* that was mailed out under the auspices of the English Catholic journal, the *Tablet,* to make invisible the role of MOI in preparing and funding it.[14] Approximately 3,400 copies of the *Catholic Bulletin* were sent out to all members of the American hierarchy, editors of Catholic newspapers and periodicals, and prominent clergymen. MOI also commissioned a book, Michael Power's *Religion and the Reich,* and posted 300 complimentary copies to a list of American Catholics believed to be influential along with a covering note that the book was a gift from a "neutral friend."[15]

Finally, the pope's denunciation of the German offensive in 1940 provided an opportunity that could not be overlooked. Circulation of this papal message was increased significantly by putting it in book form under the title of *The Pope Speaks* and paying Harcourt Brace a discreet subsidy to publish and promote it.[16]

Indeed, as developed in late 1940 and throughout 1941, the propaganda program organized by the British to reach and influence American Catholics was impressive. Much material had to be prepared, and many activities coordinated. Propaganda materials were either prepared in Britain or in America by British academics and writers with specialized knowledge of their targeted audience.

However, by design, interpreters and presenters of materials thus prepared and activities thus organized were Americans only. Through interventionist friends in New York and through membership in Fight for Freedom, Inc., Notre Dame's Francis E. McMahon became the most active and notorious of these interpreters and presenters in the Midwest.

— ii —

For O'Brien and other political conservatives in America First, the German invasion of Soviet Russia seemed almost like a providential event. The prospect of these two despised totalitarian regimes destroying one another was a fortuitous one indeed. O'Brien and his friends in America First were in no hurry to support American aid programs for the Soviet government in its life and death struggle against Germany. The necessity of keeping America out of this widened European war seemed now more urgent than ever. Thankfully, the undeserved accusation of fellow-traveling with Communists in the anti-war movement was at long last lifted from America First. American Communists now became as strong for intervention as they had been formerly for peace. O'Brien and other members of America First could now oppose both the war and damn the Communists with equal vigor. There was no longer any fear of political contamination from Communists by associating with them in the anti-war cause.

For those Americans enlisted in the interventionist cause and surprised by the German invasion of Russia, MOI had some words of caution. Four days after the war in the East began, Campbell argued that careful consideration must be given to the line taken by the pope and the Catholic Church on the German invasion of the Soviet Union. The official papal line on this question would be very important in the United States because of the large number of Catholics there.[17]

After thinking for two weeks about the problem of finding a propaganda line that would not offend American Catholics, Campbell concluded that all references to the international aspects of Communism had to be avoided when addressing the issue of aiding the Russian war effort. Instead, heavy emphasis should be put upon the nationalist and patriotic sides of the conflict.[18]

Generally, McMahon and others in the interventionist movement agreed with Churchill that "the enemy of my enemy is my friend" and willingly followed the Campbell line, emphasizing the nationalist and patriotic aspects of Russian resistance. Publicly, McMahon embraced Russian participation in the war against Hitler, but not the Soviet government or social system. As a full belligerent in the war, and at the present moment facing the full fury of three invading German army groups, McMahon and other like-minded interventionists believed that Russia deserved as much aid as Britain and the United States could spare. Very quickly, most of the interventionist leaders supported extending Lend-Lease aid to the Soviet Union.

If American aid began flowing to the Soviet Union, there was a real question whether American Catholics could or would in conscience support such a policy.[19] American Catholics had been forbidden to collaborate in any way with Communism, a government and social system understood to be totally evil. Pope Pius XI's condemnation of Communism, *Divini Redemptoris* (1937), had been so complete and unambiguous that no one could mistake his meaning—"No one may collaborate with it in any undertaking whatsoever."[20]

No collaboration clearly meant no collaboration under any circumstances. As Monsignor Frederick W. Freking, editor of *Cincinnati Telegraph-Register,* pointed out in his column on October 6, 1941, Communism was evil incarnate; no collaboration was permissible, not even in a cause as sacred as saving Christian civilization from destruction by Nazi armies.[21] To be sure, not all members of the American Catholic hierarchy were as strictly constructionist on this issue as Monsignor Freking, but a great many of them were. Maneuvering room in this matter had to be found and found very quickly. If extension of Lend-Lease to Russia or other forms of aid were approved by Congress, as matters presently stood, American Catholics would be obliged in conscience to oppose such aid programs, which were a new and important part of American foreign policy. How many would actually take such a course and what they would actually do, no one could know.

A few members of the American Catholic hierarchy believed that American Catholics should not be pushed into such a difficult and potentially dangerous position. One such bishop was Joseph P. Hurley of St. Augustine. Using material in part prepared by the United States Department of State in a radio speech delivered on July 6, Hurley employed a distinction used by Pius XI in his encyclical *Mit Brennender Sorge* (1937). In that pronouncement, the pope had distinguished between the German people and the German government. One could love the former while rebuking the latter. Hurley tried to apply that distinction to the present situation regarding aid to Soviet Russia, namely, that aiding the Russian people was not collaboration with a Communist government. By such means Hurley hoped to provide a rationale that would allow conscientious Catholics to support their country's foreign policy of extending Lend-Lease aid to the Soviet Union.[22]

In the summer of 1941, Hurley was indeed a solitary voice in the wilderness. His episcopal brethren did not find his way out of a difficult situation appealing. Cardinal O'Connell and Archbishops Curley and Beckman publicly denounced Hurley's position, and Archbishop Spellman repudiated it in a private letter to Pius XII.[23] The vast majority of the hierarchy seemed to be content to ignore the problem or at least wait for Rome to find a way out for them. Fortunately for all concerned, Rome acted quickly. Archbishop Amaletto Cicognani, the apostolic delegate resident in Washington, D.C., took charge of the matter.

After discussions with leading members of the hierarchy, Cicognani decided to assign the task of preparing a pastoral letter on the subject of American Catholics cooperating with a Communist government in the war to Archbishop John T. McNicholas, O.P., of Cincinnati. McNicholas was a small man in physical stature but very large in influence. He was a most ardent Thomist and reputed to be the strongest intellectual and best theologian among the archbishops. Moreover, McNicholas was very mindful of having earned that reputation. He was a man of strong opinions on most subjects and did not take unsolicited advice or criticism easily from anyone, bishop, priest, or layman—especially from laymen. McNicholas could become stubborn and willful when confronted by opposition and was not temperamentally disposed to forgive and forget or turn the other cheek. Among other things, McNicholas was Monsignor Freking's boss at the *Cincinnati Telegraph-Register.*

In politics, McNicholas was an admirer of Senator Robert A. Taft, scion of a prominent Cincinnati Republican family and a leading isolationist. McNicholas shared Taft's isolationist views and most of his anti-Roosevelt sentiments. Because McNicholas was not known to be a Roosevelt man, Cicognani believed that reputation qualified him all the more to draft a pastoral that the Roosevelt administration would like. The assignment was a highly confidential one, and when it was completed and released on October 30, 1941, it abandoned completely the strict constructionist position that Monsignor Freking had been asserting in the *Cincinnati Telegraph-Register* earlier in the month.

McNicholas' pastoral incorporated much of what Bishop Hurley had suggested in July about making a distinction between helping the Russian people and aiding the Soviet government. The heart of the pastoral was an exhortation for charity in matters of political opinion and a conclusion that the well-known passages in *Divini Redemptoris* forbidding cooperation with Communism did not apply to the present moment of armed conflict.[24] The pope's condemnation of Communism should not be taken as a moral direction to refuse aid in a war of defense. Moreover, the Holy Father's words should not be viewed as having laid out a course of action appropriate for the United States or any other country in every future circumstance.[25] It would be difficult to imagine a more forceful repudiation of Monsignor Freking's strict constructionist position published in the *Cincinnati Telegraph-Register* three weeks earlier. Yet the full text of McNicholas' pastoral was printed in the same newspaper without editorial comment or any explanation for what must have appeared to the faithful as an extraordinary reversal of opinion.[26]

It would appear that the confidentiality of McNicholas' assignment was not well kept. Francis J. Beckman, archbishop of Dubuque, a man of extreme isolationist views, apparently got wind of what was happening and in a radio broadcast stated his opposition to extending Lend-Lease aid to Russia no matter what sorts of distinctions were offered to justify it. Beckman made that broadcast even though the apostolic delegate had personally urged him to stop publicly airing his foreign policy differences with other bishops.[27] In general, apart from one favorable news story about the pastoral in the *New York Times,* McNicholas' pastoral does not seem to have immediately affected American Catholic opinion on the morality of aiding the Soviet Union in its struggle with Germany one way or the other.

However, in a report sent to the Foreign Office about a year later on the state of American Catholic opinion, an observer noted that under pressure from the Vatican the Jesuit periodical *America* had abandoned all past advocacy of isolationism, a most proper thing to do after the Japanese attack on Pearl Harbor. *America*, he continued, "now cooperates by admonishing its readers to distinguish between the Russian people and Communist ideology."[28] In addition to the mission of Father Coffey, one of those Vatican pressures had to be McNicholas' pastoral letter.

At Notre Dame, the German invasion of Soviet Russia effected subtle changes in the advocacy activities of O'Brien and McMahon. Both spoke more often, added new subjects to their respective agendas, and on occasion tended to run ahead of the advocacy organizations in whose service they had enlisted. Clearly, public advocacy to both O'Brien and McMahon had become more important and certainly more exciting and interesting than teaching philosophy of religion or Thomistic metaphysics.

O'Brien was perhaps more disposed to branch out on his own. He added strident anti-Communism to his anti-war and anti-Roosevelt speaking repertoire to such an extent that the Communist newspaper *Daily Worker* took notice of it, and styled O'Brien as "Red baiting and pro-appeasement."[29] Overall, O'Brien was much encouraged by the results so far obtained from his anti-war speaking and writing. A public opinion poll of all Catholic clergy in the United States taken by the Catholic Laymen's Committee for Peace in September 1941 and financed by the America First Committee showed that American Catholic clergy overwhelmingly opposed United States participation in a shooting war outside of the United States and providing aid to Soviet Russia.[30] To be sure, credit ought to be taken when credit was due. O'Brien appeared to be making a difference.

In the months following the German invasion of Soviet Russia, McMahon's local and regional notoriety as an interventionist advocate increased. For the first time in his life McMahon had achieved local celebrity status, and he enjoyed it. Nonetheless, with the memory of recent difficulties with O'Donnell much in mind, McMahon moved very warily into full-time interventionist advocacy during the summer months. He did not want to disturb or antagonize O'Donnell needlessly and possibly jeopardize his employment at Notre Dame. He was fearful of incurring such risks, at least not until his celebrity status was so secure that he could easily move to another university if for any number of understandable reasons O'Donnell decided not to renew his annual contract.[31] Therefore, whenever trouble seemed likely to occur, McMahon tried to warn O'Donnell of that possibility early and explain what had happened or what was about to happen.

One continuing source of trouble for any interventionist advocate in the Midwest was of course Colonel Robert R. McCormick's strongly isolationist *Chicago Tribune.* The editors seemed to delight in misquoting and distorting meaning. For example, in an account of a speech delivered by McMahon at a South Bend rally on July 19, 1941, the *Chicago Tribune* reported that McMahon urged the U.S. Navy to engage in a shooting war to clear the Atlantic sea lanes and that he had used harsh words against Father Charles E. Coughlin. That report in the *Chicago Tribune* was read by a Catholic window-and-door manufacturer in Dubuque, Iowa, who telegraphed a complaint to O'Donnell. Mr. George H. Most complained, incorrectly in this instance, that according to the *Chicago Tribune* McMahon had described Father Coughlin as uncharitable and criminal.

McMahon explained to O'Donnell that the *Chicago Tribune* reporter had fabricated both statements. The only reference to Coughlin in the entire speech was in association with Wheeler and Lindbergh, whom McMahon had described as "practioners of political black magic who try desperately to revivify the decaying corpse of isolationism."[32] O'Donnell's secretary responded to the window-and-door manufacturer with the standard reply that McMahon spoke for himself and only the president of Notre Dame could speak officially for the university.[33]

In mid-August, McMahon spoke in Chicago at a rally for increased aid to the Soviet Union and received favorable notice in the Communist newspaper, the *Daily Worker.* He urged all-out assistance to the Soviet Union to defeat Hitlerism. "Russia's enemy," he declared, "is our enemy, even though the cause of Stalin is not our cause." Hitler is the immediate danger to all free people, the number-one menace to religion, culture, and American liberty. We should help Russia resist Hitler, McMahon concluded, adapting a line from Roosevelt's Lend-Lease speech, "as we might help any Communist to put out a fire that menaces both our houses." [34]

After the fall term had begun, McMahon accepted an appointment as Indiana state chairman of Fight for Freedom, Inc. The time demands of that job were such that O'Donnell should have been consulted before McMahon accepted the post. O'Donnell first heard about the appointment from a story in the *South Bend Tribune.* After the fact of acceptance and public announcement, McMahon informed O'Donnell of what had happened and made not the slightest pretense of asking advice about the propriety of accepting such a post while a full-time employee of the university. In a letter to O'Donnell, McMahon simply described the job, minimized the time demands of it, and observed, "Confidentially the organization has the approval of the national administration unof-ficially, and the work performed here will be watched with greatest interest." [35] Clearly, McMahon thought himself to be a big man, getting bigger every day, and it would be best for O'Donnell to know that and appreciate it.

While impressing upon O'Donnell the importance of this appoint-ment to head Fight for Freedom, Inc., in Indiana, McMahon assured the president that his main job was still teaching at Notre Dame. Because a paid field organizer would be sent out to handle most of the detail work, McMahon did not expect that the quality of his teaching would suffer in the least. He expected to be giving perhaps three or four informal talks a month to outside groups. [36]

There is no doubt that O'Donnell greatly disliked being told, not asked, how and when McMahon was going to fulfill his contracted teach-ing obligations to the university, but he did nothing. He did not even reply to McMahon's letter of explanation. O'Donnell was in a very deli-cate situation, and he knew it. The public relations debacle of May was not easily forgotten, and no doubt O'Donnell was a bit leery about re-sorting so soon to another display of vigorous presidential authority.

With the matter of the state chairmanship of Fight for Freedom, Inc., settled and McMahon's stature increased thereby, he accepted speaking dates all over the Midwest, hoping that with the help of colleagues in the philosophy department he would be able somehow to cover his classes as well as meet his speaking engagements.

— iii —

During the summer of 1941, most of the war news, especially the news from the Russian front, was universally bad. Perhaps the only positive news related to the war that summer was the dramatic extension of the Western hemisphere eastward across the Atlantic when American naval forces unexpectedly seized control of Iceland on July 8. Occupation troops arrived in early October.

Though not encouraging for the British cause, those summer months were a very busy time for America First. According to reports obtained by BIS which were described as German propaganda successes in the United States, Senators Nye and Wheeler went off on speaking tours arranged by America First and attracted large audiences, particularly in the western parts of the country. Consequently, isolationist sentiments, anti-British attitudes, and the conviction that Britain was all but defeated increased significantly. [37]

In addition to America First's usual stable of celebrity isolationist speakers, the leadership of the organization had some special projects in the works. One strongly advocated by John T. Flynn, chairman of the New York City chapter of America First, columnist for the *New Republic*, and spokesman for the liberal wing of America First, was an investigation of the motion picture industry for pro-war activity.[38] Flynn believed that he had collected evidence that the Roosevelt administration had made direct requests to the industry to produce a certain percentage of pro-war films. He believed that a congressional hearing exposing this situation could be arranged.[39]

Another project involved mounting a maximum effort to defeat a bill scheduled for legislative action on August 12 intended to extend the present one year of service required from draftees to an additional eighteen months. Understandably unpopular with men drafted into the army for a year and expecting to be released in the fall, Senator D. Worth Clark (R-Idaho) advised Lindbergh on August 10 that if a vote were taken on that day, the bill would not pass the House. Senator Clark feared that before the vote the president might be able to twist a few arms and perhaps gain sufficient votes to pass the bill.[40]

What neither Senator Clark nor anyone else in America First could have known was that Roosevelt would be in Argentia, Newfoundland, meeting with Churchill and not on the scene to twist any arms at all. If the senator had known where the president would be on August 12, he would have taken heart. Loss of the draft extension bill would have allowed the new army to melt away, turned the entire American preparedness effort upside down, and stopped the interventionist movement cold. It would have been a humiliating loss, and it almost was. Only a strict application of House rules and some heavy-handed gaveling by Speaker Sam Rayburn of Texas enabled the bill to pass, 203 to 202.[41]

In addition to almost losing the critical vote on the draft extension bill on August 12, Roosevelt's presence at the Argentia meeting at that time contributed significantly to America's deteriorating relations with Japan. For over a year, the president had been trying to avoid a confrontation over that country's increasingly aggressive behavior in southeast Asia. Roosevelt believed that some sort of arrangement with Japan was essential in order to gain the time required to train our expanding armed forces and mobilize American industry for war materials production. Only then would it be possible to achieve the main foreign policy objective of the American government, which was destruction of the Hitler menace in Europe. Japanese ambitions in the Pacific were a distraction, albeit a serious one, but a distraction nonetheless.

The United States simply did not have a navy large enough to confront and block the Japanese in the Pacific and deal with what was universally perceived in Washington to be the more pressing problems in the Atlantic. Informal talks between the State Department and Japanese officials in July concerning possible schemes to neutralize Indochina and Thailand on a Switzerland model proceeded without result. According to British Foreign Office reports, the Japanese gave an evasive negative response to such ideas and then moved troops into Indochina in mid-July.[42]

In retaliation for this aggressive move, the president froze Japanese assets in the United States, closed the Panama Canal to Japanese ships, and placed an embargo on high octane aviation fuel. However, while Roosevelt was meeting with Churchill in Argentia, subordinates in Washington broadened that embargo to include oil products of every type. Upon returning to Washington, the president discovered that the embargo had been expanded, but decided to let that action stand. He could not rescind what had been done without appearing to have appeased Japan. For its part, the Japanese government could not tolerate a total embargo of American oil and began developing ways of resolving their problems with the United States by means other than diplomacy.[43]

In Argentia, the president and prime minister discussed at length future Anglo-American relations with Japan. Churchill was ready to take a very hard line with that country and prepared to say so publicly. Roosevelt wanted no bellicose joint declaration at this time and agreed only to issue a unilateral warning to Japan.[44]

Besides Japan, other trouble spots in the world were discussed as well. For example, the importance of German influence in Iran was recognized and an Anglo-Russian move into Iran to eliminate it was approved.[45] Anglo-Russian forces actually moved into Iran on August 26.

From the British point of view, the most important result of the Argentia meeting were Roosevelt's promises to provide naval escorts for convoys to points east of Iceland and to attack German U-boats as far away from convoys as two hundred miles. According to Churchill's report to his cabinet upon returning from Argentia, the president had promised to wage war at sea but not declare it. Everything would be done, Churchill reported on August 24, 1941, to force an incident with the U-boats that would bring America into the war.[46] Even Churchill had to learn that in the Roosevelt administration promises of action were one thing, action actually taken was another.

Once the very important but secret strategic and tactical decisions had been made, the president and prime minister completed work on documents to be released to the public. Long hours and heated discussions were devoted to preparing for posterity an articulation of the Roo-sevelt/Churchill vision of a better world at war's end. This intended dramatic public relations conclusion to the Argentia meeting was cast in the form of joint declaration known as the Atlantic Charter.

When released, the Atlantic Charter was the first formal statement of British war aims released since the war began. The statement was jointly announced by the president and the prime minister. Though Britain was at war and technically America was at peace, both countries jointly declared no territorial ambitions, respect for self-determination, a determination to restore sovereignty to the conquered peoples of the world, and commitments to open access for all to the world's natural resources, to free trade, and to work for disarmament and a permanent system of world security.[47] The Atlantic Charter, the president and prime minister hoped, would be accepted as proof positive that the present war was more than a struggle between competing imperialisms as German propaganda had represented it to be.

More than that, the Atlantic Charter was intended to be evidence that American and British interests were one and the same and that a new world was aborning. The American people were asked to believe that this idealistic new world of egalitarianism and humane values would arise out of a terrible war that Britain would fight, somehow win, and then magnanimously share management of the peace with the great arsenal of democracy. The Atlantic Charter was largely the president's work, with the prime minister not objecting. Roosevelt expected a great public relations triumph out of the Atlantic Charter but did not get it.[48]

War news was so bad in August and September and the possibility of an Axis defeat was so remote that the ringing rhetoric of the Atlantic Charter seemed almost irrelevant. While the charter certainly defined Anglo-American relations at a critical time, it did not capture the imaginations of many Americans. America First speakers largely ignored it. Once reported, the Atlantic Charter's staying power as a front-page story or as an editorial subject was minimal. Stories about rising tensions between America and Japan dominated the news in late August and September.

There were some American reporters in London, however, who believed that more had been decided at the Argentia meeting than had been revealed. One of them, Frederick R. Kuh of the United Press, set about trying to discover what really had happened at Argentia.

Kuh was forty-six years old and had worked as a foreign correspondent in Europe since 1919. He had joined United Press in 1924 and had served in Berlin, Moscow, and London. An experienced foreign correspondent who knew his way around London, Kuh had developed a list of confidential sources who trusted him. Among the community of working American print journalists in London at that time, Kuh was one the best.

Kuh obtained information about some of the secret agreements reached at the Argentia meeting and filed two stories about them out of London through the United Press on August 22 and 23. These stories described Churchill's commitment to Roosevelt that Britain would automatically declare war on Japan if that country, because of aggressive actions in the Pacific, became involved in a war with the United States. Kuh's stories also described Roosevelt's full understanding of the present crisis in Iran and his approval of Churchill's plan to move troops into that country in cooperation with the Russians to purge the region of German influence.[49] Another story filed by Kuh out of London through the United Press on September 11, 1941, revealed that the president had given a severe warning to the Japanese government. All three of these stories had been passed by British censors.[50]

When these stories appeared in the American press, Secretary of State Hull became almost apoplectic. He complained bitterly to the Foreign Office about leaks relating to the Argentia talks and other confidential matters coming out of London and could not understand why British censors had passed them.[51] Anthony Eden immediately charged Sir William Ridsdale to investigate the leaks and try to discover their source. As director of the Foreign Office news department, Ridsdale had earned the confidence of the American journalist community and through his many contacts with them quickly identified a source of the leaked information.

Ridsdale reported to Eden on September 15. He was certain that at least one of leaks leading to Kuh's United Press reports came from Captain Elliott Roosevelt, the president's son. Elliott Roosevelt had attended the Argentia meeting with his father and knew as much about what had been discussed there as anyone.[52] Two American journalists in London disclosed to Ridsdale that Elliott Roosevelt had talked about the Argentia talks to them on an off-the-record basis.[53] Ridsdale surmised that Kuh either had obtained information about the Argentia talks from Elliott Roosevelt himself or from journalists who had received it from the captain. In any case, the information was obtained, and Kuh did not consider himself bound by any off-the-record agreement. The source was so credible and the story so important that he wrote it quickly and, without any attribution of sources, filed it through United Press.

Ridsdale recognized clearly the delicacy of the situation. As he saw matters, the United States ambassador, John G. Winant, on instructions from Washington had protested the action of British censors "in passing a cable, embarrassing to the President and State Department, which was compiled by a correspondent as the result of information received from the President's own son." Appropriately, Ridsdale added, "This seems a little hard."[54] Eden agreed, noting on Ridsdale's report, "It does indeed, but I suppose that I must not even hint anything of the kind to the U.S. Ambassador."[55] Eden did not.

Nonetheless, something had to be done. More leaks of this sort could impact severely on the willingness of the State Department to share information with the Foreign Office if Hull believed that such information would soon appear in the American press under a London dateline. To avert such a situation, Ridsdale urged Eden to discuss with Ambassador Winant some of the problems bedeviling British censorship while making no mention of the "Elliott Roosevelt thing."[56]

Because of earlier stupidities committed by British censors, Ridsdale explained, American journalists had managed to defeat British censorship. Among American journalists, badgering ministers of information had become an all-around sport, that is badgering them with implied threats that the United States Embassy fully supported whatever a particular American journalist had written. Since checking the truth of all such assertions was impractical, few were checked. The end result of all of this successful badgering was that British censorship had lost practical power to stop transmissions from American journalists, even transmissions inconvenient for the State Department.[57]

Ridsdale recognized that given Britain's most pressing war aim—getting America into the war—any journalist's transmission embarrassing to the president and State Department ought to be stopped. In the world as it was, that was an utterly unrealizable ideal. However, Ridsdale observed, even Ambassador Winant would probably admit that no leak could be more damaging to the president and State Department than news that Winant "had protested to us because we had not imposed sufficiently firm restrictions upon the messages of American correspondents in London."[58]

Ridsdale's solution to the problem of leaks and the impracticality of censoring American journalists was simple. Since almost all of the recent troublesome messages had been the work of Frederick R. Kuh of the United Press, Ambassador Winant could do one of two things. First, the ambassador could talk to Kuh and try to persuade him into more cooperative and responsible behavior. Second, Winant could try and get this "annoyingly brilliant collector of news" transferred to some better post elsewhere, "so that his abilities could embarrass the Axis rather than ourselves."[59]

Throughout the rest of 1941, British officials in the American divisions of MOI and the Foreign Office continued to worry not so much about Kuh as about the probability of more and perhaps even greater American journalistic indiscretions. Until conditions changed as they did after America formally entered the war in Europe after the Japanese attack on Pearl Harbor, MOI and Foreign Office officials despaired of finding any practical way of preventing them from happening.[60]

What Winant did about the Kuh problem in London in September 1941, if anything, is unknown. Kuh did not disappear. He remained with the United Press until 1942 when he joined the *Chicago Sun* as London correspondent and served in that capacity all through the war and up until 1949. He stayed with the *Chicago Sun* which by then had become the *Chicago Sun-Times*, returned to the United States, and served as one of their correspondents in Washington until his death in 1971.

— iv —

Reactions to press reports out of London that the Roosevelt administration had behaved as a co-belligerent with Britain in high-level meetings while still professing non-belligerent status raised popular anxiety levels hardly at all. As a matter of fact, the summer public opinion polls indicated that while a large number of Americans opposed immediate intervention, a larger majority wanted British convoys to be protected by the U.S. Navy and an amazing 85 percent of those polled thought that war with Germany was inevitable.[61] Moreover, on September 17, 1941, when asked the question: Which was more important, staying out of the war or defeating Germany? 70 percent of those polled chose defeating Germany and only 30 percent answered for isolationism.[62]

To be sure, given the level of polling sophistication in the United States at that time, responses depended as much on where the poll was taken as on the forms of questions put. Yet it seems clear that during the last half of 1941 isolationism was losing support. A major cause of that trend was easy to identify. The conflict between interventionists and isolationists had become nasty and increasingly personal. Both sides perceived that a bad cause was being led by bad men.

The president and Harold L. Ickes, secretary of the interior, were particularly skilled at making that point by implication. Their principal target was Lindbergh, a popular person but an extraordinarily vulnerable and predictable opponent. At times, the man seemed totally bereft of any ability to anticipate or willingness to repair public relations damage. Against Roosevelt and Ickes, Lindbergh was grossly overmatched.

Ickes lost no opportunity to remind Americans that Lindbergh had accepted a medal—Order of the German Eagle—from Reichsmarshal Herman Goering in Berlin in 1938 and had not given it back.[63] The president took the matter a bit further. In a press conference on April 25, 1941, Roosevelt alluded to Lindbergh's advocacy of a negotiated peace with the Axis powers as Britain's only hope for survival by comparing him to Clement Vallandigham, a leader of Union army renegades during the Civil War known as "copperheads," who wanted to make peace with the Confederacy. If that were not enough, Roosevelt also likened Lindbergh to those so-called "sunshine patriots" at Valley Forge who urged George Washington to surrender.[64]

Believing himself to be dishonored by the president's remarks, Lindbergh declared himself unable to serve under a commander-in-chief who doubted his loyalty. Lindbergh resigned his commission as a colonel in the Army Air Force Reserve on April 28, only three days after the president's accusatory press conference. Editorial writers quickly noted that Lindbergh had kept his German medal, but found service in an American uniform under Roosevelt as commander-in-chief dishonorable. On this occasion as on another in the near future, Lindbergh did not and could not repent an action done in haste that damaged himself and by association other leaders in the isolationist cause. As events were soon to demonstrate, Lindbergh had become more dangerous as a colleague than as an opponent.

Recognition of a definite public opinion shift away from isolationism drove the America First organization to counterattack by initiating a new activity and intensifying some old ones. First, John T. Flynn's project to expose the heavy pro-war bias of the Hollywood film industry proceeded apace. Actually, Hollywood had been slow to adopt a pro-Allied stance in released films. Until Warner Brothers released *Confessions of a Nazi Spy* in 1939, the industry had been very careful not to offend anyone and thereby possibly jeopardize their foreign markets. Since 1939, however, Hollywood films had presented a consistently anti-Nazi and anti-Fascist message.

With this recent history clearly in mind, on August 1, 1941, Senator Wheeler charged on the Senate floor that the motion picture industry was embarked on a major pro-war propaganda effort. The Senator had learned from his son that studios were forcing employees to attend pro-war rallies. Darryl Zanuck had led a group of extras from Twentieth Century Fox to provide an audience for Wendell Willkie speaking at an interventionist meeting in the Hollywood Bowl.[65]

Next, Wheeler, a Democrat and chairman of the Senate Interstate Commerce Committee, engineered an ingenious method of mounting a senatorial investigation of pro-war propaganda activities by the Hollywood film industry without obtaining formal Senate approval. Senator Bennett Clark (D-Missouri) introduced a resolution on behalf of himself and Senator Nye (R-North Dakota) on August 1, calling for an investigation of attempts "to influence public sentiment in the direction of participation by the United States in the present European war."[66]

Clark's resolution was referred to Wheeler's Interstate Commerce Committee. Thereupon, Wheeler appointed Senator D. Worth Clark (D-Idaho) as chairman of a subcommittee to consider whether such an investigation ought to be proposed to the full Senate for approval. Wheeler and Clark then chose two Democrats—Bone of Washington and McFarland of Arizona—and three Republicans—Nye of North Dakota, Tobey of New Hamshire, and Brooks of Illinois to serve on the subcommittee. Along with Chairman Clark, Nye, Bone, Tobey, and Brooks formed a bipartisan team of confirmed isolationists who were all opposed to the president's foreign policy. Only McFarland, a freshman senator, was a Roosevelt loyalist. When the composition of the subcommittee was announced, the New York Times pointed out that the full Senate had never debated or approved the investigation and editorialized that the manner of establishing the subcommittee and its composition suggested that no objectivity was intended.[67] Clearly, Wheeler had stolen a march on the Democratic leadership of the Senate and had demonstrated what a master of rules and procedures he was.

Meanwhile, when Bennett Clark introduced his resolution on August 1, Nye was in St. Louis delivering a speech to an America First rally there wherein he offered a rationale for investigating the pro-war bias of the Hollywood film industry. Nye took the industry to task for propagandizing people who had paid money to be entertained and then involuntarily received generous doses of politics as well. Once in a motion picture theater, Nye asserted, people could not get out without hearing at least one speech "designed to make you believe that Hitler is going to get you."[68] All of this was nonsense, Nye added; real dangers to America from the war were lessening. Americans need not send their boys to bleed and die to make the world safe for the British Empire and Communism.

Nye believed that at least two sinister forces were responsible for the production of pro-war pictures. One was the Roosevelt administration, which he insisted had pressured Hollywood to glorify war in order to encourage public acceptance of intervention. The other was a near-monopoly control of movie making, distribution, and exhibition by a handful of men with their own financial and political agendas. Because of this monopolistic situation, a small group of movie producers were positioned to feed pro-war propaganda to the 80,000,000 Americans attending their theaters every week.

Consequently, Nye declared, American film producers had become operators of a giant war propaganda machine that was seemingly directed from a central source, implying of course the president of the United States. At least twenty pictures produced during the last year, Nye continued, were "all designed to drug the reason of the American people—to rouse them to a war hysteria."[69] Next, Nye named the men and companies that he believed dominated the industry and were most heavily involved in disseminating pro-war propaganda in their films. The names provided were familiar to all Americans who bothered to read credits when attending movies. Not only did these names belong to the country's best-known film entrepreneurs, most of these names were distinctively Jewish.

According to Nye, these well-known American movie makers enthusiastically produced pro-British films because British Commonwealth markets were so financially lucrative for them. In his opinion, the film industry had "a stake of millions of dollars annually in Britain winning the war."[70] American boys should not be sent off to die in Europe, Nye proclaimed in St. Louis, "to make the world safe for this industry and its financial backers."[71] Arthur Krock tried to explain what Nye and others on the committee were up to and why they were willing to risk flirting a bit with prejudice. If critics of the film industry, wrote Krock in his *New York Times* column "In the Nation," can rouse prejudice by linking the production, distribution, and exhibition of pro-war films "to direct orders from Jewish executives, naturally bitter against the Nazi regime, they would be delighted."[72] Yet seeking public relations advantage through appeals to prejudice however subtly orchestrated was a dangerous game that many more than one could play. By attacking the leaders of the American film industry as pro-war propagandists, Nye opened himself to the charge of attacking Jews.

Hollywood moguls knew what was coming and had ample time to prepare for it. Encouraged by Sydney Bernstein, a British film entrepreneur in the United States that summer of 1941 on behalf of MOI, studio executives resolved to take an aggressive stand against the Clark committee.[73] To help them do so, Bernstein and others persuaded them to hire Wendell Willkie for a fee of $100,000 to act as counsel for the film executives summoned to appear before the committee.

Arrangements with Willkie were completed by September 1, and he immediately managed to obtain a postponement of hearings until September 9. Willkie needed that much time to prepare a case. Preparation of this case consisted of mounting a public relations assault on the committee. The place to start was with Nye's St. Louis speech. Among the first into the fray was Ulric Bell of the Fight for Freedom organization. On September 7, Bell released an open letter to Congress with sixty-three signers describing the forthcoming Clark committee hearings as "the most barefaced attempt at censorship and racial persecution which has ever been tried in this country."[74]

According to Bell, Wheeler, Nye, and Clark were attempting "to mark a particular section of our national community as propagandists for war." By picking on Jewish filmmakers, Bell continued, Nye, aided and abetted by Wheeler and Clark, "knowingly or not, play the role of Hitler's advanced guard." The objective of these hearings appears to be that of preventing "the American public from being told anything by radio, motion pictures, eventually we must suppose the press, which might make us love freedom more and hate its enemies."[75] Indeed, this was Bell at his best or at his worst. In the St. Louis speech, Nye had provided opponents with a public relations opportunity too good to let pass. The anti-Semitic spin put on Nye's St. Louis speech would stick.

The day after Bell released his open letter to Congress and the day before the Clark committee began its hearings, Willkie publicly attacked Nye and his rationale for investigating the film industry. Willkie put his own special spin on Nye's St. Louis speech. He rephrased some of Nye's prose and made explicit some of the things implied in that speech and then proceeded to denounce the senator for saying what he attributed to him. Willkie denied that pro-British propaganda had been put into Hollywood films "at the instigation of the president and that the racial origins of many of the leading film producers made questionable the motives inspiring their productions." Such reasoning, Willkie concluded, "is contrary to the American way of thinking."[76]

Bell and Willkie wanted to put Nye and the entire committee on the defensive before the hearings began and succeeded grandly in doing so by directly raising and interjecting accusations of anti-Semitism into the committee's proceedings. As the first witness to testify before the committee, Nye had to begin by defending himself from charges of anti-Semitism. However, the more he tried to put matters aright and explain what he had meant to say, the more outrageously anti-Semitic he appeared to be.

With a senatorial investigation of the Hollywood film industry now firmly established and with opposition to it of the nastiest sort building, the leadership of America First reexamined some of its other activities and decided to expand its speakers' program. In September, Lindbergh was booked solid. Senators Nye and Wheeler spoke almost whenever and wherever invitations could be arranged. As the most well-known

Catholic America First speaker in the Midwest, Father John O'Brien was much in demand and spent most of the time before classes began in mid-September away from campus.

Wherever America First speakers appeared in the Midwest during September, they attracted enthusiastic audiences, sometimes large and sometimes not. Despite the shrinkage of isolationist support across the country, Midwesterners came out to see and hear these speakers because they were celebrities and because the president lately had given them some new powerful emotion-laden issues to address.

At the Argentia meeting, Roosevelt had promised Churchill that the U.S. Navy would escort British convoys across the Atlantic to points east of Iceland. However, by early September the president had not yet disclosed this new policy to the American people. A German U-boat attacked an American destroyer, USS *Greer,* in the North Atlantic on September 4. That incident provided an occasion for the president to explain the new policy of escorting convoys and to try and mobilize support for it.

Roosevelt delivered a major radio address to the nation on September 11. In this speech, the president claimed that the German U-boat had fired first on a vessel whose American identity was very clear. Actually, the circumstances of the encounter between the *Greer* and the U-boat were not as clear as Roosevelt had made them. A British patrol plane had attacked the U-boat with depth charges and then alerted the *Greer* that a German submarine was nearby. The *Greer* proceeded to stalk the U-boat which then turned on its pursuer and fired a salvo of torpedoes that missed. The destroyer responded with a depth charge attack that also missed. After a chase of about three hours, the *Greer* dodged another salvo of torpedoes and broke off the chase. Neither the destroyer nor U-boat suffered damage, and there was no evidence that the U-boat commander knew that the destroyer stalking him was American.[77]

In the rest of this speech the president compared German U-boat activities in the Atlantic to the behavior of rattlesnakes poised to strike. The rattlesnakes of the Atlantic had to be dealt with as such, that is, destroyed before they could strike. He announced the new policy of escorting British convoys across most of the Atlantic and his order to the navy to "shoot on sight" any German or Italian raiders entering an American defensive zone. A majority of Americans (62 percent) polled on the "shoot on sight" policy accepted it because there appeared to be no other way of protecting American ships on the high seas.[78] The shooting war in the Atlantic had begun, and in September and October it was not going well at all.

On September 19, an American freighter, *Pink Star,* loaded with food, machine tools, and war materials was sunk off Greenland. A month later, October 16, a newly commissioned destroyer, *Kearney,* was torpedoed off Iceland. Eleven crew members were lost. Then on October 31, another destroyer, *Reuben James,* was sunk west of Iceland with 115 sailors going down with her. It was clear to the president and the Navy Department that unless the sea lanes could be kept open, Lend-Lease would fail and the war would be lost. The American naval command had no special plans in their files to deal with the highly successful German U-boat wolf pack tactics, but they were anxious to try. The present rate of losses could not continue.

As the president considered the present situation in the North Atlantic, the time had come to repeal those parts of the neutrality laws remaining that prevented the arming of American ships and routing them to belligerent ports through combat zones.[79] Roosevelt announced on October 10 his intention to ask Congress to amend the neutrality laws and give him authority to arm American merchant vessels. If the president succeeded in getting the neutrality laws amended, there would be nothing left of them. The country would be only one very small step away from expanding the present undeclared war in the Atlantic against Germany into full-scale belligerency. Leaders in Washington, London, and Berlin all had no doubts that such a step would be taken. They just did not know when.

Strident opposition to any revision of the neutrality laws turned out to be the last major anti-war effort mounted by the America First organization. In early September 1941, the leadership of America First did not imagine that such would be the case, but events intervened that began turning their world upside down.

— vi —

On September 9 in Washington, Senators Clark and Nye began the first day of public hearings on the pro-war bias of the film industry. Fearing the mounting wave of opposition to the committee's intended work and intimidated by Willkie's much-reputed skill as a cross-questioner, at the outset of the hearings Senator Clark laid down a set of very limiting committee procedural rules. According to those rules, Willkie was not allowed to examine his own witnesses, cross-question others, or even privately counsel his own witnesses while they were being questioned.[80] Cheerfully, Willkie retired into a corner with microphone in hand ready for banter and distant verbal badgering of witnesses and committee members.[81]

Thus protected, Nye began the proceedings by speaking from a prepared statement of forty-one pages. He denied that the hearings were motivated by anti-Semitism, insisting that his only objective was to prevent American intervention in a foreign war. The men named in his St. Louis speech, Nye continued, did in fact control the motion picture industry, and it was only coincidence that most of them were Jews. It was their war propaganda that was objectionable, not their religion.[82]

Nonetheless, Nye kept returning to his point about the dominant role of American Jews in the film industry. He believed that support by American Jews of a foreign policy directed against oppressors of European Jews was quite natural, but tactlessly added that the interests of the Jewish race were not necessarily the interests of United States foreign policy.[83] In addition to the factors of religion and race in accounting for the film industry's pro-war bias, there was always the matter of money. According to Nye, leading filmmakers had selfish interests to protect: "Sales to Britain represent the difference between profit and no profit in the entire year's business. If Britain goes down, they lose sales."[84]

Nye regretted the interjection of charges of anti-Semitism into this investigation but claimed that was not his doing. That issue had been raised, he suggested, by interventionists as a public relations tactic. Then, in an observation that won no friends in the American Jewish community, Nye attributed the charges of anti-Semitism against him to "Jews who were feeding their own persecution complex."[85]

Many people seemed to have assumed, Nye concluded, that our Jewish citizenry would willingly have our country and its sons taken into the present war. It was better to have such "whisperings" out in the open. After Nye's testimony to the committee was completed, they were.

During the course of his long presentation, Nye was particularly scornful of Warner Brothers for producing some of the most blatant examples of pro-war propaganda. He mentioned such films as *Sergeant York, The Great Dictator, Escape, Convoy, Flight Command,* and *I Married a Nazi* as needing committee scrutiny. Newsreels should not be overlooked, especially *The March of Time.* During most of this first day, Willkie did not have much to do except to let Nye continue to talk. The senator provided more substance to the charges of anti-Semitism against him than Willkie could ever manufacture.

On the next day, Senator D. Worth Clark, chairman of the committee, testified about the near-monopolistic character of the film industry. With production concentrated among four or five companies, the senator believed there was basis for an anti-trust prosecution if the Justice Department could be persuaded to undertake one. John T. Flynn appeared on September 11 and addressed the issue of monopoly from another perspective. Flynn considered the present condition of near-monopoly control of the film industry as dangerous. It was dangerous because it had imposed a crude but effective system of censorship on the film-viewing public. This censorship followed not from government directives nor from interest-group pressure. It was internal censorship imposed by the industry or by the industry's moral watchdogs in the Hays Office.[86]

According to Flynn, the effects of this censorship were clear enough for all to see. Contemporary Hollywood films were characterized by the reiteration of a single point of view. Monopolistic control had prevented production of anti-Fascist films before 1939. During the last two years, monopolistic control had prevented production of a single foot of film showing the anti-war side.[87] Flynn's solution to the problem of internal censorship was simple and straightforward: break up the monopoly.

Though Flynn had tried to make a serious point in his testimony about how social and political messages in commercial films were determined, Willkie did not treat it as such. After two days of relative silence, Willkie grabbed the microphone and berated the committee for not producing anything that remotely would lead to legislation. All that had happened so far, Willkie insisted, was a vague suggestion that the industry should produce pictures showing both sides of international questions.[88]

Willkie disposed of Flynn's testimony about the power of monopoly in the film industry by observing that Flynn's speech "was a redraft of Senator Clark's of yesterday or perhaps John Flynn wrote them both."[89] On Flynn's specific point about the dangers inherent in Hollywood's reiteration of a single point of view, Willkie managed to dispose of that one with humor. Because Chaplin had made a laughable caricature of Hitler, Willkie suggested, all could be set aright if "the industry was forced to employ Charles Laughton to do the same on Winston Churchill."[90]

Discrediting the motives of the isolationists on the committee and exposing their abysmal ignorance of the film industry was easily done. What strict committee procedural rules prevented Willkie from doing to Nye and other witnesses inhibited Senator McFarland not at all. As a committee member, McFarland was able to question Nye closely about the story lines and characters in the films denounced in his St. Louis speech. In so doing, McFarland forced Nye to admit that he had actually seen only one or two of the pictures denounced as British propaganda and had based his criticism of them on information provided by others.[91]

Nye's strictures on the dominating influence of American Jews in the film and broadcasting industries did not fade away. Those people offended by what Senator Nye had said about Jews in those industries were of no mind to forgive or forget while those persons agreeing with him wanted to hear more. Very soon that latter group would have more to hear.

Two days after Nye's long presentation to the committee in Washington with so many well-reported negative comments about Jews, Lindbergh raised and addressed directly the issue of the role of American Jews in the interventionist movement in a nationally broadcast speech at an America First rally in Des Moines, Iowa. In the Des Moines speech, Lindbergh went far beyond what Nye had said about a small group of Jewish filmmakers. Lindbergh indicted American Jews as one of the major groups in the country working hardest to bring America into the war.

On September 11, the same night that the president delivered his "shoot on sight" speech to the nation, Lindbergh and a large America First audience waited patiently but not quietly in a packed Des Moines meeting room until Roosevelt finished his radio address before beginning an evening of speeches of their own. In a short speech delivered that night, also broadcast nationally, Lindbergh identified American Jews as one of four major groups intent upon bringing the United States into the war.

According to Lindbergh, those four groups were the Roosevelt administration; the British government; capitalists, Anglophiles, and intellectuals enamored of everything British; and the Jews. Lindbergh asserted that the strong Jewish commitment to the interventionist cause posed "a great danger to this country because of their ownership and influence in our motion pictures, our press, our radio, and our government."[92] This representation of Jews as warmongers which his wife urged him to delete,[93] coming as it did close upon Nye's observations on Jewish influence in the film industry, touched off a media uproar that Lindbergh had not expected and could not understand. However, it must be said that the Des Moines speech was no momentary abdication of common sense. He had been moving toward some sort of public statement about a perceived Jewish problem in the United States for some time.

As early as May, Lindbergh wrote in his journal a preview of what he would say in the Des Moines speech four and a half months later.[94] In his entry for May 1, 1941, he complained about American Jewish interests being pro-war and controlling much of the media. With very sharp but critical looks at how the Morrow family had made their money in international finance through a partnership in J. P Morgan & Company and at brother-in-law Aubrey Morgan's activities at BIS, Lindbergh made a point of noting in his journal how strongly international bankers favored intervention and that British agents were allowed free rein.[95]

Certainly, Lindbergh's relationship with his wife and his in-laws was complex and probably not psychologically healthy, and one can infer much about his attitudes toward Britain and the war from it. Yet the basis of his political behavior during 1941 seems to have been rooted elsewhere, that is, in the fact that he admired the Germans for their contributions to aviation technology, for their apparent efficiency, and most of all for their demonstrated military prowess. Lindbergh refused to condemn the Germans before, during, or even after the war.

Lindbergh had lived in England and had visited Germany. He could not imagine how Britain could ever possibly defeat Germany with or without massive assistance from the United States. Lindbergh believed absolutely that after the Germans had overrun the Soviet Union, Britain's only hope for survival was a negotiated peace with Hitler. For Lindbergh, that was realism.

With regard to anti-Semitism, Lindbergh was probably no more of an anti-Semite in thought and speech than were others in his social circle. He had Jewish acquaintances and certainly did not believe himself to be anti-Semitic. At the same time, he had listened sympathetically to complaints of Fulton Lewis, Jr., an anti-Roosevelt and anti-interventionist radio commentator for the Mutual Broadcasting System (MBS), about Jewish advertising firms threatening to remove advertising from MBS if one of Lewis' feature stories was not taken off the air.[96] Lindbergh had seen or heard about Hollywood films that were blatantly pro-war and certainly knew that his brother-in-law was a British agent, working night and day to bring America into the war. In the Des Moines speech, Lindbergh simply said publicly what he had been discussing privately and writing in his journal for the past two years.

In Des Moines, Lindbergh and other America First speakers encountered the most unruly and unfriendly audience of the past month. The crowd had come to hear Lindbergh but first had to listen to the president's radio speech. According to Lindbergh, local opposition had been organized and paid shouters had been strategically placed around the hall.[97] The first speaker of the evening, Janet Ayer Fairbank of Chicago, a novelist and member of the national committee of America First, struggled to be heard.

A second speaker, Hanford MacNider, an Iowa manufacturer and former national commander of the American Legion, did better, leaving the audience generally orderly for Lindbergh, who spoke next. Lindbergh spoke only for twenty-five minutes and did not move his audience until he named the Roosevelt administration; the British; Anglophile intellectuals and international financiers; and finally, the Jews as the four main groups agitating for war. At that point, according to Lindbergh, the entire audience stood up and cheered. Moreover, after the speech dozens of people came to the Fort Des Moines Hotel to praise Lindbergh for a splendid effort.[98]

On September 12, Lindbergh left Des Moines confident that he had delivered a well-received speech. Upon arriving in New York in the morning of September 13, he learned otherwise. The *New York Times* carried bitter attacks on Lindbergh and the Des Moines speech from Jewish groups; CDAAA; Norman Thomas, a Socialist supporter of America First; and a wide range of organizations around the country.[99] Stephen Early, Roosevelt's press secretary, compared Lindbergh's Des Moines speech to the regular "outpourings from Berlin."[100] Willkie affected to be utterly shocked by the Des Moines speech, calling it the "most un-American talk made in my time by any person of national reputation."[101]

One early reaction to the Des Moines speech was a fierce determination by Jewish filmmakers in Hollywood not to be bullied by isolationist senators investigating their alleged pro-war bias. To be sure, casting Hollywood moguls in a new role of defending freedom of speech required leaps of faith that most informed observers of the industry were unable to make, and Willkie did not try. The film industry, Willkie insisted, produced anti-Nazi pictures because Nazism was a totally evil force in the world. Hollywood had produced pictures that were reasonably accurate portrayals of Nazi cruelties. Willkie denied that anti-Nazi films had been produced at the behest of the Roosevelt administration and successfully coached Harry Warner in an eloquent defense of the film *Sergeant York* as a story of the greatest American hero of the last war.[102]

When Harry Warner testified before the Nye Committee on September 25, he denied every charge of warmongering, film by film, displaying his own patriotism, and revealing Nye's ignorance of the subject. By September 26 when the hearings ended, the members of the committee were in full flight, looking generally ignorant of the subject investigated, appearing too cavalier about what consequences for America might follow from a German victory in Europe, and possessed by thoroughly anti-Semitic attitudes. The hearings adjourned the next day and were not resumed.[103] Though sometime later Congressman Karl Mundt (R-South Dakota) attacked the *March of Time* film news series for pro-war bias, like so much else in America First the investigation of Hollywood's pro-war activity was a casualty of Lindbergh's Des Moines speech.

By September 15, the controversy over the Des Moines speech had become so intense that Robert Wood decided to hold a special meeting of the America First board in Mrs. Fairbank's home in Chicago on September 18.[104] Several situations drove Wood to call this meeting. First, there was the great personal strain put upon him from running Sears, Roebuck, and Company and directing the many activities of America First. The time demands of the two jobs were more than Wood could handle. More than that, the controversy over the Des Moines speech threatened serious damage to Wood's character and reputation as well as possible economic reprisals against Sears and Roebuck. However, even more serious than those possible threats was a full-scale attack on Lindbergh's Des Moines speech by the Hearst newspapers and a message from that corporation to America First either to repudiate that speech or face repudiation by the Hearst newspapers.[105]

As uncovered by the British consul in New York and reported in a secret dispatch to the Foreign Office, the Hearst attack on Lindbergh and the Des Moines speech resulted from pressure put upon Hearst by John Haynes, former assistant secretary of the treasury and "now responsible to the banks for Hearst's interests."[106] According to information received from an unnamed confidential source, Haynes told Hearst that the time had come when he had to stand up and be counted. Hearst was either for "this kind of talk such as promoting racial hatred, starting civil war, or you are not." Haynes was reported as stating further that he would be obliged to sever his relationship with Hearst unless Hearst severed his relationship with Lindbergh. Moreover, Hearst's repudiation of Lindbergh had to be complete. That the man stood for the right principles but had made a mistake was unacceptable.[107]

No wonder Robert Wood was a troubled man when he met with Lindbergh in Chicago on September 17 to prepare a strategy for the America First board meeting on the following day. At this meeting, Wood did not lecture Lindbergh about the stupidity of the Des Moines speech. However, he surprised Lindbergh by suggesting that perhaps it would be appropriate for the America First organization to adjourn all activities for the time being, giving everyone a needed respite. His reason for suggesting an adjournment, not to be understood as a dissolution, was recognition that the president had already involved the country in a shooting war in the Atlantic. Given that fact, America First gained nothing by continuing advocacy activities at this time and ought to adjourn until the campaign season for the congressional election of 1942 began in September of that year.[108]

Apparently, Lindbergh grasped the subtlety of Wood's argument but would have no part of it. He rejected out-of-hand Wood's adjournment idea. In his view, the times required strength not weakness. Encouraged by a flood of telegrams supporting the Des Moines speech from America First chapters everywhere in the country, except in New York City, Lindbergh urged Wood to continue America First activities for the present time until public opinion about the war showed a more definite trend. He preferred to go down fighting for their beliefs, if indeed they went down at all.[109]

However, Lindbergh had grasped what Wood was trying to say to him and offered a concession of sorts. Though unwilling to modify or repudiate any part of the Des Moines speech, he would issue a statement that the speech represented his personal opinions only and was not a policy statement by America First's national committee. Lindbergh did not think that such a statement was advisable, but promised to issue one if the national committee asked him to do so. That was all that Wood had to take to the national committee meeting. Unwilling or unable to argue Lindbergh's case for him, Wood had a subordinate ask the man to attend the national committee meeting and speak for himself.[110]

On the morning of September 18, before the afternoon board meeting, Lindbergh went to the Chicago Club to discuss events since the Des Moines speech with two very important Catholic supporters of America First—Francis J. Beckman, archbishop of Dubuque and John T. Flynn, chairman of the New York City chapter of American First. Ever since delivering a speech in Oklahoma City in late August and meeting several Catholic priests there who assured him of their support, Lindbergh increasingly viewed Catholics as perhaps the most committed anti-war and anti-Communist group in the country. His conference with Archbishop Beckman confirmed that opinion.

As has been noted earlier, Archbishop Beckman was a man of very strong convictions, usually ready to act upon them. Brought into America First by Father O'Brien, the archbishop enthusiastically used the prestige of ecclesiastical office and his own considerable energy on behalf of that cause. He had regularly and publicly attacked interventionists and Communists. For example, on July 27, in a radio address carried by CBS, Beckman called for an end to this "abominable game of aid to Britain and Bolshevism." He claimed that the country was tired of false hysterics and manufactured crises. According to the archbishop, Americans wanted no war, undeclared or declared, and urged his listeners to write to their respective congressmen making that point crystal clear.[111]

With regard to Communism and Communists, Beckman believed that any alliance with the Soviet Union or any degree of cooperation with Communism imperiled American democracy.[112] He saw evidence of Communist machinations everywhere. Every "responsible branch of our government" had Communists working as bureaucrats. According to the archbishop, these "unmolested commissars" were disciples of a "New Order" who wanted war in order to increase their power over our lives. Today the mask is off, concluded Beckman, "It is Communism, Communism, Communism everywhere gaining ground."[113]

Of course, Archbishop Beckman had his critics among fellow bishops and among Catholics generally, but very little of that criticism was public. One exception was William Agar who released to the press through the Fight for Freedom organization the text of a telegram signed by him and sent to Beckman.

In this telegram, Agar urged the archbishop to retract statements made in his radio address of July 27. According to Agar, retraction was appropriate because the speech resonated with echoes of Christian Front and Coughlinite *Social Justice* patter.[114] Messages of any sort from the likes of Agar signified nothing more to the archbishop than impudence. Beckman retracted nothing.

Despite differences in age and religion, Beckman and Lindbergh had much in common. They both loathed the president of the United States, the archbishop probably even more intensely than Lindbergh. Archbishop Beckman had convinced himself that the country was in a terrible state of crisis, and Roosevelt was the cause of it.

According to Beckman, the nature of this crisis was the sad fact that one-man-government now dominated our country. The Roosevelt regime had become "a parody of fuehrerism." It was "not Christian but an abominable reversion to pagan slavery." When corruption, deceit, and Communism had so entrenched themselves in government, the archbishop warned, it was time for religion to step in and stop this wholesale betrayal of our nation.[115] Believing strongly that Lindbergh was a great American hero, a strident anti-Communist, and a selfless patriot, Beckman dismissed the media furor over the Des Moines speech as more of the same from the other side. Meeting with Lindbergh at the Chicago Club at that moment was one way for religion to step in.

On September 18, when the archbishop met with Lindbergh, if aware of the storm of anti-Semitic charges showering upon the man, Beckman took no notice of them. He certainly exhibited no fear of guilt by association and had no reservations about meeting with Lindbergh or of being identified as one of his supporters. At the same time, Lindbergh's attitude toward the archbishop was appreciative and positive. They conferred for an hour about finding ways to reach Catholics and involve more of them in the anti-war cause.[116]

After a satisfying meeting with the archbishop, Lindbergh next met privately with John T. Flynn who had also been invited to attend the afternoon national committee meeting. Lindbergh tried very hard not to dislike the chairman of the New York City chapter of America First. However, he could not understand why Flynn, an absolutely committed anti-war activist, was so disturbed over the Des Moines speech.

Politely but firmly, Flynn pointed out to Lindbergh that complaints about Jewish influence in American radio broadcasting and in the motion picture industry in private conversations was one thing but denouncing Jews as warmongers on a public platform was quite another. No one could do that without incurring the stigma of religious and racial bigotry. Whether real or imagined, Flynn continued, that sort of bigotry was poison for any person or organization touched by it.[117]

Flynn's argument moved Lindbergh not at all. He remained convinced that his Des Moines speech had been a careful and moderate treatment of a serious situation. Lindbergh wrote in his journal that Flynn "would rather us get into the war than mention in public what the Jews are doing, no matter how tolerantly and moderately it is done."[118] For Lindbergh, Flynn's distinction between private conversations and public statements was hypocrisy pure and simple, and he would have no part of it.

What began in this morning meeting between Flynn and Lindbergh continued in the afternoon meeting of the national committee. Lindbergh came late to the meeting but quickly, though informally, took charge of it. He offered to issue a public statement that the Des Moines speech reflected his opinions alone and not those of the America First national committee. That offer was considered, a vote was taken, and everyone opposed issuing such a statement except Flynn. Though clearly dispirited by the media frenzy over the Des Moines speech, the idea of temporarily adjourning activities at this time had no support. Most of the board believed that Roosevelt's determination to amend the Neutrality Law at this time made continuation of vigorous America First activity absolutely necessary. While Flynn may have been fearful of the great influence of the Hearst newspapers in New York City turning against Lindbergh and against America First, the others were not. In any case, the national committee decided to continue events planned or scheduled. Lindbergh and the national committee would stand or fall together.

Satisfied with the national committee's reaffirmation of support and believing that the media uproar over his Des Moines speech was much ado about nothing, Lindbergh went off to Martha's Vineyard to prepare a speech for his next speaking engagement at an America First meeting on October 3 in Fort Wayne, Indiana. In that strongly isolationist area, even after the Des Moines speech and media coverage given it, Lindbergh was confident that the audience there would be friendly. He was not to be disappointed.

In one respect, however, Lindbergh must have been disappointed since his appearance in Des Moines. Notwithstanding the intended very clear message of that speech, the immense amount of negative media coverage given to it, and the charges of anti-Semitism levied against him because of it, public opinion had not been changed very much one way or the other. A Gallup poll released on October 24 found that only one in sixteen agreed with Lindbergh's analysis and explanation of what groups were most committed to bringing America into the war and what groups were working hardest to keep us out. The results were surprising.

According to the Gallup findings the most determined advocates of intervention were (1) the Roosevelt administration, (2) big business and profiteers, (3) British organizations and agents, (4) American organizations with pro-British sympathies, and (5) American Jews. The most resolute champions of keeping the country out of the European war were (1) Lindbergh, Wheeler, and Nye, (2) America First, (3) the Roosevelt administration, (4) Nazi agents and fifth columnists, and (5) church groups and organizations.[119]

American Jews were perceived to be as committed to intervention as Church groups were devoted to isolationism and peace. Surprisingly, the Roosevelt administration ranked very high as an advocate of both intervention and of peace. Perhaps the most startling finding of all—attributable to Willkie's interventionism and Wheeler's isolationism—was that fewer than 2 percent of those polled regarded the Republican party as being more actively committed to keeping the country out of war than were the Democrats.[120] After a year of strident conflict between interventionists and isolationists, the Gallup findings suggest that the public mind had been more confused than enlightened by it. Over the next two months, that confusion would dissipate rapidly, and American public opinion would be ready for war when it came on December 7, 1941.

— 6 —

The War Controversy: Isolationism and Interventionism in the Country and at Notre Dame, October to December, 1941

During September, interventionist and isolationist activity intensified in the country generally and especially so in the South Bend area after the president's "shoot on sight" radio broadcast and Lindbergh's Des Moines speech, both delivered on September 11. The day after the Des Moines speech, Notre Dame was a very busy place. Francis McMahon had listened to both speeches on the radio and immediately turned Lindbergh's styling of the Jews as warmongers and his attack on their presence and influence in the media into a campus cause celèbre.

McMahon drafted a protest statement forthwith and sent it to the *New York Times* on September 12, denouncing the speech as an un-Christian and un-American attack on the Jewish people. In a telegram sent to Lindbergh but also published in the *New York Times,* McMahon accused Lindbergh of "fomenting anti-Semitism at a moment when the Jewish people sustain one of the supreme agonies of their history." He also accused Lindbergh of "leading astray from their Christian obligations to humanity and country, citizens of my own faith." McMahon ended by declaring "Conscience left me no course save to challenge you to defend your prejudices, errors, and sophisms in a public forum against me."[1]

Lindbergh had no time for a publicity-seeking upstart, as McMahon must have appeared to him. He ignored McMahon's telegram and his challenge; no such debate ever occurred. However, McMahon wrote an article attacking Lindbergh that appeared in *Liberty* magazine on January 3, 1942. Issuing the challenge and publishing this article made McMahon a famous person in some circles and infamous in others.

There were, of course, Catholic anti-Semites in the country, and one extremely virulent and possibly deranged one wrote immediately to McMahon's boss, Father O'Donnell. The writer insisted that on the subject of Jews, McMahon did not know what he was talking about and had no business attacking our country's greatest hero and patriot. Next, he proceeded to denounce Bishop Hurley, Archbishop Spellman, and the late Cardinal Mundelein for profaning religion on behalf of the New Deal and the Red Rascal in the White House.[2] Perhaps shocked by the venom of this letter, O'Donnell filed it and told his secretary to send the usual reply: McMahon had spoken only for himself and not the university in the matter of Lindbergh's Des Moines speech and thanked the writer for his continued interest in Notre Dame.[3]

For McMahon, much more than publicity seeking had been involved in his attack on Lindbergh. McMahon had been very seriously worried for some time about the disposition of some American Catholics, particularly Irish American Catholics, to be easily led into anti-Semitism. Aware of the strength of anti-Semitism along with isolationism and traditional Catholic anti-Communism among the followers of Father Coughlin across the country and shocked by the activities of the Christian Front and Christian Mobilizers organizations in New York City, McMahon had not been slow to condemn them and the anti-Semitism they preached.

In publicly denouncing the anti-Semitism of the Christian Front and the Christian Mobilizers, McMahon found himself drawn into the fierce inter-ethnic and inter-religious conflicts then raging in New York.[4] By speaking out against anti-Semitism instead of attacking alleged anti-Catholic appointments and activities of the La Guardia administration, McMahon appeared to many Irish Americans in that city to be supporting the wrong side in a bitter struggle then raging between Jewish Americans and Irish Americans for status and political power.[5] By doing so, in the eyes of some of his ethnic brethren in New York, he had become a traitor to his own race.

Very quickly, however, in the country at large, McMahon emerged as one of the best-known Catholic layman actively opposing anti-Semitism in the United States. Exposing and attacking anti-Semitism wherever he might find evidence of it, especially among American Catholics, became a regular and frequent public activity. Combating anti-Semitism for this Irish American Catholic became a life-long commitment. Indeed, for McMahon it was, as the Irish rebel ballad proclaimed, a cause that never died.

While Lindbergh's Des Moines speech gave McMahon a new cause and a new direction to his advocacy career, it also profoundly influenced John A. O'Brien. During August and September, the priest from Notre Dame had served America First well, speaking throughout the Midwest whenever and wherever audiences could be found. He had spoken harshly of President Roosevelt, opposed the draft extension bill, opposed aid to Russia, and insisted that the war could not be won. However, O'Brien, the great convert maker turned anti-war advocate, though notoriously reckless in speech, was not and had never been anti-Semitic in thought and speech. For him, Lindbergh's Des Moines speech was a terrible mistake, inexplicable and indefensible. Good soldier for America First that he was, after witnessing the stupidity of that address and aware of how much the anti-war cause had been damaged by it, O'Brien began thinking that perhaps it was time for him to distance himself from the leadership of that organization and serve the cause on his own.

While O'Brien was moving away from the leadership of America First, another well-known political conservative and strong isolationist from Notre Dame had agreed to join it. Following the Des Moines speech several key America First chapter leaders had resigned.[6] In order to find strength somewhere for an organization clearly faltering but whose national committee lately had decided to continue present activities, Robert Wood turned toward Catholics for support and resources at this most critical time. In October, Wood contacted and then recruited Clarence P. Manion, dean of the Notre Dame Law School, for a place on the national committee of America First. As unconcerned about anti-Semitic fallout from the Des Moines speech as had been Archbishop Beckman and unaware of how dispirited the leadership of the organization had become, Manion accepted Wood's invitation and became a member of the national committee.

Manion must have shared the nature of Wood's communication to him with either Cavanaugh or O'Donnell and probably with O'Brien as well. Neither Cavanaugh nor O'Donnell offered any objection to having an academic officer of the university join the national committee of an organization now perceived by many as anti-Semitic. What advice O'Brien gave, if any, is unknown. In any case, with the usual public relations fanfare, Manion joined the board of an organization that unbeknown to him had only two months to live.

Before striking out on his own as an anti-war movement organizer, O'Brien had America First speaking commitments to fulfill, one of which was to share a platform with Lindbergh at an America First meeting in Fort Wayne on October 3. Before that, however, O'Brien had engagements in Cincinnati, Chicago, and Indianapolis. O'Brien went to Cincinnati on September 18 to appear at an America First rally on the same platform as Senator Gerald P. Nye. In a sense, both Nye and O'Brien revisited two of the points Lindbergh had made in his Des Moines speech a week earlier. They attacked Roosevelt and Churchill as the men most determined to bring America into the war, but neither made any reference to Jewish interventionist advocacy. Clearly, a lesson had been learned over the past seven days.

However, one untoward and very embarrassing incident did follow from O'Brien's Cincinnati speech. The report of the speech published in the *Washington Evening Star* on September 19 carried the headline, "Head of Notre Dame and Nye Criticize Roosevelt and Churchill." O'Donnell sent a letter to the editor that the critic in question was the Reverend John A. O'Brien, a member of the Notre Dame faculty and not the president of the university, Reverend J. Hugh O'Donnell, C.S.C. The editor cheerfully accepted O'Donnell's explanation and printed a correction stating that Father O'Donnell had been in no way involved with the meeting or with the criticism of Roosevelt and Churchill expressed at it.[7]

O'Brien spoke next on September 25 in Chicago in the Marshal Field Auditorium and then on October 2 traveled to Indianapolis where he spoke in Caleb Mills Hall. In Indianapolis he was billed as speaking against President Roosevelt's effort to get Congress to repeal the Neutrality Law. After the subject and date of O'Brien's appearance had been announced, local America First organizers were overwhelmed with ticket requests, many coming from as far away as fifty miles. O'Brien spoke to a packed house, declaring that repeal of the Neutrality Law would be another step toward war. He urged his audience to thunder their protests against repeal of a law that 83 percent of the American people wanted retained and enforced.[8]

From Indianapolis, O'Brien traveled to Fort Wayne where he appeared with Lindbergh on the evening of October 3 in a large Protestant church auditorium, Gospel Hall, with the Fort Wayne Catholic Bishop John F. Noll seated with the platform party. In Fort Wayne, the America First chapter was one of the strongest in the country. Mayor Harry Baals was solidly anti-war and not embarrassed at all to stand on the platform next to Lindbergh. The local press was supportive and Bishop Noll's very strong isolationism was reflected in the Catholic press.

Of the 8,000 people crowded into Gospel Hall, there was not a single heckler among them.[9] Janet Ayer Fairbank spoke first, warming up the audience for the featured speaker.[10] After an introduction by the mayor, Lindbergh spoke for a half hour, concentrating on his perception of the president's determination to say or do anything to bring the country into the war. According to Lindbergh, the president had consistently evaded constitutional checks and balances in order to draw more dictatorial power into his own hands.[11]

Sadly, Lindbergh continued, the present generation of Americans had lost their constitutional heritage. Freedom of speech was under constant attack. Smear campaigns against himself and others in the anti-war movement were widespread. Only propaganda from Moscow seemed to have ready access to our newspapers. Because of the growing strength of censorship, Lindbergh feared that this speech in Fort Wayne might be his last.[12] However, there was one new element worked into this speech that was not vintage Lindbergh.

Giving a new twist to Robert Wood's idea about adjourning America First activities until the congressional elections of the following year, Lindbergh told his Fort Wayne audience that dictatorship in America was at hand, because the president was treating Congress "more and more like the Reichstag under the Nazis." In Lindbergh's judgment the president was "moving toward" cancellation of the congressional elections of 1942.[13] He concluded by asserting that not a single public statement made by himself over the last two years had been proved false.[14] That conclusion was perhaps the only reference, direct or indirect, to his Des Moines remarks in the entire Fort Wayne speech.

In the Fort Wayne speech, Lindbergh reached precisely the position on the war that he had attributed to Roosevelt. While the president had demonstrated often enough a readiness to say or do anything to bring America into the war, Lindbergh demonstrated in Fort Wayne that he would say or do the same to keep us out.

After Lindbergh's warning about the prospective end of democracy in the United States, O'Brien's message, though spiritedly delivered, was almost anti-climactic. The Notre Dame priest repeated the substance of his Indianapolis speech given the night before. O'Brien emphasized the critical importance of the president's decision to repeal the Neutrality Law. Repeal of that law would be the final step toward war. All peace-minded Americans should work as hard as possible to defeat the president on this issue.

After the meeting had ended, Lindbergh and O'Brien met with well-wishers in their hotel until after midnight. However, during a few moments of private conversation, O'Brien showed Lindbergh the results of a poll of the American Catholic hierarchy indicating that 90 percent of them were opposed to entering the war.[15] O'Brien took personal credit for that result. Whatever America First leaders had been doing wrong in the present public relations war, the priest from Notre Dame had elected to follow his own instincts, not theirs, and had achieved much greater success. He knew that, why should not they. Euphoric from their experience in Gospel Hall, both Lindbergh and O'Brien left Fort Wayne to prepare for separate major events in New York a month hence, Lindbergh in Madison Square Garden on October 30 and O'Brien at the Hotel Commodore on November 2, the day after the Notre Dame-Army football game.

— ii —

Back at Notre Dame, McMahon discovered that the publicity following his challenge to debate Lindbergh had made him increasingly attractive to midwestern audiences. He read about the performances of Lindbergh and O'Brien at Fort Wayne and decided to do as well or better in engagements booked for late September and October.

McMahon began his new campaign with a radio talk on foreign policy over station WHIP in Chicago on September 21. His point was the now familiar one of all possible assistance to the nations struggling against Hitler or else allow them to collapse and then later face the enemy alone.[16] After Chicago, McMahon accepted a speaking date at a luncheon meeting of the Cincinnati chapter of Fight for Freedom, Inc., on October 1. As the hometown of Senator Robert A. Taft, Cincinnati was one of the most intensely isolationist cities in the country. O'Brien had shared a platform with Senator Nye there a few weeks earlier. Together, they had savaged Roosevelt and Churchill to a highly enthusiastic crowd that clamored for more.

McMahon saw the speaking opportunity in Cincinnati as a major challenge. He decided to preach his anti-Hitler and interventionist gospel to the unconverted majority in Cincinnati in the style to which they were accustomed. That is, communicate in the manner of O'Brien's all-out anti-Roosevelt attacks reinforced by substantial amounts of guilt-by-association. McMahon had moved in that direction with his Lindbergh statements issued earlier in September and intended to improve upon that performance in Cincinnati. He doubted not at all that Taft and other prominent isolationists were as vulnerable to this style of attack as any other elected politician.

From the beginning, nothing in the Cincinnati venture worked right. On the drive from South Bend to Cincinnati, McMahon's car broke down. He had to beg a ride from a passing truck to reach the luncheon site on time to deliver his speech.[17] In his speech, McMahon declared that in reality the country was already at war. He attacked isolationists as obstructionists of national policy, meaning such men as Senators Nye, Wheeler, Taft, Father Coughlin, and Lindbergh, accusing them of being "engaged in nothing but treason."[18] That rhetorical extremism was enough for the press and for most of the people in Cincinnati, but McMahon did not stop. He urged maximum assistance for the Soviet Union and then offered a special message to the Catholics of that city.

In speaking to the Catholics of Cincinnati, McMahon borrowed arguments from Monsignor John A. Ryan of the National Catholic Welfare Conference and Bishop Hurley about the morality of aiding Russia. Ryan had argued that the meaning of Pope Pius XI's text prohibiting collaboration with Communism had been twisted by those unable to understand the absolute necessity of keeping Russia in the war against Hitler. McMahon restated Ryan's point and mentioned Bishop Hurley's distinction that aiding the Russian people in their moment of great emergency was not the kind of collaboration with Communism that the pope had condemned.[19]

McMahon's essay into an O'Brien-style all-out attack on the persons and principles of the other side turned out to be counterproductive. The local press reported the speech and found nothing to praise and much to blame in it. More important, the archbishop of Cincinnati, John T. McNicholas, O.P., read newspaper accounts of the speech and reacted to them with embarrassment and anger. That a Catholic educator would resort to such name-calling in a speech delivered anywhere in the archdiocese was extraordinary. That a Catholic layman, no matter how well educated, would presume to explicate Catholic morality publicly in this archdiocese without the prior consent of the official public teacher of Catholic morality here was unforgivable. At once, the archbishop took steps to insure that in his city a like event would not soon reoccur.

Monsignor Edward A. Freking, editor of the *Cincinnati Telegraph-Register*, attacked McMahon in his column, "The Observer." Freking denounced McMahon's name-calling, particularly his treatment of

Father Coughlin and Lindbergh. McMahon's reckless attribution of treason to persons of opposite points of view about the war was at once shameful, undemocratic, and an abuse of free speech. However, the worst part of McMahon's performance in Cincinnati was his posturing as a Catholic moralist.

As a philosopher, McMahon might know a great deal or nothing, but whatever the extent of his philosophical knowledge, he was neither qualified nor authorized to speak about matters of conscience or of moral theology. There were religious leaders, Freking insisted, "trained for that end and religious superiors appointed to speak authoritatively on Christian morality and obligations of conscience."[20] In this case, neither McMahon nor his mentor Monsignor John A. Ryan were included among them, and their arguments about the morality of giving aid to Soviet Russia were rooted in misinterpretation and were unacceptable. Until an official public teacher of Catholic morality, someone such as Archbishop McNicholas, had formally declared that collaboration with the Soviet Union in this war was right, it was wrong for Catholics subject to his moral authority to do so or even to advocate doing so.[21] Therefore, by his performance in their city, Freking concluded, McMahon had done himself a great disservice and "certainly reflected no credit on the University of Notre Dame . . . so highly regarded in the Archdiocese of Cincinnati."[22] McMahon would not be welcome back soon.

The extent and intensity of Freking's attack on McMahon was a reflection of the archbishop's anger with the interventionist speaker from Notre Dame. What McMahon did not know was that McNicholas had been charged by the apostolic delegate to prepare a pastoral on the morality of aiding the Soviet Union in its war with Germany. As noted earlier, this project was a highly confidential one and was not completed until October 30. Moreover, McMahon had used some of the same arguments that McNicholas was working into his pastoral. It so happened that this particular archbishop was extremely loathe to have anyone, especially a layman, try to steal his ecclesiastical thunder, hence, the emphasis that Freking had placed on McMahon's free and easy explication of Catholic moral principles on the issue of aiding Russia in the war.

McNicholas and Freking did not let the McMahon matter rest with the attack published in the *Cincinnati Telegraph-Register*. Freking wrote to O'Donnell in early October complaining about McMahon's behavior in Cincinnati and enclosed clippings of his column on the subject, including the reference to McMahon discrediting the university. O'Donnell understood clearly that Freking had written on behalf of the archbishop and knew that the standard form letter response would not do.

Ever solicitous of and responsive to ecclesiastical authority, O'Donnell replied with a rousing letter to Freking intended to satisfy the archbishop that the situation regarding McMahon at Notre Dame was well in hand. O'Donnell assured Freking that he had known nothing about McMahon's "crusading mission to the Queen City." He affected to find humor in McMahon's physical handicap, his automobile breakdown, and the truck ride into Cincinnati. "It is just too bad," O'Donnell observed, "that the truck didn't break down, because if the Doctor had to walk, he would have missed the luncheon." Please tell His Grace, O'Donnell concluded, "that I am sending for this gentleman today. After I have finished with him, perhaps he will not be so anxious to *drive* to Cincinnati in the future."[23] This was a letter written from one old buddy to another and calculated to put the archbishop's mind at ease which it appears to have done.

O'Donnell met with McMahon probably on October 10 or 11. Whether he also met with O'Brien at this time is unclear. He probably did not. From O'Donnell's perspective, O'Brien was too valuable to the university to discipline, even if he was of a mind to do so. Not only was O'Donnell genuinely fond of O'Brien, but in the short time that this good-natured, wealthy priest had been at Notre Dame, he had become a regular and substantial contributor to university fund drives.[24]

The only surviving record of this meeting with McMahon is O'Donnell's undated notes indicating what he intended to say. According to these notes, O'Donnell went over much of the same ground covered the previous April and May, mentioning that he had asked McMahon to refrain from addressing mass meetings in South Bend and elsewhere. Since that last discussion, McMahon had spoken at many such meetings. Next, O'Donnell disclosed that he had received "innumerable letters of protest about such participations and I am now convinced that the university is being misrepresented by your occasional appearances and as a result its interests are being jeopardized."[25] O'Donnell did not say that one of those innumerable letters of protest had come from an assistant to the archbishop of Cincinnati.

At this point, O'Donnell intended to become very presidential. He advised McMahon that as president of the university, he was invoking the clause of his employment contract relating to faculty behavior that menaced the good name or reputation of the university. Formally, he instructed him "to stop immediately appearing at public mass meetings and assemblies or any gathering not in keeping with your status as a member of the faculty of the university."[26] Even though the purpose and context of the particular contractual clause invoked by O'Donnell related to angry faculty striking students—that was the sort of behavior in the meaning of this clause that menaced the good name and reputation of the university—O'Donnell attempted to apply it to a freedom of speech situation.

What McMahon said to O'Donnell at this meeting is unknown, but there were no more letters from him professing strong loyalty to the university and personal affection for its president. Most likely, McMahon said as little as prudence and good manners would allow and ended the meeting as soon as possible. Of course, McMahon knew that he had been attacked by Monsignor Freking in the *Cincinnati Telegraph-Register* and must have suspected that Freking's column was the cause of O'Donnell's obviously agitated state. If a hostile column by a monsignor in an archdiocesan newspaper had made O'Donnell that threatening to a Notre Dame faculty member of eight years' standing, McMahon may have wondered what would happen if he ever received a complaint from a really important ecclesiastic.

Brooding over hopeless people or lost causes was unhealthy and pointless. The possibility of being dismissed from Notre Dame was a fact of life that any layman working there had to face. McMahon had made a decision to face that fact and did not worry about when this endemic possibility would become probable or even certain. At the present moment, the likelihood of dismissal was somewhere between high probability and near certainty. He knew the risks of public advocacy in the Notre Dame environment but was willing to stay the course he had chosen. McMahon was well known in the Midwest, not yet a person of universally recognized celebrity status but well on the way to becoming so. Moving to another university or even to another career was becoming more feasible every year.

After the meeting with O'Donnell, McMahon could think of at least one consolation. It was a fact that at the present time, October of 1941, he was bigger, more respected, perhaps more disliked, but certainly more widely known than the insecure priest threatening to fire him for exercising his constitutional rights of free speech on political issues. In any case, the anti-Hitler cause had become more important than the goodwill of his clerical bosses. The great war, as well as his personal one, against Hitlerism had to be waged.

— iii —

America First's campaign against arming merchant ships and amending the Neutrality Law received a serious setback on October 16, when a German U-boat torpedoed the USS *Kearney* off Iceland. The *Kearney* had joined a convoy as an escort, picked up a submarine contact, and dropped several depth charges. The U-boat responded by firing a salvo of three torpedoes at the *Kearney,* with only one finding its target. Heavily damaged and with eleven sailors killed, *Kearney* managed to reach Reykjavik under its own power on October 20.[27]

Public reaction to that incident was severe, swift, and unmistakable. Secretary of State Hull described the attack as "more piracy." Senator Claude Pepper (D-Florida) demanded revenge, calling for two sinkings of theirs for every one of ours.[28] Within twenty-four hours of the attack on the *Kearney,* the House of Representatives voted 258 to 138 to authorize the arming of American merchant ships.

Immediately after that vote, John T. Flynn issued a statement in New York that the war parties in the government and in the country were determined to convince the people that our ships were being wantonly attacked. Interventionists were "praying for the sinking of American vessels in order to raise war fever."[29] There was no question, Flynn stated, that the employment of American warships to hunt down German submarines in the North Atlantic was a policy designed and carried out by the Navy Department to bring America into the war. According to Flynn, the Roosevelt administration was deliberately manufacturing incidents at sea for war-making purposes. The American people must realize, Flynn concluded, "that they are victims of a conspiracy to hurry them into war."[30]

Flynn, Lindbergh, other America First leaders, and Father O'Brien believed that at the present moment there were three wars to worry about. First, there was, of course, the undeclared war in the North Atlantic, which was killing American seamen, and had to be stopped. Second, there was the declared war in Europe that the country must avoid. Finally, there was the public relations war against the interventionists at home that would decide the outcomes of the other two.

America First's public relations war with the interventionists reached a climax in late October and early November over the proposed amendment to the Neutrality Law. Congressional debate on this measure began on October 29 and lasted until November 13. For isolationists, the issue of peace or declared war with the Axis powers as well as the future of the America First movement and isolationism in general all seemed to turn on how the Senate and House would vote on this amendment.

Realization that a strategic moment was at hand inspired America First to make a maximum effort. A major peace rally at Madison Square Garden in New York City with Lindbergh as the featured speaker was scheduled for October 30. In addition, O'Brien participated on November 2 in a special anti-war event organized largely by Catholics at the Hotel Commodore in the same city. However, congressional debate on repealing the Neutrality Law would be more profoundly influenced by grim news from the North Atlantic than by anything that either Lindbergh or O'Brien might say in New York. The loss of 115 American sailors when the USS *Reuben James* was sunk on October 31 while protecting a convoy west of Iceland cast a very long shadow over the proceedings in Washington.[31] Was a vote against the amendment to the Neutrality Law a vote for peace or a vote against dead American sailors?

In New York, Lindbergh and O'Brien did their best to promote their cause. In Madison Square Garden, Lindbergh intended to be himself, that is, present an apologia explaining why he had taken the isolationist road over the last two years. In the Hotel Commodore, O'Brien offered a new direct action remedy to stop the Neutrality Law amendment. With regard to Lindbergh and the others appearing at Madison Square Garden, Stephenson and other BSC operatives attempted to create some special problems for speakers appearing there and in so doing managed to overreach themselves.

Clearly, the America First meeting in Madison Square Garden as organized by Flynn was intended to be a grand event. Lindbergh described it as the most successful America First meeting ever.[32] BSC tried to disrupt the proceedings by issuing counterfeit tickets to produce confusion and acrimony over assigned seating[33] and by deploying agents provocateur inside the Garden to disrupt and demonstrators outside to intimidate.[34]

The counterfeit ticket strategy failed completely, having no other effect than to increase the size of the audience. The few agents provocateur carrying signs and shouting "Hang Roosevelt" who managed to get inside were applauded and provoked only greater crowd enthusiasm.[35] The demonstrators outside identified themselves as members of the First to Fight Volunteers. They read statements and handed out flyers describing Lindbergh as "America's Number One Nazi."[36] However, the police detail of 725 patrolmen assigned to the event for that night did their work extremely well. Not only were demonstrators kept a safe distance from Garden access points, but even bus traffic running past the building was rerouted for the evening.[37]

Police estimated the crowd to be 20,000 inside the Garden with another 20,000 outside jamming the sidewalks and streets for two blocks. All of the speakers took turns going outside of the Garden to speak briefly to the crowds there from a wooden platform erected for that purpose.[38] Crowd enthusiasm was so intense that almost anything said from the platform occasioned thunderous applause. Flynn had planned a grand event and certainly delivered one.

The list of speakers and the platform party that night included just about every active America First celebrity from the New York/Washington region. However, there was one noteworthy absence. Though scheduled for an appearance in New York three days after the America First Madison Square Garden event, the popular priest from Notre Dame, John A. O'Brien, was not there. The reasons why are not clear.

On the one hand, ever since Lindbergh's Des Moines speech, Flynn had been arguing strongly for more organizational control over what speakers said at America First–sponsored events. Clearly in charge of the Madison Square Garden meeting, Flynn may have been fearful that a notoriously loose cannon like O'Brien would not comply with any limitations. Flynn must have decided that the risks of having O'Brien speak at this carefully orchestrated event were greater than any representational or rhetorical contribution he might make by being there.

On the other hand, O'Brien had a remedy in mind for preserving the Neutrality Law that he must have suspected Flynn and others in the New York Chapter of America First would regard as too extreme. Whatever the reasons, O'Brien did not appear at Madison Square Garden and was not missed.

When the Madison Square Garden meeting was called to order, Flynn delivered a short speech about the practical problems of getting the antiwar message out to the American people. According to Flynn, the prowar bias of the radio networks was overwhelming. During the past few weeks, by Flynn's count, the major radio networks and broadcast chains had offered 127 programs laden with interventionist propaganda compared to only six carrying an isolationist message, hence, the importance of this meeting which he hoped would be fairly and widely reported.[39]

After Flynn's remarks, Senators Nye and D. Worth Clark stood up for recognition and made brief speeches. Then Senator Wheeler rose and severely denounced Roosevelt claiming that the president had allowed British and American staff officers to set a date when America would enter the war. Fortuitously, that deadline had passed because the administration had been unable to manage events to meet it. For good measure, Wheeler turned to Wendell Willkie and savaged the former Republican presidential nominee for assuming the leadership of the war party.[40]

Next up to the microphone was John Cudahy, former ambassador to Belgium, who managed to bore most of the audience, urging the president to call for a peace conference now, which in his heart of hearts he believed Hitler would accept. At last, it was Lindbergh's turn. When he strode to the speaker's podium, the crowds both inside and outside of the auditorium roared into action, greeting him with a massive ovation that lasted six minutes.[41] This was the man that the people had come to see and hear. Lindbergh did his best not to disappoint them.

Lindbergh began by explaining the several public positions he had taken on the situation in Europe since 1938. Reflecting perhaps the increasing importance of anti-Communism in his own thinking, Lindbergh made some new points about the failure of pre-war Anglo-French diplomacy. Appeasement had been correct; it had just not been carried far enough. Britain and France, he declared, should have allowed Germany to expand east through Czechoslovakia and Poland and even to have acquiesced in an undeclared war against the Soviet Union.[42]

If Germany had been permitted to throw her armies against Russia in 1939 instead of waiting until 1941, Lindbergh insisted, Europe would be far different today. Whether Germany would have turned against the West after defeating Russia, he continued, is debatable. If Germany had turned west, it would have been a Germany weakened by the campaign in Russia facing a stronger England and France.[43] So much for the failures of pre-war Anglo-French diplomacy.

Next, Lindbergh spoke about the war and about how America would be affected by its outcome. He saw no great danger to our security or to our prosperity from a German victory. Reporters noted that in this speech, unlike in Des Moines, Lindbergh made no references whatsoever to the religion or race of perceived warmongering groups in the country. He directed all of his rhetorical energy against the president and his advisors. In Lindbergh's view, those utterly unscrupulous men had brought us to the brink of war and had suppressed traditional constitutional safeguards in the process.

Lindbergh insisted that the president had steadfastly refused to tell the American people the truth about the war and about our interests in it. Moreover, Roosevelt and his crowd had behaved as super-hypocrites, preaching democracy but practicing dictatorship. The fundamental issue facing the country today, Lindbergh continued, was not war or peace. It was integrity, that is, the integrity of the leadership of the country. There was no danger to America from without, Lindbergh concluded, there was danger only from within.[44]

The meeting broke up at 11:00 P.M. Lindbergh, other speakers, and the platform party went directly to an America First reception where they shook hands and received congratulations for two hours.[45] Indeed, the event in Madison Square Garden had turned out to be as grand as Flynn had planned. However splendid the moment or thunderous the applause, that sort of public relations effort could not blunt the effect of the dreadful news about the sinking of the *Reuben James* and the terrible loss of life on October 31. The cheering in Madison Square Garden may have turned some congressional heads about resisting the Neutrality Law amendment but not enough to succeed. Flynn's spectacular public relations effort was a casualty of the undeclared war in the North Atlantic and really changed nothing.

Because the Lindbergh speech on October 30 was such a major news event, the *New York Times* immediately published a special editorial about it. It was, the editors wrote, "A Speech Berlin Can Cheer." There was not one reproach in it for Nazi perfidy, insolence, blasphemy, or cruelty.[46] Be that as it was, the significance of one very important occurrence in Madison Square Garden noted by the *Times* reporter covering the event was totally missed by the editorial writers. The reporter pointed out that in the audience that night was a group of about forty Japanese sitting together.[47]

There is no doubt that Japanese officials in America watched the escalating conflict between isolationists and interventionists with as much attention as their German counterparts. Ever since the imposition of the American oil embargo in August, Japan and the United States were on a collision course. As a matter of fact, American trade sanctions against Japan were having a serious effect. Rice was being rationed, and after April, general rationing had been imposed on the six largest Japanese cities.[48] On September 4, 1941, the Japanese premier, Prince Konoye, warned his countrymen that Japan faced the greatest emergency in modern history.[49]

The center of that emergency was the oil shortage. Neither the Japanese economy nor the country's war machine could function without adequate supplies of oil. If oil supplies could not be purchased from America, then the Japanese military leaders were prepared to risk war with the United States by seizing oil wells and refineries in the Dutch East Indies.[50] The gravity of the oil crisis in Japan strengthened the resolve of the military leaders to take charge of their country's destiny. On October 16, the day of the U-boat attack on the *Kearney*, General Hideki Tojo replaced Konoye as premier. Tojo gave Japanese diplomats a deadline of November 30 to work out an arrangement with the United States that would end sanctions.[51]

In order to facilitate such an outcome, however unlikely it may have appeared at the time, Tojo dispatched special envoy Saburu Kurusu to Washington in the first week of November to assist Ambassador Nomura in negotiations with Hull and other State Department officials. If those negotiations failed, war would begin in early December. In the meantime, preparations proceeded apace for a massive air attack on Pearl Harbor and for the dispatch of invasion forces south into the Philippines, Malay States, and Dutch East Indies.

Whatever the Japanese attending Flynn's grand event in Madison Square Garden reported to their superiors in the Washington embassy or to Tokyo directly about America's readiness for war is unknown. From a group of forty Japanese in the auditorium that night, however, certainly something must have been reported. Lindbergh's main point of the evening that America was more threatened from within than from without could have been collected from any large metropolitan newspaper. However, those Japanese actually present in Madison Square Garden and experiencing the euphoria of that greatest of all isolationist moments could have come away with a dangerously misleading impression of the state of the country.

For those Japanese witnessing Lindbergh's reception by the cheering crowds in Madison Square Garden, an inference too easily drawn was that those Americans present and others who thought like them were more determined to fight their own government than some distant foreign enemy. That inference, if reported, would have heartened the Japanese war party at home as well as the negotiators in Washington. Standing firm against the American government would win oil supplies one way or the other.

— iv —

When O'Brien traveled to New York at the end of October to address a largely Catholic peace rally at the Hotel Commodore on November 2, he expected to enjoy a typical Notre Dame football weekend of vicarious athletic triumph and a lot of sociability. Frank Leahy brought his undefeated team into Yankee Stadium to play Army before 76,000 people. Outweighing Army players by fifteen pounds a man and led by a brilliant passer, Angelo Bertelli, and two fine running backs, Steve Juzwik and Clarence "Dippy" Evans, the Notre Dame team was a strong pregame favorite. However, by game time a steady cold rain and oceans of mud took away most of Notre Dame's offensive advantages. The game became a defensive brawl and a punting duel between Evans and Army's Hank Mazur.

The combination of terrible weather and an inspired Army defense held Notre Dame to a total of only ninety-six yards. Bertelli managed to

complete three passes for only ten yards. Leahy tried just about every formation in his play book—box, single wing, and occasionally even the
new Chicago Bears' T—but could not score. The offensive performance
of Earl Blaik's Army team was no better. The game ended in a scoreless
tie. Both Leahy and Blaik were first-year head coaches at their respective
institutions. Thus began a seven-year rivalry between these two formidable coaches and their respective teams that produced some of the best
football games ever played and some of the worst examples of intercollegiate football sportsmanship.

Leahy's unexpected failure to defeat Blaik's Army football team was a
harbinger of bad news for O'Brien's new personal crusade for peace. It
was clear to O'Brien that once the Neutrality Law was amended the next
step was war. For that very compelling reason, what was left of the Neutrality Law had to be preserved. Peace depended on it. Paradoxically, as
the dreadful weather in Yankee Stadium had prevented Notre Dame's
superior football offense from overrunning the Army team, the terrible
news about the *Reuben James* stopped O'Brien's efforts as well as those of
others to save the Neutrality Law. However, even that news did not discourage him from trying.

Insofar as anti-Roosevelt rhetoric was concerned, O'Brien reached the
highest level in his public advocacy career in the speech at the Hotel
Commodore on November 2. He began by identifying himself as a
Catholic priest and as a professor of philosophy of religion from Notre
Dame. Having done that, O'Brien stated explicitly that he spoke as an
ordinary private citizen, not for the Catholic Church, not for Notre
Dame, and not for the America First Committee that he had sometimes
represented. The war in Europe was a terrible thing, O'Brien declared,
and if the American people were driven into this war, it "should be called
by one name, Roosevelt's war."[52] Moreover, if our country actually entered the war, it would be a case where one man surrounded by a clique
yelling for war had violated his solemn promises and dragged 110 million
Americans into a war that was contrary to all of their instincts and legitimate self-interests.[53]

With an eye on the present congressional debate over the Neutrality
Law, O'Brien called for a special kind of peace offensive now. O'Brien
borrowed an idea developed in June 1941 by the African American civil
rights leader, A. Philip Randolph, to force the president to issue an executive order banning discrimination in defense industries. Randolph
obtained such an executive order by threatening to organize a march on
Washington by 25,000 African Americans to protest job discrimination
in defense plants. If such a tactic worked in the area of race discrimination by unions and defense contractors, why not try it on behalf of peace?

What O'Brien had in mind was a series of coast-to-coast mass demonstrations against American involvement in the war culminating in a great anti-war convention in Washington.

O'Brien's dream of masses of anti-war demonstrators descending upon Washington and forcing the president and Congress to come to their senses about the war got absolutely nowhere. Few people outside of those in the Hotel Commodore that night ever heard about it. Whereas the full text of Lindbergh's speech in Madison Square Garden had been published in the *New York Times* and coverage of that event started on the front page, O'Brien's address at the Hotel Commodore appeared in the *Times* as a four-inch column note on page 5. Whether this idea was good or bad, practical or impractical, was irrelevant. Once the House and Senate began voting on the amendment to the Neutrality Law, the time for it had passed.

Debate on the amendment to the Neutrality Law in the Senate lasted eleven acrimonious days. The debate was acrimonious because over the entire proceedings hovered the ghosts of dead American sailors. Some opponents attacked the provision that allowed American merchant ships to travel through German-declared combat zones to English ports as the equivalent of a declaration of war.[54] On this point, an observer from the British Embassy reported to the Foreign Office that supporters of the amendment "were less profuse than usual with claims that it was a peace measure, though of course they denied it was a declaration of war."[55]

In an effort to exorcise the ghosts of sailors lost on the *Reuben James,* other opponents directly accused the administration of deliberately provoking incidents at sea in order to outrage public opinion and then ask Congress for a declaration of war. According to others, this amendment increased the likelihood of more incidents at sea and made inevitable our entry into the war. Senator Bennett Clark claimed that opponents of the amendment had a twenty-vote majority on November 7. The president's men worked the telephones all night to change votes and succeeded in doing so.[56] When senators cast their votes for final passage on November 8, the amendment carried by thirteen votes, the smallest winning margin on any major foreign issue since the start of the war.

The amendment's journey through the House was equally rough. Most of what had been said in the other body was repeated in the House and none of it meant very much. The president obtained a majority in the House only by pledging to move decisively against John L. Lewis and the United Mine Workers union to end a crippling coal strike.[57] Finally on November 13, the amendment passed the House, 212 to 194. The president signed the measure into law four days later. In the end, neither speeches in Congress nor grand anti-war public relations events in New

York mattered. It was the ghosts of dead American sailors and a presidential promise to end the coal strike that carried the amendment.

Interpretations of these two critical votes in the Senate and House differed widely. Roosevelt's advisors appear to have been chastened by the narrow margins of victory and believed they could go no further without help from some unanticipated dramatic event.[58] British officials in Washington tended to agree with their friends in the administration but were more cynical about congressional performance. They viewed the very close win on the Neutrality Law amendment as another example of very familiar behavior by congressional isolationists. Measures violently attacked by congressional isolationists on the grounds that they would inevitably lead to war, encountered little further opposition in either body once they were enacted. The political meaning of this situation was that strong congressional opposition to similar measures ought to be expected, but not defeat.[59]

The view of a British operative, Graham Hutton, working in the Midwest on the political consequences of the successful revision of the Neutrality Law was much less cynical than that of his Washington and New York colleagues. Reporting from Chicago, Hutton observed that with the Neutrality Law now revised, the interventionists had won their battle with the isolationists. Formal American intervention in the war would be very soon, and there was nothing that the isolationists could do to prevent it. All that remained for isolationists was a hopeless rearguard action.[60]

Both public opinion polls and decisions by America First's leadership supported Hutton's assessment. A poll taken on November 19 reported that 72 percent of the respondents regarded defeating Nazi Germany as the biggest job facing the country.[61] Robert Wood and other members of the national committee of America First, including Lindbergh, agreed with what the polls were saying. The trend of American public opinion had been steadily moving away from isolationism, and no end of that trend was in sight. Enactment of the Neutrality Law amendment created a major policy crisis for America First. At a meeting in Chicago on November 14, Wood and the national committee decided that activities already scheduled, such as a speech by Lindbergh in Boston in December, would proceed but no new activities would be initiated. Wood's old plan to adjourn America First for the time being and then reactivate the organization as a non-partisan player in the congressional elections of 1942 was proposed anew and was approved by Lindbergh and the others on November 15.[62] Indeed, the active life of the America First organization was over. However, dedicated and determined interventionists were not so sure.

— v —

Among those interventionists in late October and early November 1941 who were not sure that the battle with isolationists was over were three young men from Harvard university: David E. Owen, an assistant professor of English history; Arthur M. Schlesinger, Jr., a junior fellow; and John C. Goodbody, a graduate student. These three young men were members of a group at Harvard under Owen's chairmanship that was working for an immediate declaration of war.[63]

Much less exultant than British operatives in America since Lindbergh's Des Moines speech over propaganda successes, this Harvard group was sharply critical of the way Sir Gerald Campbell's MOI organization conducted its business in the United States. Recognizing that some propaganda coups had been managed, these young men believed that the success achieved was not commensurate with the time and money expended. It could be done much better, and these two graduate students were not shy about telling important people how to do it better.

In a chance meeting in Boston in late October with T. North Whitehead of the American section of the Foreign Office, who was on a fact-finding tour of the eastern United States at that time, Schlesinger and Goodbody complained to Whitehead that Campbell's propaganda programs were far too stereotypically British for American audiences. For his part, perhaps Whitehead was too eager to listen to criticism of Campbell and of MOI's management of British propaganda in America. In any case, North Whitehead asked Schlesinger and Goodbody to prepare a memorandum detailing their criticism of Campbell's programs and how the situation could be improved. The two young men worked all night and drafted a handwritten document which they presented to North Whitehead at the airport.

Though these two young men confessed horror at some of things they had put into this memorandum, there was no time for revision so the document was passed on as it had been written. Hastily prepared as it was and not without factual errors, North Whitehead was much impressed by the maturity and intelligence of what the young men gave him—so impressed that he included about eight pages of it in the final printed report of his tour.[64]

In North Whitehead's judgment, the Schlesinger/Goodbody memorandum was not important for its details. It had been prepared by firm friends of Britain and reflected a basic mood and attitude toward Britain that existed in America at that time. It was an attitude that could profoundly affect Anglo-American cooperation once America entered the war. The attitude that Whitehead found informing the Schlesinger/Goodbody memorandum derived from resentment over the fact that so many British representatives in the United States displayed a disconcerting condescension and intellectual inflexibility, while exhibiting small will to try to understand the peculiarities of the American scene. Those representatives had their own notions of what America is and ought to be; neither facts nor experience seemed able to alter them.[65]

Moreover, according to the Schlesinger-Goodbody memorandum, some British representatives affected to profess a greater knowledge of American public opinion than professional pollsters and disliked being told anything that conflicted with their unchallenged assumptions and theories. If British representatives could not act within the limitations of the American situation without expecting that situation to conform to their specifications, then they should return to Britain as soon as possible. While Schlesinger and Goodbody probably did not know Sir Gerald Campbell, director general of BIS in New York, well enough to have used him as a model in their memorandum, North Whitehead saw the resemblance at once and put it into his report, hoping his bosses in the Foreign Office would also see it. Apparently, they did.

In any case, in the spring of 1942 Campbell was moved out of MOI's New York operations to Washington, where he served under the watchful eyes of embassy-based Foreign Office officials. Aubrey Morgan took over Campbell's duties in New York. Later that same year, Campbell was transferred to an MOI assignment in Britain. He was replaced in Washington by Harold Butler, who presided over a new expansion of British publicity in wartime America.[66]

When America finally came into the war, the entire Anglo-American relationship changed significantly and immediately. Henceforth, America and Americans would run the war. It was clear to many in MOI and in the Foreign Office that Campbell was not the man to deal with these new circumstances. How much influence the Schlesinger/Goodbody memorandum had on the removal of Campbell can only be guessed. Certainly, North Whitehead used it for that purpose. The original hand-written draft of the Schlesinger/Goodbody memorandum passed into an appropriate Foreign Office file, where it remained closed for the next fifty years.

Among still other interventionists not so sure that the battle with isolationism had been won was Notre Dame's Francis E. McMahon. Less strategically situated than the young men at Harvard to influence important people, and laboring under severe restrictions in a different and sometimes hostile environment, McMahon was determined to carry on his personal war against Hitlerism and isolationism any way he could. Angry with O'Donnell for prohibiting further public policy advocacy work, McMahon devised an alternative way of serving the interventionist cause without speaking at public meetings or writing for newspapers and magazines. As a working Thomist philosopher, McMahon had not forgotten how to extricate himself from logical conundrums by redefining terms and drawing new distinctions. To be sure, O'Donnell had banned McMahon from making public speeches and imposed restrictions on what he could write but had said nothing about disseminating the work of others.

In his capacity as state chairman of the Fight for Freedom organization, McMahon collected a packet of anti-Hitler materials prepared by BIS and a Catholic argument for sending military aid to Russia for distribution to all Notre Dame students. After the episode of the student antiwar petition of last May, there was no doubt in his mind that many Notre Dame students needed to see and study what he had collected. Perhaps moved by the announcement of Dean Manion's appointment to the national committee of America First, or perhaps not, McMahon mailed from the campus post office to all Notre Dame students on November 26 copies of a "Hitler Wanted for Murder" flyer; *The Enemy Is Hitler,* reprinted from the Voice of Austria by BIS; and Monsignor John A. Ryan's pamphlet, *Is It Ethical to Aid Russia?* O'Donnell was furious over this unauthorized campuswide distribution of obvious war propaganda material.[67] He communicated his displeasure to McMahon but did nothing more.

— vi —

Negotiations between Hull and the Japanese envoys in Washington dragged on. At a cabinet meeting on November 14, much discouraged and cynical about the intentions of the other side, the secretary of state informed the president that talks with the Japanese had reached an impasse.[68] At the center of the impasse was China. Hull insisted on troop withdrawals from Indochina and China as the price for lifting the American embargo. The Japanese government expressed a willingness to remove troops from Indochina and to promise no further military moves south if the embargo was lifted. Indeed, there were some hints from the Japanese negotiators about possibly reducing troop strengths in China but a complete withdrawal of troops was non-negotiable.

Pressured from the Nationalist Chinese leader Chiang Kai-shek and by Churchill to stand firm, the American position hardened. In effect, the American government delivered an ultimatum to Japan by stating that agreement was impossible without a complete withdrawal of Japanese troops from China.[69] Nye and others in America First disagreed sharply with the president's very hard line against Japan over China.

Nye declared on November 20 that the United States could end the Japan/China war at once. All that was needed were some minor face-saving concessions for Japan, such as allowing them to retain two or three air bases in China. According to Nye, concessions of this nature were not offered because the Roosevelt administration was determined to keep war fever in the country as high as possible.[70] Thus matters stood in the last two weeks of November with no movement in sight by either side. At that point, events began happening automatically.

On November 25, a large Japanese naval task force left its northern bases for a long Pacific crossing to launch a massive air strike against Pearl Harbor. The following day American naval intelligence learned that an escorted convoy of Japanese troop transports departed Shanghai, heading south. On November 26 the president issued a general alert to the American armed forces. Four days later in Tokyo, Premier Tojo delivered an uncompromising speech calling on Japan "for the honor and pride of mankind" to take immediate steps to eliminate United States and British exploitation of the Far East.[71]

Wheeler followed events in the Far East with increasing anxiety. After reading published reports of Tojo's speech, he declared on the floor of the Senate on December 2 that the "only excuse for a war with Japan would be to protect the British Empire."[72] Clearly, even Wheeler believed that something was about to happen in the South China Sea.

Then, suddenly, two days later Senator Wheeler and the *Chicago Tribune* turned public attention away from the Pacific to Washington. The newspaper published the text of a document delivered to them by Senator Wheeler purporting to be a secret military staff memorandum prepared by the Joint Army/Navy Board and dated September 11, 1941. Known as the Victory Plan, Wheeler had obtained it from a dissident Army Air Force officer.

According to those parts of the plan published in the *Chicago Tribune*, the Roosevelt administration planned to raise an army of ten million men with half of that total to be assigned to a prospective American expeditionary force intended for an invasion of Germany through occupied Europe. Army planners believed an expeditionary force of that size would be required because without it Germany and her allies could never be defeated. Britain and the Soviet Union simply could not do it on their own.[73]

More important, the plan estimated that the five million man expeditionary force would not be available until July 1943. That meant Germany would have a free hand for eighteen months to defeat the Soviet Union. When America finally entered the war, Germany would be the principal enemy and should be defeated first. In the event of hostilities with Japan, the plan recommended employment of unspecified strategic means against that country while our main forces were engaged with Germany.[74]

Before the authenticity of the document could be verified or the culpability for releasing it assigned, the press carried reports that a Japanese invasion of the Malay States was at hand. On December 5, the BBC reported two large, heavily escorted Japanese convoys headed into the Gulf of Siam. Moreover, fresh troops had been observed moving into Indochina all week.[75] A day later, Japanese troop ships were sighted off Cambodia steaming toward the Kra Isthmus.[76] The next day, December 7, planes from the undetected Japanese task force attacked Pearl Harbor. Formal declarations of war followed quickly, the United States against the Empire of Japan on December 8 and Germany and Italy against the United States on December 11. Life as it had been lived in America was over.

— vii —

After the Japanese attack on Pearl Harbor and the German and Italian declarations of war upon the United States, the American isolationist world collapsed slowly, unrepentantly, but in the end completely. So distrustful of the Roosevelt administration's credibility were isolationist leaders generally that many of them were suspicious of the first reports of the Japanese attack on Pearl Harbor. They wanted verification of the event before rallying behind the American government at this moment of national emergency.

Speaking for himself privately to Lindbergh after hearing the news of the attack, the head of America First, Robert Wood, commented that at long last the president had managed to get the country into the war through the back door.[77] Speaking publicly for himself and for the America First organization, Robert Wood declared on December 7, 1941, that if Congress declared war, he would support America's entry into the war.[78] Indeed, after Congress declared war on December 8, Wood issued a statement two days later urging all Americans to give full support to the war effort. He announced also that all America First activities would be suspended and that the organization would dissolve forthwith.

Flynn closely followed Wood. Upon first hearing reports of the attack on Pearl Harbor, Flynn refused all public comment until he knew what had really happened there. After telephone conversations with Wood, he endorsed his leader's statement, adding that duty obliged every citizen to stand behind the government. Flynn indicated, not too enthusiastically to be sure, that at this grim and uncertain moment he was ready to do his duty.[79]

Lindbergh was in West Tisbury, Massachusetts, on December 7 and initially reacted to reports of the attack by refusing to see newsmen or accept any messages. The next day Lindbergh promised full support, stating in an awkwardly phrased press release buried on page 44 of the *New York Times* that we must respond to this national emergency as "united Americans regardless of our attitudes in the past toward the policy our government has followed."[80]

Within a week of his statement of support for the war effort, Lindbergh wrote a private letter to General Henry H. Arnold offering his services to the Army Air Force. Upon his own authority, Arnold immediately released Lindbergh's private letter to the press.[81] When Roosevelt was questioned about Lindbergh's offer, he affected to know nothing about it and would not comment.[82] Nonetheless, the editors of the *New York Times* were moved by Lindbergh's timely patriotic act and published an editorial that doubted not at all that in the interests of national unity the offer should and would be accepted.[83] It was not.

Lindbergh had said and done too much for Roosevelt and his advisors ever to forgive. In view of the role that the man had played in public affairs over the last several years, placing Lindbergh in any sort of command position in the Army Air Force was impossible. Indeed, in time Lindbergh was able to find a way briefly to participate in the air war in the South Pacific, but it would be as an aircraft manufacturer consultant, not as an air force officer.

Nye was speaking at an America First rally in Pittsburgh during the afternoon of December 7 when news of the attack was announced by a member of the audience. Nye dismissed the report as unverified, watched the man who had made the announcement being ejected from the auditorium, and continued with his speech. However, confirmation of the Japanese air strike was quickly delivered to the podium. Nye cut short his speech, ending with the observation that a "Jap attack on Pearl Harbor was just what Britain had planned for us."[84] Nye returned to Washington immediately and voted for the declaration of war.

Unlike other isolationist leaders, Wheeler responded to the news of Pearl Harbor forthrightly and without hesitation. The senator called on all parties to support the administration and urged an immediate declaration of war.[85]

As for Catholic isolationists, Archbishop Beckman, the most perfervid and sharpest anti-Roosevelt critic of all American prelates, issued no public statements about the attack on Pearl Harbor or about rallying behind the government that were nationally reported. Not far behind Beckman in isolationist fervor and anti-Roosevelt rhetoric was O'Brien's old nemesis, Archbishop Michael J. Curley of Baltimore and Washington. Archbishop Curley had made some outlandish statements about the probable course of the war in Europe on December 3 and another about events in the Pacific on December 7 that he hoped would be quickly forgotten.

On December 3, Archbishop Curley had astounded reporters with a proposition that Stalin was so utterly evil and devious that coming to terms with Hitler and standing against the United States after Britain was defeated was a distinct possibility.[86] Even more bizarre was his response to a reporter on December 7 when questioned about the war in the Pacific. Unaware that Pearl Harbor had been attacked, Curley stated that the United States had no greater reason for fighting in the Pacific than in Europe. After these two well-publicized gaffs, the archbishop had severe public relations damage to repair, which he proceeded to do in a lusty fashion on December 14.

Through the press, Curley publicly offered the president a pledge of devoted and willing service by himself and by the half-million Catholics living in his archdiocese. Regardless of all past public policy differences, the archbishop assured the president that the Catholics of Baltimore and Washington were "ready to do their duty at the call of their country and offered . . . [themselves] to the nation's defense."[87] It was much the same in other Catholic areas. Patriotism and unity before a common enemy were values well understood by American Catholics. Archbishop Curley and other prelates promptly displayed and then vigorously acted upon them. American Catholics were in the war and solidly behind the war effort.

At Notre Dame, the conflict over interventionism and isolationism was over. As happened with other prominent isolationists, O'Brien put on his best and most forthright patriotic face. In his judgment, the president had been wrong, terribly wrong, but war had come to America and the task of all good men and women was to rally round the flag and make all sacrifices necessary to achieve victory and a better world.

In a supreme irony that went unrecognized by most of the Notre Dame community, the outbreak of the war brought political peace to the campus. As president of the university, O'Donnell had to put the past behind him and consider a whole set of new but more manageable problems than had beset him over the past year. Enlistments in the armed forces and the draft would probably reduce the student population below financially sustainable levels. Many faculty would be called up for military service, and as had occurred in past wars, Holy Cross priests would go off as volunteers to the military services as chaplains.

To be sure, a naval ROTC unit on campus since September most likely would be expanded, and the probability that other naval or marine training groups would be established at Notre Dame was high. Early in 1942 that probability was realized. On February 10, 1942, O'Donnell announced that beginning on April 15 a U.S. Navy V-7 program would be installed at Notre Dame, and a corps of a thousand midshipmen would commence academic and professional training in two-month and four-month programs ending in commissioned rank. The presence of this naval officer training program at Notre Dame and others established later insured institutional survival. Certainly, Notre Dame would have to adapt to wartime conditions, and campus life would change accordingly. After the controversies and negative publicity of the past year, O'Donnell was anxious to identify himself and the university with patriotic causes. He was anxious to bury the past and join the war effort, even if that included toleration of McMahon's continuing presence at Notre Dame, instances of cooperation with him, and even an occasional compliment for his good work undertaken during this critical period of national emergency.[88]

After Pearl Harbor, O'Brien withdrew from the exciting world of foreign policy advocacy. America First had begun the process of dissolving its organization on December 11, 1941. With the demise of that organization and the spread of war fever throughout the country, not many former members or sympathizers wanted to be reminded of their past affiliation. O'Brien was such a reminder; speaking invitations on war-related issues were very sparse indeed. Except for denouncing the doctrine of unconditional surrender as proclaimed by Roosevelt and Churchill at the Casablanca Conference in early 1943 as contrary to Christian ethics, O'Brien neither wrote nor said much about the war that was widely reported.[89] On the conduct of the war or war aims, the notorious isolationist priest from Notre Dame was no longer newsworthy. He gave up some, but not all, of his celebrity status and returned to teaching, religious pamphlet writing, and, like most Americans, waiting for the end of the war.

For McMahon, the outbreak of hostilities, especially the declarations of war by Germany and Italy, was a vindication. He had been right all along about Nazi and Fascist threats to America. Unlike America First, Fight for Freedom did not dissolve but remained in place and continued to provide forums for speakers. Unlike O'Brien, McMahon did not withdraw from public affairs activity. As a matter of fact, his personal war against Hitlerism intensified.

Excluded from military service by his physical handicap of polio as a child, the only personal contribution to the war effort that he could make was as a public advocate of righteous causes. While at Notre Dame during the next three years, there were not many righteous causes of the liberal sort that he missed. There was, however, a major difference between McMahon's public advocacy activities before Pearl Harbor and what he did subsequently. Before Pearl Harbor, McMahon had been one of two strident voices speaking out of Notre Dame on different sides of a highly divisive public issue. After O'Brien withdrew from foreign policy advocacy, McMahon was alone in the field. His point of view, rather than that of the president of the university, was the one most frequently heard and reported in the regional and national press. McMahon was far more newsworthy than O'Donnell.

Being an established, well-recognized, though often an unrepresentative voice speaking out of Notre Dame on controversial public issues was a most extraordinary status for an associate professor of philosophy at this university to achieve. Increasingly disposed to equate his own newsworthiness with campus status and influence, in the months after Pearl Harbor, McMahon no longer seemed to care what university administrators thought about his outside activities. He surmised, correctly and accurately, that there would be no more nonsense about restricting or monitoring his outside speaking and writing activities. At the same time, McMahon simply did not appreciate the depth of resentment and hostility which university administrators and many members of the Congregation of Holy Cross now held for him. McMahon did not realize, and probably did not care, how vulnerable his position at the university had become.

— 7 —

NOTRE DAME AND
WARTIME AMERICA
DURING 1942

Fresh from a visit to Washington and from several satisfying meetings with President Roosevelt, Churchill broadcast a triumphant address to the world on February 15, 1942. The present great world conflict was very far from being over, but with the United States finally in the war, it was now winnable. In a moment of extraordinary candor, Churchill described the entry of America into the war as an event he had "dreamed of, aimed at, and worked for."[1] From the perspective of American politics, the prime minister's choice of words was unfortunate, and Lord Halifax writing from Washington to Eden in London tried to tell him so. In effect, Churchill had publicly confirmed a principal tenet of American isolationism, namely, that Britain had maneuvered America into this war as she had done in the last one. Indeed, in the weeks before Pearl Harbor, both Wheeler and Nye had been developing the theme of British pressure on the American government as a cause of its increasingly hard line against Japan.

The problem of publicly confirming former isolationist positions at this time was that isolationism might be an absolutely spent force in American politics but isolationists were alive and well. The mistrust of British motives and actions so characteristic of prewar isolationist rhetoric was not diminished by post-Pearl Harbor patriotism. That mistrust found expression in mounting criticism of Britain's contribution to the war effort and in demands for more aggressive American actions in the Pacific. A cloud of mistrust and suspicion surrounded the post-Pearl

Harbor Anglo-American partnership. British officials and operatives in this country worked diligently to dispel it.

— ii —

In the early months of 1942, most Americans did not share Churchill's ecstatic sense of deliverance now that their country was in the war. Americans were very angry about how they had been brought into the war and wanted to punish their enemies. In January and February, news from the battlefronts was bad but also inspiring. War fever swept over the entire country. For American men of draft age, patriotism and adventurism combined to banish all uncertainty about their next jobs. Rich or poor, employed or out of work, college man or corner boy, khaki or navy blue would be in the near future of most able-bodied young American men. At Notre Dame the expansion of the campus naval ROTC unit, the arrival of 1,000 midshipmen for the V-7 training program, the rapid construction of a naval drill hall and a combined classroom and office building, the appointment of Father James D. Trahey, C.S.C., prefect of discipline, as an official university contact person for naval training units on campus, the opening of evening training opportunities for war workers, and the announcement of undergraduate programs to accelerate completion of degree requirements were all indications that the university had joined the war effort.

For those lay faculty members not facing immediate induction into the armed forces, the impending arrival of a midshipmen training unit at Notre Dame would mean major changes in the way they lived and worked. Because the V-7 program ran twelve months a year, the probability of summer employment at regular academic year pay scales for those faculty desiring it was very high. More money was always welcome, but with it came uncertainties. The Notre Dame faculty would be dealing with a very different type of student. Most of the midshipmen had attended colleges elsewhere, many of which under traditional Catholic definition were state-supported, godless institutions. Few of the midshipmen were Catholic, and fewer still had experience with Catholic education on any level. It was clear from the start that both hosts and visitors would have to make adjustments and special efforts to get along.

For most lay faculty, however, there were aspects of life and work at Notre Dame that special efforts of any sort were not likely to improve. In the bleak winter of 1942, lay faculty did not appear to have been a very contented lot. To be sure, distressing war news was a major source of anxiety for everyone, but very long-standing and systemic causes of worry in some cases and perceptions of mistreatment in others afflicted many of the lay faculty. The basis for such worry was twofold: the insecurity of annual employment contracts and the general exclusion of lay faculty from university governance and decision making.

Because the university was owned and operated by the Congregation of Holy Cross, it was the vision and interests of influentials in the congregation as well as its internal politics that determined how Notre Dame would develop. As the university had grown and become a more complex organization, it had acquired a few of the characteristics of a family-owned business. There were the owners—members of the congregation—and there were employees—the lay faculty. To be sure, as in a family-owned business, not all members of the family shared equally in management, but most family members had expectations of being provided for and of playing some sort of role in the operation of the business. In the case of Notre Dame, a relatively small number of influentials in the congregation actually managed university affairs and made important decisions, but all members of the congregation had expectations of spending some part of their professional lives at Notre Dame. In addition, most members of the congregation were situated within an informal information network and regularly heard rumors and gossip about what was intended and what had been decided. They were in most instances the first to know.

Few lay faculty could ever aspire to a higher status than that of an employee, sometimes a very highly valued employee, but only an employee and as such generally expendable. Very few lay faculty during this period could be insiders. Even the long-serving and highly placed lay administrator James A. McCarthy, dean of the College of Commerce and sometime protégé of O'Hara, stood far outside the ring of decision making and insider information. Though a serving dean, as a layman, McCarthy "realized perfectly" that he had no right to interfere in "purely administrative affairs" and had no authority whatsoever to negotiate faculty salaries.[2] Being outside of that inner ring was a fact of life for laymen at Notre Dame. Some were not troubled by it, but many others were.

The dean's respectful embrace of clerical administrative prerogatives was more than just a way to build a long and successful career at Notre Dame, which McCarthy did. It was expected behavior before administrative authority. Formality and subordination, as well as occasional unhealthy displays of flattery and hypocrisy, tended to characterize relations between many lay faculty and upper-level administrators. An insight into the pervasiveness of this behavior is provided by an unsigned letter sent to O'Donnell in May 1942 from a young faculty member completing his first year of teaching at Notre Dame. Though unsigned, O'Donnell carefully preserved this letter and shared its contents with his vice president and director of studies.[3]

If this anonymous correspondent can be believed, lay faculty morale was terrible in the College of Arts and Letters. Neither the director of studies nor the dean was perceived by lay faculty as a fair and objective person. Flattery and hypocrisy were necessary survival skills. Cronyism was rampant. Lay faculty in the College of Arts and Letters were so persuaded that these conditions prevailed that when tongues were loosened by drink many provided personal horror stories to document their own cases. At Notre Dame, the correspondent continued, mutual admiration masqueraded as cooperation. Consequently, if one was accepted by the dean or director of studies, he would have nothing to worry about "regardless of . . . [a] lack of scholarship or ability to teach."[4] All a man needed to insure his future here, he added, "is a glib tongue and histrionic proclivities."[5]

To obtain salary increases or good courses, this correspondent insisted, lay faculty had to learn how to become opportunists and dispense flattery when and where it would do the most good. Standards generally recognized in the outside world, such as seniority of service and conscientious application to duty, were rarely encountered here. The principles underlying most academic and personnel decisions appeared to be those of expediency and whim. For that reason, complaints to the president were of little use. One priest rarely ever overturned the decision of another.

A rule that lay faculty always obeyed was never to speak of justice to anyone in authority. Signing a letter of petition, the young man concluded, will doom you. The administration will resent any sort of petition or protest "because they want you to consider them as being unable to commit any injustice."[6] It is never safe here "to express a just opinion. Constructive criticism spells death. The clergy will resent it, and one will be made to pay dearly for it in the end."[7] Disenchanted lay faculty sometimes described Notre Dame as the last and only surviving example of absolute monarchy in the Western hemisphere, a highly deferential "Yes, Father, no, Father," subculture wherein laymen were underprivileged and powerless. This correspondent did not want to believe that all of these things were true and had no advice for the president about how to change them if they were. He simply wanted to share his disillusionment with someone who might be able to do something.

Morale problems of another sort troubled the College of Science. It is clear that O'Hara's recruitment of research-oriented faculty for that college had been neither tension-free nor universally applauded. The old guard resented the presence of these new men and had persuaded themselves that research activity would take time away from teaching and inevitably lower the quality of science instruction at the university. That resentment quickly escalated into hostility when long-serving, well-reputed non-doctorate teachers of popular introductory science courses had courses taken away and given to research-oriented new faculty with doctorates, that is, the old hands were made victims of "a nefarious new order."[8]

This new order at Notre Dame, where research and publication were to be expected and required faculty activities, was already too well established in several critical academic departments to be seriously discouraged or displaced. In time, with the encouragement of the administration it would spread to other academic departments and eventually inform the entire university. It would appear that the disillusioned young teacher was unable to recognize the painful, sometimes humiliating realities of institutional growth and change.

To be sure, the pace of institutional change was to be a gradual one. It would be twenty years before upper-level administrative posts at the university were open to laymen and before the faculty gained any formal participation in departmental, college, or university governance. However, that was the way the best American universities were developing, and that was the way this Catholic university had to go if it were to make any sort of mark on American higher education.

— iii —

During the grim winter and spring of 1942, anxieties over the rate, impact, and nature of institutional change at Notre Dame were not much discussed. Winning the war was. The best-known university expert and busiest public speaker and writer on that subject was Francis E. McMahon. Early in February, McMahon turned his attention once again to the matter of Ireland's neutrality. Gallup polls taken during 1941 revealed that Irish American public opinion on the issue of Ireland's denial of ports to the Royal Navy was shifting significantly toward allowing such use. Sometime in late October or November 1941, the Fight for Freedom organization of New York provided funds to create the American Irish Defense Association (AIDA).[9] The purpose of this new organization was to try to change public opinion on that issue a bit faster.

After the attack on Pearl Harbor and formal American entry into the European war, AIDA's objective changed. It attempted to persuade the

Irish government to abandon neutrality and join the United States in the war against Hitlerism.[10] When AIDA had been founded and continuing throughout its active life of about a year, it was a shell organization consisting of officers with virtually no rank-and-file membership.[11] In early 1942, McMahon assumed the title of Midwest chairman of the American Irish Defense Association, a group of about nine members of the New York branch of Fight for Freedom. On February 2, 1942, McMahon released to the press the text of a cable that he had sent to Prime Minister DeValera appealing to him to support the cause of the United States and enter the war.[12]

In that cable, McMahon appealed to DeValera and the Irish people to make common cause with twenty million Americans of Irish descent against the forces menacing the Christian religion and culture in Europe. Ireland's neutrality was incomprehensible while nation after nation was being crucified by a satanic nihilism. Your lot, he assured the prime minister, is with us in this fight for freedom.[13]

McMahon followed up this cable with an article, "Is Ireland's Continued Neutrality Justifiable?" published on April 15 in *PM*, a very liberal, anti-fascist New York newspaper that few New York Catholics ever read. What was most offensive to New York Catholics about this article was not so much what McMahon had said, but how he said it. It seemed that some of the old familiar arguments usually directed at atheistic Communism were now being turned against Irish American Catholics. McMahon had used moral and ethical arguments against holy Catholic Ireland. Ireland's continued neutrality in this enormous struggle to save religion and Christian civilization, McMahon insisted in the *PM* article, was more than bad policy. It was unreasonable, unethical, and wrong. As a Christian country, Ireland had obligations to this great cause that in conscience could not be avoided. Ireland must do what was right and join with America in this most necessary and just war.

This sort of discourse was at once unfamiliar and mysterious to most of *PM*'s regular readership. To many Irish American Catholics in New York who recognized the arguments, however, McMahon's application of them to condemn Irish neutrality on ethical and moral grounds was absolutely infuriating. This professor at the country's best-known Catholic university had tried to enlist St. Thomas into the sordid service of British imperialism. Surely, there was near blasphemy in that.

One furious Irish American woman was shocked to discover that a professor at Notre Dame would even consider writing for a paper as "unsavory as *PM*." She asked, perhaps anachronistically but bitterly, where were all of your Christian ethics arguments when Ireland was being persecuted during the last seven centuries?[14] This woman seemed to be almost as angry at O'Donnell and the university as she was at McMahon. Along with others who wrote to the president at this time, she believed that this professor was a problem that the priests in charge of this Catholic university should have resolved but had not.

Apparently DeValera was neither impressed by McMahon's logic nor by his claim as Midwest chairman of the American Irish Defense Association to represent majority opinion of the great American Irish diaspora on this matter. As a matter of fact, the Irish ambassador visited the State Department and advised Secretary Hull that tactless attempts of private citizens to bring Irish American pressure on the Irish government could adversely affect relations between Ireland and the United States.[15] The Irish American press in New York and other local Irish American organizations, especially the Friends of Irish Neutrality headed by Paul O'Dwyer, attacked AIDA severely and often as an unrepresentative shell organization.[16] Letters, mostly from New York and inspired by those attacks, berated McMahon as a warmongering propagandist and condemned the university for not repudiating his views. One irate priest even threatened "This conduct on the part of Notre Dame University will not be easily forgotten."[17]

Clearly, O'Donnell did not like receiving such mail. He responded to these increasingly severe attacks on McMahon and on the university for allowing him to speak out on such matters with the usual disclaimer that the professor spoke for himself alone and not for the university. O'Donnell surely hoped that somehow very soon McMahon would change his ways or perhaps even leave the university, but he took no action against his most renowned professor of philosophy. O'Donnell did nothing because he was fearful of transforming what was already a difficult situation into an impossible one.

Even when a student complained to the prefect of discipline about what the young man believed was an irrational outburst by McMahon against perceived on-campus opponents of the war effort, O'Donnell did nothing more than discuss the incident with his vice president, director of studies, and other members of the congregation. According to the student's complaint, McMahon flew into a rage during a class discussion, declaring that there were priests and laymen on campus who dared to criticize the war effort and in doing so verbally sabotaged it. Those who engaged in such loathsome activity, he asserted, were "guilty of an immoral act which in my estimation is worse than fornication." This is a just war, he continued, and I want you boys to enter the service and fight with every known means to defeat the enemy. According to the prefect of discipline, who interviewed the student, he was uncertain whether this outburst was directed at Father O'Brien or not.[18]

Whether the student was reliving in his mind a scene from the film *All Quiet on the Western Front,* or if the incident actually happened as reported, no one will ever know. Neither the prefect of discipline nor the president took the time and trouble to investigate the matter further. McMahon was never asked about it. Both of these officials, however, were prepared to believe that it had happened, and both agreed that at the moment nothing could be done to prevent a recurrence.

For his part, McMahon had become frustrated and unhappy in his role as Irish American critic of DeValera's neutrality policy. On any scale of important war issues, DeValera's intransigence was a small matter indeed. Moreover, efforts to change that policy were hopeless. McMahon had encountered abundant evidence that majority Irish and Irish American opinion on Ireland joining any alliance with England for any reasons was so hardened that arguments, no matter how ingenious or emotional, from him or anyone else simply would not make a difference. Enough time had been wasted on it. In the waging of this war and in the shaping of postwar America, McMahon wanted very much to be able to make a difference. He decided to turn his attention and energy to combatting anti-Semitism in the United States and urging greater collaboration with Soviet Russia in the war against Hitler and in arranging a postwar settlement.

McMahon made this decision in 1942 because most American Catholic lay and clerical leaders were reluctant to condemn anti-Semitic activities and incidents occurring in the United States and because many of those same leaders seemed overly eager to denounce Soviet Communism as a world menace and oppose maximum collaboration with the Russian government in the war. Archbishop McNicholas' recent pastoral arguing that the late pope's strictures against cooperating with Communism were not applicable to the circumstances of the present war had very little effect on Catholic opinion. The inherent evil of Communism and the immorality of collaborating with it so clearly defined by Pius XI simply could not be explained away by the expediency of the present moment. Not even an archbishop as respected and learned as McNicholas could do that. When McMahon took up those two causes seriously in 1942, he had no idea how quickly in certain Catholic circles he would be identified as a renegade and as a Communist sympathizer.

— iv —

Actually, McMahon had begun his personal war against anti-Semites in September 1941 when he challenged Lindbergh to defend his views that

American Jews were actively working to involve the United States in the war. At that time and later, McMahon frequently stated publicly his fears that Catholics were being led into anti-Semitic beliefs and activities by persons such as Lindbergh and Father Coughlin. In mid-March 1942, McMahon wrote a letter to newspapers in the St. Paul-Minneapolis area condemning Coughlin and his newspaper, *Social Justice,* for publishing anti-Semitic material. McMahon berated Father Coughlin for fomenting racial and religious antagonisms and for attempting to turn Americans against the Jewish people at this moment of unbelievable agony for them. It was tragic, he concluded, to think that some people actually believed the damnable anti-Christian nonsense published in *Social Justice.* He reminded Catholics in the Twin Cities that Pope Pius XI had condemned all forms of anti-Semitism.[19]

For at least two Catholic residents of St. Paul, McMahon's strong words against Father Coughlin and *Social Justice* were not appreciated. They wrote to O'Donnell claiming that thousands of St. Paul citizens, many being patrons of Notre Dame, were indignant over McMahon's letter attacking Father Coughlin and urged the university or someone in authority there to publish an immediate retraction of McMahon's "false philosophy."[20] O'Donnell responded with the usual form letter reply.

On the issue of collaboration with the Soviet Union in war and later in peace, McMahon announced his position at the end of May. He did so after personal experiences in April convinced him that prominent Catholic leaders and foreign policy experts were absolutely wrong about the relative strengths of the Nazi and Communist threats to America. The full force of this realization struck McMahon when he attended the sixteenth annual conference of the Catholic Association for International Peace in New York in early April.

At that time, McMahon was vice president of the association, and on April 8 he was elected president. Archbishop Robert E. Lucey of San Antonio was chosen as vice president and Father Raymond L. McGowan of the National Catholic Welfare Conference was renamed executive secretary.[21] In a speech and in private conversations at this conference McMahon made the point that Nazi propagandists and apologists were intent upon trying to divert American attention away from the true enemy, Germany, toward Soviet Russia. As McMahon interpreted world events in April 1942, Communism was clearly a lesser menace to America than German armies.

At this conference and many times thereafter, McMahon was reminded that, notwithstanding Archbishop McNicholas' pastoral about collaborating with Russia in the present war, the view that Communism was only a minor menace was clearly contrary to the papal encyclical *Divini Redemptoris*. McMahon simply could not understand how rational people could maintain such a position, given the state of the world and the course of the war. As he wrote in greater detail a few weeks later, the Axis coalition was the enemy and every American ought to thank God that our enemy was being successfully resisted by the peasant soldiers of Russia who fought not to preserve a pernicious government and hateful social system but "to save the soul of their Fatherland."[22]

McMahon went public with a fully developed statement of his position in an article "Hitler against God," published in the *Washington Post* on May 31, 1942. In this article, later placed in the *Congressional Record* by Congressman John D. Dingell (D-Michigan), McMahon argued that a German victory and triumph of Nazi ideology would be more destructive of Christianity and European Christian civilization than a Europe dominated by Soviet Communism.

The stark materialism of a Stalin, McMahon declared, was not as deceiving as the satanic mysticism of a Hitler. While Communism strove to eliminate the notion of divinity, it did not bestow divinity upon a mythical master race. When faced with a choice between Nazism and Communism, he added, the latter was clearly the least detestable. One of the supreme ironies of modern history, McMahon concluded, was that the victory of Soviet Russia would help preserve all that we hold dear in religion and culture.[23]

Sometime after that article appeared, McMahon attended a Latin American seminar at Georgetown University in the company of other Catholic lay and clerical foreign-policy experts. During the course of this seminar, the formidable Father Edmund A. Walsh, S.J., vice president of Georgetown and founder of the Georgetown School of Foreign Service, attacked the proposition that Communism was a minor menace and criticized McMahon for publicly advocating that it was.

Walsh knew Soviet Russia very well both as a scholar and as a visitor. He had headed a papal relief mission there in 1922–23 and had come away from that experience a perfervid anti-Communist. Walsh's experiences on that mission trying to deal with Soviet ministers as well as personal research and scholarship had convinced him that Communism was the greatest political plague of the twentieth century. He doubted not at all that the present Soviet leadership intended to export their system of totalitarian stateism through the world at war's end. Walsh believed fervently that Communism was the implacable enemy of religion and Christian values and that no collaboration with it was morally acceptable at any time under any circumstances. He was absolutely certain of those propositions in 1942 and continued to believe in them firmly and absolutely until his death in 1956.

On this occasion, however, McMahon was not overwhelmed by Walsh's erudition and enormous store of knowledge. Two other participants in the seminar, Archbishop Lucey and Monsignor John A. Ryan, interposed. They spoke up immediately and defended McMahon's position, pointing out that the philosopher from Notre Dame was by no means the only Catholic scholar who had recognized the need for cooperating with Russia in order to win the war and to secure a lasting world peace.[24] Believing himself to have escaped from his encounter with Father Walsh relatively unscathed and persuaded that Walsh's views were widely shared by many American Catholics, McMahon undertook a new task. As McMahon said later, he assumed the role of a self-appointed Catholic public advocate of greater cooperation with Soviet Russia in the war and also of creating a better climate of understanding between our country and Russia for the sake of a peaceful postwar world.[25]

The task of creating a better understanding between the United States and the Soviet Union in 1942 was a difficult one. A major source of that difficulty was the deep distrust and inveterate hostility to cooperation with the Soviet government by former leaders and activists in the now disgraced isolationist movement and by American Catholic leaders. As the war progressed, more and more of the old combatants in their fight against Roosevelt's prewar foreign policy found a new and increasingly appealing cause in anti-Communism.

The shift from isolationism to anti-Communism was perhaps more a change of emphasis than a new departure. Anti-Communism had been actively present in the America First Committee from its inception, notwithstanding the brief but embarrassing period of cooperation given to the isolationist cause by American Communists before the German invasion of Russia. There was a growing fear among old isolationists and American Catholic leaders that America was expending its blood and treasure in a war to make Europe and the world safe for Communism. Both the *Chicago Tribune* and the *New York Daily News*, even before the attack on Pearl Harbor, had editorialized that the defeat of Hitler, the great European bulwark against Communism, might force the United States into a war against Russia.

In the fall of 1944, Father James Gillis, editor of the *Catholic World*, developed these sentiments further in an article, "Getting Wise to Russia," published in his magazine in October 1944. Gillis identified Russia as the greatest potential menace to permanent peace in the world. Earlier that same year, Senator Robert A. Taft (R-Ohio) made speeches accusing

Roosevelt of pursuing an appeasement policy toward Stalin. At the same time, Senator Arthur H. Vandenberg (R-Michigan) asserted in private letters that the Atlantic Charter had been torn to shreds and that the governments of Russia and of Great Britain had already agreed upon the division and spoilation of the postwar world.[26] To be sure, the movement of American opinion toward anti-Communism, increasingly evident in 1944, was only a drift in the dark wartime days of 1942. However, in 1942 McMahon observed that drift and considered it as undermining the war effort. He determined to do whatever was necessary to check it.

— v —

After classes had ended at Notre Dame and graduation ceremonies were completed at the end of June 1942, McMahon appeared as one of several featured speakers at the annual four-day convention of the Tamiment Economic and Social Institute in Camp Tamiment, Pennsylvania. Founded in 1921, this organization supported and publicized a wide range of labor-oriented, anti-Fascist causes through public forums and publications. On this occasion, with an eye on the forthcoming congressional elections in November, McMahon addressed directly the subject of the role of former isolationists in the public life of the country. He suspected that former isolationists were responsible for the general escalation of anti-Communist and anti-Russian statements and activities presently underway. Tragically, he argued, the escalation of such statements and activities occurred at the very moment when the Russian people needed all of the support they could get as the main German summer offensive approached the Volga near Stalingrad and another army group moved south toward the Maikop oil fields and the Caucasus.

McMahon affected not to question the patriotism of those men who before Pearl Harbor had supported an isolationist foreign policy. However, such persons had clearly demonstrated no capacity to interpret world trends and ought to be retired from public life.[27] According to McMahon, the person most deserving of such a retirement was Congressman Martin J. Dies (D-Texas), chairman of the House Un-American Activities Committee. In McMahon's judgment, Dies' attempt to smear members of the Union for Democratic Action as Communist sympathizers was more un-American than anything his committee had investigated.[28] McMahon was himself a member of the Chicago chapter of that organization. The Union for Democratic Action was an interventionist group organized in New York in April 1941 with the eminent Protestant theologian Reinhold Niebuhr as national chairman. Moreover, before the German invasion of Soviet Russia, the Union for Democratic Action enjoyed the dubious distinction of being attacked by the *Daily Worker* as "the fifth column of the Wall Street empire."[29] By 1942 the Union for Democratic Action had adopted for its official slogan, "A two-front fight for democracy—at home and abroad."

It is not clear that Dies knew about McMahon's speech or if he did that he was much intimidated by it. He remained in Congress and in place as chairman of the committee for two more years. In May 1944 Dies announced his intention to leave Congress. He pleaded poor health and a desire to enter private business. Others pointed out that Dies faced a very difficult and costly re-election campaign.[30]

What McMahon had begun at Camp Tamiment at the end of June, he expanded later into a full-scale denunciation of all defeatists and so-called unconscious traitors at work and at large in the United States at this most critical time of the war. He was invited to speak at the summer forum presented by the Springfield Massachusetts Education Council on August 15. Organized and directed by A. Abbott Kaplan, this public forum had a local reputation for advocating left-wing causes and presenting radical speakers. As a matter of fact, the advertisement of McMahon's appearance as a forum speaker was something of a coup for Kaplan. Professors from Catholic universities rarely ever appeared. That advertisement produced an immediate reaction among some of the politically conservative Catholics in the area.

On August 10, 1942, Charles P. Foley, a conservative Catholic living in Springfield, wrote to O'Donnell in order to explain what he believed was the radical nature of the summer forum and to warn the president about the dangers of allowing one of his faculty to speak there. Two weeks earlier, Foley wrote, Michael J. Quill, president of the Transport Workers Union in New York City, spoke at the forum and had berated Ireland for not joining the war against Hitler, described the outcome in Spain as the Spanish mistake, and demanded the launching immediately of a second front in Europe to relieve the Russians. According to Foley, Quill was known in the Springfield area and in New York City as a committed Red.[31]

On a previous occasion, Foley continued, Professor Hans Kohn from Smith College had spoken at the forum. Last Saturday, Professor Frederick L. Schuman from Williams College was the featured speaker. Foley claimed that Schuman had a long Red record which was detailed on page 320 of *The Red Network,* an account of Communism in the United States recommended by the American Legion Ladies' Auxiliary and the National Daughters of the American Revolution. He had no doubts that the philosophy espoused by Professor Schuman was that of Marx and Engels.[32]

Foley explained that he had taken the trouble to write to O'Donnell in the hope that, as McMahon's employer, he would intervene and prevent a faculty member from Notre Dame from appearing at the forum. Only by such an intervention, he stated, would the Jewish Communists running the forum be denied the opportunity of displaying a professor from a Catholic university and publicly identifying him with a cause that the Holy Father had condemned.[33] Unfortunately for Mr. Foley's peace of mind, his letter arrived at Notre Dame when O'Donnell was away from campus. O'Donnell's secretary acknowledged receipt of Foley's letter and repeated the routine disclaimer that when addressing public issues faculty members spoke for themselves alone and only the president could speak for the university. As events were soon to demonstrate, that was not the sort of response that Foley had expected or wanted.

McMahon came to Springfield and his performance there fulfilled Mr. Foley's worst fears. McMahon lashed out at Coughlinites, Christian Fronters, anti-Semites, and anti-British elements in this country that he believed were playing Hitler's game. McMahon described the Coughlinites and other groups, including the *Chicago Tribune, New York Daily News,* and *Washington Times-Herald,* as unconscious traitors and compared them to the internal enemies responsible for the fall of France. Returning to the ideas expressed at Camp Tamiment and again looking toward the fall congressional elections, McMahon declared that only those people who knew what the war was about and comprehended its fundamental nature should be in public office during the course of this great struggle for freedom in the world. Those persons not absolutely committed to winning the war and fighting for freedom for all men ought to be retired from public life. Americans should never forget that German dive-bombers and storm troopers did not defeat France. It was the Fascist elements in positions of power in France who caused their country's downfall.[34]

Touching on another now familiar theme, McMahon insisted that Nazism was a far more invidious doctrine than Communism. While Communism was a doctrine of stark materialism, Nazism enslaved men and tried to substitute a false religion for Christianity. There was really no danger to the United States from Communism, he added. We have had Communism in our colleges for twenty years, but we never had to raise a large army and navy until Hitler came to power. Compared to Fascism, Communism was a minor menace to this country and to our way of life.[35] Russia's cause today is not our cause, McMahon concluded, but her enemy is our enemy. In the present war, the Russian people are not fighting for the Communist party. They are fighting for their fatherland and to preserve the Russian soul.[36]

McMahon's speech was widely reported in Springfield newspapers, and very quickly O'Donnell was informed about everything his best-known professor of philosophy had been saying. Charles P. Foley wrote immediately to O'Donnell after reading newspaper accounts of McMahon's speech. He complained bitterly that despite his warning letter of August 10, 1942, about the radical Communist nature of the summer forum, O'Donnell had done nothing to prevent his now infamous professor of philosophy from speaking there. As a matter of fact, Foley berated O'Donnell for not taking the matter seriously. He accused the president of not deeming the appearance of a professor from a Catholic university at such a meeting of sufficient importance even to acknowledge the warning letter personally, leaving that task to a secretary. It would appear that neither O'Donnell nor McMahon had any idea of the intensity and depth of inter-ethnic hostility currently raging in New York and elsewhere in the Northeast between Irish American Catholics and American Jews. What O'Donnell did not know in depth or detail, he was soon to learn.[37]

McMahon had come and gone, wrote Foley. Thanks to this professor of philosophy, he stated, the Jewish Communists in charge of the forum had their holiday at the expense of the Catholics. Our people were scandalized, he continued, that a man like McMahon, whose Catholic connections were emphasized in forum advertisements, could be guilty of such wild statements. He regarded McMahon's attacks on the Coughlinites and the Christian Front as slanderous. At least those much-abused Catholics had "not sold out to Jewish Gelt."

Foley reminded O'Donnell that no less an ecclesiastical dignitary than Bishop John F. Noll of Fort Wayne, the diocese in which Notre Dame was located, had urged in *Our Sunday Visitor* the organization of Christian Front branches in every diocese in the country. In this regard, however, Foley neglected to mention or did not know that Bishop Noll's endorsement of the Christian Front occurred in 1938 in a context of forming a general alliance of all Christians against Communism and two years before seventeen Christian Fronters were indicted and tried for sedition in Brooklyn in 1940.[38] When Noll naively endorsed the Christian Front in 1938, the organization was not yet the near exclusively Irish American Catholic collection of anti-Semites that it had become in New York by 1942.

According to Foley, when McMahon condemned the Christian Front, he was also condemning Bishop Noll. Similarly, when McMahon asserted that there was no danger in Communism, he was contradicting the Holy Father. Foley informed O'Donnell that local newspaper accounts of McMahon's speech, including the attacks on the *Chicago Tribune, New York Daily News,* and *Washington Times-Herald,* were being sent to Bishop Noll, the *Chicago Tribune,* and *Brooklyn Tablet.*[39] If Foley had intended to chastise O'Donnell, he succeeded. The president could not help thinking that neither he nor the university deserved the public relations damage being done to them. Yet O'Donnell did not know what he could do to stop it without risking even more serious consequences. At the moment, doing nothing seemed more prudent than trying to do something. However, others were far less uncertain about proper remedies and were anxious to communicate recommendations to the now increasingly beleaguered and frustrated president of Notre Dame.

Patrick Walsh of New York City wrote to O'Donnell in early September complaining that whenever McMahon spoke in public, for reasons known best to himself, he seemed to delight in smearing the Irish and the Catholics. Walsh referred to McMahon's Springfield speech and observed that the attacks on Father Coughlin and the Christian Front were gratuitous and mistaken. If Coughlin's advice had been followed, Walsh insisted, the youth of our country would not be in the four corners of the world fighting to preserve the exploiting British Empire and the Communist government of Russia.[40]

More to the matter of McMahon's perceived disgraceful conduct, for Walsh the proper course of action was clear. "It is time to take Professor McMahon out of Notre Dame," he insisted, "if you want to keep it as a Catholic institution of learning." Walsh explained this point further by pointing out that American Catholics had made and were making great financial sacrifices to support Catholic schools. "Catholics pay a double tax," he added, "to send our children to Catholic schools from kindergarten to the university." Because of this financial sacrifice, American Catholics had a right to expect an education that was different from what was available in public schools and universities. "We want and expect," he concluded, "different teachers in our Catholic schools than Professor McMahon and his ilk."[41] O'Donnell filed this letter but did not answer it.

McMahon knew very well that complaints about his public positions had been directed to O'Donnell. Many of the complaints had sent him copies of their letters to the president. Later, McMahon referred to those complaints as originating among anti-British, anti-Semitic, and anti-

Communist zealots in the Catholic community and generally accepted them as inevitable consequences of public advocacy activities.[42] Certainly, he was in no way intimidated or deterred from his course because persons outside of the university sent hostile letters to his boss. In one sense, McMahon respected O'Donnell and was grateful to him for not capitulating to such outside pressures. Yet, by mid-1942, in another sense McMahon had ceased to care about what O'Donnell thought about his activities or to be genuinely concerned about how intense outside pressures against him became. He was simply too important as a public figure to worry about job security. Moreover, it was a fact that McMahon enjoyed celebrity status and was properly thrilled by reports in the *New York Times* of his own speeches, statements, and interviews. Publicity of the sort that he had experienced during the past two years had become addictive. Colleagues at Notre Dame had noticed how much he appeared to crave it.[43] McMahon himself had made clear on many occasions how committed he was to front-page living. As he was wont to say almost whenever asked, whatever the personal consequences to him might be, the fight for freedom as he was waging it would continue.

— vi —

In late September 1942 McMahon mounted what was for him to date the most spectacular publicity effort on behalf of greater collaboration between the United States and the Soviet Union in the war. The German offensive had been stopped near the Volga, and by September the battle for Stalingrad had assumed the character and proportions of the most decisive land battle of the war. The Russians had massed more than a million men in three army groups in the region north of Stalingrad and were poised for an attack that by late November would have encircled 350,000 troops of the German Sixth Army. At Stalingrad, initiative in the war would pass out of Hitler's hands, never to return.

McMahon sensed that great things were happening in Russia and were about to happen in North Africa. He wanted very much to make a contribution and in some small way be a part of this vital historic moment. On September 24, 1942, McMahon dispatched a cablegram to General Secretary Joseph Stalin in the name of millions of Americans of Irish descent. McMahon found authority to speak for Americans of Irish descent by resurrecting the American Irish Defense Association and issuing the cablegram in his capacity as Midwest chairman. Copies of the cablegram were sent to all of the major newspapers and in the publicity attendant upon it, McMahon was mistakenly identified as Reverend Francis E. McMahon, associate professor of philosophy at the University of Notre Dame and Midwest chairman of the American Irish Defense Association. To much of the world, it appeared that a Catholic priest from Notre Dame had sent a congratulatory and supportive message to the head of the Communist party in Soviet Russia. At least that was how the incident was represented in the Communist newspaper, the *Daily Worker*.[44] For the next week, O'Donnell was very busy issuing denials and offering explanations.

In the cablegram, McMahon testified to the admiration that millions of Americans of Irish descent had for the Russian people in their great struggle for the life and soul of their country. He implied that a second front somewhere would soon be a reality and assured the general secretary that the full power of the United States was "engaged in the historic effort to insure respect for the natural rights of all nations and of all men."[45] McMahon claimed later that he sent the cablegram to Stalin without any expectation that the general secretary would ever see or respond to it. The purpose of the cablegram was to alert Americans, especially American Catholics, to the enormous human cost being paid by the Russian people to win this war and to bring the Russian and American people together.[46]

Reactions to the cablegram were predictable. Four days after news of it broke, letters attacking McMahon for his latest publicity stunt began arriving at Notre Dame. One complainant expressed feelings of disgust over the cablegram. Catholics, he wrote, should never forget what the Communists did in Russia and in Spain and should thank God for the Holy Father's guidance about never collaborating with Communism under any circumstances. He condemned "Father McMahon for casting a shadow over the good name of Notre Dame."[47] Others outside of the Catholic community reacted differently. Some were genuinely impressed by McMahon's moxie.

McMahon received two invitations that could not be refused. One was from Corliss Lamont of J. P. Morgan Company, who was chairman of the Congress of Soviet-American Friendship, asking him to speak at a large luncheon meeting of the congress at the Hotel New Yorker on November 8, 1942. McMahon would appear on the same program with Corliss Lamont; Joseph E. Davies, former ambassador to the Soviet Union and leading advocate of Soviet-American cooperation in war and peace; Senator Claude D. Pepper (D-Fla.); Professor Ralph Barton Perry of Harvard; and Arthur Upham Pope of the Committee of National Morale. The other invitation came from Soviet officials who requested McMahon's appearance in New York at the mid-November celebration of the twenty-fifth anniversary of the Russian Revolution. McMahon was flattered by the celebrity status which these two invitations bestowed. He accepted both of them at once, said nothing to officials at Notre Dame, and set to work on a speech that he hoped would be well received and widely reported. Depending on perspectives, these November appearances in New York were the high or the low points of his public advocacy career.

The Congress of Soviet-American Friendship luncheon at the Hotel New Yorker was a grand affair. More than a thousand guests had come to hear the speakers. Proceedings began with the reading of a special message from General Eisenhower. The featured attraction was Ambassador Davies, who called for better and fuller understanding between the people of the United States and the Soviet Union. He chided those in this country who regarded the Soviet alliance as a disagreeable necessity. Davies warned of a German peace offensive in which subversive elements in America would certainly take part.[48] Such subversive elements were, of course, those deluded Americans who opposed and attacked maximum collaboration with the Soviet Union in this war.

McMahon spoke after the ambassador and called for an immediate second front in Europe. Any unnecessary delay, he declared, would be a crime against humanity, culture, and religion.[49] After that declaration, his speech was interrupted by applause so loud and prolonged that it even surpassed the ovation given to Ambassador Davies. When his audience quieted, McMahon continued, insisting that some people sought to divide Americans from the Russian people and were content to let the Nazis overrun the soil of Russia. We must never allow that spirit to spread and "not be taken in by Nazi propaganda that Hitler is a crusader against the Red peril." He finished by making a point that few in the audience had ever considered and were surprised to hear. McMahon recalled that Pope Pius XII had not been deceived by that sort of propaganda and had refused to endorse Hitler's aggression against Russia. That refusal, he concluded, was one of the most important incidents of the war.[50]

Not many in the audience attached much importance to McMahon's point about Pius XII not endorsing the German invasion of Russia or even tried to understand why he had made it. They could not know how much easier reconciliation of one's loyalty to the Catholic Church with personal commitments to liberal causes became if the pope had not specifically endorsed or condemned them. About this particular Catholic problem, McMahon said nothing further for the present. Certainly, he did not raise it in New York at the anniversary celebration of the Russian Revolution. He enjoyed Russian champagne and caviar at the Russian Consulate with the rest of the official guests and returned to South

Bend and Notre Dame feeling very good about himself. After all, no other lay faculty member in the history of the university had ever rubbed shoulders and mingled so familiarly with so many important public men as he. As one of the foremost Catholic spokesmen for liberal causes in the country, McMahon must have wondered toward the end of 1942 about what he would do next and how long he would remain at Notre Dame.

After McMahon's appearances at Soviet Russian events in New York, some Catholics living there were appalled by what he had done and said. These outraged Catholics had great difficulty believing that a practicing Catholic would celebrate such an event as the Russian Revolution. One woman wrote to O'Donnell and described McMahon as a "publicity-seeking social pest."[51] Brazen effrontery toward Catholics, she added, was a way of life for him. McMahon's speeches and attitudes in the past demonstrated "his Communist leanings and should have been warning enough." Imagine a Communist teaching in a Catholic college, she concluded; "He should have been removed long ago."[52]

O'Donnell knew very well that McMahon had no affection whatsoever for Soviet Communism and paid no heed to complaints alleging that he did. Nonetheless, the president was increasingly worried and depressed by what he perceived to be the impact of McMahon's public advocacy activities on the reputation of the university. That some persons in the Catholic community seriously considered that Notre Dame would actually employ a Communist sympathizer as a philosophy professor alarmed O'Donnell. When personal friends sent clippings from conservative Catholic newspapers ridiculing McMahon or attacking him as an "impertinent, rash, highly intolerant, conceited publicity seeker,"[53] O'Donnell was embarrassed and hurt. To be sure, there were moments when O'Donnell agreed with such characterizations of his celebrity philosophy professor. However, the present situation at Notre Dame was unprecedented, and O'Donnell was extremely fearful of doing anything that the general public might not understand or could possibly misconstrue.

O'Donnell filed some difficult letters without answering them and advised friends that affairs at Notre Dame were not as bad as might appear. He put his faith not in action but in patience, believing that in time deliverance would come. Modern concepts of academic freedom were simply not highly valued by a majority of American Catholics, and Catholic colleges and universities were not places where parents, students, alumni, or faculty expected to find them. O'Donnell wanted to do the right thing in this McMahon business, but in late 1942 he did not know what the right thing was.

— vii —

During the fall of 1942, along with other American colleges and universities, Notre Dame was deeply committed to the war effort. Academic life had been changed significantly by the effects of conscription on both faculty and students and by the on-campus presence of a thousand navy trainees whose educational objectives and cultural values were so different from those of traditional Notre Dame students. However, one very important aspect of university life during that grim autumn seemed almost untouched by the exigencies of the war effort. Despite rationing and wartime shortages of everything, Notre Dame increased its football schedule during 1942 from nine to eleven games, playing before 472,000 people and making one railroad trip each to the east and west coasts.

Notre Dame's first wartime football season in twenty-four years began with very great expectations. Coming off an undefeated season and selection as coach of the year, Leahy had decided to abandon Rockne's traditional offensive sets and adopt the new T formation. This decision was highly controversial. Nonetheless, Leahy proceeded with it because he had convinced himself that the advantages of a wide-open passing offense over Rockne's speed and deception-oriented running attacks had been demonstrated often enough during the Layden years. Moreover, in Angelo Bertelli, one of the country's premier passers, Leahy believed that he had a quarterback sufficiently skilled to manage the complexities of the T formation.

Though only 23,000 people turned out to watch Leahy's much-bruited new offense challenge a talent-laden Wisconsin team in Madison on September 26, the eyes of the intercollegiate football world were on Camp Randall football stadium that afternoon. Notre Dame supporters attending the game were shocked by what they saw. The new Notre Dame offense did not work. The game was a typical season opener performance. Both teams missed several scoring opportunities with Notre Dame rallying in the third quarter to achieve a 7 to 7 tie. The very hard-charging Wisconsin line defended very well against the T formation, allowing Bertelli only four pass completions out of thirteen attempts. On the other side, Wisconsin's Pat Harder and Elroy Hirsch ran almost at will between the two twenty-yard lines, but once in scoring territory the Notre Dame defense toughened and would not break. Hirsch scored Wisconsin's only touchdown.[54]

While Notre Dame finished the game with better overall statistics than Wisconsin, it was clear that both the coach and the team had been surprised by the brilliant running abilities of Harder and Hirsch. In any case, a tie was not a loss, and redemption would be possible a week hence when Georgia Tech, a team without players of the star quality of Harder and Hirsch, visited the Notre Dame stadium.

Only 20,000 people went out to Notre Dame stadium to see Leahy's redemption and instead witnessed catastrophe. Georgia Tech fielded few players known outside of their region and in fact played several unknown freshmen, who after the game were unknown no longer. The freshmen running backs ran through and around the Notre Dame defenders. Though the first quarter ended scoreless, Georgia Tech had managed a thirteen-point lead early in the fourth period. Notre Dame scored a late final-quarter touchdown, avoiding a shut-out. As had been the case against Wisconsin, the Yellow Jackets' relentless line stopped Bertelli and neutralized the T formation. Bertelli completed only four passes out of thirteen attempts and threw four interceptions. Again, Notre Dame ended the game with all statistical advantages except in scoring.[55]

Suffering its first defeat in thirteen games and poorest performance in early season play in recent memory, the Notre Dame team experienced a brief crisis of confidence. Doubts about the wisdom of changing offensive systems were inevitable. Leahy added to the team's uncertainty by complaining of severe neck and back pains and left the university after the Georgia Tech game for a two-week stay in the Mayo Clinic. He gave team preparation responsibilities to assistant coach Edward McKeever for games against a weak Stanford squad on October 10 and the collection of former college players and professionals who were enrolled in the Iowa Pre-Flight naval program on October 17.

McKeever must have savored his two weeks of media attention because under his leadership the Notre Dame team performed brilliantly, rolling over Stanford 27 to 0 and defeating Iowa Pre-Flight, 28 to 0. Against Iowa Pre-Flight, Bertelli made his mark as a T-formation quarterback, completing six passes out of thirteen attempts with one touchdown. Leahy praised McKeever and the team from his hospital room at the Mayo Clinic. With neck and back pains much improved, he returned to South Bend forthwith to take charge of a team whose fortunes clearly had turned around during his absence.[56]

Leahy traveled with the team on October 24 to Champaign and won a close game with Illinois, 21 to 14. A week later, the team managed to defeat a stubborn Navy squad, 9 to 0, in Cleveland before 60,000 people. After Cleveland, Leahy and the team went to Yankee Stadium in New York City for the annual game with Army on November 7. The press and ticket scalpers had proclaimed this game to be the season's premier football event in the East.

Military and political celebrities joined a crowd of 75,000 to watch a typical Notre Dame/Army football performance. Both teams played very aggressively. For the coaches, this football encounter had become much more than a game. For Leahy and Blaik, this contest was serious business indeed and the outcome was a matter of personal honor for both of these intensely ambitious coaches. The Army team looked for its first victory over Notre Dame since 1931 and its first score against them since 1938. Although Notre Dame managed a win, 13 to 0, the game was poorly played by both sides.

Neither team was able to mount much of an offense. The hard-charging Army line was not much fooled by the T formation and turned the first half into a defensive battle with neither team able to score. In the third period, Notre Dame recovered an Army fumble on the thirty-five yard line and drove for a touchdown and an extra point to take the lead. Though Army was never in the game offensively, rushing for only seventy-nine yards, the game was not put away until the final ten seconds, when Notre Dame added another touchdown.[57]

Blaik's defense limited Bertelli to only four completed passes out of eighteen attempts for a total of twenty-two yards.[58] Clearly, the T formation was not invincible and was not working as well as Leahy had hoped. A week later in South Bend, Leahy's new offense would be severely tested against Michigan in a game that revived a historic football series suspended since 1909.

The attraction of a powerful Michigan team coming to Notre Dame after such a long absence was great enough to fill the stadium for the fourth time in history. To beat Michigan, Notre Dame would have to score quickly and often. Consequently, during the week before the game Leahy drilled his squad relentlessly in offensive preparations.

By game time on November 14, Leahy was confident that his team could score on the formidable Michigan defense. That confidence was confirmed by Notre Dame's performance during the first half. At the end of that half Notre Dame led Michigan, 14 to 13. In the third quarter, however, the Notre Dame defense collapsed with Michigan scoring nineteen points and putting the game out of reach. Though Notre Dame scored a touchdown in the final period, Michigan won the game, 32 to 20.

Game statistical advantages belonged to Michigan as well. Wolverine running backs gained twice as many yards as did those of Notre Dame. Bertelli completed six passes, including one for a touchdown, but also threw three interceptions.[59] Described as a "romp" for Michigan in the *New York Times*,[60] the loss to Michigan was a bitter disappointment for Notre Dame supporters around the country. However, amends of a sort for the poor performances against Army and Michigan were possible because there were still three more games to play in this prolonged season.

The next game against Northwestern, played at home on November 21, drew a crowd only half the size that had turned out for Michigan but it was a game worth watching. Notre Dame played well and despite a few defensive lapses defeated the Wildcats, 27 to 20. Next came the long trip to Los Angeles for a game against Southern California, the last between these two teams for the duration of the war. The enormous appeal of Notre Dame football in the Los Angeles area was evident. More than 95,000 people crowded into the Coliseum to see an ordinary Notre Dame team with a gifted quarterback challenge a somewhat better performing Southern California squad and defeat them 13 to 0.

The long season finally ended on a very cold Saturday, December 5, in a game against the Great Lakes Naval Training Station played at Soldier Field, Chicago, before only 19,000 lonely people. Paul Brown's Great Lakes team was a well-coached collection of former college stars and professionals, including the great Bruce Smith of Minnesota, Heisman Trophy winner in 1941, and Bernie Bellichick, an All-American from Western Reserve. This game was not one that Notre Dame was expected to win, and by the end of the first half, it appeared that they would not. The passing and running of Smith and Bellichick had given the sailors a lead of 13 to 0.[61]

However, during the third period, with Smith out of the game with an injury, Notre Dame managed a stunning comeback on long touchdown runs by Corwin Clatt and Creighton Miller. Unfortunately, Bertelli missed an extra point kick, and the game ended in a 13 to 13 tie. Apart from the missed extra point, Bertelli had a good day as a passer, completing eleven out of twenty-five attempts. Notre Dame led in all game statistical categories except scoring. Nonetheless, coming from behind to gain a tie against a quasi-professional team such as Great Lakes was a moral victory of a sort. For Notre Dame, this disappointing and frustrating season had ended a bit better than it had begun and on a positive note.

Disappointing as the team's performance had been during 1942, overall attendance during the long eleven-game season was the highest since Rockne's last year. However, attendance at home games continued to be below expectations. Except for Michigan, the other home games had been played in a half-filled stadium. (Only visits by strong Southern California, Minnesota, Northwestern, and Michigan teams had attracted enough people to fill the Notre Dame Stadium during the Layden and late Rockne years.)

In order to keep the Notre Dame football program solvent, the number of games in a season was set at ten. However, only three home games were scheduled for 1943 and 1945 and no more than four games were played at home until 1953. The long trips to play Southern California in the Los Angeles Coliseum and Army in New York's Yankee Stadium as well as the game against Navy in the large Cleveland Municipal Stadium were financially essential both for the football program and for the university. Given the importance of football profits to the university and the facts that travel restrictions would affect scheduling and that draft and armed-services requirements were taking away players and coaches, no one could be certain what kind of squad Leahy could field the next year or even if Leahy would be at Notre Dame to field one.

— viii —

Though the football season had been financially successful for the university, by Notre Dame football standards overall team performance had been mediocre. Disappointing also were the results achieved by Notre Dame's other celebrity performer, Professor Francis E. McMahon. This formerly very active interventionist was now a very active apologist for the Roosevelt's administration's management of the war. During the spring of 1942 and especially in the fall congressional election campaigns, McMahon, along with other members of the Fight for Freedom organization, spoke out strongly about the patriotic necessity of driving former isolationists out of public life.

This message of turning out former isolationist congressmen and rallying behind the president at this most critical moment was broadcast vigorously across the country by radio and in speeches and articles. In the end, that effort appears to have had little effect mainly because, during the first half of 1942, there was not much to praise about the president's management and prosecution of the war. Moreover, by the early spring when the shock of the Pearl Harbor attack had diminished, former congressional isolationists made abundantly clear their intention to stay their course and try to influence how, when, and where the war would be fought. During 1942 McMahon and other spokesmen for the administration found themselves virtually powerless to change voters' minds about elected officials who had been so utterly wrong about foreign affairs before Pearl Harbor.

British officials and agents in the United States were baffled by the isolationists' political durability and vitally concerned about how those men might shape the war effort and influence where American military and naval assets would be deployed. Consequently, British officials in this country pursued two strategies during this congressional election year. First, they urged their friends in Fight for Freedom and in other pro-British organizations to speak out in support of the president's leadership and policies. Second, they dispatched several British celebrity intellectuals and scholars of American politics to talk with American influentials, collect information about the state of public opinion here, and make informed judgments about the probable results of the fall congressional elections.

As early as mid-February 1942, British Embassy officials were alarmed by what seemed to them to be deliberate campaigns by the *Chicago Tribune* and by the Hearst newspapers, especially the *New York Daily News*, to depreciate Britain's contributions to the common war effort. Embassy officials suspected the existence of an organized plot among groups hitherto assumed friendly to separate British interests from those of her allies and dominions as well as to divide American interests from those of Britain.

According to embassy officials, the major participants in this plot to disparage Britain's contribution to the war effort were none other than the accredited representatives of the Allies and dominions working in Washington. These representatives added much to the rising tide of criticism of Britain in order "to get a greater share of American support for their fronts."[62] In addition, many influential members of the Roosevelt administration made no secret of their intention to place control of the entire war effort in American hands.[63]

Given the enormous disparity in resources between the two countries, such developments were inevitable. Nonetheless, embassy officials and MOI operatives in the country did their best to minimize them in the hope of being able to wage the war where the British government wanted it waged and to secure a strong voice for their government in the shaping of the postwar world.

On the basis of a secret report on American attitudes toward their wartime partners prepared by Colonel William Donovan's intelligence unit (not yet named Office of Strategic Services [OSS]) and passed on to the British, Americans were deeply suspicious of Britain, Russia, and China. Donovan had concluded that the principal source of distrust was the old World War I war debt issue.[64]

In February, Sir Gerald Campbell reported a somewhat different cause of American doubts about Britain's role in the war. He attributed the rising tide of alarm about Britain's contributions to the war effort now sweeping across the United States to the humiliating British military and naval disasters in the Far East.[65] Whatever the cause, Donovan's report stated that Britain was "a shade less thought of than Russia by Americans, except on the matter of cooperating with the United States after the war." Even on that point, Britain lagged behind China.[66]

Whether undertaken by British spokesmen, by friends in Fight for Freedom, or by other pro-British groups, current propaganda in the United States had failed to generate much American sympathy for the British cause.[67] Campbell recommended that future propaganda strategies "must combat deliberate misrepresentations . . . [by] unfriendly writers and speakers."[68] Friends in the Roosevelt administration have to be supplied with materials to counter the present raging criticism of the British war effort that all agree is doing great damage to the common cause. British spokesmen and their friends in Fight for Freedom, Campbell concluded, must explode the myth that England is sitting down comfortably behind three and a half million bayonets, leaving dominion troops and other Allies to do the fighting and suffer heavy losses.[69]

To find arguments to persuade ordinary Americans to think better of Britain, the Foreign Office dispatched an extraordinary English intellectual to the United States in early March to conduct a fact-finding tour. Upon arriving at the embassy in Washington, the eminent labor-oriented economist, R. H. Tawney, discovered that the staff there knew nothing whatsoever about his mission, that is, what he was supposed to do, where he should go or whom he ought to see.[70] That was not a good beginning.

Left on his own, Tawney read American newspapers and observed proceedings in Congress. He visited academic friends and acquaintances at universities in the Northeast and discussed with them the progress of the American war effort and the present state of American opinion about the war and the Allies. All in all, Tawney formed a generally negative impression of the American government's management of war production and of home-front politics and morale.[71]

According to Tawney, munitions production was a bright spot. At long last, it was improving, but that was about the only bright spot he could find. In his view, psychologically the American people were not yet fully committed to the war. Most alarmingly, he did not find that Americans were a united people. Tawney gave the president and a group around him credit for knowing the truth about the war and how dangerous the present situation was on every front, and he believed that they were doing their best with what they had. Congress was another matter. To Tawney, congressional behavior was inexplicable. They seemed to be wasting time on trivialities and exhibited an extraordinary talent for labor baiting.[72]

Tawney was particularly dismayed by the durability of isolationism. It would not go away. Put down temporarily by post-Pearl Harbor patriotism, he believed that isolationism had revived in the form of endless criticism of Britain, pleas for an all-out war in the Pacific while leaving the Atlantic on hold, and sermons on British misrule in India. Tawney described the American press, with a few exceptions, as "less malignant than silly." Consequently, as Tawney read the public mind, most Americans were "more ignorant of everything to do with the war than a European child" and were "at the mercy of charlatans." Vested interests, dislike of the president and the New Deal all distracted from the essential tasks of mobilizing the country for total war.[73]

No doubt, Tawney concluded, "the mass of American people are a much sounder lot than many of those who profess to speak for them. So all of this may not be as bad as it sounds." Despite that final optimistic hope, Tawney's report did little to relieve Foreign Office anxiety about the spread of negative American attitudes about Britain and provided no insights about how to change them.

Indeed, Tawney was a famous economist and intellectual but had no special expertise in American politics. He did not understand the conventions and realities of American politics and liked not at all what he could not understand. He had been a very poor choice for a mission intended to develop a better appreciation of American affairs and admitted as much to the Foreign Office.[74]

Though Tawney's mission failed, the need for finding ways of changing American opinion about Britain's contribution to the war effort remained, as did a need for understanding American politics in a critical congressional election year. In June, Dennis W. Brogan, one of Britain's most knowledgeable young scholars of American affairs, was assigned to examine in depth the current American political situation and report his assessment to the Foreign Office as soon as possible.

Unlike Tawney, Brogan spoke with Democratic and Republican public officials and political leaders at both national and state levels. From those talks, he was able to develop an understanding of what was happening in current American politics and an appreciation of the complexities of the system. Brogan agreed with Tawney and other British observers that isolationism was by no means a spent force in congressional electoral politics. It simply did not follow that because of post-Pearl Harbor patriotism "some of the most violent and near treasonous" congressional isolationists would be defeated in the fall elections.[75]

Brogan referred specifically to Congressman Clare Hoffman from southwest Michigan, a near neighbor of the University of Notre Dame.

According to Brogan, Hoffman's "virulent philippics" against the president and against Britain continued apace after Pearl Harbor and were freely used by German propaganda agencies. Most certainly in November, Brogan forecast, Hoffman would be re-elected, and he was.[76]

Brogan believed that Republican congressional and senatorial candidates were likely to do very well across the country. He looked very closely at Massachusetts and predicted that Henry Cabot Lodge, Jr., would be easily reelected there. Lodge had so skillfully cultivated Irish American voters and labor leaders in that state that he seemed to be a sure winner. Helping Lodge also, Brogan stated, was the serious discredit that had fallen upon the other serving senator, Democrat David I. Walsh.[77] Though Walsh was not up for re-election until 1946, a scandal surrounding him touched all Democrats, especially unmarried ones, running for office. The intensity of the scandal was also a measure of the serious conflict raging in Massachusetts and in New York between Catholics and Jews for control of local and state Democratic politics and patronage.

As Brogan told the Walsh story, this unmarried Irish American Catholic United States senator was attacked by the *New York Evening Post*, "a Jewish-controlled paper," for homosexual activity. The Walsh case was severely troubling for both the Roosevelt administration and the Catholic hierarchy. At the same time, according to Brogan, another New York paper, *PM*, "though not Jewish-owned, markedly Jewish in tone," had been running a campaign against former Catholic isolationist leaders such as Father Charles E. Coughlin, Father Edward Lodge Curran, and Congressman Barry. Most of the practical politicians speaking to Brogan wished that the attack against Walsh and the campaigns against former Catholic isolationists "had less of a Jewish/Catholic aspect and were conducted by more competent people."[78]

Brogan reported grave concern expressed by Edward Flynn, chairman of the New York State Democratic Committee, and by Frank Walker, postmaster general and chairman of the Democratic National Committee, that these attacks by newspapers perceived to be Jewish-owned or Jewish-controlled would produce a backlash among Catholics against Democratic candidates who were Jewish and against domestic and international causes perceived as strongly supported by Jews.[79] That would not be good Democratic politics in a congressional election year.

With Roosevelt's management of the war encountering severe criticism in Congress and in the press, Democrats needed party unity above all else to preserve their majorities. In key Eastern states, they did not get it. As Brogan and as most American political pundits had forecast, the Republicans did very well at the polls in November 1942.

The congressional elections took place in a political climate lately turned very unfavorable for the Roosevelt administration. Recent war news from the South Pacific was depressing. The first American offensive in that area had been launched against Guadalcanal in the Solomon Islands in August and had encountered fierce opposition. Fighting raged on that island and in the seas around it throughout August, September, and October with alarmingly high losses in men and ships. With the public unaware of preparations for the invasion of North Africa scheduled to begin five days after the election, Americans were disappointed by the apparent lack of movement toward a second front somewhere against the Germans.

On the home front, people from all regions and all classes had much to complain about. In order to conserve supplies of rubber for war production, gasoline rationing and a thirty-five miles an hour speed limit was imposed on the country in September.[80] Food prices had risen sharply during the year while wages had been fixed. Most politically damaging of all was the announcement from the Office of Price Administration on October 31, three days before the election, that in three weeks time coffee would be rationed at the rate of one cup a day for each person over fifteen. For a country of eighty-three million coffee drinkers, that announcement was a shock. Virtually every adult in the country would be affected. As election day approached, newspapers confidently predicted a Republican clean sweep.

While voter turnout was light, many of those taking the time and trouble to vote in an off-year election were frustrated and irritated, if not angry with the Roosevelt administration, and they showed it. The results proved the pundits wrong but not by very much. It was not a Republican clean sweep but was, nonetheless, a clear protest against the president's management of the war. Republicans elected nine new senators and returned forty-four new members to the House while capturing several governorships as well. In the Senate, the previous comfortable Democratic majority of twenty-eight was reduced to nineteen. In the House, where more damage had been done, the Democratic majority shrunk to only nineteen.[81]

Neither the president nor most of his most ardent supporters who had campaigned against former isolationists were pleased by the election results. The president made hardly any mention of it in his post-election press conferences, expressing at them only his confidence that the new Congress would be as determined to win the war as their old president.

In any case, a major step toward winning the war occurred days after the election and pushed explanations and analyses of it off newspaper front pages. Indeed, the invasion of North Africa was not the beginning of the end for the war in Europe, but it was a beginning. Certainly, all Americans took heart in that at the end of 1942. The next year, 1943, promised to be better. It would have to be better because no public person could imagine how it could possibly turn out to be worse than the year just passed.

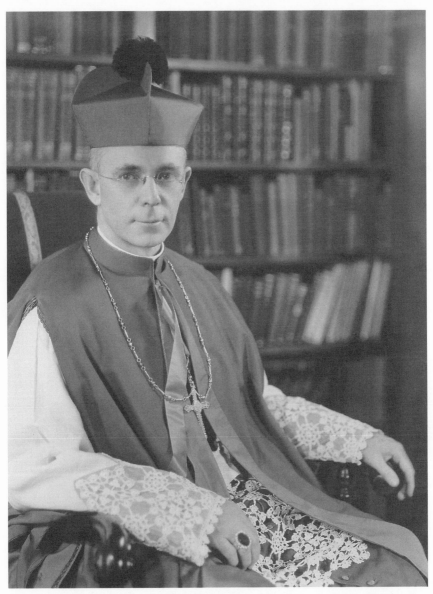

John F. O'Hara, Notre Dame president 1934–40, later became the Cardinal-
Archbishop of Philadelphia.

University of Illinois President A. C. Willard, Illinois Governor Henry Horner, Newman Club chaplain John A. O'Brien and Notre Dame President O'Hara at the 1937 Illinois–Notre Dame game in Champaign

University of Michigan's Fielding Yost with Notre Dame's Elmer Layden, named head football coach in 1934

Philip S. Moore, C.S.C., dean of the Graduate School and later vice president for academic affairs

Two of the European scholars
who came to Notre Dame in
1937, Waldemar Gurian of the
department of politics and
Karl Menger of mathematics

J. Hugh O'Donnell, Notre Dame president 1940–46

Coach Frank Leahy was wooed away from Boston College in 1941.

Heisman trophy winners, quarterback Angello Bertelli, 1943, top, and quarterback Johnny Lujack, 1948

Francis McMahon with philosophy class

McMahon at the podium on Tribute to Russia Day, 1943

Archbishop
Amaletto Cicognani,
apostolic delegate to
the United States

Below: M. A. Fitzsimons,
Thomas T. McAvoy, C.S.C.,
and Frank O'Malley

The senior class presents the flag at the 1942 commencement exercises.

Vincent Fagan of
the department
of architecture

Willis Nutting of
the history
department

Clarence P. Manion, dean of the Law School

James A. McCarthy, dean of the College of Engineering

John A. O'Brien

Franklin Delano Roosevelt
with Postmaster General
Frank Walker

John J. Cavanaugh, C.S.C., Notre Dame president from 1946 to 1952, chose Theodore M. Hesburgh, C.S.C., as executive vice president in 1949.

— 8 —

The Great Crisis over
Academic Freedom
at Notre Dame, 1943

I n contrast to Father O'Donnell's deep uncertainty and
pessimism about how the university would fare in 1943
and during the rest of the wartime years, McMahon was
optimistic about the future. At the end of 1942, the results of the recent
congressional elections notwithstanding, McMahon had no doubts or
second thoughts about the value and importance of his public advocacy
activities. Nothing but good could follow from them. This was his way
of contributing to the war effort, and in early 1943 that war seemed to
be going rather well. By mid-January, the seventeen months' siege of
Leningrad had been broken, and the enormity of the German military
disaster at Stalingrad was apparent. Similarly, since the opening of the
British offensive at El Alamein in late October and the Anglo-American
invasion of North Africa in early November 1942, the war news coming
out of that theater had been good. Although there would be a brief
American setback at Kasserine Pass in late February 1943, Axis resistance
in North Africa would be completely crushed in early May when Allied
forces captured Tunis and Bizerte.

Because of the extraordinary changes in the military situation, President Roosevelt met for ten days with Prime Minister Churchill in January
1943 at Casablanca with the French leaders Generals Giraud and De
Gaulle in attendance. The Allied leaders met to survey the entire field of
the war throughout the world theater by theater, allocate resources, and
determine strategy for final victory. Nothing like this prolonged discus-

sion between Roosevelt and Churchill and their respective staffs had ever taken place before. In a final communique on the conference released January 26, 1943, the president stated that he and Churchill were determined to accept nothing less than unconditional surrender of Germany, Japan, and Italy.[1] For McMahon, this policy of unconditional surrender was entirely appropriate and ethically defensible. Moreover, it defined war aims in ways that all Americans could understand and put an end to prospects for a negotiated peace and the possible survival of Hitlerism.

With regard to the state of affairs at the university, O'Donnell's anxieties about the reputation of Notre Dame in conservative Catholic circles touched McMahon not at all. If asked about the concerns of many of O'Donnell's correspondents, McMahon most likely would have urged the president to ignore them, insisting that the anti-British, anti-Communist, and anti-Semitic utterances of such people required correction from university leaders, not consideration. Increasingly during 1943 McMahon devoted time to providing such correction when needed. Time and energy thus expended, he believed, was neither misspent nor inappropriately diverted from classroom preparation. It was what philosophers had always done. Moreover, it would appear from articles and editorials published in the *Cincinnati Telegraph-Register* in early 1943 that the editor, Monsignor Edward A. Freking, certainly and perhaps even Archbishop John T. McNicholas, O.P., needed a bit of such correction. McMahon was ready, perhaps even anxious, to provide it.

McMahon had no reason to be solicitous about Monsignor Freking. The man's nasty, demeaning attack upon McMahon in the Cincinnati archdiocesan newspaper for advocating aid to Russia in October 1941 was not something quickly forgotten or easily forgiven. From time to time thereafter, McMahon regularly examined the *Cincinnati Telegraph-Register* and did not like what he found in it. By March 1943, he had convinced himself that on at least three occasions between January 22 and March 12, 1943, the paper had published material that reasonable persons would regard as being tasteless at best and at worst as anti-Semitic.

For some inexplicable reason Monsignor Freking felt compelled to provide Catholic theological commentary for an unconfirmed story on January 22, 1943, about a possible mass suicide for virtue's sake by ninety-three Jewish girls and women in Warsaw.[2] According to a letter from Warsaw allegedly received by a rabbi living in New York City, these Jewish women had chosen suicide rather than enslavement as prostitutes for German troops in Warsaw. Neither the unnamed New York rabbi nor Monsignor Freking knew whether or not such a scheme had been proposed or carried out. The rumor of such a possibility was sufficient to inspire Freking to offer the faithful of the Archdiocese of Cincinnati a clarification regarding the morality of suicide in such dreadful circumstances.[3]

According to Freking, Catholic theology recognized no circumstances when men or women could decide to end their own lives. Only God could determine that. In the case of the Warsaw Jewish women, as in all other cases, the true test of morality ought to be the cold light of natural law, not emotionalism. There was no doubt that deliberate self-destruction was contrary to natural law. Furthermore, if directly intended suicide was permissible under any circumstances, Freking concluded, "the bars would be down for many types of it,"[4] and presumably many more people would choose that form of escape from hopeless situations.

A month later in the same column, Freking addressed the general issue of anti-Semitism in a fashion perhaps not as simple-minded as his observations on the moral problem of the Warsaw Jewish women but no less offensive. He reported that a Jewish newspaper, *American Hebrew,* had accused Congressman Martin J. Dies and his Un-American Activities Committee of anti-Semitic statements and actions.[5] Freking could not say whether or not Dies and the committee had been anti-Semitic. However, he was certain that the work of Dies and the committee had been an anathema to the many Jewish readers of the *Nation, New Republic, PM,* and other left-wing publications. Dies' exposure of "Pinkos in government" [6] had been necessary and long overdue. While Freking reminded his readers that Pope Pius XI had condemned anti-Semitism in 1938, he doubted that many Catholics would regard the revelations of the Dies committee as anti-Semitic activity.

Finally, on March 12, 1943, Freking published an editorial which McMahon perceived as being so offensive to American Jews that something had to be done. Freking reported a story out of New York that several prominent rabbis and Jewish writers had complained about the harmful influence on Christian-Jewish relations of alleged anti-Semitic passages in the New Testament. Such an allegation so outraged Monsignor Freking that he could not let it pass. Any propaganda by Jews, he wrote, about what they "wrongly consider anti-Semitic passages in the New Testament will rebound against the Jews with the most serious consequences."[7] To Catholics the New Testament is the inspired word of God, he continued, and "Jews will certainly be misguided if they arouse the Catholics of the United States on the question of the divinity of Christ and on the inspired word of God found in [the New Testament]."[8]

McMahon read Freking's editorial as a villainous threat that some responsible Catholic religious authority ought to repudiate. He waited about a month for someone to speak out. When nothing happened, he drafted two letters. McMahon's first letter, a polite complaint about articles and commentary offensive to Jews published in the *Cincinnati-Telegraph Register,* was sent to Archbishop John T. McNicholas probably sometime in early April. The second letter was sent to Archbishop Robert E. Lucey of San Antonio, a personal friend and ideological soul mate, about the same time.[9] McMahon informed Lucey about what Monsignor Freking had been publishing about Jews, explained what he had written to McNicholas, and asked for advice about what to do next.

Lucey's response was very clear and forthright. An analysis of the situation at the *Cincinnati Telegraph-Register,* wrote Lucey, was not difficult to work out. "A bishop gets exactly what he wants in his diocesan paper," he added. "The sort of stuff which has been published in Cincinnati would not have been published in Cincinnati if the archbishop had told Father Freking where to get off." That members of the hierarchy "should have almost absolute power in their dioceses is very helpful in the field of faith and morality," Lucey continued, "but when we come to the field of economics or foreign affairs the thing does not work out so well. Only a bishop can stop that sort of thing and when he is not so minded the abuse continues."[10]

About Archbishop McNicholas, Lucey observed, His Grace "has made a great deal of progress in the last five or six years and is not only highly intelligent but a very saintly man. Just why he permits this sort of vicious dribble to be published in his paper is beyond me." About what to do next, Lucey was extremely candid. "Since you have brought to his attention what is going on, I think that you have done all that you reasonably can," Lucey concluded. "Further action should be left to the Jewish groups themselves."[11]

Whether McMahon pressed Archbishop McNicholas any further or whether any Jewish group complained to the archbishop is unknown. There is also no evidence available that McNicholas ever responded to McMahon's letter. However, the probability that His Grace of Cincinnati had some conversations with Monsignor Freking about this matter is very high. As early as June 18, 1943, Freking noted in his "Our Comments" column that one could not be a good Catholic and harbor anti-Semitic sentiments.[12] In this instance, McMahon had taken a very important stand, albeit a very private one, against anti-Semitism. In the months ahead, such stands would be frequent, forceful, and much more public.

— ii —

Because of past public criticism of Father Coughlin and of Lindbergh, by early 1943 McMahon's reputation in the American Jewish community as a leading Catholic opponent of anti-Semitism was well established. Consequently, when accounts of the terrible plight of European Jews under German control began appearing in the American press, McMahon was approached to serve as vice chairman of the Chicago chapter of the Emergency Committee to Save the Jewish People of Europe. He accepted that post and also an invitation to appear as a featured speaker at the Emergency Conference to Save the Jewish People of Europe organized by Max Lerner in New York City in late July. Headquartered in the Hotel Commodore, this conference was planned as a major event and such it turned out to be. Special statements from President Roosevelt and Secretary of State Cordell Hull in the form of telegrams to Lerner were read to the conferees and a telephone speech from former President Herbert Hoover was presented live in a plenary session. McMahon was joined by several other speakers including the celebrated novelist Sigrid Unset and the mayor of New York City, Fiorello LaGuardia.

President Roosevelt's message was brief but intended to be reassuring. He promised the conferees that their government would never cease its efforts to save those who could be saved.[13] Hull's message was a bit longer but equally unspecific about plans and projects. The secretary assured the conferees that the rescue of the Jewish people as well as others marked for slaughter by Nazi savagery was under constant examination by the State Department. Any and all suggestions calculated to achieve that end would be gladly considered provided they were consistent with the destruction of Nazi tyranny and the final defeat of Hitler. Hull informed the conferees that an intergovernmental agency had been created to deal with this crisis and that cooperation with the British to initiate practical measures appropriate for wartime conditions was underway.[14]

By phone from San Francisco Hoover urged development of alternatives to Palestine as safe havens and future homes for the oppressed minorities of Axis-dominated Europe. He recommended the uplands of central Africa for refugee resettlement. Unset told the conferees what most of them believed and wanted to hear, that is, the future of the Jewish people would be secure only after they had become an independent nation in possession of a national stronghold with all of the institutions of a national life.[15] LaGuardia's remedy for the current desperate situation was simple, direct, and one that he had proposed several times during recent months. He called upon the American government and its allies to serve notice on the Axis that all persons responsible for the deaths of Jews and non-Jews would be tried for murder at the end of the war. For the present, however, all of those Jews desiring to emigrate from Europe and resettle elsewhere ought to be allowed to do so as soon as conditions would allow them to leave.[16]

McMahon did not speak until July 25; when he did, many of the conferees were pleased but some must have been mystified. McMahon began well. He characterized the plight of the Jewish people in Europe under Hitler as "the most terrible single tragedy of the present war." Passive acquiescence to these frightful events, he declared, "will make us moral participants in the crimes of the Nazis."[17] However, as he had done in other speeches several times, McMahon shifted from the moral responsibility of all Christians for what was happening to the European Jews to alleged heroic efforts by Pope Pius XII to save them. The pope's good works on behalf of European Jews could not be told now, he concluded, but would be disclosed at war's end after Germany had been defeated and conquered.[18]

As a public relations event the conference was a great success, and McMahon was very proud of his role in it. His commitment to assail anti-Semitism wherever he found evidence of it had been strengthened by the experience. Strengthened also during the early months of 1943 as much by audience reactions to his speeches as by the progress of the war was McMahon's determination to defend the war policies of the president. McMahon had been delighted by the published reports of the decisions made at the Casablanca conference in January 1943, and he became a powerful advocate of the policy of unconditional surrender.

Immediately after the Casablanca conference most of the old isolationists offered little criticism of the unconditional surrender policy. Only after the Red Army began its offensive into Eastern Europe in January 1944 did many of the old isolationists seriously attack unconditional surrender for prolonging the war and opening much of Europe to Soviet domination.[19] One exception to this general pattern of delayed reaction was Father John A. O'Brien, McMahon's colleague at Notre Dame and former adversary during the isolationist-interventionist controversies of 1941. In speeches on campus and elsewhere and in an article that appeared in the *Catholic Worker,* a Catholic pacifist journal published in New York City, O'Brien argued that the doctrine of unconditional surrender was difficult to justify when measured against Christian ethical standards or American national interests.[20]

Always fearful that O'Brien's foreign policy views would be taken as representative of American Catholics as a whole, McMahon felt a special obligation to respond and refute the priest's foreign policy statements whenever possible. Consequently, in speeches delivered throughout 1943, whenever his context would permit McMahon insisted that unconditional surrender was an ethically justifiable policy because of the unprincipled character of the enemy. He also drafted and sent off to the Associated Press a formal refutation of O'Brien's argument which never found its way into print.[21]

In a speech delivered at the Princeton Club in New York City on April 24, 1943, McMahon declared that "at least 99 percent of the Catholics of this country are wholly behind the unconditional surrender aim of the Allies."[22] Then in an interview after the speech, a *New York Times* reporter questioned McMahon about rumored peace feelers coming out of Spain and how he thought American Catholics would react to them. McMahon had no doubts at all about American Catholic opinion on the prospects for a negotiated peace. Catholics, he insisted, were "wholly unsympathetic to recent peace feelers by Spanish authorities." Moreover, "Franco's fascism is now apparent to all," he added. "Many Catholics who formerly supported the Spanish dictator have now turned away." Only an infinitesimal fraction of Catholics in this country, McMahon concluded, "favor peace unless the Axis powers surrender unconditionally to the Allies."[23]

When this brief story appeared, McMahon was identified as president of the Catholic Association for International Peace and as a professor of philosophy at Notre Dame.[24] It would appear that because of McMahon's remark about Franco reported in this story, someone in the Spanish consulate in New York clipped it from the *Times* and put it in the next dispatch bag bound for Madrid. Thus began a course of events that in four months would turn the protected world of McMahon and Father O'Donnell into a battleground.

— iii —

Related to the peace feelers allegedly coming out of Spain in April were persistent reports in February and March about the prospects of a separate peace with Italy worked out through the good offices of the Vatican. These reports were given a small degree of credibility by Archbishop Spellman's clandestine visit to Rome in February 1943. Clearly, the archbishop of New York had gone to Rome at considerable personal risk to talk with his close personal friend Pius XII about something important.

Though scarcely any observers of Italian affairs believed for a moment that the German forces in Italy would allow such an event to occur so long as their military power was intact, Spellman's visit to Rome inspired speculation in the liberal press about what might happen in Italy. A major article and several letters by Gaetano Salvemini, a renowned Italian anti-Fascist and anti-clerical writer and scholar, published in the *New Republic* set a tone and advanced an argument about Pius XII and Fascism that American Catholic publicists, including McMahon, could not let pass unchallenged.

Salvemini argued that the pope simply could not deliver a separate peace with Italy until the Nazi military machine had broken down. The purpose of the Spellman visit, he speculated, was to talk about what would happen in Italy after that breakdown had taken place. According to Salvemini, the issue was when and how to replace the present pro-German-with-Mussolini clerical fascism in Italy with a pro-Allied-without-Mussolini clerical fascism.[25]

Salvemini was well aware of what the Catholic press would try to do to anyone who publicly asserted that Pius XII's past and current policies were pro-Fascist, but he proceeded anyway. The main points of his article were that the Italian people would never accept a new edition of Fascism without Mussolini and that by associating himself with any attempt to rescue the Fascist regime without Mussolini at its moment of collapse, the pope would himself become the first victim of such a policy. Indeed, Salvemini was attacked by the Jesuit weekly *America* as well as other Catholic papers and by a few letters published in the *New Republic*.[26]

To be sure, Salvemini had said nothing explicitly about pro-Fascist sympathies being endemic in the American Church. However, others were ready and willing to indict American Catholics for such an un-American political disposition and then try to document that accusation from the usual Coughlinite, Christian Front, anti-Communist, and pro-Franco sources.

McMahon first entered the controversy over the relationship between Catholicism and Fascism in the correspondence pages of the *New Republic* in April. Monsignor John A. Ryan had been attacked by a correspondent for alleged undemocratic passages in his *The State and the Church* and for toadying to the *Brooklyn Tablet*. In an explication of the Catholic position on religious toleration in predominantly Catholic countries presented in *The State and the Church*, Ryan acknowledged that full freedom to proselytize was not accorded, and properly so, to non-Catholic religious groups. With regard to the *Brooklyn Tablet*, a letter from Ryan to a Catholic couple criticizing the *Tablet* had found its way into a featured article in *PM*. Ryan sent a formal apology to the *Tablet* for the appearance of his personal letter in *PM* and then described the *Tablet* "as one of our most useful Catholic newspapers."[27]

McMahon responded to this attack on Ryan in the correspondence pages of the *New Republic* by insisting that this eminent priest's forty-year record as a political democrat was absolutely unblemished. Ryan's observations about religious toleration in a predominantly Catholic state were theoretical and hypothetical with no real relevance to any foreseeable actual situation, especially in the United States. With regard to the *Brooklyn Tablet,* McMahon distinguished between the *Tablet's* political side and its religious side, asserting that Ryan would no more endorse the former than he would think of questioning the strict orthodoxy of the latter.

On the larger question of the relationship between Catholicism and Fascism, McMahon responded to a letter published in the *New Republic* from Professor Lawrence W. Beals of Williams College contending that Catholicism, Communism, Fascism, and emperor worship were all equally totalitarian and opposed to historic American ideals of freedom. According to Beals, Catholics believed that the proper form of society and the blueprint for the good life had been revealed. This being the case, Catholics proclaimed the freedom of the individual only up to the point where one's own thought challenged that revelation. In the last analysis, Beals stated, the principles on which earthly institutions were founded could not be criticized. Where in America, Beals questioned, were the responsible spokesmen of Catholic Christendom who declared their belief in the ultimate authority of individual men to question freely every control established over them.[28] In Beals' judgment, there were none.

McMahon's spirited reply to Beals' letter was published in the *New Republic* on June 7, 1943.[29] Not again! he wrote, regarding the accusation that Catholicity and Fascism are identical. How often must that hackneyed liberal calumny be uttered? Professor Beals' letter was only the last and by no means the best in a long series of similar diatribes. McMahon wrote in high anger, declaring that twenty million American Catholics were a suspect lot because they belonged to an allegedly crafty, scheming, seditious organization known as the Catholic Church. What do you liberals want of us? he asked. Do you want us to abandon our faith? We will never do that. Do you want us to pack up our belongings and leave the country? This land is as much ours as it is yours. You liberals have a serious problem, McMahon concluded; have the intelligence and courage to face it. Tell us in clear and simple language what you are after.[30]

Neither McMahon nor anyone else had to wait long or look far for an answer to the Notre Dame professor's challenge. It came in the form of editorial comment in the same number of the *New Republic* that published the challenge. The editors of the *New Republic* refused to believe that a man as intelligent as McMahon would deny that in its ultimate theology the Catholic Church was authoritarian and therefore anti-liberal. Having said that, the editors admitted no necessary relationship between that fact and support of political and military totalitarianism in Germany, Italy, or Spain. In supporting Franco and Mussolini and in carrying on a disarmed truce with Hitler in Germany, the editors continued, the Catholic Church had acted not as a religious body but as an economic and political corporate entity with huge possessions and enormous spiritual and emotional stakes in those countries. In the past the Church had been wrong in such matters and could be wrong again.[31]

Regardless of final theological beliefs, the editors believed that the majority of American Catholics have always been loyal citizens of a democratic regime. However, there is a lunatic fringe among them who insist on importing into this country ideas alien to the democratic tradition and to the views of a majority of their fellow Catholics. The decent majority of American Catholics should do far more at present than reduce the influence of the Coughlinites and Christian Fronters who are Fascists at heart and whose practices should have no place in a free America.[32]

Specifically, in reply to McMahon's question, decent Catholics should reconsider their policy of trying to enact Catholic doctrine into federal, state, and municipal law. Catholics should confine their disciplines to their own community, instead of trying to force everyone in the country to live up to their precepts, especially in the matter of contraception.[33]

There were, of course, problems with Catholic censorship of motion pictures. Also, Catholic economic pressure on newspapers, magazines, and radio stations had the effect of discouraging public discussion of the social and political programs and policies of the Church in this country. The close identification of the Catholic Church with corrupt urban political machines ought to be broken. Similarly, good Catholics ought to persuade the bad ones to abandon anti-Semitic activities everywhere, especially in Brooklyn and Boston.[34]

The editors were particularly hopeful that good Catholics would find some way of raising the level of Catholic journalism in the country. They estimated that 90 percent of the Catholic press in this country was pitched at the level of the lowest 10 percent of the Catholic community. Finally, the editors wished that good Catholic political democrats such as Dr. McMahon would not always exhibit such hypersensitivity about public discussions of Church policies. The editors could not understand why so many good Catholics did their best to silence public discussion of

Church interests by insisting on treating the Church as a monolithic whole, defending its good and bad aspects with equal vigor. Because of the universality and intensity of this attitude, the editors concluded, serious public discussion of the Catholic question in the United States was impossible.

The list of anti-democratic behaviors and attitudes which the editors of the *New Republic* believed to be the heart of the Catholic question in America was a formidable one indeed. It took McMahon about a week to penetrate and sort out this extraordinary editorial collage of well-intentioned advice, condescension, and effrontery to prepare a measured but informative and dignified response.

McMahon described the *New Republic* editorial comments as clear, forthright, sincere, but not always reasonable or directed toward the main point of the presumed linkage of the Catholic Church to Fascism. That presumed linkage had been the sole reason for initiating the present epistolary exchange. Moreover, the charge that such a linkage was operative had been made openly or indirectly in editorials, articles, and letters appearing in liberal papers all over the country. Such a charge was a reflection on the patriotism of 20 million American Catholics and was untrue.[35]

According to the *New Republic* editorial, a majority of American Catholics were loyal citizens in spite of their membership in an authoritarian religious organization. McMahon insisted that American Catholics were loyal citizens *because* of their religion. The Church was indeed authoritarian in character but not totalitarian or fascist. Membership in an authoritarian religious organization did not imply that Catholics preferred authoritarian forms of government in the political order. The Church's insistence upon the dignity of the individual soul, the essential equality of all men, and respect for legitimate authority, McMahon stated, "fructifies *logically* on the political plane into democracy."[36] It was a thoroughly Thomistic response. For those who might question this position or who wanted more of the same style of argument, McMahon referred them to *Christianity and Democracy*, written by his personal friend, the distinguished Thomist philosopher, Jacques Maritain.[37]

As to totalitarianism, McMahon continued, one simply could not be at once a good Catholic and a good Nazi or Fascist. One or the other allegiance must eventually disappear unless reason had fled. He noted also that, in his opinion, the liberal press on the whole had been unfair to those Catholics who have intelligently and profoundly assessed the role of the Catholic Church in the modern world and assessed it in a spirit of healthy criticism of the laity and clergy. He wished greater media attention had been given to recent numbers of the *Dublin Review* and the *Review of Politics.* In those periodicals could be found evidence aplenty that hypersensitivity to criticism of a temperate and judicious quality was not characteristic of good political democrats professing the Catholic faith.[38]

McMahon addressed the other specifics in the editorial either by citing his own record, as in the case of anti-Semitism, or by referring to Monsignor John A. Ryan's article on "Contraception and Censorship" published in the *New Republic,* and Bishop John F. Noll's statement on the Catholic Church and post office censorship of so-called indecent literature. He also cited the efforts of John A. Lapp and Jerome G. Kirwin to defeat the corrupt politicians who had disgraced the Catholic name in urban affairs. McMahon concluded by admitting that while American Catholics had their faults, well reported ones, liberals had theirs as well and not always so well reported. A proper stance in the years ahead would be for Catholics and liberals to make a strong effort to minimize tensions between them and effect the greatest possible unity of effort against the common foe.[39]

Generally, the editors of the *New Republic* were pleased by McMahon's response. In their view, he was perhaps insufficiently opposed to all of the various forces of obscurantism in his Church, but he was extraordinarily fair and reasonable. If more of American Catholics were of the same mind and disposition as McMahon, the editors stated, liberals would find far less to criticize in Church policies and interests.[40] While the complex question of the relationship between the Catholic Church and Fascism had not been resolved, McMahon's contributions to this lengthy exchange had done much to diminish it. A new fearless layman defender of the Catholic faith in America with media accessibility had emerged. Those of an anti-Catholic turn of mind had better beware, and archbishops and bishops would be wise to take notice.

— iv —

As the prospects of an Allied victory appeared more certain during 1943 and notwithstanding his emergence as a Catholic champion, McMahon began to devote more thought and energy to the kind of peace that this victory would bring. Upon returning to the university after the Princeton

Club speech and interview, McMahon became increasingly convinced that any sort of lasting peace in the postwar world would depend upon continuing cooperation between the United States and the Soviet Union.

On the vitally important matter of present and future cooperation between the United States and the Soviet Union, American Catholic opinion had to be changed. McMahon had no illusions about how difficult and painful effecting such a change would be. He convinced himself that there was nothing in Catholic doctrine that forbade working with a great power that happened to have a Communist government in order to achieve and maintain world peace. That message needed to be heard, and he set himself to the task of finding ways to insure that it was.

From time to time, McMahon had discussed with like-minded Catholic friends the possibility of mounting a project—organizing a conference perhaps in New York or preparing a publication—wherein prominent Catholic academics, church leaders, or public men could address all aspects of the problem of cooperating with the Soviet Union in war and peace. Critical to the success of any such project would be the support and involvement of some bishops or archbishops with open minds on the subject. Such prelates would have to have more than open minds. They would also have to be sufficiently knowledgeable to be able to discuss the subject and sufficiently courageous to be willing to assist clarification of whether Catholic doctrine did or did not conflict with a public policy of cooperating with the Soviet Union. Friends prevailed upon McMahon to draw upon his long-standing relationship with Archbishop Lucey of San Antonio and try to persuade that prelate to become part of this project and thereby provide the credibility it needed to succeed.

McMahon wrote Archbishop Lucey on March 23, 1943, to explain what he and others had in mind and to ask for His Grace's active support.[41] To be sure, Archbishop Lucey shared most of McMahon's views about the importance of cooperation between the United States and the Soviet Union in the war and after. He was also very critical of the way this matter had been treated in the Catholic press.[42] Nonetheless, the archbishop refused to join McMahon and his friends in this project in any public way: "I think it would be the part of prudence for me to abstain."[43]

Lucey feared that his advocacy of cooperation and appearance at such a conference in New York or elsewhere outside of San Antonio would be regarded by eastern bishops as an intrusion into their jurisdictions. To McMahon, the meaning of that point was clear enough. As he had learned so painfully after his Cincinnati speech in early October 1941,

American Catholic bishops tended to view the question of cooperating with the Soviet Union as an issue of Catholic morality rather than as a straightforward morally neutral public policy matter.

As Monsignor Freking had so vigorously phrased this issue in the *Cincinnati Telegraph-Register* eighteen months earlier,[44] once an official Catholic public teacher of morality in a given area, a local bishop, had formally determined the morality of an issue, such as cooperating with the Soviet Union, the matter was closed. Henceforth, it would be wrong for anyone subject to a bishop's moral authority, that is, all Catholics living in his diocese, to advocate a contrary position. In Archbishop Lucey's mind, that prescription against advocating moral positions contrary to the determination of the local bishop in that bishop's diocese applied as much to visiting prelates from other parts of the country as it did to mere laymen. This point was clearly made. "The measure of Catholic public opinion on collaboration," Lucey continued, "should be set, they believe, by themselves and not by bishops in far off Texas."[45]

Opposition to any intrusion by outsiders into diocesan affairs was so strong among American Catholic bishops that Lucey did not have to think twice about challenging it for any secular cause, no matter how important that cause might appear to be. About the substantive issue of cooperation with the Soviet Union, Lucey believed that many of his fellow bishops were mistaken in their opposition, but he did not know what should or could be done about it.

"Neither our laity or hierarchy, not to mention our clergy," Lucey wrote, "has learned completely that Russia is doing a good job against one of our enemies and in a certain sense is saving Western Civilization until we can gather our forces for the ultimate triumph. You . . . know this but others do not."[46] This present situation is regrettable, Lucey said, but the worst is yet to come. "When peace comes I await the awful mistakes that will be made by many sections of the Catholic press whose editors," he concluded, "are only waiting for the armistice to permit them to reveal their profound spirit of isolationism and opposition to Mr. Roosevelt's policies, which are largely the policies of the Vatican."[47] At this moment, the archbishop advised McMahon, "I guess there is nothing we can do except to plug along and hope for the best."[48]

Lucey had declined to be the point man in a campaign to change American Catholic opinion about cooperating with Soviet Russia, but he had not abandoned the cause of cooperation. In a sermon delivered at the sesquicentennial celebrations of the Archdiocese of New Orleans on May 12, he sharply criticized those Catholic editors and writers who insisted on publishing simple-minded views on international affairs, much to the disservice of the Church. These good men, he said in his New Orleans sermon, had the courage of their ignorance, and it was very difficult to keep them quiet. In a letter to McMahon, the archbishop confessed that as originally written that line read, "the courage of their stupidity, but at the last moment, I weakened and made the statement softer,"[49]

It is unlikely that McMahon was surprised by Archbishop Lucey's response to his request for public support in a campaign to try to increase the level of tolerance among American Catholics for Soviet Russia. The idea of such an organized campaign was dropped, but McMahon decided to do what he could for that cause as an individual by addressing the issue of cooperation whenever and wherever he could. His most important effort on behalf of this cause was a speech given in late June 1943, under the auspices of Russian War Relief to an audience of over a thousand people in a Masonic temple in Scranton, Pennsylvania.

As was his usual practice, McMahon did not have a prepared manuscript. He spoke from notes and held the attention of his audience for nearly an hour. Advance publicity about the speaker and the subject matter was sufficiently broadcast to attract a reporter from *Newsweek* magazine who published a brief account of it and him in the religion section under the title "McMahon's Mission" on July 12, 1943. If McMahon had not already achieved celebrity status in the small world of American religious writers and thinkers, this *Newsweek* article acquired it for him. The article accomplished something else as well. It got him into serious trouble with university authorities. The nationwide reporting of perhaps no more than three or four lines of this largely extemporized speech would in time generate a complaint from a person that the president of Notre Dame could not ignore.

In Scranton, McMahon spoke first about the heroic struggle and enormous sacrifices of the Russian people in the present war. He insisted that Russians fought for their land and their culture, not for totalitarian Communism. He dwelt next upon the nature of the postwar world and future threats to world peace. A new world order based on President Roosevelt's Four Freedoms was aborning. The old order of spiritual bankruptcy, national selfishness, and economic chaos was gone and could never be re-established. The one indisputable fact about the future world order, McMahon insisted, was that Russia could not be left out of it. The country was too large and too important to be isolated like a social and political leper. The American government would have to devise some form of collaboration with postwar Russia or face the prospect of another war.

About the form that postwar collaboration would take, McMahon was marvelously unspecific. We simply had to find a way to get along. Too many people had perished in this terrible war and too much was at stake not to try. All of us, especially Catholics, he declared, must work for world peace. To Catholics once again he said that he knew of nothing in Catholic doctrine that conflicted with a policy of cooperating with Soviet Russia in order to secure and preserve world peace. McMahon had no illusions about the present Soviet regime. It was a totalitarian monstrosity. Yet, he saw some basis, not much to be sure, for hoping that realism of a sort might prevail among present Soviet leaders so that concessions toward a freer, if not free, exercise of religious worship and possession of private property might be forthcoming.

McMahon ended by assuring his audience that American ideals were stronger and more resilient than anything advocated by Communist theorists. Communism flourished only when social and economic injustice was widespread. Therefore, McMahon concluded, Americans had only to be true to themselves. If we were faithful to the great ideals of life, liberty, and the pursuit of happiness, that is, to equality of opportunity and a just measure of material goods available to all, then we need not fear Communism and could face the future with confidence.[50]

This speech was vintage McMahon. He said nothing in Scranton that he had not said many times before. What was different about this speech and what made its content appear to some as being new was the way *Newsweek* magazine reported the speech and what it said about the speaker. Of the speech itself, the magazine mentioned only McMahon's observations that securing and maintaining peace in the postwar world required cooperation with Soviet Russia, that Communism was a danger only to a world rife with social and economic injustice, and that nothing in Catholic doctrine conflicted with a policy of working with Russia in order to preserve world peace.[51]

The rest of the article focused on McMahon's new and special mission which was explained as "a self-appointed task of reconciling his fellow Catholics to a greater tolerance of Russia."[52] He was described as a person of progressive opinions, "a lean, energetic associate professor of philosophy at the University of Notre Dame," and also as the president of the Catholic Association for International Peace. McMahon was quoted as saying that the views of this association represented "a large minority of Catholic thought" on international affairs.[53] Implied throughout the article was the notion that although McMahon spoke as an individual, he represented a growing liberal influence in a generally conservative American Catholic community. Here was a new voice, and a Catholic layman's voice at that, claiming to speak out authoritatively on an important foreign policy question that most bishops and a majority of Catholic lay people considered to be a moral issue. To be sure, McMahon did not claim to be speaking for the Catholic Church in America in any official way. The constituency he claimed to represent was at the moment only a large minority of American Catholics. However, he believed that minority was increasing in size and influence within the Church every passing month. The appearance of such a liberal influence in American Catholic affairs at this time was regarded by the editors of *Newsweek* as a new phenomenon and worthy of special notice in the religion section of their national news magazine.

— v —

Within a week of the publication of the *Newsweek* article featuring McMahon, a major incident in the war made American Catholics even more newsworthy. That event was the heavy American air raid on Rome on July 19, 1943. Virtually every American newspaper and major news magazine published accounts of the raid accompanied by stories detailing the reactions of prominent American Catholics to it.

The Italian government had steadfastly refused to declare Rome an open city because it was the heart of the country's railway system. All rail traffic between northern and southern Italy with the exception of what was routed directly from Bologna to east coast points such as Foggia and Bari passed through Rome's two large Littorio and San Lorenzo marshaling yards.[54] There was simply no way for German forces fighting in Sicily since the Allied invasion on July 10 to be supplied without extensive use of those two important marshalling yards. This circumstance was well known to the Allied high command, and after some hesitation they targeted Littorio and San Lorenzo for a major bomber attack.

Because Rome was the eternal city, the seat of the pope, and the center of the Catholic world, every precaution had to be taken to bomb only targets of military importance. As many available Catholic pilots as possible in the Ninth Air Force were selected for this mission. Air crews were carefully trained. On July 19, 1943, more than five hundred heavy and medium bombers attacked the Littorio and San Lorenzo yards in the morning and the Ciampino airfields in the afternoon, dropping about a thousand tons of bombs.[55]

Correspondents who went on this mission reported heavy damage to the military objectives. Only one major religious structure was severely damaged, the Basilica of San Lorenzo outside of the walls and its cloisters, located about five hundred yards from one of the rail centers.

Accounts of the raid were released promptly and all of them stressed the limited nature of the objectives and the care taken to strike military targets alone.[56] In addition, a dramatic but largely symbolic Allied political objective was achieved within a week of this extraordinary air action. On July 25, Benito Mussolini and his Fascist government was dismissed by the king and replaced by Marshal Pietro Badoglio, who opened negotiations with the Allied command in Algiers for an armistice and unconditional surrender. Immediately, German forces in Italy began seizing strategic points and occupying major cities, including Rome.

Reactions of American Catholic leaders to the bombing of Rome were mixed. Most laymen and a majority of the bishops questioned about the raid regretfully accepted the argument of military necessity. Archbishop Mooney of Detroit deplored the bombing but faulted the Italian government for not preventing it by declaring Rome an open city.[57] The sharpest critics of the raid were William Cardinal O'Connell, archbishop of Boston, and Bishop Joseph P. Hurley of St. Augustine. Both of these men had spent many years living and working in Rome as Vatican officials.

O'Connell had not been persuaded by the argument of military necessity. Hurley was outraged by what he described as "the obscene chorus of approval . . . registered in the regimented press."[58] A case in point was the clumsy effort by the Office of War Information to justify the devastation of the Basilica of San Lorenzo by enumerating the churches destroyed by Axis forces in Britain, Poland, Yugoslavia, Greece, and Manila.[59]

Newsweek magazine not only reported statements by bishops about the raid, but the editors also provided a sampling of reactions from the Catholic press, in effect giving national exposure to limited circulation Catholic newspapers and periodicals. *Newsweek* quoted the *Brooklyn Tablet's* complaint that Nazis and Fascists bomb churches. Americans had no business copying them. *Newsweek* also quoted from an editorial in *Commonweal,* which was described as one Catholic periodical that "openly approved the military necessity of bombing the city."[60] The *Commonweal* editorial insisted that there could not be one justice for Rome and another for all other cities in the world. The zone of faith was not bounded by the walls of Rome, and Catholics should make no distinction between the bombing of Rome and of the most miserable Calabrian village. In the measure that Catholics have the faith of Peter, *Commonweal* concluded, "they can stand the threat to Peter's tomb."[61]

Back at Notre Dame, reactions of the people there to the bombing of Rome were similar to those of Catholics in other parts of the country. They accepted the argument of military necessity. McMahon echoed the views of the *Commonweal* editorial in a story about the raid carried in *PM.*[62] Though the *South Bend Tribune* carried a full account of the raid and damage to the Basilica of San Lorenzo, no local comment on the raid had been solicited. An editorial fully accepted military necessity justification of the attack. The editors hoped that the bombing of Rome would encourage the Italian people to act positively and take their country out of the war as a Nazi ally.[63] O'Donnell could not have been pleased by this editorial. He was very worried about the increasing number of air raids in the Rome and Naples areas because his sister, married to an Italian aristocrat, lived near Siena. For most people in the Notre Dame community, however, the bombing of Rome was not the most newsworthy that summer. Of more immediate importance was the much anticipated announcement by Father Thomas A. Steiner, C.S.C., provincial of the Congregation of Holy Cross, on August 3, 1943, that Father O'Donnell had been reappointed for another three-year term as president of the university and local religious superior.

McMahon closely followed campus gossip as well as the news from abroad. O'Donnell's reappointment was certainly no surprise. What surely did surprise McMahon, however, was a letter from the director of studies, Father J. Leonard Carrico, dated August 10, 1943, summoning him to a meeting with Father O'Donnell in the president's office at 10:00 A.M. on August 16. In this letter Carrico did not indicate the purpose of the meeting but asked McMahon to bring with him copies of his speeches delivered at Springfield the previous summer, a recent one given at Scranton, and the text of a cablegram sent to Stalin in September 1942.[64]

It would appear that McMahon's one-man campaign to reconcile American Catholics to a greater tolerance of Soviet Russia had achieved some sort of result. As McMahon gathered his papers for the meeting with O'Donnell, there is no doubt that he had a fair idea of what that result was and why he had been summoned to the president's office in such a fashion. After all, he had been there before. He prepared himself accordingly.

— vi —

It was evident to McMahon that O'Donnell was reconsidering his policy of patience and forbearance toward public advocacy activities operative at the university since America's entry into the war. It was a fact, however, that the prohibitions imposed on McMahon in mid-October 1941 against appearing at public meetings "not in keeping with your status as a member of the faculty of the university" formally had never been rescinded. But something important must have happened to start O'Donnell thinking about reimposing limitations on outside speaking engagements.

Indeed, something had happened, something too important for O'Donnell to ignore or deliberately put aside. For the first time in his life, O'Donnell had received an official communication from Archbishop Amleto G. Cicognani, the apostolic delegate. In a letter dated August 3, 1943, and marked confidential, Cicognani advised O'Donnell that a formal complaint against McMahon had been lodged with His Eminence Luigi Cardinal Maglione, papal secretary of state.

According to Cicognani, the cardinal secretary of state had informed him in a letter dated June 20, 1943, that the Spanish ambassador had protested to the Holy See, alleging that McMahon—identified as president of the Catholic Association for International Peace and as a member of the department of philosophy of the University of Notre Dame—had engaged in anti-Spanish propaganda in the United States. Especially displeasing to the ambassador had been McMahon's assertions that General Franco was a Fascist and an accomplice of the Axis. To those complaints of the Spanish ambassador, Cicognani added two of his own, namely, McMahon's recent address on cooperation with Soviet Russia and his exaggerated observations on the bombing of Rome.

The apostolic delegate affected to understand that McMahon had spoken only for himself and did not reflect in any way the opinion or policy of the university. Nevertheless, Cicognani continued, McMahon's connection with the university was always mentioned, and he feared that many persons would not be able to distinguish between the views of the speaker and those of the institution. The apostolic delegate believed that the university should not be exposed to danger because of what may prove to be objectionable or embarrassing statements by its faculty members.

For those reasons, Cicognani concluded, "I would ask you to take whatever measures may be dictated by prudence and charity to obviate a recurrence of these difficulties."[65] In addition, Cicognani asked O'Donnell to inform him about what steps had been taken in this matter so he could make a suitable report to the cardinal secretary of state.[66]

The apostolic delegate's English was very good, and the meaning of his letter was perfectly clear. On the matter of Communism being a minor menace and on the bombing of Rome, the professor had crossed a line. McMahon had said things at a critical time in Italian affairs that Vatican authorities did not want to hear from a Catholic spokesman anywhere. While Cicognani appears to have had neither any knowledge nor appreciation of McMahon's long-standing role as a defender of papal policies or of his recent emergence as a respected apologist for Catholic policies and interests in American liberal circles, he was aware that the American press accepted him as an authority of a sort on Catholic affairs. For that reason, something had to be done about him at once.

Some other points expressed or implied in the apostolic delegate's letter were also very clear if one took the trouble to read it carefully. One such point was an assumption about the status of lay faculty in American Catholic universities. Archbishop Cicognani, Cardinal Maglione, and the Spanish ambassador all assumed that the president of the university of Notre Dame possessed sufficient authority over his lay employees to put an end to something like the McMahon problem one way or another. They also assumed that as an obedient religious, the president of the university would exercise that authority when asked to do so by someone of a higher status in the Roman Catholic religious hierarchy than himself. In the end, both of those assumptions turned out to be true. None of these eminent men appear to have given a moment's thought to the possible effect of such action upon either McMahon or the university.

Also in this letter, McMahon's alleged culpability was simply asserted. Truth did not appear to have been an issue. O'Donnell was not asked to look into the matter and try to discover what McMahon had said or even intended to say about Franco, cooperating with Russia, or the bombing of Rome. None of the parties making a case against McMahon had ever heard or read a single word of any of his off-campus speeches delivered in 1942 and 1943. The case rested entirely on a half-dozen lines in a *New York Times* report of an interview following his Princeton Club speech in April 1943, the way *Newsweek* styled the Scranton speech in late June 1943 as part of McMahon's mission to increase tolerance among American Catholics for more cooperation with Russia, and a few observations in *PM* about the bombing of Rome in July 1943.

Still another point clearly implied in the apostolic delegate's letter was His Grace's utter failure to appreciate the value of free speech on public policy matters in an American academic setting. Orthodox or specious theology was not an issue here, though McMahon's habit of appearing to speak for the magisterium of the church in a public way must have displeased the apostolic delegate. The danger to be avoided, as Cicognani saw it, was public dissemination of faculty statements on public policy possibly viewed as objectionable by some Catholic religious authorities or as embarrassing to a Catholic university administration. The only way to protect against that sort of danger was for faculty employed at Catholic universities to say nothing at all in print or in public speeches about public policy issues. Such matters were better left to those vested with the authority to deal with them.

Newsweek's reporting of McMahon's mission must have annoyed the apostolic delegate in a special way. The praise heaped upon McMahon, a mere layman, in the religion section of *Newsweek* for his so-called mission must have struck Cicognani as overdone and misplaced. In any case, when the apostolic delegate decided to write to O'Donnell in early August, McMahon's insistence that Communism was a lesser menace than Hitlerism and that military necessity justified massive air attacks on Rome must have struck His Excellency as a hopelessly naive and dangerous oversimplification.

— vii —

Conditions in Europe had changed radically since October 1941 when Cicognani prevailed upon Archbishop McNicholas to draft and issue a pastoral explaining that Pius XI's condemnation of Communism was never meant to apply to a war of defense or intended to be a moral direction for every possible set of future circumstances. The reality of politics and military affairs in Italy during the summer of 1943 was far more complicated and worrisome than McMahon's generalities would allow. To persons with family and friends in Rome at that time, Communism would certainly not have been considered as a minor menace.

Within a week of the American air raid on Rome on July 19, Mussolini was turned out of power. Immediately thereafter, a very uncertain situation developed in Rome. The Allied campaign in Sicily was not yet completed. The only Allied force capable of reaching the city was the Ninth Air Force, and no one wanted to see them again. Romans did not know what was going to happen next.

During July and August, the pope and other Vatican officials were extremely anxious to have Rome recognized by the Allies as an open city and spared future air attacks. They were also fearful of the new situation in Italy and were of a mind to interpret the overthrow of Fascism as a victory for Communism.[67] Vatican diplomats consistently overestimated Communist strength in and around Rome and often described all anti-Fascist groups operating there as being pro-Communist.[68]

During August, the fear of Communist-inspired disturbances in Rome bordered on near hysteria.[69] Diplomatic notes sent by the apostolic delegate in Washington to the State Department reflected the Vatican mood of fear and intense anxiety. For example, less than three weeks after the apostolic delegate wrote to O'Donnell about McMahon, he advised the State Department that any disturbances occurring in Rome would also engulf the Vatican.[70] Two days later, Cicognani sent a memorandum to the State Department citing the demonstrations following Mussolini's fall as evidence that Italian Communists were well organized, adequately armed and financed, and ready to move.[71] Reports were also sent to Washington from Rome about the insufficiency of police protection in Rome and the presence of Communists bands outside of the city.[72] Images of burning Russian and Spanish churches as well as memories of victimized priests and nuns came easily to minds disposed to expect the worst.

Very soon, however, German forces began moving into the major Italian cities. For many in Rome, they could not establish themselves in their city too quickly. Field Marshal Albert Kesselring, commander in chief of German Forces in Italy, was reputed to be a good Catholic and a disciplinarian. With Kesselring in charge, there would be few problems with German troops in Rome and fewer still with Italian Communists.

Anxiety and fear over what might happen in Rome when the Fascist regime collapsed no doubt inclined Cardinal Maglione in June to try and help the Spanish ambassador resolve a small problem with a lay professor employed at a Catholic university in the American Midwest. Later, he spoke anxiously to the German ambassador to the Vatican about the Communist danger threatening the clergy of Rome whenever the city might pass out of German control.[73] Considerations of that sort certainly persuaded Archbishop Cicognani in early August to add statements about cooperating with Communism and justifying the bombing of Rome to the list of McMahon's offending public remarks.

There is no doubt that during August, Cicognani was extremely concerned about the possibility of Communist-led disturbances occurring in Rome. At the same time, he was deeply involved in a major campaign to persuade the American government to cease all air attacks on Rome. The apostolic delegate's letter to O'Donnell about McMahon must be read in the context of that concern and of that campaign. The circumstances inspiring Cicognani's intrusion into the internal affairs of the University of Notre Dame were most extraordinary. It was not a piece of history that would be easily repeated. However, that intrusion occurred when it did only and precisely because Notre Dame was a Catholic university.

O'Donnell acknowledged receipt of the apostolic delegate's letter on August 11, 1943. He said nothing whatsoever about McMahon's well-established media prominence as a defender of Catholic policies and interests in America. O'Donnell simply informed Cicognani of his intention to confer with "the man in question" as soon as possible in the hope that the gentleman could be persuaded to mend his ways and cease making statements embarrassing to all concerned. "Naturally," he added, "no mention will be made of your letter." O'Donnell promised to send a full report after the conference had been held and concluded by observing that "in my opinion the individual in question is suffering from a Jehovah complex which often times characterizes cripples."[74]

— viii —

O'Donnell discussed Cicognani's letter with Fathers Cavanaugh and Carrico. Together, the president, vice president, and director of studies developed a set of procedures whereby McMahon would be required to obtain permission from Father Carrico before accepting an outside speaking engagement. In addition, the thesis to be presented at each outside speaking engagement also would have to be submitted to Father Carrico for approval.[75] O'Donnell and his counselors chose to call these procedures a *modus agendi,* not censorship. In their view, this *modus agendi* would become censorship only when and if permission to speak was denied or changes or deletions from McMahon's texts were required.[76] This narrowly drawn distinction defining where O'Donnell's *modus agendi* ended and censorship began may or may not have been philosophically defensible, but for most American academics of that time such a distinction was meaningless, an unpersuasive and unacceptable rationale for censorship. Nonetheless, O'Donnell and Carrico were determined to proceed with it and decided to meet with McMahon on August 16 and explain the new *modus agendi* to him.

According to McMahon's memorandum of this meeting, the session lasted about fifty minutes. O'Donnell was calm and kindly throughout, whereas Carrico was belligerent and insistent that something had to be done to check McMahon's "imprudent talk."[77] O'Donnell began by saying that the time had come to review McMahon's activities because during the past year his office had received a great many complaints about him. O'Donnell talked first about the cablegram sent to Stalin and wondered why he had sent it. McMahon answered that he had sent it for the sake of bringing the Russian and American people together. Whether or not Stalin ever read it was unimportant.[78]

Next, O'Donnell passed to the Franco matter. He asked McMahon what he had said, and shocked the professor by admitting that he had not seen the item in the *New York Times,* where the offending remarks had been reported. As a matter of fact, O'Donnell had even neglected to ask McMahon to bring a clipping of that item to the meeting. Notwithstanding the president's admitted ignorance in this matter, he raised a question that stuck in McMahon's mind as being most curious.

O'Donnell asked McMahon whether or not he had ever considered the possibility that his statements about Franco might have a bad effect on delicate international negotiations. McMahon responded by insisting that such a possibilty had been considered but had been dismissed as extremely unlikely. McMahon's purpose in speaking about Franco had been straightforward and simple. He merely wanted to demonstrate that American Catholics had not been deceived by the current propaganda line of the Spanish government. Then McMahon asked O'Donnell how his attention had been brought to the Franco matter. O'Donnell stated simply that a high official had informed him about it. McMahon noted in his memorandum of this meeting that O'Donnell had not said the person in question was a high government official.[79]

O'Donnell changed the subject and asked McMahon where he got the authority to presume to speak for American Catholics on such important policy matters. McMahon responded by claiming his judgments about the views of American Catholics were derived from informal surveys, personal interviews, and his reading of the Catholic press. At this point Carrico entered the discussion. He accused McMahon of complimenting Communism by saying, in his Springfield speech of the previous year, that it was only a minor menace to the world. He added that McMahon must stop his imprudent public remarks or quit the faculty. When McMahon asked which of his remarks were imprudent, Carrico mentioned describing Franco as a Fascist as one example. McMahon responded heatedly that he had given the matter some study, and, in his opinion, Franco was a Fascist.[80]

O'Donnell intervened and took charge of the discussion. He explained his proposed *modus agendi*. Because of the sharp exchanges between Carrico and McMahon, the president must have had some second thoughts about the intended role of Carrico in the *modus agendi*. In any event, O'Donnell only asked McMahon to think over the procedures just explained before making a decision. The president even suggested that perhaps McMahon himself might be able to come up with an alternative set of procedures that would work better. The purpose of this entire process was not censorship. It was to find some effective mechanism for disassociating McMahon's controversial public policy positions from the good name of Notre Dame. After expressing great disappointment over what was happening to him and to the university, McMahon left O'Donnell's office. He went directly home and set to writing a memorandum on what had transpired.[81]

— ix —

McMahon thought about what O'Donnell and Carrico had said to him at the meeting for about a week before responding. It is not clear at this time how many Notre Dame people he took counsel from, but Father Philip S. Moore, C.S.C., head of the philosophy department, appears to have been one. Also at this time, McMahon wrote to Archbishop Lucey indicating that he was in serious trouble with the university administration over his public advocacy work and that his career at Notre Dame might be ended very soon.[82] In any case, whether on his own or upon advice of others, McMahon concluded that heavy pressure from one or more American prelates had been applied to O'Donnell to silence or otherwise limit his public advocacy activities. That type of pressure had been applied by Archbishop McNicholas in the fall of 1941, and now in the summer of 1943 McMahon assumed that the present crisis was probably more of the same.

There is no evidence at this stage of affairs that McMahon suspected the source of the pressure was the pope's representative in America. Moreover, as a thorough-going papalist and consistent defender of papal policies in most situations, the possibility that the apostolic delegate would be against him was unimaginable. Consequently, McMahon picked up on O'Donnell's suggestion about offering an alternative procedure to the president's *modus agendi*. He decided to try and neutralize conservative complaints against him by obtaining endorsements of his activities from liberal bishops and monsignors as well as from prominent citizens.[83]

With that end in view, McMahon wrote to O'Donnell on August 20, stating first that he could not submit to the conditions laid down in the president's *modus agendi*. He described those conditions as "humiliating censorship" and discriminatory because no other lay faculty member was to be subjected to them. In any case, he could not take seriously the contention that his efforts to win the war and bring about a better world order conflicted with the interests of the university. If the present difficult situation was just a matter of negative letters sent to the president's office, he would be happy to ask friends from all over the country and from all walks of life to have 1,000 supportive letters sent to the university within a month's time.

However, as an alternative proposal, McMahon offered to ask Archbishops Lucey and Stritch, Monsignors John A. Ryan and Francis Haas, the Honorable Joseph E. Davies, Thomas Lamont, Marshall Field, Harold Ickes, and Claude A. Pepper to wire O'Donnell their respective judgments about the effect of his public advocacy activities on the well being and good name of the Catholic Church, the United States, and the university. Of course, O'Donnell could contact any of these men directly. If any of those reverend gentlemen, distinguished public servants, and private citizens gave an unfavorable judgment on his work, he would resign at once. If their responses were favorable, then he should be free to continue his activities as before. McMahon concluded by mentioning a recent speech of his wherein he had pleaded for a major effort to save the Jews of Europe. He suspected that O'Donnell had probably already received letters "denouncing me for having sold out to the Jews."[84] In a letter dated August 25, O'Donnell thanked McMahon for sending him an alternative proposal but rejected it. In the president's judgment, McMahon's proposal did not provide the kind of protection for the good name of Notre Dame that he was duty-bound to ensure. Moreover, there was no need to try this matter before the bar of national opinion. The present case was between a faculty member and the president of the university and should be resolved there.[85]

Also in this letter, once again O'Donnell tried to explain the position of the university in the entire matter. First, O'Donnell denied any intention to curtail McMahon's exercise of free speech. His concern was no more and no less than to keep the name of Notre Dame as much as possible out of the controversies with which McMahon had become identified. O'Donnell wanted both sides, "you or those opposed to you," to cease employing the name and influence of Notre Dame on behalf of their respective causes. Notwithstanding Carrico's earlier observations about McMahon's imprudent talk, O'Donnell insisted that neither the prudence, validity, or nonvalidity of McMahon's positions were at issue. Notre Dame had been in the past and was in the present being associated in the public mind with McMahon's positions and that association was what O'Donnell wanted to break.[86]

O'Donnell asked McMahon to reconsider the original *modus agendi* in the hope that he could see his way clear to accept the conditions set down in it. The president invited McMahon once again to come to his office for another conference, and then concluded with the hope that he would not "take a stand in opposition to what I consider to be a fulfillment of duty."[87]

Before sending his letter of August 25 to McMahon, O'Donnell gave a copy of it to Carrico for advice about possible amendment or improvement. In this instance, Carrico was not much help. He clearly disliked McMahon and was not disposed toward compromises of any sort. Carrico believed that "in view of possible developments," O'Donnell's letter "dealt with the case as well as one could." He doubted whether the letter would "get a proper response and serve the delicate purpose intended."

This failure, Carrico concluded, "will be no fault of yours and this letter will be evidence of your utmost efforts to clear up the difficulty."[88]

O'Donnell sent off the letter as written, and two weeks later he had another conference with McMahon. On this occasion, McMahon moved a bit toward a compromise. He presented a second counterproposal. McMahon offered to send all of his press releases to the president's office or to anyone that O'Donnell might suggest. Also, he offered to meet occasionally with Father William A. Bolger, C.S.C., professor of economics, and discuss with him questions relating to his public advocacy activities. McMahon professed great respect for Bolger as a priest, a member of the Congregation of Holy Cross, a friend, and most of all for his judgment on political and social matters. From seeking the counsel of man like Father Bolger, McMahon expected only profit. Of course in the end, only McMahon would have responsibility for the content of his own public pronouncements. Bolger's role would be only that of a valued consultant.[89]

O'Donnell asked McMahon to submit a written memorandum to him detailing this counterproposal, and O'Donnell promised to take it up with his counselors. Next, O'Donnell and McMahon discussed the charges against the professor, and O'Donnell attempted to explain how the general character of his work jeopardized university interests. McMahon made clear that any review procedure involving Carrico would be difficult.[90] During this discussion, McMahon kept asking precisely how his speaking and writing on war and peace issues jeopardized university interests, and O'Donnell kept asserting that it had. After about forty minutes of desultory conversation of this sort, O'Donnell ended the meeting. McMahon went off to draft his second counterproposal.[91]

Shortly after this second conference with McMahon, O'Donnell received a strong but carefully worded letter from Archbishop Lucey. The archbishop admitted to being very disturbed by what was happening to his friend at Notre Dame. He praised McMahon for maintaining the essence of the papal peace program during a time when the pitiful spirit of isolationism and reprehensible antipathy toward the English people and toward other races characterized the thinking of many American Catholic leaders.

Lucey noted that the Jesuit fathers through their weekly periodical *America* had given an unfortunate leadership to Catholics in this country in years past. They had been thinking very poorly in the fields of industrial relations and international politics. Some of their editorials before Pearl Harbor had embodied abominable theology and poor patriotism. Of late, however, the good fathers appear to have undergone a reformation and have seen the light at long last.[92] The archbishop hoped that the priests and brothers of Holy Cross at this late date would not achieve a reformation that faced the wrong way. Prestige had come to Notre Dame because McMahon was working there. The vast majority of intelligent Catholics, he warned, would condemn you if McMahon were forced to leave. He hoped that no drastic action had already been taken and that there was still time to work out a formula that would satisfy both parties.[93]

O'Donnell responded to Lucey promptly.[94] O'Donnell argued that censorship was not involved in any aspect of this controversy. O'Donnell stated that his sole purpose was to develop a *modus agendi* that would separate McMahon's personal views on controversial public issues from the university and thereby protect the good name of Notre Dame from identification with controversy. The conditions set down in that *modus agendi*, O'Donnell insisted, were reasonable. Resolution of the matter now rested entirely with Dr. McMahon. If the good professor, O'Donnell added, accepted the conditions of the *modus agendi*, he could remain a member of the faculty. Otherwise, the president concluded, "he automatically excises himself in accordance with [a] clause in his official contract."[95] Clearly, there was nothing that the archbishop could do for his friend at Notre Dame.

Unaware of the Lucey-O'Donnell exchange and of how unlikely the prospects were for genuine compromise, McMahon completed his second counterproposal and sent it off to O'Donnell on September 14. In this proposal he was as firm in his position as O'Donnell had been in his letter to Lucey. McMahon made very clear that he would not even "entertain the thought of submitting my future public pronouncements to censorship."[96] He explained the role that Father Bolger or someone like him would play as a friendly consultant and expressed hope that this proposed arrangement would prove satisfactory. Moreover, if for some reason Bolger was unwilling or unable to take on this role, McMahon had three other Holy Cross priests in mind as possible alternatives—Fathers Philip S. Moore, C.S.C., head of the philosophy department; John C. McGinn, C.S.C., also a colleague in the philosophy department; and James H. MacDonald, C.S.C., of the English department.[97]

McMahon concluded the memorandum by pointing out that during ten years of teaching at Notre Dame no complaints had ever been made against him until he spoke out against the Nazis, Fascists, and anti-Semites abroad and at home. My enemies are powerful and endowed with great subtlety, he wrote; it "is to the credit of the authorities at Notre Dame that they have resisted all pressures—however powerful—up to the present."[98] He had no idea how accurate this assessment of O'Donnell's situation was.

Because a well-respected Holy Cross priest had been introduced into the McMahon problem, O'Donnell had to think seriously and carefully about McMahon's second counterproposal before responding to it. As a matter of fact, he took ten days to prepare a reply. McMahon's scheme to use Father Bolger as an occasional consultant on his public advocacy activities was clearly an effort toward compromise, which O'Donnell recognized and appreciated. However, as envisaged by McMahon, the consultative role assigned to Bolger was no solution for O'Donnell's problem with McMahon's numerous and well-reported outside speaking engagements. That problem was how to develop a procedure that would prevent recurrence of incidents such as the anti-Franco interview reported in the *New York Times* and statements in *Newsweek* about the morality of American Catholics supporting public policies of cooperating with Soviet Russia for the sake of world peace. O'Donnell had promised the apostolic delegate that the McMahon problem would be resolved. Employment of Bolger in an occasional consultative role would not and could not obtain the assurance against recurrence that O'Donnell required. Only an acceptance by McMahon of censorship or his departure from the university could provide that.

On September 24, O'Donnell sent off an answer to McMahon's counterproposal. He thanked McMahon for his suggestions about Father Bolger but respectfully declined to accept them. While Father Bolger was an excellent priest and an admirable gentleman, he was not a member of the university administration. In O'Donnell's judgment, only a member of the university administration was in a position to pass judgment on the "fundamental proposition," namely, protection of the good name of Notre Dame.[99]

Reacting perhaps to Archbishop Lucey's letter of September 10, 1943, O'Donnell added that because he wanted McMahon to continue teaching at Notre Dame, he was prepared to designate Father John J. Cavanaugh, vice president, in place of Father Carrico, as his representative in the *modus agendi*. For O'Donnell, that was the absolute limit of compromise in this matter. He concluded his letter by insisting that the proposed *modus agendi* was no threat to academic freedom. Notre Dame was a privately controlled university where "academic freedom, in the right sense of the phrase, has been and always will be maintained."[100]

Fearful of what McMahon may have heard or suspected or perhaps just protesting too much, O'Donnell added that no pressure group or individual will have "any influence on me, or my representative, when it comes to dictating what is best for the interests of the university and the protection of her good name."[101] As this business moved toward final resolution, O'Donnell tried very hard to convince McMahon and those members of the faculty giving him counsel that no outside agencies were involved.

With this letter of September 24, O'Donnell in effect brought this matter to a conclusion. McMahon was profoundly disappointed. His ten-year career at Notre Dame was about to end. He made a copy of O'Donnell's letter and sent it to Father Moore with a notation that he could not accept the president's modified *modus agendi*. "I know nothing of Father Canvanaugh's views on political questions," he wrote. "His position [as vice president] would make the thing official censorship."[102] There was not much more that anyone could say or do except to try to seek clarification of precisely what the modified *modus agendi* required.

McMahon wrote to O'Donnell on October 5 regretting that his proposal involving Father Bolger had been rejected. He confessed complete confusion about just how his work had injured the name of Notre Dame. If the content of his opinions was not the problem, as he had been told, why had it become so necessary for an official representative of the president of the university to review and approve his speeches before he could deliver them?[103]

More important for the moment, however, were the practicalities of the *modus agendi*. Before deciding one way or the other about the future, McMahon wanted to know for certain, first, whether all of his speaking engagements had to be approved by O'Donnell's representative, and, two, whether all of his speeches had to be approved as to their content by the same representative. Clarification came at once. McMahon was correct in his understanding of the *modus agendi*. All speaking engagements had to be approved as did the content of all speeches and press releases. "Now," O'Donnell concluded, "there should be no doubt in your mind about my official instructions."[104] There was none.

McMahon considered his situation and discussed it with friends for about three weeks until October 22, when he gave O'Donnell his final answer to the president's plan to regulate his public activities. The conditions laid down, McMahon wrote, "are violative of free speech and academic freedom. I would have, frankly, small respect for the college professor who would submit to them."[105] He sent off with this letter copies of press releases for two forthcoming speeches in Milwaukee and St. Louis. "That is all," he concluded, "I can honorably do."[106]

— x —

While awaiting a response from O'Donnell, McMahon turned his attention to what he called the continuing fight for freedom in America.

Sporadic anti-Semitic incidents had been occurring in the Northeast for about eighteen months, but charges of organized anti-Semitic activity in Boston were made by the attorney general of Massachusetts in October. Anxious to become the next governor of the state, the attorney general demanded several immediate corrective measures including removal of the present chief of police of Boston.[107] Details of about forty incidents occurring during the past year and a half had been widely reported in the Boston press. However, a feature story about anti-Semitism in the city published in *PM* on October 18, 1943, created a political uproar in Boston.

The *PM* story alleged that an organized campaign of terrorism was in progress against Jewish boys and girls in the Dorchester section of the city. The article implied that a full-scale pogrom was about to overwhelm the Jewish community of Boston. The *PM* story charged further that this campaign of terrorism had been underway for eighteen months without interference from civic authorities, that is, the governor, the mayor, and the police department had maintained a hands-off policy despite numerous protests.[108]

Governor Saltonstall challenged the veracity of the *PM* story and actually ejected the author of it from a press conference.[109] He instructed John F. Stokes, state commissioner of public safety, to head a commission of prominent Protestant, Catholic, and Jewish leaders to inquire into all of the allegations and report their findings. The Stokes Commission worked quickly and reported its findings on November 9, 1943. The commission reported no evidence of an organized campaign of violence against Jews in the Boston area. The average age of participants in the incidents investigated was 16.5. However, the widespread circulation of anti-Semitic literature in the city certainly suggested organized activity of another sort. The police were criticized for lax and occasional improper performance of their duties.[110]

McMahon had followed developments in Boston largely through articles and stories carried in the *New York Times* and *PM* rather than from a reading of the Boston press. He appears to have accepted the charges as presented in *PM* as facts. In any case, McMahon decided to intervene in the Boston situation directly and immediately. He sent a strong letter condemning anti-Semitism from a Catholic perspective to the *Boston Herald*. The paper published McMahon's letter on November 4, 1943, five days before the Stokes Commission reported.

Under a headline of "Anti-Semitism a Blot and a Stain" and signed with his name and identification as an associate professor of philosophy at the University of Notre Dame, McMahon expressed profound shock about the anti-Semitic outbursts occurring in Boston. While recognizing that only a small minority of Bostonians were culpable as participants, he wondered about the motivations of the unfortunate people responsible for such actions. McMahon insisted that anti-Semitic behavior of the sort reported in Boston was contrary to the principles of Americanism and to the dictates of the Christian religion.[111]

Next, McMahon quoted from Pope Pius XI's unequivocal statement of 1938 that anti-Semitism was a movement in which Christians could take no part whatsoever. He argued further that one could encourage the evil of anti-Semitism not only by outward action but also by silence when one should speak. It was this general silence in Boston that McMahon found more frightening than overt anti-Semitic actions. Conscience required that he stigmatize the incidents in Boston for what they were— a blot not merely upon Boston, but upon America, and a stain upon all Christendom.[112] While in this instance McMahon's attack on the city of Boston was based upon inadequate local knowledge and perhaps even misinformation, it was total and unsparing. At least, it was perceived that way by many Catholics, both lay and cleric, throughout the city. Several letters protesting McMahon's uninformed intervention into Boston religious and racial affairs were soon on their way to South Bend.

However, what captured local attention at Notre Dame in early November 1943 was not letters received by O'Donnell. It was a letter sent by the president of the university, after lengthy consultation with his advisors, to McMahon on November 5, 1943, and which immediately became public. In this letter of November 5, O'Donnell employed almost the same language used in his letter sent to Archbishop Lucey on September 16. O'Donnell stated that on the basis of McMahon's letter of October 22 to him, "it is clear . . . that you are automatically withdrawing from the faculty of the University of Notre Dame. It is with regret, therefore, that I accept your resignation, and, in doing so, I wish you well in your future endeavors." O'Donnell enclosed a check for $308.90, which covered McMahon's salary until December 6, a full month of severance pay.[113]

The next day, November 6, McMahon responded with a telegram stating, "Have not resigned . . . must assume that I have been discharged because of refusal to accept conditions."[114] The McMahon problem had not been resolved, only transformed. A firestorm of negative publicity, the worst public relations disaster in the history of the university, was about to begin.

— 9 —

FIRESTORM

B y the fall of 1943, over 85 percent of the men enrolled at Notre Dame were navy trainees. None of those trainees nor the few hundred civilian students returning to the campus, nor most of the faculty and staff suspected that Notre Dame would shortly become the center of an intensely negative and sometimes hateful publicity storm. That publicity storm would severely damage the reputation of Notre Dame in American academic circles for years and would even impugn the patriotism of the university's leadership. To be sure, when the fall semester began, all Notre Dame students, faculty, and staff had reasons to expect that national publicity might be sharply focused upon them but not because of a dispute between their president and a professor. Rumors and reports from the Cartier football practice field strongly suggested that Leahy's team in 1943 would be the best since Rockne's last year. War or no war, a national championship for the Notre Dame football team was a distinct possibility. That was news, that was important.

During the first six games, the team played so well that all preseason expectations were surpassed. As a T-formation quarterback and as a passer, Bertelli was brilliant, throwing ten touchdown passes in six games. Under Bertelli's direction, Notre Dame overran Pittsburgh, 41 to 0. The previous year's defeat by Georgia Tech was avenged, 55 to 13. Mighty Michigan was humbled, 35 to 12. Wisconsin was put aside easily, 50 to 0. Next, Illinois was routed, 47 to 0. Then, on October 30 in Cleveland before 78,000 people, Bertelli's strong arm and powerful running by a freshman halfback, Bob Kelly, disposed of a strong Navy team, 33 to 6. However, after that game the road to national championship glory suddenly became obstructed. Bertelli had played his last football game in Notre Dame uniform. The Marine Corps transferred Bertelli to active duty in San Diego.

Sportswriters speculated that with Bertelli gone, Notre Dame's string of one-sided victories over all previous opponents would end. Moreover, the moment of truth for the Notre squad without Bertelli was at hand. Leahy's men would have to confront an excellent Army team in Yankee Stadium on November 6 with a young, untested quarterback, John Lujack. For Leahy, for Coach Blaik of Army, and especially for Lujack, this game in Yankee Stadium would be an occasion for great personal emotion and an afternoon of high drama. It would be such a day because in the spring of 1941, Lujack had accepted an appointment to West Point to enter the military academy and play football for Blaik. Under controversial circumstances and at the last moment, Leahy persuaded Lujack to come to Notre Dame and play for him. Ironically, Lujack's first game appearance was against Blaik and the West Point team.

In Notre Dame football lore November 6, 1943, was a day to remember. For Coach Blaik, it was a day he would never forget. Lujack's debut as a T-formation quarterback was exceptional. While he did not persuade Notre Dame supporters to forget about Bertelli, they surely did not miss him. Notre Dame could win football games against strong teams without their star quarterback because they had another star waiting to replace him. Notre Dame defeated Army handily before 75,000 people in Yankee Stadium in a lopsided game, 26 to 0.

Lujack completed eight out of sixteen passes and was personally responsible for scoring three touchdowns, two by passes and one by running. Bob Kelly was unstoppable, running through the Army line and around it almost at will. The huge Notre Dame line so harried Army's celebrated running backs—Glenn Davis, Max Minor, and Douglas Kenna—that the team managed only 119 yards rushing against Notre Dame. Moreover, all game statistical advantages went to the South Bend team. Blaik's West Pointers were outplayed and outcoached.

As Allison Danzig told the story of the game in the *New York Times*, Notre Dame "had humbled one of the best Army teams in years."[1] Clearly at the end of the day on November 6, Notre Dame possessed the best intercollegiate football team in the country. Back in South Bend, Fathers O'Donnell and Cavanaugh were able to take considerable comfort from that but in the weeks ahead from not much else.

— ii —

McMahon must have contacted the editors at *PM* on Friday, November 5, only moments after he had received O'Donnell's termination letter and final paycheck. He told them about what had happened at the university, and they agreed to do a major story on it. James T. Howard was assigned the job, and he set himself to the task at once.[2] Howard interviewed McMahon by telephone and in the course of that interview McMahon simply read to Howard portions of the memoranda that he had written after his August and September meetings with O'Donnell.

After finishing with McMahon, Howard immediately contacted the the Notre Dame publicity office and asked for a statement explaining the university's position in the matter. The publicity office was unprepared for any such inquiry and refused to say anything to Howard about the event.[3] That inquiry from Howard set off two days of frenetic activity in the administration building. James Armstrong, director of the publicity office, pressed O'Donnell to prepare a statement that would clarify the university's position, and the two of them worked frantically over the weekend to complete a statement for release on Monday, November 8, in time for publication in most papers on November 9. For these reasons, Howard's story, published in *PM* on November 8, appeared without any input from the university.

PM was the first paper to publish a detailed account of the event. It scooped the *New York Times* and all other national newspapers by a full day and had its story out before the Notre Dame publicity office released O'Donnell's statement about the case.[4] Generally, Howard's story represented McMahon as a victim of an irrational speaker's policy unfairly administered. He contended it was unfairly administered in the sense that isolationist and conservative faculty such as Father O'Brien and Dean Manion had been allowed to speak their minds in public freely, whereas McMahon had been frequently admonished to stop his public advocacy activities, sometimes harassed, and in the end fired for exercising his constitutional right of free speech. The only new information in the Howard account was McMahon's disclosure that his connection with Notre Dame was definitely ended. For the future, he planned to catch his breath and then start over somewhere else.[5]

From O'Donnell's perspective, the most annoying aspect of *PM*'s coverage of this case was not what Howard had said in the story, because O'Donnell in effect confirmed much and contradicted none of it in his statement prepared over the weekend and released on the day the article appeared. The most threatening aspect of *PM*'s involvement was what the paper might print next. Somehow, somewhere, the editors of *PM* had heard rumors that the Holy See was behind the effort by university authorities to censor McMahon's public pronouncements. The editors wasted no time seeking out confirmation.

On Monday, November 9 *PM* sent telegrams to O'Donnell and to the superior general of the Congregation of Holy Cross in New York City requesting a confirmation or denial that the Holy See had requested university authorities to censor McMahon. The source of this rumor is unclear, but it was not Notre Dame. At the university, the roles of the cardinal secretary of state in Rome and of the apostolic delegate in Washington in initiating university action against McMahon was a well-kept secret.[6] Most likely, the source of the rumor was the apostolic delegate himself or someone on his staff.

It is clear that the interest of the Holy See and the action of the apostolic delegate in this case was known to at least one member of the staff of the National Catholic Welfare Conference in Washington.[7] The problem of how to prevent public disclosure of the involvement of Vatican officials and of Cicognani was discussed at a meeting on November 28 between Father Christopher O'Toole, C.S.C., superior of the Holy Cross House of Studies in Washington and Father Raymond McGowan of the National Catholic Welfare Conference, a longtime friend of McMahon and colleague in the Catholic Association for International Peace.[8] McGowan suggested to O'Toole, that under the right circumstances and if approached by a priest he knew and trusted, McMahon might be persuaded to cooperate in preventing public disclosure of a direct Vatican involvement in this matter.[9]

It is extremely unlikely that McGowan ever approached McMahon with such a proposition for the very good reason that by the end of November, O'Donnell was sick to death of the matter and refused to worry about more bad publicity. Matters would just have to run their course.[10] That McMahon had heard the rumor about the involvement of the Vatican in his problems at Notre Dame is fairly certain. The editors at *PM* would have told him about the rumor if he had not heard of it from other sources. Whether McMahon would have believed such a rumor without further confirmation is another issue. Ardent papalist that he was and continued to be after leaving Notre Dame, he was more disposed to consider General Franco or perhaps some American prelates rather than the Holy See as the true authors of his difficulties.

For O'Donnell, deciding how to respond to the *PM* telegram was perhaps the most anxiety-laden moment of the entire crisis. The superior general, Father Albert F. Cousineau, was no help. From his office in New York City he simply sent O'Donnell his copy of the *PM* telegram without any recommendation, trusting that the president would do what the situation required and what was best for the university.[11] O'Donnell had promised the apostolic delegate complete confidentiality in this matter, so he could not tell the truth. At the same time, O'Donnell could not lie directly because he did not know what the editors of *PM* actually knew about Vatican involvement or what sort of confirmation they might have. He had to deny Vatican involvement categorically without risking possible disclosure as a discovered liar. O'Donnell's chosen way out of this moral and practical dilemma turned out to be clever, if not entirely honest. In his telegram to *PM*, O'Donnell simply stated that "No one but myself responsible for position university has taken in the McMahon case."[12] While he gave no explicit answer to the *PM* request for a confirmation or denial of the rumor, the editors accepted O'Donnell's response as a denial and followed this aspect of the story no further.

In this instance, O'Donnell's interior coping mechanisms had been severely tested. The anxiety levels of the last few days had been very high, and stress began to take its toll. When O'Donnell wrote to Cousineau on November 12 to explain how the *PM* matter had been handled, he included a copy of the official statement of the university's position in the McMahon case that he and Armstrong had drafted over the weekend and released on Monday, November 8. Believing that this statement would clarify the university's position and effectively counter whatever McMahon and his friends at *PM* or elsewhere might say against Notre Dame, he slipped in a vicious joke about McMahon's physical handicap. With the official university statement now released, O'Donnell noted to Cousineau, "Now he hasn't even a good leg to stand on, and I use this expression with utmost charity."[13] The strain of developing the response to the *PM* telegram showed.

In addition to contributing information for the Howard story in *PM*, McMahon prepared a statement giving his version of the reasons of why he had been dismissed from the university. That statement as well as the one prepared by O'Donnell and Armstrong was released on November 8. Both statements appeared in the *New York Times* and in other newspapers on the following day, with McMahon claiming that he had been discharged while O'Donnell asserted that his most newsworthy faculty member had resigned.[14]

Stating that he had refused a demand by university authorities to submit texts of his speeches and press releases for prior approval before delivering or releasing them, McMahon insisted that such conditions violated the principles of free speech and academic freedom. Because they believed that his efforts to win the war and the peace had in some fashion harmed the good name of the university, McMahon continued, Notre Dame authorities had discharged him. Next, he recounted details of the negotiations between himself and O'Donnell over the previous three months and stated directly that no issues of Catholic faith or morals had ever been involved. While he would cast no aspersions upon the personal integrity or patriotism of the university authorities responsible for this end result, he questioned seriously their judgment about the meaning of academic freedom and their interpretation of the effect of his public advocacy activities on the good name of the university. He questioned also their appreciation of political factors in world affairs.[15]

McMahon recognized that over the past few years powerful pressure had been exerted on university authorities to silence him. He was grateful to the administration for having resisted such pressure for so long. The specific accusations against him, he added, were vague and insubstantial, namely, that he had called Franco a Fascist and had declared Communism a minor menace to the world compared to Nazism. University authorities had told him that they did not want the name of Notre Dame associated with the promulgation of those views. "There was no personal animosity involved," he concluded, "simply a difference in the meaning of free speech."[16]

O'Donnell's statement was in effect a response to questions about the affair put to Armstrong by Howard on November 6 but unanswered at that time. Howard's inquiry had forced O'Donnell and Armstrong to prepare a statement and release it as soon as possible. O'Donnell had a difficult case to argue and he knew it. He anticipated what the reactions of the general American academic community to the circumstances of McMahon's departure from the university would be and refused to worry about them. Similarly, when preparing his statement, he gave virtually no thought to probable reactions of the Notre Dame faculty or to possible responses by them to a most extraordinary mid-term dismissal of one of their own. Faculty docility in this entire affair was assumed.

The audience to which O'Donnell directed his statement was the American Catholic community at large. He wanted to convince them that in this matter university authorities had done the right thing. Moreover, he employed a mode of argument that they would recognize, understand, and accept. He tried to defend and justify his actions by redefining some of the key terms in the controversy with McMahon and by drawing distinctions.

O'Donnell began his statement by insisting that "obviously there was no intent to violate freedom of speech or academic freedom, rightly understood, by an institution which has fostered these freedoms for a hundred years."[17] Also obvious, he continued, vigorous and prudent efforts to win the war and the peace were not out of harmony with the policies of an institution noted for its traditional patriotism and which today was devoting three-quarters of its energies and facilities to the war effort. According to O'Donnell, a rising volume of protests for some months indicated that, wittingly or unwittingly, Dr. McMahon's public pronouncements on matters that many Americans considered to be controversial were being fortified by his identification with the university and in many instances had been interpreted as university positions. Furthermore, it has been a longstanding policy at Notre Dame that only the president of the university "may appropriately express the university's position on such matters whenever expression was considered advisable."[18]

University authorities, O'Donnell continued, have always regarded Dr. McMahon as a competent professor of philosophy and like all other faculty members, he was entitled to make personal opinions and expressions. However, "Our efforts to separate the University's identity on these questions from his own" made it "necessary to ask for his cooperation." The kind of cooperation requested, O'Donnell explained, was simply for Dr. McMahon "to submit a list of his speaking engagements, an account of his press releases, and the content of his addresses so that precautions might be suggested by the university administration for separating the name and influence of Notre Dame from Dr. McMahon's position. This single purpose of the procedure was made thoroughly clear to Dr. McMahon."[19]

Differences of opinion about McMahon's interpretations of Franco, Fascism, and Communism were really incidental to the primary issue, that is, "Notre Dame's unwillingness to continue to sponsor, by implication at least, such individual views of a faculty member." Dr. McMahon chose to withdraw from the faculty, O'Donnell concluded, "rather than to cooperate in employing the precautionary procedures suggested to him."[20]

Howard's story in *PM* and the published statements of McMahon and O'Donnell inspired other newspapers to send correspondents to South Bend for follow-up stories. Victor Riesel, staff correspondent for the *New York Post*, went to South Bend on Wednesday, November 10. He spent a day talking to McMahon, collecting facts and rumors from faculty, and seeking useable quotes from members of the Board of Lay Trustees assembled on campus for a scheduled meeting prior to attending the Saturday Notre Dame-Northwestern football game in Chicago.[21]

Riesel's story appeared in the *New York Post* on Friday, November 12, and like Howard's account, it depended heavily on McMahon's memoranda of the August and September meetings with O'Donnell. Riesel recounted the substance of those meetings and reported the widely held faculty opinion that Carrico had been responsible for persuading O'Donnell to take action against McMahon. Moreover, Riesel reported that neither McMahon nor his friends felt any bitterness toward O'Donnell. The president was generally perceived as an amiable, well-intentioned administrator caught between his own sincere desire for an atmosphere of academic freedom at Notre Dame and pressure from many alumni and isolationists who revered Rockne's memory and preferred a university renowned for football prowess.[22]

According to Riesel's campus sources, O'Donnell had been worried by what was described as a "mysterious Washington influence." The source and nature of this "mysterious Washington influence" was never identified. The basis for campus speculation about it was O'Donnell's widely known comment to McMahon at the August meeting—that the professor's remarks about Franco reported in the *New York Times* might have a bad effect on delicate international negotiations.[23]

Faculty interviewed by Riesel expected no strong pressure for McMahon's reinstatement from undergraduate students. Approximately 2,800 of the 3,200 students on campus were United States Navy trainees and under strict Navy discipline. The other 400 civilian students were principally young men under the draft age and more interested in football than academic freedom.[24]

Riesel's efforts to get interviews from some of the trustees were unsuccessful. James Armstrong kept Riesel away from them and issued a statement declaring that because the trustees were so busy rushing through their routine work and preparing to leave for the game in Chicago, they had no time for interviews about the McMahon case. Riesel concluded that the lay trustees were of the same mind as the civilian undergraduates, namely, "much too excited over tomorrow's crucial Notre Dame-Northwestern football game in Chicago to take time out to discuss civil liberties on campus."[25]

Indeed, Riesel's journalistic points about the apparent disinterest of Notre Dame lay trustees in the McMahon case and then attributing to them a preference for getting to a football game on time over answering a reporter's questions about civil liberties on campus were well made, but unfairly so. No one knows how the trustees felt about the case or about O'Donnell's handling of it because Armstong had so successfully isolated them from reporters.

The trustees understood clearly, even if Riesel did not, that their personal or collective views on the McMahon case were irrelevant. At Notre Dame a dispute between the president and a professor was an internal matter that only the president was empowered to resolve. Trustees had no authority, formal or informal, to interfere in the university's internal affairs and did not. Moreover, as a practical matter, trustees had no formal voice in the selection of a president and could not so long as this office was combined with that of local religious superior.

Consequently, there was simply no way for trustees to compel a president of Notre Dame to change his mind about anything or to try to discipline him if they had a mind to do so. In this case, there is no evidence of such a mind among any of the trustees. If outraged by O'Donnell's management of this affair, trustees could resign. None of them did.

However, Riesel was certainly correct about the high level of campus excitement about the Notre Dame/Northwestern football game on November 13. In view of campus aspirations for an undefeated season and possible selection as intercollegiate football national championship, this game was crucial. Many students, some faculty and staff, and some trustees traveled to Chicago to attend the game. All who went were delighted by the team's performance. Hopes for a national championship were kept alive when Notre Dame defeated Northwestern decisively, 25 to 6.

— iii —

Though McMahon had stated publicly several times that he had made no moves for reinstatement and would make none if freedom of speech was in any way compromised, Riesel did not think that all had been lost at Notre Dame. The cause of freedom of speech here, he believed, had two chances for vindication. First, many faculty believed that the embarrassment of this affair was too great for the country's most powerful Catholic leaders to endure. Faculty holding this opinion expected strong pressure from the hierarchy to resolve the matter in a more acceptable manner would force O'Donnell to reinstate McMahon. Second, other faculty believed salvation would come more readily from political princes than ecclesiastical ones. Faculty of this turn of mind intended to seek support for reinstatement from Frank Walker, chairman of the Democratic National Committee, postmaster general of the United States, confidant of President Roosevelt, and a Notre Dame lay trustee. Those faculty could not imagine that the man who had managed the silencing of Father Coughlin would not try to help McMahon and rally to the cause of preserving academic freedom at Notre Dame.

Faculty hoping for intervention from the bishops were disappointed. Strong public statements in support of McMahon were issued from the dioceses of Milwaukee, Pittsburgh, and St. Augustine but that was all. The well-known and always newsworthy archbishops of the East and Midwest, the great powerbrokers of the American Catholic Church, maintained a careful public silence on the matter. They did so either because they knew something about the cause of the problem that others did not, or because as outside agents in this matter they believed that intervention through public statement would be pointless and possibly even counterproductive.

This archepiscopal and episcopal silence appears to have been private as well as public. O'Donnell's correspondence during the time of this crisis contains no letters or news cuttings from bishops that were critical and only one cutting and one letter that were supportive of the university's position.

According to a news cutting from the *Catholic Courier* of Rochester, New York, James E. Kearney, bishop of Rochester, gave the the University of Notre Dame a vote of confidence for its handling of the McMahon affair. Speaking before guests at a Catholic high school who were assembled to hear a talk by Coach Frank Leahy, Bishop Kearney championed the academic reputation of the university in the McMahon matter.[26]

The bishop disclaimed any detailed knowledge of the case and tried to make his point with logic rather than with facts. He insisted that the university had behaved properly and correctly in dismissing its celebrated associate professor of philosophy. Academic freedom in a Catholic university such as Notre Dame, Bishop Kearney argued, could not mean unlimited freedom of speech. As a Catholic university, Notre Dame was committed to definite principles in philosophy, theology, and in the interpretation of history. Given this sort of commitment, professors at Notre Dame or at other Catholic institutions could not be left unbridled and permitted to speak as they wished on any subject. Commitment to definite principles, Bishop Kearney concluded, made criticism of the university's action in the McMahon matter illogical and unjust.[27] So much for factless logical arguments.

Bishop Gerard O'Hara of Savanah-Atlanta thanked O'Donnell for providing him with tickets for the Notre Dame-Northwestern football game and expressed "heartfelt sympathy regarding the McMahon affair."[28] We are all on your side in this unfortunate controversy he wrote, "and deplore the spirit shown by Professor McMahon." Then, perhaps emboldened by distance and ignorance, the bishop tried to console

O'Donnell with the thought that "Men of that strap are not real Catholics. They certainly haven't the mind of the Church. No wonder God hates pride so much."[29]

Of those few bishops who spoke out publicly for McMahon through their diocesan newspapers, their conception of the mind of the Church was far different from that offered by his excellency of Savanah-Atlanta. Bishop Hugh C. Boyle of Pittsburgh, speaking through an editorial in the *Pittsburgh Catholic,* condemned the dismissal of McMahon and described O'Donnell's publicly admitted capitulation to outside protests as a "sinister pronouncement indeed."[30]

The editorial raised what had become in recent days a most obvious question and for which no true answer would be forthcoming, namely, "From what sources did the protests come? What made them so weighty as to induce the university to impose censorship restrictions on one member of its faculty which it has not, as far as is known, placed on others?" Father O'Brien and the weekly periodical published at Notre Dame, *Ave Maria,* (described as a mouthpiece for the reactionary views of the *Chicago Tribune* and the Hearst publications) were cited as two such examples. By its official statement, the university had put itself in the indefensible position of having acted in this matter on behalf of certain unnamed forces.[31]

The editorial insisted further that McMahon's political positions were an open book. His views that Communism was a lesser menace to the world than Nazism at the present moment or that General Franco was a Fascist violated no Catholic teaching. As a matter of fact, McMahon had distinguished himself many times by his vigorous defense of the Church and its doctrines, the exchange of letters in the *New Republic* in June about the relationship between Catholicism and Fascism being the most recent example. It was a sad, perhaps even frightening, moment indeed to see McMahon's connection with one of the country's leading Catholic educational institutions ended because he stood honestly and bravely for Catholic ideals.[32]

The voice of Bishop John. J. Hurley of Saint Augustine on the McMahon affair was heard loud and clear in an editorial, most likely written by the bishop himself, in the *Florida Catholic* on November 20, 1943. This editorial was briefer than the one in Pittsburgh but was no less trenchant. It had the advantage of being picked up by the *New York Times* and read throughout the Northeast. The editorial condemned McMahon's dismissal and described him as a "champion of the best interests of this country."[33]

McMahon's many forthright addresses and writings made him anathema, the editorial continued, to the "Crypto-Fascists in our midst. That of course is to his credit." That these "Crypto-Fascists" had succeeded in getting McMahon dismissed was a serious matter, all the more serious because an important Catholic university will be left in the undisputed possession of a "sorry assortment of peace-at-any-price voters, of America Firsters, and bitter anti-government men."[34]

Faculty hoping to enlist the persuasive powers of Frank Walker on behalf of McMahon's reinstatement were even more disappointed than those hoping for a major episcopal intervention. As Riesel reported on November 12, Walker had "given no aid as yet to McMahon's fight for academic freedom"[35] and gave none thereafter. To be sure, Walker met secretly in the Oliver Hotel with some of McMahon's friends on the morning of November 12. At this meeting, he was presented with what Riesel styled as "official documentary evidence" of university efforts to censor McMahon's attacks on General Franco and his anti-Nazi speeches.[36] The material presented to Walker consisted of portions of O'Donnell's correspondence with McMahon. Walker examined it but raised no hopes after reading it. He stated unequivocally that he could not and would not do anything about this case at the meeting of lay trustees scheduled for later in the day.[37]

As postmaster general, Walker had moved directly and decisively against Father Charles E. Coughlin, a bitter opponent of the Roosevelt administration, by banning his weekly news magazine *Social Justice* from the U.S. mail. Apparently, silencing an anti-Semitic, stridently isolationist Catholic opponent of the Roosevelt administration was one matter. Rescuing a devoted supporter and frequent public apologist for Roosevelt administration policies who happened to be in trouble with his clerical employers was something else entirely. Walker said nothing publicly and did nothing privately.

However, Walker's absolute neutrality and determined non-involvement turned out to be far less harmful to the cause of reinstatement than the private stance of his predecessor as chairman of the National Democratic Committee, James A. Farley. Farley wrote to O'Donnell on November 9 to thank him for supplying tickets to the Notre Dame-Army football game in New York. In his letter, Farley mentioned that he had been following the newspaper accounts of the McMahon case with interest and thought that O'Donnell's statement about it as reported in the papers was "appropriate and timely."[38]

It was probably fortuitous that neither Walker nor any of the archbishops were disposed to press for reinstatement of McMahon, because O'Donnell was absolutely determined that his decision in this matter would stand. As president of the university, he really had no choice. As his hiring of Coach Frank Leahy away from Boston College three years previously had demonstrated, at Notre Dame there were no precedents and certainly no institutional disposition for public admission of administrative error. That was never done. McMahon could not be reinstated without doing what was never done. The massive publicity surrounding the case had made reinstatement impossible.

O'Donnell tried to explain to one supportive alumnus about the finality of administrative actions and the current status of the case. He wrote, "Once an official decision has been reached in any case at Alma Mater she will not recede 'what though the odds be great or small.'"[39] In such a situation as this, O'Donnell continued, whenever the good name of Notre Dame was involved, "I defy anyone to challenge my right to take measures to protect it. With Sorin of old, I stand like the 'moveless rock,' firmly convinced that I have taken the proper action."[40]

Given this mindset, there was not much that anyone could say or do that would make a difference. O'Donnell had nailed his colors to the mainmast and would simply wait out the storm. He intended to stand by his public statement and would make no others. There would be no further explanations or clarifications, and he absolutely refused to be drawn into further controversy with anyone, publicly or privately, about any aspect of the case. After the appearance in the press of his statement and of the Howard and Riesel stories, for O'Donnell the matter was closed.

—   iv   —

At Notre Dame, scarcely any of the lay faculty were able to comprehend the depth of O'Donnell's intransigence in the McMahon case. Many believed that he could be moved. The statements issued by McMahon and O'Donnell and the news stories written by Howard and Riesel about what had happened were important news. Both statements and stories were widely read by faculty, carefully analyzed, and much discussed. O'Donnell's public admission that he had been persuaded to act against McMahon because of outside pressure inspired much speculation about the sources of that pressure. Some attributed McMahon's difficulties to local former-isolationist Republican businessmen.[41] Others suspected that conservative alumni or perhaps an offended prelate or two were behind it all. Despite the speculation as reported by Riesel about a "mysterious Washington influence," no one outside of O'Donnell's closest advisers would have reckoned the apostolic delegate as a precipitating cause.

As events were quick to show, O'Donnell's statement did not stand up well to a close reading. McMahon's history of difficulty with the president and with the director of studies over outside speaking activities were well known to many of the faculty. Anyone familiar with the Chicago press in May 1941 was aware that McMahon had been ordered by O'Donnell to cease addressing war issues at public meetings. The restraints imposed on McMahon in October 1941 as well as the threat to discharge him at that time were by no means secrets well kept. While McMahon's summary discharge certainly shocked faculty at Notre Dame at this time, it could not have surprised them. What surely surprised the faculty were the reasons O'Donnell offered for McMahon's dismissal. The president had said things in his statement that every member of the faculty knew were untrue. If O'Donnell indeed had fired McMahon for the reasons publicly stated, the president had crossed a line.

Freedom of speech and academic freedom, rightly understood or not, in 1943 were not highly valued in American Catholic colleges and universities generally or at Notre Dame in particular. Certain books were prohibited for theological, philosophical, or moral reasons. Certain subjects were not studied or discussed. To be sure, instances of official censorship in Catholic higher education were relatively rare because the rules and regulations relating to prohibited books and subjects were usually obeyed. Censorship for theological, philosophical, or moral reasons was largely self-imposed. Censorship of that sort were conditions of life and work in American Catholic higher education, and there was nothing particularly secretive or perceptibly oppressive about it.

However, censorship of political, social, or economic opinions perceived by university authorities as embarrassing or as politically incorrect was another matter entirely, especially in the midst of a great war waged against totalitarian tyranny. O'Donnell's attempted redefinition of political censorship as a request for cooperation or as precautionary procedures or as trying to distinguish between versions of academic freedoms, one rightly and the other wrongly understood, outraged many Notre Dame faculty. So many felt this way in fact that the assumed docility of the group utterly and immediately dissolved. What O'Donnell had done and said in this affair so embarrassed and demeaned the faculty and the university in American academic circles that no matter how risky to personal job security, some of the faculty decided to respond. For the first time in the history of the university, a group of faculty organized themselves in order to try to reverse a major administrative action. This organization turned out to be interdisciplinary and intercollegiate. Only the small and largely part-time law school faculty under the leadership of their very conservative dean and former isolationist, Clarence P. Manion, abstained.

When a report of McMahon's involuntary departure from the university appeared in the *South Bend Tribune* on November 8, friends and many colleagues immediately communicated their great sense of shock at what had happened and promised solidarity with him in the days ahead. One of the first of McMahon's friends to write was Vincent T. Fagan, a very devout Catholic, a man of strong Democrat political opinions, and a professor in the department of architecture. Fagan was deeply disturbed by O'Donnell's action and expressed the depth of that despair in a brief but moving letter to his friend.

Fagan could not believe that a man of such cultivated intelligence and deep religious faith as McMahon could be turned out of a Catholic university. "Your scholarship," Fagan continued, "has always been at the command of the Church and I cannot recall at any time when your voice was silent or hypocritical in matters of faith or of any of the truths implied in it." The present situation was deplorable, Fagan concluded, "and I would give a great deal to see it rectified."[42]

A few days later, November 12, when the firestorm of protest had begun to grow, Fagan wrote again attempting to assess the damage already done to the reputation of the university and to find some explanation for O'Donnell's behavior. Fagan complained that the bad publicity already generated only four days after the event had set back the university twenty-five years. In the short time since the first news stories appeared in the national press, Fagan had received four letters "ridiculing any ND pretense toward intelligence or ordinary honesty in matters academic or scientific." We all recognize, he added, that pressure was put on O'Donnell "from the anti-New Deal champions of the status quo, who expect to restore the old fashioned Hoover-Harding-Coolidge pattern—men like Bernie Voll, Pat Manion, Bishop Noll, Ernie the Medici and that ilk."[43]

If Notre Dame wanted an academic reputation, Fagan continued, the people here had to act in responsible ways. In Fagan's judgment, most of the Notre Dame faculty were willing and able to do just that. If a shortsighted, headstrong chap insisted on grabbing the bit in his teeth, Fagan concluded, "it will injure our task immeasurably—but it will not destroy the great facts of the main body of truth. If Luther didn't do it—Pepper [O'Donnell] can't. I grant you that both have tried. . . . Upon that rock it was built and neither the gates of hell nor the antics of clerics will prevail against it."[44] Fagan wrote with that tinge of bitterness that only disappointed and embarrassed true believers can know.

Fagan was, of course, wrong in his identification of a precipitating cause for the public relations disaster visited upon the university. In his mind, the cause had to be an important one, like the ambitions of an assumed local reactionary financial-industrial-clerical complex. Neither Fagan nor anyone else at Notre Dame at that time could have imagined how utterly trivial and unexamined by anyone in authority at the university the actual precipitating causes were.

Fagan's hope that the present deplorable situation regarding McMahon could be remedied was shared by many other Notre Dame faculty. Centered in the departments of history, English, politics, and philosophy in the College of Arts and Letters, a group of twenty-nine lay professors and a few clerical faculty members set about organizing a campaign to get McMahon reinstated.[45] As Dr. Willis Nutting of the history department, one of the leaders of this faculty protest group, explained to a clerical friend in Chicago, the group intended "to put on what pressure we can to change the situation. . . . We would like the authorities [here] to realize that they have touched a buzz saw."[46]

To set that buzz saw turning as fast as possible, Nutting and his friends pursued two strategies, one that was local and another of outreach. First, the local strategy was intended to force O'Donnell to face up to the absurdity of his publicly stated justification for discharging McMahon. They attempted to do this by sending a letter to the president formally requesting a clarification of just how much freedom of political expression Notre Dame faculty could expect to enjoy. Second, to secure maximum outreach for their campaign, individual members of the protest group contacted friends and acquaintances throughout the country who were prominent in Catholic affairs. They also approached men and women working in Catholic higher education, colleagues in private and public colleges and universities, as well as persons presumed to be sympathetic and influential in labor and professional organizations. This protest group asked for letters, especially letters from priest-professors. They wanted letters from Catholics and from prominent non-Catholics. They wanted letters to the press, letters to the university administration, and letters to themselves that could be shown in the proper quarters.[47]

M. A. Fitzsimons of the history department drafted the faculty protest letter, and twenty-nine lay professors drawn from all four colleges agreed to sign it. The signers were: E. W. Carey, James A. Corbett, Jose Corona, S. Leonard Dart, B. Finnan, M. A. Fitzsimons, W. Gurian, E. Guth, W. H. Hamill, Louis Hasley, F. A. Hermens, H. Lee Hope, Raymond P. Kent, Joseph Landin, A. N. Milgram, F. E. Moran, John F. Nims, Willis Nutting, Daniel Pedtke, L. E. Peterson, S. R. Price, A. S. Ryan, Rufus

298 — *Being Catholic, Being American*

Rauch, Philip Riley, Yves Simon, Richard Sullivan, W. Roy Utz, George S. Wack, and M. John Walsh.

One name conspicuous by its absence from the protest letter was that of Frank O'Malley. While O'Malley agreed absolutely with McMahon's foreign policy positions and had been appalled by his firing, he refused to sign the protest letter. He did so because of O'Donnell's personal kindnesses to him. O'Donnell had written several letters of recommendation for O'Malley to the Naval Department seeking a waiver of physical examination requirements so the young professor could become a commissioned officer in the U.S. Navy. O'Malley's eyesight was so poor that the waiver was never given. Yet, being the kind of man he was, O'Malley simply could not be publicly critical of a person who had tried so hard to get him into the navy. O'Malley's friends understood why he could not sign the protest letter and never faulted him for it.[48]

The letter was dated November 16, 1943, and expressed grave concern over university action against McMahon. It declared that none of the signers would have accepted the conditions of censorship which the precautionary procedures offered to McMahon implied. The signers asked for clarification of two points. First, they wanted to know how personal convictions could be expressed so that such convictions would not be identified as university positions. What was demanded beyond the usual disclaimer that one spoke only as an individual citizen and not for the university? Second, the protest group wanted to know what protection was available to faculty against outside complainants who, despite such a disclaimer, insisted on misrepresenting personal convictions as university positions.[49]

Believing from press statements that university action against McMahon had been taken because of mutual misunderstanding, the group urged the university to reconsider its decision. They concluded by declaring that the signers of this letter had acted out of a concern for their integrity as citizens of a democracy and as teachers in a great university. Moreover, determined to observe the university chain of command in this matter, the signers presented their letter addressed to Father O'Donnell as president to Father Carrico as director of studies for transmittal.[50]

Father Carrico read the letter but refused to accept it on the grounds that it was not an authentic letter. The names of the signers had been typed at the bottom of the page, not signed individually. Fitzsimons had to prepare another copy of the letter, obtain twenty-nine signatures, and then deliver this second signed copy to the director of studies. Father Carrico accepted this signed copy of the letter. However, O'Donnell and Carrico refused to run into the trap of attempting to define the limits of freedom of expression at Notre Dame that Fitzsimons and his friends had set. The president stayed firmly with his decision of trying to contain and end the controversy by refusing to engage in any more of it. No written acknowledgement of receipt of the letter or written response was ever sent.[51]

At the same time, an effort was made by persons outside of the university who were friendly to the local protest group to draw the naval officer training units operating at Notre Dame into the controversy. It was a fact that the university was completely dependent for economic survival on the revenues provided by these programs. Pressure from the navy on the university administration on behalf of McMahon and for the cause of free speech, it was thought, might be more effective than a protest letter from part of the lay faculty. It was a tactic worth trying.

However, the navy refused to become involved. As early as November 14, the officer in charge of the training units advised O'Donnell that the navy's only interest in Notre Dame was obtaining full compliance of its contract to provide educational services for the training programs in place here. So long as McMahon was replaced by a qualified and technically competent teacher, the navy's interest was protected.[52]

All Holy Cross priests assigned to Notre Dame were forbidden to make public statements or comments about the entire McMahon matter.[53] Only the president was authorized to speak for the university about the case. Virtually all of the Holy Cross priests closed ranks and rallied around the president at this moment of great crisis. Father Cousineau, the superior general, had sent a brief note of support and sympathy as early as November 10, 1943.[54] Father Raymond L. Murray, C.S.C., worried about the timing of McMahon's dismissal. He was fearful that some of the public might assume that McMahon's public and locally unpopular intervention into allegations of organized anti-Semitic activity in Boston would be considered as one of the causes of the dismissal. Murray had material which he believed would effectively counter any attempt to smear the university as being anti-Semitic.[55]

Father Cornelius Haggerty, C.S.C., a priest with very strong Irish nationalist and anti-British opinions and a colleague of McMahon in the philosophy department, congratulated O'Donnell for getting rid of him. According to Haggerty, McMahon had been a great detriment to the school, "both in his influence on the boys in the school and on our reputation abroad." Haggerty's Irish friends would be delighted with McMahon's departure. "This was well done."[56]

Only one Holy Cross priest at Notre Dame came close to breaking the ban on public comment on the McMahon case. Father Philip S. Moore, head of the philosophy department, managed to communicate his dissatisfaction with O'Donnell's action to a friend at another Catholic college without making an explicit statement to that effect.

Father E. C. Garvey, head of the philosophy department, and Father J. S. Murphy, registrar at Assumption College, Windsor, Ontario, long-standing friends of Moore, sent him a telegram on November 11, 1943, expressing their amazement and profound regret at the unfavorable light which the dismissal of McMahon had put upon Catholics and Catholic higher education. Moreover, Garvey insisted that Jacques Maritain, a recent visitor at Assumption College, shared their view. McMahon's positions regarding Fascism and Communism, Garvey continued, were similar to those of the leading integral humanists among the hierarchy. Surely, he added, Catholic educators should be free to apply Catholic principles to social and political fields. Unless some important disclosures had been concealed from the press, it would seem that a dangerous precedent was being established. If there is more to it, Garvey concluded, please let us know as we are getting in touch with McMahon.[57]

Moore responded by telegram at once. He promised to convey Garvey's strongly worded message to O'Donnell and stated that further disclosures, if any, would have to come from the president because no one else was authorized to speak. He concluded by declaring that he had no further facts, having been ignored by both sides during the transaction.[58] Of course, Garvey was absolutely right. An important disclosure had been concealed from the press, but O'Donnell had promised not to reveal it. The president gave no thought to answering Garvey's telegram. He simply filed it and tried to forget it, something he would be doing very often over the next three months. However, he would not forget Moore's reply to his friends in Canada. The president wanted to know what Moore had meant when he used the word "ignored" in his telegram to Garvey. Through his secretary, O'Donnell asked Moore for a further explanation.[59] Evidently Moore provided one that was satisfactory.

Not all of the lay faculty were sympathetic to McMahon or to the sending of a protest letter to the president. For example, the eminent mathematician Karl Menger informed O'Donnell that he shared many of the views expressed by McMahon. He had not joined the protest group because he had enjoyed complete freedom of speech at Notre Dame.[60] Others were deeply dismayed by the serious public relations damage being done to the university, and of course O'Donnell had some friends among the lay faculty. Also, there were men on the faculty who wanted the president to perceive them as a friend.

Professor T. Bowyer Campbell wanted to separate himself from the stances of three of his colleagues in the history department—James E. Corbett, M. A. Fitzsimons, and Willis Nutting. As a loyal and long time member of the Notre Dame family, Campbell expressed to O'Donnell grave concern over the very bad publicity presently being visited upon the university. He assured O'Donnell "as only one member of the lay faculty" of his abiding love for Notre Dame and of his intention to do his utmost for the progress and prestige of the institution. It was time, he concluded, for those of us most intimately concerned for the university "to close ranks and stand by Notre Dame, looking beyond the present to the future."[61]

John H. Sheehan, head of the economics department, informed Carrico that after three meetings with South Bend non-Catholic businessmen he was able to persuade them to call off a public meeting organized to discuss the McMahon case. Sheehan claimed to have convinced these businessmen of the "unwisdom" of such a meeting and that university action in this matter had been proper and fair.[62] O'Donnell responded with "God bless you" letters to both Campbell and Sheehan.

Other reactions to the McMahon case from the South Bend area, mostly likely inspired by the faculty protest group, were not so fortuitously turned aside. Prominent members of the local Jewish community sent O'Donnell letters protesting McMahon's dismissal.[63] Because of McMahon's standing with Jewish groups locally and nationally, the president was fearful that any response of his to such letters probably would be misunderstood. So none were sent. Letters of protest and resolutions condemning university actions were received from Local 65 of the United Rubber Workers of America in Mishawaka and from the large Studebaker Local 5 of the United Auto Workers and the Indiana Council—CIO. Local 5 denounced McMahon's dismissal as a "definite violation of free speech, academic freedom, and the democratic principles for which the people's war is being fought."[64]

By no means were all South Bend reactions to the dismissal negative ones. O'Donnell received some supportive letters from the local community. Probably inspired by Dean Manion of the Notre Dame Law School, a member of a well-known local law firm active in the St. Joseph County Bar Association and some local lawyers who were alumni of the law school and active in city and state Republican politics all sent supportive letters to O'Donnell.[65] More important, Gerald E. Cosgrove, associate editor of the *South Bend Tribune,* sent O'Donnell "hearty congratulations on your administration's procedures in the McMahon case."[66]

The outreach aspect of the faculty protest group's campaign to obtain McMahon's reinstatement concentrated on Chicago and New York City. In Chicago, Monsignor Daniel M. Cantwell of St. Mary of the Lake Seminary and friends in the Chicago Jewish community and at the University of Chicago all played roles in damning O'Donnell and the university for disregarding academic freedom and freedom of speech. Cantwell's response was the most thoughtful, Cifford K. Rubin's was the most indignant, while that of Herman L. Meyer, Jr., was the most personal.

Cantwell wrote a letter to O'Donnell dated November 11, 1942, that was published in the *Chicago Sun* on the following day. Unaware that negotiations between O'Donnell and McMahon had run on for over two months, Cantwell suspected that the university had imposed an impossible arrangement on McMahon in order to drive him from Notre Dame. "No honest person could have accepted the conditions laid down for his continuance at the university," he wrote. "You must have been pretty sure that Professor McMahon would not violate his integrity by submitting to such an arrangement."[67]

Cantwell insisted that O'Donnell's publicly stated reasons for the dismissal were not convincing. He questioned the meaning of the president's notion of freedom of speech rightly understood. He wondered what Notre Dame's alleged traditional patriotism had to do with the action taken against McMahon. He doubted whether any sane person actually identified McMahon's pronouncements on controversial issues with university stands. He even questioned whether a university could have any positions on such matters or even how a university president, when speaking, could express a view that accurately reflected a university position on anything.[68]

The position that would have given Notre Dame real glory, Cantwell continued, would have been to protect "the right of anyone at Notre Dame to speak his mind, offering such protection especially in the face of organized opposition." Moreover, if the majority of faculty at Notre Dame had expressed opinions on some of the controversial issues addressed by McMahon, he hoped that the opinions expressed would coincide with those of Professor McMahon on "Franco, anti-semitism, race discrimination, the rights of workers, and the threat of Nazism and Fascism to the world." About McMahon's most recent controversy over the doctrine of unconditional surrender, Cantwell admitted that he personally did not agree with his friend's position, but there was no doubt that he had a right to express it.[69]

Finally, Cantwell concluded, what the university asked of McMahon made no sense. If he had complied, his future remarks would have received official approval and therefore could be interpreted as reflecting the opinion of the university administration. Such remarks would have been passed by the university censor and would be no longer his. Cantwell ended by asserting that this letter did not represent the position of St. Mary of the Lake Seminary, because insofar as he knew, it did not have one.[70] O'Donnell neither acknowledged receipt nor wrote a reply.

Clifford K. Rubin, a West Washington Street Chicago lawyer, wrote to O'Donnell on November 9, 1943, stating that he could not imagine that anyone would have understood that McMahon's speeches and public statements in any way reflected official university positions. O'Donnell's contention that such was the case would not stand examination. That statement, therefore, was an "obvious subterfuge to cover what is an act unworthy of you or of Notre Dame."[71]

When a university fired a professor for speaking his mind, Rubin insisted, that was no mere family quarrel. It was "a blow against the very freedom of every American." In discharging Professor McMahon you "have brought more discredit, yes shame, upon your institution than it would be within the power of a professor to bring in a lifetime." In the Middle Ages, Rubin concluded, "they burned at the stake those who differed with the rulers; Hitler and Franco shoot them; you at Notre Dame fire them: the principle is the same, the difference is only in the degree."[72]

Herman L. Meyer, Jr., was a professor of mathematics at the University of Chicago. He was a man obviously touched in no small way by anti-Catholic prejudice and much endowed with a gift for pompous expression. Meyer combined that prejudice and gift into a vicious verbal assault upon O'Donnell beyond what the president deserved, nor did the crisis at Notre Dame require it. According to Meyer, the dismissal of McMahon had been an arbitrary misuse of administrative power of the sort that Catholic authorities were so famous for. It was a violation of McMahon's academic freedom and civil rights. Moreover, Meyer charged that O'Donnell's statements, where they are "free from confusion and double meaning, bespeak a mockery of common sense and principle."[73]

Meyer doubted whether O'Donnell even understood the meaning of freedom and argued that his action in the McMahon case underscored "again in every American mind the vast ambiguities of Roman Catholic policy as it pertains to the efforts for war and for peace, of our country and our allies." Next, he claimed to have written to the War Department protesting the training of officers and men at an institution whose atmosphere contributed so little to the understanding of American ideals. For O'Donnell personally because of his role in this "disservice to man and country and God," Meyer hoped for the strictest and sternest measure of personal disadvantage.[74] Meyer had been nasty and personal but at least it was private. Worse was yet to come, and when it did, it would be public.

— v —

The outreach of the Notre Dame faculty protest group to New York City looked first to George N. Shuster, a former Notre Dame faculty member who had severely criticized the educational and pastoral programs operative at Notre Dame in 1925 in two articles published after he had left the university. In 1943 Shuster was president of Hunter College and a member of the board of directors of Freedom House. Through Shuster, approaches were made to McMahon's friends at Freedom House to organize a massive celebrity protest of his dismissal. The board of directors of Freedom House endorsed the project, and a large part of the eastern liberal academic and literary establishment reachable by Freedom House responded. Shuster joined with Harry D. Gideonse, president of Brooklyn College and chairman of the board of directors of Freedom House, and William Agar, acting president of Freedom House, to draft a public letter addressed to O'Donnell urging reinstatement of McMahon. Headed by Albert Einstein, sixty-seven celebrity academics, educators, scientists, writers, journalists, critics, and union leaders agreed to sign what was in fact a public indictment of O'Donnell's performance as a university president.

The Freedom House letter began by praising McMahon for his courage and patriotism. Long before Pearl Harbor, they wrote, McMahon had been in the forefront of the fight against Hitler and against the forces of Fascism and reaction within America as well as beyond her borders. Shuster and his colleagues applauded McMahon's opposition to anti-Semitism, racial and religious discrimination at home, his strong stands for preparedness, aid to Britain, and intervention as well as aid to and understanding of Russia.[75]

While McMahon's dismissal had been a shock, the publicly announced justification for it was astonishing. The university had chosen to penalize McMahon for doing the very things that merited acclaim. Furthermore, the letter continued, by taking the action that it did, the university appeared to have placed itself "in open opposition to views which conform to the best American and Christian traditions and which have been fully justified by events."[76]

On the matter of the public identifying McMahon's views with official positions of the university, the letter pointed out that McMahon never claimed to speak for Notre Dame. In any case, the university was always at liberty to disclaim responsibility for anything that McMahon might say. The alternatives of censorship or dismissal was an unwarranted interference with his basic natural right of freedom of expression. Moreover, if McMahon's public pronouncements were, as O'Donnell had said, considered controversial by many Americans, Notre Dame "has tolerated and is still tolerating under its banner the other side of this same 'controversial' question."[77]

Shuster, Gideonse, and Agar concluded by recognizing how difficult it was to correct a mistake made in the full glare of publicity. Nevertheless, they urged O'Donnell to reconsider his action and "prove Notre Dame University courageous enough to admit and redress a wrong done to one of its faculty."[78] Coming from Shuster, whom many clergy at Notre Dame regarded as a renegade, this letter was particularly hurtful. O'Donnell reacted to that hurt by consistently referring to this Shuster-inspired letter in correspondence with friends and off-campus sympathizers as emanating from those "crack-pot liberals from Freedom House."[79] He neither acknowledged receipt nor responded to the Freedom House letter.[80]

The Freedom House letter was only one of many indicators that the buzz saw which Nutting and others in the faculty protest group had set turning was running out of control. The academic reputations of O'Donnell and of the university were being shredded. Professional associations and special interest groups aided the process. First into the fray, as early as November 9, was the Committee on Academic Freedom of the American Civil Liberties Union (ACLU) located in New York. Shuster was a member of their executive committee.[81]

While this committee normally did not concern itself with conduct of private institutions, they decided in this instance to express their deep regret over the dismissal of Professor McMahon for refusing to submit to censorship. According to the executive secretary, Karl N. Llewellyn, the committee was fearful of the influence that this most serious incident would have on other institutions. In the past, the committee always intervened in cases in public institutions where teachers were dismissed without charges or a hearing before a jury of their peers. The principle of academic freedom, Llewellyn concluded, "would seem to us to apply equally to a private institution in which the public has some concern on moral grounds."[82]

On November 16, the *Chicago Sun* carried a story that the American Association of University Professors (AAUP) intended an investigation of the McMahon case, even though he was not a member of the association. Professor Anton J. Carlson, professor of physiology at the University of Chicago, a member of the executive council of the AAUP, and a former president of that organization, made the announcement.[83] O'Donnell's reaction to the communication from the ACLU and the proposed intervention by the AAUP was predictable. He stated to supportive correspondents that those two organizations could do whatever they pleased. Notre Dame did not accept the principles of those associations and never would.

— vi —

The intended AAUP inquiry was long delayed. The general secretary, Ralph E. Himstead, did not officially contact O'Donnell until June 13, 1944. At that time, Himstead described the purpose of the inquiry as one of clarifying the facts of McMahon's termination. He explained the nature and purpose of the AAUP and stated that in evaluating the facts of academic freedom or tenure situations, the association was guided by the principles of good academic practice observed in accredited institutions of higher education. He enclosed copies of official statements of AAUP principles and procedures.[84]

Himstead advised O'Donnell that McMahon's length of service, ten years, was more than sufficient to entitle him to continuous tenure as defined by the principles mentioned above. According to those principles, a teacher entitled to continuous tenure should not have been dismissed except for justifiable cause determined at a hearing in which all of the facts were carefully canvassed. The fact that the concept of continuous tenure was not recognized at Notre Dame was not mentioned.

Next, Himstead recounted information relating to the dismissal process collected from McMahon. If the facts as stated by McMahon were accurate—that certain of his public statements constituted the principal reason for his dismissal—then, "it would seem that the termination of his services presents an issue of academic freedom."[85]

Himstead referred O'Donnell to a portion of the 1940 Statement of Principles on Academic Freedom and Tenure which in effect provided a basis for taking action against McMahon. According to this section of the Statement of Principles, university teachers had responsibilities as well as rights. Among these responsibilities was an obligation to be accurate in all public statements, show appropriate restraint, respect the opinions of others, and make every effort to indicate that he is not an institutional spokesman.[86]

Himstead concluded by asking for O'Donnell's judgment about whether McMahon as a faculty member of the university had complied with those portions of the principles cited above. He hoped that the president would respond and indicate "with particularity in what ways and at what times Dr. McMahon's conduct was not in accord with these principles."[87]

O'Donnell was much impressed by the studied fairness and balance of Himstead's approach to the case. O'Donnell had not encountered much fairness or balance from anyone on either side of this case since November. The AAUP clearly recognized a right of a university to protect itself from inaccurate and unrestrained public statements by faculty. To O'Donnell, recognition of that right by an organization such as the AAUP was extremely satisfying. He saw in that recognition a near vindication of his role in the affair. After all, it was upon an assumed right of institutional self-protection that the public justification of his action against McMahon rested. To be sure, he would not find much sympathy for the dismissal process employed in this case, but at least the principle of institutional self-protection was recognized as a valid one by an organization that O'Donnell hitherto had always regarded as an enemy. After six months of public criticism and abuse that was something to be grateful for.

After thinking about Himstead's inquiry for a few days and taking counsel on it, O'Donnell decided that a detailed reply would be inappropriate. By June 1944 the case was no longer newsworthy. The capture of Rome and the long-awaited Allied invasion of Europe dominated the news. O'Donnell saw no useful purpose in saying or doing anything that might revive public interest in the case. He responded briefly but politely and cordially to Himstead on June 19. O'Donnell sent Himstead a copy of his official statement released on November 9, indicating the information requested could be found in it.[88] The AAUP proceeded no further with the case. After the announcement of the proposed investigation of the dismissal by the AAUP appeared in the *Chicago Sun* in mid-November, O'Donnell heard from J. Raymond Walsh, director of education and research for the Congress of Industrial Organizations (CIO) located in Washington, D.C.[89] Walsh wrote to O'Donnell as an officer in the CIO and as a Catholic. Walsh stated his admiration for McMahon's "honest and candid espousal of the labor cause." For better or worse, Walsh continued, McMahon had come to be identified with democratic positions on any number of domestic and international questions. Walsh suggested that much more was at stake in the McMahon case than conditions of academic freedom at a Catholic university or the personal hardship of an undeserved loss of employment. McMahon's dismissal would be taken by many in the country as "a deplorable indication of the reactionary drift among many leaders of our church."[90]

This reactionary drift was deplorable, Walsh argued, because it ran against values that were "central to a democratic and Catholic civilization." McMahon's dismissal, Walsh feared, would encourage a fierce reaction against the Catholic Church in the minds of a majority of Americans. For this most compelling reason, Walsh believed that O'Donnell owed "a wide public an explanation concerning this quasi public matter beyond any that has come from your office." Dr. McMahon should be reinstated at the earliest possible moment.[91]

O'Donnell must have begun to wonder what on earth he had really done. A spokesman for the Brooklyn chapter of Fight For Freedom, Inc., characterized O'Donnell's action against McMahon as encouraging all of the anti-democratic forces in the country.[92] With regard to a possible reaction against the Catholic Church, in American opinion events seemed to be showing that Walsh's fears were well-founded. Within a month of the appearance of the Howard and Riesel stories and of O'Donnell's official statement, public interest in the issues raised by the McMahon case had begun to shift. More important than academic freedom or freedom of speech in a Catholic university was a growing suspicion, particularly in New York City, about reactionary, anti-democratic principles and attitudes informing the leadership and directing the behavior of many members of the Catholic Church.

The widespread regional and national publicity generated by the McMahon dismissal along with O'Donnell's firm resolution to say nothing publicly about the case beyond his statement of November 9 combined to revive old but not forgotten anti-Catholic prejudices. In some quarters the American Catholic Church was perceived as a homogenous, authoritarian, foreign-dominated organization. To persons of this persuasion Catholic beliefs and practices appeared to be incompatible with, and perhaps even a threat to, American democratic values and institutions.

O'Donnell received both simple-minded and sophisticated statements of this point of view during the McMahon firestorm. One polite and measured example of the latter came from E. K. Brown, professor of English and chairman of the English department at Cornell University. Brown either was or had been a Catholic. He opposed any administrative restraints on expression when matters of faith or morals were not involved. He much regretted the suggestion communicated to the public by this affair "that the educational instruments of the Catholic Church are based on a philosophy wherein the ideas of freedom were different from that which obtains in a university such as Cornell." Brown regretted further anything tending "to drive a wedge between the Catholic citizens of this country and the others." He wrote this letter as a sincere friend and well wisher of Notre Dame.[93]

Another more severe and not so measured expression of this point of view was received from Stanford Clinton, who described himself as chairman of the Council for Democratic Action, a non-partisan political reform interest group composed of ministers, businessmen, university educators, and professional men in Evanston, Illinois. Very few of the members of this group, if any, were Catholics.

Clinton protested not so much the dismissal of McMahon as the conditions that led to it. While the evident absence of academic freedom at Notre Dame was to be regretted and condemned, Clinton and his group were concerned about something more fundamental and more important. The Council was appalled that the administration of a great American educational institution was entrusted to people who could not distinguish between Fascism and democracy, who were unable to recognize Franco as a Fascist, who could not understand that Russia was our ally and Nazi Germany our foe, and who tried to gag and then destroy one who spoke out for America and denounced the country's enemies.[94]

Clinton and his associates were especially alarmed over O'Donnell's failure to respond to innumerable editorial demands to "reveal the identity of the individuals and groups which you publicly stated brought pressure to bear on you and forced the dismissal of Dr. McMahon." Moreover, Clinton concluded, "it is in the public interest that it be known whether these groups were within or without the Catholic Church, or both." The burden of providing evidence that clericalism and education for democratic living were reconcilable was on O'Donnell.[95] The president's secretary acknowledged receipt of this letter, but the president did not reply.[96]

By dismissing McMahon, admitting that he had done so because of outside pressure, and then refusing to identify the sources of that pressure, O'Donnell had opened up one of Pandora's oldest boxes. What came out of it were old prejudices about the compatibility with American freedom of an assumed authoritarian Catholic power directed by like-minded bishops and lay leaders. Press coverage of the McMahon case had made more people willing to express degrees of those old prejudices both privately and in public. What persons as unalike as Brown, Clinton, Rubin, and Meyers expressed to O'Donnell could be heard in many parts of the country, but especially in New York City.

Ironically, the person perhaps most immediately concerned about the revival of such old prejudices and the first publicist to try to deal with it was McMahon himself. From his friends at *PM*, McMahon knew well the depth of suspicion of Catholic power held by many in New York left-wing circles. He also must have read the frequent criticisms of Archbishop Spellman's activities and policy statements appearing in that pub-lication.[97] In any event, McMahon published an article in *PM* on Novem-ber 22, entitled "Catholics and Isolationism" that carried a banner, "A Defense of Catholic Liberalism by Anti-Fascist Professor Ousted by Notre Dame." His thesis was simple: All Catholics were not the same, they all did not think alike, and they were divided in their interpretations of world affairs.[98]

McMahon divided pre-war American Catholic opinion into three groups. First, the majority of Catholic journals were isolationist before Pearl Harbor. Well-known Catholic periodicals such as the *Catholic World, Sign, Ave Maria,* and *America* clamored loudly on behalf of the non-interventionist cause. Even *Commonweal,* McMahon insisted, wavered between a sentimental pacifism and a sickly neutrality. Archbishops Beckman of Dubuque, Curley of Baltimore, and Cardinal O'Connell of Boston were only three of the many prelates, followed by most of the clergy and many laymen, who associated themselves with and publicly advocated the foreign-policy positions of the America First Committee. That was majority American Catholic opinion.[99]

Second, opposed to that majority were the voices forthright and true of Archbishop Robert E. Lucey of San Antonio and Bishop Patrick J. Hurley of St. Augustine, followed by some clergy and increasing num-bers of laymen. This articulate substantial minority of American Catho-lics, McMahon claimed, consistently pleaded for support of the national policy against Hitlerism.[100]

Third, there was a small but vocal minority of American Catholics stridently opposed to national policy at home and abroad. Largely com-posed of Coughlinites, Christian Fronters, anti-Semites, and irrational Irish nationalists, this segment of the American Catholic community dis-graced themselves and disgusted the country. Their story, McMahon stated, was quite distinct from that of mainstream Catholic America and was a tale of stupidity, ignorance, and viciousness.[101]

In this article McMahon's principal concern was not the lunatic fringe. He wanted to explain why so many Catholic educators, editors, and clergy of both high estate and low had been either neutral or hostile to the national policy during the gravest crisis in human history. He began by describing what these people were not. In his judgment, they were neither unpatriotic nor unconsciously fascist. They surely loved their country in their own peculiar way. Such people had been misguided by an inherited suspicion of British imperialism, great fear of and hostility toward Soviet Communism, and a deep distrust of our national leader. For them, American involvement in the war was too great a price to pay for preventing Nazi domination of Europe. That was what had made them the way they were. McMahon assured the readers of *PM* that neither theology nor religious practices had much to do with it.[102]

For McMahon, the world of 25 million American Catholics was a diverse and complex place. In his judgment, American Catholics formed a heterogeneous political community, and except on issues of faith and morals, a universally acceptable Catholic point of view on almost anything was difficult to find.[103] Whether McMahon managed to persuade many of *PM*'s readers that American Catholics really were as diverse in political attitudes as he claimed and that they understood the meaning of freedom and valued it as much as other Americans was unlikely. He was living proof of what Catholic power could do.

For many academic friends of the university in the Northeast, O'Donnell's steadfast refusal to explain why McMahon's public speeches were considered more damaging to the good name of Notre Dame than the public speeches of O'Brien and Manion was incomprehensible. O'Donnell's initial denial that the content of McMahon's public speeches were issues in this case was not believed. By maintaining a continuing silence on this point, O'Donnell had managed to turn a shameful administrative action into a disaster in academic reputation.

Helen C. White, professor of English at Vassar and a recent recipient of Notre Dame's prestigious Laetare Medal, was one academic friend of the university thus bewildered. She urged reinstatement as the only salvation for the university's academic reputation. To a Catholic, she stated, "there is no shame in the acknowledgement of a mistake but honor in its reparation, and that honor I covet for a great university."[104] Carl J. Friedrich, director of the School for Overseas Administration at Harvard University was another. Friedrich wrote not just for himself but "for those of us at Harvard who have come to admire various members of the faculty of Notre Dame in the course of the last few years." All in this group were greatly troubled by the event, and all hoped that the president could find a basis for reinstatement.[105]

Expressing grave concern about the impact of the dismissal on the quality of instruction and research at Notre Dame, Edmund A. Stephan, class of 1933, berated O'Donnell for misunderstanding and corrupting the mission of a university. An important part of that mission was to encourage the widest possible discussion of vital public issues. It now appears, wrote Stephan, that no member of the faculty, except the football coach and the president, may express an opinion to the public on anything controversial without fear of reprisal, unless he first obtains approval of his intended remarks from university officials. This was a long step backward for Notre Dame; in the long run it could only mean a second-rate faculty. The university could neither afford to lose first-class intellects nor to deter men of independent mind from joining its faculty, he concluded, and this it had effectively done.[106] This devoted alumnus wrote with a prescience and passion commensurate with the kind of man he was. Twenty-four later years, Edmund A. Stephan became the first chairman of a new Board of Trustees for the university. He served with distinction in that post for fifteen years.

— vii —

As the firestorm of negative publicity against the university raged on during the final weeks of 1943, O'Donnell looked for solace where he could find it. The performance of the Notre Dame football team during the season of 1943 and the honors bestowed upon it provided sportswriters, if not reporters and editorial writers, with something to praise about the university. During the first eight contests in a ten-game season, as the lyrics of the Notre Dame fight song proclaimed, Notre Dame had won over all and convincingly so. The Notre Dame football team had won all of its first eight games, outscoring all eight opponents by the astonishing point total of 312 to 37.

However, the last two games played against Iowa Pre-Flight on November 20 and against Great Lakes on November 27 were another story. These naval service teams were blessed with excellent coaches and a roster of former college stars and professionals. How much the negative publicity against the university during November and the published aspersions about the patriotism of university leadership depressed Notre Dame team performance or inspired the play of these two service teams could only be guessed. Both Iowa Pre-Flight and Great Lakes were not at all intimidated by Notre Dame's record and played extremely well against the team reputed to be the best in the country.

Once again the eyes of the sports world were focussed on South Bend. Almost 50,000 people went out to the Notre Dame stadium to watch their team challenge an Iowa Pre-Flight squad led by Dick Todd, a strong running back from the Washington Redskins. Todd's running gave Iowa Pre-Flight a lead of 7 to 0 by halftime. However, an injury took Todd out of the game in the second half. Lujack's passing and running enabled Notre Dame to score a touchdown and an extra point in the third and in the fourth periods. Iowa Pre-Flight responded with a touchdown and a missed extra point in the final quarter giving Notre Dame a narrow lead of 14 to 13 near game's end. Leahy's men secured their victory only after Iowa Pre-Flight missed a last second field-goal attempt.[107]

Both teams played well with game statistical advantages slightly favoring Iowa Pre-Flight. Lujack played the entire game and managed seven pass completions out of fifteen attempts, a good but not a great performance. Though poor place kicking by Iowa Pre-Flight handed Notre Dame its ninth win of the season, the team remained undefeated and still very much a contender for the intercollegiate football national championship.

The season ended a week later on a cold Saturday in a game against Great Lakes before a small crowd of only 23,000 in Soldier Field. The Great Lakes sailor players were well prepared for this game and ironically started two outstanding former Notre Dame players, Steve Juzwik and Emil Sitko. Juzwik had earned varsity monograms playing for Layden in 1940 and for Leahy in 1941. Sitko had been recruited by Leahy in 1942 and had played on the Notre Dame freshmen team in that year before entering the navy. Playing for Great Lakes in 1943, Sitko was the star of the game, a portent of what he was to do for Notre Dame after the war.[108]

Notre Dame scored a touchdown in the first period and enjoyed a lead of 7 to 0 at halftime. During the third period, Sitko's hard running led to two Great Lakes touchdowns, giving the sailors the lead, 12 to 7. Notre Dame responded in the final period with a touchdown and an extra point, going ahead, 14 to 12. That two-point lead appeared to be enough until the final thirty seconds of the game, when Lach completed a desperation pass to Anderson covering forty-six yards for a game-winning touchdown. Great Lakes kicked the extra point upsetting Notre Dame, 19 to 14. Game statistics followed the score and favored Great Lakes. Lujack completed seven passes out of fourteen attempts but threw two interceptions.[109]

Despite losing the final game of the season in the last thirty seconds, the Notre Dame team's performance in 1943 had been excellent. A majority of coaches and sportswriters agreed that Notre Dame had the best intercollegiate football team in the country and had earned the honor of national champion. At the same time, though playing only six games in 1943, Angelo Bertelli, now on active duty with the U.S. Marines, was awarded the Heisman Trophy as the most outstanding player in intercollegiate football.

For Fathers O'Donnell and Cavanaugh, the accolades for the football team and for Bertelli could not have come at a more opportune time. They both needed a psychological lift. For the past month, apart from Saturday football scores, the only times Notre Dame had been mentioned in the national press was in the context of the McMahon affair.

Recognition for football glory alone might not count for much in some American academic circles but for the president and vice president of Notre Dame at this moment, it was a pride-restorer and a much appreciated respite.

However, this respite was to be of very brief duration. In time, of course, the McMahon affair would cease to be newsworthy and the press would drop it, but that fortuitous occasion was not to be soon. More bad publicity would come from it, and some disreputable allies would be embraced. For O'Donnell, there was a long and very rough course that had to be stayed.

— 10 —

Reprise

Though most Catholic educators simply averted their eyes from the crisis at Notre Dame and avoided public comment of any sort on it, some Catholics in other lines of work congratulated O'Donnell for dismissing McMahon. For them, the dismissal was a necessary action long delayed. Not surprisingly, most of the favorable comment on the event received from outside of the South Bend area came from Holy Cross priests offering moral support to a beleaguered comrade who surely needed it. Positive letters came also from personal friends, both lay and clerical. Monsignor Thomas M. Conroy, chancellor of the Cathedral of Immaculate Conception in Fort Wayne, Indiana, congratulated O'Donnell for dissociating McMahon from the university and assured him that resentment over this action would soon pass and that all reasonable people would understand why the professor's departure from the university had become so necessary.[1] Support of another type came from veterans of the bitter interethnic conflicts currently raging in the circulation area of the *Brooklyn Tablet.*

When the news of McMahon's dismissal appeared in the *New York Times* on November 8, one of the first to applaud O'Donnell's action was Arthur O'Leary, the New York lawyer and advocate for Franco Spain.[2] O'Leary had warned O'Donnell in May 1941 that McMahon's public statements about opening southern Irish ports for use by the Royal Navy were likely to be misinterpreted as official university positions. O'Donnell acknowledged O'Leary's letter and thanked him for supporting the dismissal.

Another person, with perhaps even stronger Irish nationalist opinions than O'Leary, and delighted to learn of McMahon's departure from Notre Dame was Father Daniel J. Fant of the American National Shrine,

Washington, D.C. According to Fant, Notre Dame was well rid of that "shallow, intolerant egoist" whose mouthing of "aggressive, obtusive, unmannerliness" disgusted people of common sense.[3] Of course, the *Gaelic American* had its say. The editors praised O'Donnell for getting rid of McMahon and congratulated the president for upholding what they described as the fine traditions of Notre Dame.[4]

Also, among O'Donnell's early respondents was the never-to-be-forgotten Charles P. Foley of Springfield, Massachusetts, who had denounced the president in August 1942 for not heeding his warning about preventing McMahon from speaking at the Springfield Summer Forum. Foley apologized for his harsh words written in anger at the prospect of a professor from a Catholic university speaking at that gathering of "Communistic Jews" in beautiful Forest Park. With McMahon gone, Foley added, "Notre Dame can once more hold its head high."[5] O'Donnell delayed five weeks before acknowledging and thanking the writer for so warmly endorsing his decision in the McMahon case.[6]

Very early in the crisis, O'Donnell must have wondered what sort of people, outside of fellow priests in Holy Cross and personal friends, were rallying to his support. In the same spirit as the Foley letter, O'Donnell received a copy of a program issued by the Marshall Committee for Racial Unity in Chicago that was sponsoring a conference on "Ways of Combatting Anti-Semitism." No cover letter, return address, or explanation of any sort was included with the program. McMahon was listed as one of five scheduled conference speakers. His name was circled, and typed across the bottom of the program was the notation, "You are well rid of that rat."[7]

Then, of course, O'Donnell heard from Boston. McMahon's letter with a Catholic and Notre Dame identification sent to the *Boston Herald* condemning anti-Semitic activity in the city was deeply resented by many Catholics there. They saw it as an unwanted and unnecessary intrusion into serious problems of which McMahon was vastly ignorant. Both O'Donnell and McMahon received responses to that intrusion that they would never forget. For example, a person identifying himself as "Broadway Notre Dame Alumnus" congratulated O'Donnell for sending McMahon on his way. The writer included in his letter a collection of clippings from the Boston press relating to the findings of the Stokes Commission on anti-Semitic incidents occurring in the city over the previous eighteen months.[8]

On the basis of the enclosed clippings, the writer insisted the Stokes Commission found no evidence of an organized anti-Semitic campaign in Boston and showed McMahon to be an uninformed, interfering meddler that the city could do without. He interpreted this lack of evidence of an organized anti-Semitic campaign as proof that there was no anti-Semitism of any significance in the city. As a matter of fact, the writer concluded, Jews did very well for themselves in Boston. Ninety percent of all black market operators in the area, he asserted, were Jewish. More than that, the Jews who operated the Coconut Grove nightclub had gotten away with murder. In the fire that destroyed that establishment, 500 people died. Every fire law on the books had been broken, he wrote, "so that there was only one exit (at the cash register) for this vast number of patrons."[9] Support of this sort must have made O'Donnell shudder. It had to get better because it could not get any worse. It did, but not very much and only very slowly.

For example, a Jesuit priest, Father Michael J. Aherne from Weston College in Weston, Massachusetts, provided a somewhat different perspective on the problems in Boston. According to Aherne, McMahon's letter to the *Boston Herald* had been stupid. He did not know anything about the outbreaks in Boston, which had been "unorganized hoodlumism pure and simple and were exercised as much against Christians as against Jews."[10] Only the incidents against Jews received front-page coverage.

However, Aherne had not written to O'Donnell for the single purpose of complaining about McMahon's letter to the *Herald*. He sent O'Donnell a letter written by Dr. Ralph Barton Perry, an eminent professor of philosophy at Harvard, who was deeply disappointed about the apparent violation of academic freedom at Notre Dame.[11] Perry knew McMahon slightly and had appeared on the same platform with him and others at the Soviet-American Friendship meeting in New York the previous year. According to Aherne, Perry was a sincere man and an ardent admirer of the work of the Catholic Church for peace.

Aherne noted that, as decent and sincere a man as Perry was, he fully accepted a very liberal notion of academic freedom. Aherne, of course, did not and was convinced that most practicing Catholics did not either. In sharp contrast to the position that McMahon was to argue in his *PM* article on November 22, Aherne believed and wanted others to believe that Catholics had a different understanding of the meaning of freedom than other Americans.

Even if O'Donnell chose not to respond to Perry about the McMahon case, Aherne intended to write to the professor to explain that "we in the Catholic Church have a principle of freedom that is not the freedom which is only another name for license."[12] He was certain that in liberal circles there was much hypocrisy about "so-called academic freedom." He claimed to know of some instances at Harvard where that hypocrisy had been displayed and was considering that perhaps now was an appropriate moment politely to remind Professor Perry of them.[13]

Whether Father Aherne communicated further with Perry about the McMahon case is unknown. If Aherne had done so, his message must have been unconvincing because Perry went public with his views about the case in a letter to the *Commonweal* on January 7, 1944.[14] Insofar as O'Donnell was concerned, he politely but firmly refused to be drawn into any sort of public or private exchange of views with Perry or anyone else.

O'Donnell insisted to Aherne that academic freedom as such was no part of the McMahon case. Censorship had never been applied to him. McMahon had refused to accept precautionary procedures intended to insure that the professor's views on controversial issues would not be identified with the university. McMahon had never been gagged. That was all that had happened. Furthermore, McMahon's immediate disclosure to the world of confidential conversations revealed the true nature of the man and how difficult dealing with him had become. In all charity, O'Donnell added, "I believe that poor man is suffering from a Messianic complex."[15] In any case, the matter was closed absolutely, and Professor Perry would have to find someone else to dispute with about it.[16]

The strongest support for O'Donnell's action against McMahon came from Brooklyn. As early as November 12, 1943, Patrick J. Scanlan, managing editor of the *Brooklyn Tablet*, sent O'Donnell a copy of the Riesel article from the *New York Post* which he described in a covering letter "as a 100% exhibit of the smearing and sneering anti-Catholic campaign being conducted by the organs of 'liberalism.'" By way of encouragement, Scanlan assured O'Donnell, "We have heard nothing but praise of Notre Dame's action in ousting McMahon."[17]

Scanlan was a much bruised and scarred, religiously conservative veteran of the many Catholic-Jewish conflicts and confrontations occurring in New York City at that time who tended to see evidence of anti-Catholic statements and activities everywhere. Efforts by prominent New York liberal Catholics and Jews to get McMahon reinstated at Notre Dame were for Scanlan proof positive that once again the liberal enemies of institutional Catholicism were up to their old tricks. He opened the pages of the *Brooklyn Tablet* to those who supported O'Donnell's dismissal of McMahon and in so doing encouraged other editors of local Catholic periodicals and newsletters to do the same.

— ii —

One local Catholic editor who accepted Scanlan's lead in this matter but not his religious conservatism or combative instincts was Father William J. Smith, S.J. Smith edited the *Crown Heights Comment,* a newsletter appearing eight times a year, and served as director of the Crown Heights School of Catholic Workmen, a strongly anti-Communist adult education facility for Catholic working people in Brooklyn.

Smith saw himself and the Crown Heights School of Catholic Workmen as being dedicated to "Christ the Worker by and for His Fellow Workers."[18] For Smith that dedication meant following a middle road between the extremes of reactionary and liberal Catholics in the New York area. According to Smith, of the two extreme parties at the present moment, reactionary Catholics were probably less disturbing to the progress of the Church in America than the liberal ones.[19] To be sure, reactionary Catholics were embarrassing and from time to time caused unnecessary disturbances. However, their influence was principally limited to unthinking people. Most important, reactionary Catholics were rarely ever co-opted by well-organized outside groups and led into specious public advocacy positions.[20]

At the other extreme, Smith maintained, liberal Catholics, of whom there were many in New York City, were a bigger problem for the Church. Experience in the New York area had taught him that liberal Catholics were subjectively sincere but could be "just as bigoted and set in their extreme ways as those they criticize." Liberal Catholics praised the pope but abused the hierarchy. They assumed that "the country must be Catholic but do little to make it so except to attack others whom they dislike."[21] They simply did not represent a healthy Catholic viewpoint and showed themselves too willing to identify with other groups "who seek to cooperate with us, usually for their own purposes."[22]

With regard to the McMahon case, Smith presented a three-page defense of the dismissal in the *Crown Heights Comment.* Smith did not know McMahon personally nor much about him, except that he had been involved in many liberal causes. Smith's defense, derived principally from the university's official published statement about the event, consisted of a restatement of O'Donnell's argument about protecting the good name of the university and an attack on Charles D. Gideonse, president of Brooklyn College, for his statement in the *Brooklyn Eagle* asserting that the dismissal at Notre Dame violated accepted standards of academic freedom.

Smith drew on his own personal experience as a an anti-Communist labor priest working in Brooklyn to clarify the nature of McMahon's transgression as presented in the official university statement. According to Smith, the university did not want its name identified with the personal opinions and individual activities of "a solitary professor whose liberalism brings him into close contact with groups and movements which the university is unwilling to sanction."[23] For Smith, contamination by association with Communists in common causes was as dangerous for Catholic universities as it was for Catholic labor organizations. Given all of McMahon's contacts with liberal and Communist causes, contamination was unavoidable. Notre Dame had "a *right* to *protect* and *keep unblemished* its own *reputation* and *good name*."[24]

In his article in *Comment*, Smith insisted that there was more to Notre Dame than football prowess. This institution represented a philosophical and theological system that had been a foundation for morals and a sublime spirituality for over four hundred years. The school's spiritual, cultural, and educational heritage was too sacred to risk. If other colleges and universities cared so little for their good names, he continued, as to allow revolutionists and intellectual nondescripts to become so identified with them that even their friends were scandalized, that was their responsibility.[25] If other institutions had become "so enamored of modern liberalism as to cast a shadow on their own traditions of fundamental Americanism by allowing Communists to bore into their faculties" under the cover of something called academic freedom, Notre Dame need not follow.[26]

Smith took Gideonse to task for his statement in the *Brooklyn Eagle*. In that statement Gideonse had pointed out that the present war was being waged against the Nazis, not against Communism. Smith went on to say that although the Soviet Union was one of our powerful allies, that circumstance implied no support for Communism or for American Communists.[27] For Smith, this part of Gideonse's statement epitomized Catholic problems with liberalism as well as Notre Dame's problem with McMahon.

According to Smith, Gideonse's statement clearly communicated a negative attitude toward Communism, but a negative attitude was not enough.

Communism was just as vicious and deadly as Nazism, Smith asserted. If Gideonse and his friends at Freedom House, including McMahon, were unwilling to denounce Communism as totally and completely as they did Nazism, he insisted, one had to conclude that they were ignorant of its nature or had sympathetic leanings toward it. In any case, American Catholics did not want an illustrious university identified with the names of men who had failed to recognize the evil of Communism and failed to condemn it.[28]

Smith's representation of McMahon as perhaps a liberal pro-Communist dupe, a fellow traveler, but definitely insufficiently anti-Communist for employment at a Catholic university got him into serious trouble with his superiors. About two weeks after the *Comment* article on the McMahon case appeared, Smith wrote to O'Donnell asking for help. His article had "stirred up a bit of a protest from the South together with a rather forceful letter from an influential person in New York City."[29] Most likely Smith's superiors had heard from Bishop Hurley of St. Augustine and Archbishop Spellman of New York.

Smith expected that he would be "on the spot shortly" and any information about McMahon that O'Donnell could send to help him would be appreciated. Smith wanted anything usable as evidence of McMahon's pro-Communist sympathies to back up the accusations published in *Comment.* He also asked for a complete list of the signers of the Freedom House letter. A measure of the seriousness of Smith's present situation was the priest's urgent request that O'Donnell send off whatever he could at once and by air mail special delivery.[30]

When Smith's letter reached Notre Dame, O'Donnell was ill with a heavy cold. He directed his secretary to send Smith newspaper clippings reporting McMahon's speeches and other activities, the issue of *Liberty* magazine containing McMahon's article "Lindbergh and the Jews," McMahon's most recent article in *PM* on "Catholics and Isolationism," and a list of the signers of the Freedom House letter. He also forwarded to Smith a number of original letters sent to him complaining about McMahon's activities. While this transaction was to remain strictly confidential, all of the material could be used as Smith saw fit, so long as the names of the writers of the personal letters were protected. O'Donnell asked that the personal letters be returned when Smith was finished with them.[31]

Smith thanked O'Donnell for promptly sending the requested material. He thought that researching the backgrounds of the signers of the Freedom House letter might lead somewhere, but as matters turned out none of the material sent to Smith was very helpful. His only hope to find support for his accusations was to research back issues of the liberal and Communist press to find statements praising McMahon's speeches.Such statements might possibly be accepted by his superiors as a form of substantiation for the charges he had leveled at McMahon in *Comment.*[32]

In the absence of any direct evidence of McMahon being sympathetic toward Communism, guilt by association was the only practical argument left for Smith. As a matter of fact, Smith suggested to O'Donnell that if the controversy continued, the president should assign someone at the university the task of examining back issues of large city newspapers and magazines for evidence linking McMahon's opinions to left-wing organizations and causes. In due course, he returned the personal letters that O'Donnell's secretary had sent to him.[33]

O'Donnell wrote Smith, thanking him for all of the support given so far and for the idea about researching back issues of large city newspapers and magazines. He stated his intention to set James Armstrong to that job. Moreover, if the director of publicity discovered anything of use to Smith, O'Donnell promised that it would be sent off forthwith. O'Donnell was not serious about pursuing this strategy. Armstrong had enough to do already, but even more important, there was no point in continuing a relationship with Smith. O'Donnell wanted no involvement in the priest's problems in New York, even if they had been caused in part by Smith's defense of Notre Dame and attack on Gideonse. O'Donnell closed his letter off as politely as he could.[34]

Having been attacked privately and publicly for the past month and being ill in early December may account in part for O'Donnell's inexcusable behavior in this Smith matter. Notwithstanding an official public statement and repeated private ones that the content of McMahon's opinions had nothing to do with the dismissal, O'Donnell cooperated with Smith in order to demonstrate that they did. O'Donnell knew positively that McMahon had no Communist sympathies whatsoever. Yet he agreed to become a partner, to be sure a silent partner, in an effort to represent McMahon as either a dupe of Communism or as an actual sympathizer. He did so in order to rescue a fellow priest from the embarrassment of having made an outrageous charge that could not be substantiated. O'Donnell had given not a moment's thought to the possible consequences for McMahon if this monstrous lie came to be widely believed or for himself and for the university if it were not and if his role in perpetrating it were uncovered.

Continuing public humiliation often leads to desperation, and desperation can make the best of men careless and drive them into reckless action. In the matter of providing information to Smith for the purpose intended, O'Donnell failed utterly as a person of honor and as a responsible university administrator. He knew better, but he did it anyway. In the end, O'Donnell was saved from himself by the futility of Smith's purpose. In this instance truth could not be altered by innuendo. Smith had to take whatever reprimands were due a man in his vocation who had assumed too much, knew too little, and publicly accused too quickly. *Crown Heights Comment* printed nothing more about the McMahon case.

— iii —

Another source of support from Brooklyn for O'Donnell's action against McMahon was Dr. Edward I. Fenlon, a teacher in the department of philosophy at Brooklyn College. Fenlon was a practicing Thomist, a conservative Catholic, a former member of the Brooklyn chapter of America First, a dedicated anti-Communist, a friend of Patrick J. Scanlan of the *Brooklyn Tablet,* and a man very unhappy with the intellectual and cultural environment of Brooklyn College at that time.

According to Fenlon, about 90 percent of the student body of Brooklyn College was Jewish, most of the students and faculty professed some sort of left-wing political persuasion, and the very young, liberal, highly opinionated president of Brooklyn College, Charles Gideonse, fancied himself sufficiently wise to address and resolve any policy issue anywhere encountered. Fenlon's way of knowing as a teacher of philosophy was Thomist, but student interest in that mode of analysis at Brooklyn College was minimal, and curriculum opportunities to demonstrate the efficacy of it were few. Moreover, after having given testimony as a friendly witness before the Dies Committee in 1938 and many times expressed strong support for the Franco cause during the Spanish civil war, Fenlon was not a popular teacher.[35] For some students and faculty at the college, Fenlon must have been viewed as the institution's resident fascist.

Fenlon's motive for involving himself in the McMahon affair seems to have arisen from the man's intense distrust and dislike of the president of Brooklyn College. Gideonse had attacked O'Donnell in the Freedom House statement for violating McMahon's freedom of speech and academic freedom, and Fenlon publicly berated Gideonse in a letter printed in the *Brooklyn Eagle* for misinterpreting the state of free speech and academic freedom at Notre Dame and for projecting his own prejudices into the situation there.[36]

Though Fenlon had very limited factual knowledge of the situation at Notre Dame, he assumed for the sake of his argument against Gideonse that McMahon had never clearly indicated to the public that his statements on controversial subjects were personal ones and not those of the university. After no little time, Fenlon argued, university officials developed a procedure to insure that clear distinctions between personal views and official university positions were made. According to Fenlon, that was the heart of the matter, not censorship. The right of the university to protect itself from public identification with the personal views of faculty members was widely recognized. He cited the AAUP's 1940 Statement of Principles on Academic Freedom and Tenure to validate his point that academic freedom and freedom of speech were rightly understood at Notre Dame.[37] Because of McMahon's well-known history of rash and imprudent public statements, Fenlon assumed that the professor had consistently neglected to preface his speeches and writings with the usual disclaimers that he spoke only for himself.[38]

It was a peculiarity of the times, Fenlon wrote, when a self-appointed coterie such as Gideonse and friends at Freedom House could sit as some long-distance panel and "often with but a shred of the facts constitute themselves accuser, jury, and judiciary." Academic freedom and free speech, Fenlon concluded, were, "in fact, every whit as recognized and observed at Notre Dame as they are at Brooklyn College, City College, Columbia University, etc."[39]

O'Donnell much appreciated Fenlon's unsolicited effort on his behalf. Public support of the president's action against McMahon from working academics outside of Notre Dame had been virtually nonexistent. He responded to Fenlon immediately and gratefully with a God-bless-you letter, describing the story in the *Brooklyn Eagle* as an intelligent and sweeping rebuke of Gideonse and his friends for their "stupid pronouncement" on the McMahon case.

O'Donnell praised Fenlon's logic as irrefutable, his expression as incisive, and in effect confirmed the man's mistaken assumption about McMahon failing to preface his speeches with appropriate disclaimers.[40] Moreover, he did so at a time when his vice president, Father John J. Cavanaugh, admitted to a friend that no one at the university had accused McMahon of wittingly or unwittingly causing "the misinterpretation by sections of the public."[41] What Cavanaugh did not say to his friend was that the apostolic delegate had stated to O'Donnell that such misinterpretation was occurring and something had to be done about it. At this stage of the crisis, O'Donnell was willing to accept support from whoever would give it. Telling the truth about the role of the apostolic delegate in this affair had never been considered; now telling the truth about what McMahon had actually said and done was no longer important.

Flattered by O'Donnell's immediate and grateful response, Fenlon decided to do whatever he could to help the president of Notre Dame weather the fierce storm of criticism presently being visited upon him. On November 24, Fenlon reported to O'Donnell the substance of McMahon's "Catholics and Isolationism" article in *PM*, condemning what Fenlon insisted were untruthful allegations of anti-Semitic propaganda appearing in Father Coughlin's news magazine, *Social Justice*. He also admitted sending another letter supportive of O'Donnell's action against McMahon under the name of John E. Williams to the Reader's Forum section of the *Brooklyn Tablet*. Fenlon acknowledged that he had an understanding with Patrick J. Scanlan to publish multiple letters from him on important subjects under assumed names.[42]

In addition, Fenlon sent along to O'Donnell a summary of the highly critical editorial from the *Florida Catholic* and mentioned the appearance of supportive comments in the *Leader* out in San Francisco. He also reported a message from Scanlan that William Agar had attacked Notre Dame over the McMahon case in a radio broadcast in New York City on December 2. Fenlon concluded his report to O'Donnell by observing that men such as Agar and George Shuster were "of a type while Gideonse is just no good."[43]

O'Donnell's responses to Fenlon's letters were prompt but also very curious. In some instances, he affected agreement with Fenlon when there could be none. In others, O'Donnell simply lied to the man when it was absolutely unnecessary to do so. For example, O'Donnell certainly knew that Father Coughlin's *Social Justice* had been banned from the United States mail and why. Frank Walker, the postmaster general responsible for implementing the ban, was a personal friend and a member of the Notre Dame Board of Trustees. Surely O'Donnell knew that for years McMahon had been one of Coughlin's severest Catholic critics. Surely O'Donnell knew that at long last the Detroit priest had been silenced by his Ordinary. Yet O'Donnell expressed surprise that McMahon or anyone else would have complained about the anti-Semitic quality of *Social Justice*.[44] Except for wanting Fenlon to believe that the president of Notre Dame agreed with him that the widely accepted allegations against Father Coughlin and *Social Justice* were unfounded, O'Donnell's response defies rational explanation.

Similarly, O'Donnell also told Fenlon that in due course he would deal with the editor of the *Florida Catholic*.[45] Disputing with a bishop was a course of action utterly out of character for O'Donnell and one that was absolutely contrary to his frequently expressed position that the McMahon case was closed and that he would not be drawn into any private or public discussion of it with anyone. Yet, in his most presidential manner, he assured Fenlon that at the proper time, this matter of the *Florida Catholic* editorial would be put aright.[46]

Finally, in what turned out to be O'Donnell's last letter to Fenlon, he expressed agreement with the professor's observations about Agar and Shuster. He also professed a strong suspicion that the fine hand responsible for one of the letters defending Notre Dame's handling of the McMahon case recently appearing in the Reader's Forum section of the *Brooklyn Tablet* belonged to Fenlon, and then thanked the man profusely for standing up for Our Lady's university. There is no evidence that O'Donnell had access to any issues of or clippings from the *Brooklyn Tablet* or that he had ever seen the letter in question.[47] All he knew about this letter was what Fenlon had written to him. O'Donnell's posturing and untruthful responses to this man are perhaps a fair measure of just how frustrated and unnerved he had become. However, by early December relief was on the way. McMahon was about to get another job.

— iv —

A few days after McMahon's dismissal became public, some of his friends at Notre Dame contacted Professor Jerome J. Kirwan in the Department of Government at the University of Chicago to inquire about employment prospects at that institution.[48] Kirwan was himself a Catholic, a respected and published scholar in his chosen discipline, well-informed about American Catholic affairs in general, and familiar with the states of scholarship and of internal politics at Notre Dame. Immediately, Kirwan approached Robert M. Hutchins, president of the University of Chicago, and urged him to offer McMahon a post in the Department of Philosophy at that institution.

Initially, Hutchins' reaction to Kirwan's suggestion was one of extreme caution. Certainly, Hutchins had no reason to feel any special affection for McMahon. The president had once encountered the man on the field of public controversy and could not have been pleased by the experience. Active in the isolationist cause before Pearl Harbor, Hutchins certainly remembered being criticised by McMahon in the *Chicago Daily News* on January 30, 1941, for Hutchins' radio address against Lend-Lease legislation. McMahon styled the university president as overly pessimistic, incurably romantic, and entirely wrong. According to Kirwan's recollection of his discussion with Hutchins, the president worried about the propriety of hiring a faculty member that a sister institution had discharged. He was also fearful that hiring McMahon forthwith might be perceived by authorities at Notre Dame as a form of interference into their internal affairs. Kirwan persuaded Hutchins to have someone phone O'Donnell and simply ask him if he had any objections to the University of Chicago offering McMahon an appointment.[49]

A Catholic chaplain attached to the University of Chicago, Father James B. Connerton, called the president's office at Notre Dame on behalf of Hutchins as early as November 12, 1943.[50] However, when the call came to Notre Dame, O'Donnell was not in his office, so Cavanaugh took it. For Cavanaugh, Hutchins' proposal seemed nothing less than providential. With McMahon employed elsewhere, perhaps now public interest in his case would diminish and institutional image repair could begin. Cavanaugh assured Connerton that Notre Dame had no objections whatsoever to the University of Chicago making an offer to McMahon. As a matter of fact, Cavanaugh actually gave his former celebrity philosophy professor a strong personal recommendation. He asked only that public announcement of the appointment be delayed until O'Donnell could be informed

Because O'Donnell was away from the campus until early December, rumors about McMahon's job possibilities circulated widely in Chicago, New York, and Washington, D.C. As early as November 28, Father Raymond McGowan of the National Catholic Welfare Conference in Washington had heard that McMahon had been offered writing positions at *PM* and at the *Washington Post,* and that there was a possibility of a teaching appointment at the University of Chicago.[51] When the University of Chicago announced on December 10 that McMahon's appointment would begin with the spring semester, press reactions were everywhere positive. McMahon followed up the announcement by releasing a statement that made very clear the Chicago appointment was in large part a vindication of his stand against censorship and for freedom of speech. He expressed great pride and honor in being invited to teach at one of the world's most renown universities and promised to continue "to write and lecture as before in behalf of the cause of freedom and democracy."[52]

The University of Chicago was universally applauded for fulfilling American ideals of academic freedom and freedom of speech. Ira Lattimer of the American Civil Liberties Committee released a telegram commending President Hutchins for giving a practical answer to this most serious challenge to academic freedom in America. It was particularly important in times like these, Lattimer concluded, "that freedom of speech by professors on controversial subjects be preserved. Notre Dame's loss is Chicago's gain."[53]

The theme of President Hutchins' striking a blow for academic freedom in America by hiring McMahon at Chicago was repeated and expanded by Norman Jay, host of the "Very Truly Yours" prime time evening radio program broadcast on station WMCA in New York City. In an open letter addressed to Robert Hutchins broadcast on December 29, 1943, at 9:30 P.M. by "America's leading Independent Station," Jay interpreted Hutchins' action as being more than a vindication of academic freedom in this country. It was a victory for freedom and free men everywhere, as much a victory as a 2,000-ton bomb raid on Frankfort, a partisan blowing up a bridge in Yugoslavia, a Red Army breakthrough at Nevel, or a Marine landing in the South Pacific.[54]

According to Jay, total victory would be the sum of many little things. Victory would never be total, he declared, until men like Dr. McMahon could raise their voices against the enemy here and abroad without fear of economic reprisal. When President Hutchins turned back the forces of reaction by hiring Dr. McMahon, he earned the thanks of all Americans who cherished the democratic way of life and were determined to preserve it.[55] Jay did not state explicitly that O'Donnell, Notre Dame, and segments of the American Catholic community were active elements in the reactionary force that Hutchins had turned back. Clearly, however, the implication was there for those wanting to receive it. In the matter of this great challenge to American democratic values and academic freedom, Hutchins had shown himself to be a hero whereas O'Donnell had acted as an unpatriotic opponent of both. Jay offered O'Donnell an opportunity to respond to his open letter to Dr. Hutchins by sending one of his own to WMCA that Jay promised to read over the air.[56] Consistent with O'Donnell's insistence that the McMahon case was closed and further public discussion of it by himself was pointless, the president ignored Jay's offer.

O'Donnell's action against McMahon had created a serious public relations problem for Notre Dame. However, the widespread negative publicity attendant upon this case had succeeded grandly in accomplishing one of O'Donnell's publicly stated objectives. Any and all connections between McMahon's well-known liberal and anti-fascist views and official university positions had been broken. Norman Jay was correct when he stated in his broadcast that in the midst of a great world war there could be no ideological middle ground. If official Notre Dame was admittedly not as liberal and anti-fascist as McMahon, what were they? To that question, O'Donnell's actions had spoken much louder than his words.

Most Americans simply could not understand how describing Franco as a fascist was sufficiently controversial to justify turning an American academic out a job of ten years' standing. Public advocacy work, considered highly controversial at Notre Dame, was not generally thought to be so elsewhere. What was regarded as freedom of speech and patriotic activity elsewhere was not perceived as such at Notre Dame. Jay's impeachment of the university's patriotism was neither new, isolated, nor limited to persons of an anti-Catholic disposition. Such charges had been made frequently and explicitly in letters sent to O'Donnell during 1941 protesting some of Father O'Brien's more spectacular isolationist and anti-Roosevelt speeches. They continued to be made even after McMahon had been hired by the University of Chicago.

C. E. Kane, a Notre Dame alumnus, an executive with the Illinois Central Railroad, a frequent correspondent, and longtime friend of O'Donnell congratulated McMahon on receiving the appointment at Chicago. With tongue in cheek, Kane stated his hope that President Hutchins' offer did not mean that the Baptist traditions of the University of Chicago were more sensitive to matters of freedom of conscience and free speech than were the Catholic ones of Notre Dame.[57] Kane wondered now whether Notre Dame could find some nice, quiet parish where Father O'Brien could work out his salvation, remote from all temptations to enlighten the world with public speeches on controversial questions. If that were to happen, perhaps the university might be able to escape further patriotic reproach for all of the unwisdom displayed there during the days before Pearl Harbor.[58]

While Kane's concern was wrapped in humor, it was serious. By dismissing McMahon for advocating controversial public policy positions and making no public mention of past advocacy activities of O'Brien and Manion, O'Donnell in effect identified official Notre Dame with the conservative domestic and foreign policy positions of those men and their associates.

In a slightly different but more public way than was possible for Kane to do, an editorial in *Commonweal* made the same point. The editors regretted that O'Donnell's action against McMahon had set "a precedent unfortunate for academic freedom in Catholic institutions of learning."[59] However, the editors regretted even more that, according to his own admission, the president of the University of Notre Dame had responded to pressure from unidentified persons and organizations outside of the university to censor the publicly expressed political opinions of one of his faculty members. It was a fact, the editorial concluded, that Catholic institutions were at present sadly sensitive to such pressure, making the Church in general seem sympathetic to the fascist tendencies of what was only a loud-mouthed minority.[60]

The well-intentioned Ralph Barton Perry approached the same problem from still another perspective in the communications section of a later number of *Commonweal*. Perry worried about what Americans at large might think about the freedom of individual Catholics to make up their own minds about controversial public issues and about cooperating with non-Catholic fellow citizens to find solutions for common social and political problems. After all, by dismissing McMahon, the university created an impression that it had official political opinions that were the reverse of those expressed by Professor McMahon.[61]

According to Perry, enemies of Catholicism insisted that Catholics were not free to take independent positions on controversial political and social issues. They were convinced also that the Church would not shrink from using its discipline to achieve self-serving political and social ends. Friends of Catholicism, Perry continued, consistently denied that such allegations were true. Nonetheless, the university's treatment of Professor McMahon seemed to have strengthened the arguments of the enemies, weakened those of friends, and jeopardized the prospects of continuing a civic comradeship between Catholic and non-Catholic Americans. At the present moment, Perry concluded, there were grave doubts, widely disseminated, that academic freedom was not rightly understood at Notre Dame.[62]

— v —

By the end of the year, everything that outsiders could say about the McMahon case had been said. All that remained was for the insiders in this affair to wrap up final details and close their files. After McMahon's appointment to the University of Chicago was announced on December 10, O'Donnell began preparing a final report for the apostolic delegate. According to O'Donnell, the McMahon case was closed, and it had been closed insofar as he was concerned since the time of the professor's resignation on October 22.[63] Everything transpiring at Notre Dame or in the press since formal acceptance of that resignation on November 6 had been irrelevant.

Next, the president described his conferences and correspondence with McMahon beginning on August 16 and ending on November 6. He repeated the substance of his own arguments but not those of McMahon. O'Donnell mentioned his proposed *modus agendi* for protecting the good name of the university but did not explain the conditions set down in it. He stated explicitly that McMahon's rejection of those unexplained conditions was interpreted as a resignation from the faculty which he, as president, accepted with regret.

In order to provide the apostolic delegate with full knowledge of the procedures followed in this case, O'Donnell included with this report copies of his correspondence with McMahon, official university statements on the case, the telegram received from *PM* about the possible involvement of the Holy See in the decision to act against McMahon, and his response to the *PM* telegram. He also included in the packet of material sent to Cicognani copies of his September correspondence with

Archbishop Lucey. In this report, O'Donnell admitted, forthrightly and without regret, that he had lied to the editors of *PM*, "Naturally, I gave categorical denial to its brazen innuendo."[64] He concluded by mentioning that McMahon had been hired by the University of Chicago.

O'Donnell said nothing in this report about his correspondence and cooperation with Father Smith and Professor Fenlon in Brooklyn. No mention was made of local or national reactions to his action against McMahon, of the enormous damage done to the academic reputation of the university, or of the suspicions raised and publicly expressed about the patriotism and commitment to democratic values of the university and of American Catholics. The report was as O'Donnell described it as succinct as possible. It was also written to please, being exactly what O'Donnell believed the apostolic delegate wanted to hear.

Cicognani required three weeks to acknowledge receipt of O'Donnell's report and enclosures. He thanked the president for providing such a "clear and comprehensive view of the recent events attendant upon the withdrawal of Dr. Francis McMahon from the university faculty."[65] The apostolic delegate assured O'Donnell that now he had sufficient information to prepare and send off his required report to the cardinal secretary of state. Cicognani agreed that the McMahon case was officially closed and confidently hoped that the repercussions of it "will not in any way interfere with the prestige of the University."[66]

Indeed, the McMahon case was now officially closed. The apostolic delegate could get on and write his report. The Spanish ambassador to the Vatican could be told that the small problem troubling him caused by a layman employee of the University of Notre Dame had been resolved. Surely, the greatest challenge to academic freedom in America at that time deserved something more thoughtful than Archbishop Cicognani's confident hope that the university had suffered no real damage. Surely, for what he had done and endured, even O'Donnell deserved something more supportive than that. But a meekly expressed confident hope was all that O'Donnell got. In one sense, the case had begun in triviality with McMahon's off-hand comment about Franco reported in the *New York Times* and ended in the same way with the apostolic delegate's spare thank you to O'Donnell.

— vi —

While the McMahon affair had begun and ended in triviality, the consequences of it for the professor as well as the Vatican anxieties and fears behind the apostolic delegate's intervention were serious. To be sure, McMahon lost his post at Notre Dame and quickly obtained another one at the University of Chicago. While there, McMahon wrote and published in 1945 his one major book, *A Catholic Looks at the World*. In that book, he developed further the themes presented in his article, "Catholics and Isolationism," published in *PM*, November 22, 1943. He touched upon his difficulties while at Notre Dame but only in an abbreviated and very measured way. The book was reviewed, but not widely so and reached only a very small audience.

With the book now behind him, McMahon began to think seriously of a career change. For reasons not evident, McMahon did not find teaching philosophy to the students at his new university very satisfying. Perhaps the exhilaration of front-page living experienced over the last three years at Notre Dame had been too exciting to give up. Certainly, McMahon had enjoyed being quoted in the *New York Times* or reading about himself there. That sort of importance was difficult to put aside.

Moreover, while at the University of Chicago, McMahon probably admitted to himself that Father O'Donnell had been absolutely right about one thing. The Notre Dame connection had made McMahon a celebrity. It was that connection that had made McMahon's interventionism in 1941 and advocacy of wartime cooperation with the Soviet Union newsworthy. In the postwar climate of an escalating cold war, there was nothing about a University of Chicago connection that could make McMahon's off-campus speeches denouncing exaggerated nationalism, pointing out the inherent evil of Communist philosophy and ideology, and strongly condemning Soviet domination of eastern Europe especially interesting.[67] Others with greater expertise than McMahon made the same points more often and more authoritatively. Consequently, in 1945 and 1947, his outside speaking engagements became fewer and farther between.

Though McMahon certainly loved the city of Chicago, he seems to have been insecure in and even bored by his situation in the philosophy department of the University of Chicago. In any case, for whatever reasons, McMahon's time there was short. He stayed one semester less than three years, leaving the university and academic life as well in the summer of 1946. He was offered a job with the *New York Post* as a columnist and foreign correspondent and took it. His first assignment in 1946 was in Spain.

As early as April 1945, the Spanish government had made special efforts to improve strained wartime relations with the United States and Britain. Anxious also to secure membership in the new United Nations organization, Spanish authorities agreed at that time to let foreign journalists file news stories out of Spain uncensored. Believing absolutely that the Franco government had played some role in effecting his dismissal from Notre Dame, McMahon was a poor choice to test the Spanish government's new policy of openness to foreign journalists. His visa was not granted quickly, but granted it was, and he arrived in Spain at the end of December 1946.

Apparently, Spanish officials had been alerted by unnamed persons prominent in American Catholic circles that McMahon was going to Spain and advised also that the man was far too politically "impassioned" to function as an objective reporter and would bear watching. Spanish authorities took this advice seriously and kept their eyes on him, hoping to find or create a situation that would justify revoking his press credentials and deportation.

McMahon filed a few stories in January and February, 1947, without incident, but he was closely watched.[68] In late March, Spanish wireless companies refused to transmit two of his stories. One of the stopped stories dealt with alleged corruption in the Spanish Foreign Office. He had based this story on an article published in a Spanish Falangist magazine and had added nothing of his own to it. The other suppressed story criticized the attitude of some Spanish Republicans toward Holy Week celebrations.[69]

Regarding those two specific articles as defamatory and displeased by the tone of others, the Spanish government decided to move against McMahon. While traveling in Seville he was arrested and relieved of his press credentials. No longer an accredited journalist, McMahon was transported to Madrid and put aboard the first New York–bound plane.

Notice of McMahon's difficulties appeared in the *New York Post* on April 3 and in the *New York Times* the following day. T. O. Thackery, managing editor of the *Post,* requested that the State Department intervene to secure McMahon's personal safety. Immediately, Philip Bonsal, U.S. charge d'affaires in Madrid, protested the Spanish government's actions and urged that McMahon's press credentials be restored.[70] The Spanish government stood firm on the matter and proceeded with the deportation.[71]

Thereupon, a spokesman for the State Department suggested that McMahon's expulsion might be a violation of the Spanish government's agreement proclaimed two years ago allowing foreign journalists to file uncensored news stories. There seemed to be a pattern operative there. A similar action had been taken against a French journalist, Raymond Hubert, in late March.[72]

Pattern or not, the State Department's interest in McMahon's problem with the Spanish government rapidly diminished. A few days after the *New York Times* quoted a Spanish official's explanation that his government had been warned against McMahon by unnamed persons prominent in American Catholic circles, the State Department announced without further explanation that the matter of McMahon's expulsion from Spain was closed. Given the escalating tensions of the cold war, apparently the need for good relations with the Spanish government to facilitate establishment of air force bases in that country was far more important to America's national interest than the plight of an expelled American journalist with an anti-Franco reputation.

After a short and unpleasant experience in Spain as a foreign correspondent and unhappy with journalism as a career and the *New York Post* as a place of employment, McMahon looked for another line of work. He took a job for a year with Americans for Democratic Action (ADA) as a United Nations observer. For McMahon, one year in New York was enough. He returned to Chicago, where his new wife was employed as a social worker.

Once settled into a small apartment on Lake Shore Drive, McMahon encountered serious difficulties finding an academic job. His widely publicized difficulties at Notre Dame effectively prevented area Catholic colleges and universities from hiring him. At the same time, local public and private colleges and universities were uninterested in a man with a reputation as a troublemaker, especially one whose academic specialty, Thomistic philosophy, had such limited appeal.

For about eleven years, stipends from lectures and free-lance articles in Catholic periodicals were McMahon's main sources of income. Nonetheless, during this long period without a regular academic job, he maintained his memberships in national and regional Catholic philosophy associations, presented papers at professional conferences, and published specialized articles in learned journals. He remained current in his field and maintained contacts with friends and colleagues working in his discipline.

Finally, in 1961 McMahon found an academic job in Chicago. He received a regular appointment in the philosophy department at the recently established Roosevelt University. Until his retirement in 1973 McMahon remained at that university, teaching Thomistic metaphysics in an institution with a high percentage of Jewish students.

At no time before retirement or after did McMahon ever try to summarize his own life or put it into a perspective. If he had, most likely he would have described himself as a relatively uncomplicated Catholic man living and working in an extraordinary time. Throughout his adult life McMahon had generally expected the best from persons and from institutions and, to his sorrow, far too often did not find it. Nonetheless, he committed himself totally to the service of what he believed were the great and noble causes of his generation, increasing papal influence in the world, expanding liberal Catholicism in America, making New Deal politics and economics work, defeating Nazi totalitarianism, cooperating with Russia in the war for the sake of better postwar world, combatting anti-Semitism everywhere, and then after the war attacking Communism as a social and political system. As a true believer and passionate devotee of such causes there was no one better.

Ironically, however, despite McMahon's enduring devotion to such causes, some of the custodians of them knew little or nothing about him and made virtually no effort to find out who he was or what he had done. They never knew how willingly and positively he had served their causes. Sadly, in the end, some of those custodians treated him shabbily. Yet there was one group that did not.

For a perceived greater good, McMahon had been victimized by the pope's representative in America in 1943. For the sake of ease and political convenience, he was abandoned by the great men of the Roosevelt administration in 1943 and again by influentials in Truman's State Department in 1947. However, American Jewish leaders in Chicago did not forget his courageous public stands against anti-Semitism in America during the war years, and in time a place was found for him teaching many of their sons and daughters in Roosevelt University. McMahon appreciated that and did it for twelve years. He enjoyed fourteen years of retirement in the city he loved. McMahon died in Chicago in 1987 at the age of eighty-one.

— vii —

What then about the reality of the fears of Vatican officials and of the apostolic delegate so often expressed about a possible Italian Communist takeover of Rome after German forces withdrew? Vatican anxieties about possible Communist actions of some sort occurring in Rome after the fall of Mussolini in 1943 were entirely appropriate. At that time, Rome was a troubled and unruly city full of black market operators, hustlers, informers, spies, double agents, escaped prisoners of war, hunted Jews, hungry people, and some haphazardly armed and trained Communist-led partisan bands.[73] For Vatican officials in the summer of 1943, there was a lot to worry about and absolutely no tolerance for Catholic spokesmen in the United States or elsewhere publicly advocating cooperation with Communists for any reason.

With the benefit of historical hindsight we know now that Italian Communists in and around Rome were insufficiently armed, organized, or numerous to take over the city in the very short time between the German departure at the end of May and the American arrival on June 4, 1944. However, Vatican officials did not know that and tended to think about their situation in worst-case scenarios.

If a major Communist coup in Rome was impossible, there were in the city Communist groups and cells sufficiently organized and disciplined to undertake terrorist attacks on German troops serving there and to provoke the most severe reprisal against innocent civilian hostages of the entire Italian campaign. All of this began on March 23, 1944, when sixteen Communist students organized into four partisan action squads and attacked an SS military police company on parade in the Via Rasella. With explosive devices and small arms, they killed thirty-two soldiers and wounded sixty others.

The German response to this attack was swift and brutal. Though both Hitler and Himmler insisted that the city of Rome had to be severely punished, it was Field Marshal Albert Kesselring, commanding general of German forces in Italy, who decided how serious that punishment had to be. In order to achieve maximum deterrence against future partisan attacks in the city, the field marshal ordered the execution of ten Italians for every German soldier killed.

In order to mitigate the horror of collecting and executing so many innocent hostages, Kesselring and his staff decided to empty local prisons and select for reprisal executions only persons already under death or life imprisonment sentences for other offences. However, there were not enough prisoners in custody to provide a ratio of ten for one. In the end, the shortfall was made up from persons rounded up near the scene of the attack and from local Jews. The selection process was quickly done. The gruesome work of executing 335 innocent hostages began in the afternoon of March 24 in the tunnels of the Christian catacombs off Via Ardeatine, twenty-four hours after the attack on Via Rassella, and required six hours and many bottles of cognac to complete.

Vatican officials and the apostolic delegate in Washington, D.C., had been right about the danger of an Italian Communist attack occurring in Rome. However, their assumptions about who would savage the people of Rome the most were entirely wrong.

The dismissal of McMahon for the reasons publicly stated was perceived by most of the American academic community as the most seri-

ous attack on academic freedom occurring in the country in years. Moreover, that dismissal produced the greatest public relations crisis in the
history of the university.

Academic freedom was assaulted at Notre Dame in 1943 precisely and
only because Notre Dame was a Catholic university. As such, the school
was embedded within an ancient but functioning arbitrary authority system that did not highly value contemporary American concepts and
applications of freedom of speech and academic freedom. Regulation by
that arbitrary authority system was a price that American Catholic clerical administrators and teachers and most lay faculty and students willingly paid in order to work and study at an American Catholic university.

As a matter of fact, within the general context of American Catholic
colleges and universities, there was nothing particularly oppressive or
limiting about the conditions of intellectual life and work at Notre Dame
at that time. George Shuster, who surely knew well of what he wrote,
observed that Notre Dame had always been a fairly generous and hos-
pitable institution, never quick to pounce on the private failings or ideological idiosyncracies of its faculty.[74]

What happened to McMahon at Notre Dame occurred because the
arbitrary authority system regulating Catholic institutions and instru-
mentalities in the United States was in good working order. No one in
the clerical chain of command of this system doubted, questioned, or
objected. The cardinal secretary of state wrote to the apostolic delegate,
who wrote to the president of the university, who in turn conferred with
his closest advisors, decided what to do, and then did it. Moreover,
O'Donnell, as president, acted forthwith and without serious consideration of possible damage to his reputation or that of the university.

The apostolic delegate precipitated this great crisis over academic
freedom at Notre Dame. That O'Donnell would have acted on his own
against McMahon in the summer of 1943 for public speeches delivered
during the previous six months is extremely unlikely. O'Donnell acted as
he did when he did because the conventions of the authority system of
which he was a part obliged him to report exactly how he had responded
to a formal request from a hierarchical superior. Surely, the strengths and
weaknesses of O'Donnell's character affected the course and intensity of
the crisis, but O'Donnell did not initiate it. What happened to McMahon
and O'Donnell could have happened at any other Catholic college or
university. Occurring as it did at Notre Dame, maximum notoriety was
assured.

Unaware of the role of the apostolic delegate in initiating the crisis at
Notre Dame, George Shuster indicted O'Donnell for presidential cow-

ardice. Shuster hypothesized that O'Donnell had capitulated to pressure from the Coughlinite crowd, that is, rabid anti-British, anti-Semitic, anti-Communist, and anti-Roosevelt Catholics.[75] To be sure, O'Donnell had heard from such people many times during the past three years and had not enjoyed the experience. However, in the summer of 1943 the president of Notre Dame had not capitulated to pressure from that group. Shuster was wrong about O'Donnell being a presidential coward. The crisis occurred and developed as it did because O'Donnell had acted out the part of a loyal, courageous, perhaps even reckless officer determined to obey orders and fulfill his mission at whatever cost.

Persons as well as institutions were victimized by this affair. Clearly, McMahon was a victim, but in the short term was perhaps the least damaged. His career went on in other places. O'Donnell was a victim also, badly used by the authority system of which he was a part. Other Notre Dame presidents might have responded more wisely or well to the situation in which O'Donnell found himself, few could have done worse, but he was a victim nonetheless, in effect forced to fight a battle he did not want. In American academic circles, for a brief time, O'Donnell's reputation as a university president was severely damaged.

In the short term, the McMahon case rendered suspect the intellectual integrity and overall quality of the type of education provided at Notre Dame and at other Catholic colleges and universities as well. Also, sadly and ungenerously in some quarters, the patriotism and commitment of American Catholics to democratic ideals was questioned. While the public relations damage to Notre Dame was severe in the McMahon case and to Catholic higher education in general less so, it was not to be long lasting. In 1944, there were few students to compete for, the case was not replicated elsewhere, and public interest in it diminished after McMahon moved to the University of Chicago. In any case, in the euphoria of victory at war's end, much of what had happened at home and abroad during the course of that conflict was quickly and happily forgotten. The educational needs of hundreds of thousands of returning veterans had to be met. Along with the rest of American Catholic higher education, Notre Dame strove mightily to do its part by expanding facilities and finding space for as many students as possible.

The last word, perhaps the best words, on the McMahon case were really some of the first ones written about it after reports of the dismissal first appeared in the press. Willis Nutting of the Notre Dame history department wrote to Monsignor Daniel Cantwell on November 12 seeking support from that influential Chicago priest for the faculty petition to reinstate McMahon. In his letter to Cantwell, Nutting observed that "we have a chance of having a really fine school here if certain elements learn that there are some things that simply cannot be done in an institution of higher learning."[76] Somewhere at Notre Dame, there must be an available slab of granite where that extraordinarily prescient and timeless bit of wisdom can be inscribed.

11

WAR'S END:
RECOVERY AND
REDIRECTION

D uring the summer of 1944, the progress of Allied forces in breaking out of Normandy and the steady advance of the Red Army toward and into Eastern Europe dominated the news. That news was not always good and the war was far from over, but by the end of the summer the inevitability of an Allied victory in Europe was clear enough. Media speculation about what the postwar world would be like and what America's role in it would be intensified. Related to such speculations was the crucial question of who would lead the country into a postwar world clouded with all sorts of political and economic uncertainties. Because 1944 was a presidential election year, that question would have to be answered in November.

Encouraged by their gains in the congressional elections in 1942, Republican leaders were optimistic about capturing the White House in 1944 whether the president ran for a fourth term or not. Those leaders were confident that in the political climate of 1944 Republicans could win if their message was right. A right message was one that successfully persuaded a majority of American voters that the federal government was in the hands of tired old men who were bent upon destroying free enterprise, were much too beholden to labor interests, and had turned blind eyes to an alleged increasing Communist influence over our domestic programs and foreign policy. To deliver that message to the American people in the fall election, Republican leaders selected two popular state governors.

At their national convention in Chicago in late June, Republicans nominated on the first ballot Thomas E. Dewey of New York for president. Dewey was a proven vote getter in New York, a state that Republicans would have to carry in order to win. For a running mate, Dewey chose his only near rival for the presidential nomination, John W. Bricker of Ohio, an older man, strongly conservative, and a former isolationist. It was a formidable team that promised a no-holds-barred campaign.

Though virtually all Democratic politicians as well as the public expected President Roosevelt to head the Democratic ticket for the fourth time, Roosevelt showed little interest in the nominating process and gave scant public attention to it during the spring of 1944. As a matter of fact, he did not formally declare his willingness to run for the presidency until July 11, five days before the opening of the Democratic National Convention, also held in Chicago.[1] Nonetheless, there was a real suspense factor for Democrats attending their convention. The state of the president's health was so precarious and obvious to all who saw him on a regular basis that Democratic leaders knew they had come to Chicago not to nominate a president and a vice president but to select two presidents.

Roosevelt did not travel to Chicago to attend the convention. Delegates arriving there were confused and uncertain about who ought to be their vice presidential nominee. Henry Wallace, the serving vice president elected in 1940, had become a serious political liability for the president and for the Democratic party. He had incurred the ire of conservative members of the Democratic party and of Southern senators and congressmen. Wallace had become a pariah among conservatives and Southerners because of his frequently expressed strong liberal principles, particularly his many public statements about the need to promote racial equality in the country.

In public statements about racial inequality in the United States, Wallace had been both general and annoyingly specific: racial discrimination in the country must end, poll taxes denying African Americans voting rights must go, equal educational opportunities must come, and equal pay for equal work regardless of race or sex must become the norm.[2] In all such matters, Wallace was clearly ahead of his time. However, because Wallace was so far ahead of his time in 1944, Democratic party leaders decided, and the president agreed, that as vice president and as a possible president Wallace was unacceptable to mainstream America and must be put aside. He was.

But putting Wallace aside was not neatly or easily done. The managers of the convention were totally in the dark about whom the president and his advisors wanted. At one point, Wallace was reported to be the chosen one. A day later, the favorite appeared to be James F. Byrnes of South Carolina, a former senator, former Supreme Court justice, serving director of economic stabilization, and well-liked by the president, but also a strong segregationist and a Catholic who had converted to Protestantism in order to marry a wealthy southern girl. In the end, the president selected Harry S. Truman, a blunt-speaking but generally well-respected senator from Missouri, to be his running mate.

The process leading to Truman's nomination had been very messy, at times throwing convention proceedings into turmoil. However, Roosevelt managed to reassure the delegates and rally them to the great cause of a fourth term with a short but moving acceptance speech delivered by radio from a railroad car in San Diego. On his way to a secret meeting with General MacArthur and Admiral Nimitz in Hawaii and though severely debilitated physically, his marvelously self-confident radio voice overpowered the delegates in Chicago.

The president simply stated what were the tasks facing his administration in 1944 and what ought to be the postelection and postwar social and economic agenda for the country. First and foremost, the war had to be won as fast and as decisively as possible. Second, international organizations had to be formed that would be able to arrange the armed forces of the sovereign nations of the world in ways that would make future wars impossible. Third, an economy for our returning veterans and for all Americans had to be built that would provide employment and a decent standard of living for all. With no one on the stage in the Convention hall or at the podium, the effect of the president's familiar booming radio voice on the delegates was astonishing. Forty thousand people rose and cheered their leader, who might have been absent physically but was in every other way with them.[3]

The president's words about providing employment and other opportunities for returning veterans were in large part promises already kept. On June 22, 1944, Roosevelt signed into law the extraordinary veteran's benefit program known generally as Public Law 346 or the GI Bill of Rights. This law established the largest, most generous, and by far most successful time-limited training and educational entitlement program mounted by the federal government in the twentieth century.

Indeed, there were a few doubtful moments for the GI Bill as it moved through the stages of legislative enactment. As a matter of fact, extraordinary measures had to be employed to report the bill out of a House committee where its southern conservative chairman, John A. Rankin

(D-Mississippi), objected to using taxpayer dollars to assist able-bodied men who ought to be able to take care of themselves. However, once the bill reached the floors of the House and Senate, it passed both houses without a single negative vote.

The GI Bill embodied a comprehensive approach to veterans' entitlements. It authorized the Veteran's Administration to administer a wide range of benefits including mustering out pay, mortgage insurance for no-down-payment home loans, payments of twenty dollars a week for up to fifty-two weeks to veterans unable to find jobs or, for that matter, even to veterans unwilling to look for work, guaranteed loans up to two thousand dollars for starting or expanding businesses, funds for constructing additional veteran's hospital facilities, and massive training and education programs for returning soldiers and sailors.

Under the provisions of the GI Bill, veterans could qualify for subsidized farm training and receive subsidized industrial on-the-job training. Between 1946 and 1956 more than two million former service men and women pursued such programs. Also, there were subsidized educational opportunities for veterans in technical and trade schools as well as payments to veterans for completion of interrupted or abandoned secondary-school education. In the decade after the war, over three and a half million ex-soldiers and sailors took advantage of these opportunities.

The most important and most far-reaching of all of the educational benefits provided by the GI Bill were the tuition subsidies and living allowances given to veterans seeking higher education. Between 1946 and 1956, more than two million veterans flooded into American colleges, universities, and graduate schools. Most of these institutions managed this unprecedented situation well, but some did not. However, for American colleges, universities, and graduate schools generally, the most crowded years, 1946 to 1952, were in every way a magic moment in the history of American higher education. No form of federal aid to colleges, universities, and graduate schools before or since has been so generous or has changed so many lives for the better.

— ii —

In the summer of 1944 at Notre Dame, neither O'Donnell nor Cavanaugh thought much about magic moments for American higher education. However, both of them thought seriously about what a postwar Notre Dame would be like. O'Donnell and his advisors assumed that a postwar growth area at the university would be in graduate programs. To cope with an anticipated "resurgence of graduate study" after the war, the president proceeded with a modest reorganization of graduate school governance. A dean and a graduate school council replaced the existing graduate school committee as the governing body of departmental graduate programs. The serving secretary of the present graduate school committee, Father Philip S. Moore, was installed as the new dean of the graduate school.[4]

In 1944, to a very great extent, university academics were being run for and by the navy. O'Donnell and Cavanaugh understood their roles as president and vice president of the university in the present state of affairs to be those of interfering as little as possible with the officers in charge of the naval training programs. Beyond the modest change in graduate school administration, there is little evidence that either O'Donnell or Cavanaugh seriously considered what impact the GI Bill might have on postwar Notre Dame. If they thought about the GI Bill at all in 1944, most likely they would have been suspicious of it.

Catholic educators generally were opposed to all forms of federal aid to education. That opposition was based upon historical experience. At various times in the not-too-distant past, state legislatures and other state agencies had attempted to severely regulate or even abolish Catholic schools in their jurisdictions. For Catholic educators, application of the separation of church and state doctrine had come to mean separation of the state from Catholic educational institutions. It would be inaccurate to assume that Catholic educators opposed federal aid to education because most forms of it would be denied to them on constitutional grounds and for that reason opposed federal aid to education for everyone. That argument was rarely, if ever, publicly stated. The most frequently offered public rationale for opposing federal aid to education was a fear that with such federal aid would come some sort of curricula control. During the 1940s that was a price for state and federal aid that Catholic school and college administrators were unwilling to pay.

It was true, of course, that the wall of separation between church and state with regard to church-related colleges and universities had never been as impregnable as it was with church-related elementary and secondary schools. Among church-related elementary and secondary schools, Catholics predominated, whereas, among church-related colleges and universities, the majority of them were Protestant. In the practical order, for whatever reasons, federal aid to church-related colleges and universities was far less controversial and politically and constitutionally more deliverable than aid to church-related elementary and secondary schools.

In any case, the formula for paying tuition to church-related colleges and universities and providing living allowances to students attending them was ingenious and successfully avoided serious separation of church and state issues. No funds were paid directly to such institutions. Benefits went to entitled individual veterans. Tuition payments were paid by the Veteran's Administration to colleges and universities, church-related or not, only when the entitled veteran enrolled and remained in academic good standing. This formula worked and the experience of how well it worked inspired many Catholic educators to reconsider their view of federal aid to education programs as inimical to Catholic higher education.

At Notre Dame, O'Donnell and Cavanaugh began to rethink that traditional Catholic view of federal aid to education earlier than most other Catholic educators. They did so because members of their physics and chemistry departments had received about a dozen contracts between 1940 and 1945 from federal government agencies for research projects carried out in Notre Dame laboratories. While the number of contracts received was small and the dollar amounts obtained—almost $450,000 over a six-year period—was minuscule when compared with what research giants like MIT, Cal Tech, Harvard, and Chicago received, it was more than went to any other Catholic university.[5]

Given that Professors Walter Miller and Bernard Waldman of the Notre Dame physics department worked on the Manhattan Project in Los Alamos and that several other Notre Dame scientists were well connected in the network of science professional associations and academic science circles generally, Notre Dame was well positioned to participate in the enormous postwar expansion of the federal government's sponsorship and support of university-based scientific research. The steps leading to the establishment of the National Science Foundation in 1950 were many and complicated, but in the person of the much-maligned Father O'Donnell, Notre Dame was present in 1944 when the first of those steps was taken.[6]

Why Notre Dame was present at the beginning of planning for the federal government's postwar support of university-based scientific research programs is clear enough. Despite all of the extremely negative publicity visited upon Notre Dame and upon O'Donnell personally from the McMahon affair, it seemed politically wise to Roosevelt's science advisors that at least one highly visible Catholic university ought to be involved in the planning of this major national effort. Since Notre Dame had the best science record of all Catholic universities at the time, that seemed to be the place to go to find support and gain influence in the

American Catholic community for using tax dollars to support scientific research in American universities.

Notwithstanding how vigorously O'Donnell had been attacked in the press during late 1943 and early 1944 and the fact that he was neither a scientist nor an active scholar in any academic field, he was invited in October 1944 to participate in a proposed study of the relation of basic research undertaken in universities to future American industrial development.[7] The invitation, which came from Dr. Karl Compton of MIT, was accepted at once. No longer a pariah among university presidents and very glad of it, O'Donnell gave much time and energy to this project during 1945 and early 1946, earning appointment to the prestigious Committee on Science and the Public Welfare.

O'Donnell met several times with this group during 1945 and fully participated in their discussions. Out of those discussions and with input from other groups and individuals in July 1945 came Vannevar Bush's celebrated report "Science—The Endless Frontier." The forms of taxpayer support for university-based scientific research justified and recommended in this report became the basis for establishing the National Science Foundation five years later. Not only did O'Donnell contribute significantly to the discussions of the Committee on Science and the Public Welfare on the many controversial issues involved in providing government funding for scientific research, he also testified before a Senate committee and lobbied legislators on behalf of Bush's vision of a new, independent, non-political scientific research agency administered and funded by the federal government.[8]

At hearings conducted by the Joint Senate Committee on the proposed new National Science Foundation in October, 1945, O'Donnell admitted that he was not a scientist by training but asserted that he had become one "by exposure and association." Unreservedly, O'Donnell endorsed the objectives of the new foundation, insisting that government-supported basic research and development programs in universities would be no less essential in peace than they had been in war. Continuing progress in pure scientific research in the United States, he concluded, was essential to achieve a lasting peace.[9]

On the broader question of muting traditional Catholic opposition to all forms of federal aid to education, O'Donnell performed yeomen service as well. While not publicly dismissing that traditional opposition, he certainly helped put it aside by observing that if the federal government's proposed scheme for funding university-based scientific research was sinful, it was only venially so in view of all of the good it could do.[10]

Indeed, in a very important public relations sense, the president of Notre Dame had done a great service to further Bush's project. Unfortunately, O'Donnell did not live long enough to see the actual establishment of the federal agency he had publicly and forthrightly supported at a very critical time. Nonetheless, when the National Science Foundation became operational in 1950, Notre Dame had a representative on its governing board and continued to have one there for the next sixteen years.[11]

On the controversial issue of federal aid for university-based scientific research, O'Donnell, with strong support in 1944 and 1945 from Cavanaugh and from the dean of his recently reorganized graduate school, Father Philip S. Moore, faced the future and enthusiastically embraced it. As a matter of fact, O'Donnell revealed just how complete that embrace was in his response to a survey of science facilities and program expansion plans. He made very clear his intention to build new chemistry, biology, and physics laboratories as soon as construction materials became available. Moreover, reflecting his experience on the Committee on Science and Public Welfare and as an advocate for improving university-based scientific research programs, O'Donnell announced plans for increasing the size of the physics department.[12]

Also in the summer of 1944, another very important part of the future confronted O'Donnell and Cavanaugh, one which they did not like but could neither avoid nor put aside. That part of the future was the general issue of racial equality in the United States and the specific one of admitting African-American students to Notre Dame.

— iii —

In 1944, Gunnar Myrdal published his classic analysis of American race relations, *An America Dilemma: The Negro Problem and Modern Democracy*. Coming as it did close upon the great Detroit race riot of the previous year, Myrdal's book initiated a new awareness of race inequality in the country and made improvement of race relations a national social imperative. The book generated much soul-searching everywhere, especially among Catholic educators.

Into the 1930s, the record of Catholic educators admitting African-American students to their colleges and universities was dismal. Only a very small number of Catholic colleges and universities actually enrolled African-American students, and most of them were northern urban institutions. By the early 1940s that overall record had improved. A survey of the race issue in Catholic colleges and universities conducted in 1944 revealed that three-quarters of the responding institutions claimed to have no restrictions on admitting African-American students. However, that same survey disclosed that at least twenty-two Catholic colleges, most but not all located in the South, still excluded African Americans as a matter of policy.[13] Notre Dame was one of those few northern Catholic universities that did so exclude.

Notre Dame administrators had enforced a policy of excluding African Americans for many years. The justification for such a policy was that few African Americans were Catholic and that fewer still ever applied for admission. When any tried, even when highly recommended by Catholic priests, they were refused. As early as 1922, Father Matthew J. Walsh, president of the university, explained the reasons for denial to a priest seeking admission of an African-American student to Notre Dame by arguing that exclusion was done for the applicant's own benefit. There are so many students at Notre Dame from the deep South, wrote Walsh, that the university had to question the advisability of "exposing a well-deserving colored boy to the prejudice that unfortunately the Southerner carries with him."[14]

As late as 1939, Father O'Hara justified exclusion of African Americans from the university on the same grounds. However a year later, a campus Catholic action group, Young Christian Students (YCS), challenged that policy by collecting signatures from students denying that admission of African-American students to Notre Dame would cause others to leave the university. This YCS effort notwithstanding, the policy of exclusion was not changed in 1940.[15]

The color line at Notre Dame was broken first by the U.S. Navy. At least two African-American trainees went through the Notre Dame V-12 program and another received his commission from the midshipman school.[16] Nonetheless, in the summer of 1944, the policy of excluding African Americans from regular Notre Dame undergraduate and graduate programs was still intact. However, on July 15, that policy was successfully challenged by an African-American applicant to the Notre Dame Law School. This application simply could not be denied because it came from an African American who happened to be an elected, sitting member of the Indiana State Legislature.

On July 24, 1944, Dean Manion of the law school informed Cavanaugh that he had received an application for admission to the law school from Jesse L. Dickinson of South Bend. Dickinson had represented the district in which Notre Dame was located in the Indiana State Legislature since 1942. In his letter of application, Dickinson described himself as "an American of African descent." Manion sent Dickinson's letter to Cavanaugh and wanted to know how he "should answer the enclosed letter from the African."[17]

Cavanaugh advised O'Donnell of the Dickinson application, discussed it with him, and together they carefully instructed Manion about how to proceed. Whether this instruction was written by Cavanaugh or by O'Donnell is not clear, but it came from O'Donnell's office and a copy of it was filed with O'Donnell's presidential correspondence. The instruction to Manion was sent on August 4, 1944, and asked the dean to investigate the case further. Then, after further investigation, if Manion was "satisfied with the background of the son of Liberia referred to in the letter of July 15 and assuming of course that he has the necessary prerequisites for entrance to our College of Law, I should not object to his enrollment, providing he does reside off-campus."[18]

Next, the president observed to Manion that since the man was the state representative for our district, "I think you will agree that it would be inadvisable to draw the color line for him." However, O'Donnell continued, "He will be the only American of African descent that you will permit to register for the next semester providing he meets the foregoing requirements." O'Donnell concluded by stating and then underlining his statement that "*Under no circumstances is any publicity to be given to this case.*"[19]

If otherwise qualified, Dickinson could be admitted to the Notre Dame Law School. The color line could be broken in the law school only for him in the fall of 1944 because of the exceptional circumstance that he was a member of the Indiana State Legislature. There is no surviving evidence indicating what Manion actually told Dickinson about his application. In any case, Dickinson did not attend the university. He remained active and popular in South Bend Democratic politics for many years and ended a long career of public service as director of the South Bend Public Housing Authority.

As for the admission of African Americans to other colleges of the university, a middle-aged local African-American minister, Rev. Edward B. Williams, was admitted to the journalism program in the College of Arts and Letters in November, 1944, and began his studies in January 1945. Also in 1945, Frazier Leon Thompson, an African-American student who had completed the V-12 program, was admitted to the university as a regular student, assigned to Morrissey Hall, and won a varsity monogram as a sprinter on the track squad. Both Williams and Thompson graduated from the university in August 1947.

Since Williams and Thompson were the first African Americans ever to graduate from Notre Dame, much was made of the event in the Negro press. Thompson was quoted as saying that while he was at Notre Dame, the only time that he knew he was colored was when he went off-campus. Coach Frank Leahy was also quoted in the same source as saying that he could imagine a time when qualified Negro athletes might even play on a Notre Dame football team.[20] The color line for undergraduates had been broken in 1945, but not many came. African-American undergraduates did not come to Notre Dame in recognizable numbers until the 1960s.

Contrary to O'Donnell's fear that negative publicity would follow from the admission of African Americans to Notre Dame, when that actually happened in the fall of 1944 there was none. Moreover, the rough handling of the Dickinson application in the summer of 1944 remained a well-kept secret. That secret was well kept because in the fall of 1944 discriminatory policies against African Americans in Catholic colleges and universities were crumbling everywhere. There were public relations advantages for those Catholic colleges and universities that had abandoned past discriminatory policies and opened their doors to African Americans who wanted to come.

For example, at a meeting of the midwestern unit of the National Catholic Educational Association (NCEA) in the fall of 1944, tales were told by representatives of Catholic colleges and universities about how far their respective institutions had moved toward non-discriminatory admission practices. Father William F. Cunningham, head of Notre Dame's Department of Education, assured NCEA members present that all was well at Notre Dame in this regard. Stretching the truth more than a bit, Cunningham explained how Navy programs had broken the color line at Notre Dame. Once that had happened, Cunningham continued, when a "Negro from South Bend entered the graduate school . . . his entrance was taken as a matter of course."[21]

Indeed, Cunningham had spoken a bit too soon. Certainly, the recollections of the Dickinson affair, if that was what Cunningham had in mind, by Manion, Cavanaugh, and O'Donnell were much different. The first African Americans to receive graduate degrees from Notre Dame— Goldie Lee Ivory, a South Bend social worker, and Joseph R. Luten, a South Bend elementary school teacher—did not do so until 1956.

Having more or less abandoned older negative attitudes toward federal aid to education and moved away from an outdated and immoral color line in admissions policies, knowingly or not, O'Donnell and Cavanaugh helped prepare the university for the new realities of postwar American higher education. Alas, those two issues, extremely important as they were, turned out to be only very small parts the great changes now bearing down on the university. In the months and years ahead, there would be many more exercises in reality acceptance that Notre Dame administrators would have to perform.

— iv —

A different but familiar sort of reality that Notre Dame administrators had to face in the summer and fall of 1944 was how the altered nature of intercollegiate football would affect the season during 1944. There were game contracts to be honored, stadiums to fill, and bills to pay, so the season had to be played through. However, wartime manpower requirements had depleted virtually every major college or university football program of experienced players. Moreover, some programs had lost coaches and staff as well.

In order to field teams in 1944, most major football programs had to rely on young eighteen- or nineteen-year-olds who were either pre-draft or draft-exempt. Only the naval and military academies at Annapolis and West Point had been able to keep their programs intact. Coaching staffs had been allowed to remain in place and experienced junior and senior football stars stayed on the playing fields and far away from active duty in Europe or the South Pacific. Other service teams, such as Great Lakes and Iowa Pre-Flight fared not quite as well as Annapolis and West Point, but transferred star players were regularly replaced by former college standouts or by experienced players from professional football teams. When the intercollegiate football season began in the fall of 1944, the playing fields were anything but level.

From such wartime exigencies, Notre Dame suffered severely. Both Coach Leahy and his starting quarterback, John Lujack, had gone off to active duty with the Navy in early 1944. Coaching responsibilities for the season of 1944 had been passed to Leahy's chief assistant, Ed McKeever. T-formation quarterback duties were taken over by Frank Dancewicz, a junior with limited playing time. While a young strong running back from last year, Bob Kelly, remained at Notre Dame, most of the experienced blockers and defensive linemen had to be replaced with younger and lighter players. The number of games played continued to be ten. But, as had been the case the previous year, the long train trip to Los Angeles was eliminated. Nonetheless, three train trips to the East Coast were authorized, allowing the Notre Dame team to play Dartmouth in Boston, Navy in Baltimore, and Army in Yankee Stadium.

Surprisingly, McKeever's team received an early season ranking of number one by running over its first three outclassed opponents, defeating Pittsburgh 55 to 0, Tulane 26 to 0, and then overwhelming Dartmouth in Fenway Park, 64 to 0. Next came a solid victory over Wisconsin, 28 to 13. The following week, against a team that Notre Dame had beaten by 47 points the previous year, McKeever's squad managed a narrow victory over a scrappy Illinois team, 13 to 7, and dropped to second place behind Army in the national rankings.

Then, only four days after President Roosevelt won re-election to an unprecedented fourth term, an inspired Navy team, ranked sixth in the country, played Notre Dame in Baltimore before 60,000 people and broke a long-standing precedent as well. For the first time since 1936, a Navy team defeated Notre Dame and did so handily, 32 to 13, dropping Notre Dame to fifth in the national rankings.

The game in Baltimore was a celebrity event with many high-ranking naval and military dignitaries traveling to it from nearby Washington, D.C. Among the military officers attending was Lt. Col. Earl Blaik. He had left the direction of his West Point squad to assistants in a game against Villanova in Philadelphia while he went to Baltimore to scout both the Notre Dame and Navy teams. Blaik was missed in Philadelphia perhaps only by Villanova. The Army team severely punished the overmatched team fielded by that Catholic school, 83 to 0.

In Baltimore, from the opening kickoff the power of the Navy line asserted itself. That line completely shackled Notre Dame running backs, limiting them to only thirty-six yards rushing in the entire game. Navy's offense, featuring Clyde Scott and Dick Duden, mounted four sustained touchdown drives of thirty-two, forty-four, sixty-five, and fifty-six yards, amassing an amazing 338 rushing yards against Notre Dame.

With the running game shut off, Frank Dancewicz threw thirty-three passes, completing fifteen. The only bright spot in an altogether dismal afternoon for McKeever's men was Bob Kelly's fierce determination to keep trying. He scored two touchdowns in the second half, when the game was already out of reach.[22] This unexpected, humiliating loss to Navy shocked Notre Dame supporters everywhere, but in no way did it prepare them for what awaited McKeever's team in Yankee Stadium against Army on Armistice Day, November 11, 1944.

In 1944, Earl Blaik's Army team was perhaps the most overpowering intercollegiate football team in modern history. The Army team's enormous football superiority during that year was founded on the wartime personnel weaknesses of its opponents. The inevitability and universality of the draft enabled Annapolis and West Point to attract, recruit, and retain the biggest, fastest, and best players in the country for three or four years.

Many of the stalwarts in the huge Army line had played college-level football elsewhere before receiving appointments to West Point. One-half of the celebrated Army backfield combination of Felix "Doc" Blanshard and Glenn Davis had previous college-level football experience. Blanshard had been a star in freshmen football at North Carolina before joining the Army Air Force and being plucked out of the ranks to attend West Point and play football there.

Blanshard's partner in football excellence, Davis, had been an All-American prep school star in football and track in California before agreeing to play four years of varsity football for Blaik at West Point. In 1944 the players fielded by Army simply battered and rolled over every team it played, outscoring opponents 504 to 35, and averaging fifty-six points a game. Against Notre Dame on Armistice Day, Army exceeded that average by three points, defeating Notre Dame, 59 to 0.

The Notre Dame team was never really in the game. Army's powerful line absolutely contained Notre Dame runners and harassed its passers all afternoon. Davis's speed and Blanshard's expert blocking for him was too much for the Notre Dame defense to handle. In short-yardage situations Blanshard was unstoppable. By halftime, Army had built its lead to 33 to 0. With the game clearly won, Blaik continued to play his starting backfield and added twenty-six points to the score at game's end. This Armistice Day massacre was the worst football defeat in Notre Dame's football history.

Alison Danzig, reporting the game for the *New York Times,* attributed the enormity of the debacle to the altered nature of wartime intercollegiate football. Because of the draft and transfers of naval trainees out of Notre Dame to active duty elsewhere, the football program there had been left dependent on younger, less-talented, and less-skilled players "who never would have made the third team on a prewar squad."[23] Indeed, that afternoon Notre Dame had been grossly and unfairly overmatched, but so was every other team played by Army during 1944. Yet one could not have watched the game in Yankee Stadium or listened to radio broadcast accounts of it without suspecting that Blaik had run up the score because he wanted to punish Notre Dame. Something more than a desire to win an important football game appears to have driven Blaik on that day.

There were many reasons why Blaik would want to run up the score and humiliate Notre Dame. Though Army had played Notre Dame regularly since 1913, victories for the Cadets had been few and, lately, far between. Army had not defeated a Notre Dame team since 1931 and had not even scored against one since 1938. Moreover, in the 1944 season, Notre Dame had exhibited no qualities of mercy toward outclassed opponents, running up a total score of 148 to 0 against Pittsburgh, Tulane, and Dartmouth. Perhaps the ever-mighty Notre Dame needed to be taught a lesson. There was also the bitter memory of Leahy spiriting Lujack away from West Point. In spite of Lujack's signed agreement to attend the military academy, Notre Dame officials allowed him to attend the university and play football.

Finally, there was a possible effect on Blaik from the great public-relations damage done to Notre Dame by the McMahon affair during the previous year. The university had been represented in the press and on radio broadcasts as an authoritarian, undemocratic institution, too friendly to Fascism in Spain and maybe elsewhere as well. Perhaps to Blaik and his staff at the time, defeating Notre Dame as decisively as the Army team did seemed a highly patriotic thing to do. Whatever Blaik's reasons, by sanctioning the Armistice Day massacre in Yankee Stadium, the long-standing football relationship between Army and Notre Dame was changed forever. Someday Leahy would return to Notre Dame. When he did, the respective Army and Notre Dame football programs would wage a war in which no quarter would be asked or given.

Humiliating as the one-sided loss to Army had been, the Notre Dame team quickly recovered its composure and mended its shattered confidence. During the final three games of the season, the Notre Dame team outplayed and easily defeated Northwestern, 21 to 0, turned back Georgia Tech, 21 to 0, and ran over a talented Great Lakes squad now coached by Lt. Comdr. Paul Brown, former head coach at Ohio State, by the convincing score of 28 to 7. Notre Dame ended this ten-game season with a record of eight wins, two losses, and ninth place in national rankings.

Except for the Notre Dame team's performances against the service academies, the team had played well enough in its other games to increase McKeever's marketability. Offered a head coaching position elsewhere, McKeever left Notre Dame in early 1945. With Leahy still in the Navy, O'Donnell and Cavanaugh had to find a coach for spring practice and the fall season and appointed Hugh Devore to serve as interim head coach until Leahy returned. A monogram winner on Hunk Anderson's teams, Devore had learned his coaching skills by working as an assistant under Leahy. O'Donnell and Cavanaugh knew that Devore was a loyal alumnus who would do his best with the talent available. Given the present state of wartime intercollegiate football, one could not ask for more than that.

— v —

The university had been embarrassed by the Armistice Day football massacre but not seriously and not for long. The president received a few nasty letters on the subject, which he did not bother to answer. However, another kind of embarrassment, cast also in the form of a nasty letter but on matters more serious than losing a football game, crossed the president's desk, and he had to deal with it. That embarrassment derived from Father John A. O' Brien's habit of putting into books and pamphlets written for ordinary people easy answers to very hard and complicated questions.

Lack of knowledge about a subject, especially a controversial one, never constrained O'Brien from addressing it and from offering judgments that severely amused or appalled persons better informed. That was his way. Embarrassments to the university from what he wrote or said were, and would continue to be, unending. They were simply a function of having him around.

Both O'Donnell and Cavanaugh liked O'Brien personally and were mindful of his repeated acts of generosity to the university, but they recognized that some way had to be found for disconnecting him from Notre Dame academics. Because O'Brien was so well known, his publications, no matter how hastily written or factually incorrect, were frequently taken in academic circles as a qualitative measure of the kind of scholarship produced by Notre Dame professors. That misperception was unfair, untrue, and damaging to the university's academic reputation.

For example, O'Brien had recently published a popular account of the causes of the sixteenth-century Protestant Reformation that was unscholarly and filled with factual errors. It was not a serious work but was taken as such by people who should have known better. For Protestant readers with serious historical interests in the Reformation era, O'Brien's treatment of the causes of that movement was outrageously bigoted and unhistorical. Moreover, he seemed to be totally unaware of just how unscholarly and offensive his essay into Reformation history was. When the little book appeared, he actually presented a signed copy of it to O'Donnell.

Over the years, O'Brien had been in trouble frequently with some Catholics, especially with theologians and philosophers. No outstanding historical, theological, or moral controversy was too big or too complex for O'Brien to explicate. He usually did so without much regard for current official views, largely because he probably did not know what the official views were. For Catholic experts in such matters, O'Brien's explication was generally out of context, too simplistic, much too liberal, and disrespectful of received authority. Indeed, O'Donnell and Cavanaugh recognized that O'Brien's free-wheeling, idiosyncratic treatment of issues better left to experts was embarrassing to the university. Something had to be done about the O'Brien problem, but nothing really unpleasant.

Criticizing Father O'Brien to his face or disciplining him in any way was extremely difficult. No one could be more charming, and, of course, O'Brien rarely missed an opportunity to be generous. The man was so devoted to Notre Dame, so friendly and anxious to please the president and vice president, that the slightest sort of reprimand seemed exceedingly misdirected.

For example, just when the wave of negative publicity from the McMahon firing was about to sweep over the university, O'Donnell sought a temporary escape by traveling to Mexico with a very wealthy potential donor. O'Brien had introduced the potential donor to O'Donnell and offered to use his connections in Mexico to arrange a visit for O'Donnell and his traveling companions with the Mexican president, Avila Comacho. O'Brien assured O'Donnell that Comacho "will welcome you with Spanish cordiality."[24] Later, O'Brien sent a check for $500 to the centenary of the university, stating that he wanted "to aid in some slight way in its noble work of Catholic education and in the salvation of souls. Would that it were much more. As usual it may be simply credited as from a friend."[25] Deeply touched by the gift and by the demeanor of the donor, O'Donnell thanked O'Brien and hoped that his bountiful heart would be forever blessed.[26]

O'Donnell's extremely positive attitude toward O'Brien was jolted in June 1944 when a long, blistering attack on the priest's recently published essay on the Reformation arrived at the president's office. Walter Whitacre, a writer with strong Protestant opinions, sent his comments directly to O'Brien at the university with a copy to the president. The essay had been published by the Paulist Press in the fall of 1943 just before the McMahon crisis became front-page news. As was the custom with Catholic religious publishing houses, this pamphlet carried an official imprimatur indicating that nothing in it was objectionable to Catholic teachings.

The pamphlet was a typical O'Brien-style piece of popular religious writing. It was a short, hastily written, but readable argument that the Reformation had been a regrettable mistake. Luther was a good man who had gone bad. Henry VIII was an evil, lustful man who could not control himself. The pamphlet was intended to persuade lightly-churched Protestants and unchurched Americans generally to think about the Catholic Church as custodian of the one and only secure road to salvation. Certainly, O'Brien was no Reformation scholar and totally unfamiliar with crucial documents from the period and with the writings of contemporary scholars on the leading issues and personalities driving the movement. O'Brien's essay was by no standard a scholarly work and in normal circumstances would not have been perceived as such by anyone familiar with the field.

However, for interfaith relations, the times were not normal. As has been seen, tensions between Catholics and Jews in urban areas had intensified. The combination of Catholic intransigence on the issue of only one true Church and fear of an increased Catholic influence in American political and social life had worsened relations with Protestant denominations. For his part, Whitacre treated the O'Brien essay as an example of Catholic aggression, an uniformed, error-filled, but nonetheless official Catholic indictment of the Reformation. For Whitacre, it was representative of American Catholic scholarship generally and of Notre Dame scholarship in particular. It was time for honest men of faith to take a stand against what he believed was nefarious published nonsense about the Reformation. He did so by writing a sharp personal attack on O'Brien, adding a spiteful disparagement of most things Catholic, and then sent a copy of it to the author's boss.[27]

In attacking O'Brien's essay, Whitacre missed few opportunities to abuse Notre Dame and diminish the status of American Catholics and their institutions. He began with a series of rhetorical questions, asking first whether the O'Brien essay was a sample of the kind of teaching that went on at Notre Dame. If so, he continued, the university's greatness must evidently be found on the football field rather than in the classroom. Next, Whitacre speculated whether there was any connection between McMahon's recent well-publicized departure from the university and the level of scholarship exhibited in O'Brien's essay.[28]

Whitacre concluded by asking why the Catholic religion needed to be perpetuated constantly by such dreadful propagandistic writing. The answer had to be that Catholicism as a religion lacked something. Whitacre finished by faulting the Catholic Church for its steady intolerance of other denominations and asserted that this pamphlet did no credit to O'Brien, to his church, or to the school that employed him.[29]

This attack was strong medicine indeed for O'Brien and underservedly so for O'Donnell. Yet both of them took it very well. Separately, O'Donnell and O'Brien imperceptibly and slowly realized that traditional scholarship was not the latter's metier. Systematic research and judgments derived from analyzed evidence were not intellectual tasks done easily or well by everyone. Certainly, O'Brien did not do them well.

It is a fact that simple interest in historical subjects does not make an expert. Interest is not and can never be a substitute for a learned competence. Much like his earlier ventures into theological controversy, O'Brien's latest essay into Reformation history was a disaster. To informed readers who took the trouble to read his pamphlet, in effect O'Brien admitted that he simply did not know what he was talking about. That was not good for his own reputation or that of the university.

From his presence on the Committee on Science and the Public Welfare and from sharing conference tables with such men as Vannevar Bush and Karl Compton, O'Donnell had acquired a deeper appreciation of the value of university-based research in science and other scholarly fields. Though he never articulated it in a formal way, O'Donnell now believed that if teaching were the heart of a modern university, in the postwar world research would be its soul. In a modern, postwar university, especially one aspiring for distinction, men and women who lacked solid scholarship would have a diminishing presence. How much of this hastening future O'Donnell and O'Brien actually understood or even recognized is impossible to know. Nonetheless, each of these two men managed to remain civil to one another and work out an adjustment.

— vi —

In early 1945, the pace of the war in Europe and in the Pacific intensified. After stopping the unexpected German offensive in Belgium in December and January, American troops advanced rapidly toward the Rhine, capturing Cologne, and actually crossing the river at Remagen on March 7. At the same time, Russian battalions swept through Eastern Europe, taking Warsaw on January 17 and Budapest on February 13. Vienna fell on April 13 and the final assault on Berlin began on April 20.

In the Pacific, American naval and military forces moved closer to the Japanese home islands. Heavy air attacks on major Japanese cities had begun in November. A massive incendiary raid against Tokyo by American bombers killed 83,000 people during the night of March 8. A week later, after killing more than 20,000 Japanese troops and suffering more than 6,000 men killed and 15,000 wounded in one of the bloodiest battles of the Pacific, American commanders declared the strategically placed island of Iwo Jima secure after five weeks of furious fighting. Though very costly in men and ships, great military successes had been achieved in both theaters. By the end of March, it was clear that victory in Europe could not be far off and that victory in the Pacific was inevitable.

However, the national leader who had directed and inspired the nation from the grim days after Pearl Harbor to the crossing of the Rhine and to the approaches to Japan would not live to see the complete triumph of American arms. While Roosevelt's deteriorating health was widely known in Washington circles and had been frequently noted by visitors, the president's death in Warm Springs, Georgia, on April 12, 1945, was unexpected by most Americans and shocked the country.

To many Americans, the death of President Roosevelt was much more than just a sad realization that a great man and incomparable national leader was gone. A secondary shock from that event was the startling recognition that Harry S Truman would succeed him. Many in Congress, the cabinet, the Washington bureaucracy, and most of the military high command had difficulty accepting the fact that this second-term Missouri senator who had never successfully run any sort of enterprize was now the president of the United States and leader of the grand alliance against the Axis powers.[30]

Truman's public persona at the time was that of an ordinary decent man who had made his way through a corrupt Missouri political system without being spoiled or tainted by it. Colleagues regarded him as an honorable man with the best of intentions and high honesty of purpose. Most senators and congressmen who knew him were very glad that Truman and not Henry Wallace was now president.[31]

In Europe, Eisenhower and Bradley believed that Truman was unqualified for his new role and were fearful that his inexperience might delay decision making and prolong the war. Patton was undisguisedly bitter about the qualifications of his new commander in chief and said so[32]. What MacArthur thought about Truman assuming the presidency is unrecorded. For most Americans, however, the question most asked about Truman did not concern his qualifications, but who was he? That question was quickly answered. He was the president of the United States and immediately acted accordingly. Over the next four months Truman made a series of historic military and diplomatic decisions that changed the world forever.

As president, Truman received his first briefing from the chiefs of staff on April 13. Either unaware that the western front was collapsing at almost every point or unwilling to say so to their new president, the chiefs presented Truman with an absolutely worst-case scenario. Even though American troops had reached the Elbe River on April 12, the chiefs advised the president that fighting could go on in Europe for six months and in the Pacific for another year and a half.[33] Truman had no time to digest or reflect upon the chiefs' dismal forecast. The rush of events made it obsolete moments after the president heard it.

Organized resistance to American and British forces in most European sectors was virtually ended by mid-April, and masses of German troops surrendered on a daily basis. Finally, American and Russian troops linked up at Torgau on the Elbe River on April 25. The extremely costly Russian attack on Berlin was proceeding through the city, street by street. The end came quickly. Hitler committed suicide on April 30, and the Russians declared Berlin secure on May 2. The German armed forces surrendered to the Allies completely and unconditionally on May 7, 1945. The war in Europe, which had run on for sixty-nine terrible months, finally was over.

At home, the end of the war in Europe inspired joyful street demonstrations and much celebrating in cities and towns across the land. One-half of the great national covenant to defeat our enemies solemnly undertaken by the president and Congress on behalf of the American people three and a half years ago had been fulfilled. Though most Americans dared hope that completion of the other half of the national commitment would be a matter of months and that millions of soldiers and sailors would be returned home soon, the chiefs of staff thought otherwise.

Nothing had happened in the Pacific theater to change this forecast of at least another year and a half of total war being required to defeat Japanese military and naval forces. The bitter struggle for the Japanese island of Okinawa, begun with great optimism on April 1, was lasting longer than military planners had estimated and after a month had exacted a terrible cost in men and ships.

The battle for Okinawa raged for almost eleven weeks, ending finally on June 21. The fighting on both land and sea was ferocious. American forces destroyed about 110,000 Japanese troops and perhaps 150,000 civilians or almost one-third of the island's population. The price of this bloody victory was over 12,000 Americans killed and 40,000 wounded. At sea, Japanese air attacks on American ships were unrelenting. Hundreds of kamikaze pilots sacrificed themselves to sink American ships and kill American sailors. By the end of the campaign, the U.S. Navy had lost thirty ships and suffered damage to 368 more. Over 5,000 sailors died and another 5,000 were wounded. If the Japanese home islands had to be invaded, Okinawa was a harbinger of terrible things to come.

Actually, plans for such an invasion had been prepared and presented to the White House for review on June 18, even before Okinawa had been secured. Indeed, Okinawa was on everyone's mind when General Marshall presented Plan Downfall, a two-phased invasion of the Japanese home islands, to the White House. The first phase, known as Operation Olympic, proposed an invasion of Kyushu, the southernmost home island, only 350 miles from Okinawa, to begin on November 1. The second and larger invasion of the main island of Honshu, known as Operation Coronet, would follow in March 1946.[34]

Preparations for the invasions of Japan were elaborate and underway. The president had authorized the chiefs of staff to move more than one million troops into position for the final attack on Japan. Thirty divisions were on their way from Europe to the Pacific. Supplies were piling up in Saipan.[35] An air bombardment of staggering weight was planned; more bombs would be dropped on Japan than had been delivered against Germany during the entire European war. With all of that, estimates of American casualties for these operations ranged from 250,000 to 500,000.[36] If Japanese soldiers and civilians fought for the home island as their troops had fought in Iwo Jima and Okinawa, the loss of American lives would exceed all of the American campaigns of the war combined. President Truman heard the presentations and approved General Marshall's Plan Downfall.[37]

There was, however, a possible alternative to invasion and to the great loss of life certain to accompany such an operation that the new president heard about for the first time on April 25. On that day Henry L. Stimson, secretary of war, and General Leslie R. Groves, head of the Manhattan Project, briefed Truman on the history and present status of the Manhattan Project. By 1945 that project, authorized by Roosevelt in 1940, had employed over 120,000 people and spent two billion dollars to develop an atomic bomb.

Stimson and Groves informed the president that within four months the United States would have such a bomb. One atomic bomb was capable of destroying an entire city. It was the most terrible weapon in human history. At this time, no one could say for sure whether the bomb would actually work, but it would be ready for testing in early July.[38] According to Stimson, Truman seemed as much concerned about the role of the atomic bomb in shaping human history as in its capacity to shorten the war. Stimson asked the president to authorize appointment of a special committee to study the implications of this new weapon and then advise the president about decisions he alone could make concerning it. Truman agreed and told him to go ahead and appoint such a committee.[39]

Besides Stimson, who served as chairman of this new all-civilian, highly secret committee, were James B. Conant, Karl T. Compton, Vannevar Bush, Ralph A. Bard, William L. Clayton, George L. Harrison, and

James F. Byrnes. Conant, Compton, and Bush were eminent scientists and educators who had been involved with the Manhattan Project from the beginning. Bard and Clayton were respectively assistant secretaries of the navy and of state. Harrison was an insurance company executive and a special assistant to Stimson. Byrnes served as the president's special representative.[40]

The committee met several times during May, including a crucial two-day session beginning on May 31. At that session, the committee was joined by an advisory council composed of four men actively involved in developing the bomb—Enrico Fermi, Arthur H. Compton, Ernest O. Lawrence, and J. Robert Oppenheimer. A wide range of subjects relating to the bomb were discussed during this final session including relations with Soviet Russia. In the end the committee and advisory council reached three unanimous conclusions: (1) the bomb should be used against Japan as soon as possible; (2) it should be used against targets where damage would be the greatest for psychological effect; and (3) it should be used without warning. These conclusions were passed on to the president, who would bear the sole responsibility for deciding whether or not the bomb should be used.[41]

However, until the bomb had been actually tested, decisions about using it against Japan were premature. That test occurred in a remote part of the Almogordo Air Base in the New Mexico desert on July 16. President Truman learned of the successful test while attending a conference with Churchill and Stalin at Potsdam. He was informed that operational use of the bomb would be possible after August 1.[42] Decisions about using the bomb could be delayed no longer and were not.

President Truman decided to use the bomb against Japan in order to shorten the war. On July 25 the general military order to the Air Force to proceed with an atomic bomb attack on Japan sometime between the date of the order and August 10 was issued. On August 6, while the president was at sea returning from the Potsdam conference, an atomic bomb was dropped upon Hiroshima that destroyed most of the city and killed about 90,000 people. On August 9, a second bomb was dropped on Nagasaki, killing 35,000 people. Japan surrendered on August 10, and the war in the Pacific was over.

Though many Americans wondered what sort of unimaginable horror had been unleashed upon the world, a wave of euphoria swept across the country. Half a million people filled the streets of Washington, D.C., in what was to be the biggest night of celebration in that city's history. Similar scenes occurred in major cities and small towns everywhere. Millions of servicemen in the Pacific or destined to go there would be coming home. It was a moment of joy, and most important it was a time of great expectations for the future.

— vii —

At Notre Dame as elsewhere in the country, the sudden end of the war in August occasioned a sense of great relief that the terrible war was over and that at long last millions of servicemen would be coming home. It also caused some local anxiety about the immediate future of the university. With the war over, the naval training programs that had sustained Notre Dame financially since 1942 would be shut down. Those anxieties were relieved somewhat, however, when the Navy authorized continuation of the midshipman program at Notre Dame until June 1946.

Nonetheless, Notre Dame administrators decided to accept applications from former students returning from military or naval service and allow them to resume their interrupted academic work in January 1946. Enough students were admitted in September and in January under this provision to raise overall enrollment close to the prewar levels. By the end of the spring semester 1946, about 3,000 students were attending the university, that is, 1,600 returning and new students, 800 midshipman trainees, and 600 veterans supported by the GI Bill.[43]

Realizing from the flood of admission applications pouring into the university during the fall of 1945 that a massive enrollment increase would occur the following September, O'Donnell announced in January 1946 that an extensive postwar expansion of Notre Dame facilities would begin with the construction of a new residence hall on the freshman quadrangle. As yet unnamed, this new facility, known later as Farley Hall, would cost about $400,000. However, it would not be ready for occupancy until September 1947.[44] Therefore, accommodating the large number of students expected to arrive on campus in September 1946 would have to be solved by using more efficiently the residential space vacated by the departing naval trainees and by resorting to off-campus housing.

Administrative anxiety over the problems of student housing and of finding faculty to teach record numbers of new students were by no means unique to Notre Dame. Every college and university in the country faced this situation. There were, however, problems—one general and one very special—troubling Notre Dame administrators that state universities and very few private ones had to face. The general problem was the reappearance of strong anti-Catholic attitudes among many Americans in the immediate postwar years.

Between 1946 and 1950, anti-Catholicism in America was stronger than at any time since 1928. Self-proclaimed spokesmen for the larger society assured their countrymen that there was a Catholic problem in America and proceeded to denounce Catholic institutions and some Catholic practices as being undemocratic, if not un-American. Persons of this mind were alarmed by a perceived growing Catholic influence in American social and political life that had to be checked. All Catholic colleges and universities had to cope with this new wave of anti-Catholicism in one way or another.

The second more specific problem troubling Notre Dame officials at war's end was largely one of public relations. It derived from the isolationist/interventionist controversies of 1940 and 1941. O'Donnell's much-publicized uneven treatment of McMahon and O'Brien at that time, followed by the dismissal of McMahon in 1943, created a public perception of Notre Dame as an authoritarian, undemocratic, anti-Roosevelt, anti-British, and pro-Franco place. The performance of Notre Dame men in the armed services, the university's commitment to training naval officers during the war years, and O'Donnell's strong public advocacy for the proposed National Science Foundation notwithstanding, in some quarters the memory of a perceived past of flawed institutional patriotism remained to be exorcised.

In the postwar years, the most frequent and persuasive displays of American patriotism were those cast into anti-Communist rhetoric. As the cold war intensified, to be publicly anti-Communist was to be an American patriot. Like most American Catholic priests of that era, O'Donnell's commitment to the anti-Communist cause was sincere and total. By identifying himself publicly as strongly anti-Communist and by firmly aligning Notre Dame with the anti-Communist cause in a newsworthy way, O'Donnell successfully exorcised whatever lingered in the public memory of past university associations with authoritarian ideologies and pro-Fascist causes. Professing American patriotism through anti-Communist rhetoric was for O'Donnell a natural and easy thing to do. He did it reasonably well and on at least one occasion memorably so.

On October 11, 1945, the *New York Times* reported that Louis Budenz, managing editor of the American Communist newspaper *Daily Worker* and president of the company that published it, had renounced Communism and formally embraced the Catholic faith. Budenz had been an active Communist party member for ten years. He had led major strikes in Kenosha, Wisconsin; Nazareth, Pennsylvania; and Toledo, Ohio, experiencing no less than twenty-one trials and no convictions for participating in strikes and labor disputes. There was little about the intentions or activities of the Communist party in America that Budenz did not know. His defection was a major event in the history of the party in America.[45]

Budenz had been raised as a Catholic and actually attended Catholic schools before converting to Communism and joining the party. He was brought back to the Catholic Church by the eminent convert-maker, Monsignor Fulton J. Sheen. Immediately after his reconversion, Budenz left the party and his employment at the *Daily Worker,* stating publicly that he had done so because Catholicism and Communism were irreconcilable. He had been a true believer in the former, but now totally devoted to the latter, and he repudiated his misguided past and all of those men and women who had shared it with him.

The *New York Times* also reported that Budenz and his family would move to South Bend immediately and that he would join the faculty of the University of Notre Dame.[46] Father Howard Kenna, director of studies, confirmed that Budenz had been appointed an assistant professor and would assume his new duties at once. Although he held a law degree, Budenz was without teaching experience of any sort. Exactly what duties he would perform were unclear. For the moment, he was assigned to the economics department.

By hiring the country's most celebrated defector from Communism, who had stated publicly that Communism and Catholicism were irreconcilable, O'Donnell hoped to make a powerful statement about the university's strong opposition to Communism at home or abroad. In the cold war, the mistakes of 1940 and 1941 would not be repeated. Never again would the university be identified in any way with views that opposed American foreign policy. Hiring Budenz was certainly no celebration of American patriotic values. Yet, in the context of the times, O'Donnell believed it was a noble and right thing to do and that perhaps a little bit of history was being repeated.

O'Donnell saw no real difference between his hiring of Budenz in 1945 and President Hutchins of Chicago's rescue of McMahon in 1943. After all, lofty principles of a sort had been involved in both situations. McMahon had refused to accept censorship of his speeches and writings and lost his job. Budenz had joined the Catholic Church, renounced Communism, and in effect lost his job for that. However, no one in the press and very few at the university saw any relationship between those two incidents. In 1943, Hutchins had been extravagantly praised in major newspapers and on the radio for hiring McMahon. O'Donnell's appointment of Budenz in 1945 was buried on page twenty-five of the *New York Times.*

Nonetheless, by hiring Budenz and publicizing that he was qualified to hold a faculty appointment at Notre Dame, O'Donnell did the man a very great service. In effect, O'Donnell absolved Budenz from all of his many past political sins and provided him with a degree of credibility and respectability hitherto unknown. If Budenz were credible and acceptable at Notre Dame, he should be creditable and acceptable anywhere in the American Catholic community. He was, and enormous career opportunities opened up for him.

Within the university, however, the Budenz appointment attracted very little praise and actually inspired a mild protest from the economics department. As a celebrity appointment, he combined very little teaching with some off-campus lecturing during the fall of 1945, but a heavy commitment to that lucrative part of his later life was still about a year away. Generally while at Notre Dame, Budenz socialized little and made few friends in the department or elsewhere in the university. In truth, he soon became bored to death with living in South Bend and decided to return to New York as soon as possible.

He resigned from the university at the end of the spring semester in 1946, stating that his family needed a change of climate to relieve conditions of chronic sinusitis.[47] Apparently, the climate of New York City was more helpful for his family's health. He accepted an appointment at Fordham University as a professor of economics in the fall of 1946 and remained there for ten years. While at Fordham, Budenz's career as an active off-campus lecturer and as a star witness at congressional committees, before loyalty review boards, and in court blossomed.

During the late 1940s and early 1950s, Budenz was a key government witness in no less than sixty proceedings against persons accused of membership or allegiance to the Communist party. In these proceedings, Budenz named scores of persons—high ranking military officers, diplomats, writers, professors, ministers, artists, actors, and others—as Communists or as fellow travelers. Budenz was the most publicly active and most notorious anti-Communist informant of his generation.[48]

In nearly every instance of alleged Communist affiliation exposed by Budenz, but not all, such allegations were denied or never actually proved. His most spectacular public denunciation involved Owen Lattimore, a State Department advisor on far eastern affairs. Budenz appeared as a surprise mystery witness in 1950 at hearings held by Senator Joseph R. McCarthy (R-Wisconsin). At those hearings, Budenz identified Lattimore as an alleged member of a Communist cell. After that public denunciation, Lattimore's career in the State Department was over. Two years later, Lattimore was indicted on a charge of lying when he denied ever having been a sympathizer or promoter of Communism.

The case against Lattimore proceeded no further than indictment. Later, the charges against him were dropped.[49]

Budenz's most accurate public denunciation was that of Gerhardt Eisler, described by him as the number one Communist spy in the United States. In due course, Eisler was indicted, convicted, and sentenced to prison for contempt of Congress and making false statements on a passport application. Freed on bail pending an appeal, Eisler made newspaper front pages by jumping bail and escaping from the country on a Polish ship. Later, Eisler surfaced as an information officer in the Communist East German government.[50]

During and after Budenz's numerous appearances as an expert on Communist activities in America, he was frequently accused of denouncing well-known people as Communists in order to get personal publicity and make money. Budenz denied these accusations vociferously, and actually addressed the matter of money-making in 1952 during a trial in New York of sixteen persons accused of Communist connections. As a witness at that trial, under cross-examination Budenz admitted earning more than $70,000 between 1946 and 1952 from lectures and writings against Communism and from giving testimony against persons alleged to be Communists.[51]

Budenz left teaching and retired from Fordham in 1956 at the age of sixty-five in order to devote more time to writing articles and preparing his memoirs. He died in 1972 at the age of eighty-one. Such was the career that O'Donnell launched by hiring Budenz in 1945.

— viii —

The public relations advantage to the university following from the Budenz hiring and from his brief time at Notre Dame was minimal. Demonstrating the patriotic and anti-Communist character of the university proceeded in other ways. In off-campus speeches, O'Donnell managed to work that message into his presentations no matter what the announced subject of his remarks happened to be.

For example, in a radio address following the annual dinner of the Notre Dame Club of New York at the Biltmore Hotel on April 29, 1946, O'Donnell spoke seriously about a lack of moral balance in contemporary American life. He attributed that lack of balance to flaws in the American system of education. The cause of the flawed system of American education, O'Donnell insisted, was secularism, meaning generally the practical exclusion of God from human thinking and living. More specifically, secularism had come to mean the displacement of traditional religion by science as a source of truth and knowledge and displacement of the Church by the state as the guardian and arbiter of social life.[52]

Protesting the perceived dominating influence of secularism in American education and the moral and social problems following therefrom was a very popular subject among Catholics and was addressed often by Catholic educators during the postwar years. That O'Donnell should criticize the evils of secularism in American education in a speech to Notre Dame alumni was not surprising at all. That he should find a way to include in such a speech references to Notre Dame's patriotic performance of training nearly 12,000 naval ensigns since 1941 was.[53] O'Donnell did not worry about forming a context in his speech for such a point; he just put it in and then went on to deliver his message about secularism.

With regard to attacking Communism in 1946, O'Donnell was only one of many prominent Catholics—including both O'Brien and McMahon—who had publicly taken up that cause. His most memorable performance was at an alumni dinner at Notre Dame during commencement week on June 19, shortly before his presidential term ended. O'Donnell began by describing Communism as a foreign ideology whose principal objective was to take America away from Americans. Individually and collectively, he continued, Communists were bent upon overthrowing our form of government and abolishing the American way of life.[54]

Americans must be alerted to the red menace, O'Donnell declared, and "not sit idly by and permit these ideological termites to destroy us."[55] In the real world after all, there was only one way to deal with termites of any species. He called upon his audience to demand that Congress "bring to the bar of justice every enemy from within who would first weaken and then destroy the American heritage. . . . What we want is action that is swift but effective."[56]

O'Donnell concluded by recommending a threefold program to combat the growth and spread of Communist thinking and influence in the United States. First, the nation must get back to God and the moral law which too many of us have forgotten. Second, we must be aggressive in our opposition to Communism, that is, be positive, remembering that the best defense in such situations always is a good offense based on a sound idea of what we stand for. Third, whenever possible, we should deport these "Red Fascists" to any land that will receive them.[57] This was a strong prescription indeed, especially when roughly delivered by a university president. O'Donnell's alumni audience listened attentively and wildly applauded what their president had said.

In this instance at the end of June 1946, four months before the congressional elections of that year in which anti-Communism became a major national issue and before Budenz had begun his career of publicly exposing alleged Communists employed by the federal government, O'Donnell was probably slightly ahead of his time in playing the anti-Communist card for public relations advantage. He was either unusually prescient about how important anti-Communism would become in American public affairs in the months and years ahead or had made an extraordinarily timely and lucky guess.

In any case, before leaving office O'Donnell successfully put out of mind memories of the university's isolationist and pro-Franco past. He did so by publicly identifying Notre Dame as a place where God and country would always be well served. The university was and would continue to be stridently anti-Communist and forever a friend to and protector of America's values and democratic institutions against all threats and challenges. O'Donnell left the presidency of Notre Dame in the summer of 1946 satisfied that the public relations damage done to the university during the isolationist/interventionist controversies of 1940 and 1941 and again during the McMahon affair in 1943 and early 1944 had been repaired.

— ix —

During the early fall of 1945, however, the athletic department was concerned with the university's football reputation, which had been severely damaged the previous year. The memory of the Army football team's 1944 Armistice Day massacre of the Notre Dame squad in Yankee Stadium was alive and strong. There was not much that the new interim head football coach Hugh Devore could do to avenge that humiliating loss. Returning veterans would not be available for Notre Dame or for any other intercollegiate football teams by the time the 1945 season began. The extraordinary player personnel advantages enjoyed by the service teams in 1944 would continue into 1945.

Hugh Devore fielded substantially the same players that McKeever had used the year before. The team's premier running back Bob Kelly was gone, but Dancewicz had returned as an experienced quarterback with monogram winners Phil Colella, Elmer Angsman, and Frank Ruggerio behind him in the backfield. The first half of the season was almost a repeat of the first five games of 1944.

Notre Dame opened the season at home on September 29 and managed to defeat Illinois, 7 to 0, in a hard-fought game before 41,000 people. The next four games were lopsided victories. Notre Dame easily turned back Dartmouth, 34 to 0, and Iowa, 56 to 0, at home and overpowered Georgia Tech, 40 to 7, and Pittsburgh, 39 to 9, away. Undefeated through five games, Notre Dame was ranked second in the country behind Earl Blaik's powerful, undefeated Army team.

Devore's squad met its first real test after the Illinois game when they played Navy, unbeaten and third in national rankings, in Cleveland before an enormous crowd of 82,000 on November 3. Anxious to avenge the one-sided loss to Navy in the past season, Notre Dame took an early lead. After intercepting a Navy pass and returning the ball to midfield, Devore's squad drove steadily down the field with Ruggerio scoring Notre Dame's only touchdown of the game.[58]

For most of the second and third quarters, the game was a bruising defensive battle with Navy never getting inside of the Notre Dame twenty yard line but able to stop Notre Dame running backs inside of the Navy five yard line. However, with only seven minutes to play in the final quarter of the game, Notre Dame's nemesis from the past year, Clyde Scott, intercepted a Dancewicz pass and ran forty yards to tie the score.

With only thirty seconds left in the game, Colella caught a pass from Dancewicz and appeared to have scored a touchdown. Officials ruled that Colella had not scored but had been pushed out of bounds. The ball was placed only inches away from the goal line. With time remaining for only one play, Dancewicz attempted a quarterback sneak and failed. Time expired immediately, and the game ended in a tie, 6 to 6.[59]

Similar to the previous year, among the many officers attending the game was Lt. Col. Earl Blaik, head coach of the Army team. He had traveled to Cleveland to scout two important future opponents. What he must have noted was that Notre Dame led in all statistical categories. The fact that Navy had been held to only sixty yards rushing and that Dancewicz had completed only four passes out of fourteen and had thrown four interceptions was a measure of how intensive the defensive play of both teams had been. What Blaik took away from this game was a firm conviction that against an aggressive defense, neither Notre Dame nor Navy were likely to score many touchdowns. With that conviction as a basis for a game plan, Blaik went back to West Point to prepare his team for their annual encounter with Notre Dame in Yankee Stadium on November 10.

Blaik's Army team was undefeated. It had rolled over all opponents, running up impressive scores against all of them. Actually, the Army team playing Notre Dame in New York City in 1945 was probably better than the one fielded in 1944. The outstanding Army line had returned almost intact, and the backfield was even stronger. In addition to Davis and Blanchard, Blaik had recruited Tom "Shorty" McWilliams, a six foot three inch All-American running back from Mississippi State. This combination of running backs had been too much for all previous opponents and was too much for Notre Dame also.[60]

After the opening kick off, Army obtained excellent field position by recovering a fumble on the Notre Dame thirty-one yard line. Davis ran two consecutive plays and scored Army's first touchdown. By the end of the first quarter, it was clear that the Notre Dame line had not fully recovered from its bruising encounter with Navy a week ago. The Army line overpowered Notre Dame defenders, allowing their running backs to mount six sustained touchdown drives, two in the second quarter and two each in the third and fourth periods. In the end, Army defeated Notre Dame, 48 to 0.[61]

All statistical advantages in the game went to Army. Davis scored three touchdowns, Blanchard managed two, and McWilliams had one. Throughout the game Notre Dame could not run successfully against the Army line. Forced to throw the football often, Dancewicz attempted twenty-three passes but completed only six. Generally, New York sportswriters were sympathetic to Notre Dame, recognizing that when compared to other intercollegiate football teams of that time the Notre Dame squad was much better than a forty-eight point loss to Army indicated.[62]

During the past two years, Army's total domination of intercollegiate football derived from the special circumstances of the war and the draft. Now, with the war over and so many former players returning to their colleges and universities after military service, all major intercollegiate programs were bound to improve, and Army's unfair recruitment advantages would end. Major intercollegiate programs mauled by Army during 1944 and 1945, especially Notre Dame, had much to pay back and looked forward to the next season, when that payback could begin. This prospect was clearly understood by both Blaik and the new superintendent of the Military Academy, General Maxwell Taylor, and in time steps would be taken to avoid it.

However at Notre Dame, before getting serious about the season of 1946, the present one had to be completed. The embarrassing loss to Army dropped Devore's team to seventh place in the national rankings. Notre Dame was expected to win all of its last three games. On November 17, Notre Dame defeated Northwestern easily, 34 to 7, before 46,000 people in Evanston. The following week, the Notre Dame team traveled to New Orleans and did the same to Tulane, 33 to 6, with a crowd of 51,000 watching. Those two convincing wins moved Notre Dame up two places to fifth in the national rankings. The final game against Great

Lakes, a three-touchdown underdog, in Chicago before only 23,000 people turned to be the one of the most surprising upsets of the year.

Because the football program at the Great Lakes Naval Training Station was being terminated, the game against Notre Dame was the last one that Coach Paul Brown's team would ever play. Although Great Lakes had not fared well during the season, losing three games before playing Notre Dame, this final game was a very special moment for both the coach and the players. Since the Army Cadets had defeated the Navy Midshipmen, 32 to 13, the previous week, defense of the Navy's football reputation had fallen upon the enlisted men playing for Great Lakes.[63]

As a matter of fact, this game meant so much to the sailors on Brown's team that discharges had been delayed for Jean Lamoure, a guard from Fresno State; Grove Klemmer, a halfback and 440 yard sprint world record holder from California; George Terlep, a former Notre Dame quarterback; and Marion Motley, the great African-American fullback from Nevada so they could play in this final game against Notre Dame.[64]

Game day was cold and damp, and few came out to watch their favorites from South Bend. Nonetheless, the Notre Dame team played the first two quarters well. To be sure, Devore's men had not played up to the standard of a three-touchdown favorite, but well enough to hold a lead, 13 to 7, at the end of the second quarter. However, during halftime Brown must have found some way to inspire his players. Great Lakes tied the game in the third period and scored an incredible twenty-six unanswered points in the final quarter, winning the game 39 to 13. With this extraordinary performance by the naval enlisted men playing for Brown at Great Lakes, the aberrant era of wartime intercollegiate football ended, and a brave new football world was aborning.

After winning the game against Notre Dame, Paul Brown and his football playing sailors savored their moment of glory. Most of them took their discharges and went separate ways. Paul Brown moved to Cleveland and became head coach of that city's new professional football team in the recently established All-American Football Conference (AAFC). Brown took Motley and Terlep from the Great Lakes team with him to Cleveland. In the AAFC, Brown's team, now known as the Cleveland Browns, won consistently and was several times league champions.

However, when the AAFC collapsed in 1950, the Cleveland Browns entered the National Football League (NFL) and continued their winning ways. In that league, Brown did more than win football games. He made history. By signing Motley to a contract in the AAFC in 1946 and by hiring other black players when his team joined the NFL, Brown helped break a color ban in professional football that had been operative in that league since 1933.

As for Devore, his future was to be less historic. He returned to Notre Dame after the Great Lakes game to learn that he was no longer head coach of Notre Dame and would have to find a coaching position elsewhere. Frank Leahy was about to be discharged from the navy and intended to proceed to South Bend forthwith to take over the Notre Dame football program. John Lujack also expected discharge in early 1946 and planned to report for spring practice. Other former players fresh out of the service were on their way to Notre Dame as well.

Leahy's spring practice player roster indicated that the Notre Dame football team in 1946 would be more experienced, older, and bigger than any in history. Circles were drawn around November 9, 1946, on athletic department calendars marking that date as the day when the best of Leahy and the best of Blaik would try to settle an accumulation of old and unforgiven accounts in their next football encounter in Yankee Stadium.

— x —

With Leahy and Lujack returning and other outstanding business of the football program settled in the spring of 1946, O'Donnell and Cavanaugh turned their attention to an academic matter of some delicacy. By the summer of 1946, opposition to O'Brien's performance as a teacher/scholar in the department of religion had become serious. The increased postwar student enrollments in all of the university's colleges had impacted severely on the Department of Religion. That department taught courses that were required in all of the colleges and experienced great difficulty staffing them. All department members taught more students in more sections than ever before, that is, all department members except O'Brien. Opposition to O'Brien's special status came largely from the Holy Cross priests who did most of the teaching in that department. To them, O'Brien seemed unwilling or unable to carry an appropriate share of departmental teaching obligations.

Opposition focused on the fact that though O'Brien was the best-known member of the department, he was no theologian. He had no degrees or advanced training of any sort in theology and was personally loathed for past controversies by the reigning authorities in the field at the Catholic University of America and elsewhere. More specifically, the subject matter of all of O'Brien's courses tended to be the same, no matter what course titles were put on them. O'Brien taught his view of God and man in the world plus whatever else popped into his mind at a given moment. Insofar as readings were assigned, they tended to be his own books and pamphlets and very little mainstream Catholic religious writing. He worried not at all about content objectives in multi-sectioned required courses, paid only scant attention to course syllabi, and scheduled few examinations. In department affairs, O'Brien was not a team player and assumed that ordinary rules did not apply to him.[65] In the end, O'Brien's bountiful heart notwithstanding, they did.

The person charged to resolve the O'Brien problem in the Department of Religion was its head, Father Roland Simonitsch, C.S.C. The particular issue that Simonitsch addressed was whether O'Brien's book *Evolution and Religion* should be used as a text or even as collateral reading in departmental courses. Simonitsch read the book and had serious doubts about its intellectual quality. He was troubled by the chapter on creation and also by O'Brien's simplistic explication of evolution theories. He passed the book for review to some local experts, "to three PhD's, two in theology and one in philosophy." All three local experts recommended against using the book in any capacity. Simonitsch advised O'Brien in writing of that judgment with copies to O'Donnell and to Father Howard Kenna, C.S.C., director of studies.[66]

This decision was a turning point in O'Brien's career in Notre Dame's Department of Religion. With his books and pamphlets all but banned from departmental use on qualitative grounds, his days of pretending that he was a theologian or a historian were over. Henceforth, his contributions to the Department of Religion would be more practical than academic and intellectual. First, O'Brien returned to what he had always done well, convert making. Next, either stung or perhaps even inspired by Whitacre's attack on himself and the man's negative perception of a growing and ever more threatening increase of Catholic influence in American social life and public affairs, O'Brien discovered another great new cause. He embraced ecumenism and became an advocate for ecumenical ideals long before it was fashionable to do so.

In 1946 when O'Brien was being pushed out of the religion department at Notre Dame, the prospects were very poor indeed that Catholics and Protestants would be able to put aside historical sources of disagreement, forgive past grievances, turn the other cheek to contemporary slights and indignities, and then cooperate in some sort of combined Christian effort for the common good. O'Brien persuaded himself that in matters of interfaith relations the future could be much better than the past. To insure that the future would be better, O'Brien assumed the public role of sectarian peacemaker and devoted the rest of his life to the noble task of bringing Catholics and Protestants together. Most of this activity would be carried on outside of the university.

While enduring the ego-bruising judgment of Simonitsch's local experts, O'Brien never faltered in his friendship with O'Donnell and in his generosity to the university. For example, the president and his advisors decided that a new chapel of perpetual adoration would be a fitting memorial to the Notre Dame men killed in World War II. Plans were drawn, a site was chosen, and an architectural model for fund-raising purposes was prepared.

O'Brien was among the first to respond to solicitations for this new chapel/war memorial. He immediately pledged $50,000 for the project and then transferred titles of seventeen of his deceased mother's rental properties and lots in Peoria, Illinois, to the university as a down payment on his pledge.[67] By mid-April over $30,000 of that pledge had been delivered, and the balance was paid before the end of the year.[68] The size of the pledge and the promptness of payment positively overwhelmed O'Donnell. He graciously commended O'Brien for his "abiding devotion to this old school."[69]

In the end, construction of the chapel/war memorial was never begun, and the project was abandoned. In order to accommodate the very large postwar student enrollment increases, the funds collected, with O'Brien's permission, were diverted to build much-needed revenue-producing dormitories. Indeed, by so doing O'Brien had rendered an extraordinary service to the university that would never be forgotten. He had become one of those special Notre Dame faculty whose "blood was in the bricks," that is, men who had served so well and done so much for Notre Dame that they would be forever a part of its history and mythology.

No matter what the future needs of the Department of Religion might require or it politics might dictate, O'Brien had secured for himself a permanent place at Notre Dame. As a matter of fact, as outside convert work and ecumenical activities increased, O'Brien actually gave up his home on Peashway Street near the university and moved into a small apartment created for him on the first floor of the Main Building. Living virtually one floor below the president's office for the next forty years, O'Brien could not be any closer to the heart of the university that was his home and heart's desire.

For his part, during the spring of 1946, O'Donnell managed to continue a friendly relationship with O'Brien while at the same time allowing the Department of Religion to try to reduce public perception of him as a Notre Dame theologian. Once again, O'Donnell found himself in a familiar but nonetheless difficult situation. The president recognized a need to disassociate the name and reputation of the university from O'Brien's embarrassingly simplistic historical writing and from present and future idiosyncratic public statements on current Catholic moral and religious issues. Both Simonitsch and O'Brien cooperated to find a solution and make the best of a difficult situation. Mutual civility made present and future moves toward such a disassociation easy. Resolving the O'Brien problem in the Department of Religion and launching the chapel/war memorial project were among the final acts of the O'Donnell presidency.

— xi —

O'Donnell's six years as president had been a very difficult time for the university and for him personally. The war affected every aspect of university life, creating problems unanticipated and requiring changes unwanted. There were times during the war years, especially in 1943, when nothing seemed to go right. Even the football team during 1944 and 1945 suffered two of the most humiliating defeats in its history. O'Donnell coped with events and circumstances beyond his control as best as he could. In the process, he exhausted himself physically and emotionally. By the time his presidential term expired in July 1946, O'Donnell was very anxious to step aside and leave the future of Notre Dame in the able, experienced hands of his close friend, John J. Cavanaugh.

In other less-perilous times, O'Donnell would probably have been remembered as a good, if not great, president. However, O'Donnell failed utterly as a crisis manager when a gifted one was needed and he must be remembered for that.His attempts to limit faculty public advocacy of aid to Britain in 1940 and of interventionism in 1941, while allowing faculty isolationists to speak and write at will, seriously affected public perceptions of the university. It appeared to be a place that was anti-British, stridently anti-Communist, and pro-Franco, a place where anti-Roosevelt rhetoric flourished and where freedom of speech and other democratic principles were lightly valued.

More damaging to the university was the handling of the McMahon affair in 1943. Pressed by the apostolic delegate to put a stop to McMahon's public advocacy of aid and cooperation with the Soviet Union in the war and in the postwar world, O'Donnell demanded prior approval of the professor's future public speeches while insisting that such a demand was not censorship. When that tactic failed, O'Donnell, as president, dismissed McMahon from the university.

At no point did O'Donnell even consider arguing with the apostolic delegate about the professor's right to speak freely on public-policy issues in his own country. The highest Catholic ecclesiatical authority in the country had spoken. For O'Donnell and for most of the Catholic clergy of his generation, once that authority had spoken, there was nothing to argue about. Dismissing McMahon satisfied the apostolic delegate but generated a massive wave of negative publicity that seriously damaged the reputations of himself and of the university.

However, as O'Donnell had hoped, that damage was not to be long lasting. O'Donnell's decision to deny absolutely that the Holy See was in anyway involved in the McMahon affair, his public assumption of sole responsibility for the action taken against the professor, and his tactic of refusing to respond publicly to questions about the incident or to attacks upon himself or upon the university succeeded in the long run. O'Donnell's patience, aided by the passage of time and by exciting war news, put the McMahon affair out of the public mind. Indeed, for O'Donnell and for Notre Dame, the worst had happened in 1943. But the worst was over by the time Rome was liberated and Allied troops had landed in Normandy in June 1944.

Within the university, however, the memory of McMahon's dismissal was not so easily forgotten. Wisely at the time, no reprisals were taken against faculty who had publicly supported McMahon. There was simply no sense in revisiting an incident that was best forgotten. Nonetheless, all aspects of the McMahon affair remained lively subjects of faculty conversation for years. It negatively impacted faculty morale and probably affected faculty recruiting for a decade. Until the university established a policy of academic tenure for the two upper professorial ranks in 1954, there were no formal university regulations insuring that something like the McMahon affair could not happen again. Since 1954, nothing like it has.

Certainly, as a member O'Donnell's contributions to the national Committee on Science and the Public Welfare in 1945 and his public testimony given on behalf of federal aid to university-based scientific research helped to improve the university's academic reputation. His work on that committee and public statements about the postwar importance of university-based scientific research reinforced public perceptions of Notre Dame as a place where science and scholarship really mattered.

No less important for improving public perceptions of postwar Notre Dame was O'Donnell's repeated public references to the university's work in training naval officers during the war and to the patriotic service of Notre Dame men in that conflict. Moreover, with the hiring of celebrity anti-Communist Louis F. Budenz in 1945 and strong anti-

Communist speeches sometimes roughly delivered in 1946, O'Donnell tried and generally succeeded in identifying Notre Dame as a Catholic institution forever patriotic in all things and uncompromisingly anti-Communist at home and abroad.

On at least one very important issue, O'Donnell had guessed right. Over the next decade a majority of Americans were ready to believe that anti-Communism was the highest form of American partriotism. In that sort of intellectual environment, as a Catholic university, Notre Dame found itself fortuitously positioned. The past was done, and the future was now.

— xii —

When O'Donnell left office in July 1946, virtually all of the naval training programs at the university had been terminated. As was happening at most other colleges and universities across the country at that time, applications from discharged veterans flooded into the Notre Dame admissions office. The university had to prepare for an enormous influx of civilian students in the fall of 1946 and somehow find new faculty to teach them. The class of 1950 entering in the fall of 1946 promised to be the largest, oldest, and most serious group of students ever to attend Notre Dame up to that time. Truly, with the class of 1950 the celebrated magic moment in American higher education had arrived at Notre Dame.

O'Donnell and Cavanaugh and other university administrators made special efforts to prepare for and accommodate the record-setting class. New faculty had to be hired. Several student residence halls were refurbished and improved. Since many of the new students were married, negotiations for war-surplus buildings were completed and thirty-nine former prisoner of war barracks were transferred from Missouri to Notre Dame. The surplus buildings were located on a site north of Cartier Field, subdivided into 117 temporary apartments for married students and appropriately named Vetville. These apartments turned out to be not so temporary with some being occupied for twenty years. When the number of married veterans declined, their places were taken by married graduate students and first-year instructors.

Among the many veterans returning to Notre Dame were, as has been noted, former as well as new aspiring football players. Coach Leahy, released from the navy in early 1946, was on campus and held spring practices in May. Leahy's star quarterback from the final games of 1943, John Lujack, also obtained his discharge from the navy and joined his coach to lead the team during the season of 1946. Despite Leahy's usual pessimistic forecasts about team prospects, reports from Cartier Field indicated that the team would have an outstanding season and perhaps even avenge the humiliating one-sided losses inflicted by Army in 1944 and 1945. That game against Army on November 9 in Yankee Stadium would be a clash of the country's football titans and was the one that Leahy and his team most wanted to win.

O'Donnell missed the frenetic activity going on at Notre Dame during the summer of 1946 not at all. Cavanaugh was welcome to it. As a matter of fact, during the last few months O'Donnell had passed more of the major decision making and most of the negotiating with government agencies to his vice president. O'Donnell's energy level had diminished and lengthy meetings exhausted him. The truth was that O'Donnell had a very serious health problem but did not know it.

The president knew, of course, that he tired easily and for that reason had limited some of his activities. He even declined O'Brien's offer to arrange a trip to Mexico with Bishop Gannon and enjoy the "princely hospitality" of one of that country's wealthiest and most influential citizens.[70] A long anticipated trip to South America, where travel and rest could be combined with congregation business, also had to be postponed.[71] O'Donnell's condition did not improve and was not positively diagnosed until after Christmas, 1946.

When informed that he suffered from an advanced stage of pancreatic cancer and should not expect to live more than a few months, O'Donnell reacted to that news with a degree of equanimity and quiet resignation that astonished his friends in the congregation. He continued to be pleasant and affable to all who attended and visited him until the end.[72] O'Donnell died on June 12, 1947.

PART III

12

Cavanaugh and Postwar American Higher Education: Opportunities and Challenges

John J. Cavanaugh, fifteenth president of Notre Dame, came to the Congregation of Holy Cross and to the university by a circuitous route. Born in Owosso, Michigan, in 1899 into a family of four children, three boys and one girl, John was the middle son. The father of the Cavanaugh children died when a young man, leaving the family financially strapped. All of the Cavanaugh children had to go to work to help support the family.[1]

While in high school, John Cavanaugh had taken business courses and through family connections was able to find employment as a teenager as an assistant to Henry Ford's private secretary. While John worked at the Ford plant, his younger brother Frank entered the Holy Cross novitiate at Notre Dame. Through his brother John met John W. Cavanaugh, then president of the university, who was sufficiently impressed with the young man to make a special arrangement for him to attend Notre Dame. If John Cavanaugh would leave his job at the Ford plant and come to Notre Dame and work as a secretary to the president for two years, he would be allowed to enroll in the university and pursue any course of studies then offered. John worked for the president for two years, and then in 1919 at the age of twenty entered the College of Commerce as a freshman.[2]

Though young Cavanaugh continued to perform secretarial duties for the new president, James A. Burns, he completed his courses in four years and graduated in 1923. Immediately, through Burns' close association with Albert R. Erskine, president of the Studebaker Corporation, Cavanaugh was hired by that corporation and quickly became an assistant advertising manager. He did not remain at Studebaker very long, however. In 1924, John Cavanaugh decided to follow his brother Frank into the Congregation of Holy Cross and entered the novitiate in early 1925.

After completing his novitiate and spending a year and a half in Moreau Seminary, Cavanaugh spent four years at the Catholic University of America, studying theology. In 1931, after ordination, he was sent off to Rome to study Thomistic theology at the Gregorian University. He enjoyed his time in Rome immensely and completed the courses there, but developed no special affection for the field of Thomistic philosophy and absolutely no passion to study it further or to spend his life teaching it.[3]

Cavanaugh returned to Notre Dame in 1933 and was appointed an assistant prefect of religion working under O'Hara. When O'Hara was appointed vice president in 1933 and then president a year later, Cavanaugh became prefect of religion. He remained in that post for five years, leaving it in 1938 to take up the post of assistant provincial. When Hugh O'Donnell succeeded O'Hara as president in 1940, Cavanaugh was appointed vice president.

O'Donnell and Cavanaugh were close friends and worked well together. Though lacking higher degrees and academic accomplishments, as vice president Cavanaugh earned a reputation in the congregation and among faculty, who knew him as an excellent troubleshooter, that is, as a man able to obtain the best result out of difficult and embarrassing situations. As had been seen, that reputation was justly deserved and demonstrated several times during O'Donnell's much-beleaguered presidency.

Not only was Cavanaugh absolutely loyal to O'Donnell during troubled times, but he successfully facilitated such difficult and embarrassing matters as the hiring of Leahy away from Boston College and the placement of McMahon at the University of Chicago. Moreover, for most of the final year when O'Donnell's energy level had dropped significantly, Cavanaugh shared decision making and general governance of the university with him.

Cavanaugh's selection as president in July 1946 surprised no one and was certainly accepted, if not wildly applauded, by all. Because he was so experienced in administrative matters and obviously so well prepared for the presidency, Cavanaugh was everyone's choice to lead the university through the uncertainties and challenges of the postwar years. He was the best man available at a critical time and most of the Holy Cross congregation and lay faculty knew it.

— ii —

Cavanaugh chose Father John H. Murphy, C.S.C., to fill the now vacant post of vice president. Murphy was bright, promising, and only thirty-four years old. He had graduated from Notre Dame in 1933, studied theology in Rome and at the Catholic University of America for several years, and had been ordained in 1938. Murphy taught languages for a while at Notre Dame but spent most of his time during the war as director of vocations and rector of Moreau Seminary. Cavanaugh chose Murphy for vice president because of managerial experience demonstrated at Moreau and because of a belief that the man had a flare for public relations. After appointing Murphy, Cavanaugh was not disposed to consider or make further changes among university administrators. He continued Howard Kenna as director of studies and kept virtually all of O'Donnell's appointees in place.

The principal immediate task confronting Cavanaugh and other Notre Dame administrators was that of finding ways to accommodate the flood of postwar students wanting to attend Notre Dame. Out of more than 10,000 applications received prior to July 1946, 4,000 were selected for admission as either returning or new students. Because of preference given to applicants returning from the military and naval services, two-thirds of the students enrolling at the university in the fall of 1946 were veterans. Taken together, returning and new students admitted to Notre Dame in 1946 constituted the largest enrollment in university history.[4]

As a group, these former servicemen now students were older, many were married, and almost half had been commissioned officers. So many veterans were able to attend Notre Dame and other colleges and universities across the country because the costs of higher education between 1946 and 1951 were easily met by the extraordinary generosity of the educational entitlement provided by the GI Bill.

Any honorably discharged veteran who had served three months in any of the armed services was entitled to twelve months of GI Bill support. Service time after the first three months received a day of support for each day of service up to a maximum of forty-eight months. Because the standard academic year lasted only nine months, any honorably discharged veteran with three years or more of service qualified for support through four academic years of undergraduate work and, if desired, for two more academic years of graduate study. Furthermore, veterans with as little as a 10 percent service-connected disability were treated even better. Disabled veterans were paid a slightly higher stipend and were supported through completion of all academic work required to qualify for their chosen vocational objective.

At a time when tuition, room, and board at Notre Dame cost $1100, veterans were allowed up to $500 a year paid directly to the university for tuition, books, fees, and a stipend of $65 a month for living expenses paid directly to the veterans. The combined tuition and stipend payments for nine months amounted to $1,175 or $75 more than the cost of tuition, room, and board at Notre Dame for one year. Tuition payments and the monthly stipend were continued as long as the entitled veteran stayed in school and in academic good standing.

The years between 1946 and 1956, when the GI Bill education programs ended, were truly magic moments in the history of American higher education. For the first time in American history large numbers of working-class students, albeit veterans who were preponderantly white and male, had equal access with middle-class students to the country's colleges and universities. For veterans during that decade, personal or parental resources simply did not affect individual decisions about seeking a higher education. In the end, over 2.2 million veterans went to American colleges and universities under GI Bill provisions during those years, with perhaps 15,000 choosing to attend Notre Dame.

By 1951, the flow of GI Bill students into Notre Dame and American colleges and universities generally was much diminished. Amazingly, however, the growth of enrollment at Notre Dame and at colleges and universities elsewhere slackened hardly at all when the numbers of entering GI students declined. The tidal wave of veterans filling up American colleges and universities in the immediate postwar years firmly established the experience of a college education as a near absolute requisite for economic security and success in America. There simply was no other easy way for ordinary people to obtain for their children access to well-paying jobs.

As gatekeepers for entry into the comforts and security of the American middle class, colleges and universities acquired a status and importance in American life during the postwar years that ensured their long-term growth and prosperity. In postwar America, college and university officials worried no longer about too few students; their enrollment problem had been transformed into one of finding room for so many. The principal postwar problem following from that transformation was how to find the intellectual, material, and human resources required to educate so many without lowering academic standards. Some did it well, others did not. Notre Dame did it well.

As the best-known Catholic university in the country, Notre Dame profited greatly from this gatekeeper phenomenon. The practical rewards of a Notre Dame undergraduate degree seemed so great and so certain in postwar America that almost any level of personal or parental sacrifice was worth making to obtain one. Indeed, while the years of the Cavanaugh presidency were the best of times for American higher education generally, for Notre Dame they were the beginning of an exciting new era of intellectual development, scientific and scholarly achievement, and facilities expansion. Moreover, all of this was managed within a very traditional context of Thomistic philosophy, required religion courses, a modest amount of curricular experimentation, and resounding football glory. Much would change during the Cavanaugh years, but also much would remain the same.

— iii —

One thing that did not change was the university's commitment to maintain a stridently anti-Communist, patriotic public image. No less than O'Donnell, Cavanaugh rarely missed opportunities in public speeches to denounce and attack Communists at home and abroad, and, in so doing, strongly assert or imply the patriotism of the university and of American Catholics generally. Cavanaugh's message was perhaps a bit less roughly delivered than had been his predecessor's, but it was rough enough, always cast in language that ordinary loyal Americans could understand and would approve.

An example of Cavanaugh's patriotic rhetoric can be found in a speech delivered to the annual dinner meeting of the National Aviation Clinic in Oklahoma City on October 16, 1946. At this event Cavanaugh shared the podium with Lt. Gen. James H. Doolittle, hero of the first American air attack on Tokyo. Doolittle had come to this meeting for a specific purpose, to argue for the creation of a single Department of Defense that would include a separate autonomous air force co-equal with the army and navy. Cavanaugh was there, first, to warn his audience against threats to American security posed by international Communism and, second, to inspire them to resist all such threats by giving a very short history lesson.

Cavanaugh declared that the United States "had better pile up armaments and build bigger and better bombs if it must deal with nations who repudiate the moral law."[5] He denounced Communists for their denial of human rights to people under their control and predicted that this new form of totalitarianism threatening the world would suffer the same fate as its German and Italian predecessors destroyed in the late war. The only language that such regimes understood, he continued, was force. History had shown "that was the language Japan knew best. We answered them at Hiroshima."[6]

This was strong language indeed for a university president to deliver in 1946, even to an audience such as the National Aviation Clinic. Cavanaugh had based his opposition to international Communism on the very high ground of Christian morality, but had then proceeded to dissociate himself and the university from current controversies about the morality of using atomic weapons against Japan. Inconsistencies notwithstanding, Cavanaugh's rhetoric on these points was widely reported. Consequently, he had clearly identified himself and the university with hard-line American cold war positions. Moreover, the serious public relations problems caused by the university's official policy of neutrality during the war controversy of 1940–41 would not be revisited. During the cold war, the University of Notre Dame would never be neutral. For the leadership of the university, there could be no degree of compromise or cooperation with Communism.

During the years of his presidency, Cavanaugh found that simply being anti-Communist was not enough to bury the past. He joined with a number of other Catholic spokesmen in a common public relations enterprise. This common enterprise involved frequent public statements and assurances that most American Catholics were and forever would be anti-Communist in all things. It also involved similar statements and assurances that as a group Catholics in this country were totally committed to the values of American democracy. Such statements and assurances were necessary because in postwar America many unchurched intellectuals and Protestant ministers believed otherwise. Once again, the so-called Catholic question became an issue in American public discourse. Postwar anti-Catholicism was intense and nasty but also short-lived.

During the war years, some Protestant writers expressed concern about the growing strength and assertiveness of the Catholic community. Articles appeared in the respectable Protestant journal *Christian Century* in late 1944 and early 1945 contending that the Catholic hierarchy was pursuing a plan calculated to increase clerical domination of American culture and in time take over the country.[7] Other Protestant writers about the same time in *Christianity and Crisis* declared American Protestants annoyed and unwilling to tolerate indefinitely the arrogance of Catholic religious and political ambitions.[8] After all, America was a Protestant country, and Protestant leaders were determined to keep it that way.

Examples of perceived Catholic arrogance were not difficult to find. Official United States diplomatic representation at the Vatican was one clear example, but most important of all was the possibility of providing public funding for parochial schools through any general scheme of federal aid to education. For the country's religious communities, no issue was more divisive. Crudely put, the prospect of giving taxpayer dollars to nuns in parochial schools was unthinkable. As a matter of fact, a new militantly anti-Catholic organization, Protestants and Other Americans United for the Separation of Church and State (POAU), was established for the principal purpose of forestalling just such an outcome.[9]

Indeed, between the end of the war and the outbreak of the Korean conflict, many Protestant leaders considered the Catholic Church as the chief threat to religious freedom in America and acted accordingly. Virtually any form of Catholic activity, no matter how innocuous or innocent it might appear, was suspicious and interpreted by some ministers from pulpits and writers in Protestant publications as undoubted examples of Catholic aggression against other religious denominations. There was not much that Catholic leaders or publicists could do to allay such suspicions, so not many tried.

To be sure, Communism as a threat to religious freedom was properly denounced as well, but the American Communist party was small, and the Soviet Union was far away, preoccupied with expanding its influence into Europe and Asia. On the one hand, the threat to religious freedom from Communism was real enough but not immediate. On the other hand, the perceived danger to that freedom from the Catholic Church was clear and present.

Protestants of this mind-set believed that the American Catholic Church was organizationally efficient, directed by determined leaders, and sufficiently endowed with resources to be capable of anything. Consequently, fear of Catholic aggression remained endemic in some Protestant circles for many years, intensifying greatly during the presidential election of 1960, only to expire as a political influence in the outpouring of national grief following the Kennedy assassination.

At the same time that Protestant leaders warned the country about the danger of Catholic aggression, liberal intellectuals—reacting to Catholic criticism of increasing secular influences in American life—seriously doubted the commitment of American Catholics and their leaders to democratic principles. As noted earlier, McMahon had tried to address this point in an exchange of letters sent to the *New Republic* in early 1943 and chided his liberal friends for too easily linking Catholicism with forms of political authoritarianism. While McMahon's arguments at that time were received with respect, they were not much believed and changed few minds. Moreover, when McMahon was fired from his position at Notre Dame that same year and the enormous firestorm of negative publicity over that event continued into 1944, arguments about an authoritarian Church respecting American principles, such as freedom of speech, lost all credibility in liberal circles.

Catholic authoritarianism and apparent disregard for freedom of speech and other civil liberties, abetted by such widely publicized incidents as the McMahon affair in 1943 and then Archbishop Francis Spellman's severe public attack in 1949 on Eleanor Roosevelt for supporting pending legislation that would deny public funds for parochial schools, alarmed liberal intellectuals. In a public statement, Spellman accused the former first lady of being anti-Catholic and of discrimination unworthy of an American mother.[10]

For liberal intellectuals Eleanor Roosevelt was a great heroine, and even though a reconciliation was effected later, the archbishop's ill-chosen words attacking her for a political position was nothing less than outrageous. In this instance, one very prominent Catholic leader seemed to have crossed an ethical line and forsaken civility in order to shock and intimidate. Moreover, Spellman's example as well as others by less prominent Catholics suggested that the increasingly frequent displays of Catholic power in American public affairs were having a corrupting effect on political processes and demeaned political values. To persons of this mind-set, it seemed self-evident that protection and preservation of democracy in America required that Catholic power be checked.

The person most determined to meet that challenge was Paul Blanshard. A twin brother of Brand Blanshard, the eminent American philosopher teaching at Yale, Paul Blanshard had pursued several different vocations before assuming the role of scourge of American Catholic aggressors. He had been trained as a lawyer and early in life had been ordained a minister in the Congregational Church. He actually served as a pastor for two years but left that calling to participate in the labor movement during the 1930s. Blanshard was an associate editor of the *Nation* for a short time, practiced law, and served in the State Department during the war. From 1946, Blanshard was a full-time writer.

First, in a series of articles in the *Nation* and then in a best-selling book, *American Freedom and Catholic Power,* published in 1949, Blanshard attacked Catholic leaders for employing pressure-group tactics to advance their own religious and moral agendas. According to Blanshard, such tactics were inappropriate for such agendas and violated traditional church-state relations. While attacking the Catholic Church as an organization, Blanshard found virtually no fault with Catholicism as a private religious faith and professed no special concern over the size of the Catholic community in the country. For Blanshard, the heart of the Catholic problem in postwar America was not beliefs or numbers, it was the extent and degree to which the Catholic hierarchy was able to direct and control the thinking and the social and political behavior of ordinary Catholics.

In effect, Blanshard revived in his articles and books a modernized version of an old standard anti-Catholic idea propagated by American and British anti-Catholic propagandists throughout the eighteenth and nineteen centuries and employed by the Ku Klux Klan with some success during its anti-Catholic campaigns in the 1920s. Simply stated, that very old, much used and abused notion was that ordinary Catholics had given their minds away to their priests and bishops. On issues perceived as moral or related to Catholic religious practices, Catholics generally did what their bishops told them to do. In Blanshard's view, that was the basis of Catholic power in postwar America.

According to Blanshard, the Catholic Church was an authoritarian, undemocratic, and intrinsically un-American institution. It was also an extremely divisive one because of its commitment to separate schools. Beyond that, Blanshard saw the Catholic Church as informed by reactionary moral positions and political principles that its hierarchical leaders imposed on their own people by fiat and attempted to impose on all Americans through boycotts, censorship, and political influence.

Blanshard did not stop there. In another book published in 1951, *Communism, Democracy, and Catholic Power,* Blanshard stretched credibility beyond the bounds of even an affected objectivity. He drew some absolutely extraordinary parallels between the hierarchical structure of the Catholic Church and the state totalitarianism of Stalin's Soviet Union. Of course, everybody knew which of those two authoritarian hierarchical organizations came first. Blandshard's message was clear enough. As a formidable, efficient, enduring totalitarian institution, the Catholic Church consistently disregarded civil liberties and seriously threatened American freedom.

American Freedom and Catholic Power was widely reviewed, reached large audiences, was commercially successful, and earned Paul Blanshard an entry in *Who's Who*. To be sure, there were Catholic responses to Blanshard's book, particularly James M. O'Neill's *Catholicism and American Freedom*, published in 1952, but they were slow in coming and did little to repair the enormous public relations damage that Blanshard's skillfully presented attack had wrought. Certainly, Vatican officials were dissatisfied with the timeliness and quality of published American Catholic replies to *American Freedom and Catholic Power*. Archbishop Giovanni Battista Montini, Vatican secretary of state, chided Archbishop Spellman about the failure of American prelates to defend the Holy See against Blanshard's attacks.

At Notre Dame, Cavanaugh did not need Paul Blanshard or anyone else to tell him that anti-Catholicism was abroad in the land. With other informed Catholics of that time, he had watched it build during the final months of the war. He could not have been surprised during the years of his presidency by the number of otherwise respectable people willing and perhaps even eager to advocate and support public policy positions offensive to Catholics. At the time, there were few social or political risks in doing so.

A great many Americans at war's end still believed that Catholics could never be absolutely American because the requirements of their religion prevented them from being so. After all, Catholics owed religious allegiance to the head of a foreign sovereign state, too willingly recognized authoritarianism in religious matters at home, and too often accepted clerical dictation on social and political issues that affected the whole country, not just themselves. Beyond that, however, Catholics as a group were not perceived to be good citizens. Their leaders had close ties to corrupt urban political bosses and generally had poor records as defenders of traditional American civil liberties. Most important, Catholic leaders were notoriously indifferent to freedom of speech for others.

What must have surprised Cavanaugh and others was that their frequent and straightforward, anti-Communistic rhetoric utterly failed to establish the patriotism of Catholics as beyond question, mute criticism of their methods of influencing public policies, or lessen verbal attacks upon their leaders. No matter how patriotic Catholic rhetoric might be, the old problem of trying to be both Catholic and American remained.

From the perspective of those suspicious or fearful of Catholics, none of the old objectionable rules and requirements had been changed. Catholics could not accept religious equality as a matter of principle and would not accept separation of church and state as a permanent constitutional arrangement. Until that was done, Catholics could not be truly American.

Cavanaugh had heard such arguments all of his professional life and was determined not to reinforce them by involving himself or the university in any sort of embarrassing civil liberties situations. He had gone through one such experience in 1943 and wanted no part of another. Cavanaugh realized that for Notre Dame to establish itself as a major university in postwar America, it had to be a place where civil liberties and academic freedom were respected and defended.

As the cold war escalated and the country became possessed by anti-Communist hysteria, especially after the congressional elections of 1946, to much of the country at large preserving civil liberties protection for all American citizens seemed much less important than uncovering Communists and removing them from positions in government and in higher education. Consequently, there were occasions aplenty during these years to offend some important part of the public either by denying or by protecting civil rights, especially the right of free speech, of American citizens who were members of the Communist Party or who had been accused of being so.

At Notre Dame, where Communist infiltration had never been a problem and where pro-Communist sentiments were never heard, Cavanaugh tried to avoid situations for the university where the events of 1943 might be remembered and Notre Dame once again publicly stigmatized as being indifferent to freedom of speech. Early in 1948 maintaining such a stance was easier said than done. Cavanaugh found himself confronted by situations where he would have to make choices on free-speech issues that would become public and decided the most prudent course for the university was not to make them.

In late 1947 and early 1948, serious freedom of speech issues were raised in the New York City university system when Communists were barred from speaking to student groups in any of the city's publicly supported colleges. Known at the time as the "outside speaker's policy" issue, this ban on Communist speakers was widely covered in the New York press and became a highly contentious issue in local politics.

In February 1948 the Committee on Academic Freedom of the American Civil Liberties Union (ACLU) took a public position against the City University's outside speaker's policy. The ACLU recognized that impressionable youth attending public universities might need some sort of protection against Communist propaganda but not at the cost of severely limiting freedom of speech. They solicited information from colleges and universities across the country about respective policies governing campus access for outside speakers.

Such an inquiry with an accompanying explanatory letter was received at Notre Dame in late February 1948. The ACLU letter explained the organization's position that no outside speaker associated with groups blacklisted by the United States Attorney General should be barred from speaking to student groups *as a matter of policy.* Speakers addressing meetings open only to chartered campus groups ought to be allowed unrestricted access. However, some limitations on campus access might be appropriate for speakers appearing before general college audiences. On the general issue of banning all Communist speakers as such, the ACLU letter pointed out that the Communist Party was a legal organization in every state. The letter also stated that from the point of view of democratic procedures, it was more useful "to discuss Communism in the open rather than suppress it."[11]

Since Notre Dame had no formal, written speaker's policy of any sort, Cavanaugh turned the ACLU materials over to Father Louis J. Thornton, C.S.C., registrar of the university, and asked for a recommendation about how the university ought to respond. After considering the possible public relations consequences of either supporting or opposing the ACLU policy, Thornton stated to Cavanaugh that since "there can be no harmony between Catholic education and the proponents of atheistic Communism," the best course was not to respond at all to the ACLU inquiry.[12]

That was precisely what Cavanaugh did, successfully avoiding any possible public relations damage from appearing to have either cooperated with Communism or disregarded freedom of speech. Courageous no, forthright no, prudent probably. As Cavanaugh saw his world in 1948, the potential public relations damage to the university for taking forthright positions on such issues was just too great to risk.

— iv —

The task of finding faculty to teach the number of veterans and returning students flooding into Notre Dame at war's end was a formidable one. In the fall semester of 1945, 3,000 students registered, twice as many as had been enrolled during 1944–45. Somehow during the summer of 1945, O'Donnell and Cavanaugh were able to combine returning faculty discharged from the services along with new hires to provide about fifty new positions throughout the university. Even with that very substantial increase in regular faculty bringing the number up to the pre-Pearl Harbor level (250), fifty new teaching assistants had to be appointed to meet the instructional needs of all the students registering at Notre Dame during the 1945–46 academic year.

With about 350 faculty and teaching assistants in place and by severely straining available permanent and temporary facilities, the university was able to manage the education of about 3,000. However, the demand by veterans for higher education became so enormous between September 1945 and September 1946 that Notre Dame's enrollment increased by 55 percent in a single year, rising to 4,671 by September 1946. During the same period the university hired additional faculty and appointed more teaching assistants, increasing the size of the total instructional staff by 16 percent or up to 406.

During Cavanaugh's six years as president, both student enrollment and faculty size continued to increase but at much less spectacular rates than in 1945 and 1946. When Cavanaugh left office in July 1952, student enrollment had passed 5,000, that is, 7 percent more than 1946. Over the same period, the instructional staff expanded 22 percent up to 495, that is, 367 faculty and 128 teaching assistants. It is important to note that during Cavanaugh's time, once the enormous enrollment increases of 1945 and 1946 had been digested, the instructional staff increased much faster than the student body. Most significant for Notre Dame, after 1946 the growth in instructional staff was largely a matter of newly hired regular faculty with advanced degrees, not teaching assistants.

While he proceeded with faculty expansion as expeditiously as possible, Cavanaugh did not consider curricular reform as an immediate priority. Except for one important project in the College of Arts and Letters, the president generally left curricular matters to the colleges and departments. In the Colleges of Engineering and of Commerce, requirements were usually set by their respective professional associations. The College of Science curriculum, then as later, was profoundly influenced by medical school entrance requirements. Only in the College of Arts and Letters were there even opportunities for serious discussions about curricular change.

Discussing curricular change was a very long step from actually doing it. Curricular change turned on the issue of required courses. Entrenched department heads were well aware that required courses were the building blocks of academic empires and would act accordingly to preserve what they had. Like so many other university presidents and administrators of that time, Cavanaugh had some deeply held ideas about what a liberal arts education ought to be, but he was of no mind to try to impose his preferences upon departments unwilling or unable to accept them.

Along with other Catholic educators in the late 1940s, Cavanaugh had become enamored of the Great Books program developed by Mortimer J. Adler and Robert M. Hutchins in Chicago, wherein students read parts or all of ancient, medieval, and modern classics and then discussed them with trained teacher/discussion leaders in small-group seminar or tutorial settings. As early as 1947, Cavanaugh had talked about the possibility of introducing a Great Books component into the curriculum of the College of Arts and Letters.[13]

Actually, the Great Books movement was first brought to the university by an alumnus in an unexpected way. Roger J. Kiley, class of 1922, a three-year football monogram winner as a starting end for Rockne's teams, 1919–21, now a judge on the Illinois Appellate Court, had participated in a Great Books seminar organized for a group of Chicago civic leaders by Hutchins in 1942. Beginning in 1945, Kiley commuted regularly to South Bend to lead a Great Books discussion group for selected students in the Notre Dame Law School. Cavanaugh and his longtime friend Dean Manion of the law school were enthusiastic supporters of Kiley's Great Books work at Notre Dame and facilitated the establishment of other activities inspired by it.[14]

First, beginning in 1947, the law school sponsored an annual series of "Natural Law Institutes" or symposia on justice-related issues addressed in the works of Plato, Aristotle, St. Thomas Aquinas, and other classic thinkers. Prominent jurists and philosophers attended these symposia and presented papers and comments later published as proceedings of the Natural Law Institute for that year. In time, these annual symposia and published proceedings evolved into a Notre Dame Law School journal, named by Manion the *Natural Law Forum*.[15] Second, law student participation in Great Books discussion programs at Notre Dame encouraged establishment of adult Great Books discussion groups in South Bend, introduced some Notre Dame faculty to the national leaders of the Great Books movement in Chicago, and led to the appointment of Cavanaugh to the board of directors of the Great Books Foundation.

Although Cavanaugh, Manion, and other Notre Dame faculty were active in Great Books work in the South Bend area during 1946–1950, formal introduction of a Great Books component into the College of Arts and Letters did not occur until 1950. With the president's blessing the General Program of Liberal Education was established as a four-year college-within-a-college. The rationale for this new academic entity administratively located within the College of Arts and Letters was to provide students with opportunities to pursue an integrated Catholic humanities-centered education. This particular style of education was to be delivered through reading and discussion of masterworks of the ancient world and of western Christian civilization in a series of seminars and tutorials set within a context of Thomistic philosophy and theology.

Dr. Otto A. Bird, one of Adler's assistants in Chicago, was hired to direct the program. In time, the General Program of Liberal Studies evolved from its original four-year college-within-a-college concept into a three-year regular Arts and Letters academic department accepting majors in the sophomore year. In the course of that evolution, the program was renamed—Program of Liberal Studies.

The Program of Liberal Studies always managed to attract able students and develop in them a highly positive esprit d'corps. To be sure, over the years, the program had its share of detractors but has ever remained popular with the students and faculty participating in it. It is now a permanent part of the Notre Dame academic landscape.

— v —

When Cavanaugh assumed the presidency in 1946, the university had instructional staff and facilities sufficient to educate about 3,000 students. By adopting more selective admissions procedures to control enrollment increases after 1946, Cavanaugh and his hard-working department chairmen by 1952 had been able to increase the size as well as raise academic standards of a faculty needed to teach 5,000 students. It was a difficult task well done.

Increasing the size of the regular faculty was only one part of the problem of trying to educate 5,000 students in facilities geared for 3,000. All existing facilities—residence halls, classrooms, and laboratories, the library, and even the theater—had to be stretched to their limits, but the shortage of teaching and laboratory space was most serious. While scheduling classes and laboratory sessions on Saturdays and in late afternoons maximized usage of available teaching space, such strategies made overcrowding endurable but did little to end it. Additional new facilities were urgently needed.

Some immediate help was obtained from government surplus buildings, cheaply obtained and quickly erected. One such surplus former army barracks placed west of the Rockne Memorial was divided into offices and classrooms, and became the social science building. It served those disciplines as their principal teaching and research facility for a decade.

Because wartime restrictions compelled the university to defer ordinary maintenance work as well as postpone needed renovations and all new construction, facilities would have been inadequate in 1945 and 1946 even without the enormous postwar enrollment expansion. O'Donnell and Cavanaugh understood clearly that whenever construction materials were released for civilian uses, there would be much to do at Notre Dame.

Consequently, during 1945 a long-range plan was developed to prepare Notre Dame for the postwar world. The major projects in that plan were a new science building with classrooms and laboratories and a new arts and letters building with classrooms, some offices, and perhaps an art gallery attached. Also included in the plan were new residence hall projects, renovation of existing facilities, and much-needed improvements to the university's infrastructure. O'Donnell and Cavanaugh estimated that no less than $25,000,000 spent over an eight-year period would be required to complete the long-range plan and ensure the future progress of the university.

On January 12, 1946, O'Donnell announced a facilities expansion plan. Though the president offered few details at the time beyond that the plan was extensive, he stated that construction of a new student residence, Farley Hall, was to be the first part implemented. In his news release, O'Donnell made no mention of a funding source for the Farley Hall project, because at that moment there was none. That really did not matter, because as a revenue-producing facility, even if no donor could be found, the project could be financed from internal sources.

Classrooms, lecture halls, and libraries were another matter. Since they produced no revenue, funds to build them would have to be raised outside of the university. Certainly, fund raising was not a new experience for the university. There were priests on campus in 1946 who remembered Father Burns' successful three-year campaign after the end of World War I to raise a million-dollar endowment for lay faculty salaries. It was quite natural for Cavanaugh and Notre Dame administrators to think that perhaps a little history ought to be repeated but on a larger scale and this time for much-needed new facilities.

However, since 1922 the university's experience with fund drives had been disappointing. A drive launched in the mid-1920s to raise a million dollars for new buildings had failed miserably. Still another campaign to raise money for the Rockne Memorial after that coach's tragic death in 1931 was stopped cold by the Great Depression. Nonetheless, even though those drives failed, costly building projects went forward anyway—

including new revenue-producing facilities such as a splendid new dining hall and the football stadium. Profits from the football program, creative financing schemes, and timely gifts from alumni and friends allowed such projects to proceed.

During the war, rationing of strategic materials deferred most renovation and new construction projects for the duration. Yet, the university continued to receive bequests and gifts from alumni and friends throughout that time. Several contributions of $100,000 for specific future projects as well as for unrestricted use were gratefully accepted during those years. Then, in 1945, P. C. Reilly of Indianapolis generously donated a million dollars to the small Notre Dame endowment for support of teaching and research in chemistry and chemical engineering.[16]

Insofar as acquisition of those generous gifts and donations had been actively facilitated by university officials, the principal facilitators were the president, vice president, and some Holy Cross priests with wealthy acquaintances. University fund raising before and during the war was largely a Holy Cross affair, a highly personalized but nonprofessional and unsystematic enterprize. If the objectives of Notre Dame's long-term facilities expansion plan were to be attained, the enormous giving potential of an increasingly affluent American Catholic community would have to be tapped. To do that, university fund raising would have to become professionalized, that is, recognized as a full-time occupation, located in a permanent administrative unit with its own budget, paid staff, and national outreach. An administrative change of such magnitude would not be managed easily or quickly. Even though such an organization was not fully operational at the university until the end of Cavanaugh's presidency, a beginning was made in late 1945.

In the fall of that year, building on experiences with the Committee on Science and the Public Welfare, O'Donnell established at Notre Dame an advisory council for science and engineering. Headed by Harold S. Vance, chairman of the board of the Studebaker Corporation, this new advisory council included among its fourteen members the president of the Mutual Broadcasting Corporation and corporate officers from Standard Oil, AT&T, and several other major companies. The advisory council met for the first time in October 1945 and heard presentations about the university's wartime research activities and about ambitious plans for expanding research in science and engineering. In these presentations, special attention was given to the estimated costs and probable time frame of such an expansion.[17]

The council members responded favorably to the presentations and agreed to provide public relations assistance and guarantee $182,000 to help the university implement the first year of its science and engineering

expansion plan. O'Donnell, Cavanaugh, and other university administrators were so pleased by the results of this first advisory council meeting that in time every college and school in the university would have one
of its own, composed of successful businessmen and wealthy potential
benefactors.

In early 1947, with assistance of public relations personnel provided by
the Mutual Broadcasting Corporation, the university published under
the sponsorship of the advisory council for science and engineering a
twenty-page brochure, *America's Stake in Science and Engineering.* This
very well-prepared brochure did what such public relations publications
were supposed to do. It stretched a few points and exaggerated others for
the sake of a good cause.

The brochure began by emphasizing the great importance of scientific
research for the future security and prosperity of the country. It then
proceeded to trumpet the extent and quality of scientific research and
graduate instruction under way at Notre Dame. Perhaps the most inspiring part of the brochure was the suggestion that even greater things in
science and engineering were about to happen at Notre Dame if only
outside financial support could be found.[18]

About seven months after the first meeting of the Notre Dame advisory council for science and engineering, the university took a major step
toward creating and establishing an administrative entity that would
evolve into the kind of permanent fund-raising organization that modern American private universities required. This new entity was the University of Notre Dame Foundation.

The justification announced on May 31, 1947, for creating the Notre
Dame Foundation was modest. It was intended to coordinate present
university outreach activities by bringing the university public relations
office into closer contact with the alumni association and with local
alumni clubs. The Notre Dame Foundation was intended to be an organization distinct from these groups but would be closely allied to them. It
would be the principal vehicle through which the public relations office
would communicate university needs to alumni throughout the country.

Part of the plan for the Notre Dame Foundation involved a reorganization of alumni clubs on a state-by-state basis. Within each state, committees would be chosen to approach local alumni and also Catholic and
non-Catholic friends of the university for financial contributions. Harry G.
Hogan, elected president of the alumni association in early 1947, estimated that if each alumnus could be persuaded to contribute $200 an-
nually for a ten-year period, the university would be able to raise the
$25 million required to complete its facilities expansion program. Direc-

tion of the Notre Dame Foundation was turned over to Father Robert H. Sweeney, C.S.C., an executive assistant to Cavanaugh in 1947. Together with Hogan and James Armstrong, director of public relations, Sweeney traveled extensively in 1947, speaking to alumni clubs all over the country. Sweeney was amazed by the responses of his audiences and by the enthusiasm with which they promised financial support to their alma mater.[19]

No matter how enthusiastically alumni club members responded to Sweeney's speeches or how inspiring Hogan's vision of thousands of Notre Dame alumni contributing small amounts to the university every year, the Hogan scheme implemented through the new foundation was impractical for meeting current facility needs. Certainly the prospect of possibly accumulating $25 million ten years hence for classrooms and laboratories needed today was encouraging but not immediately helpful. To be sure, small contributions always had been and would continue to be very important to the university, but the scale of facilities expansion envisaged for the postwar years required large contributions promptly delivered if projects were to go forward.

In the postwar years, the wealth of the American Catholic community increased enormously. During the 1940s and 1950s affluent American Catholics were at once more visible in the country and much more willing to contribute to higher education than had been the case in previous decades. Some of these Catholic affluents were beneficiaries of old money well managed while others were newly rich. Some were Notre Dame alumni; many were not.

Identification of potentially large contributors to the university from among these old and new Catholic affluents quickly became an on-going task for local alumni club members. Once potential large contributors were identified, they would be approached by Sweeney or by some other Notre Dame official during the early years of Foundation activities and after 1951 by paid university staff fund raisers. The form and nature of such approaches would vary according to circumstances, but generally potential contributors would be asked to help the university complete a particular building project.[20] During Cavanaugh's presidency, special fund-raising drives for particular projects were regular occurrences.

The first major project undertaken by the new foundation was a special fund drive launched in late 1947 to pay for a new science building.[21] Cavanaugh estimated that $1,750,000 would be required for the building and an additional $250,000 would be needed to equip it. This fund drive clearly demonstrated the effectiveness of the new foundation organization. In less than two years, over $1,240,000 had been contributed for the new science building to be named for Father Julius A. Nieuwland, C.S.C., a celebrated Notre Dame botanist and chemist. With more than half of the total project costs in hand and with excellent prospects that the needed balances would be collected within a year, Cavanaugh announced on April 9, 1949, plans to construct Nieuwland Science Hall along with three other major projects during 1950–51.[22]

For the additional projects announced by Cavanaugh, no special fund drives were necessary. Individual donors had agreed to provide funds for two revenue-producing facilities—a two-story on-campus inn costing $1,000,000 and a four-story residence hall housing 200 students and costing $750,000—and also for a new liberal and fine arts building with classrooms and offices estimated to cost $1,500,000.[23] It would appear that the new foundation organization was succeeding grandly. The large contributors needed to begin implementing the university's postwar facilities expansion plan had been found among alumni and also in the larger American Catholic community.

The need for an on-campus inn had been obvious for years. In addition to the crowds coming to South Bend on football weekends, there were conferences, parental visits, graduation ceremonies, and special events which brought thousands of people to South Bend every year and many thousands of dollars to local hotels and restaurants. Building a comfortable on-campus inn would have the double effect of providing a great convenience to the ever-increasing number of university guests and visitors and of diverting many of those visitors' dollars to Notre Dame.

A local Presbyterian alumnus, highly successful financier, banker, philanthropist, longtime benefactor of the university, sometime Indiana State Republican party activist, and personal friend of Cavanaugh, Ernest M. Morris, class of 1906, recognized the need and the wisdom of building an on-campus inn and agreed to provide the funds to do so.[24] Construction began on what was to be named the Morris Inn in 1950. The new facility opened and received its first guests in the fall of 1952, just in time for a football weekend. Another donor, Fred J. Fisher, Jr., provided funds for a new ultramodern student residence hall and chapel. Named the Fred J. and Sally Fisher Memorial, construction began in 1951. The new hall opened its doors as a residence for seniors in 1953.

The extraordinary generosity of Notre Dame alumni and friends demonstrated in the fund drive for Nieuwland Hall and in the wonderful gifts provided by the Morris and Fisher families was at once gratifying and surprising to university officials. They were simply not used to this level of giving. As had been demonstrated in these instances, Notre Dame's alumni were enthusiastic about contributing funds to expand

and improve the university. Moreover, that enthusiasm would continue in the years ahead and alumni generosity would grow far beyond anything that Cavanaugh could have imagined in 1949.

Yet there was much more to come. By 1950 Notre Dame also had acquired many very affluent friends in the American Catholic community who were enthusiastic about contributing to the mission of the university. One such person was the highly successful industrialist and active Catholic philanthropist from St. Paul, Minnesota, I. A. O'Shaughnessy.

O'Shaughnessy was president of the Globe Oil and Refining Company of St. Paul, Minnesota, and headed two other energy companies as well. He was a man who had managed to combine extraordinary business success with a deep personal commitment to the Catholic faith. Seriously concerned about what he perceived to be a growing emphasis upon material success in American social and cultural life, O'Shaughnessy believed that the social and cultural influence of Christian intelligence and ethics could be reinforced significantly through Catholic philanthropy.[25]

O'Shaughnessy was generous to his alma mater, St. Thomas College, and to the Archdiocese of St. Paul. For that generosity, he was rewarded with papal titles and honors. In the early 1940s, both Mr. and Mrs. O'Shaughnessy were attracted to Notre Dame, and in 1943, 1944, and 1945 they made gifts of $100,000 to the university to endow a fine arts foundation in the College of Arts and Letters.[26] Funds thus endowed were intended to finance the acquisition and display of the great artistic achievements of a society informed by the intelligence and ethics of Christian culture. O'Shaughnessy received an honorary doctor of law from the university in 1947 and was placed on the Board of Lay Trustees shortly thereafter.

As plans for a new arts and letters building developed during 1948 and 1949, O'Shaughnessy was kept apprised of them. By late 1949, Mr. and Mrs. O'Shaughnessy had been persuaded that a new arts and letters building with a connected art gallery bearing their name would be an appropriate fulfillment of their fine arts interests and Catholic philanthropic goals. On May 10, 1950, the university announced reception of a gift of $1,500,000 from O'Shaughnessy for construction of a liberal and fine arts building and art gallery.[27] Ground-breaking began immediately in space south of the commerce and science buildings and east of the law and engineering buildings. When this new large structure was completed, it would cap a quadrangle running west to the Rockne Memorial. O'Shaughnessy Hall with its connected art gallery opened for use in February 1953. Appropriately, in that year the university awarded O'Shaugh-nessy its Laetare Medal.

In addition to the Nieuwland Science building, Morris Inn, and the Fisher student residence, Cavanaugh ended his construction program by making improvements to the LaFortune Student Center, breaking ground for a new power plant, and cooperating in the completion of the Fatima Shrine. Altogether, during Cavanaugh's presidency, more than $8 million was spent on new buildings and on the renovation of existing ones. Cavanaugh stands well in the company of Presidents Walsh, Charles L. O'Donnell, and O'Hara as a builder of new facilities at Notre Dame.

However, putting up new buildings was only part of Cavanaugh's con-tribution to the physical expansion of Notre Dame. He did more than raise and spend $8 million on facilities. Indeed that was a major achieve-ment, but perhaps even more important for the future growth and devel-opment of the university was his prescient establishment of the Notre Dame Foundation and his decision to begin transforming that fledgling organization into a large full-time, professional, extremely effective fund-raising/public relations organization. To be sure, this transformation took about twenty years to effect and was done in large part by Cava-naugh's successor, but the change started with him.

This enormously important change began in June 1951 when Cava-naugh hired James W. Frick, a young bright enthusiastic naval veteran lately graduated from Notre Dame, as the first university employee to engage exclusively in fund raising and development work. With one full-time fund raiser in place, early successes ensured that others would follow. A threshold had been crossed, and no return to the part-time amateurism of Notre Dame's previous approaches to fund raising would ever be possible. In about twenty years' time, Frick and others managed to create one of the country's most successful money-raising machines. By comparison, even Rockne's fabled football profits during the late 1920s appear insignificant. In the late twentieth-century history of Notre Dame, Frick has earned a very significant place.

Frick was important to Notre Dame as much for his vision of what the university could become and his inspired recognition of the astonishing scope and depth of the postwar American Catholic community's willing-ness to give to church-related educational institutions as for his personal fund-raising achievements. Frick learned from Cavanaugh that the best American universities were the ones with the largest financial endow-ments. Raising the university's small endowment of about $6 million became for Frick a long-term objective. However, for the time being that objective had to be deferred in order to meet immediate facility needs.[28]

Yet to approach that long-term objective or, for that matter, even to find ways of raising the large amounts of money for much-needed facilities required new strategic thinking about the role of fund raising in university development. Frick argued that fund raising at Notre Dame should be a permanent and continuous program, not just periodic activities targeted for specific projects. It should also be direct and personal. Affluent persons with past associations or with present interests in Notre Dame should be approached directly and simply asked to contribute to the improvement of the university.

According to Frick, this new university strategy for fund raising began without fanfare or public announcement in the fall of 1951. Cavanaugh allowed Frick to visit alumni industrialists and Notre Dame football enthusiasts in Milwaukee and Chicago. Frick traveled to Milwaukee first. He visited his prospect in the man's office and delivered a half-hour presentation about what Notre Dame had to do in order to become a major American university. Without any further persuasion, this alumni industrialist wrote and handed Frick a check for $500 while promising to do more in the months ahead. Next, Frick traveled to Chicago and the result there was the same. He visited two prospects and returned to Notre Dame with checks totaling $1200 for three days' work.[29]

Cavanaugh was amazed by what Frick had accomplished. The president decided then and there that Frick's notion of a permanent and continuous Notre Dame fund-raising program was both viable and appropriate. According to Frick, those visits to Milwaukee and Chicago were the beginning of serious professional fund-raising at Notre Dame. Once begun, there would be no turning back. It was like finding a long lost treasure above ground waiting to be discovered. Within the increasingly affluent postwar American Catholic community resided enormous charitable resources for religious works. Moreover, at that time American Catholics were willing, many were anxious, to give to Catholic higher education. However, in order to give, first they had to be asked. The challenge for Cavanaugh, Frick, and others involved in the Notre Dame Foundation was to do the asking.[30]

Over the next forty-five years, two Notre Dame presidents ably assisted by Frick and his successor, William P. Sexton, did a lot of asking. During that time, the Notre Dame Foundation expanded enormously and was completely transformed. It grew from one full-time paid employee, Frick, in 1951 into a major university division by 1996, headed by a vice president with more than forty variously titled professionals reporting to him. Though Cavanaugh headed the Notre Dame Foundation for a time after leaving the presidency in 1952 and another Holy Cross priest succeeded him, most of the growth and transformation of the Notre Dame Foundation into a full-scale university division of development and public relations was managed by Frick.

Frick worked very well with Cavanaugh and came to enjoy even greater presidential confidence with Cavanaugh's successor, Father Theodore M. Hesburgh, C.S.C. The Hesburgh-Frick relationship turned out to be a most fortuitous and long-lasting combination of political and public relations skills that did wonderful things for the university. As president, Hesburgh appointed Frick to the post of director of development in 1961 and, four years later, chose him to be vice president of public relations and alumni affairs. As vice president, Frick was the first layman ever to hold such a position at Notre Dame and the first layman to serve as an officer of the university. Together Hesburgh and Frick managed four major fund campaigns between 1960 and 1972, raising over $300 million. By the time Frick left the university in 1983, Hesburgh and he had put up forty buildings and increased the university endowment from $9 million to over $200 million.

Needless to say, an achievement of this magnitude could not be accomplished by telephone. Hesburgh and Frick were on the road constantly. During that time, Frick estimated that he was away from home 300 days in any given year. Hesburgh was rarely on campus for more than ten consecutive days at any time during those campaigns. Both men were blessed with boundless optimism, persuasive on virtually any subject in all situations, and possessed with the extraordinary physical and intellectual energy required to achieve what previous university presidents and vice presidents had not even imagined. Having said that, however, one must also say that it was Cavanaugh who recognized the promise and ability of these two men and put them into posts where they could change the course of university history.

As Cavanaugh had recognized ability and potential in Frick as a fund raiser, he saw in Hesburgh the kind of leadership qualities needed to manage the university and make the most of the challenges and opportunities of the postwar world. Indeed, Cavanaugh had considered at least two others before deciding that Hesburgh should be his successor. However, those two others were founding wanting in some essential qualities that Cavanaugh believed to be necessary for the Notre Dame environment at that time and were sent off to the University of Portland.

— vi —

Theodore M. Hesburgh was born in Syracuse, New York, in 1917, the second of five children. He was raised in a devout middle-class Catholic family and attended parochial schools in his native city. He first learned about the Congregation of Holy Cross in grammar school at the age of thirteen. His desire and determination to become a priest developed early and intensified during his high school years. After graduating from high school, he enrolled at Notre Dame as a seminarian in 1934.

Although Hesburgh distinguished himself as a student and attracted the attention of Father James A. Burns, C.S.C., former president of the university then serving as provincial, Hesburgh remained at Notre Dame until 1937, when Burns decided to send him to Rome for the next eight years to pursue doctoral study in theology and also in Thomistic philosophy at the Gregorian University.[31]

Indeed, Rome was a great spiritual and intellectual adventure for the young priest. In particular, Rome provided an opportunity for him to develop his natural gift for learning languages, whereupon he became fluent in Italian, French, Spanish, and comfortable in German. However, his very ambitious study plan to obtain two doctorates in Rome was curtailed by the outbreak of World War II.

In May 1940, Hesburgh and other American seminarians studying in Rome were advised to return to the United States at once or risk being left there until the end of the war. He embarked on the SS *Manhattan* out of Genoa on June 1, arriving in New York six days later. Allowed to visit his family in Syracuse for two weeks, he proceeded thereafter to the Holy Cross House of Studies in Washington, D.C., and to the Catholic University of America, where he resumed doctoral work in theology.

Hesburgh spent most of the war years in Washington, returning to Notre Dame in 1943 to be ordained. While in Washington after ordination, 1943 to 1945, he completed his doctoral studies in theology but abandoned all intentions of obtaining a second doctorate in Thomistic philosophy. He did so because pastoral activities left him no time for such an academic ambition. Hesburgh helped out in local parishes, worked in United Services Organizations, served as a chaplain to inmates of the National Training School for Boys, and found time to write and publish some well-received religious pamphlets for servicemen and women.[32]

While completing course work and finishing his dissertation at the Catholic University of America, Hesburgh had some unforgettable encounters with the formidable Monsignor Joseph C. Fenton, then one of the reigning theological authorities and most indefatigable protectors of theological orthodoxy in the American Catholic Church. Undaunted by Fenton's determined enforcement of rules and precedents for their own sake, Hesburgh appears to have resolved at that time never to become that sort of theologian or that type of person. After receiving his degree, Hesburgh was directed to return to Notre Dame and take up new duties as an instructor in the Department of Religion and as chaplain to those married veterans studying at the university who were living in Vetville, the former prisoner-of-war barracks turned into temporary housing for married students.[33]

Hesburgh began teaching religion courses during the summer session of 1945. He discovered quickly what the president and department head already knew. For teachers of required religion courses, there were virtually no standards about content, readings, or tests. Each priest teaching a religion course simply talked about whatever interested him, assigned little reading, and gave few tests.[34] Required religion courses were not regarded as serious intellectual activities either inside or outside of the university. As a matter of fact, if Notre Dame students transferred to state or private universities elsewhere, credits earned in required religion courses did not transfer with them.

Father Roland Simonitsch, head of the department, was well aware of the situation and had already taken some remedial action. With President O'Donnell's backing, he had managed the very delicate task of moving Father John O'Brien out of teaching. Next, with President Cavanaugh's support, he undertook the even more delicate task of directing Holy Cross priests teaching required religion courses to follow a common syllabus, use common readings, and schedule the same number of papers and tests.

Simonitsch chose Hesburgh and Father Charles E. Sheedy, C.S.C., also lately returned from graduate studies at the Catholic University of America, to be his agents of reform. He asked Hesburgh to prepare a syllabus for the required course in Catholic dogma and asked Sheedy to do the same for moral theology. In addition, Simonitsch asked Hesburgh and Sheedy to prepare teaching notes to accompany their new syllabi. After a semester to work all of this out, Hesburgh's notes and Sheedy's sheets were distributed to the priests teaching required courses in Catholic dogma and moral theology.[35]

While the reactions of the experienced priest teachers in the religion department to the reform efforts of these two young energetic new doctors of theology is unrecorded, it can be imagined. However, those reactions, whatever they were, did not matter. The most important person at the university was impressed by what Hesburgh and Sheedy had done and responded in a surprising way. Cavanaugh approached Hesburgh in the spring of 1948 and asked him, an instructor with only three years of teaching experience, to accept the post of dean of the College of Arts and Letters. Moreover, the political impracticality of such a sudden upward jump at Notre Dame was intensified by the fact that the priest to be displaced by Hesburgh was none other than the president's brother, Father Francis P. Cavanaugh, C.S.C.

Despite youth and undisguised ambition, Hesburgh was wise enough to realize that the prospect of a priest instructor with very little teaching experience and virtually no serious scholarly publications becoming dean was a prescription for disaster. Displacing the president's brother was bad enough, but moving into a position where he would have to interact with powerful department chairmen and some faculty who were unaccustomed to receiving academic direction from anyone could end only one way.[36]

Hesburgh told Cavanaugh kindly but firmly that he did not want to be a dean or any other sort of administrator. He was happy as a teacher of religion and enormously satisfied with his work as chaplain to married veteran students. After reflecting on the devilish situation almost created, Cavanaugh appreciated Hesburgh's obvious political wisdom and abandoned what was clearly a bad idea. Cavanaugh admired his now well-established protégé even more. Very soon, however, there would be another administrative opening that Hesburgh could not refuse.

Simonitsch had asked for and had received leave from his administrative and teaching duties to return to the Catholic University of America to complete his doctoral studies. With Simonitsch on leave, the post of head of the Department of Religion was open, and Cavanaugh offered it to Hesburgh. He accepted the post forthwith, reciting no litany of complaints about not wanting to be an administrator. Hesburgh took the post and even agreed to give up his pastoral work in Vetville, principally because Cavanaugh insisted that he do so but also because he believed that as head of the Department of Religion he could make a difference.

In 1948, when Hesburgh was appointed head of his department, there was a tradition at Notre Dame of strong presidents, weak deans, and some very powerful department heads. Indeed, for those in charge of academic departments at Notre Dame, the descriptive term, head, instead of chairman was entirely appropriate. Department heads were appointed by the president, not elected by their departmental colleagues.

Moreover, heads of departments had no defined terms. They served until the president became sufficiently troubled by their behavior to want them out.

Long-tenured priest department heads—ten or fifteen years in some cases—achieved an autonomy that neither Cavanaugh nor his predecessor had been anxious to challenge. It was a fact that at the time within the several colleges there were some near absolute long-tenured priest department heads that were more influential in setting college academic policies than were their respective deans. Hesburgh was certainly aware of the importance of powerful priest department heads in college affairs and may have aspired to emulate them. Certainly, there were models enough to inspire emulation.

Father Henry J. Bolger, C.S.C., long-serving head of the physics department, was one such model and Father Thomas T. McAvoy, C.S.C., head of the history department since 1939, was another. By hiring European émigré scientists and young men with advanced degrees from prestigious American universities, Bolger, a supreme autocrat, had built up an excellent department that he fiercely protected from encroachment, interference, or dilution by anyone, that is, other department heads, his dean, the director of studies, or even the president. Bolger was so autonomous that, in effect, he ran his own admissions program. He personally reviewed all admissions applications to the College of Science from prospective physics majors and decided who would be admitted to the college and who would not.

McAvoy was hardly less autocratic, assertive, or contemptuous of academic authorities at Notre Dame than was Bolger. Dean Cavanaugh could not cope with him and stopped trying. McAvoy was a serious, respected, well-published scholar. He built up a very strong department by hiring Catholic war veterans with doctoral degrees from Ivy League institutions who were expected to do research and publish. He made all departmental decisions, great and small.

McAvoy was a true believer in the discussion mode of instruction, common syllabi, and departmental examinations for introductory courses. He saw no conflict between regular research and good teaching. In his view, the latter followed from the former. McAvoy had little patience with faculty who tried to justify an abandonment of scholarly research and publication by proclaiming themselves to be singularly devoted to teaching. He absolutely loathed the expression "great teacher" and was suspicious of all faculty in the College of Arts and Letters thus popularly acclaimed. Faculty in his department were expected to teach responsibly and well, but they were also expected to do research and publish. Most did; those who did not were obliged to leave.

For an ambitious young new doctor of theology determined to make a difference in a department needing improvement, the Bolger and McAvoy models were at hand to emulate. Whether Hesburgh aspired to follow either of those models or find a way of his own to create a distinguished department is unknown. It is clear, however, that Hesburgh was comfortable in the role of head of the Department of Religion. It was a large department with perhaps forty full- and part-time members, but in one important respect, the Department of Religion was easier to administer than either physics or history. Because most of the men in the Department of Religion were Holy Cross priests, Hesburgh would not have to interact with lay faculty. Moreover, what was true for priest department heads was not the case for priest teachers. The priests in the Department of Religion would either take Hesburgh's directions and follow them or would soon find themselves in new assignments elsewhere. In 1948, that was the way religious obedience worked and that was the way things were done.

Just how ruthlessly Hesburgh would have employed the autocratic authority available to him or how far he would have reached outside of the Holy Cross community to try to re-create the Notre Dame Department of Religion can only be guessed. Certainly, the idea of such a re-creation was in his mind at the time and actively remained there for the next thirty-five years. However, he did not remain department head long enough to move it very far. Hesburgh was destined for greater things, and with a sharp push from Cavanaugh, destiny moved very quickly.

Also in 1948, Cavanaugh began thinking seriously about ways of modernizing the administrative structure of the university. That structure of a president and a vice president assisted by a director of studies, a director of student welfare, a business manager, and advised by a university council composed of sixteen administrators and three elected faculty representatives had been in place and unchanged since 1919. Clearly, by contemporary American university governance practices in 1948, this antiquated structure was obsolete and much in need of reform.

In the summer of 1948, Cavanaugh took the first of two steps toward reform by renaming the university council. All he did was rename it, nothing else. Henceforth, this advisory body, still completely dominated by presidential appointees, became known as the Academic Council. Then in the following year, Cavanaugh took another step. He decided to try to modernize the upper levels of his administration and at the same time identify and prepare a successor to take over the presidency when he left office in July 1952.

At first glance, Cavanaugh's modernization scheme appeared to be a very modest one indeed. He changed the names of several high-level administrative offices but kept the same people in them. In 1949, Cavanaugh's top administrators were all Holy Cross priests. John J. Murphy was vice president, Howard J. Kenna served as director of studies, John J. Burke was business manager, and Joseph A. Kehoe held the office of director of student welfare. Cavanaugh abolished the posts of director of studies, business manager, and director of student welfare but reappointed all three incumbents respectively to the new offices of vice president for academic affairs, vice president for business affairs, and vice president for student affairs.

Next, Cavanaugh created two entirely new offices. Murphy was moved to a new post of vice president for public relations and Hesburgh was named executive vice president. The now vacant office of head of the Department of Religion was given to Hesburgh's friend and close collaborator in that department, Father Charles E. Sheedy, C.S.C.[37] Moreover, by raising Hesburgh to the second highest office in the university after he had served only one year as head of the Department of Religion, Cavanaugh, in effect, designated this energetic, relatively inexperienced priest, barely thirty-two years of age, as his choice to be the next president of the University of Notre Dame. With this decision made in the summer of 1949, Cavanaugh believed that he had settled the course of university leadership for the next nine years. At the time he did it, Cavanaugh could not have imagined how far into the future of Notre Dame the consequences of this decision would reach.

13

The End of One Era
and the Beginning
of Another

Reflecting on the circumstances of his appointment as executive vice president many years after the event, Hesburgh insisted that Cavanaugh's decision was a total surprise to him.[1] Apparently at the time, it surprised the other vice presidents as well. When Cavanaugh explained to Hesburgh that the primary function of the executive vice president was to oversee and manage the other vice presidents, then charged him to revise the Articles of Academic Organization promulgated by Hugh O'Donnell in 1941, and following that to prepare new articles of administration for the other vice presidents to live by, resentment surfaced.

O'Donnell's Articles of Academic Organization was the only published body of rules and regulations governing the academic operations of the university. It was a brief document amounting to only fourteen double-spaced typewritten half-pages. Within these very few pages, the authority of the president over every aspect of university life was unambiguously asserted. The duties of deans and department heads were enumerated as twelve for the former and as ten for the latter. The composition of the university council was specified as consisting of the president, vice president, director of studies, registrar, the five deans, and five faculty members elected by the colleges and the law school for two-year terms. The functions of this fourteen-person body were limited to the general academic matters of the undergraduate school.[2]

With regard to institutional expectations for faculty performance, the Articles of Academic Organization made clear, albeit in ponderous prose, precisely what faculty behaviors would lead to termination of employment. Since the success of the university's educational mission depended on the efficiency of individual faculty members, O'Donnell had written, inefficiencies such as indifference by a teacher to his work, lack of preparation in the subject matter of his courses, and irregularity in the teaching of classes would not be tolerated at Notre Dame. Beyond those professional failings, an inability to get along with students, persistent disregard of academic regulations, failure to attend academic meetings, and lack of cooperation with his department head, dean, or other university officials singly or in combination justified termination of employment as well, disqualifying such a person for "the responsible work of educating the young" at Notre Dame.[3]

Hesburgh's revisions of O'Donnell's articles turned out to be neither intellectually challenging nor time-consuming. He did not waste time trying to improve them. He simply added to the list of duties assigned to deans and department heads and increased the size of the body now known as the academic council to seventeen by adding two more administrators and one elected faculty member.[4]

Most important and highly indicative of Hesburgh's future actions, he excised from the articles all of O'Donnell's ponderously presented, professionally demeaning justifications for termination of employment. Believing that such strictures were more appropriate for high schools than for a developing university with great aspirations and convinced that they would discourage quality faculty from even thinking about coming to Notre Dame, Hesburgh simply did away with them. In the administrative environment of Notre Dame at that time, no one reporting to him objected.[5]

Preparing articles of administration for the other vice presidents was not so easily or quickly done as was the revision of O'Donnell's Articles of Academic Organization. Hesburgh's undisguised eagerness to write job descriptions, set lines of authority, and define areas of responsibility for all of the vice presidents was more than Father John J. Burke, vice president for business affairs, could stomach. He told Hesburgh to his face that he was too naive and inexperienced even to think about trying to reorganize the division of business affairs at the university.[6]

Hesburgh responded to Burke's candor by telling him to take his complaints, if he had any, to Cavanaugh. For his part as executive vice president he intended to complete what the president had charged him to do.

To make very clear to Burke and anyone else the strength of his relationship with Cavanaugh and how certain he was of his own authority, Hesburgh delayed not at all in addressing the problem of Father Francis Cavanaugh's ineffectiveness as dean of the College of Arts and Letters. The man was the president's brother, but he needed help whether he wanted it or not. In late July 1949, he got it.

Hesburgh and Kenna installed Father Paul E. Beichner, C.S.C., lately returned from Yale with a doctorate in medieval English literature, as a new assistant dean in the College of Arts and Letters.[7] Indeed, Hesburgh's exchange with Burke severely strained relations between these two men and made communication difficult. However, Beichner's appointment to assist Dean Cavanaugh sent a message about who was the new boss at the university that Burke could not misunderstand. According to Hesburgh, the vice president for business affairs accepted reality. He cooperated, albeit reluctantly, with his now recognized new boss and helped prepare new articles of administration for the division of business affairs.[8] Hesburgh came out of this unpleasant encounter with a diminished respect for the value of experience and seniority in any university job that truly never left him. After all, Hesburgh was young and inexperienced, Sheedy was young and inexperienced as an administrator, Beichner was also young and inexperienced, but as Hesburgh saw the world at that time, bright energetic people like himself could do anything or could learn very quickly how to do anything.

Thus matters stood between the executive president and vice president for business affairs, but not for very long. Within two years, Burke was given an extended leave of absence from the university for the publicly stated reason of health. He was replaced by Father Edmund P. Joyce, C.S.C., a young accountant, lately returned to Notre Dame after a year at Oxford.[9]

At the same time, Kehoe gave up the wearying and thankless, largely disciplinary post of vice president for student affairs to Father Charles J. Carey, C.S.C., and went back to teaching. Kenna had already left the office of vice president of academic affairs to become assistant superior of the Congregation of Holy Cross in 1950, being replaced by Father James E. Norton, C.S.C. By the middle of 1951, of the original four vice presidents only Murphy, vice president for public relations, remained. After Cavanaugh, Hesburgh was by far the most powerful priest in the university administration. As the second most powerful man in the university, it was fitting that Cavanaugh should give him the task of controlling and regulating the best-known and most charismatic person at Notre Dame, Coach Frank Leahy.

— ii —

The football players fielded by Leahy in the fall of 1946 were some of the most talented ever to play for Notre Dame. Most of these players were war veterans. They were older, bigger, and stronger than any players in recent memory. As a matter of fact, Leahy had men representing seven different undergraduate classes playing for him. Over thirty-five members of this team went on to play professional football. Lujack at quarterback was a strong contender for All-American honors as were linemen George Connor and Bill Fischer. Actually, the performance of the Notre Dame defense in 1946 was record-setting. During the entire season, opponents managed to score only twenty-four points against Notre Dame. No opponent scored more than six points, and in five of the nine games played that year, opponents were scoreless. It was a season where only one Notre Dame game was really competitive; that was the celebrated scoreless tie with Army in Yankee Stadium on November 9.

Though the Army team was undefeated and stood first in national rankings in 1946 when they played Notre Dame, who stood second, the West Point squad of that year was not as strong in depth as their great team of 1945. To be sure, Davis and Blanshard and most of the linemen were back, but Shorty McWilliams was not. Clearly, the wartime advantages that had enabled West Point to dominate intercollegiate football in 1944 and 1945 were lost.

It was sad but true that there were cadets with political influence or outstanding athletic ability attending West Point during the war years who had sought and obtained appointments to the academy in order to avoid the draft and possible combat duty.[10] By the end of 1945 and early 1946, most of those cadets were trying to find ways to get out of the academy and out of the army. The easiest way out was to fail academically. Those who preferred to keep their academic records respectable could either try to resign or demonstrate negative attitudes or inappropriate conduct that would lead to separation.[11]

In 1946 and 1947 both routes were taken. In the academic year ending in June 1946, no less than 185 cadets either resigned or were separated for attitudinal or behavioral problems. A year later that number dropped to 172 and continued to drop significantly in subsequent years.[12] By no means were most of these departing cadets athletes, but a few were and among them was Shorty McWilliams.

McWilliams had one brilliant year of varsity football at Mississippi State University in 1944. Faced with the certainty of being drafted, McWilliams agreed to accept an appointment to the academy and play football for

Blaik at West Point in 1945. Once at the academy, he performed superbly as a wing back in the same backfield with Blanshard and Davis. However, with the war over for almost a year, in June 1946 McWilliams tried to resign from West Point and return to Mississippi State.

During this difficult period when so many cadets were trying to leave West Point, Major General Maxwell Taylor, superintendent of the United States Military Academy, denied McWilliams' request to resign and publicly stated that this cadet had received "a particularly lucrative financial offer from a certain quarter" to leave.[13] Totally ignoring the West Point football program's dismal history of recruiting violations during the 1920s and early 1930s and forgetful of what draft and combat avoidance had done for that same program in 1944 and 1945, sportswriters praised Taylor for attacking and disclosing the corruption and hypocrisy of intercollegiate football recruiting practices in general and of Mississippi State in particular.[14]

Coach Allyn McKeen of Mississippi State was outraged by Taylor's charges and demanded publicly that the superintendent of the United States Military Academy either retract or provide proof for what he had said about McWilliams and Mississippi State. Taylor would not retract but could not prove his charges. However, within three weeks of McKeen's demand, McWilliams was allowed to resign from West Point.[15] Indeed, McWilliams went back to Mississippi State and played brilliantly there for three seasons, being named to the all Southeastern Conference team for each of those years. He played professional football for the Los Angeles Dons and Pittsburgh Steelers until a knee injury ended his professional career in 1950. In retrospect, McWilliams was one of the best athletes ever to play football for Mississippi State.[16] That was the young man whom Taylor tried but failed to keep at West Point for the football season of 1946.

On the day of Army's game with Notre Dame in Yankee Stadium, the Army team, seeking its twenty-sixth consecutive victory, was the favorite. Though Blaik was able to field a highly publicized and genuinely excellent first team, the Army squad lacked the overall depth of Notre Dame. Both Blanshard and starting quarterback Arnold Tucker played most the game hurt. Blaik and Leahy, who liked one another not at all, were determined to win. In a game between teams of this quality, the surest way to win was to avoid mistakes. Consequently both coaches followed very conservative offensive strategies.

Notre Dame mounted the only sustained drive of the day, moving eighty-five yards only to be stopped on the Army three-yard line. The Cadets marched once to the Notre Dame twenty-six yard line and once to the twenty yard line. Notre Dame's Terry Brennan had the longest run from scrimmage, twenty-two yards. Blanshard had one run of twenty-one yards and appeared on his way to score a touchdown until brought down by Lujack's brilliant open field tackle. Davis was unable to gain much yardage by running either outside or inside. Final game statistics gave Notre Dame a slight advantage. Notre Dame rushed for 173 yards to 138 for Army. Lujack completed six out of seventeen passes while Tucker completed five out of sixteen.[17] Indeed it was a close game, declared by the *New York Times* to be an "epic game." For those playing in the game or attending it, the experience was a memorable one. The game was made even more memorable by the fact that it brought the long uninterrupted Army/Notre Dame football series to an end.

In 1946, Notre Dame went on to win its last three games handily, allowing only one of those opponents to score against them, and ending the season with a record of eight wins, no losses, and one tie. Army also won its remaining games but not handily, winning a very close final game, 21 to 18, against a Navy team with only one win for the entire year. Consequently, though Army and Notre Dame had identical records of 8-0-1, Notre Dame won recognition as the national champion of intercollegiate football, but Blaik was named coach of the year and Glenn Davis won the Heisman Trophy.

With Davis, Blanshard, and many other varsity letter winners graduating and because outstanding football prospects were no longer interested in attending West Point, it was clear to Taylor and Blaik that the glory days of West Point football were over. Simply stated, the requirement of three years of military service after graduation made recruitment of athletes with apirations to play at the professional level virtually impossible. In the future, Army teams could not expect to be able to compete with major intercollegiate football powers. Moreover, future West Point football squads had absolutely no business playing a team with the skilled players and bench strength of Notre Dame. What Blaik's teams had done unmercifully to so many wartime draft-depleted intercollegiate football teams in 1944 to 1946 would now be done to them. Indeed, there was much to remember and much to pay back.

Taylor and others at West Point reasoned that such an outcome would be embarrassing to West Point, to the army, and possibly even bad for the country. It was time to escape from this long-standing football relationship with Notre Dame that, notwithstanding the lopsided victories in 1944 and 1945, had allowed Army teams only eight wins in thirty-six years. Steps to discontinue the series began shortly after the end of the Army/Notre game of 1946, while the West Point football program still enjoyed high repute. Actually, preliminary discussions about suspending or terminating the Army/Notre Dame football series were underway at West Point at least a month before the two teams played to a scoreless tie on November 9, 1946. Perhaps triggered by the McWilliams affair in June, athlete recruitment problems evident in the fall, and much driven by Blaik's perception of Leahy as an unscrupulous and even unsportsmanlike coach who would do anything to win, the Academy's Athletic Council unanimously recommended that the football series with Notre Dame be ended.[18] Also driving this recommendation was the bitter memory of Leahy's highjacking of Lujack away from West Point in 1942. A memorandum on that subject from the athletic council to the superintendent in the fall of 1946 indicated just how long and painful the memory of that incident was for the West Point athletic council. The council memorandum concluded by noting that "today, he [Lujack] is their greatest star."[19] That point was reinforced grandly by Lujack's touchdown-saving tackle of Blanshard in Yankee Stadium on November 9.

Taylor agreed with the recommendation of the athletic council but wanted to get the support of General Eisenhower before initiating steps to "dump" Notre Dame from the Army schedule. Taylor wrote to Eisenhower on October 21, 1946, almost three weeks before the game with Notre Dame, seeking advice on the issue of ending the football series with the Catholic school from South Bend. It was not something easily or hastily done. There were serious public relations matters to consider.

In his argument for ending the series, Taylor offered three reasons for doing so. First, playing Notre Dame every year limited flexibility in scheduling. Second, except for the extraordinary circumstances of wartime intercollegiate football, Notre Dame had usually played and in the future would continue to play football "out of the Cadets' class."[20] Finally, the game had become so partisan and such an anticipated public event that for a very large number of people it pitted West Point against the Catholic Church.[21] Taylor noted also that because of this popular association of American Catholics with Notre Dame football fortunes, West Point coaches and players had been flooded with threatening and sometimes scurrilous letters and postcards from so called Notre Dame "subway alumni," that is, a species of rabid Notre Dame supporters who had no connection with the university other than an emotional one. Some of these letters and postcards were jokes, but others, Taylor believed, were not.[22]

Eisenhower agreed that the series ought to be suspended but suggested that a final game be played either in 1947 or 1948. With Eisenhower's approval in hand, Taylor drafted a letter to Cavanaugh wherein he touched upon the many public relations problems generated by the extreme partisanship of this game and proposed justifying suspension of the series on the grounds of scheduling problems. Taylor emphasized also in his letter to Cavanaugh that the matter at issue was only suspension of the series, not termination.[23]

Clearly, Cavanaugh was distressed by Taylor's letter. He did not appreciate being dumped by anyone. Yet he could not have been surprised. More than anyone else at Notre Dame, Cavanaugh appreciated the depth of anger shared by West Point officials over the Lujack highjacking and their sense of outrage over that young man's brilliant intercollegiate football debut against them in 1943. He could also understand why Blaik unmercifully ran up his team's scores against Notre Dame in 1944 and 1945. Understanding those circumstances, however, did not make acceptance of Taylor's decision any easier. Cavanaugh, however, was in no position to do anything except cooperate with the superintendent of West Point.

During November and December, relations between Cavanaugh and Taylor were strained but remained polite. They worked together to prepare a believable press release explaining the reasons for suspending this much-awaited sports event. Both the president and the superintendent were determined to say as little as possible and thereby minimize public relations damage to both schools. Though leaks about a possible suspension of the series appeared in the press before Christmas, the joint Taylor/Cavanaugh statement was not released until December 31, 1946.

When released, the statement was pleasantly disingenuous. It was a need-to-know document only, and in the opinion of both Taylor and Cavanaugh, not many needed to know. Both Taylor and Cavanaugh said very nice things about each other and about their respective institutions. They justified suspension of the series on two grounds. First, the game had grown out of all proportions as a sports event and was in danger of escaping from the control of the two schools. Second, as a national institution, West Point needed greater flexibility in scheduling.[24]

Generally, sportswriters regretted the passing of what they regarded as a classic American football series. Most sportswriters suspected that there was more involved in the mutual decision to suspend the series than had been admitted publicly but agreed that the full story, the true story, probably would never be known.

Arthur Daley of the *New York Times* was certain that the initiative for the suspension had come from West Point. Building on Taylor's public statement released when McWilliams first tried to resign from the academy the past June, Daley speculated that the leadership at West Point had been appalled by the undisguised commercialism presently enveloping intercollegiate football and believed that by dropping Notre Dame from their schedule the academy would be in some degree separated from it. Daley also suggested that the game with Notre Dame had become too big psychologically for the corps of cadets to bear. Defeating Notre Dame had become more important to the cadets than a victory over their traditional rival, Navy.

With regard to Notre Dame, Daley blamed the raucous behavior of the university's so called "subway alumni" for persuading Cavanaugh to support suspension of the series. According to Daley, the "subway alumni" were not alumni at all but rowdy Notre Dame supporters who went out to the game with a blue and gold pennant in one hand and a flask in the other to celebrate New Year's Eve two months ahead of time. There were also the matters of ticket scalpers asking and getting as much as $200 for a ticket and misgivings about the millions of dollars reportedly being wagered on the game. Behavior of this sort, Daley suggested, deeply offended the leadership at Notre Dame, a place where religion and respectability were very important.[25]

Neither Daley nor any other sportswriter suggested or implied that the coaching behaviors of Blaik and Leahy might have had anything to do with causing this break in Army/Notre Dame football relations. Of course, no sportswriter mentioned the Lujack affair or the very high probability that West Point would never win another football game against Notre Dame as long as Leahy was coach.

For Cavanaugh and Leahy, public relations consequences from the West Point decision to end the Army/Notre Dame series continued into the new year. Public interest in discovering the actual reasons why the two schools had agreed to suspend their very long football relationship did not abate as quickly as hoped. Speculation went on and on. The reasons why are clear enough.

In four seasons (1941, 1942, 1943, and 1946), Leahy's teams had won two national championships and lost only three games. That record seemed to some in the press and to others concerned with the over-commercialization of intercollegiate football as too good to be true. Building on the widely accepted assumption that West Point had dumped Notre Dame for good and honorable reasons, critics implied that Leahy was careless about rules compliance and coached overly aggressive physical play in order to intimidate opponents and win football games no matter what.

In mid-January 1947 Cavanaugh spoke out against such critics and their innuendos. He defended the Notre Dame football tradition and absolutely denied that Leahy-coached teams had won games by playing "dirty football."[26] He complained that the Notre Dame football program seemed to be fated once or twice a generation to be singled out for unfair criticism because their teams were such consistent winners. Cavanaugh denounced those critics of American sports who were ever-suspicious of winners merely because they were winners. That species of criticism, Cavanaugh concluded, simply ignored the many fine qualities that had made intercollegiate football so inspiring and came close to advocating mediocrity as a virtue.[27] To be sure, Cavanaugh had not persuaded many critics of Notre Dame football to rethink their judgments about it, but he had publicly professed his loyalty to the program and confidence in its coach at a time when they needed it.

The final game in the Army/Notre Dame series played in South Bend in 1947 was anti-climactic. The prowess of the Notre Dame football team during that entire season, and especially the squad's performance against Army, confirmed the wisdom of Taylor and Blaik to suspend the series. The talent and depth of Leahy's squad in 1947 was so extraordinary that no less than forty-two of them played professional football for at least one year. The team defeated every opponent handily; only Northwestern was able to score more than one touchdown against them.

In the final game of the Army/Notre Dame series, Blaik's team, ranked ninth in the country but playing without the great stars of the last three years, was never really in it and lost convincingly, 27 to 7. At season's end, Leahy gloried in winning his third national championship, and Lujack received the Heisman Trophy. With the now-celebrated Army/Notre Dame football series suspended, Leahy rescheduled Nebraska to replace Army for the following year. Ironically, it was Nebraska that Father Walsh had forced Rockne to drop from the schedule in 1925 because of anti–Irish American and anti-Catholic crowd behavior during a game at Lincoln. Indeed, time had healed a very old wound and had left no scars.

For Taylor and Blaik, the decision to drop Notre Dame from the Army football schedule had been driven by very special circumstances. That action was not part of broader policy decisions either to de-emphasize intercollegiate football at West Point or to seek out less formidable opponents. Taylor and Blaik dumped Notre Dame because they did not want to play against Leahy-coached teams. Nothing else on their schedule changed. As a matter of fact, after a season of five wins, two losses, and two ties in 1947, with Notre Dame no longer an annual opponent, Blaik's teams had undefeated seasons in 1948 and 1949 and lost only one game in 1950.

Then, in 1951, the academic and athletic worlds of West Point were turned upside down when ninety cadets were discharged from the academy because of a massive cheating scandal. Moreover, thirty-seven of the discharged cadets were varsity football players, including Blaik's son, who was the starting quarterback for that year. At the heart of the matter was the foolish practice in a school operating on an honors system of giving identical tests on different days.[28]

Under such circumstances, opportunities and temptations to cheat on examinations were too numerous and powerful to be put off at that time by exhortatory slogans about the value of personal honor. At West Point at that time cheating was just too easy. Blaik was devastated personally by the scandal but rejected the easy option of resignation. He decided to remain head football coach at West Point, try to rebuild the program, reclaim his reputation, and at an appropriate time retire with dignity and honor. Whatever Blaik had done or countenanced in years past, in 1951 he was no summer soldier.

Rebuilding could not begin until 1952 and was a painfully slow and frustrating process thereafter. During the season of 1951, Blaik's depleted team won only two games while losing seven. In the following season, Army managed to win only four games, losing four, and tying one. Indeed, Blaik achieved impressive winning seasons in 1953 and 1954 and then experienced mediocre ones in 1955 and 1956. However, over the next two years, Army's football fortunes improved dramatically.

A measure of that improvement was the reappearance of Notre Dame on Army's schedule in 1957 and 1958. Notre Dame had been rescheduled because Leahy had been forced to resign as head football coach in January 1954 and because the teams fielded by his successor were much less formidable opponents. In their first meeting in 1957 after a ten-year hiatus, Notre Dame managed to defeat Army in a close game in New York, 23 to 21 but finished the season with three losses while Army finished with only two. The next year, 1958, Army defeated Notre Dame 14 to 2 in South Bend, finished the season undefeated, and their brilliant halfback, Pete Dawkins, won the Heisman Trophy. Blaik's moment of justification had arrived. Now, he had repaired all past damage, redeemed the reputation of the West Point football program, and could retire as a winner with the dignity and honor that meant so much to him.

Leahy, after defeating Army easily in 1947, finishing that season undefeated, capturing his third national championship, and watching Lujack receive the Heisman Trophy, had reached the pinnacle of his football coaching career. Indeed Leahy continued to win many football games for Notre Dame. As the season of 1948 unfolded, Leahy seemed well on his way to a third consecutive national championship. Except for a very narrow victory over Purdue, 28 to 27, at home on opening day and a close game against Northwestern, 12 to 7, on November 13, Notre Dame ran over all other opponents, running up huge scores against them until the final game against Southern California in Los Angeles on December 4. That hard-fought game ended in a tie, 14 to 14, assuring that Michigan would be chosen national champion.

So many victories so easily won intensified even more the widely held public perception of Notre Dame as a football school. During the spring of 1949, Cavanaugh must have regretted his strong public defense of Leahy and of the football program made two years previously. He had misgivings over Leahy's much-publicized fanatical devotion to football perfectionism at whatever cost and over rumors that assistant coaches bullied players unmercifully.

Cavanaugh must have suspected that all was not well with the internal management of the athletic department generally and of the football program specifically. The men in charge of athletic department business affairs and football ticket distribution had been in place for years. Cavanaugh certainly heard the same stories well known to faculty members about how the business offices of the athletic department were transformed at Christmas time into virtual department stores by a near obscene deluge of gifts from favored ticket holders and from those wanting to be favored. In all of this, however, there was one aspect of the current football program management situation at Notre Dame about which Cavanaugh could have no doubts.

Cavanaugh's serving vice president, Father John H. Murphy, the person formally in charge of the football program at the university, could not control or even manage Leahy. With Murphy as a boss, Leahy simply did whatever he wanted without serious concern about reprimands or consequences. Awareness of this situation certainly influenced Cavanaugh's decision to reorganize the upper levels of the Notre Dame administration in 1949. That reorganization moved Murphy to the new post of vice president for public relations and placed the newly created executive vice president, Father Theodore M. Hesburgh, in charge of the entire Notre Dame football enterprise.

At the very moment when Leahy was fielding some of the greatest teams in Notre Dame football history, when Notre Dame football glory was winning over all, Cavanaugh asked Hesburgh to initiate a full-scale reform of everything going on in the athletic department. Indeed, everything meant everything: installing an athletic director over Leahy who would report directly to Hesburgh; preparing new articles of administration for the athletic department; and updating all statutes dealing with finances, schedules, eligibility requirements, number of players on traveling squads, and the authority of the team physician.[29] Leahy was both athletic director and head football coach, master of the entire football enterprise and under Murphy was really answerable to no one. Under Hesburgh, all of this would change.

Ironically, it was Cavanaugh who had recruited Leahy away from Boston College in 1940 and then had allowed him to reign as the absolute monarch of Notre Dame football. Now in 1949 Cavanaugh directed his ambitious protégé, now heir apparent to the presidency, to undo what he had himself wrought.

Hesburgh knew that persuading Leahy that rules and regulations prepared by the young, relatively unknown executive vice president were real and were intended to be enforced absolutely would be difficult. After preparing and issuing new articles of administration, Hesburgh planned to attend every game played at home or away during the season of 1949 in order to observe personally how well or badly the new regulations were being enforced.[30] After the first home game, Cavanaugh had to decide who was more important to the university, his executive vice president and heir apparent or his highly successful and very popular head football coach.

Since assuming the office of executive vice president in July 1949, Hesburgh had been actively making his presence and authority known throughout the athletic department. He required Herb Jones, business manager of the athletic department, to prepare an accounting of total monies received and spent over the past ten years and then insisted that henceforth every check requisition drawn on an athletic department account required his initials indicating approval. In addition, Hesburgh tried to reform some of the most serious abuses of the football ticket distribution system by limiting the issuance of complimentary tickets to persons or organizations approved by himself or by the president.[31] He did nothing about reducing athletic department insider influence in determining stadium seating locations or in obtaining tickets for nominally sold-out games at home or away. Consequently, the deluge of gifts into athletic department offices at Christmas time from favor receivers and favor seekers continued unabated. The virtual department store that appeared in the athletic offices during the holiday season remained intact and thrived for many years to come.

Hesburgh's new articles of administration for the athletic department, directed primarily at Leahy and at the football program, were accepted as they had to be but grudgingly so. Determined to separate the posts of head football coach and athletic director presently held by Leahy, Hesburgh persuaded Edward "Moose" Krause, former two-sport monogram winner, to take what promised to be a thankless job of being in between the hammer of the executive vice president and the anvil of the head football coach. Krause clearly had the personality and patience to survive in such a situation. He strove valiantly over the next few years to keep peace between the two protagonists and generally succeeded.[32]

Clashes between Hesburgh and Leahy were inevitable. Given the nature of the administrative environment of Notre Dame at that time, when such clashes occurred, notwithstanding the national celebrity status of the head coach, all advantages lay with the executive vice president. Indeed, Leahy accepted without comment Hesburgh's regulation that the team physician had absolute authority to determine whether or not an athlete was physically fit to play. When Hesburgh stopped cold a lightly disguised effort to increase the number of football-grants-in-aid, Leahy accepted that defeat with equanimity. However, when Hesburgh decided to impose the Big Ten Conference rule governing the number of players on traveling squads, Leahy balked.

Big Ten Conference rules limited traveling squads to thirty-eight players. Leahy intended to bring forty-four players on the long train trip to Seattle for a game against the University of Washington. When Leahy informed Hesburgh two days before departing for Seattle that he was too busy on the practice field to find the time to prepare a list of the names of the players on the traveling squad, Hesburgh exploded. He told Leahy, through Herb Jones, that only thirty-eight players would be approved for excused class absences, leaving six without such permission and therefore subject to dismissal from the university if they went to Seattle with the team.[33] Hesburgh immediately advised Cavanaugh about his rapidly developing situation with the coach. He made very clear to Cavanaugh that if Leahy took forty-four players to Seattle, the president would have to find a new executive vice president or get a new head football coach.[34] Cavanaugh promised absolute support in this matter, stating that Leahy would comply or be asked to resign.

Indeed, Leahy complied and took only thirty-eight players to Seattle. Thereafter, relations between Hesburgh and Leahy were strained, sometimes tense, but always polite. Neither man liked the other very much and complete mutual trust was impossible, but both men tried very hard not to show their mutual dislike and distrust in a public way. Leahy accepted the absolutely indisputable fact that Hesburgh was the boss. Out in Seattle with only thirty-eight players and experiencing some glaring examples of unfair officiating, Notre Dame won the game easily, 26 to 7, but Leahy's sharp on-field criticism of the officiating was widely reported. Rallying behind his coach, Hesburgh publicly defended Leahy's sideline behavior as justified and not as poor sportsmanship.

Tensions between the executive vice president and the head coach, notwithstanding, Leahy's team played brilliantly during the season of 1949, defeating all opponents except one by at least three touchdowns and finishing the season undefeated and untied. Once again, Leahy captured a national championship, his fourth, and his superb All-American end, Leon Hart, won the Heisman Trophy. It was a great team with many excellent players but it was to be the last one of such extraordinary quality for a while.

With so many star quality players graduating and with Notre Dame increasingly unable to recruit the biggest and fastest prospects from the country's Catholic schools, the talent pool for the next season declined significantly. The season of 1950 was Leahy's worst ever as well as the worst in modern Notre Dame football history up to that time. Though ranked first when the season began, Leahy's team managed only four wins while suffering four defeats and one tie. That poor team performance had the effect of muting much of the outside criticism of the Notre Dame football program and of demonstrating to the sportswriting establishment that even supercoach Leahy could not win games without highly talented players.

After the dismal season of 1950, the football situation at Notre Dame could only improve, and it did. In 1951, Leahy's team overwhelmed Indiana, the University of Detroit, Pittsburgh, Purdue and Navy. The team won close games against North Carolina and Southern California, lost a close game against Southern Methodist, was overwhelmed by Michigan State, and managed a tie with Iowa. A record of seven wins, two losses, and one tie would have been regarded as respectable in most of the country's major football programs but was not at Notre Dame. Leahy certainly knew that in early 1952. He knew also that Father Cavanaugh would be out of office in the summer of that year and that a sometime adversary, Father Hesburgh, was almost certain to be the next president of the university.

If Leahy had not begun to think seriously about what his future at Notre Dame might be after the change of presidency occurred, he should have. The old order at Notre Dame was about to be shaken up in virtually every aspect of institutional life. Henceforth for the athletic department, intercollegiate football rules' compliance and maintaining as much integrity as possible in the Notre Dame football program would be more important than winning overall. Hesburgh had made clear enough to anyone within earshot that if and when he became president of the university, there would be absolutely no tolerance of personal or coaching behavior in the Notre Dame football program that publicly embarrassed the university. Hesburgh and those around him believed Notre Dame could win and maintain its integrity while doing so.

Leahy was very much a part of that old order and would have to adjust to both the athletic ideals and athletic fantasies of the new men about to take charge of Notre Dame or find some dignified way of leaving the scene with his reputation intact. Neither of those options had much appeal.

— iii —

After coping with the personalities and successfully managing the recurring minor crises of the football program, Hesburgh addressed other university problems with perhaps more self-confidence than his age and academic experience warranted. In later reflective moments, Hesburgh would describe his administrative style during the years as executive vice president as one of keeping Cavanaugh informed about current and intended actions, basing administrative decisions and actions on what he believed was best for the university, and then, once a decision had been made, having no second thoughts and proceeding immediately to the next matter at hand.

There is no doubt whatsoever that Hesburgh enjoyed the role of boss and administrator. Power and the exercise of it burdened him hardly at all. Moreover, he enjoyed his work immensely because he had such an enormous physical and psychological capacity for it. Cavanaugh had recognized early on just how large that capacity was and passed more and more of the day-to-day details of running the university to him. For Hesburgh, no job was too large, too complicated, or one too many.

Of course, all jobs were not equal, and certainly some jobs required more consideration and energy than others. At that time, the most frequently voiced complaint from those reporting to Hesburgh was that far too often he failed to distinguish adequately between importance and triviality. When that happened, routine matters could escalate into major confrontations, whereas some very important ones would be approved without comment. Whether calculated or not, this particular aspect of working for and always under Father Hesburgh frustrated some deans and department heads, casting a shadow of unpredictability over what would be allowed and what would not.

With that said, virtually all of the serving deans and department heads of those years would also admit to no memory of a time when more administrative energy had been expended by any Holy Cross priest charged with running the university. Hesburgh's response time to correspondents was then and continued to be absolutely astonishing. Matters sent to him were always acknowledged. Moreover, he took great pride in making decisions quickly and in being able to explain them succinctly and easily when asked to do so. Those were qualities that Cavanaugh admired and believed profoundly that Notre Dame needed at this critical time in its history. Enormous new opportunities for developing the university intellectually, physically, and financially were everywhere in postwar America. Cavanaugh was wise and prescient enough to realize that his young protégé was a Holy Cross priest blessed with the determination and stamina to make the most of them.

Building on Hesburgh's commitment to travel to all football games played away, Cavanaugh introduced him to the world of benefactor relations. While at games played in New York, Cleveland, Los Angeles, New Orleans, and Detroit, Hesburgh attended prearranged meetings of friends of trustees, past donors, local alumni leaders, and non-alumni interested in Notre Dame. Almost from his first appearance in such settings, Hesburgh was enormously successful. He was never crass about the university's needs for additional resources, even though the list was a very long one. Indeed, in his presentations, Hesburgh projected candor, honesty, and unvarnished enthusiasm for the university and for its mission. He also talked about his vision of Notre Dame becoming a great Catholic university.

For those persons hearing Hesburgh's passionate exposition of this noble vision for the first time, the experience could be extremely moving. He admitted readily that there were many distinguished universities in this country and in Europe as well but stated unambiguously that there was not and had not been a great Catholic university anywhere since the Middle Ages. He told his audiences that the possibilities for Notre Dame becoming a great Catholic university, "the greatest in the world,"[35] were enormous.

When finally realized, he suggested, this great Catholic university would be a place where deeper understanding of the meaning of religious faith in the modern world could be discovered and where Catholic thought and influence in this country could be advanced. There was absolutely nothing defensive in his presentation. Past spokesmen for the university had not talked about Notre Dame in such a visionary way. His message delivered in city after city received enthusiastic responses. Audiences were moved, and promises of future support were freely given.

Inspired in turn by the reception of his message, Hesburgh fine-tuned it. The goal of becoming a great Catholic university was a long way off in 1950 but was achievable before the end of the century. One moved toward that goal by being honest about where the university was now. Facilities were inadequate, Hesburgh wrote in a grant application to a foundation, the faculty was at best ordinary, academic programs were old-fashioned, and students generally lacked intellectual curiosity. At the same time, he continued, deans and department heads were complacent, and the administration had been insufficiently proactive, but the football team consistently won national championships.[36]

To change all of this and become truly a great Catholic university, he wrote, administration, faculty, and students must all find within themselves a kind of spirit which inspires cooperation and an institutional ambiance wherein all members of the university community believe themselves embarked together in a common enterprise. None of the needed steps toward fulfilling the mission of Notre Dame could be taken without a substantial endowment and continuing support from generous benefactors. The move to this spirit, Hesburgh believed, was already present in some members of the university community and could be cultivated in others. All the rest, he convinced himself, had to come from leadership within the university, from new faculty recruited from elsewhere, and from massive infusions of foundation funds and monies from benefactors old and new.[37]

While being educated in the conventions and realities of fund raising, Hesburgh also experienced the exhilaration and anxieties of spending large amounts of money very fast. Cavanaugh put him in charge of supervising the five major building projects in various stages of development. Hesburgh's knowledge of architecture, design, and construction was minimal. To be sure, he was a very quick study in most things and learned very fast. However, in these areas Hesburgh needed help and got it by hiring a young engineer, Vincent Fraatz, to provide trustworthy technical advice.[38]

Relying heavily on Fraatz's technical expertise and knowledge of construction industry practices, Hesburgh ended up hiring three different architectural firms to design four buildings in order to get the best designs at the lowest prices. He also stopped the long-standing university practice of contracting with builders on a cost-plus basis. Instead, Hesburgh invited builders to submit sealed bids on specific projects in order to obtain lower prices. Notwithstanding the outbreak of the Korean War and the rationing of strategic materials that followed, Hesburgh went to Washington and managed to obtain the necessary permits to buy steel and copper tubing so that the construction projects could go forward.[39]

During 1950 and 1951, Cavanaugh's admiration for Hesburgh's amazing energy and industry grew. More important, the president's confidence in his protégé's judgment became absolute. At times during summers, when Cavanaugh was away from the university on Holy Cross congregation business or on vacation, Hesburgh was in charge of everything. On such occasions, Cavanaugh demonstrated absolute confidence by not calling or inquiring about the state of things while he was away. Finally, in January 1952 when Cavanaugh developed health problems and had to escape from the severe northern Indiana winter by spending two months in Florida, Hesburgh ran the university as an informal acting president for most of the last six month's of Cavanaugh's presidency.[40]

After having demonstrated determination and firmness with the athletic department, exhibiting an extraordinary aptitude for benefactor relations, and mastering the skills of negotiating with architects and contractors, Hesburgh turned next to what he described as the problem of ineffective deans and department heads.[41] Actually, during his three years as executive vice president, Hesburgh had acquired a low opinion of most Notre Dame deans, some department heads, and many faculty members.

As has been noted earlier, Hesburgh had tried to improve a poor leadership situation in the College of Arts and Letters. Leadership in the dean's office was not only very weak but corrective actions of any sort had to be very carefully considered. That was because the dean, Father Frank Cavanaugh, was the brother of the president and because of the possible reactions of other Holy Cross priests to the removal of a priest as likeable as Frank Cavanaugh. With the president's support, Hesburgh had tried to deal with this very delicate problem cautiously, that is, by keeping the man in place but installing an assistant, Father Paul Beichner, to perform the unpleasant tasks of saying no and reestablishing the dean's authority over some overmighty department heads.

According to Hesburgh, after the College of Arts and Letters the academic unit most needing a leadership change was the Notre Dame Law School. The situation there was delicate only in the sense that the serving dean, Clarence E. Manion, had been a faculty member since 1924, dean of the law school since 1941, a long-standing personal friend of the president, and recipient from Cavanaugh's hand of the third annual Notre Dame Faculty Award in 1950. He was, however, a layman, and though he had many friends among Holy Cross priests, congregation politics did not affect his situation nor did the outstanding faculty member award of 1950. Negotiations to obtain the dean's resignation began before Cavanaugh left for Florida, but the move to force a resignation from Manion had Hesburgh's fingerprints all over it.[42]

Manion was generally popular with the law school faculty and students. That popularity derived from his recognized teaching ability and from the fact that the law school was small enough for him to know personally every student and faculty member in it. Because the law school was so small, managing it was more analogous to running a department than a college. Moreover, there was much about the law school at that time suggestive of a gentlemen's club, that is, a gentlemen's club whose like-minded members were generally politically conservative practicing Catholics.

As Catholic gentlemen-to-be, students were not pushed. Few papers were required, and course examinations were infrequent. To the faculty, Manion provided a much-appreciated libertarian administrative style. Paperwork and bureaucratic requirements were minimalized. He imposed few time demands on faculty other than meeting classes. Moreover, the operative principle of class scheduling was faculty convenience, and there were no faculty research and publication expectations at all.

In 1951, the Notre Dame Law School was a pleasant, if undistinguished place, where one could experience the pleasure of teaching in an undemanding curriculum while enjoying the financial advantages of a partnership in a South Bend law firm. As dean, Manion had set a prosperous example of how easily all of that could be managed. Other law school faculty either followed the dean's precedent or aspired to do so when circumstances permitted. All of this aggravated Hesburgh immensely.

What appears to have aggravated Hesburgh even more than Manion's toleration of academic laxity in the law school was the dean's very full schedule of outside activities. Time spent in his downtown law office or in court certainly took Manion away from Notre Dame during working hours but did not publicly embarrass the university in any way. However, Manion's other outside activities did. Like so many other active isolationist opponents of the Roosevelt administration before Pearl Harbor, Manion totally committed himself to a strident, absolutely unrelenting and politically profitable anti-Communist ideology in the postwar years.

For Manion and those of a like mind, the slogan "better dead than red" described accurately the emotional depth of their brand of anti-Communism. As they saw the world, Soviet Communism in whatever forms or guises was inherently evil, and no compromise with evil was possible. Manion doubted not at all that Communist mischief was behind all contemporary national and international crises in the world and that Communist influences informed many, if not most, of the agencies of the United States federal government and affected policy decisions of every sort. Moreover, he was convinced that those influences had to be discovered and then eliminated as quickly and completely as possible.

For all of these reasons, Manion was highly supportive of the anti-Communist investigations undertaken by Senator Joseph R. McCarthy (R-Wisconsin), Senator William E. Jenner (R-Indiana), and others. Manion admired McCarthy as an exemplary product of Catholic education and as an American Catholic politician doing a great service to his country. With Jenner, Manion had no special ethnic or religious ties. However, as an Indiana Republican party activist, Manion had known him personally for several years. In addition to Jenner's fierce anti-Communism, Manion shared completely the senator's abhorrence of the New Deal and of any sort of federal intervention into local economic, social, or educational affairs.

It should be no surprise, therefore, that when Jenner attributed the Communist victory in China to policy advice given by General George C. Marshall and then described him as "a front man for traitors" and "a living lie" in a Senate debate during the fall of 1950, Manion did not dissent or in any public way repudiate this gross defamation of America's architect of victory during World War II. Whatever Jenner or any other senator said on the floor of the Senate was constitutionally protected and therefore immune from liable actions in the courts. What Jenner did to Marshall on the floor of the Senate was an example of a political tactic know at that time as "McCarthyism" or making unfounded and never proved public accusations against individuals while protected from liable actions by senatorial or congressional immunity.

McCarthyism was named for its most celebrated practitioner, Senator Joseph R. McCarthy, who regularly reported true or assumed past Communist affiliations of government officials, some military officers, and educators and then charged them publicly with being either agents or dupes of an international Communist conspiracy. It was a political tactic widely used by Republican politicians to try to end almost twenty years of Democrat party control of the White House and of Congress. Jenner's attack on Marshall was a variation of the classic McCarthyite mode. Even Jenner dared not accuse Marshall of ever having been a Communist or of sympathy for their cause. According to Jenner, Marshall's mistake was to have been fooled by the Communists.

McCarthyism in its many forms, practiced at all levels of federal and state governments, produced many casualties but few prosecutable cases. Nonetheless, widespread use of McCarthyite tactics deeply divided the country. Much like the isolationist/interventionist conflict during the pre-war years when in speeches and public appearances Father O'Brien and McMahon had identified the university with extremist positions on one side or the other, Manion seemed to be doing much the same in late 1950 and 1951. Always identified in the press as dean of the Notre Dame law school, Manion's anti-Communist and anti–Truman administration speeches and statements had the effect of identifying the university in the media with extreme McCarthyite positions.

That problem was exacerbated by the fact that Manion's ultraconservative voice was the only one being widely reported. There was no McMahon to offset an O'Brien. Cavanaugh had been very much in the eye of such a storm before in 1943 and was not about to repeat that experience again.[43] He allowed Hesburgh to move against a longtime friend for a perceived greater good of the university much as he had once encouraged his protégé to replace Cavanaugh's own brother as dean of the College of Arts and Letters. Many years later when all of the principals had died, the arguments Hesburgh employed to justify the move against Manion were not those of embarrassing the university with extremist speeches or by supporting McCarthyite campaigns against prominent and not so prominent public officials. The ground chosen in 1990 on which to justify ridding the university of a problem dean in early 1952 was the very safe and secure plain of academic laxity.[44]

Discussions between Hesburgh and Manion were probably completed in early January 1952, and the resignation was announced on January 11. Manion represented the resignation as his own decision, made because of "the pressure of private business" and because of a "constant lengthening schedule of writing and speaking engagements."[45]

Manion's resignation had been neatly managed with minimal public relations fanfare and made newspapers' front pages only in South Bend. Nonetheless, the Manion resignation communicated an unintended message to the university community that the present and future leadership of the university was determined to disassociate the name of Notre Dame from the conservative political causes championed by Manion. Within a year, some local consequences of that unintended message would challenge and stretch to the limit all of Hesburgh's considerable political instincts and public relations skills.

To replace Manion as dean of the Notre Dame Law School, Cavanaugh and Hesburgh settled on a well-known lawyer from Columbus, Ohio, Joseph O'Meara. O'Meara had been admitted to the Ohio Bar in 1921, had worked for corporations, and practiced law in Columbus for over thirty years. Except for a brief three-year stint as a lecturer in tax law at the University of Cincinnati during the war, O'Meara had no full-time teaching or law school administration experience.

One could hardly imagine a man more different from Manion. Indeed both men were strong Catholics, but O'Meara was small in stature, no orator, and absolutely bereft of a sense of humor. Not only was O'Meara an inexperienced teacher, but he had no patience at all with students perceived by himself to be lazy or not serious about studying law. More to the point, O'Meara was in politics a Democrat and a proud member of the American Civil Liberties Union (ACLU). In addition to all of that, O'Meara was also a complete martinet and very soon after being installed as dean exhibited some of those qualities.

According to Hesburgh, after studying the academic state of affairs in the Notre Dame law school, O'Meara advised Cavanaugh and himself that what they had on campus was an evening law program being run in the daytime.[46] He told Cavanaugh and Hesburgh to their faces that with him as dean, changes would be numerous, swift in coming, and probably offensive to many. Cavanaugh and Hesburgh promised their support. O'Meara took the job and was as good as his word about the number and extent of changes initiated.

First, O'Meara expelled about half of the student body, dismissing those who had failed two or more courses. He raised entrance requirements, reformed the curriculum, and mandated more frequent examinations. Next, he issued a host of new rules regulating faculty classroom performance, out-of-class advising, and attendance at faculty meetings. As O'Meara had forecast, some faculty and students were offended by the substance and tone of the new dean's reforms and departed.[47]

Among faculty in other colleges, Joe O'Meara stories and anecdotes abounded. Anything severe or silly attributed to him was believed. It was not true as some alleged that he had paraphrased King Louis XIV by telling a complaining faculty member that after all, the Notre Dame Law School, it is I. It is also not true that at one point, he considered installing time clocks in the law school faculty lounge.[48] However, it was absolutely true that after three years O'Meara was the absolute monarch of the Notre Dame Law School, and both faculty and students knew it and acted accordingly. He was a man who had made a great difference in a very short time.

Most important of all, in Hesburgh's judgment O'Meara had been a great success, as he so often said, in "jacking up" the law school. O'Meara became for Hesburgh a model of what a determined person could do to improve a stalled or declining academic unit. In the years ahead, Hesburgh would search diligently for other Joe O'Mearas who could come in from outside Notre Dame and "jack up" an operation. He rarely ever found them.

As for Manion, his career was by no means cut short by being forced out of the law school. Once out of Notre Dame, he was able to pursue his business interests full-time and tend to his ideological ones as he saw fit. In 1954, Manion founded a weekly series of politically conservative radio commentaries and local television presentations known as the Manion Forum. In the same year, as a reward for many years of service to the Indiana Republican party, President Eisenhower appointed Manion to the chairmanship of the Intergovernmental Relations Commission.

In an era when big government was believed necessary to wage the cold war, Manion was very much ahead of his time by urging a dismantling of the New Deal social safety net and reducing the size and scope of the federal government. Then in 1958, Manion became a member of the board of the very conservative John Birch Society located in Indianapolis. For the rest of his life, Manion remained committed to, active in, and a contributor to conservative causes of all sorts. He died at the age of eighty-three in 1979.

— iv —

With Hesburgh in charge of the university during Cavanaugh's absences in Florida and with his succession to the presidency in July assured, faculty did not have to speculate about what kind of presidency his would be. He had been an activist executive vice president, exhibiting the enormous self-confidence of youth and inexperience. As president, he would still be young, only thirty-five years old, but no longer inexperienced.

Based on Hesburgh's record as executive vice president, most observers of the man in the university community expected that his presidency would be activist as well. Many things were about to be changed in the law school, and the same had to be expected in the other colleges as well. There were rumors about an intended revision of the university's articles of administration and preparation of a new faculty manual with a general thrust toward adoption of the academic and professional standards and administrative procedures presently operative in the best American universities. Such changes would probably involve revision of existing faculty contracts, extending contract times from one to three years for new hires, and introducing some form of permanent academic tenure provisions for selected current faculty.

There was, of course, the near probabilty of a major effort to modernize the curriculum, which had been basically untouched for twenty-eight years. The late 1940s was a time of intense curricular study and innovation throughout American higher education. At Notre Dame, a good beginning would be to reexamine all university course requirements with a view to dropping some and adding others more reflective of current Catholic thinking about the value of an integrated curriculum and also of the general education models lately introduced at Harvard and Columbia.

If all of these rumored projects actually occurred at Notre Dame under a new president, clearly the new leadership would be trying to move the university into the mainstream of American higher education. How all of this would work out in the years ahead in an institution as traditional as Notre Dame was not clear, but that there would be unforeseen and unanticpated consequences was certain.

Also certain was that however the articles of administration, faculty contracts, or the curriculum might be changed, Holy Cross priests would continue to be in charge of everything at Notre Dame. Any other arrangement was unthinkable at that time. Moreover, not only was Hesburgh extremely Holy Cross community-minded, but he really did not know many lay faculty well enough even to think about moving any of them into upper- or lower-level administrative positions. There were, of course, lay deans and department heads in the Colleges of Science, Engineering, and Commerce. They would remain in place, because few, if any, technically trained Holy Cross priests were available to replace them.

In the College of Arts and Letters, the situation was very different. An impressive cohort of bright young Holy Cross priests lately had returned to the university with brand new doctorates in hand from the most prestigious graduate schools in the country. Very quickly, these men would find themselves in college leadership positions. That was the script that most lay faculty expected the new president to follow.

When the spring semester of 1952 ended and the time for Cavanaugh's departure approached, speculation focused on who the new president's supporting university officers would be. By June, Hesburgh knew the men he wanted, and Father Mehling, provincial of the Congregation, agreed to assign them. For executive vice president, Hesburgh chose Father Edmund P. Joyce, a certified public accountant and acting vice president for business affairs, now a very close friend and trusted confidant. To replace Joyce, Hesburgh selected Father Jerome J. Wilson, another friend who was also experienced in business affairs. Next, Hesburgh decided to leave Father John H. Murphy in his post as vice president for public relations and move Father James E. Norton, presently vice president for academic affairs, to student affairs.

For the important post of vice president for Academic Affairs, Hesburgh chose the dean of the graduate school and the congregation's academic elder statesman, Father Philip S. Moore. To replace Moore in the graduate school, Hesburgh named Father Paul E. Beichner, presently the assistant dean in the College of Arts and Letters. Hesburgh asked for and obtained the resignation of Father Frank Cavanaugh as Dean of that college and replaced him with his close friend and former reform collaborator in the religion department, Father Charles E. Sheedy. For the time being, all other college deans were untouched. That was Hesburgh's management team, and all of these new men entered their respective offices with prioritized lists of things to do and charged to get on with the business of the university and of their offices at once.

When the actual moment of presidential power transfer occurred, it was quietly done. There were no convocations, installation ceremonies, or celebrity speakers. Cavanaugh simply gave Hesburgh the keys to the president's office from which he had not even bothered to remove books and personal items. He asked the new president to take over a scheduled speaking engagement at a campus meeting of the Christian Family Movement and then left immediately for New York. That was all there was to it. Hesburgh decided to retain Helen Hosinski, Cavanaugh's personal secretary, as his own and then undertook the first official act of what was to be a very long and much praised presidency by giving an impromptu speech to a Christian Family group that had been expecting Cavanaugh.[49] That was the way one important era in Notre Dame history ended and a new and even more expansive and transforming one began.

— v —

As for Cavanaugh, he removed himself from the university to California for six months where he worked with Robert M. Hutchins and helped launch the Ford Foundation's Fund for the Republic. At Hesburgh's request Cavanaugh then returned to Notre Dame to take charge of the Notre Dame Foundation and manage a new fund-raising campaign.[50] He remained at the foundation for about six years, resigning in favor of a young, promising Holy Cross priest marked by Hesburgh as a possible successor to the office of vice president for academic affairs. Once out of the Foundation, Cavanaugh took up campus ministry work at Saint Mary's College and provided friendship and counseling to religious sisters pursuing graduate studies at Notre Dame. He continued that sort of campus ministry work until retiring from regular assignments in 1968. During those years Cavanaugh counseled Hesburgh whenever asked, but perhaps his most engaging activity at this time was that of being a very close friend and virtual personal chaplain to Ambassador Joseph Kennedy and to other members of the Kennedy family.

The Cavanaugh/Joseph P. Kennedy relationship was a long-standing one about which very little is known.[51] Cavanaugh probably met Kennedy through O'Brien when the Ambassador delivered a commencement address at Notre Dame and received an honorary degree in the spring of 1940. Cavanaugh also had occasion to meet and associate with Kennedy during Kennedy's tenure as a member of the Board of Trustees. The principal reason so little is known about the depth of this relationship by Notre Dame people was because Cavanaugh was so protective of it.

All during Cavanaugh's six years as president of Notre Dame and six more at the foundation, he absolutely refused to exploit his friendship with Kennedy for the benefit of the university or of other Catholic causes. For Cavanaugh, Kennedy was a close personal friend, not a potential donor. He refused to ask Kennedy for money, an experience quite new and unusual for the ambassador.

Kennedy appears to have appreciated Cavanaugh's genuinely sincere friendship with no disguised agendas at all and reciprocated with candor and trust. After Cavanaugh left the presidency and the foundation, Notre Dame faculty members recollect him being almost constantly at the beck and call of the ambassador, visiting him often in both Hyannisport and Palm Beach. What role, if any, Cavanaugh played in John F. Kennedy's presidential campaign in 1960 or in the run up to it or what advice he gave to the family during those critical years can only be guessed.

What is known for certain is that Cavanaugh was present at the Kennedy compound in Hyannisport on election day in 1960 having dinner with the Kennedy family and with two other close friends of the ambassador while watching the televised reporting of the election returns throughout the evening and into the early hours of the next morning.[52] It is also true that Cavanaugh celebrated a Requiem Mass for President John F. Kennedy, with the widow and Kennedy family attending, in the East Room of the White House on November 23, 1963, the morning after the assassination of President Kennedy in Dallas. The close relationship between Cavanaugh and Joseph P. Kennedy continued after the assassination through the rest of the tumultuous years of that decade, lasting until the ambassador died in 1969.

Cavanaugh's close relationship with the Kennedy family during the 1960s brought him nothing but disappointment and grief. After enduring the trauma of Robert Kennedy's assassination in June 1968, the shock of Jacqueline Kennedy's marriage to Aristotle Onassis in October 1968, Senator Edward Kennedy's shameful public embarrassment over the tragedy at Chappaquiddick in July 1969, and finally the not unexpected death of the ambassador four months later, Cavanaugh stayed away from Hyannisport and Palm Beach. That part of his life was over.

While in semi-retirement during the 1960s, like so many other Catholic priests of that time, Cavanaugh was touched and challenged by the reforms of the Second Vatican Council, the Vietnam War, the student revolution, and most of all by the civil rights struggle. Observing the course of that struggle during 1964 and 1965 from the security of the Notre Dame campus, Cavanaugh was shocked by televised accounts of the brutal confrontation between state and local Alabama authorities and civil rights marchers led by Martin Luther King, Jr., at the Pettus Bridge outside of Selma. When a Unitarian minister from Boston, James J. Reeb, died from a beating at the hands of segregationist thugs, Cavanaugh wanted to join the pilgrimage of concerned students, teachers, and clergymen traveling to Selma to show solidarity with the civil rights protestors.

In order to obtain permission for such a trip to Selma, Cavanaugh called upon his old friend Father Howard Kenna, then serving as provincial of the congregation. Because of the risks involved in going to Selma at this time, Kenna was reluctant to allow his friend to go. He pointed out that Selma, Alabama, in the midst of intense civil strife was no place for a sixty-six-year-old Catholic priest to visit, that it was a very dangerous place and even life-threatening for someone like him.[53]

Cavanaugh responded by pointing out that the mother of the governor of Massachusetts, some years older than himself, had joined the pilgrimage to Selma. Then, possibly feeling some personal guilt for the color line that had governed Notre Dame admissions policy for so many years, he told Kenna that the dangers in going to Selma frightened him not at all. In any case, Cavanaugh concluded, considering some of the things he had done over the years, if the worst happened to him, perhaps he deserved it. With Cavanaugh in that sort of mood, Kenna could say no more and gave permission for his friend to go to Selma, which he did.[54] Having made a small but deeply personal contribution to the popular outcry against racial injustice that forced enactment of the Voting Rights Act of 1965, Cavanaugh believed that at last he had done something important.[55]

Cavanaugh retired eventually to the tranquility and security of living with other elderly Notre Dame priests at Holy Cross House, where his ageless sense of humor and endless supply of stories never failed to cheer and entertain those around him. He died in December 1979 at the age of eighty, surviving Manion by five months and being survived by his brother, Frank. In and out of Notre Dame, John Cavanaugh's was an extraordinary life.

Notes

1. Notre Dame during the 1930s

1. Rockne had been given a ten year contract and paid a salary of $12,500. However, the coach's many outside business activities raised his annual income to over $75,000. Rockne's highest paid assistant earned $8,500.

2. Clauses were added to annual faculty contracts during the first fund drive, 1920–1922, warning faculty against activities that might offend donors. The contract of John P. Tiernan, a professor in the law school for seven years and the highest paid faculty member at the university other than the football coach was not renewed for 1921–1922 because of a divorce scandal.

3. O'Hara to Brierly, July 3, 1937, UPOH, General Education Board File, AUND.

4. Recollection of Frank Moran, a member of the Notre Dame English department during O'Hara's presidency. The person thus admonished was Father Cornelius Hagerty, C.S.C.

5. Arthur J. Hope, C.S.C., *Notre Dame: One Hundred Years,* revised edition, introduction by Thomas J. Schlereth (South Bend: Icarus Press, 1978), 459–61.

6. Thomas T. McAvoy, C.S.C., *Father John F. O'Hara of Notre Dame: The Cardinal Archbishop of Philadelphia* (Notre Dame, Ind.: University of Notre Dame Press, 1967), 102.

7. Ibid., 101, 171.

8. Ibid., 122.

9. Ibid., 112.

10. Ibid., 101, 159.

11. Ibid., 122–23.

12. Ibid., 101, 171.

13. Ibid., 171.

14. Ibid., 122.

15. Fathers Henry Bolger, C.S.C., and Philip S. Moore, C.S.C.

16. Interview by Arnett of Burns and O'Hara, September 16, 1935, UPOH, General Education Board File, AUND.

17. Ibid.

18. O'Hara to Brierly, July 3, 1937, UPOH, General Education Board File, AUND.

19. Murray Sperber, *Shake Down the Thunder: The Creation of Notre Dame Football* (New York: Henry Holt and Company, 1993), 446.

20. Ibid.

21. Ibid., 447.

22. Hope, 416–18.

23. Hope, xvii–xix.

24. Ibid.

25. McAvoy, 178.

26. Hope, 480–81.

27. O'Hara to Brierly, July 3, 1937, UPOH, General Education Board File, folder 4, AUND.

28. McAvoy, 177.

29. O'Hara to Mitchell, October 12, 1937, UPOH, Box 71, 1937–38, AUND.

30. Sheed to O'Hara, February 5, 1935, and Sheed to O'Hara, February 25, 1936, UPOH, Box 70, folder Sheed and Ward, 1934–37, AUND.

31. O'Hara to Sheed, July 27, 1937, UPOH, Box 70, folder Sheed and Ward, AUND.

32. Hannah Arendt, "The Personality of Waldemar Gurian," *Review of Politics,* January 1955, 37.

33. Thomas Stritch, "After Forty Years: Notre Dame and *The Review of Politics,*" *Review of Politics,* January 1978, 438.

34. Waldemar Gurian, "The Catholic Publicist," trans. M. A. Fitzsimons, *Review of Politics,* January 1955, 11–13.

35. M. A. Fitzsimons, "Die Deutschen Briefe: Gurian and the German Crisis," *Review of Politics,* January 1955, 47.

36. Gurian, 12–13.

37. Stritch, 438–39.

38. O'Hara to Gurian, July 29, 1938, UPOH, Box 71, folder Gr–Gz, 1937–38, AUND.

39. O'Hara to Gurian, July 29, 1938, UPOH, Box 71, folder Gr–Gz, 1937–38, AUND.

40. Ibid.

41. John W. Nef, "The Significance of the *Review of Politics,*" *Review of Politics,* January 1955, 31.

42. McAvoy, photograph caption between pp. 258–59.

43. O'Brien to O'Hara, May 19, 1939, UPOH, O, 1938–39, 76/11–12, AUND.

44. O'Hara to O'Brien, May 22, 1939, UPOH, O, 1938–39, 76/11–12, AUND.

45. John A. O'Brien, ed., *Catholics and Scholarship* (Huntington, Ind.: Our Sunday Visitor Press, 1939), 128–29.

46. O'Brien to O'Hara, June 1, 1939, UPOH, O, 1938–39, 76/11–12, AUND.

47. O'Brien to O'Donnell, March 18, 1940, UPOH, OA to OK, 1940, #2, AUND.

48. O'Brien to O'Hara, June 1, 1939, UPOH, O, 1938–39, 76/11–12, AUND.

2. Father John A. O'Brien and His Bishops, 1916–1939

1. John A. O'Brien, ed., *The White Harvest: A Symposium on Methods of Convert Making* (New York: Longmans, Green, & Company, 1927), 3.

2. John A. O'Brien, *Modern Psychology and the Mass: A Study in the Psychology of Religion* (New York: Paulist Press, 1927), 26.

3. Ibid., 31.

4. Ibid., 26.

5. Ibid., 8.

6. Ibid., 5.

7. Ibid., 27.

8. Ibid., 1.

9. John Whitney Evans, *The Newman Movement: Roman Catholics in American Higher Education, 1883–1971* (Notre Dame, Ind.: University of Notre Dame Press, 1980), 78.

10. O'Brien, "A Ghost and Its Flight," address to the State Convention of the Knights of Columbus, Springfield, Illinois, May 12, 1925, John A. O'Brien Personal Papers, COBR 8/14, AUND.

11. Ibid.

12. Ibid.

13. The title of this campaign in the Chicago area was suggested by, if not patterned after, "The Five Hundred Thousand Dollar University of Notre Dame Development and Endowment Fund Campaign" operating out of offices in the Congress Hotel. See Walsh to Burns, March 30, 1922. Folder M. J. Walsh, Box 48, UPBU, AUND. See also, Catholic Foundation at the University of Illinois, John A. O'Brien Personal Papers, COBR 8/14, AUND.

14. O'Brien, "A Ghost and Its Flight."

15. Evans, 79.

16. Claude H. Heithaus, S.J., "Catholics at Non-Catholic Universities," *America* 33, August 22, 1925, 455–46; "Morals of Non-Catholic Universities" 33, August 29, 1925, 479–80; "Courses at Catholic Universities" 33, September 18, 1925, 552–53; "Are Catholic Universities Inferior?" 33, September 26, 1925, 576–78; "Catholic Colleges for Women," 33, October 3, 1925, 599–600; "A Reply to Mr. Quinlan" 34, November 7, 1925, 81–83; "A Catholic Foundation Unmasked" 34, December 19, 1925, 226–28; "Catholic Foundations and Canon Law" 34, January 2, 1926, 277–78.

17. Evans, 80.

18. Ibid., 81.

19. John A. O'Brien, "Catholics on Secular Campuses," *America*, April 8, 1961, 52–56.

20. Evans, 80.

21. "The Catholic Foundation Plan," editorial, *America* 35, March 20, 1926, 337.

22. Ibid., 538.

23. Evans, 80.

24. "The Catholic Foundation Plan," 337.

25. Evans, 80.

26. This suspension seems to have been out of deference to a major fund drive undertaken by the University of Notre Dame in the Chicago area and scheduled for completion by July 1922. Burns to O'Brien, February 14, 1922, UPBU, Box 46, and Walsh to Burns, March 30, 1922, UPBU, folder M. J. Walsh, Box 48, AUND.

27. Receipts for loans from the Franklin Insurance Company signed by Bishop Dunne on June 15, 1927, found their way into O'Brien's possession. Folder: Royalty Series, Box 28, John A. O'Brien Personal Papers, AUND.

28. Folder: Financial and Legal Records, 1928–1940, Box 10, John A. O'Brien Personal Papers, AUND.

29. Proceedings for Corporate Reorganization under Section 72-B of the Bankruptcy Act in folder: Financial and Legal Records, 1928–1940, Box 10, John A. O'Brien Personal Papers, AUND.

30. At that time O'Brien deposited $6,000 in the bank servicing the notes and debentures. That sum was insufficient to redeem all of the coupons presented, so the bank paid no interest and placed O'Brien's deposit in a special account and awaited resolution of the problem. See Proceeding for Corporate Reorganization in folder: Financial and Legal Records, 1928–1940, Box 10, John A. O'Brien Personal Papers, AUND.

31. See folder: Bartley, Box 1, Restricted, John A. O'Brien Personal Papers, AUND; folder: Financial and Legal Records, 1928–1940, Box 10, John A. O'Brien Personal Papers, AUND.

32. O'Brien to Benzinger Brothers, April 10, 1934, folder: Benzinger Brothers, COBR 2/38, John A. O'Brien Personal Papers, AUND.

33. Receipts for amounts paid on this loan from 1935 to 1938 by Bishop Schlarman have been preserved in O'Brien's legal and financial records. See folder: Financial and Legal Records, 1928–1940, Box 10, John A. O'Brien Personal Correspondence, AUND.

34. See Proceedings for Corporate Reorganization under Section 72-B of the Bankruptcy Act in folder: Financial and Legal Records, 1928–1940, Box 10, John A. O'Brien Personal Papers, AUND.

35. See Statement of the Plan of Extension in folder: Financial and Legal Records, 1928–1940, Box 10, John A. O'Brien Personal Papers, AUND.

36. See Joseph Bartley to O'Brien, March 12, 1936, and John W. McMahan to O'Brien, March 14, 1936, in folder: Financial and Legal Records, 1928–1940, Box 10, John A. O'Brien Personal Correspondence, AUND.

37. Joseph Bartley to O'Brien, March 12, 1936, folder: Financial and Legal Records, 1928–1940, Box 10, John A. O'Brien Personal Correspondence, AUND.

38. See Joseph Bartley's references to extending and revamping the mortgage indebtedness of the Newman Foundation. Bartley to O'Brien, January 9, 1948, in

folder: Bartley, Box 1, Restricted, John A. O'Brien Personal Correspondence, AUND.

39. The amount of money transferred in 1936–1937 must have been substantial. A dozen years later when the Diocese of Peoria sought to purchase Newman Hall from O'Brien, his financial advisers urged him as president of the Newman Foundation Corporation to produce as evidence that the money transferred at that time had been a loan rather than a donation. With such notes in hand, the adviser believed that O'Brien could recover $200,000 from the proceeds of the sale of the building. See Whitmore to O'Brien, January 29, 1948, in folder: Bartley, Box 1, Restricted, John A. O'Brien Personal Correspondence, AUND.

40. Schlarman made certain that copies of receipts for interest and principal payments on the mortgage loan held by the Metropolitan Life Insurance Company were sent to O'Brien. See folder: Financial and Legal Records, 1928–1940, Box 10, John A. O'Brien Personal Correspondence, AUND.

41. O'Brien, ed., *The White Harvest,* 4.

42. Ibid., 3.

43. Ibid., 7–8.

44. Ibid., 9, 11.

45. Ibid.

46. John A. O'Brien, "The Moral Causes of Catholic Leakage," *Homiletic and Pastoral Review,* April 1933, 693.

47. John A. O'Brien, "Did We Lose Half a Million Catholics Last Year?" *American Ecclesiastical Review,* December 1931, 589.

48. Rev. Gerald Shaughnessy, S.M., "The Alleged Leakage of 1930," *American Ecclesiastical Review,* March 1932, 280–81.

49. O'Brien, "Moral Causes of Catholic Leakage," 693–701.

50. Ibid., 693.

51. See Frank A. Smothers, "New Light on Birth Control," *Commonweal,* March 8, 1933, 511–13.

52. Quoted in John A. O'Brien, "Birth Control and Catholic Leakage," *Homiletic and Pastoral Review,* May 1933, 822.

53. O'Brien, "Moral Causes of Catholic Leakage," 700.

54. O'Brien, "Birth Control and Catholic Leakage," 813.

55. Ibid., 925.

56. Very Rev. John A. Ryan, S.T.D., "The Moral Aspects of Periodical Continence," *American Ecclesiastical Review,* July 1933, 29.

57. Ibid., 30.

58. Ibid., 35.

59. John A. O'Brien, "Rightly Handling the Word of Truth," *American Ecclesiastical Review,* December 1930, 579–90.

60. Ibid.; *Evolution and Religion* (New York: Paulist Press, 1930); *Evolution and Religion,* Century Catholic College Text series (New York: The Century Company, 1932).

61. Jacob W. Gruber, *A Conscience in Conflict: The Life of St. George Jackson Mivart* (New York: Published for Temple University Publications by the Columbia University Press, 1960), 188.

62. O'Brien, *Evolution and Religion* (Paulist Press), 5.

63. Ibid., 7.

64. Ibid., 21, n. 13.

65. Ibid., 23

66. Joseph Mendez to O'Brien, November 21, 1930, John A. O'Brien Personal Papers, COBR (1), AUND.

67. Gruber, 70, 188. The American clerical writer required to submit and recant was Father John Zahm, C.S.C., a former vice president of the University of Notre Dame and recently appointed provincial of his order.

68. Joseph Mendez to O'Brien, November 11, 1930, John A. O'Brien Personal Papers, COBR (1), AUND.

69. Archbishop Hayes certainly knew about O'Brien's difficulties with Archbishop Curley and appears to have been unwilling to have anything to do with O'Brien. Hayes took the same position again in 1934 about an imprimatur for another of O'Brien's books, *Lawful Birth Control.* He referred the publisher, Benzinger Brothers, to Bishop Schlarman for the approval.

See Joseph Mendez to O'Brien, November 11, 1930, John A. O'Brien Personal Papers, COBR (1), AUND; Benzinger Brothers to O'Brien, June 1, 1934, John A. O'Brien Personal Correspondence, COBR 2/38, AUND.

70. Ibid.

71. O'Brien, *Evolution and Religion,* Century Catholic Text series, 47, viii.

72. Ibid., 82–89.

73. O'Brien, review of Rev. Ernest C. Messenger, *Evolution and Theology: The Problem of Man's Origin* (New York: Macmillan, 1932) in *Commonweal,* March 9, 1932, 526–27.

74. O'Brien thanked Cooper for his suggestions and stated that he followed them all, "eliminating the last chapter on the soul entirely and modifying every reference to theologians which might be construed to be critical." O'Brien to Cooper, October 22, 1931, John A. O'Brien Personal Papers, COBR (1), Evolution (1), AUND.

75. O'Brien, "Origin of the Soul," 1–16, see p. 1 and p. 4; folder: Evolution (2), no date, Box 14, John A. O'Brien Personal Correspondence, AUND.

76. Ibid., 5.

77. Ibid., 22.

78. O'Brien to Rev. Thomas O'Shea, October 10, 1931, John A. O'Brien Personal Papers, COBR (1), AUND.

79. Rev. William A. Begin, C.S.V.; Rev. Charles L. Sonvay, C.M.; Doctor Henry Baldwin Ward.

80. J. Elliot Ross, review of John A. O'Brien, *Evolution and Religion,* in *Commonweal,* September 14, 1932, 472–73.

81. See folder of personal correspondence on *Evolution and Religion,* John A. O'Brien Personal Papers, COBR (1), AUND.

82. John A. O'Brien, "A Sane Treatment of Hell," *Homiletic and Pastoral Review,* June 1934, 966–69.

83. Ibid., 969.

84. Francis J. Connell, C.Ss.R., "Is the Fire of Hell Eternal and Real?" *Homiletic and Pastoral Review,* September 1934, 1250.

85. Ibid., 1255.

86. Ibid., 1250.

87. Ibid., 1251.

88. Ibid., 1260.

89. St. George Mivart, "Happiness in Hell," *Nineteenth Century* 32: 899–919; "The Happiness in Hell: A Rejoinder," ibid., 33: 320–38; "Last Words on the Happiness in Hell," ibid., 637–51; "The Index and My Articles on Hell," ibid., 34: 979–90; "Roman Congregations and Modern Thought," *North American Review,* 170: 562–74.

90. John A. O'Brien, "Father Connell's Ideas of Hell," *Homiletic and Pastoral Review,* October 1934, 31–39.

91. Ibid., 37–38.

92. Francis J. Connell, C.Ss.R., "Again the Doctrine of Hell," *Homiletic and Pastoral Review,* January 1935, 368.

93. Ibid., 371.

94. Ibid., 380.

95. Ibid., 381.

96. Albert A. Chevalier, O.M.I., "The Eternity of Hell Fire," *Homiletic and Pastoral Review,* February 1935, 517–18.

97. Ibid.

98. John A. O'Brien, "Reply to Father Chevalier," *Homiletic and Pastoral Review,* April 1935, 751–52.

99. See note accompanying John A. O'Brien, "Are Lost Souls Eternally Tortured?" *Homiletic and Pastoral Review,* April 1935, 604.

100. Ibid., 603.

101. Ibid., 604.

102. Ibid., 610.

103. Connell, "Again the Doctrine of Hell," 382–83.

104. O'Brien, "Statement," *Homiletic and Pastoral Review,* August 1935, 1129–30.

105. See David Kinley to O'Brien, June 1, 1939, John A. O'Brien Personal Papers, COBR (1), AUND.

106. James Cardinal Gibbons, *The Faith of Our Fathers,* 92d edition (Baltimore: John Murphy Company, 1917), 121–22.

107. O'Brien, *The Faith of Millions,* 2d ed. (Huntington, Ind.: Our Sunday Visitor Press, 1938), 124.

108. O'Brien's financial records on deposit in the Archives of the University of Notre Dame are closed. This judgment about O'Brien's wealth rests on the extent of his real estate holdings in Peoria (twenty-one houses in one period), the frequency and size of his contributions to university fund drives (Hope, 475) and his very large final bequest to the university. At the time of this writing, three endowed chairs are funded out of John A. O'Brien bequests. Two of those chairs were given to the theology department and one was placed in the philosophy department.

In view of O'Brien's many difficulties with the American Catholic theological establishment and the Holy Office and recalling his very sharp words about scholastic philosophers, the decision of the Notre Dame administration to use his very large bequests in this way from one point of view might seem supremely ironic. However, given the causes and positions advocated by O'Brien during the later part of his life—vernacular liturgy, birth control, optional celibacy for priests, ecumenism—from another point of view perhaps that allocation of O'Brien's bequests will appear entirely appropriate.

See also O'Brien's statement in a letter to Bishop Pursley in the course of a dispute over publishing a more ecumenical, post–Vatican II version of *The Faith of Millions* that between 1938 and 1973 that book had sold over 800,000 copies in the United States alone and had earned for Our Sunday Visitor Press over $100,000. O'Brien to Pursley, February 1, 1973, John A. O'Brien Personal Papers, COBR (1) AUND.

109. John A. O'Brien, ed., *Catholics and Scholarship* (Huntington, Ind.: Our Sunday Visitor Press, 1939), 30–33.

110. Ibid., editor's foreword and 104.

111. Ibid., 21.

112. Ibid., 23.

113. Ibid.

114. Ibid.

115. Ibid., 24.

116. Ibid., 25.

117. Ibid.

118. Ibid., 52.

119. Ibid., 59.

120. Ibid., 155–56.

121. Ibid., 156.

122. Ibid., 158.

123. Ibid., 160–61.

124. Ibid., 161.

125. Ibid., 163–64.

126. *American Ecclesiastical Review,* April 1939, 375–76.

127. Virgil R. Stallbaumer, O.S.B., review of John A. O'Brien, ed., *Catholics and Scholarship,* in *Homiletic and Pastoral Review,* 1939–1940, Part I, 455–56.

128. O'Brien to O'Hara, October 9, 1939, UPOH, OA to OK, 1940 #2, AUND.

129. O'Brien to O'Hara, November 25, 1939, UPOH, OA to OK, 1940 #2, AUND.

130. Ibid.

131. Ibid.

132. Helen and Charles Bruce-Jones to O'Brien, June 28, 1940, John A. O'Brien Personal Papers (1), AUND.

133. O'Brien to O'Donnell, March 8,1940, UPHO, OA to OK, 1940 #2, AUND.

134. O'Donnell to O'Brien, April 30, 1940, UPHO, OA to OK, 1940 #2, AUND.

3. Britain at War and Isolationism in America, 1939–1940

1. R. Butler, D. Dakin, M. Lambert, et al., eds., *Documents on British Foreign Policy* (DEBFP), 2d series, vol. 17 (London: HMSO, 1979), 792.

2. Ibid., 801.

3. Nicholas J. Cull, *Selling War* (New York: Oxford University Press, 1995), 6.

4. Ibid., 28.

5. Ibid., 29.

6. Quoted in Cull, 10.

7. Ibid., 30–31.

8. Darvall to Colwell, December 18, 1939, FO 371/24227, 62, PRO.

9. Ibid., 33.

10. Ibid., 40.

11. Darvall to Balfour, January 9, 1940, FO 371/24223, 16, PRO.

12. T. North Whitehead Confidential Memorandum, July 22, 1940, FO 371/24230, 279–84, PRO.

13. Cull, 141–42.

14. Ibid., 16.

15. Darvall to Balfour, January 9, 1940, FO 371/24227, 17–18, PRO.

16. Cull, 102.

17. Ibid., 104.

18. Ibid., 107.

19. Ibid., 105.

20. Ibid., 105–6.

21. Ibid.

22. Ministry of Information Notes on Broadcasting, December 13, 1939, FO 371/24277, 26–27.

23. Ibid.

24. Ibid.

25. M. R. Perlzweig to R. A. B. Butler, report on his tour of America, January 17 to March 30, 1940, FO 371/24228, 187.

26. Lord Lothian to Halifax, Memorandum on Sir George Paish, August 28, 1940, FO 371/24231, 241–43.

27. Ibid.

28. Ibid.

29. Ibid., 150.

30. Ibid., 259.

31. Ibid., 241–43.

32. Ibid.

33. Ibid.

34. See Lothian's Weekly Summary of American Affairs for the Foreign Office, October 8, 1940, FO 371/2421, 91, PRO.

35. Cull, 53.

36. Lothian's Weekly Summary of American Affairs for the Foreign Office, October 8, 1940, FO 371/2421, 91, PRO.

37. Ibid.

38. Ibid., 92.

39. Ibid., 91.

40. Hansard, October 23, 1940, 1097.

41. Cull, 60.

42. H. Hessell Tiltman's Report, December 7, 1939, FO 371/24277, 397, PRO.

43. Tiltman Report, December 3, 1939, FO 371/24277, 114–37.

44. Ibid.

45. Ibid.

46. Ibid.

47. Ibid.

48. Ibid.

49. Ibid.

50. Doris Kearns Goodwin, *No Ordinary Time: Franklin and Eleanor Roosevelt: The Home Front in World War II* (New York: Simon & Schuster, 1995), 112.

51. Ibid., 112–13.

52. J. O. Perowene's Minute, March 11, 1940, FO 371/24251, 5.

53. Ibid.

54. Ibid.

55. Ibid.

56. Lothian to Scott, February 20, 1940, FO 371/24277, 380–85.

57. Cull, 65.

58. T. North Whitehead's comment on Reports from the British Embassy in Washington, June 3, 1940, FO 371/24279, 169.

59. Ibid.

60. Ibid.

61. Cull, 66–67.

62. Ibid., 68.

63. Darvall to Monckton, May 1940, Memorandum of Rae Smith of the J. Walter Thompson Agency to MOI, FO 371/24229, 255.

64. Ibid.

65. Cull, 71.

66. Memorandum of Rae Smith of J. Walter Thompson Agency, May 30, 1940, FO 371/24228, 74.

67. Ibid.

68. Ibid.

69. *New York Herald-Tribune,* May 31, 1940.

70. Cull, 71.

71. Cypher Telegram to Lothian, June 25, 1940, FO 371/24230, 156.

72. Ibid.

73. Lothian to the Foreign Office, June 26, 1940, FO 371/24230, 155.

74. Ibid.

75. Lothian to the Foreign Office, June 27, 1940, FO 371/24230, 162.

76. Churchill to Lothian, June 28, 1940, FO 371/24230, 166–67.

77. Ibid.

78. Ibid.

79. Ibid., 77.

80. Ibid.

81. Lothian to Scott, June 3, 1940, FO 371/ 24229, 35.

82. Ibid.

83. Lothian to the Foreign Office, June 26, 1940, FO 371/24230, 158.

84. Lothian to Scott, June 3, 1940, FO 371/24229, 35.

85. Cull, 80–81.

86. Ibid., 179–80.

87. Ibid., 80–81.

88. Ibid.

89. Ibid.

90. Ibid.

91. Ibid.

92. Goodwin, 66.

93. Ibid.

94. Ibid.

95. Cull, 82.

96. Ibid., 134.

97. War Cabinet Minute, June 28, 1940, FO 371/24230, 273–76.

98. Cull, 131–32, 179.

99. Ibid., 98.

100. Goodwin, 44.

101. Ibid., 449.

102. *Congressional Record,* 76th Cong., 3rd session, May 13, 1940, 5947; May 15, 1940, 6163. (Hereafter cited as *CR.*)

103. *Vital Speeches,* 1940, vol. 6, 485–86.

104. *New York Times,* May 21, 1940, 12.

105. Goodwin, 48.

106. Ibid.

107. Mark Lincoln Chadwin, *The Warhawks: American Interventionists before Pearl Harbor* (New York: W.W. Norton, 1970), 3.

108. Gallup Polls, October 1939 to November 1940, *South Bend Tribune,* December 1, 1940, 2:1.

109. Ibid.

110. Ibid.

111. Chadwin, 17, 20–21.

112. Ibid., 21

113. Wayne S. Cole, *Charles A. Lindbergh and the Battle against American Intervention in World War II* (New York: Harcourt Brace Jovanovich, 1974), 128.

114. Chadwin, 22.

115. Wayne S. Cole, *America First: The Battle against Intervention 1940–1941,* (Madison: University of Wisconsin Press, 1953), 7.

116. Michele Flynn Stenehjem, *An American First: John T. Flynn and the America First Committee,* (New Rochelle, N.Y.: Arlington House, 1976), 13.

117. For a hostile local reaction to this campaign, see the *South Bend Tribune,* December 2, 1940.

118. Williams to Lothian, October 4, 1940, FO 371/24231, 218.

119. Ibid.

120. Ibid.

121. Duff Cooper to Lothian, October 13, 1940, FO 371/24231, 221.

122. Cole, *America First,* 7.

123. Ibid.

124. Chadwin, 79.

125. Ibid., 38.

126. Ibid., 34.

127. Ibid., 279–80.

128. Ibid., 37.

129. Ibid., 41, 49.

130. Ibid., 40.

131. Ibid., 43–45.

132. Ibid., 44–45.

133. Ibid., 160–61.

134. Ibid., 161–62.

135. Ibid., 170.

136. Ibid., 171.

137. Ibid.

138. Ibid., 261.

139. Cole, *America First,* 11–12; Justus D. Doenecke, *In Danger Undaunted: The Anti-Interventionist Movement of 1940–1941 as Revealed in the Papers of the America First Committee,* (Palo Alto, Calif.: Hoover Institution Press, Stanford University, 1990), 7.

140. Doenecke, 17.

141. Ibid.

142. Ibid., 12.

143. Ibid., 12–15.

144. Ibid., 15–16.

145. Stenehjem, 18.

146. Ibid., 16.

147. Ibid., 26.

148. Ibid., 30.

149. Ibid., 32.

150. *Congressional Record* (hereafter *CR*) 86, part 7, June 12, 1940, 8053–56.

151. Ibid., part 11, September 26, 1940, 12451; 12646–47.

152. Ibid., part 8, July 11, 1940, 9497–99.

153. Ibid., part 7, June 12, 1940, 8055, 8057.

154. Chadwin, 115.

155. Ibid., 116.

156. *CR,* 86, part 11, September 26, 1940, 12651–52.

157. Chadwin, 116–18.

158. *CR,* 86, part 11, September 26, 1940, 12628.

159. Ibid., 12649.

4. The War Controversy: Isolationism and Interventionism at Notre Dame, May 1940 to June 1941

1. Peter Fleming, *Operation Sea Lion* (New York: Simon and Schuster, 1957), 90–91.

2. Ibid., 91.

3. Ibid.

4. Helen and Charles Bruce-Jones to O'Brien, June 28, 1940, John A. O'Brien Personal Papers, (1), AUND.

5. *New York Times,* July 4, 1940, 3:7.

6. Helen and Charles Bruce-Jones to O'Brien, June 28, 1940, John A. O'Brien Personal Papers (1), AUND.

7. Fleming, 93.

8. Ibid.

9. *New York Times,* July 6, 1940, 2:1.

10. Ibid., July 4, 1940, 3:2; July 6, 1940, 2:3.

11. Ibid., July 3, 1940, 3:3.

12. Winston S. Churchill, *Their Finest Hour* (Boston: Houghton Mifflin, 1949), 646, n. 1.

13. *New York Times,* July 3, 1940, 3:3.

14. Ibid., June 21, 1940, 1:4; 13:1.

15. Ibid., July 6, 1940, 2:6.

16. Goodwin, 99.

17. *New York Times,* July 6, 1940, 2:6.

18. Ibid., July 4, 1940, 3:2.

19. Ibid., July 6, 1940, 2:1.

20. Helen and Charles Bruce-Jones to O'Brien, June 28, 1940, John A. O'Brien Personal Papers (1), AUND.

21. Ibid.

22. Ibid.

23. Ibid.

24. Ibid.

25. Ibid.

26. Ibid.

27. Fleming, 94.

28. Ibid.

29. *New York Times,* September 23, 1940, sec. 1, p. 1.

30. Ibid., p. 5; September 27, 1940, sec. 1, p. 1.

31. Fleming, 94.

32. *New York Times,* September 26, 1940, sec. 1, p. 3.

33. Ibid., September 24, 1940, 3:1.

34. Ibid.

35. O'Donnell to Barry, September 12, 1940, UPHO, OA to OK, 1940, #2, AUND.

36. O'Donnell to Congressman Raymond S. McKeough, January 22, 1942, and O'Donnell to Father John Ryan, C.S.C., January 22, 1942, UPHO, 91/18, Mc–Mz, AUND.

37. Arthur J. Hope, *Notre Dame: One Hundred Years,* rev. ed. (South Bend, Ind.: Icarus Press), xix.

38. Murray Sperber, *Shake Down the Thunder: The Creation of Notre Dame Football* (New York: Henry Holt and Company, 1993), 468.

39. Ibid.

40. Ibid., 470.

41. Ibid., 471.

42. Ibid., 474.

43. Ibid., 476–77, 608.

44. Ibid., 487.

45. Ibid., 488.

46. Ibid.

47. Ibid., 481.

48. Ibid., 481–82.

49. Maurice V. Dullea, S.J., to Albert F. Cousineau, C.S.C., June 26, 1941, UPHO, folder: Boston College, AUND.

50. John M. Taylor, *General Maxwell Taylor: The Sword and the Pen* (New York: Doubleday, 1989), 152–53.

51. Ibid.

52. Ibid.

53. Cole, *America First,* 104–5. See also the *Chicago Tribune* December 1, 1940, and December 15, 1940.

54. *South Bend Tribune,* December 1, 1940, 8.

55. Ibid.

56. Ibid.

57. Weekly American Survey, Lothian to the Foreign Office, November 29, 1940, FO 371/26217, 211, PRO.

58. *South Bend Tribune,* December 17, 1940, 1, section 2.

59. Michael R. Beschloss, *Kennedy and Roosevelt: The Uneasy Alliance* (New York: W. W. Norton, 1980), 213.

60. Ibid., 217–18.

61. Ibid., 218, 221.

62. *New York Times,* October 30, 1940, 1.

63. Beschloss, 220.

64. Ibid., 221.

65. Peter Collier and David Horowitz, *The Kennedys: An American Drama* (New York: Warner Books, 1984), 126.

66. William H. Tuttle, Jr., "A Reappraisal of William Allen White's Leadership," *Journal of American History,* March 1970, 856.

67. Beschloss, 232.

68. Joseph P. Kennedy to O'Brien, December 24, 1940, John A. O'Brien, Personal Papers, K, Box 1, folder 37, AUND.

69. The Joseph P. Kennedy Papers are deposited in the Kennedy Presidential Library in Boston but are not open to the public. Some scholars have been allowed to inspect parts of the collection but others have been denied access. A routine telephone inquiry to the Kennedy Library for the purpose of ascertaining whether O'Brien had ever responded to Kennedy's letter of December 24, 1940, was unanswered on the grounds that the papers were closed.

70. Beschloss, 232.

71. Goodwin, 192.

72. Ibid., 193.

73. Ibid., 196.

74. *New York Times,* January 7, 1941, 4.

75. Beschloss, 235–37.

76. *New York Times,* January 19, 1941.

77. *New York Herald-Tribune,* January 22, 1941, 17.

78. Beschloss, 238.

79. *New York Times,* January 22, 1941, 4:6–7.

80. Beschloss, 239.

81. Ibid., 210.

82. Robert M. Ketchum, *The Borrowed Years, 1938–1941: America on the Way to War* (New York: Random House, 1989), 578.

83. Mark Lincoln Chadwin, *The Hawks of World War II* (Chapel Hill: University of North Carolina Press, 1968), 147.

84. For a newspaper clipping about this letter as well as a negative reaction to it, see James N. McTighe to O'Donnell, December 11, 1940, UPHO, War Correspondence #2, AUND.

85. *South Bend Tribune,* December 20, 1940, sec. 2, p. 1.

86. Ibid.

87. Ibid.

88. *Chicago Tribune,* December 27, 1940. The signers of this letter were S. R. Price, George B. Collins, John J. Fitzgerald, Stephen Ronay, Rufus Rauch, Dan O'Grady, Francis E. McMahon, Bernard Waldman, Edward A. Coomes, Thomas F. Power, Richard Baker, M. A. Fitzsimons, Henry Rago, Willis D. Nutting, Daniel H. Pedtke.

89. *Scholastic* 73, no. 2 (September 29, 1939): 9, 21.

90. Ibid.

91. Francis E. McMahon, *The Rights of the People,* Catholic Association for International Peace, 1940, printed in the *Scholastic* 74, no. 5 (October 18, 1940): 10.

92. *South Bend Tribune,* December 27, 1940.

93. *New York Times,* December 31, 1940, 5:1.

94. *South Bend Tribune,* December 27, 1940.

95. Wilkins to Ellis, February 24, 1941, Ellis Papers, Box 2, Archives of the Catholic University of America. This reference was provided by Professor J. Philip Gleason.

96. *Dubuque Telegraph-Herald,* March 5, 1941, p. 1.

97. Herring to O'Donnell, March 13, 1941, UPHO, War Controversy #2, AUND.

98. Ibid.

99. *New York Times,* March 13, 1941, p. 1.

100. Item dated April 16, 1941, UPHO, War Correspondence 32, AUND.

101. Julia Robinson to O'Donnell, April 20, 1941, UPHO, War Controversy #2, AUND.

102. Undated handwritten notes, modus agendi for Dr. O'Brien and Dr. McMahon, UPHO, McMahon File, folder 3, AUND.

103. Ibid.

104. Ibid.

105. Ibid.

106. O'Brien to Herring, April 24, 1941, UPHO, War Correspondence #2, AUND.

107. Cull, 143.

108. *U.S. News and World Report,* May 2, 1941, 22.

109. *South Bend Tribune,* May 2, 1941.

110. *Chicago Daily News,* May 19, 1941, under byline of Frank Smothers.

111. Ibid.

112. *South Bend Tribune,* May 2, 1941.

113. To O'Donnell, May 5, 1941, UPHO, War Controversy #2, AUND.

114. Ibid.

115. Ibid.

116. *Chicago Daily News,* May 19, 1941, under the byline of Frank Smothers.

117. *Chicago Tribune,* May 21, 1941, sec. 1, p. 9; *South Bend Tribune,* sec. 2, p. 1.

118. *South Bend Tribune,* May 21, 1941.

119. Trahey to Cavanaugh May 21, 1941, UPHO, War Controversy #2, AUND.

120. *Chicago Tribune,* May 21, 1941, sec. 1, p. 9; *South Bend Tribune,* May 20, 1941, sec. 2, p. 1.

121. T. North Whitehead Memorandum on Present Shipping Losses, FO 371/26217, 147, PRO.

122. Chadwin, *The Hawks of World War II,* 148.

123. Ibid.

124. *New York Daily News,* May 6, 1941.

125. Ibid.

126. Muriel Benziger to O'Donnell, May 15, 1941, UPHO, War Controversy #2, AUND.

127. Ibid.

128. Ibid.

129. Ibid.

130. Secretary of O'Donnell to Benziger, May 20, 1941, UPHO, War Controversy #2, AUND.

131. Arthur O'Leary to O'Donnell, May 12, 1941, UPHO, War Controversy #2, AUND.

132. Ibid.

133. Ibid., attachment.

134. *Chicago Daily News,* May 19, 1941, under byline of Frank Smothers.

135. Ibid.

136. McMahon to O'Donnell, May 18, 1941, UPHO, War Controversy #2, AUND.

137. *Chicago Daily News,* May 19, 1941, under byline of Frank Smothers.

138. McMahon to O'Donnell, May 18, 1941, UPHO, War Controversy #2, AUND.

139. Ibid.

140. *New York Times,* June 3, 1941, sec. 1, p. 20.

141. *New York Times,* May 25, 1941, sec. 1, p. 2; Joseph P. Kennedy's address at Oglethorpe University, *CR,* 87, 1941, A2510.

142. Ibid.

143. Goodwin, 238.

144. Ibid.

145. *New York Times,* June 2, 1941, sec. 1, p. 20.

146. Commencement Address delivered at the University of Notre Dame by the Honorable Joseph P. Kennedy, June 1, 1941, 10 pp., AUND.

147. Ibid.

5. The War Controversy: Isolationism and Interventionism in the Country and at Notre Dame, June to October 1941

1. Foreign Office Minute, April 15, 1941, FO 371/26184, 169, PRO.

2. Halifax to Foreign Office, May 31, 1941, FO 371/26185, 84, PRO.

3. Ibid.

4. Weekly Guidance for Campbell, September 1, 1941, FO 371/26187, 169, PRO.

5. Savary to Roberts, October 4, 1940, FO 371/24231, 69, PRO.

6. The Rommen to Nathaniel Micklem, Mansfield College, Oxford, November 19, 1942, FO 371/30666, 146–152, PRO.

7. Ibid.

8. Ibid.

9. Ibid.

10. Confidential Memorandum to Hugh Balfour, July 4 1941, FO/26186, 86, PRO.

11. Ibid.

12. Ibid.

13. Ibid.

14. Cull, 54.

15. Ibid.

16. Ibid., 163.

17. Campbell to the Ministry of Information, June 24, 1941, FO 371/26186, 42, PRO.

18. Campbell to the Ministry of Information, July 12, 1941, FO 371/26186, 47, PRO.

19. Gerald P. Fogarty, *The Vatican and the American Hierarchy from 1870 to 1965* (Stuttgart: Anton Hiersemann, 1982), 272–73.

20. See "The Observer," *Cincinnati Telegraph-Register,* October 4–6, 1941.

21. Ibid.

22. Fogarty, 272.

23. Ibid.

24. Ibid., 274.

25. *New York Times,* October 31, 1941, sec. 1, p. 6.

26. *Cincinnati Telegraph-Register,* October 31, 1941.

27. Ibid.

28. Comment on Catholic Opinion in the United States and Vatican Policy, The Rommen, November 19, 1942, FO 371/30666, 146, PRO.

29. *Daily Worker,* August 19, 1941.

30. Ronald H. Bayor, *Neighbors in Conflict: The Irish, Germans, Jews, and Italians of New York City, 1929–1941* (Baltimore: Johns Hopkins University Press, 1978), 111 and note 8, 202.

31. The possibility of non-renewal was never out of McMahon's mind. In April of 1942, when his contract was delayed coming out of the president's office, he sent a registered letter to O'Donnell inquiring as to "what interpretation I am to place on that fact." O'Donnell pleaded oversight in his office, sent off the usual contract, and praised McMahon for doing "good work for Notre Dame during this critical period of our country." McMahon to O'Donnell, registered letter, no date; O'Donnell to McMahon, April 15, 1942, J. Hugh O'Donnell Presidential Correspondence, McH–Mz, AUND.

32. McMahon to O'Donnell, July 23, 1941, UPHO, War Controversy #2, AUND.

33. Secretary to the president to George H. Most, July 25, 1941, UPHO, War Controversy #2, AUND.

34. *Daily Worker,* August 19, 1941.

35. McMahon to O'Donnell, September 1941, UPHO, War Controversy #2, AUND.

36. Ibid.

37. Butler to Scott, June 17, 1941, Report on German Propaganda in the United States, FO 371/26214, 27–29, PRO.

38. Charles A. Lindbergh, *The Wartime Journals of Charles A. Lindbergh* (New York: Harcourt Brace Jovanovich, 1970), 524.

39. Ibid.

40. Ibid., 525.

41. Goodwin, 268.

42. Foreign Office Minute on Leaks of Confidential Information to the Press, September 17, 1941, FO 371/26274, 9, PRO.

43. Goodwin, 283.

44. Ibid., 266.

45. Sir William Ridsdale Foreign Office Minute, September 15, 1941, FO 371/26274, 27A, PRO.

46. Churchill to the War Cabinet, August 24, 1941, PREM 3/476, 3, PRO.

47. Cull, 152–53.

48. Ibid., 153.

49. Sir William Ridsdale to Eden, September 15, 1941, FO 371/26274, 27A, PRO.

50. Foreign Office Minute on Leaks of Information to the Press, September 17, 1941, FO 371/26274, 2, 15, PRO.

51. Sir William Ridsdale to Eden, September 15, 1941, FO 371/26274, 27A, PRO.

52. Ibid.

53. Ibid.

54. Ibid.

55. Ibid.

56. Ridsdale to Eden, September 19, 1941, FO 371/26274, 28, PRO.

57. Ibid.

58. Ibid.

59. Ibid.

60. Butler to Darvall, November 13, 1941, FO 371/26274, 24, PRO.

61. Cull, 143.

62. Ibid., 241, n. 131.

63. Joyce Milton, *Loss of Eden: A Biography of Charles and Anne Morrow Lindbergh* (New York: Harper Collins Publishers, 1993), 397.

64. Ibid.

65. *New York Times,* August 1, 1941, 1:7.

66. *New York Times,* September 5, 1941, editorial, 20:2.

67. Ibid.

68. Clayton R. Koppes and Gregory D. Black, *Hollywood Goes to War: How Policies, Profits and Propaganda Shaped World War II Movies* (New York: The Free Press, 1987), 40.

69. *New York Times,* August 2, 1941, 18:6.

70. Wayne S. Cole, *Senator Gerald P. Nye and American Foreign Relations* (Minneapolis: University of Minnesota Press, 1962), 187.

71. Koppes and Black, 40.

72. *New York Times,* September 10, 1941, 22:5.

73. Cull, 183.

74. *New York Times,* September 8, 1941, 6:4.

75. Ibid.

76. *New York Times,* September 9, 1941, 25:1.

77. Goodwin, 277–78.

78. Ibid., 278.

79. British Embassy, Washington to the Foreign Office, November 20, 1941, FO 371/26213, 193, PRO.

80. *New York Times,* September 10, 1941, 1–2.

81. Koppes and Black, 43.

82. Cole, *Senator Gerald P. Nye and American Foreign Relations,* 188.

83. Ibid., 183.

84. *New York Times,* September 10, 1941, sec. 1, pp. 1–2.

85. Ibid.

86. Koppes and Black, 46.

87. *New York Times,* September 12, 1941, sec. 1, p. 24.

88. Koppes and Black, 43.

89. Ibid.

90. Ibid.

91. Ibid., 45.

92. Milton, 400.

93. Ibid., 401.

94. In his journal for May 1, 1941, Lindbergh stated that pressure for war was mounting even though the people were against intervention. The administration was hell bent for war. "Most of the Jewish interests in the country are behind war, and they control a huge part of our press and radio and most of our motion pictures." Ibid., 481.

95. Ibid.

96. Ibid., 245.

97. Ibid.

98. Ibid., 538.

99. *New York Times,* September 13, 1941, sec. 1, p. 1.

100. Ibid.

101. *New York Times,* September 14, 1941, sec. 1, p. 20.

102. Ibid.

103. Cull, 183–84.

104. Ibid., 540.
105. Secret message from the British Consul in New York to MOI, September 19, 1941, FO 371/26188, 25.
106. Ibid.
107. Ibid.
108. Lindbergh, 540.
109. Ibid.
110. Ibid., 541.
111. *New York Times,* July 28, 1941, sec. 1, p. 20.
112. Ibid., October 20, 1941, sec. 1, p. 9.
113. Ibid.
114. Ibid., August 4, 1941, sec. 1, p. 6.
115. *Chicago Tribune,* November 12, 1941.
116. Lindbergh, 541.
117. Milton, 401.
118. Lindbergh, 541.
119. *New York Times,* October 25, 1941, sec. 1, p. 7.
120. Ibid.

6. The War Controversy: Isolationism and Interventionism in the Country and at Notre Dame, October to December 1941

1. *New York Times,* September 15, 1941, sec. 1, p. 2.
2. James J. McKenna to O'Donnell, September 15, 1941, UPHO, War Controversy #2, AUND.
3. Ibid.
4. Ronald H. Bayor, *Neighbors in Conflict: The Irish, Germans, Jews and Italians of New York City, 1929–1941* (Baltimore: Johns Hopkins University Press, 1978), 106–7.
5. Ibid., 28–29.
6. Milton, 402.
7. O'Donnell to McKelway, October 1, 1941, UPHO, McH–Mz, AUND.
8. *Scholastic* 75, no. 3 (November 10, 1941): 11.
9. Lindbergh, 544.
10. Ibid.
11. *New York Times,* October 4, 1941, sec. 1, p. 1.
12. Ibid.
13. Ibid. See also Milton, 402.
14. *New York Times,* October 4, 1941, 1:4.
15. Lindbergh, 544.
16. *Scholastic* 75, no. 1 (September 26, 1941): 6.
17. *Cincinnati Telegraph-Register,* October 3, 1941; see column entitled "The Observer."
18. Ibid.

19. Ibid.
20. Ibid.
21. Ibid.
22. Ibid.
23. O'Donnell to Freking, October 7, 1941, UPHO, McH-Mz, AUND.
24. Hope, 475.
25. Undated handwritten notes, UPHO, McMahon File, folder 3, AUND.
26. Ibid.
27. *New York Times*, October 18, 1941, sec. 1, p. 1; November 2, 1941, sec. 1, p. 1.
28. Ibid., October 18, 1941, sec. 1, p. 1.
29. Ibid., 3:4.
30. Ibid.
31. Ibid., November 1, 1941, sec. 1, p. 1.
32. Lindbergh, 551.
33. Cull, 169.
34. *New York Times*, October 31, 1941, sec. 1, p. 1.
35. Cull, 169; Lindbergh, 551.
36. *New York Times*, October 31, 1941, sec. 1, p. 1.
37. Ibid.
38. Lindbergh, 551.
39. *New York Times*, October 31, 1941, sec. 1, p. 1.
40. Ibid.
41. Ibid; Lindbergh, 551.
42. *New York Times*, October 31, 1941, text of the speech on sec. 1, pp. 4–5.
43. Ibid., sec. 1, p. 4.
44. Ibid., sec. 1, pp. 4–5.
45. Lindbergh, 552.
46. *New York Times*, October 31, 1941, sec. 1, p. 22.
47. Ibid., sec. 1, p. 4.
48. Cull, 155.
49. *New York Times*, September 5, 1941, sec. 1, p. 1.
50. Goodwin, 265.
51. Ibid., 283.
52. *New York Times*, November 3, 1941, sec. 1, p. 5.
53. Ibid.
54. Goodwin, 283.
55. Washington to Foreign Office, November 20, 1941, FO 371/26213, 20, PRO.
56. *New York Times*, November 14, 1941, sec. 1, p. 14.
57. Ibid.
58. Goodwin, 283.
59. Washington to Foreign Office, November 20, 1941, FO 371/26213/193, PRO.
60. Cull, 185.
61. Ibid.
62. Lindbergh, 557.

63. British Publicity in the United States, Appendix A, October 30 to November 15, 1941, FO 371/26188, 72–118, PRO.

64. Ibid.

65. Ibid.

66. Cull, 191.

67. Note and enclosures, November 26, 1941, UPHO, War Controversy #1, AUND.

68. Goodwin, 284.

69. Ibid., 283–84.

70. *New York Times,* November 21, 1941, sec. 1, p. 5.

71. Ibid.

72. Ibid., December 3, 1941, sec. 1, p. 5.

73. Ibid., December 5, 1941, sec. 1, p. 3.

74. Ibid.

75. Ibid., December 6, 1941, sec. 1, p. 1.

76. Cull, 186.

77. Lindbergh, 557.

78. *New York Times,* December 8, 1941, sec. 1, p. 6.

79. Ibid.; also December 9, 1941, sec. 1, p. 44.

80. Ibid., December 9, 1941, sec. 1, p. 44.

81. Ibid., December 31, 1941, sec. 1, p. 3.

82. Ibid.

83. Ibid., sec. 1, p. 16.

84. Ibid., December 8, 1941, sec. 1, p. 6.

85. Ibid.

86. Ibid., December 4, 1941, sec. 1, p. 3.

87. Ibid., December 14, 1941, sec. 1, p. 38.

88. O'Donnell to McMahon, April 15, 1942, J. Hugh O'Donnell Presidential Correspondence, 91/18, AUND.

89. Justus D. Doenecke, *Not to the Swift: The Old Isolationists in the Cold War Era* (Cranbury, N.J.: Associated University Presses, Inc., 1979), 38. (See O'Brien's article in *Collier's* magazine in May 1943.)

7. Notre Dame and Wartime America during 1942

1. Charles Eade, ed., *The Speeches of the Rt. Hon. Winston S. Churchill,* vol. 2 (London: Cassell, 1952), 151.

2. McCarthy to Walsh, May 5, 1925, Matthew Walsh Presidential Correspondence, Box 49, Miscellaneous, McA–McD, AUND.

3. Anonymous to O'Donnell, May 2, 1942, J. Hugh O'Donnell Presidential Correspondence, 3/34, AUND.

4. Ibid.

5. Ibid.

6. Ibid.

7. Ibid.

8. Ibid.

9. Bayor, 112; see also notes 11 and 12.

10. *New York Times,* February 2, 1942, sec. 1, p. 5.

11. William J. McLaughlin to O'Donnell, February 2, 1942, UPHO, 91/18, AUND.

12. *New York Times,* February 2, 1942, sec. 1, p. 5.

13. Ibid.

14. Miss Dorothy Talbot, April 16, 1942, UPHO, War Controversy #2, AUND.

15. Chadwin, 148.

16. Bayor, 112.

17. William J. McLaughlin to O'Donnell, February 2, 1942, and Rev. Daniel Cahill to O'Donnell, March 1, 1942, UPHO, War Controversy #2, AUND.

18. R. H. McAuliffe to Father Lane, April 17, 1942, UPHO, War Controversy #2, AUND.

19. Bonham to O'Donnell, April 6, 1942, UPHO, War Controversy #2, AUND

20. Ibid.

21. *New York Times,* April 8, 1942, sec. 1, p. 6.

22. F. E. McMahon, "Hitler against God," in the *Washington Post,* May 31, 1942, Extension of Remarks, John D. Dingell of Michigan, Tuesday, June 2, 1942, *CR* 88, part 9, A2027.

23. Ibid.

24. Memorandum by McMahon of a conference with Rev. Hugh O'Donnell, C.S.C., president of the University of Notre Dame and with Rev. J. Leonard Carrico, C.S.C., director of studies, held in the office of the president on Monday, August 16, 1943. Monsignor Daniel M. Cantwell Correspondence, Box 1, 5025, folder Cantwell, Daniel M., 1–3, 1940–1943, Chicago Historical Society, Chicago, Illinois. Hereafter cited as CHS.

See also, O'Donnell to Cicognani, December 15, 1943, UPHO 9/78, AUND.

25. *Newsweek,* June 1943.

26. For the relationship between isolationism and anti-Communism, see Justus D. Doenecke, *Not to the Swift,* 30–31 and *passim.*

27. *New York Times,* June 29, 1942, sec. 1, p. 4.

28. Ibid.

29. Walter Goodman, *The Committee* (London: History Book Club, 1968), 134.

30. Ibid., 161.

31. Charles P. Foley to O'Donnell, August 10, 1942, UPHO, War Controversy #2, AUND.

32. Ibid.

33. Charles P. Foley to O'Donnell, August 16, 1942, J. Hugh O'Donnell Presidential Correspondence, War Controversy #2, AUND.

34. Ibid.; see clippings reporting McMahon's speech enclosed with Foley's letter.

35. Ibid.

36. Ibid.

37. Ibid.

38. Charles J. Tull, *Father Coughlin and the New Deal,* (Syracuse, N.Y.: Syracuse University Press, 1965), 191, 221–23.

39. Charles P. Foley to O'Donnell, August 16, 1942, UPHO, War Controversy #2, AUND.

40. Patrick Walsh to O'Donnell, September 7, 1942, UPHO, War Controversy #2, AUND.

41. Ibid.

42. Memorandum, August 16, 1943, CHS; McMahon to O'Donnell, September 14, 1943, Cantwell Correspondence, Box 1, 5025, folder 1–3, CHS.

43. Raymond L. Murray, C.S.C., to O'Donnell on Father Miltner's observation, November 9, 1943 (misdated as October 9), UPHO, McMahon Files 110/folder 3, AUND.

44. *Daily Worker,* September 25, 1942.

45. Cablegram to Joseph Stalin as reported in the *Daily Worker,* September 25, 1942, clippings, UPHO, War Controversy #2, AUND.

46. Memorandum, August 16, 1943, CHS.

47. Richard Smythe to O'Donnell, September 29, 1942, UPHO, War Controversy #2, folder 1.

48. *New York Times,* November 8, 1942, sec. 1, p. 36.

49. Ibid.

50. Ibid.

51. Agnes L. Byron to O'Donnell, November 20, 1942, UPHO, War Controversy #2, folder 2, AUND.

52. Ibid.

53. Joseph Scott to O'Donnell, November 27, 1942, UPHO, War Controversy #2, AUND.

54. *New York Times,* September 27, 1942, sec. 5, p. 1.

55. Ibid., October 4, 1942, sec. 5, p. 1.

56. Ibid., October 18, 1942, sec. 5, p. 1.

57. Ibid., November 8, 1942, sec. 5, p. 1.

58. Ibid.

59. Ibid., November 15, 1942, sec. 5, p. 1.

60. Ibid.

61. Ibid., December 6, 1942, sec. 5, p. 1.

62. Darvall to Butler, February 12, 1942, FO 371/30655, iii.

63. Ibid.

64. King's Notes on the Secret Report on U.S. Attitudes towards Her Allies, May 11, 1942, FO 371/30724, 2, PRO.

65. Campbell to the Ministry of Information, February 20, 1942, FO 371/30668, 4–5.

66. King's Notes on the Secret Report on U.S. Attitudes towards Her Allies, May 11, 1942, FO 371/30724, 2, PRO.

67. Ibid.

68. Campbell to Ministry of Information, February 20, 1942, FO 371/30668, 4–5, PRO.

69. Ibid.

70. R. H. Tawney's Report, March 22, 1942, FO 371/30669, PRO.

71. Ibid.

72. Ibid.

73. Ibid.

74. Ibid.

75. Dennis W. Brogan's Report on the American Political Situation, June 13, 1942, FO 371/30653, 85, PRO.

76. Ibid.

77. Ibid.

78. Ibid.

79. Ibid.

80. Goodwin, 358–59.

81. *New York Times,* November 4, 1942, sec. 1, p. 1; November 5, 1942, sec. 1, p. 1.

8. The Great Crisis over Academic Freedom at Notre Dame, 1943

1. *Foreign Relations of the United States: The Conferences at Washington, 1941–42 and Casablanca, 1943,* (Washington, D.C.: Government Printing Office, 1968), 841.

2. *Cincinnati Telegraph-Register,* January 22, 1943, "Listening In."

3. Ibid.

4. Ibid.

5. Ibid., February 20, 1943, "Listening In."

6. Ibid.

7. Ibid., March 12, 1943, "Our Comments."

8. Ibid.

9. Neither of these letters is available. Their content must be inferred from Lucey's response to McMahon, May 17, 1943. McMahon Papers, CZBE, AUND.

10. Ibid.

11. Ibid.

12. *Cincinnati Telegraph-Register,* June 18, 1943, "Our Comments."

13. *New York Times,* July 26, 1943, sec. 1, p. 19.

14. Ibid.

15. Ibid.

16. Ibid.

17. Ibid.

18. Ibid.

19. Doenecke, *Not to the Swift,* 38.

20. Interview with McMahon in a clipping from *Chicago Daily News,* November 1943, Cantwell Papers, Box 1, 5025, folder 1–3, 1940–43, CHS.

21. Ibid.

22. *New York Times,* April 25, 1943, 25:5.

23. Ibid.

24. Ibid.

25. Gaetano Salvemini, "Pius XII and Fascism," *New Republic,* March 8, 1943, 305.

26. See *America,* March 27, 1943 and *New Republic,* April 6, 1943, 567; May 31, 1943, 735; June 14, 1943, 797–98.

27. See under "The Catholic Issue," *New Republic,* April 5, 1943, 448.

28. Lawrence W. Beals, "Catholics and Communists," *New Republic,* May 24, 1943, 702–3.

29. Francis E. McMahon, "The Catholic Issue," *New Republic,* June 7, 1943, 765.

30. Ibid.

31. Editorial, "Catholics and Liberals," *New Republic,* June 7, 1943, 751.

32. Ibid.

33. Ibid., 752.

34. Ibid.

35. Francis E. McMahon, "Catholics and Liberals," *New Republic,* June 21, 1943, 831–32.

36. Ibid.

37. Ibid.

38. Ibid.

39. Ibid.

40. Ibid.

41. McMahon's letter to Lucey, March 23, 1943, is unavailable. The content of it must be inferred from Lucey's response. Lucey to McMahon, March 26, 1943, CBZE, McMahon Papers, AUND.

42. Lucey to McMahon, May 17, 1943, CZBE, McMahon Papers, AUND.

43. Lucey to McMahon, March 26, 1943, CZBE, McMahon Papers, AUND.

44. *Cincinnati Telegraph-Register,* October 3, 1941. See column entitled "The Observer."

45. Lucey to McMahon, March 26, 1943, CZBE, McMahon papers, AUND.

46. Ibid.

47. Ibid.

48. Ibid.

49. Lucey to McMahon, May 17, 1943, CZBE, McMahon Papers, AUND.

50. McMahon's notes for a speech at Scranton, Pennsylvania, June 1943, UPHO, McMahon File 110/folder 2, AUND.

51. *Newsweek,* July 12, 1943, 68–69.

52. Ibid.

53. Ibid.

54. For the air raid on Rome, see the *New York Times,* July 21, 1943, 4; *Newsweek* August 2, 1943, 66–69; Wesley Frank Craven et al., ed., *The Army Air Forces in World War II Europe: Torch to Pointblank, August 1942–December 1943,* vol. 2 (Chicago: University of Chicago Press, 1949), 463–64.

55. Ibid.
56. Ibid.
57. *New York Times,* July 21, 1943, 4.
58. *Washington Post,* July 22, 1943.
59. Ibid., July 27, 1943.
60. *Newsweek,* August 2, 1943, 66–69.
61. Ibid. See also the editorial "Rome" in *Commonweal,* July 30, 1943, 360–61.
62. See the article by James T. Howard, *PM,* November 8, 1943, 4.
63. *South Bend Tribune,* July 20, 1943, "Bombing of Rome," 4.
64. Carrico to McMahon, August 10, 1942, Cantwell Papers, Box 1, 5025, folder 1–3, 1940–1943, CHS.
65. Cicognani to O'Donnell, August 3, 1943, UPHO, 97/8, AUND. Appended to the four letters that make up the Cicognani-O'Donnell correspondence in AUND was an undated typewritten note with the typed signature, J. Cavanaugh. This note and the Cicognani-O'Donnell correspondence was sent to AUND after O'Donnell had died in 1947. The notes states: "As you know, Father Hugh left me the job of sorting, destroying or retaining his personal 'stuff.' The enclosures belong in your office, I think."
66. Ibid.
67. Robert Katz, *Death in Rome,* (New York: Macmillan, 1967), 11.
68. Ibid., 12.
69. Ibid.
70. *Foreign Relations of the United States, Diplomatic Papers, 1943,* volume 2, Europe (Washington, D.C.: United States Government Printing Office, 1964), 944.
71. Ibid., 946.
72. Ibid., 950.
73. Katz, 16.
74. O'Donnell to Cicognani, August 11, 1943, UPHO, 97/8, AUND.
75. Memorandum by McMahon of conference with Rev. Hugh O'Donnell, C.S.C., president of the University of Notre Dame, and with Rev. J. Leonard Carrico, C.S.C., director of studies. Held in the office of the president, on Monday, August 16, 1943, at 11 A.M., Cantwell Correspondence, Box 1, 5025, folder 1–3, 1940–1943, CHS. Hereafter cited as McMahon Memorandum, August 16, 1943.
76. John Cavanaugh to Rev. Charles Lee, December 29, 1943, UVOC, Dr. Francis E. McMahon Case, 7/68, 1943–1944, AUND.
77. McMahon Memorandum, August 16, 1943, CHS.
78. Ibid.
79. Ibid.
80. Ibid.
81. Ibid.
82. See Lucey to O'Donnell, September 10, 1943, J. Hugh O'Donnell Presidential Correspondence, 1943, McMahon File, folder 4, AUND.
83. McMahon to O'Donnell, August 20, 1943, Cantwell Correspondence, Box 1, 5025, folder 1–3, 1940–1943, CHS.

84. Ibid.

85. O'Donnell to McMahon, August 25, 1943, Cantwell Correspondence, Box 1, 5025, folder 1–3, 1940–1943. A copy of this letter is also in McMahon File, 9/78, UPHO, 1943, AUND.

86. Ibid.

87. Ibid.

88. Carrico to O'Donnell, August 25, 1943, UVAA 37/Department of Philosophy, 1942–1955, AUND.

89. McMahon Memorandum of Conference with Father O'Donnell, September 10, 1943, Cantwell Correspondence, Box 1, 5025, folder 1–3, 1940–1943, CHS. See also McMahon to O'Donnell, September 14, 1943, loc. cit.

90. O'Donnell to Lucey, September 16, 1943, UPHO, 1943, McMahon File, folder 4, AUND.

91. Ibid.

92. Lucey to O'Donnell, September 10, 1943, UPHO, 1943, McMahon File, folder 4, AUND.

93. Ibid.

94. O'Donnell to Lucey, September 16, 1943, UPHO, 1943, McMahon File, AUND.

95. Ibid.

96. McMahon to O'Donnell, September 14, 1943, Cantwell Correspondence, Box 1, 5025, folder 1–3, 1940–1943, CHS.

97. See a copy of O'Donnell's letter to McMahon, September 24, 1943, that McMahon sent to Father Moore with a notation on it, UPHO, Box 105/127, 1945–1946, AUND.

98. McMahon to O'Donnell, September 14, 1943, Cantwell Correspondence, Box 1, 5025, folder 1–3, 1940–1943, CHS.

99. O'Donnell to McMahon, September 24, 1943, Cantwell Correspondence, Box 1, 5025, folder 1–3, 1940–1943, CHS.

100. Ibid.

101. Ibid.

102. Copy of letter of O'Donnell to McMahon September 24, 1943, and sent to Father Moore with an undated notation. This copy was sent to Father Thomas T. McAvoy, C.S.C., archivist in 1966 when Father Moore vacated his office and retired. UPHO, Box 105/127, 1945–1946, AUND.

103. McMahon to O'Donnell, October 5, 1943, Cantwell Correspondence, Box 1, 5025, folder 1–3, 1940–1943, CHS.

104. O'Donnell to McMahon, October 7, 1943, Cantwell Correspondence, Box 1, 5025, folder 1–3, 1940–1943, CHS.

105. McMahon to O'Donnell, October 22, 1943, Cantwell Correspondence, Box 1, 5025, folder 1–3, 1940–1943, AUND.

106. Ibid.

107. *Boston Post,* November 6, 1943, 1.

108. *New York Times,* October 19, 1943.

109. Ibid.

110. *Boston Post* November 10, 1943, 1.

111. *Boston Herald,* November 4, 1943. See also a clipping from the *Boston Herald,* November 4, 1943 in J. Hugh O'Donnell Presidential Correspondence, 1943, McMahon File, folder 4, AUND.

112. Ibid.

113. O'Donnell to McMahon, November 5, 1943, Cantwell Correspondence, Box 1, 5025, folder 1–3, 1940–1943, CHS.

114. McMahon to O'Donnell, November 6, 1943, Cantwell Correspondence, Box 1, 5025, folder 1–3, 1940–1943, CHS.

9. Firestorm

1. *New York Times,* November 7, 1943, sports sec. p. 1.

2. *PM,* November 8, 1943, 4.

3. Ibid.

4. Ibid.

5. Ibid.

6. Interview with M. A. Fitzsimons.

7. O'Toole to O'Donnell, November 29, 1943, UPHO, 97/14–15, O files (2), AUND.

8. Ibid.

9. Ibid. McGowan's words as reported by O'Toole to O'Donnell were that he, McGowan, "might be able to do something for or with him, particularly in view of the possible publicity connecting the Holy See or the Apostolic Delegate with the case."

10. Ibid.

11. Cousineau to O'Donnell, November 10, 1943, UPHO, McMahon File, AUND.

12. O'Donnell to National Desk, *PM* November 10, 1943 (telegram), UPHO, McMahon File, AUND.

13. O'Donnell to Cousineau, November 12, 1943, UPHO, McMahon File, AUND.

14. *New York Times,* November 8, 1943, sec. 1, p. 23.

15. Ibid.

16. Ibid.

17. Ibid.

18. Ibid.

19. Ibid., 23–24.

20. Ibid., 24.

21. *New York Post,* November 12, 1942, sec. 1, p. 4.

22. Ibid.

23. Ibid.

24. Ibid.

25. Ibid.

26. *Catholic Courier,* December 9, 1943, UPHO, 1943, McMahon File, folder 3, AUND.

27. Ibid.

28. O'Hara to O'Donnell, December 7, 1943, UPHO, McMahon File, AUND.

29. Ibid.

30. Editorial, *Pittsburgh Catholic,* clipping, UPHO, McMahon File, AUND.

31. Ibid.

32. Ibid.

33. *New York Times,* November 21, 1943.

34. Ibid.

35. *New York Post,* November 12, 1943.

36. Ibid., November 13, 1943, under the by line of Victor Riesel and under the headline "Walker Spurns Plea to Help McMahon."

37. Ibid.

38. James H. Farley to O'Donnell, November 9, 1943, UPHO, McMahon File, AUND.

39. O'Donnell to Craugh, December 8, 1943, UPHO, McMahon File, AUND.

40. Ibid.

41. Vincent Fagan to McMahon, November 8, 1943, Fagan Papers, Box 4, folder McMahon Correspondence, AUND.

42. Ibid.

43. Fagan to McMahon, November 12, 1943, Box 4, Folder McMahon Correspondence, AUND.

Bernard J. Voll was a local industrialist, a graduate of the university and a frequent and valued benefactor of Notre Dame. Clarence P. Manion was dean of the Notre Dame Law School and had married into one of the prominent local industrial families. John F. Noll was bishop of the Diocese of Fort Wayne, holding episcopal jurisdiction over the South Bend area. Ernest J. Morris was a prominent local financier and banker, a graduate of the Notre Dame Law School, and a frequent and generous benefactor of the University.

44. Ibid.

45. Nutting to Cantwell, November 12, 1943, Cantwell Correspondence Box 1, 5025, Folder 1–3, 1940–1943, CHS.

46. Ibid.

47. Ibid.

48. Twenty-nine faculty members to O'Donnell, November 16, 1943, UPHO, McMahon File, AUND; interview with M. A. Fitzsimons.

49. Ibid.

50. Interview with M. A. Fitzsimons

51. Ibid.

52. Womble to Meyer, November 14, 1943, copy to O'Donnell, UPHO, McMahon File, folder, 3, AUND.

53. See telegram from Philip S. Moore, C.S.C., to E. C. Garvey, C.S.B., November 11, 1943, UPHO, McMahon File, AUND.

54. Cousineau to O'Donnell, November 10, 1943, UPHO, McMahon File, AUND.

55. Murray to O'Donnell, November 8, 1943, UPHO, McMahon File, AUND.

56. Haggerty to O'Donnell, November 9, 1943, UPHO, McMahon File, AUND.

57. E. C. Garvey and J. S. Murphy to Moore, November 11, 1943 (Telegram) UPHO, McMahon File, AUND.

58. Moore to Garvey and Murphy, November 11, 1943 (Telegram) UPHO, McMahon File, AUND.

59. O'Donnell's secretary to Moore, November 15, 1943, UPHO, McMahon File, AUND.

60. Menger to O'Donnell, November 19, 1943, UPHO, McMahon File, AUND.

61. Campbell to O'Donnell, December 4, 1943, UPHO, McMahon File, AUND.

62. Sheehan to Carrico, November 29, 1943, UPHO, McMahon File, AUND.

63. Benjamin Piser to O'Donnell, November 9, 1943, UPHO, McMahon File, folder 1 and Frederick K. Baer to O'Donnell, November 12, 1943, UPHO, McMahon File, folder 1, AUND.

64. Local 65, United Rubber Workers of America, Mishawaka to O'Donnell December 7, 1943 and Local 5, UAW-CIO December 4, 1943, UPHO, McMahon File, AUND.

65. Vitus G. Jones to O'Donnell, November 9, 1943, UPHO, McMahon File, folder 3, AUND.

66. Cosgrove to O'Donnell, November 8, 1943, UPHO, McMahon File, AUND.

67. Cantwell to O'Donnell, November 11, 1943, J.Hugh O'Donnell Preidential Correspondence, 1943, McMahon File, AUND.

68. Ibid.

69. Ibid.

70. Ibid.

71. Rubin to O'Donnell, November 9, 1943, UPHO, McMahon File, AUND.

72. Ibid.

73. Meyer to O'Donnell, November 13, 1943, UPHO, McMahon File, AUND.

74. Ibid.

75. Shuster, Gideonse, and Agar to O'Donnell, November 24, 1943, UPHO, McMahon File, AUND.

76. Ibid.

77. Ibid.

78. Ibid.

79. One example of which there are many in O'Donnell's correspondence is O'Donnell to Craugh, December 8, 1943, UPHO, McMahon File, AUND.

80. O'Donnell to Smith, December 14, 1943, UPHO, McMahon File, AUND.

81. Karl N. Llewellyn to O'Donnell, November 9, 1943, UPHO, McMahon File, AUND.

82. Ibid.

83. *Chicago Sun,* November 16, 1943.

84. Himstead to O'Donnell, June 13, 1944, UPHO, McMahon File, AUND.

85. Ibid.

86. Ibid.

87. Ibid.

88. O'Donnell to Himstead, June 19, 1944, UPHO, AUND.

89. Walsh to O'Donnell, November 30, 1943, UPHO, McMahon File, AUND.

90. Ibid.

91. Ibid.

92. *PM,* November 18, 1943.

93. Brown to O'Donnell, November 28, 1943, UPHO, McMahon File, AUND.

94. Clinton to O'Donnell, February 4, 1944, UPHO, AUND.

95. Ibid.

96. Secretary to the president to Clinton, February 16, 1944, J. Hugh O'Donnell, 1943, McMahon File, AUND.

97. See critical stories about Spellman and about policy statements of the bishops in *PM,* October 18, 1943; November 8, 1943; and November 15, 1943.

98. *PM,* November 22, 1943.

99. Ibid.

100. Ibid.

101. Ibid.

102. Ibid.

103. Ibid.

104. Helen C. White to O'Donnell, November 27, 1943, UPHO, McMahon File, folder 2, AUND.

105. Friedrich to O'Donnell, November 23, 1943, UPHO, McMahon File, AUND.

106. Stephan to O'Donnell, November 20, 1943, UPHO, McMahon File, AUND.

107. *New York Times,* November 21, 1943, secs. 3 and 5, p. 1.

108. Ibid., November 28, 1943, secs. 3 and 5, p. 1.

109. Ibid.

10. Reprise

1. Conroy to O'Donnell, November 11, 1943, UPHO, McMahon File, folder 3, AUND.

2. O'Leary to O'Donnell, November 9, 1943, UPHO, McMahon File, AUND.

3. Fant to O'Donnell, no date, UPHO, McMahon File, AUND.

4. *Gaelic American,* November 13, 1943, UPHO, McMahon File, folder 3, AUND.

5. Foley to O'Donnell, November 9, 1943, UPHO, McMahon File, AUND.

6. O'Donnell to Foley, December 13, 1943, UPHO, AUND.

7. Program issued by the Marshall Committee for Racial Unity for a conference scheduled for Sunday, December 5, 1943, UPHO, McMahon File, AUND.

8. Broadway Notre Dame Alumnus to O'Donnell, letter and clippings, no date, UPHO, McMahon File, AUND.

9. Ibid.

10. Aherne to O'Donnell, November 14, 1943, UPHO, McMahon File, AUND.

11. Ibid.

12. Ibid.

13. Ibid.

14. Ralph Barton Perry, "Reply to Better to Grin and Bear It," *Commonweal,* January 7, 1944, 304.

15. O'Donnell to Aherne, November 17, 1943, UPHO, McMahon File, AUND.

16. Ibid.

17. Scanlan to O'Donnell, November 12, 1943, UPHO, McMahon File, AUND.

18. *Crown Heights Comment,* vol. V, no. 7 (November 16, 1943), UPHO, McMahon File, AUND.

19. Smith to O'Donnell, December 4, 1943, UPHO, McMahon File, AUND.

20. Ibid.

21. Ibid.

22. Ibid.

23. *Crown Heights Comment,* vol. V., no., 7 (November 16, 1943), UPHO, McMahon File, AUND.

24. Ibid.

25. Ibid.

26. Ibid.

27. Ibid.

28. Ibid.

29. Smith to O'Donnell, November 29, 1943, UPHO, McMahon File, AUND.

30. Ibid.

31. O'Donnell to Smith, December 3, 1943, UPHO, McMahon File, AUND.

32. Smith to O'Donnell, December 4, 1943, UPHO, McMahon File, AUND.

33. Ibid.

34. O'Donnell to Smith, December 14, 1943, UPHO, McMahon File, AUND.

35. Fenlon to O'Donnell, November 24, 1943, UPHO, McMahon File, AUND.

36. *Brooklyn Eagle,* November 21, 1943. See also *Brooklyn Tablet* November 27, 1943, for the complete public letter.

37. Ibid.

38. Ibid.

39. Ibid.

40. O'Donnell to Fenlon, November 24, 1943, UPHO, McMahon File, AUND.

41. Cavanaugh to Rev. Charles Lee, C.S.C., UVOC, 7/68, Executive Vice Presidents, H. O'Donnell and J. J. Cavanaugh, AUND.

42. Fenlon to O'Donnell, December 3, 1943, UPHO, McMahon File, AUND.

43. Ibid.

44. O'Donnell to Fenlon, November 24, 1943, UPHO, McMahon File, AUND.

45. Ibid.

46. Ibid.

47. O'Donnell to Fenlon, December 3, 1943, UPHO, McMahon File, AUND.

48. The following account of Kirwan's role in obtaining an academic post at the University of Chicago for McMahon is based on an interview with Professor Emeritus John J. Kennedy of the Department of Government at the University of Notre Dame. Kennedy was a student and friend of Kirwan and what follows is Kennedy's recollection of what Kirwan told him.

49. Ibid.

50. O'Donnell to Connerton, November 12, 1943, UPHO, McMahon File, folder 2, AUND.

51. O'Toole to O'Donnell, November 29, 1943, UPHO, 97/14–15, General Correspondence "O" Files (2), AUND.

52. *New York Times,* December 11, 1943, sec. 1, p. 16.

53. *Chicago Daily News,* December 11, 1943.

54. Jay to O'Donnell, December 30, 1943, with copy of Open Letter, UPHO, McMahon File, AUND.

55. Ibid.

56. Ibid.

57. Kane to McMahon, December 5, 1943, copy sent to O'Donnell, UPHO, McMahon File, AUND.

58. Ibid.

59. "Better to Grin and Bear It," *Commonweal,* November 19, 1943, 108.

60. Ibid.

61. Ralph Barton Perry, "Better to Grin and Bear It," *Commonweal,* January 7, 1944, 304.

62. Ibid.

63. O'Donnell to Cicognani, December 15, 1943, UPHO, 97/8, AUND.

64. Ibid.

65. Cicognani to O'Donnell, January 7, 1944, UPHO, 97/8, AUND.

66. Ibid.

67. See reports of McMahon's speeches to Temple Emanu-El, February 4, 1946, and to the United Railroad Workers, CIO, March 19, 1947, *New York Times,* February 4, 1946, p. 17; March 19, 1947, p. 19.

68. *New York Times,* April 16, 1947, p. 13.

69. Ibid.

70. Ibid., April 6, 1947, p. 53

71. Ibid., April 9, 1947, p. 7.
72. Ibid., April 6, 1947, p. 53.
72. Ibid., April 15, p. 4.
73. The account of the situation in Rome and of the Ardeatine massacre is taken from Robert Katz, *Death in Rome* (London: Macmillan, 1967), *passim.*
74. George Shuster, "Why Notre Dame Got Scared," *New Leader,* January 5, 1944, p. 5.
75. Ibid.
76. Nutting to Cantwell, November 12, 1943, Cantwell Correspondence, 5025, 1940–1943, Folder 1–3, CHS.

11. War's End: Recovery and Redirection

1. Goodwin, 524.
2. David McCullough, *Truman,* (New York: Simon & Shuster, 1992), 315.
3. Goodwin, 529–30.
4. *New York Times,* August 27, 1944, sec. 4, p. 9.
5. Philip Gleason *Contending with Modernity: Catholic Higher Education in the Twentieth Century,* (New York: Oxford University Press, 1995), 216.
6. Ibid.
7. Ibid.
8. Ibid., 216–17.
9. *New York Times,* October 20, 1945, sec. 1, p. 26.
10. Ibid.
11. Gleason, 217.
12. *New York Times,* October 5, 1945, 38:1.
13. Gleason, 236.
14. Walsh to Rev. S. J. Kelly, July 14, 1922, UPWL, folder 9, Kea-Kem, AUND.
15. Gleason, 161; 367, n. 59.
16. Ibid., 214.
17. Manion to Cavanaugh July 24, 1944, UPHO, 102, AUND.
18. O'Donnell or Cavanaugh to Manion, August 4, 1944, UPHO, 102, AUND.
19. Ibid.
20. Folder, "African Americans at Notre Dame," AUND.
21. Gleason, 236.
22. *New York Times* November 5, 1944, secs. 3–5.
23. Ibid., November 12, Sports, p. 1.
24. O'Brien to O'Donnell, October 27, 1943, UPHO, 97/14–15; O'Donnell to O'Brien, March 22, 1946, UPHO, 105/33, O-Og; O'Brien to O'Donnell, March 28, 1946, UPHO, 105/33, o-Og, AUND.
25. O'Brien to O'Donnell, December 14, 1944, UPHO, 100/53, AUND.
26. O'Donnell to O'Brien, December 26, 1944, UPHO, 100/53, AUND.

27. Whitacre to O'Donnell, May 30, 1944, UPHO, 100/53, AUND.

28. Ibid.

29. Ibid.

30. McCullough, 349.

31. Ibid.

32. Ibid., 349–50.

33. Ibid., 354.

34. Ibid., 401.

35. Ibid., 438.

36. Ibid., 401–2.

37. Ibid., 401.

38. Ibid., 377.

39. Ibid., 378.

40. Ibid., 390–91.

41. Ibid.

42. Ibid., 437

43. *New York Times*, January 13, 1946, sec. 4, p. 9.

44. Ibid.

45. Ibid., October 11, 1945, sec. 1, p. 25.

46. Ibid.

47. Ibid., July 9, 1946, sec. 1, p. 15.

48. Ibid., April 28, 1972, Obituaries, p. 44.

49. Ibid.

50. Ibid.

51. Ibid.

52. Gleason, 264.

53. *New York Times*, April 30, 1946, sec. 1, p. 16.

54. Ibid., June 30, 1946, sec. 1, p. 21.

55. Ibid.

56. Ibid.

57. Ibid.

58. Ibid., November 4, 1945, Sports, p. 1.

59. Ibid.

60. Ibid., November 11, 1945, sec. 5, p. 1.

61. Ibid.

62. Ibid.

63. Ibid., December 2, 1945, Sports, pp. 1–3.

64. Ibid.

65. This account of O'Brien in the Notre Dame Department of Religion is derived from an examination of departmental offerings and from recollections of contemporaries.

66. Simonitsch to O'Brien, July 2, 1946, UPHO, 105/52, O-Ob, AUND.

67. O'Brien to O'Donnell, February 2, 1946, UPHO, 105/33, O-Og, AUND.

68. O'Donnell to Haley, April 12, 1946, UPHO, 105/33, O-Og, AUND.

69. O'Donnell to O'Brien, February 5, 1946, UPHO, 105/33, O-Og, AUND.

70. O'Brien to O'Donnell, August 17, 1946, UPHO, 105/33. O-Og; O'Donnell to O'Brien, August 18, 1946, UPHO, 105/33, O-Og, AUND.

71. Hope, 470.

72. Ibid.

12. Cavanaugh and Postwar American Higher Education: Opportunities and Challenges

1. Hope, 472–73.

2. Ibid.

3. Ibid.

4. *New York Times,* July 28, 1946, sec. 4, p. 9.

5. Ibid., October 17, 1946, sec. 1, p. 19.

6. Ibid.

7. Gleason, 263.

8. Ibid.

9. Ibid.

10. Joseph P. Lash, *A World of Love: Eleanor Roosevelt and Her Friends, 1943–1962* (New York: Doubleday, 1984), 303–4.

11. Letter from the Committee on Academic Freedom of the American Civil Liberties Union, February 17, 1948, UPCC, AUND.

12. Ibid.

13. Gleason, 254.

14. Ibid.

15. Ibid.

16. Hope, 474.

17. Gleason, 218.

18. Ibid.

19. Hope, 475.

20. Gleason, 218–19.

21. Ibid., 219.

22. *New York Times,* April 9, 1949, sec. 1, p. 17.

23. Ibid.

24. Ibid., April 22, 1949, sec. 1, p. 21.

25. Hope, 474.

26. Ibid.

27. *New York Times,* May 11, 1950, sec. 1, p. 43.

28. Interview with James W. Frick.

29. Ibid.

30. Ibid.

31. Theodore M. Hesburgh, C.S.C. with Jerry Reedy, *God, Country, Notre*

Dame, (New York: Doubleday, 1990), 25–26. (A second edition was published in 1999 by the University of Notre Dame Press.)

32. Ibid., 44–45.
33. Ibid.
34. Ibid., 47.
35. Ibid.
36. Ibid., 54.
37. *New York Times,* October 4, 1950, sec. 1, p. 19.

13. The End of One Era and the Beginning of Another

1. Hesburgh, 56–57.
2. Articles of Academic Organization for the University of Notre Dame, March 1941, PNDP, 1000, AUND.
3. Ibid.
4. Academic Organization, c.a., 1951, PNDP, 1000, AUND.
5. Ibid.
6. Hesburgh, 58.
7. *New York Times,* July 26, 1949, sec. 1, p. 25.
8. Hesburgh, 58.
9. *New York Times,* June 22, 1951, sec. 1, p. 12.
10. Taylor, 150.
11. Ibid.
12. Ibid.
13. *New York Times,* January 11, 1997, sec. 1, p. 39.
14. Ibid., January 1, 1947, Sports, 2.
15. Ibid., January 11, 1947, 39.
16. Ibid.
17. Ibid., November 10, 1946, sec. 5, p. 1.
18. Taylor, 153.
19. Ibid.
20. Ibid.
21. Ibid.
22. Ibid.
23. Ibid.
24. *New York Times,* December 31, 1946, sec. 1, p. 21.
25. Ibid.
26. Hope, 484.
27. Ibid., 485.
28. Taylor, 154.
29. Hesburgh, 77.
30. Ibid., 57.
31. Ibid., 78.

32. Ibid.
33. Ibid., 79.
34. Ibid.
35. Ibid., 64.
36. Ibid., 65.
37. Ibid., 64.
38. Ibid., 58–59.
39. Ibid., 59.
40. Ibid., 60.
41. Ibid., 66.
42. Ibid.
43. Because the Manion file in Cavanaugh's presidential correspondence is closed to researchers, the influence of Manion's very conservative public policy positions on the decision to force his resignation must be inferred from the public record or considered from recollections of retired Notre Dame faculty members. Between the spring of 1950 when Cavanaugh gave Manion the Notre Dame faculty award and December 1951 when Hesburgh pressed for the dean's resignation, nothing extraordinary occurred in law school affairs to precipitate such a reversal of judgment about Manion's value to the law school and to the university.

To be sure, Cavanaugh and Hesburgh agreed that reforms were needed in the law school, and that Manion was not the man to initiate and implement them. They also agreed that reforms were needed in the College of Commerce and that Dean James E. McCarthy was not the man to carry them out either. However, Manion was asked to resign and McCarthy was not. Both men had very long service at the university, both had been active isolationists before the war, both were well connected in Indiana Republican politics, and both were political conservatives. The difference was that Manion was much more public and more reckless about his public policy advocacy than McCarthy. It appears to have been Manion's many widely publicized, highly controversial public policy positions that persuaded Cavanaugh and Hesburgh to seek the dean's resignation when they did.

Moreover, there is no doubt that Manion as well as others at the university believed Hesburgh to be principally responsible for forcing the resignation. In later years, Mrs. Manion would not forgive Hesburgh for what she believed he had done to her husband. When Manion died in 1979 at the age of eighty-three, Father Hesburgh was in his twenty-seventh year as president of the university. Mrs. Manion refused to deposit her husband's considerable collection of personal papers in the Notre Dame archives. Instead, she gave the Manion Papers to the Chicago Historical Society and imposed no restrictions on access.

44. Hesburgh, 66.
45. *New York Times*, January 12, 1952, sec. 1, p. 9.
46. Hesburgh, 66.
47. Ibid.

48. The source of these Joe O'Meara anecdotes was Professor Anton Herman Chroust, then a member of the law school and College of Arts and Letters faculties.

49. Hesburgh, 60–61.

50. Ibid., 64.

51. Very little is known about the Cavavanagh/Joseph P. Kennedy relationship because the surviving letters and personal papers detailing it are closed to researchers. Though deposited in the Kennedy Presidential Library, the Joseph P. Kennedy Collection is closed. Doris Kearns Goodwin was granted access to this collection for her book *The Fitzgeralds and the Kennedys*, but other researchers have been routinely denied access.

There is a file of about 145 Cavanaugh/Kennedy letters ranging in time from 1941 to 1956 in the Cavanaugh presidential correspondence in the Notre Dame Archives, but that file is closed as well. Though normally operating on the principle of allowing access after fifty years on the grounds that the dead can take care of themselves, the rationale offered by the Notre Dame archives in 1997 is that living people are mentioned or discussed in these letters. In view of the fact that someone forty years old in 1955 would be eighty-two in 1997, these protected few must be very long-lived indeed.

For the period after 1956, additional Cavanaugh/Kennedy correspondence may reside somewhere in a file in the university archives or perhaps in the provincial archives, but no one knows for certain. In any case, during the period after 1956 most of the communication between Cavanaugh and the ambassador probably would have been by telephone or in person.

52. Doris Kearns Goodwin, *The Fitzgeralds and the Kennedys* (New York: Simon & Schuster, 1987), 804.

53. This account of Cavanaugh's discussion with Kenna in March 1965 is based on what Cavanaugh told Sister Elaine Des Rosiers, O.P., some years after the event. Interview with Sister Elaine Des Rosiers, O.P.

54. Ibid.

55. Ibid.

Bibliography

Manuscript Material

Archives of the University of Notre Dame

Vincent T. Fagan Papers
Manuscript Material in the Archives of the University of Notre Dame (AUND)
Vincent T. Fagan Papers
Francis E. McMahon Papers
John A. O'Brien Personal Papers

Presidential Correspondence

James A. Burns, C.S.C., 1919–1922 (UPBU)
John J. Cavanaugh, C.S.C., 1946–1952 (UPCC)
Theodore M. Hesburgh, C.S.C., 1952–1987
Charles L. O'Donnell, C.S.C., 1928–1933 (UPCO)
J. Hugh O'Donnell, C.S.C., 1940–1946 (UPHO)
John F. O'Hara, C.S.C., 1934–1940 (UPOH)
Matthew J. Walsh, C.S.C., 1922–1928 (UPWL)

Chicago Historical Society

Monsignor Daniel M. Cantwell Correspondence, 1940–1943
Clarence P. Manion Papers

Archives of the Catholic University of America, Washington, D.C.

John Tracy Ellis Papers

Public Records Office, London

Foreign Office Correspondence, FO 115, 371, 395, 1940–1943

Interviews

Anton-Herman Chroust
Sister Elaine Des Rosiers, O.P.
James W. Frick

Printed Sources located in the University of Notre Dame Archives

Notre Dame Alumnus
The Dome
The Observer
The Scholastic
Religious Bulletin
Religious Survey

Newspapers

Boston Herald
Boston Post
Brooklyn Eagle
Catholic Courier
Daily Worker
Dubuque Telegraph-Herald
Chicago Daily News
Chicago Sun
Chicago Tribune
Cincinnati Telegraph-Register
New York Herald-Tribune
New York Post
New York Times
Pittsburgh Catholic
PM
South Bend Tribune
Washington Post

Magazines and Newsletters

America
Collier's Magazine
Commonweal
Crown Heights Comment
New Leader
Newsweek
New Republic
Review of Politics
U.S. News and World Report
Vital Speeches of the Day

Government Publications

Congressional Record, 76th Congress, 3rd Session, 1940.
Foreign Relations of the United States: The Conference at Washington, 1941–42 and Casablanca, 1943, 1968.
Foreign Relations of the United States: Diplomatic Papers, 1943, vol. II, *Europe*, 1964.
R. Butler, D. Dakin, M. Lambert et al., eds., *Documents on British Foreign Policy* (DEBFP), 2nd series, vol. 17, London: HMSO, 1979.

Books

Bayor, Ronald H. *Neighbors in Conflict: The Irish, Germans, Jews, and Italians of New York City, 1929–1941*. Baltimore: Johns Hopkins University Press, 1978.
Beschloss, Michael R. *Kennedy and Roosevelt: The Uneasy Alliance*. New York: W. W. Norton, 1980.
Chadwin, Mark Lincoln. *The Hawks of World War II*. Chapel Hill: University of North Carolina Press, 1968.
———. *The Warhawks: American Interventionists Before Pearl Harbor*. New York: W. W. Norton, 1970.
Churchill, Winston S. *Their Finest Hour*. Boston: Houghton Mifflin, 1949.
Cole, Wayne S. *America First: The Battle Against Intervention, 1940–1941*. Madison: University of Wisconsin Press, 1953.
———. *Senator Gerald P. Nye and American Foreign Relations*. Minneapolis: University of Minnesota Press, 1962.
———. *Charles A. Lindbergh and the Battle against American Intervention in World War II*. New York: Harcourt Brace Jovanovich, 1974.

Collier, Peter, and David Horowitz. *The Kennedys: An American Drama*. New York: Warner Books, 1984.

Craven, Wesley Frank, et al., eds. *The Army Air Forces in World War II Europe: Torch to Pointblank, August 1942–December 1943*, vol. 2. Chicago: University of Chicago Press, 1949.

Cull, Nicholas J. *Selling War*. New York: Oxford University Press, 1995.

Doenecke, Justus D. *Not to the Swift: The Old Isolationists in the Cold War Era*. Cranbury, N.J.: Associated University Presses, 1979.

———. *In Danger Undaunted: The Anti-Interventionist Movement as Revealed in the Papers of the America First Committe*. Palo Alto, Calif.: Hoover Institution Press, Stanford University, 1990.

Eade, Charles, ed. *The Speeches of the Rt. Hon. Winston Churchill*. Vol. 2. London: Cassell, 1952.

Evans, John Whitney. *The Newman Movement: Roman Catholics in Higher Education*. Notre Dame, Ind.: University of Notre Dame Press, 1980.

Fleming, Peter. *Operation Sea Lion*. New York: Simon & Schuster, 1957.

Fogarty, Gerald P. *The Vatican and the American Hierarchy from 1870 to 1965*. Stuttgart: Anton Hersemann, 1982.

Gibbons, James Cardinal. *The Faith of Our Fathers*. 92d edition. Baltimore: John Murphy Company, 1917.

Gleason, Philip. *Contending with Modernity: Catholic Higher Education in the Twentieth Century*, New York: Oxford University Press, 1995.

Goodman, Walter. *The Committee*. London: The History Book Club, Ltd., 1968.

Goodwin, Doris Kearns. *The Fitzgeralds and the Kennedys*. New York: Simon & Schuster, 1987.

———. *No Ordinary Time: Franklin and Eleanor Roosevelt: The Home Front in World War II*. New York: Simon & Shuster, 1994.

Gruber, John W. *A Conscience in Conflict: The Life of St. George Mivart*. New York: Published for Temple University Publications by Columbia University Press, 1960.

Hesburgh, Theodore M., C.S.C. *God, Country, and Notre Dame*. New York: Doubleday, 1990. (A 2d ed. has been published by University of Notre Dame Press, 1999, but page numbering differs.)

Hope, Arthur J., C.S.C. *Notre Dame One Hundred Years*, revised ed. Introduction by Thomas J. Schlereth. South Bend, Ind.: Icarus Press, 1978.

Katz, Robert. *Death in Rome*. New York: Macmillan, 1967.

Ketchum, Robert M. *The Borrowed Years, 1938–1941: America on the Way to War*. New York: Random House, 1989.

Koppes, Clayton R., and Gregory R. Black. *Hollywood Goes to War: How Policies, Profits, and Propaganda Shaped World War II Movies*. New York: The Free Press, 1987.

Lash, Joseph P. *A World of Love: Eleanor Roosevelt and Her Friends, 1943–1962*. New York: Doubleday, 1984.

Lindbergh, Charles A. *The Wartime Journals of Charles A. Lindbergh.* New York: Harcourt Brace Jovanovich, 1970.

McAvoy, Thomas T., C.S.C. *Father John O'Hara of Notre Dame: The Cardinal Archbishop of Philadelphia,* Notre Dame, Ind.: University of Notre Dame Press, 1967.

McCullough, David. *Truman,* New York: Simon & Schuster, 1992.

McMahon, Francis E. *A Catholic Looks at the World.* New York: Vanguard Press, 1945.

Milton, Joyce. *Loss of Eden: A Biography of Charles and Anne Morrow Lindbergh.* New York: Harper Collins, 1993.

O'Brien, John A. *Modern Psychology and the Mass: A Study in the Psychology of Religion.* New York: Paulist Press, nd.

―――. *The White Harvest: A Symposium on the Methods of Convert Making.* New York: Longmans, Green, 1927.

―――. *Evolution and Religion.* New York: Paulist Press, 1930.

―――. *Evolution and Religion.* New York: Century Catholic College Text Series, 1932.

―――. *The Faith of Millions.* 2d edition. Huntington, Ind.: Our Sunday Visitor Press, 1938.

―――. *Catholics and Scholarship.* Huntington, Ind.: Our Sunday Visitor Press, 1939.

Sperber, Murray. *Shake Down the Thunder: The Creation of Notre Dame Football.* New York: Henry Holt and Company, 1993.

Stenehjem, Michele Flynn. *An American First: John T. Flynn and the America First Committee.* New Rochelle, N.Y.: Arlington House Publishers, 1976.

Taylor, John M. *General Maxwell Taylor: The Sword and the Pen.* New York: Doubleday, 1989.

Tull, Charles J. *Father Coughlin and the New Deal.* Syracuse, N.Y.: Syracuse University Press, 1965.

Articles

Arendt, Hannah. "The Personality of Waldemar Gurian." *Review of Politics,* January 1957.

Beals, Lawrence W. "Catholics and Communists." *New Republic,* April 5, 1943, 702–3.

Chevalier, Albert A., O.M.I. "The Eternity of Hell Fire." *Homiletic and Pastoral Review,* February 1930.

Connell, Francis J., C.S.S.R. "Is the Fire of Hell Eternal and Real?" *Homiletic and Pastoral Review,* September 1934.

―――. "Again the Doctrine of Hell." *Homiletic and Pastoral Review,* January 1935.

Editorial. "The Catholic Foundation Plan." *America* 35, March 20, 1926.

Fitzsimons, M. A. "Die Deutschen Briefe: Gurian and the German Crisis." *Review of Politics*, January 1955.

Gurian, Waldemar. "The Catholic Publicist," trans. by M. A. Fitzsimons. *Review of Politics*, January 1955.

Heithaus, Claude H., S.J. "Catholics at Non-Catholic Universities." *America* 33, August 22, 1925.

———. "Morals at Non-Catholic Universities," *America* 33, August 29, 1925.

———. "Courses at Non-Catholic Universities." *America* 33, September 18, 1925.

———. "Are Catholic Universities Inferior?" *America* 33, September 26, 1925.

———. "Catholic Colleges for Women." *America* 33, October 3, 1925.

———. "A Reply to Mr. Quinlan." *America* 33, November 7, 1925.

———. "A Catholic Foundation Unmasked," *America* 34, December 19, 1925.

———. "Catholic Foundations and Canon Law." *America*, January 2, 1926.

McMahon, Francis E. "The Catholic Issues." *New Republic*, June 7, 1943: 765.

———. "Catholics and Liberals." *New Republic*, June 21, 1943: 831–32.

Mivart, St. George. "Happiness in Hell." *Nineteenth Century* 32: 899–919.

———. "Statement." *Homiletic and Pastoral Review* August, 1935, 1129–30.

———. "The Happiness in Hell: A Rejoinder." *Nineteenth Century* 33: 320–38.

———. "Last Words on the Happiness in Hell." *Nineteenth Century* 33: 637–51.

———. "The Index and My Articles on Hell." *Nineteenth Century* 34: 979–90.

———. "Roman Congregations and Modern Thought." *North American Review* 70: 562–74.

———. "Catholics and Liberals" (editorial). *New Republic*, June 7, 1943: 751.

Nef, John W. "The Significance of the *Review of Politics*." *Review of Politics*, January 1955.

O'Brien, John A. "Rightly Handling the Word of Truth." *American Ecclesiastical Review*, December 1930.

———. "Did We Lose Half a Million Catholics Last Year?" *American Ecclesiastical Review*, December 1931.

———. Review of Rev. Ernest C. Messenger's *Evolution and Theology: The Problem of Man's Origin*, New York: Macmillan and Company, 1932, in *Commonweal*, March 8, 1932: 526–27.

———. "The Moral Causes of Catholic Leakage." *Homiletic and Pastoral Review*, April 1933.

———. "Birth Control and Catholic Leakage." *Homilectic and Pastoral Review*, April 1933.

———. "A Sane Treatment of Hell." *Homiletic and Pastoral Review*, June 1934.

———. "Father Connell's Idea of Hell." *Homiletic and Pastoral Review*, October 1934.

———. "Are Lost Souls Eternally Damned?" *Homiletic and Pastoral Review*, April 1935.

———. "Reply to Father Chevalier." *Homiletic and Pastoral Review*, April 1935.

————. "Catholics on Secular Campuses." *America*, April 8, 1961.

Ross, J. Elliot. Review of John A. O'Brien's *Evolution and Religion*. *Commonweal*, September 14, 1932.

Ryan, Very Rev. John A. "The Moral Aspects of Periodic Continence." *American Ecclesiastical Review*, July 1933.

Salvemini, Gaetano "Pius XII and Fascism." *New Republic*, March 8, 1943.

Shaugnessy, Rev. Gerald, S.M. "The Alleged Leakage of 1930." *American Ecclesiastical Review*, March 1930.

Smothers, Frank A. "New Light on Birth Control." *Commonweal*, March 8, 1933.

Stallbaumer, Virgil R., O.S.B. Review of John A. O'Brien, ed. *Catholics and Scholarship* in *Homiletic and Pastoral Review*, 1939–40, part I: 455–56.

Stritch, Thomas. "After Forty Years: Notre Dame and the *Review of Politics*." *Review of Politics*, January 1978.

Tuttle, William H., Jr. "A Reappraisal of William Allen White's Leadership." *Journal of Modern History*, March 1970.

Index